RAPE AND SEXUAL ASSAULT

GARLAND REFERENCE LIBRARY
OF SOCIAL SCIENCE
(VOL. 203)

ABOUT THE EDITOR

Ann Wolbert Burgess, R.N., D.N.Sc., is the van Ameringen Professor of Psychiatric Mental Health Nursing at the University of Pennsylvania School of Nursing and Associate Director of Nursing Research at the Department of Health and Hospitals, Boston, MA. She received her B.S. and D.N.Sc. from Boston University and her M.S. from the University of Maryland. She is former chairperson of the Advisory Committee to the National Center on the Prevention and Control of Rape and was a member on the 1983–84 U.S. Attorney General's Task Force on Family Violence. Her prior co-authored books in the field of victimology include: *Rape: Crisis and Recovery*, *Sexual Assault of Children and Adolescents*, *The Victim of Rape: Institutional Reactions*, and *Child Pornography and Sex Rings*.

RAPE AND SEXUAL ASSAULT
A Research Handbook

Ann Wolbert Burgess, *editor*

GARLAND PUBLISHING, INC. • NEW YORK & LONDON
1985

Library of Congress Cataloging in Publication Data
Main entry under title:

A Handbook of research on rape and sexual assault.

(Garland reference library of social science ;
vol. 203)
    1. Rape—United States—Prevention—Addresses, essays,
lectures. 2. Rape victims—United States—Addresses,
essays, lectures. 3. Rapists—United States—Addresses,
essays, lectures. 4. Violence in mass media—United
States—Addresses, essays, lectures. I. Burgess, Ann
Wolbert. II. Series: Garland reference library of
social science ; v. 203.
HV6561.H36 1985   362.8'83'0973   83-48217
ISBN 0-8240-9049-7 (alk. paper)

Cover design by Laurence Walczak

Printed on acid-free, 250-year-life paper
Manufactured in the United States of America

CONTRIBUTING AUTHORS

Albert J. Belanger, B.S., Health Science Research Staff, Boston City Hospital, Boston, MA

Lucy Berliner, M.S.W., Sexual Assault Center, Harborview Medical Center, Seattle, WA

Nancy Brekke, Ph.D., Department of Psychology, University of Virginia, Charlottesville, VA

Eugene Borgida, Ph.D., Department of Psychology, University of Minnesota, Minneapolis, MN

Ralph B. D'Agostino, Ph.D., Department of Mathematics, Boston University and Senior Research Scientist, Department of Health and Hospitals, Boston, MA

Roger L. Depue, M.S., Unit Chief, Behavioral Science Unit, FBI Academy, Quantico, VA

John E. Douglas, M.S., Supervisory Special Agent, Director of the Criminal Profiling Program, Behavioral Science Unit, FBI Academy, Quantico, VA

David Finkelhor, Ph.D., Associate Director, Family Violence Research Program University of New Hampshire, Durham, N.H.

Theresa S. Foley, R.N., Ph.D., School of Nursing, University of Michigan, Ann Arbor, MI

Linda Gordon, Ph.D., Department of History, University of Wisconsin, Madison, WI

Renee Gould, R.N., M.A., Beth Israel Hospital, Boston, MA

Jean Guio, R.N., Tri-County Mental Health, St. Vincent's Stress Center, Indianapolis, IN

Michael V. Guio, B.S., Special Agent, FBI, Indianapolis, IN

Judith Herman, M.D., Department of Psychiatry, Harvard Medical School (Cambridge, Hospital), and Founding Member Women's Mental Health Collective, Somerville, MA

Lynda Lytle Holmstrom, Ph.D., Department of Sociology, Boston College, Chestnut Hill, MA

Raymond A. Knight, Ph.D., Department of Psychology, Brandeis University and Department of Psychology, Massachusetts Treatment Center, Bridgewater, MA

v

Mary Ann Largen, Consultant, Women's Policy Studies, Washington, D.C., and former Legislative Committee Chairperson for the National Coalition Against Sexual Assault

Mary Hanemann Lystad, Ph.D., Chief, Center for Mental Health Studies of Emergencies, National Institute of Mental Health, Department of Health and Human Services, and former Chief, National Center for the Prevention and Control of Rape

Neil Malamuth, Ph.D., Communications Studies, University of California, Los Angeles, CA

Joseph Marolla, Ph.D., Department of Sociology, Virginia Commonwealth University, Richmond, VA

William H. Masters, M.D., Director, Masters and Johnson Institute, St. Louis, MI

Caroline Montan, B.A., Research Assistant, Health Sciences Research Staff, Boston City Hospital, Boston, MA

Paul O'Keefe, University of Massachusetts, Downtown Campus Boston, MA

Judith A. Reisman, Ph.D., Department of Education, American University, Washington, D.C.

Robert K. Ressler, M.S., Supervisory Special Agent, Director of the Criminal Personality Research Program, Behavioral Science Unit, FBI Academy, Quantico, VA

Eileen E. Rinear, R.N., Ph.D., Director, Community Health Education Department, North Penn Hospital, Lansdale, PA

Ruth Rosenberg, Ph.D., Department of Psychology, Brandeis University, and Department of Psychology, Massachusetts Treatment Center, Bridgewater, MA

Mark S. Schwartz, Sc.D., Director, Sex & Marital Clinic, Westbank Center for Psychotherapy, New Orleans, LA

Diana Scully, Ph.D., Department of Sociology/Anthropology, Virginia Commonwealth University, Richmond, VA

T. Richard Teseyge-Spates, Ph.D., Director of the Psychological, Diagnostic, Treatment and Research Center, Lansing, MI

Beth A. Schneider, Ph.D., Department of Psychology, Brandeis University and Department of Psychology, Massachusetts Treatment Center, Bridgewater, MA

Carolyn T. Swift, Ph.D., Director of the Stone Center, Wellesley College, Wellesley, MA

Hollis Wheeler, M.A., Doctoral student, Department of Sociology, University of Massachusetts, Amherst, MA

Kersti Yllö, Ph.D., Department of Sociology/Anthropology, Wheaton College, Norton, MA

CONTENTS

Preface   xi

I. Introduction
  1. The Anti-Rape Movement: Past and Present
       by *Mary Ann Largen*   1
  2. The National Center for the Prevention and
       Control of Rape
       by *Mary Hanemann Lystad*   14

II. Victims
  3. The Mental Health Needs of Victims
       by *C. Richard Tsegaye-Spates*   35
  4. Rape Trauma Syndrome and Post Traumatic Stress Response
       by *Ann Wolbert Burgess* and *Lynda Lytle Holmstrom*   46
  5. Violence in the Home: A Public Problem
       by *Mary Hanemann Lystad*   61
  6. The "Normality" of Incest: Father-Daughter Incest
       as a Form of Family Violence. Evidence from Historical
       Case Records
       by *Linda Gordon* and *Paul O'Keefe*   70
  7. Father-Daughter Incest
       by *Judith Herman*   83
  8. Sexual Abuse of Boys
       by *David Finkelhor*   97
  9. Investigation of Sex Crimes Against Children:
       A Survey of Ten States
       by *Ralph B. D'Agostino, Ann W. Burgess, Albert J.
       Belanger, Michael V. Guio, Jean J. Guio, Renee Gould,
       and Caroline Montan*   110
 10. Sexual Victimization of Adolescents
       by *Ann Wolbert Burgess*   123

vii

11. Sexual Assault and the Handicapped Victim
    by *Eileen E. Rinear*   139
12. Marital Rape
    by *Kersti Yllö* and *David Finkelhor*   146

III. Family and Legal Response to the Victim
13. Family Response to Rape and Sexual Assault
    by *Theresa S. Foley*   159
14. The Criminal Justice System's Response to the
    Rape Victim
    by *Lynda Lytle Holmstrom*   189
15. The Child and the Criminal Justice System
    by *Lucy Berliner*   199

IV. The Aggressor
16. Rape and Rape Murder: One Offender
    and Twelve Victims
    by *Robert K. Ressler, Ann W. Burgess*, and
    John E. Douglas   209
17. Classification of Sexual Offenders: Perspectives,
    Methods and Validation
    by *Raymond A. Knight, Ruth Rosenberg*, and
    Beth Schneider   222
18. Rape and Vocabularies of Motive: Alternative
    Perspectives
    by *Diana Scully* and *Joseph Marolla*   294
19. Psycholegal Research on Rape Trials
    by *Eugene Borgida* and *Nancy Brekke*   313
20. Criminal Profiling Research on Homicide
    by *Robert K. Ressler, Ann W. Burgess, John E.
    Douglas*, and *Roger L. Depue*   343
21. Treatment of Paraphiliacs, Pedophiles, and
    Incest Families
    by *Mark F. Schwartz* and *William H. Masters*   350

V. Mass Media, Prevention, and the Future
22. Mass Media and Civil Rights
    by *Judith A. Reisman*   365

Contents

23. Pornography and Rape: A Feminist Perspective
    by *Hollis Wheeler*   374
24. The Mass Media and Aggression Against Women:
    Research Findings and Prevention
    by *Neil Malamuth*   392
25. The Prevention of Rape
    by *Carolyn Swift*   413

Index   427

PREFACE

The public's consciousness has been raised in the past decade to the serious social problem of rape and sexual assault in the United States as well as to the impact that such victimization has on the lives of victims, their families, and their communities. Concurrent with this educative impetus has been a burgeoning of research into a multitude of factors interwoven with sexual violence and its aftermath. In the early 1970s the professional literature related to rape victimology was quite meager. In 1977, after the first infusion of research monies to the professional community, Stanley Brodsky and Marcia Walker prepared on microfiche over 1450 annotated articles from 5,000 citations on the subject. In 1984, it seemed timely to review the progress made to the mid-1980s and to update the citations and compile a research reference book on rape and sexual assault.

This book represents many perspectives of the field of sexual violence. The authors have made substantial contributions to the field through their research and represent a large number of disciplines and backgrounds including the behavioral sciences, communications, criminal justice, criminology, history, education, law enforcement, medicine, nursing, psychiatry, psychology, social sciences, social work, victimology and women policy studies.

The book is divided into five sections. Part One includes two chapters that provide both the historical background and current efforts and products from federal initiatives in the rape victimology field. In the first chapter, Mary Ann Largen, former Coordinator of the National Task Force on Rape for the National Organization for Women, traces the historical aspects of the anti-rape movement of the 1970s starting with the period 1967–1972 when the consciousness-raising groups were organizing a strong grassroots network. In these groups, the experience of being sexually assaulted was told over and over by many of the women. In 1971 the New York Radical Feminists sponsored the first Speak Out on Rape. Then small protest groups began forming throughout the country, usually in the wake of a rape or series of rapes in local communities. It was within these groups that the anti-rape movement fully emerged and that the formal war against rape was born through the organization of rape crisis centers under the name "Women Against Rape—WAR." In February 1973, at the Sixth Annual NOW meeting, the National Organization for Women established the National Task Force on Rape and identified their short-term goals. In bringing us up to the 1980s, Largen identifies the structure that is carrying on the goals of the anti-rape movement, the National Coalition Against Sexual Assault.

In Chapter Two, Mary Hanemann Lystad, former Chief of the National Center for the Prevention and Control of Rape, presents the research priorities, research portfolio, and products of the Center. The Center began operations in 1976 with its mandate to support research studies into the causes of rape, laws dealing with rape, the treatment of victims and the effectiveness of existing programs to prevent and control rape.

Victims of rape and sexual assault include all ages, gender, social class, education and occupations. Part Two includes chapters on victims' needs, the impact of the rape, and the various population groups. C. Richard Tsegaye-Spates, in Chapter 3, presents the interactional dimensions of personal victimization as central to the impact injury and subsequent trauma. He reviews the clinical literature on victimization, with a specific emphasis on the mental health needs of victims of violence. Chapter 4 by Ann Wolbert Burgess and Lynda Lytle Holmstrom develops the relationship of the concept of rape trauma syndrome to the official diagnostic nomenclature of Post Traumatic Stress Response in the DSM-III of the American Psychiatric Association. This inclusion of rape trauma syndrome recognizes rape as a traumatic event creating disruption in normal life activities in its immediate crisis impact and continuing the life pattern upheaval for months and years afterward.

Mary Hanemann Lystad, in Chapter 5, directs attention to the phenomenon of family violence and provides an overview of studies on the incidence of violence, causal studies looking at the aggressor, the social situation in which violence occurs and the norms and values which sanction the violence, intervention techniques and prevention strategies. In Chapter 5, Linda Gordon and Paul O'Keefe, reporting on their findings on incest from an historical study of family violence in the Boston area from 1880 to 1960, corroborate some of the findings of recent clinical studies on incest, notably its frequency and the predominance of father-daughter incest as a social problem. The historical cases also suggest that such incest is usually coercive, thus appropriately to be considered as a form of family violence. Comparison of incestuous families with those experiencing other forms of family violence shows that the former are by no means more stressed nor the individuals in them more pathological and that incest victims are no more willing participants than are child victims of nonsexual abuse.

Judith Herman, in Chapter 7, challenges not only the incest taboo but many myths of the family constellation of the incestuous family. She suggests that the family structure represents a pathological exaggeration of generally accepted patriarchal norms and calls for serious attention by mental health professionals to this social problem.

Two additional chapters deal with the sexual abuse of children. David Finkelhor, in Chapter 8, raises important questions for further study in the area of the sexual abuse of boys, a topic that has been quite neglected in the literature. He compares available data with findings from his survey research on the sexual abuse of boys and suggests the incidence is higher than commonly believed, that the perpetrators are usually males and non-family members, and that the abuse, when reported, is more likely to be reported to police than to a hospital or child protective agency. In Chapter 8, Ralph D'Agostino and research staff report the findings of a survey of law enforcement agencies from ten states as to sex crimes against children including the use of children for pornography manufactured in their state, the sale of child pornography, possession of child pornography, child and adolescent prostitution, child sexual assault and law enforcement attitudes concerning appropriate sentences for first offender convicted sexual criminals, the seriousness of sexual crimes and the use of drug therapy on sexual criminals. This survey was conducted after the passage of the 1978 federal statute prohibiting the sexual exploitation of children through pornography. Findings support the high interest in boy as well as girl pornography and prostitution, and the low arrest rates for suspects.

Two chapters deal with high-risk victim populations. In Chapter 10, Ann Wolbert Burgess identifies some of the special problems that can occur when an adolescent is sexually victimized and explores some of the reasons the adolescent is so reluctant to report the rape. In Chapter 11, Eileen E. Rinear argues that both case finding and research efforts be increased in the area of sexual assault of the handicapped victim because of the lack of information for ways to be of assistance to the victim. In Chapter 12, Kersti Yllö and David Finkelhor review the evidence on the incidence of forced sex in marriage. Their chapter reports some initial findings from a study of the victim of forced marital sex including that such incidents seem to occur both in generally violent and in violence-free relationships, often near their end, and that the offender's goal in many instances appears to be to humiliate and retaliate against his wife.

Part Three includes chapters on family response to rape and the response of the criminal justice system. In Chapter 13, Theresa S. Foley reviews the research in the area of family response to rape and the victim, focusing on the beliefs and attitudes of the family that can impact on the victim. Responses that aid the victim as well as those that act as barriers to recovery are discussed. In Chapter 14, Lynda Lytle Holmstrom reviews the research over the past decade in terms of the criminal justice system's reaction to the rape victim specifically for its effect on those victims who report; for its effect on the accused rapists, and for the general statement it makes about the community's stance on rape. In Chapter 15, Lucy Berliner discusses the child and the criminal justice system and the changes that have been made in attitudes, procedures, and policy. She then challenges the basic premise of the legal system which seems to operate in a way which benefits the accused and discounts and traumatizes the child victim.

Part Four discusses the aggressor. Research on sexual aggression has expanded from the traditional psychiatric or pathological model to include sociological, physiological as well as the offender perspectives. Research is also underway on trial strategies and jurors' beliefs in the prosecution of rape cases. In Chapter 16, Robert K. Ressler, Ann Wolbert Burgess and John E. Douglas, writing on rape and murder, analyze one case of an adolescent offender who raped 7 women and raped and murdered 5 additional women when he was seeing both a probation officer and a psychiatrist. The use or relinquishment of violence was found to be dependent on subtle interpersonal factors. In Chapter 17, Robert A. Knight, Ruth Rosenberg and Beth Schneider present an exhaustive review of descriptive studies on sexual offenders that provides the basis for their systematic investigation of typologies of sexual offenders. The aim of their research has been the creation of empirically based typologies that will facilitate investigation into the causes, courses, and prediction of sexual violence, leading, one hopes to differential intervention techniques. In Chapter 18, Diana Scully and

Joseph Marolla critically analyze the psychopathological model and suggest an alternative model in which rape can be examined as a form of extreme, yet normative, male role behavior. Their intent is that the analysis will demonstrate the importance of understanding the inherent biases in any perspective that is allowed to dominate on a social problem. In Chapter 19, Eugene Borgida and Nancy Brekke focus on the prosecution of rape cases and the importance of perceived victim credibility and its role in the prosecution of rape cases and review two approaches to preserving victim rights that seem to affect victim credibility in the courtroom: statutory reform and countering rape myths through the use of expert testimony.

The creation of a new National Center on the Analysis of Violent Crime at the FBI Academy in Quantico, Virginia is reported in Chapter 20 by Robert K. Ressler, Ann Wolbert Burgess, John E. Douglas, and Roger L. Depue. They also outline a research project involving a new investigative tool in law enforcement called "criminal profiling." This technique has been used at the Behavioral Science Unit at the FBI Academy since the early 1970s and assists in focusing an investigation and locating possible suspects in criminal cases.

Chapter 21 by Mark F. Schwartz and William H. Masters reports on a demonstration project designed to measure outcome behaviors following treatment of sex offenders. The Masters and Johnson Treatment model is described in work with paraphiliacs, pedophiles, and incest families. An emphasis is made on the need for follow-up studies of effectiveness of treatment programs.

Part Five includes four chapters addressing media, prevention and the future. In Chapter 22, Judith A. Reisman outlines some of the critical research questions in the area of mass media and civil rights as they relate to the exploitation of children and youth and the relationship of sex and violence. In Chapter 23 Hollis Wheeler presents the feminist perspective on pornography and rape as but one element in a system of violence against women that reflects the larger social system of male dominance and female subordination. Neil M. Malamuth, in Chapter 24, describes findings from a research program on the cultural and individual causes of aggression against women and suggests that the findings shed light on the roots of aggressive acts that come to the attention of legal and mental health agencies. Malamuth also identifies key research areas and emphasizes the important role of the researcher in providing scientific data to assist in efforts to prevent aggression against women. In the final chapter Carolyn Swift observes that although progress and awareness of the problem of rape and sexual assault have occurred, there have been no achievements in reducing the incidence. She suggests the application of primary prevention concepts to rape, reviews activities traditionally cited as preventive for the field, and evaluates research bearing on the effectiveness of these activities.

The first decade of serious research in the field of rape victimology has provided some initial insights as to the victim, the aggressor, and the nature and extent of the crime of rape and sexual assault within a cultural context. As we move toward the twenty-first century, one goal is to reduce the number of victims in an appreciable way. I hope that some of the research findings in this volume will assist in that goal.

This book has profited from the enthusiasm and cooperation of the contributing authors. Not only was the "call for chapters" invitation promptly addressed by the researchers, but within a year the 25 chapters were received from a total of 35 contributors, launching the book into production. From the thoughtful and dedicated work of these contributors rests the hope for the decades to come.

I wish to acknowledge the foresight of former Garland Editor-in-Chief Arthur H. Stickney who originated the idea for a reference volume on rape. I also am appreciative of the conscientious editorial assistance of Julia Johnson of Garland Publishing, Inc.

AWB
Boston

Rape and Sexual Assault

PART I

INTRODUCTION

Two important forces were responsible for bringing the problem of rape to the attention of the United States in the late 1960s. First, primary credit must be given to the women's movement for initiating the consciousness raising groups and then the "speak outs," where women began saying publicly what they had not dared say before about rape.

Second, in response to a rising crime rate and the growing community concern over the problem of rape, Senator Charles Mathias of Maryland introduced a bill in September, 1973, to establish the National Center for the Prevention and Control of Rape. The purpose of this bill was to provide a focal point within the National Institute of Mental Health from which a comprehensive national effort would be undertaken to research, develop programs, and provide information leading to aid for the victims and their families, to rehabilitation of the offenders, and, ultimately, to curtailment of rape crimes. The bill was passed by overwhelming vote in the 93rd Congress, vetoed by President Ford, and successfully reintroduced. The National Center was established through Public Law 94-63 in July, 1975.

CHAPTER 1

THE ANTI-RAPE MOVEMENT Past and Present

Mary Ann Largen

There is a history to the anti-rape movement. This chapter traces the objectives of the women's rights movement and outlines the background of the anti-rape issue, its organizational structure, and its place in the 1980s.

THE PAST

The feminists have been the primary motivating force in focusing national attention on the growing problem of rape and probably the greatest single force in activating other sectors of society ... toward seeking solutions.

June Bundy Csida and Joseph Csida[1]

The developmental history of the anti-rape movement in the
United States occurred within the context of the contemporary women's
rights movement. That movement has undergone a number of births,
phases and rebirths since the beginning of the nineteenth century.
Initially, the movement concerned itself with legal recognition of
women in order to secure their rights to own and control property, to
participate in public affairs, and to vote. The movement in the
twentieth century began by focusing on equal employment, educational
opportunities, and the impact of sexism on women's lives. In particular, the movement objectives of the late 1960s broadened to include
giving women control of their own lives. For a growing number of
feminists, however, this freedom meant more than a choice of nontradi-
tional roles, lifestyles, and jobs; for many it meant confronting restrictions on women's personal lives. Identification and analysis of
these restrictions began to emerge from the dialogue of "consciousness
raising" groups.

Consciousness raising, or CR groups as they were commonly called,
were a major new organizing tool of the women's rights movement in the
late 1960s and involved informal groups of women discussing the problems of being female in modern society. Frequently viewed by the
public as hotbeds of radical feminism, the reality was that simply
attending such a discussion group was the most assertive act many
women of that day were capable of taking. Nonetheless, the issues
emerging from the meetings were far more volatile than those of equal
employment and education. Within the intimate and supportive environment of the CR groups, women found the courage to share private experiences they had never shared before, such as childhood incest and
adolescent and adult rapes.

These disclosures of former victims had a profound effect on
their listeners. The revelations represented an unprecedented breakthrough of the silence which had surrounded the subject of rape for
centuries. Silence, that is, on the part of the victim. The act of
rape, as an inherent part of women's lives throughout recorded history, was described by authors Cathleen Schurr and Nancy Gager as " ...
a theme of poetic dimension as common to literature and art as war."[2]
It was an act which other feminist writers, such as Susan Brownmiller,
linked inextricably with war itself, as well as with race and class
struggles.[3] An act which contemporary society tended to view more
through the mocking eyes of *Playboy* magazine. At best, it was a subject considered too delicate to raise. At worst, a subject which
generated derision, blame, or distrust of the victim. Indeed, the
victim who acknowledged her experience to others risked censure,
scorn, indifference, or loss of credibility.

In the 1970s, victims spoke out publicly for the first time.
The stories they told of verbal abuse and insensitive treatment by
police, doctors, lawyers, and the courts were the same stories sometimes still told today. Yet while public disclosures today may speak
to the same sense of fear and anguish, they are not laden with the
extreme sense of humiliation, isolation, and helplessness which characterized the experience of outspoken victims from 1967 to 1971.

Institutional Response

Throughout the 1970s it became a well documented fact that society and its institutions contributed to the total victimization
experience of rape victims. As early as 1973, a study by a Prince

George's County, Maryland, commission stated:

> "All too often the rape victim is treated at
> best as an object, a piece of evidence, and at
> worst, as a criminal who ... must face the
> incredulity of the police, the impersonality
> of the hospital, and then must defend herself
> in court."[4]

This government report spoke of the psychological impact of
rape, but said little about mental health services because, at that
time, the mental health profession offered nothing specific in the
way of psychological counseling services for the victims of rape.
Concurrently, independent studies were initiated by feminists in the
local chapters of the National Organization for Women in 1972 and
1973. It was indicative of the times that women, be they NOW members
or female county officials, were the driving forces behind the investigative studies. Equally significant, neither the Prince George
county nor later government investigations differed from feminist
groups in their conclusions about the institutional treatment of
rape victims.

The problems identified in the studies included the biased and
indifferent attitudes on the part of health, mental health, and criminal
justice personnel. The studies demonstrated a link between attitudes
and practices; biases and misconceptions permeated these systems and
caused systemic abuses of victims. Though specific criticisms would
vary from jurisdiction to jurisdiction, some were almost universal in
nature. Police disbelief or intimidation of complaining witnesses
was one; indifferent or antagonistic treatment of victims by emergency
room physicians and staff was still another. Also criticized was a
long-standing disregard of the psychological implications of rape by
professional mental health workers. Complaints about criminal laws
designed to persecute, rather than protect, rape victims were voiced
first by feminists and later by government commissions.

Of perhaps greater concern to feminists than to the governmental
study groups was the fact that laws and social systems reflect the
attitudes and biases of the society they serve. Most governmental
commissions viewed the problems primarily in terms of institutional
practices which needed correcting. Feminists, on the other hand,
felt that reforms would be best achieved in conjunction with a positive change in social attitudes toward the crime and its victims.
Such changes would not only garner greater public support for the reforms, but would also translate into greater interpersonal support
for victims within their own family and social circles.

With the CR groups disclosures came a growing awareness of the
oppressive role sexual assault plays in the lives of all women--victims
and potential victims alike. It was recognized how the fear of sexual
assault impinges upon the freedom of movement and lifestyle choices of
women. And, it became clear that the policies and practices of both
the so-called helping systems and the criminal justice systems did
not work for the victimized. This new-found awareness, and the outrage generated by it, spawned what would come to be known as the anti-
rape movement. A movement which, in the beginning, would not be separate from the broader women's rights movement, but would be an adjunct arm of that movement.

The philosophy of the emerging anti-rape movement was but a
simple extension of the philosophy of most women's rights issues.

Generally stated, it was that rape is a universal problem for all
women, not an individual problem for some, and that rape serves a
social and political function in society by keeping women powerless.
The philosophy itself was not controversial within the broad ranks
of the women's movement, but the timing of confronting the issue was.
Publically raising the issue of rape at that precise moment in movement history was viewed with alarm by some feminist leaders. Some
feared that an issue like rape would create an explosive schism between men and women, making it more difficult to achieve the less
controversial legal and social gains being sought. The concern was
not without some basis in fact. Rape was viewed as an act committed
exclusively by men against women, and the issue had already generated
enough mass outrage to demonstrate its potential for divisiveness.
However, it was that very sense of outrage which could not be reined
in by movement leaders.

The mood of the late 1960s was almost prophetically described in
1870 by Susan B. Anthony when she wrote " ... I do pray ... for some
terrific shock to startle the women of this nation into self-respect
which will compel them to see the abject degradation of their present
position."[5] Once the silence which had surrounded rape throughout
the centuries had been broken, the effect which Anthony so desired
could be seen--an effect which was best described by Philadelphia
WAR cofounder, Jody Pinto, in 1973: "We can no longer accept fear as
a way of life. We can no longer accept definitions of rape as sexual
encounters. We are developing a greater community sense of outrage,
and for women this is a wonderful phenomenon. Because, in order to
feel outrage, women must first think well of themselves."[6]

It was a sign of the times that women *were* beginning to think
well of themselves, give vent to their pain and frustrations, and refuse to be reined in by the more cautious and conservative among them.
And, it was against this backdrop of expressionism that anti-rape
organizing activities would begin.

The Radical Feminists

As the more conservative women's rights organizations debated
their own involvement, small groups of feminists--primarily self-
identified "radical feminists"--proceeded to take the initiative.
After months of quiet organizing, the first public activity of any
kind took place in New York City in 1971. Sponsored by the New York
Radical Feminists, the first public "speak out" on rape was held at
St. Clement's Episcopal Church in Manhattan. The speak out attracted
an overflow crowd of more than 300 and a great deal of media and
press attention. Not unexpectedly, the disclosures of the former
victims who had volunteered to tell their stories generated the same
sense of outrage in attendees as had the CR group disclosures. Viewed
as a definite success in terms of both attracting public attention
and recruiting new women for the "cause," that rally became a model
for similar speak outs in months to come.

In addition to speak outs, other actions also began taking place
in 1971. In scattered locations throughout the country, small groups
of women banded together under the name of "Anti-Rape Squads." These
squads dedicated themselves to such activities as public speaking,
teaching self-defense, and conducting "Sisters-Give-Rides-to-Sisters"
campaigns. A few demonstrated their own sense of outrage by such acts

as picketing the homes and workplaces of known or alleged rapists, or by distributing leaflets in areas in which rapes had occurred. Though such tactics were not widely endorsed by most women's groups, they were a source of vicarious enjoyment by all. In a melodramatic way, they were symbolic of the widespread conviction that the system did not work for women, and that women must take care of themselves.

As the sense of outrage and determination characterized the spirit of the early anti-rape movement, so did provocative rhetoric characterize the public image of it. "Disarm the Rapist" became a rallying cry, and "Raped by the Courts" was a classic reference to the criminal justice system. Calls for the publication of a "Who's Who in Sex Offenders" were reported with glee by the public press, while "Rape Is Violence, Not Sex" served to garner both public attention and controversy. The latter slogan would, in addition, prove to be an effective tool for changing public attitudes about the nature of the crime itself. Within a few years the rhetoric ceased, but left in its wake a somewhat extremist image of the movement, an image which probably could not have been avoided under any circumstance. The nature of the issue itself was a provocative one.

The Rape Crisis Centers

Despite this early extremist image of the emerging anti-rape movement, the issue attracted women from all walks of life and political persuasions. The diversity manifested itself most in the strategies selected by individual groups in dealing with the issue. Anti-rape squads continued to flourish in some locales for a few years, but by 1972 new concepts and strategies were beginning to emerge. The first was the creation of the self-help program now widely known as the "rape crisis center."

The first such center in the United States was founded in Berkeley, California, in early 1972. Known as BAWAR, or Bay Area Women Against Rape, the Berkeley center represented the establishment of the first crime victim assistance program in the United States. Within months of the opening of the Berkeley center, similar centers were established in Ann Arbor, Michigan; Washington, D.C.; and Philadelphia, Pennsylvania. By the end of the decade, over 400 centers existed nationwide and, the crisis center model was adopted by women's groups in England and Canada.

The earliest centers were founded primarily by feminists and former rape victims, many of whom were both. Although volunteer ranks tended to include a large number of university students and instructors, they also included many working women and homemakers. The volunteer makeup usually reflected every age, race, socio-economic class, sexual preferences, and level of political consciousness. Volunteers were, however, exclusively women. In essence, many women viewed male involvement in rape crisis centers in much the same way as many blacks viewed white involvement in the civil rights struggles of the 1960s. Among the women themselves, the most common denominators were a commitment to aiding victims and to bringing about social change.

Centers were designed to meet both these goals. They were structured to provide emergency crisis intervention services to rape victims and to provide a programmatic channel through which activists could focus their anti-rape energies. Victim services were designed to meet the objective of the individual and collective strengthening of women, while public education services were designed for the long-term objective of eradicating rape through social change. The administrative structure was that of a volunteer collective in which each member participated fully in decision making. The services, offered free to the community, included hotlines, individual and group counseling, information, and referrals, as well as literature and a speakers' bureau.

Counseling services were based on the premise that the rape victim had undergone a life crisis. Like any life crisis, it could be reconciled and the victim returned to her pre-crisis state. The ensuing disruption in her life, her feelings of vulnerability and loss of control were viewed as normal reactions to the rape experience. Counseling objectives were to assure victims of the normalcy of those reactions and to aid victims in regaining their sense of control. Among the counseling techniques chosen to meet those objectives were the sharing of information about other victims' experiences, and encouraging victims to make their own decisions and take action on their own behalf. The analysis of victim needs and appropriate counseling response was based primarily upon the experiences of former victims. Traditional doctor/patient role models were rejected as perpetuating dependency, and paternalistic attitudes toward victims were firmly rejected as demeaning to women. These traditional mental health crisis intervention techniques were replaced by peer support groups.

It was not until the 1974 publication of *Rape: Victims of Crisis*[7] that any systematic documentation and analysis of the rape trauma syndrome existed. Thus, for the first two years, centers functioned without any research or documentation to validate their conclusions and techniques, a fact which made them suspect in the eyes of many medical and mental health professionals. The 1974 publication not only made center theories and practices more credible, but also contributed to the growing willingness of some medical and mental health professionals to provide their own form of victim services.

Nevertheless, there were still tensions between the public institutions whose traditional role was to provide services to crime victims and the newly emerging rape crisis centers. The centers represented a rejection of public institutions as being unresponsive to the needs of victims. The earliest centers saw themselves euphemistically as "alternatives" to the system, and some carried the idea to an extreme by refusing to interact altogether with public agencies. Most, however, saw themselves simply as advocates within the system. Regardless of what interactive role centers chose to play, their insistence that victims make their own decision about reporting the crime caused them to be labeled "anti-establishment" in the early and even later years.

Public acceptance of rape crisis centers was far easier to achieve than professional acceptance in the early 1970s. The fact that centers were predominantly outside the mainstream of community services did nothing to thwart the increasing numbers of rape victims seeking counseling services, not the increase in victims' families and friends seeking help for themselves. Established primarily to aid adult victims, centers soon found themselves filling in the wide gap which existed in services for victims of incest and molestation. By the end of the decade, many were receiving counseling requests from male sexual assault victims and victims of still other forms of violent crimes. A few even found themselves counseling sex offenders or would-be sex offenders who voluntarily contacted the rape hotlines. Unquestionably, the increase in service demands throughout the 1970s was attributable in part to the success of the centers' community outreach programs. However, it was an even more poignant demonstration of the success of the anti-rape movement in changing public attitudes toward crime generally and toward female victims of crime specifically.

As with their counseling services, the founding centers had no role models for their community education efforts. Yet their innovative attempts to increase public awareness, combat ignorance and misperceptions, and improve the treatment of rape victims proved to be a success in ways both anticipated and unanticipated. They had hoped for success, but were unprepared for it. Thus, by the late 1970s, the ever-increasing demands for personal and community services severely strained their meager resources and threatened the very existence of many.

The founding of rape crisis centers reflected the view of many that public policy on the issue had traditionally followed the prevailing values of the elite, rather than the desires of the masses. Rape crisis centers represented a rejection of elite control over policy on the matter--a rejection which would have serious economic consequences in the years to come. Most centers received little or no support from community social service and criminal justice agencies in their initial operation phases. Most began their operations without a sound financial base; their only true resource being the human resources of their volunteers. It was not, in fact, uncommon in the early 1970s for centers to pay administrative expenses from such traditional fundraising activities as bake sales, or to rely on volunteers to pay their own costs. Churches, YWCAs, or similar community groups could frequently be counted on for free or low-cost housing, although the transiency of these arrangements left many without a permanent facility for many years. Under those conditions, a number of centers existed for only a few years and then disbanded. Most, however, rode out the early years with a dogged persistence almost unheard of for voluntary services similarly situated. While later centers benefitted from the established reputation of founding centers and were able to secure facilities and other resources for their initial operations, few could obtain the financial support necessary to meet the increasing demands for their services. In time, many centers found themselves competing with public agencies for the ever-decreasing social service and criminal justice service dollar. It was an unequal competition against programs which had been created and sustained with a wealth of financial, material, and staffing resources. Attempts to coalesce with these agencies, rather than compete with them, met with little success.

Where criminal justice agencies were concerned, the major barrier to consortiums was primarily ideological. Rape crisis centers, with their conviction that victim needs deserved to be met primarily for humane reasons, ran into conflict with the criminal justice view that victim needs should be met only in proportion to the benefit derived by the criminal justice system. This, in turn, created a conflict between the centers' adherence to counseling techniques that allowed victims to make their own decision about reporting a crime and the criminal justice system's desire for increased reporting. Although some successful coalitions were constructed for purposes of obtaining

federal crime prevention funding, the unwillingness of both entities
to compromise handicapped most coalition attempts.

The centers' view that the health and mental health needs of
victims were the priority needs should have led to more successful
attempts at health and mental health coalitions. However, this was
seldom the case. While centers were, without exception, supportive
of quality medical care for victims, they were frequently critical of
many of the policies and procedures of local emergency rooms. Where
these criticisms were accepted as constructive, successful cooperative
efforts were formed. In some jurisdictions, the local hospital even
became the sponsoring agency of the center. Few hospitals, however,
saw rape treatment as a priority in the face of shrinking public
health dollars. Similarly, community mental health centers rarely
viewed rape services as a priority in comparison to other community
service needs--a factor which led most to offer only minimal services,
or to drop whatever specialized services they had sponsored when funding levels were low. Thus, absorption into the mainstream of community services was never a viable option for rape crisis centers even
had it been universally desired.

Financial Support of Victim Services

Throughout the 1970s, it remained clear that rape was a priority
only to the affected class, victims and their advocates; a group which
rarely had the financial means to provide any significant support for
the services themselves. Without economic support from the served
population, and with minimal, if any, support from public institutions,
many centers sought funding from public donations and private foundations. Such entities, however, with their abysmal track record in
funding women's services, made no exception for rape services. A few
community-based and community-service oriented foundations made small
operational grants available to some centers, but significant financial support was lacking from either major foundations or large public funds. Though delighted to have the services within their communities, the general public in both the 1970s and the 1980s has managed
to maintain a detached view of the problem; rape is generally seen as
representing a problem for others. Even today, private donations constitute a small percentage of crisis center budgets.

Adding to the financial strain that centers were feeling as
early as the mid-1970s was an unusually high volunteer turnover rate.
A major factor in the turnover resulted from volunteer burnout. Crisis intervention is an intense form of service to provide even on a
limited basis and, where the demand is high, counselor burnout tends
to be high also. Complicating the volunteer turnover problem was the
fact that the traditional volunteers of America--i.e., women--were
beginning to enter the workforce in greater numbers, with far less
time for volunteerism. Still another factor was that the centers'
founders were growing older; many of these primary people had been
young (e.g., students) or unemployed (e.g., homemakers). It was inevitable that the demands of new jobs and new parenthood would outweigh the commitment to volunteer services. By the mid-1970s, it became clear that all-volunteer programs were no longer a viable option
for most centers, and the quest for funding was intensified. This
quest ultimately led to great changes in center structures and goals.

In order to become viable candidates for public or private
revenues, most centers were forced to drop their collective structures.

Such a non-traditional, collective decision-making was not viewed as a responsible form of organization by traditional funding agencies. Likewise, many centers were forced to recruit and hire staff whose academic or professional credentials were more acceptable to funding sources. In many cases this meant placing responsibility for rape crisis center administration in the hands of those who knew little or nothing about the issue and did not subscribe to the centers' philosophies. This fact alone contributed to the high volunteer turnover rate.

Over the years, many became almost exclusively oriented to service, rather than to social change. By the end of the decade, rape victim advocacy--as opposed to providing services--became a minor or nonexistent feature of most centers. The pressure to conform to the expectations of funding sources intensified, but even conformity could not bring the desired level of support for most centers. While a growing number of centers obtained small public service contracts from local governments and statewide rape crisis center coalitions secured a place in seven states' budgets, this was too little, too late. Approximately 30 percent of the previous 400 rape crisis centers did not survive the transition from all volunteer to partially staffed programs. Another approximately 25 percent underwent a severe reduction in services, with many becoming merely community hotlines. It was not until the 1981 congressional approval of minimal federal funding for the dying centers that the trend was halted. That federal aid, once again authored by Senator Charles Mathias of Maryland, was the proverbial "shot in the arm" for rape crisis centers nationwide. Grants as small as $5,000 kept many centers from closing, and larger grants helped some retain their range of services without reduction. Perhaps more significant than the money itself was the acknowledgement by government policy makers that rape victims were worthy of public support--an acknowledgement which renewed hope for the future and generated new interest in victim services.

In retrospect, it can be seen that the history of rape crisis centers in the United States has been one of enormous struggle--struggle to overcome apathy, indifference, changing social trends, and lack of stable resources, yet a struggle willingly engaged in from the belief in the rightness of their cause; a cause which, despite the struggles, has had its share of successes. Feminists of over a decade ago clearly identified a social need and a way of responding to it. Centers, begun without role models to adopt, became role models themselves for other women's and other crime victim services. Though never having reached the ultimate goal of eradicating rape through social change, they nonetheless were the instigators of social change essential to the rights of women. Then, as now, they represented a unique and innovative phenomenon in volunteer community services.

National Organization for Women

Rape crisis centers were not alone, however, in achieving social gains in the 1970s. They were but one, albeit the longest lasting, component of what was known as the anti-rape movement. Another, much shorter-lived but nonetheless successful arm of the anti-rape movement was the first major national organizing effort by the National Organization for Women.

Long before the national NOW leadership had given official sanction to NOW's involvement in the issue, many local NOW chapters had been setting up investigative units known as rape task forces. These groups took it upon themselves to document the needs and problems of rape victims in their respective communities. Armed with that documentation, they pressed for changed or new public policies to benefit rape victims. Like the rape crisis centers, NOW groups selected public education as the most effective means of achieving social change; in fact, many NOW chapters worked with other women's groups in founding many of the rape crisis centers themselves. By 1973, grassroots NOW involvement had grown to the extent of forcing national NOW involvement. And so it was that the NOW National Rape Task Force was established by unanimous consent of the 1973 conference body.

The NOW effort was based on many of the same goals and philosophies as the rape crisis center movement. NOW, however, concentrated on the achievement of short-term, rather than long-term, goals. The national NOW role was to aid nationwide organizing efforts through the establishment of the first national communications network, the development of material resources to aid NOW chapter task forces, and the conduct of educational campaigns and other so-called national actions geared toward increasing public awareness and bringing about institutional reforms.

The NOW public image as a conservative or middle-of-the-road feminist organization contributed to its myriad of successes on the rape issue. The press, lawmakers, and government officials tended to take more seriously the actions of an organization with over 90,000 members. And the NOW network, extending beyond United States boundaries, promoted similar organizing efforts in countries such as England, Canada, Australia, Italy, France, Belgium, Ireland, and even South Africa; thus, for a while, fostering an international anti-rape movement.

The ultimate NOW goal was the reform of institutional policies and practices. In this regard, NOW members were encouraged to work cooperatively with public agencies to bring about the improved treatment of rape victims. Academic institutions were encouraged to establish courses to aid in the professional development of those who would later come into contact with rape victims in their work. Strategic and intensive lobby campaigns were conducted for purposes of achieving major reform of the states' criminal statutes. And, where relevant, NOW engaged in support of highly publicized rape trials, such as that of the 1975 Joan Little trial.

By the end of 1976, the NOW national network included more than 300 chapter task forces which had been successful in achieving many of their short-term goals. The wave of criminal code reform begun in 1973 resulted in the achievement of major criminal statute changes in fifty states by the end of the decade. And, perhaps most important to NOW activists, the centuries-old silence which had shrouded the subject had given way to intense public dialogue.

Just as rape crisis centers provided a model for women's services, NOW task forces provided a model for several hundred governmental task forces set up to achieve many of the same reforms that NOW sought. Attention to the problem of rape initially produced a federal rape research unit under the auspices of the National Institute of Mental Health. In 1976, it also led to changes in federal rules of evidence similar to those enacted by the states.

The late 1970s saw the founding of still a second nationwide
organizing effort on the rape issue. With NOW dropping all task
force support to concentrate on passage of the Equal Rights Amendment,
a gap in nationwide communications existed from 1974 to 1977. Rape
crisis centers, then constituting the last vestiges of the anti-rape
movement, had never had an independent national network of their own.
Many had belonged to the NOW network which no longer existed; some
subsequently joined the new National Organization for Victim Assistance (NOVA). Neither network, however, had met the centers' total
professional development needs. And, at a time when the federal government was funding research, instead of services, the financial
struggles left them feeling vulnerable and isolated from each other.

National Coalition Against Sexual Assault

The decision to bridge this gap occurred at the 1977 NOVA conference in St. Paul, Minnesota. There, an ad hoc committee of rape crisis center representatives formed in order to create a new national
structure for centers. This association, called the National Coalition Against Sexual Assault (NCASA) held its first conference at Lake
Geneva, Wisconsin, in 1978. The conference attracted attendees from
centers in over thirty states—most of whom came from centers still
too poor even to finance their trips. Still they came; the desire of
meeting with others to share information and moral support outweighed
all other considerations. Once there, many of the old tensions between activists, researchers, and "helping" professionals resurfaced.
Similarly, tensions arose between activists who wanted to maintain
the rigid political stance of the past and those who desired more
flexibility in dealing with current problems. Yet, despite the shaky
beginning, the Coalition concept was a success. By 1983, the NCASA
membership included more than 300 centers and an assortment of individuals dedicated to rape crisis advocacy.

THE PRESENT

The anti-rape movement of the past decade no longer exists if
defined as a series of organized activities by people working con-
certedly toward the same goal. Coalitions of community activists
still exist or sporadically organize in response to some event but no
national effort with a specific, short-term focus has arisen to replicate the 1970s NOW effort. Rape crisis centers remain, but many are
largely changed today. A few still exist which see their mission as
including social change or victim advocacy in the old sense of the
word, but most are content to focus on providing quality services to
victims and their communities. This latter focus has led to better
services in most communities and created a more mainstream public
image of rape crisis centers. However, many of the problems of the
past remain unsolved; while renewed interest in victim services has
revived many languishing centers, little momentum in the nationwide
development of more centers has been seen.
This lack of new centers is unquestionable related to the
general decline of volunteer community services over the past decade
and the special difficulties of running community crisis intervention
services with little funding. And, while public agencies are increasingly willing to move into the service fields of family violence

and child victimization, the sexual abuse of adult women remains a
priority concern only to those affected.

Nevertheless, the activities of the former anti-rape movement
have generated greater interest in many aspects of the problem by a
wide range of social service providers, researchers, and criminal
justice systems. Most visible is the proliferation of professional
training and academic coursework which has continued into the 1980s.
Equally encouraging has been the founding of NCASA. At a time when
problems such as press release of victims' names and addresses, the
refusal of emergency room physicians to do evidentiary examinations,
and the jailing of rape crisis center counselors for refusing to release confidential victim information are beginning to resurface,
centers are in need of a strong support network. As an advocate for
rape crisis centers, NCASA can provide not only that network, but
also a new means for influencing public policy.

NCASA has already shown itself to be successful in the latter
endeavor. In 1981, NCASA's four-year effort to achieve federal funding for centers succeeded. In 1982, the organization supported successful congressional legislation designed to sensitize the federal
criminal justice system to victims' rights and needs, provide more
legal protection from harassment and intimidation of witnesses, and
provide a model for similar state legislation. In 1983, it worked
to secure legislation to create a federal Crime Victim Assistance
Fund and participated in a drive to protect the confidentiality of
clients of rape and domestic violence services.

Such successes do, of course, represent aid for crime victims,
rather than an end to crime itself. However, they reflect a dramatic
change in the way the public and public lawmakers view the victims of
crime. For rape victims, it is a far cry from the prejudice and indifference of no more than a decade ago. The 1970s anti-rape activists deeply wanted society to acknowledge its own role and responsibility for the victimization of women. In many ways, that acknowledgement is beginning to be seen in this decade. Social change is
occurring. Not in the bold, dramatic way of the 1970s, but in a more
subtle way. Change which, regardless of its external appearance,
would not have occurred without the phenomenon known as the anti-rape
movement.

The history of the anti-rape movement in the United States is
one replete with the courage and sacrifice of women working alone
and together. It is a history equally replete with struggle and
accomplishments. Today, the face of the movement, like the face of
rape crisis centers, has largely changed. The makeup of the movement
now includes more men, more activist professionals, and more minorities than at any point in its previous history. Its members are more
sophisticated in the art of public policy making and enjoy the dedicated support of many public legislators and administrators. As a
social change movement, it is more entrenched in maintaining past
gains than seeking new ones, but more determined to survive than
ever. What shape or form that survival will take remains to be seen.
Yet, whatever the future might bring, one fact remains certain: most
individuals whose lives have been touched in some way by the movement tend to carry their new awareness into all facets of their later
years. Ultimately, that individual and collective awareness may
prove to be the most incontrovertible social change of all.

REFERENCES

1. Csida, J.B. and J. Csida. *Rape: How to Avoid It and What to do If You Can't.* Chatsworth, California: Books for Better Living, 1974.

2. Schurr, C., and N. Gager. *Sexual Assault: Confronting Rape in America.* New York: Grossett and Dunlap, 1976.

3. Brownmiller, S. *Against Our Will: Men, Women and Rape.* New York: Simon and Schuster, 1975.

4. County Council of Prince George's County, Maryland. *Report of the Task Force to Study the Treatment of Victims of Sexual Assault.* March, 1973.

5. Anthony, S.B. From a letter to a friend, Summer, 1870.

6. Pinto, J. *Introduction to Rape.* New Canaan, Connecticut: Tobey Publishing Co., 1974.

7. Burgess, A.W., and L. L. Holmstrom. *Rape: Victims of Crisis.* Bowie, Maryland: Brady Company, 1974.

CHAPTER 2

THE NATIONAL CENTER FOR THE PREVENTION AND CONTROL OF RAPE

A Federal Research Agenda

Mary Hanemann Lystad

The National Center for the Prevention and Control of Rape (NCPCR) is the focal point in the National Institute of Mental Health (NIMH) for research, training, and public education activities in the area of rape and sexual assault of children and adults. Section 231 of Public Law 94-63 established NCPCR within NIMH in 1975 in recognition of rape and sexual assault as serious crimes resulting in severe emotional trauma and other mental health consequences for victims, their families, and their communities. In 1980, section 601 of Public Law 96-398 renewed the original authority of the Center and, in 1981, the authority was further amended by section 902 of Public Law 97-35 (42 U.S.C. 9511). The legal mandate of the Center has always included knowledge building and knowledge transfer. It has never included funding of services to victims of sexual assault, which is now provided to states directly under separate legislation.

The NCPCR initiated in April, 1976, supports research on the causes of rape and sexual assault, mental health consequences of such acts of violence, treatment of victims and offenders, and effectiveness of programs designed to prevent and reduce such assaults. Broad research priority areas were derived from the law which created the Center. Specific research questions within these areas were arrived at through careful review of the field by staff and through continuing consultation of staff with the National Rape Prevention and Control Advisory Committee.

Placement of NCPCR within the context of a large research funding organization, NIMH, was advantageous for its research program in several ways:

> --It permitted Center staff to consult with other NIMH staff knowledgeable about social problems, women's issues, and health/mental health care.

> --It permitted Center use of the larger National Clearing-house of Mental Health Information of NIMH. This Clearinghouse, established in 1963, is the focal point in this country for the collection, storage, retrieval, and dissemination of scientific information in areas of mental health concerns. Mental health information collected for the Clearinghouse files is abstracted from world wide sources, and about 35,000 abstracts are added to the files annually.

> --Through the NIMH review mechanism, it permitted impartial critique of grant applications by specialists in this field.

Because of its mandate to disseminate knowledge as well as to collect information on the problem of sexual assault, NCPCR has been one of the most active units within NIMH for publication and dissemination of relevant research findings. The Center disseminates not only its own final research reports but also a host of other research reports in the area of sexual assault.

NCPCR RELATIONSHIPS TO OTHER GROUPS
CONCERNED WITH SEXUAL ASSAULT

The NCPCR has from the beginning maintained long-term relationships with other groups concerned about the problems of rape and sexual assault and about the need for services to assist victims and to treat offenders. In the last few years, the staff has engaged in the following educational activities with other organizations, making use of their own and other research findings:

--Staff consulted with the Indian Health Service, Department of Health and Human Services, in terms of their revisions of Indian Health Service policy regarding treatment and examination of victims of criminal sexual assault.

--The Center helped to develop resource materials for the Department of the Army's worldwide rape prevention campaign, which took place in 1981. This campaign used a multi-media approach including radio, posters, and articles in military publications. Also in consultation with the NCPCR, the Armed Forces Information Service produced a series of radio and television public service announcements regarding myths about sexual assault and sexual offenders; these are still broadcast to all active-duty military and their families overseas.

--The Center provided the Bureau of Medicine and Surgery of the National Naval Medical Center a copy of its training film, "Rape--Caring for the Adult Female Victim," which the Navy has reproduced in video cassette form for distribution to naval medical centers throughout the country.

--The Center works with community mental health centers by responding to their requests for information about sexual assault, the extent of the problem, and mental health consequences.

--The Center is sharing prevention/intervention materials and technological approaches with the American Red Cross, which plays a major role in crisis intervention from the private sector.

--Center staff as well as Advisory Committee staff actively collaborate with other related community agencies: the National Organization for Victim Assistance (NOVA), the National Coalition Against Sexual Assault (NCASA), and the American Bar Association's Victim's Rights Committee.

The National Rape Prevention and Control Advisory Committee is composed of distinguished researchers, service workers, and educators in the area of sexual assault. Members serve for a three-year term; by law the majority of members are women. Those persons who have served, or are serving now, on this Committee are as follows:

Anthony M. Alcocer, Ph.D.
California State University
Northridge, California 91231

Linda Anderson
Field Representative
National Congressional Club
Statesville, North Carolina 28677

Marilyn Tyler Brown, Ed.D.
Assistant Superintendent for
  Student Services
District of Columbia Public
  Schools
Washington, D.C. 20012

Ann Wolbert Burgess, D.N.Sc.
Boston City Hospital
Boston, Massachusetts, 02118

Phyllis Old Dog Cross, R.N., M.S.
Regional Mental Health Program
Indian Health Service
Rapid City, South Dakota 57701

A. Nicholas Groth, Ph.D.
Director, Sex Offender Program
Connecticut Correctional Institute
Somers, Connecticut 06071

William Heiman, J.D.
Assistant District Attorney
Chief, Rape Unit
Philadelphia District Attorney's
  Office
Philadelphia, Pennsylvania 19104

Mary Ann Largen
Consultant, Center for Women Policy
Washington, D.C. 20036

Magdalena Lona-Wiant
Field Representative
Office of State Senator Alex P.
  Garcia
Los Angeles, California 90012

George J. McCall, Ph.D.
Department of Sociology
University of Missouri
St. Louis, Missouri 63121

Florence McClure
Director
Community Action Against Rape
Las Vegas, Nevada 89101

Mary Ann Montgomery, M.D.
Barnes Hospital
St. Louis, Missouri 63130

Neal Peden
Director, Administrative Services
Republican National Committee
Alexandria, Virginia 22314

Jane Robinson
Director
Division of Consumer Services
Department of Agriculture
Tallahassee, Floria 32304

Loretta M. Ropella, M.S.W.
School of Social Welfare
University of Wisconsin-Milwaukee
Milwaukee, Wisconsin 53201

Jose Santiago, M.D.
Department of Psychiatry
Kino Community Hospital
Tucson, Arizona 85713

Frances F. Saunders
Staff Associate
National Center for Health Educa-
  tion
San Francisco, California 94108

Joanne W. Sterling, Ph.D.
Director, Bernalillo County
  Mental Health/Mental Retardation
  Center
University of New Mexico School of
  Medicine
Albuquerque, New Mexico 87106

RESEARCH PRIORITIES

The research program of NCPCR is best described by the research program notice of the Center, which is distributed widely to researchers in academic and service settings. This notice runs, in part, as follows:

"The Center supports research on the causes of rape and sexual assault, mental health consequences of such acts of violence, treatment of victims and offenders, and effectiveness of programs designed to prevent and reduce such assaults. In order to be accepted for review, applications must: 1) Propose a clearly discernable research activity, involving hypotheses generation, testing, or other bases for generalizability; 2) Articulate clear and direct relevance to the mental health of victims and/or offenders, their families or significant others, or to populations distinctively at high risk of sexual assault; 3) Substantiate the risk with literature references or data on vulnerability if dealing with populations at high risk. Service programs and/or demonstrations are not supported.

"Within this context, the Center is concerned with projects with substantive emphasis in any one or more of the following five areas:

1. Research on the Causes of and Factors that Encourage Rape and Sexual Assault.
   a) Studies of incidence and prevalence in different population subgroups in order to establish differential risk.
   b) Studies of psychosocial and/or biological factors antecedent to rape or sexual assault.
   c) Studies of specific causes and conditions leading to rape and sexual assault in environments where populations are at high risk; for example in residential settings such as mental hospitals, prisons, and other like institutions.

2. Research on the Mental Health Implications of Rape and Sexual Assault for Victims of All Ages and Their Significant Others.
   a) Studies of both the immediate and long-term mental health impact of rape and sexual assault.
   b) Studies of the mental health effects of extreme fear of rape.
   c) Studies of the mental health consequences of treatment of victims by such entities as hospitals, police, and courts.
   d) Studies of differential mental health sequelae in population subgroups.

3. Research on the Designing, Implementation, and Evaluation of Mental Health Service and Treatment.
   a) Studies of both crisis and long-term care mental health treatment and service delivery modes for victims of all ages and/or their significant others.
   b) Studies of mental health treatment and service delivery modes for offenders and/or their significant others.
   c) Studies of integrative services among mental health, social, and/or legal agencies dealing with victims and offenders in cases of rape and sexual assault.

4. Research on Prevention of Rape and Sexual Assault and on Intervention in Mental Health Problems of Sexual Assault.
   a) Studies of strategies and interventions--focused on interpersonal situations and/or institutional arrangements-- for preventing rape or sexual assault. Such research must focus on populations where there is documented evidence of high risk and must have appropriate knowledge base.
   b) Studies of interventions for reducing or ameliorating emotional trauma and long-term consequences of rape and sexual assault.
   c) Studies of ways to identify and intervene with potential offenders and potential repeaters.

5. Research on Methodologies and/or Techniques Required to
   Advance Research in the Above Areas.

"Unless explicitly focused on mental illness or mental health, the Center does not support studies of security arrangements, safety programs, the criminal justice system, the legal system, the media, sex roles/relationships, cultural values, and other general social factors that may influence rape."

THE RESEARCH PORTFOLIO OF THE CENTER,
AS RELATED TO RESEARCH PRIORITY AREAS

Research on the causes of and factors that encourage rape and sexual assault:

RO1 MH27928
Project Period: 6/15/76-6/30/79
"Rape: The Public View--The
  Personal Experience"
Department of Sociology
Trinity University
715 Stadium Drive
San Antonio, Texas 78284
Principal Investigator: Joyce E.
  Williams

RO1 MH28868
Project Period: 9/20/76-2/28/79
"Forcible Rape in England and
  Sweden"
Program in Social Ecology
University of California at Irvine
Irvine, California 92717
Principal Investigator: Gilbert
  Geis

RO1 MH 28960
Project Period: 6/21/76-3/31/79
"The Prevalence of Rape and
  Sexual Assault"
Scientific Analysis Corporation
2408 Lombard Street
San Francisco, California 94123
Principal Investigator: Diana E.
  H. Russell

RO1 MH28978
Project Period: 6/21/76-3/31/79
"The Socio-Cultural Context of
  Rape: A Cross-Cultural Analysis"
Department of Anthropology
University of Pennsylvania
3451 Walnut Street, Franklin
  Building
Philadelphia, Pennsylvania 19174
Principal Investigator: Peggy R.
  Sanday

RO1 MH29023
Project Period: 6/25/76-6/30/78
"Attitudes Supportive of Rape in
  American Culture"
Minnesota Center for Social Re-
  search
University of Minnesota
1114 Social Science Tower
Minneapolis, Minnesota 55455
Principal Investigator: Martha
  R. Burt

RO1 MH29620
Project Period: 4/1/77-8/31/81
"Attitudes Toward Rape and
  Adaptive Behaviors"
Northwestern University
Center for Urban Affairs
2040 Sheridan Road
Evanston, Illinois 60201
Principal Investigators: Margaret
  T. Gordon and Stephanie Riger

RO1 MH30193
Project Period: 9/29/77-10/31/80
"Psychological Factors in
  Battered Women"
Department of Psychology
University of Pittsburgh
Pittsburgh, Pennsylvania 15260
Principal Investigator: Irene
  H. Frieze

RO1 MH30620
Project Period: 4/1/78-6/30/80
"Evaluation of Outreach to
  Minorities"
YWCA Sexual Assault Crisis Service
135 Broad Street
Hartford, Connecticut 06105
Principal Investigator: Donna
  Landerman

RO1 MH30655
Project Period: 9/29/77-6/30/81
"Non-Stranger Rape: The Role of
Sexual Socialization"
Department of Psychology
University of California at Los
Angeles
Los Angeles, California 90024
Principal Investigator:
Jacqueline D. Goodchilds

RO1 MH30702
Project Period: 7/15/78-9/30/80
"Perception of Rape: Influences
on Casual Attributions"
Department of Psychology
University of North Carolina
Charlotte, North Carolina 28223
Principal Investigator: James W.
Selby, III

RO1 MH30720
Project Period: 6/1/78-2/28/81
"Expressed Attitudes About Rape:
Preliminary Study"
Neuropsychiatric Institute
University of California at Los
Angeles
760 Westwood Plaza
Los Angeles, California 90024
Principal Investigators: Linda
Bourque and Joshia S. Golden

RO1 MH30939
Project Period: 5/1/78-7/31/80
"Incest and Family Sexual Abuse"
Department of Sociology
University of New Hampshire
Durham, New Hampshire 03824
Principal Investigators: Murray
Straus and David Finkelhor

RO1 MH31618
Project Period: 9/25/78-2/28/81
"Hidden Rape on a University
Campus"
Department of Psychology
Kent State University
Kent, Ohio 44242
Principal Investigator: Mary P.
Koss

RO1 MH31751
Project Proposal: 7/1/78-1/31/83
"Sexual Assault Among Adolescents:
A National Survey"

Behavioral Research Institute
2305 Canyon Boulevard
Boulder, Colorado 80302
Principal Investigator: Suzanne
S. Ageton

RO1 MH32309
Project Period: 4/1/80-3/31/83
"Subtyping of Sexual Offenders"
Department of Psychology
Brandeis University
Waltham, Massachusetts 02154
Principal Investigator: Raymond
A. Knight

RO1 MH32970
Project Period: 9/1/79-8/31/81
"Sex and Sexual Violence in Fic-
tion: Content and Control"
Department of Sociology
American University
Washington, D.C. 20016
Principal Investigator: Muriel
G. Cantor

RO1 MH33013
Project Period: 9/1/80-2/28/83
"Incarcerated Rapists: Exploring
a Sociological Model"
Department of Sociology/Anthro-
pology
Virginia Commonwealth University
820 West Franklin Street
Richmond, Virginia 23284
Principal Investigators: Diana H.
Scully and Joseph Marolla

RO1 MH33264
Project Period: 7/1/79-6/30/82
"Sexual and Family Violence: An
Historical Case Study"
Department of History
University of Massachusetts
Boston, Massachusetts 02125
Principal Investigator: Linda
Gordon

RO1 MH34430
Project Period: 5/1/81-4/30/82
"Sexual Aggression: Constructing
a Predictive Equation"
Clarke Institute of Psychiatry
250 College Street
Toronto, Ontario, Canada
Principal Investigator: Ronald A.
Langevin

R01 MH35733
Project Period: 2/1/82-1/31/84
"Rape of Confined Mental Patients:
  A Sociological Study"
Institute for the Study of Sexual
  Assault
401 Ashbury Street
San Francisco, California 94117
Principal Investigator: Camille
  LeGrand

R01 MH36629
Project Period: 9/30/81-8/31/84
"The Rapist: Social Background
  and Criminal Career"
National Council on Crime and
  Delinquency
411 Hackensack
Hackensack, New Jersey 07601
Principal Investigator: James
  L. Galvin

Research on the mental health implications of rape and sexual assault:

R01 MH27830
Project Period: 2/1/76-5/31/79
"Rape Reporting: Causes and Con-
  sequences"
Department of Psychology
University of Washington
Seattle, Washington 98195
Principal Investigator: Shirley
  A. Feldman-Summers

R03 MH29406
Project Period: 5/1/77-4/30/78
"Father-Daughter Incest: A Clini-
  cal Study"
Research for Social Change
1010 Wisconsin Avenue, N.W.
Washington, D.C. 20007
Principal Investigators: Judith
  L. Herman and Lisa Hirschman

R01 MH29713
Project Period: 8/15/77-6/30/80
"Rape Impact and Treatment of
  Victims and Families"
Hennepin County Medical Center
701 Park Avenue
Minneapolis, Minnesota 55415
Principal Investigator: Linda E.
  Ledray

R01 MH29727
Project Period: 3/1/78-12/31/80
"Structural Analysis of Jurors'
  Verdicts of Rape Trials"
Department of Sociology
Indiana University
Bloomington, Indiana 47401
Principal Investigator: Barbara
  F. Reskin

R01 MH29750
Project Period: 9/29/77-7/31/81

"Rape-Induced Depression: Inci-
  dence and Treatment"
Psychology Department
University of Georgia
Athens, Georgia 30602
Principal Investigator: Karen S.
  Calhoun

R01 MH29968
Project Period: 9/29/77-8/31/82
"Entrance into Juvenile Prostitu-
  tion"
Department of Psychiatry and Be-
  havioral Sciences
University of Washington
Seattle, Washington 98195
Principal Investigator: Jennifer
  James

R18 MH30315
Project Period: 7/1/77-6/30/79
"An Examination of Critical Process
  and Outcome Factors in Rape"
University of Pittsburgh
School of Social Work
2209 Cathedral of Learning
Pittsburgh, Pennsylvania 15260
Principal Investigator: Barbara
  K. Shore

R01 MH31711
Project Period: 7/1/78-6/30/82
"The Attrition-of-Justice Phenome-
  non in the Processing of Rape/
  Sexual Assault Cases"
Department of Sociology
Southern Methodist University
Dallas, Texas 75275
Principal Investigators: Vicki
  McNickle Rose and Susan Carol
  Randall

RO1 MH32761
Project Period: 7/1/79-6/30/81
"A Cross-Jurisdictional Analysis
  of the Prosecution of Rape
  Cases"
Institute of Law and Social
  Research
1125 15th Street, N.W., Suite 625
Washington, D.C. 20005
Principal Investigator: Toni Clark

RO1 MH33216
Project Period: 7/1/79-6/30/81
"Sequelae of Chemical-Involved
  Sexual Assault"
Sexual Assault Center
325 Ninth Avenue
Seattle, Washington 98104
Principal Investigator: Doris
  Stevens

RO3 MH33402
Project Period: 8/1/79-7/31/81
"Rape Victims' Behavioral/Charac-
  terological Self-Blame"
Department of Psychology
University of Massachusetts
Amherst, Massachusetts 01003
Principal Investigator: Ronnie
  Janoff-Bulman

RO1 MH33603
Project Period: 1/1/83-12/3/83
"Experiences of Afro-American
  Women"
University of California, School
  of Medicine
Neuropsychiatric Institute
405 Hilgard Avenue
Los Angeles, California 90024
Principal Investigator: Gail E.
  Wyatt

RO1 MH37102
Project Period: 9/28/82-8/31/83
"Victim Reaction to Marital Rape
  and Battering"
Policy Research and Planning
  Group
8250 Glen Echo Drive
St. Louis, Missouri 63121
Principal Investigator: Nancy M.
  Shields

Research on the design, implementation, and evaluation of mental
health services and treatment:

RO1 MH28969
Project Period: 6/25/76-6/30/79
"Alternative Interventions of
  Sexual Assault Victims"
University of Washington,
Harborview Medical Center
Seattle, Washington 98104
Principal Investigators: Karil S.
  Klingbeil and Doris Stevens

RO1 MH28975
Project Period: 6/25/76-6/30/79
"Marital Counseling for Rape
  Victims"
Marriage Council of Philadelphia,
  Inc.
4025 Chestnut Street
Philadelphia, Pennsylvania 19104
Principal Investigator: William
  R. Miller

R18 MH28990
Project Period: 6/25/76-8/30/78
"Evaluation of Outreach and
  Companion Effectiveness"
Rape Crisis Center of Raleigh
P.O. Box 5223
Raleigh, North Carolina 27607
Principal Investigator: Virginia
  G. Cogwell

R18 MH28996
Project Period: 6/28/76-1/31/79
"Evaluation of a New Community
  Rape Treatment Center"
Family Hospital
2711 West Wells Street
Milwaukee, Wisconsin 53208
Principal Investigator: Conrad
  L. Sobczak

R18 MH29019
Project Period: 6/25/76-7/30/77
"Rape Education to Care-Givers
  in Three Rural Counties"
Community Mental Health Center,
  Inc.
3375 U.S. Route 60 East
Huntington, West Virginia 25705
Principal Investigator: Nancy
  Matthews

R18 MH29022
Project Period: 6/28/76-9/30/77
"Evaluation of Rape Crisis Train-
  ing and Education"
YWCA of the Hartford Region, Inc.
135 Broad Street
Hartford, Connecticut 06105
Principal Investigator: Elizabeth
  Karl

R18 MH29025
Project Period: 6/25/76-6/30/78
"Rape Response: A Research-
  Demonstration Project"
Cedars-Sinai Medical Center
8720 Beverly Boulevard, Box 48750
Los Angeles, California 90048
Principal Investigator: Susan
  Brown

R18 MH29308
Project Period: 6/25/76-9/30/78
"Community Rape Prevention
  Project"
Didi Hirsch Community Mental
  Health Center
4760 South Sepulveda Boulevard
Culver City, California 90230
Principal Investigator: Vivian
  B. Brown

RO1 MH29602
Project Period: 4/1/77-11/30/82
"Treatment of Fear and Anxiety
  in Victims of Rape"
Medical University of South
  Carolina
171 Ashley Avenue
Charleston, South Carolina 29401
Principal Investigators: Dean G.
  Kilpatrick, Lois J. Veronen,
  and Patricia A. Resick

RO1 MH29692
Project Period: 4/1/76-5/31/85
"The Rape Victim: Her Response
  and Treatment"
Western Psychiatric Institute
3811 O'Hara Street
Pittsburgh, Pennsylvania 15261
Principal Investigators: Ellen
  Frank and Samuel M. Turner

RO1 MH31259
Project Period: 7/1/78-3/31/81
"Institutionalized Rape Inter-
  vention Project"
Kansas City Police Department
Kansas City, Missouri 64106
Principal Investigator: Jeanie
  K. Meyer

RO1 MH32669
Project Period: 5/1/79-3/31/81
"Evaluating Sex Offender Treat-
  ment Programs"
Evaluation Research Group, Inc.
Lane Building, Suite #201
474 Willamette Street
Eugene, Oregon 97401
Principal Investigator: Mark
  Weinrott

RO1 MH32782
Project Period: 9/1/79-2/28/82
"Sexual Assault of Prostitutes"
Delancey Street Foundation, Inc.
2563 Divisadero Street
San Francisco, California 94115
Principal Investigator: Mimi H.
  Silbert

RO1 MH32841
Project Period: 9/1/78-3/31/80
"The Evaluation and Treatment of
  Sexual Aggressiveness"
New York State Psychiatric Insti-
  tute
722 West 168th Street
New York, New York 10032
Principal Investigator: Gene G.
  Abel

RO1 MH32982
Project Period: 9/25/79-1/31/82
"Sexual Dysfunctions in Rape
  Victims"

School of Medicine
Columbia University
722 W. 168th Street
New York, New York 10032
Principal Investigator: Judith
  V. Becker

R18 MH33068
Project Period: 8/1/79-8/31/82
"R & D Center for Rape Prevention
  and Treatment"
Didi Hirsch Community Mental
  Health Center

4760 South Sepulveda Boulevard
Culver City, California 90230
Principal Investigator: Vivian
  B. Brown

R18 MH34835
Project Period: 6/1/81-5/31/83
"Assessing the Impact of Rape
  Victim Support Programs"
Urban Institute
2100 M Street, N.W.
Washington, D.C. 20037
Principal Investigators: Martha
  R. Burt and Karen Pittman

Research on prevention of rape and sexual assault and on intervention
in mental health problems of sexual assault:

RO2 MH25121
Project Period: 2/1/77-3/31/78
"Adoption of New Knowledge in
  Mental Health Services"
American Institutes of Research
P.O. Box 1113
Palo Alto, California 94302
Principal Investigator: Judith
  K. Larsen

R18 MH29003
Project Period: 6/25/76-6/30/78
"Rape Consultation and Education
  Research Grant"
Northern Arizona Comprehensive
  Guidance Center, Inc.
611 North Leroux
Flagstaff, Arizona 86001
Principal Investigator: Maurice
  W. Miller

R18 MH29038
Project Period: 6/25/76-9/30/79
"Consultation in the Area of
  Sexual Child Abuse"
Wyandotte County Mental Health
  and Guidance Center, Inc.
Eaton at 36th
Kansas City, Kansas 66103
Principal Investigator: Carolyn
  F. Swift

RO1 MH29045
Project Period: 9/29/76-10/31/79
"Victim Response to Rape:
  Alternative Outcomes"

Bureau of Social Science Research,
  Inc.
1990 M. Street, N.W., Suite 700
Washington, D.C. 20036
Principal Investigator: Jennie
  McIntyre

R18 MH29049
Project Period: 6/28/76-8/31/80
"Community Action Strategies to
  Stop Rape"
Women's Action Collective, Inc.
East Woodruff Avenue
Columbus, Ohio 43201
Principal Investigator: Caroline
  H. Sparks

R18 MH29260
Project Period: 6/28/76-8/31/78
"Consultation/Education Demonstra-
  tion on Rape Services"
Region Seven Mental Health/Mental
  Retardation Commission
P.O. Box 1567
Starkville, Mississippi 39759
Principal Investigator: John R.
  Hutcherson

RO1 MH29311
Project Period: 9/20/76-8/31/79
"Avoiding Rape: A Study of Victims
  and Avoiders"
University of Illinois Medical
  Center
Chicago, Illinois 60680
Principal Investigator: Pauline
  B. Bart

RO1 MH29532
Project Period: 7/1/77-12/31/79
"Law Reform in the Prevention
and Treatment of Rape"
Institute for Social Change
University of Michigan
Ann Arbor, Michigan 48109
Principal Investigator: Nathan
Caplan

RO1 MH29762
Project Period: 7/15/77-12/31/78
"Study and Prevention of Sexual
Assault in Jails"
Center for Homosexual Education
Evaluation and Research
San Francisco State University
San Francisco, California 94132
Principal Investigator: John P.
DeCecco

RO1 MH30724
Project Period: 9/29/77-7/1/80
"Evidence in Rape Trials: A
Socio-Legal Analysis"
Department of Psychology
University of Minnesota
Minneapolis, Minnesota 55455
Principal Investigator: Eugene
Borgida

RO1 MH32677
Project Period: 6/1/79-5/31/81
"Rape Case Processing: Evaluation
of Legal Reform"
Social Science Research Institute
University of Southern California
Los Angeles, California 90007
Principal Investigator: Mary B.
Deming

RO1 MH34109
Project Period: 8/1/80-1/31/83
"Parents' Attitudes and Responses
to Sexual Abuse"
Department of Sociology and
Anthropology
University of New Hampshire
Durham, New Hampshire 03824
Principal Investigator: David
S. Finkelhor

RO1 MH37133
Project Period: 6/1/82-5/31/85
"The Impact of Sexual Abuse on
Children"
School of Social Service Adminis-
tration
University of Chicago
969 East 60th Street
Chicago, Illinois 60637
Principal Investigator: Jon R.
Conte

R18 MH37549
Project Period: 9/29/82-8/31/85
"Prevention of Sexual Victimiza-
tion"
Worcester Area Community Mental
Health Center, Inc.
162 Chandler Street
Worcester, Massachusetts 01609
Principal Investigator: Michael
C. Klein

T31 MH15664
Project Period: 7/1/83-7/30/80
North Carolina Rape Crisis Associ-
ation
Chapel Hill, North Carolina 17514
Principal Investigator: Debra Kay

T31 MH16760
Project Period: 7/1/82-6/30/84
Children's Hospital
National Medical Center
Washington, D.C.
Principal Investigator: Joyce
Thomas

HIGHLIGHTS OF RECENT RESEARCH FINDINGS

Following are research findings on the causes of and factors that
encourage rape and sexual assault, the mental health consequences of
sexual assault, evaluation of mental health sources and treatment,
and prevention measures for avoidance of assault.
Causes of Abuse

Straus and Finkelhor, researchers at the University of New Hampshire, collected data on incest cases from students at six colleges
and universities in the New England area. [3], [12] The goal of the project ("Incest and Family Sexual Abuse," MH30939) was to obtain information about the causes of family sexual abuse, its incidence, and
the nature of the problem. It was anticipated that such information
would be important in drawing attention to the problem of sexual
abuse and in formulating public policy for dealing with the problem
and preventing its occurrence in the future.

Using a broad definition of "sexual experience" to include experiences that range from any instance in which a child was kissed,
hugged, or fondled in a sexual way by an older person to instances of
actual intercourse, some of the major conclusions of the study are as
follows:

> --A large number of children have had childhood sexual ex-
> periences with adults. Of the student population surveyed,
> 19 percent of the women and 9 percent of the men revealed
> such experiences.
> --A majority of the sexual experiences were with older persons
> who were well known to the child victims, and in the case
> of girls, nearly one-half were with older family members.
> --Almost all of the childhood sexual experiences were not re-
> vealed when they occurred.
> --The aspect of the experience most likely to result in
> trauma for the child was whether or not force was used by
> the offender.
> --Girls from lower socioeconomic groups and girls with step-
> fathers were more vulnerable to sexual victimization. Other
> factors which placed a child at greater risk of abuse in-
> cluded whether the child lived without a mother, whether a
> child had a mother who was sick or incapacitated or a mother
> who had a substantially lower education than her husband,
> and whether the child had a sexually punitive mother, or re-
> ceived little physical attention from the father, or had
> few friends during childhood.

These findings have important implications for public policy.
For example, the widespread existence of sexual victimization indicates that mental health and medical professionals need to recognize
such experience and need to ask their clients and patients routinely
about their sexual contacts with children and adults. The fact that
so few experiences are reported would suggest that we need to take
steps to increase the number of providers, parents and other adults,
who are comfortable with the subject and who are able to talk to
children about such experiences. This latter aspect of child sexual
abuse is being investigated in another study by Finkelhor which NCPCR
is currently runding ("Parents' Attitudes and Reponses to Sexual
Abuse," MH34109).

A recent study by Sanday of the University of Pennsylvania ("The Socio-Cultural Context of Rape," MH28978) investigated the incidence, meaning, and function of rape in tribal societies.[11] She hypothesized that the incidence of rape varies cross-culturally and that high incidence of rape is embedded in a distinguishably different cultural configuration than a low incidence of rape. In this study, societies were classified as rape prone if there were social use of rape to threaten or punish women and/or a high incidence of rape either of the society's own or of other women. Societies were classified as rape free if rape were reported as absent or as being a rare occurrence. In rape-prone societies, female power and authority was low and women did not participate in public decision making, while in rape-free societies, women participated in all aspects of social life including religion, politics, and economics. Both interpersonal and intergroup relations in rape-free societies were marked by mildness as opposed to the violence which frequently erupts in rape-prone societies.

Sanday concludes that rape in tribal societies is a part of a culture of violence and an expression of male dominance. Male dominance evolves in societies when factors such as depleting food resources or migration contribute to a growing dependence on male destructive capacities as opposed to female fertility. The male role is accorded greater prestige and females are perceived as objects to be controlled in order to control population levels.

Mental Health Consequences of Abuse

James, in her study of the early sexual history of female prostitutes and non-prostitutes, found significant differences between the two ("Entrance into Juvenile Prostitution," MH29968).[6] Her subject population consisted of forty-six juvenile prostitutes and fifty juvenile non-prostitute delinquents from twelve to eighteen. The prostitute population was contacted in the Youth Service Center or on the street. The comparison population was drawn from the female delinquent population at the Youth Service Center.

A major finding was that negative early sexual experience significantly increases the possibility of entrance into prostitution. Prostitutes reported significantly more negative early sexual experiences than non-prostitutes. Negative sexual experiences were defined to include: 1) coercion at first sexual experience, 2) coercion at first sexual experience with a male, 3) sexual assault/rape, 4) molestation, and 5) incest.

Only 6 percent of the control group (n=50) had been sexually exploited. Sixty-three percent (n=46) of the prostitutes had negative sexual experiences. The figure for the prostitutes increases to 83 percent if attempted sexual assaults are added. This variable significantly discriminates between prostitutes and non-prostitutes and has predictive potential.

Another study by Herman and Hirschman focussed on the mental health consequences of incest ("Father-Daughter Incest: A Clinical Study," MH29407).[5] The sample consisted of two groups of twenty adult women, selected from a population of outpatients in psychotherapy. The first group reported a history of incestuous relations with their fathers or stepfathers; the comparison group reported a relationship which was perceived as seductive and "special," but which stopped short of genital contact. The groups were roughly matched in terms of demographic criteria.

In terms of mental health consequences, incest victims showed an adult pattern of impairment in intimate relations, low self-esteem, and negative identity formation. They appeared to be at risk for continued victimization and abuse. Women who had grown up in seductive families also suffered from low self-esteem and some disturbance in intimate relations. However, identity formation was usually ambiguous or confused rather than purely negative; women in this group spoke of leading "double lives" or having a good and bad self.

A few women in each sample appeared to have reached adult life relatively unscathed by the incestuous or seductive experience. In each case, a significant factor appeared to be a protective, warm relationship with an admired older woman during childhood or adolescence.

Several women in both samples reported that their brothers had developed quite similarly to their fathers; within the family they were permitted to be tyrannical, demanding, and in some cases violent toward their mothers and sisters. Three brothers were reported to have sexually abused either their sisters or other women. Four brothers in the seductive families were violent, either with their sisters, brothers, or present wives.

Mental Health Services and Treatment

The clinical research studies supported by NCPCR are principally concerned with the effects of rape on the victims' psychological functioning and on the effectiveness of various types of behavior therapy.

Early descriptive studies reported that fear and anxiety were the most salient problems for rape victims. Following this lead, Kilpatrick, Veronen, and Resick ("Treatment of Fear and Anxiety in Victims of Rape," MH29602) were able to test a social learning theory model which focuses primarily on the development of fear and anxiety responses subsequent to a rape experience.[7] For example, any stimuli present during the rape such as being alone, or darkness, or a man's physical appearance can become associated with the fear response through classical conditioning. To test the learning theory model, forty-six rape victims and thirty-five non-victims matched for age, race, and neighborhood were assessed at (1) six to ten days, (2) one month, (3) months, and (4) six months. The outcome assessment at the intervals noted above supported the hypotheses subsumed under the learning theory model, namely, that victims are more fearful than non-victims as indicated in a high overall fearfulness score, that the magnitude of fear changes over time, and that the situations which victims fear but non-victims do not fear are clearly rape-related. One important finding is that interactions with the criminal justice system remained anxiety producing throughout the six-month post-rape period.

As a result of their findings that rape produces marked effects that persist at six months, the investigators initiated a second phase study to examine one-year post-rape adjustment. The participants in this study were recent victims referred from People Against Rape, Charleston, South Carolina, matched with non-victimized women from the same neighborhood and of the same age and race. Standardized psychological assessments were conducted at six to twenty days, three months, six months, and at one year and two years post-rape. As noted earlier, the first phase study indicated a pattern of recovery, that is, at one month, there is generalized distress and at three to six months the initial distress has diminished. However, victims continued to be more fearful and anxious than non-victims. At one year most victims have difficulty with fear and anxiety. An equally important finding is that not all do remain fearful and anxious. Between 20 to 25 percent of the untreated victims were relatively symptom free and some victims report functioning better at one year.

The researchers believe behavior therapy offers a treatment consonant with the nature of the victim's problems. They are currently testing a stress-inoculation model wherein women are trained to utilize cognitive and behavioral coping skills to reduce anxiety.

Early in the study by Frank and associates ("The Rape Victim: Her Response and Treatment," MH29692), the investigators noted that fear and anxiety tended to be emphasized as the predominant response to sexual assault in the major studies of psychological response to sexual assault in the major studies of psychological response to rape conducted since 1970. However, they were also impressed with the extent to which the women in their rape victim study "evidence depressive symptoms and, in some cases, exhibit a full depressive syndrome." In their assessment of thirty-four recent rape victims for depressive symptomatology, the investigators found fifteen women to be moderately or severely depressed. A closer examination revealed that eight were suffering from a major depressive disorder.

The investigators state that the data suggest depressive symptoms are both prevalent and clinically important among recent victims of sexual assault. While recognizing the limitations of the sample size in the initial study, the research team believe it is important to alert counselors to the possibility of the presence of depression in their at-risk group.

In the context of the same study, the investigators examined the relationship between specific aspects of the rape situation and immediate post-rape measures of depression, fear, anxiety, and social and interpersonal functioning in fifty recent victims of sexual assault. The data failed to reveal any significant relationship between the characteristics of the rape situation--for example, stranger versus known assailant, weapon versus no weapon, sexually experienced versus inexperienced--and the nature or severity of the victim's psychological response. The investigators note that the lack of significant relationship between specific aspects of the rape situation and measures of depression, fear, anxiety, social functioning, or interpersonal functioning contradict clinical lore in previous reports concerning the reaction to rape. The investigators suggest that the disparity may be accounted for by the use of standardized measures in this study, in relation to subjective data in other studies, and may also be related to the fact that the initial assessment was made within a few days to a few weeks after the assault. The importance of the finding for counselors is the caution to look not only at the woman's response to the rape situation but to also try to understand as thoroughly as possible her current life situation and current problems.

Since the circumstances of the rape itself did not account for the variation in response to sexual assault, the investigators began to look at other factors which might be associated with difficulty in recovery. One possibility was the impact of previous psychological distress. To explore this issue, Frank, et al. (1981)[4] studied fifty recent sexual assault victims and a comparison group of twenty-two non-victims who volunteered to respond to a psychiatric history, interview schedule, and to provide a number of self-report inventories.

While the researchers are cautious about the representativeness of the sample, they state that the data do suggest that the variability in intensity of response to sexual assault can, in part, be attributed to what the victim brings to the situation. Indicators of serious psychological difficulties in the past, including having been given psychotropic medication, having made a suicide attempt, or having had suicidal ideation do seem to predict a severe response.

Frank and her colleagues have chosen two behavioral treatment approaches in helping victims of sexual assault. Systematic desensitization, a procedure designed to reduce or eliminate maladaptive anxiety, appears to be optimal for phobic reactions which develop subsequent to a rape experience. Cognitive therapy, directed toward changing maladaptive behavior patterns, appears particularly appropriate for women who are depressed.

Becker chose to explore another dimension of the impact of rape, that is, the incidence and type of sexual dysfunction which may be attributed to the rape experience. In her NCPCR supported study ("Sexual Dysfunctions in Rape Victims," MH32982), Becker assessed 402 femal sexual assault victims, including victims of rape and attempted rape, incest, and child molestation.[2] A total of 100 women who had never been sexually assaulted served as a control group. The referral sources for the victims and non-victims were media, clinical staff, project staff, and others. Of the total sample, 83 sexual assault victims volunteered to be interviewed regarding their sexual histories to determine the incidence and types of sexual dysfunctions. For the majority, the assault had taken place three or more years prior to the study while for the minority the assault occurred less than three months before. Becker reports that almost 39 percent were sexually dysfunctional, and they attributed their dysfunction to rape (22 were adult rape victims and 23 were incest victims). The majority of rape-related dysfunctions fall into the category of fear of sex, arousal dysfunction, or desire dysfunction. These researchers urge counselors to be aware of the severity and chronicity of sexual dysfunction for some women.

Prevention

Two final reports of research projects have considerable implications for prevention. Both explored the ways in which women have successfully avoided rape. One, conducted by Bart of the University of Illinois Medical Center ("Avoiding Rape: A Study of Victims and Avoiders," MH29311), utilized data gathered from a self-report questionnaire and interviews with a sample of fifty-one women who had been attacked and avoided being raped and a sample of forty-three who had been raped, all from the Chicago metropolitan area.[1] Some of the findings are that the women who avoided being raped were more likely to 1) be taller and heavier; 2) have played football or another contact sport, often in childhood; 3) engage in sports regularly; 4) have been attacked between midnight and 6 a.m.; and 5) live alone. An important finding was that a woman significantly increases her chances of avoidance of rape by attempting physical resistance, which, at most, moderately increases her chances of being beaten; in only two cases could a definite linkage be made between the women fighting back and additional physical damage by assailants. The study indicates that changes in sex role socialization of women, especially socialization to sports and to physical resistance in the threat of danger, would reduce the probability of being raped. Overt training in physical resistance might also reduce such a probability.

The second study, which systematically compared the factors that differentiate the outcome from a rape avoidance, is by McIntyre of the Bureau of Social Science Research in Washington ("Victim Response to Rape: Alternative Outcomes," MH29045).[9] It investigated the factors that differentiate a sample of 128 women who had been attacked and avoided being raped from a sample of 192 women who had been raped in the Washington, D.C., metropolitan area. Analysis of the victim and assailant behavior in sequence shows that victims who are initially aggressive when they first perceive the problem increase the likelihood of their own subsequent aggressiveness and, most importantly, reduce the probability of being raped later in the encounter. Other findings are that 1) intervention or potential intervention of others can be a decisive factor; 2) the assailant's possession of a weapon, particularly a gun, decreases but does not eliminate a victim's chances of escape; and 3) talking, crying, making oneself less desirable, or appealing to the sympathy of the assailant are generally not useful victim behaviors. It also appears that serious injury is generally not a consequence of victim resistance. The study indicates that behavior increasing physical resistance--including fighting, screaming, and attempting to flee--reduce the probability of being raped.

Information from both these studies is potentially useful to educators, law enforcement personnel, and the general public. NCPCR plans further analysis of these findings in relation to those of other research studies on this topic.

Caplan and associates addressed the issue of prevention from a societal rather than an interpersonal point of view. His project ("Law Reform in the Prevention and Treatment of Rape," MH29532) set out to describe procedures used to handle sexual assault cases in the criminal justice system in Michigan, and to examine the impact of Michigan's Criminal Sexual Conduct Statute.[8]

Findings reveal that the law in Michigan has been implemented such that the goal of "normalization" was achieved; that is, the procedures used in sexual assault cases are in many ways similar to those used for other crimes:

   --Respondents report that the frequency with which police decide to seek warrants and the prosecutors decide to issue warrants is the same for sexual assault and equally serious crimes.

   --Respondents report that the frequency with which cases are plea bargained is about the same in sexual assault and equally serious crimes.

However, many aspects of criminal justice processing are left untouched by the law. For example:

   --The credibility of the victim is a more salient factor in sexual assault cases.

   --Respondents describe using polygraphs more frequently in sexual assault cases.

   --Respondents estimate that there are more fabrications in sexual assault reports.

   --The majority of defense attorneys and prosecutors report that the law has not forced them to change the way in which they prepare for cases.

   --Despite specific prohibitions on sexual history evidence written into the law, respondents report judges often rule this evidence admissible.

--Although respondents report that the law has limited the extent to which judge's discretion can control the outcome of the trial, a majority report that judges can still influence the outcome (e.g., through their demeanor or through rulings on admissibility of evidence).

In terms of impact of the law, the effectiveness of Michigan's Criminal Sexual Conduct law can be documented directly in terms of the tangible goals that have been achieved:

--Convictions for criminal sexual conduct in the first degree have increased substantially as a result of the reformed law.

--Respondents perceive that prosecutors' chances of winning convictions have increased.

--Prosecutors are able to win more types of cases than they were in the past, suggesting that the law is protecting more groups of people (e.g., those with prejudicial sexual histories, or male victims).

--Respondents feel that the victim's experience in the criminal justice system, while difficult, is less onerous than it was in the past.

Thus, from the perspective of those who implement it, there is considerable evidence that the law has achieved the goals of exerting some control on decision-makers in the criminal justice system and has brought the legal standards for cases more in line with those used for other violent crimes.

CONCLUSION

It is important to note that the research portfolio of the Center is a melding of three factors: 1) research interests of the field, which prompt application to NIMH, 2) peer review of the scientific merit of these applications, which allows funding; and 3) Center priorities in funding, as developed by NCPCR staff in collaboration with its National Advisory Committee. There continues to be both private and public input into these activities. Readers who wish more information on the review system of NIMH, should obtain the Research Support Program notice of the Institute.[10]

There have been changes in the portfolio over the seven years of the Center's existence. Recent years have seen more concern with basic studies on the causes of and factors that encourage rape and sexual assault. These studies are needed in order to adequately design effective intervention and prevention programs. There is also increased recent concern with the offender, with his social history and his criminal career, and with offender treatment programs. There is more concern now with children, with how they learn about sex and sexual abuse, the impact of sexual abuse on them, and prevention measures to avoid any such victimization.

The long-range plan of the Center continues to include the five areas of research mandated by law, with concern for the child as well as adult victim, and for treatment of offenders. Two areas in particular will be focussed on:

--Research on the design, implementation, and evaluation of mental health services and treatment.

--Research on prevention of rape or sexual assault and on intervention in mental health problems of sexual assault.

The research program of NCPCR does not stand alone. Two clinical training grants of the Center have benefitted from research findings.

The Center's first training grant was conducted by Kay of the North Carolina Rape Crisis Association. This grant focused on leadership training for rape crisis center staff in North Carolina. Participating rape center staff, drawn from about twenty mostly rural areas, were able to meet regularly for self-development activities, management training experiences, and sharing of problems and successful strategies. The women, on their own initiative, also developed a network for lending and borrowing expensive materials such as public education films. Isolation of rural centers was reduced, program development was enhanced, and a permanent interactional network was established.

The Center also funded a grant to Thomas of Children's Hospital National Medical Center, Washington, D.C., to develop mental health training programs for non-mental health professionals who deal with sexually victimized children and their families. The training program will focus on improving legal, medical, and social service procedures faced by young victims of sexual abuse so that emotional trauma is reduced. The medical center will offer three-day intensive workshops based on experience gained from the hospital's work with sexually victimized children. The hospital plans to export the training program to other urban areas. Other program goals include teaching case-finding techniques to prevent initial and repeated sexual victimization and to encourage adoption of training program components into regular curricula of medical, nursing, legal, police, social service, and child care training programs.

The NCPCR mandate also includes dissemination of research, training, and other pertinent information on sexual assault to service providers and the general public. Consequently, NCPCR sends complimentary single copies of these prevention publications to persons requesting information:

    --*How to Protect Yourself Against Sexual Assault*
    --*He Told Me Not to Tell* (booklet for parents regarding child
      sexual assault)
    --*Rape and Older Women: A Guide to Prevention and Protection*

Reports on Center research findings are published six times a year in the magazine *Response to Family Violence and Sexual Assault*. This magazine, a project of the Center for Women Policy Studies, has a subscription list of 5,000; most of the subscribers are service providers.

In addition, responding to requests by medical personnel for training material to assist them in working with sexual assault victims, the Center is making available to the public free of charge a new training film, *Rape: Caring for the Adult Female Victim*. The film is designed to help doctors, nurses, counselors, and other medical and social service personnel respond appropriately to the psychological, legal, and medical needs of sexual assault victims. Research has shown that a sexual assault victim's emotional recovery is largely determined by the way people respond to her. The care given to the victim in the hospital is crucial because it is given at a time when she is psychologically most vulnerable. *Rape: Caring for the Adult Female Victim* presents a model environment in which to treat the victim's physical injuries, developed by the Center, in a sensitive, supportive, and non-threatening manner. The film suggests that medical personnel may need to examine their own emotional responses to sexual assault before they can provide supportive care to a rape victim.

Rape: Caring for the Adult Female Victim is one of three films made available by NCPCR on a five-day, free-loan basis. *Acquaintance Rape Prevention*, a series of four short discussion films for teenagers, examines the problem of non-stranger rape. *Rape: Victim or Victor* is a rape prevention education film appropriate for general audiences, teenage through adult. All of these films may be obtained by contacting the NCPCR distributor: Modern Talking Picture Service, 5000 Park Street North, St. Petersburg, Floria 60062, (813) 541-6661.

Finally, the Center answers about 600 requests a month for information on sexual assault. The principal requesters are school administrators who request the loan of films. Health and mental health professionals, particularly those in a community mental health center setting, are also requesters for materials. Rape crisis center workers call in for various types of service-related information. And the general public, including adolescents as well as adults, look to the Center for knowledge and understanding of this major public health problem.

The NCPCR is only one of a number of organizations concerned with knowledge building in the sexual assault field (the National Center for Child Abuse and Neglect and NIMH's Center for Studies of Crime and Delinquency, for example, have also funded in this area). But the Center is gratified by the responsiveness of its funded researchers and looks forward to continued funding of, and dissemination of information about, sexual assault. NCPCR supported researchers have produced major books and scientific articles for use by their research colleagues and by human service workers. They have also provided the general public--through appearances on national news shows and through articles in popular magazines--information on the extent and nature of the problem, and intervention and prevention strategies for controlling it. Through such knowledge transference the American people are made more aware of the crime and its consequences, and are provided a firmer basis for taking necessary actions to address the individual and societal issues involved.

REFERENCES

1. Bart, P.B. "Rape as a Paradigm of Sexism in Society--Victimization and Its Discontent." *Women's Studies International Quarterly* 2 (1979): 347-357.

2. Becker, J.V., L.J. Skinner, G.G. Abel, and E.C. Treacy. "Incidence and Types of Sexual Dysfunction in Rape and Incest Victims." *Journal of Sex and Marital Therapy* 8 (1982): 65-74.

3. Finkelhor, D. *Sexually Victimized Children.* New York: Free Press, 1979.

4. Frank, E., S. Turner, B. Duffy Stewart, M. Jacob, and D. West. "Post Psychiatric Symptoms and the Response to Sexual Assault." *Comprehensive Psychiatry* 22 (1981): 479-487.

5. Herman, J., and L. Hirschman. "Families at Risk for Father-Daughter Incest." *American Journal of Psychiatry* 138 (1981): 967-970.

6. James, J., and J. Meyerding. "Early Sexual Experience as a Factor in Prostitution." *Archives of Sexual Behavior* 7 (1978): 31-42.

7. Kilpatrick, D.G., L.J. Veronen, and P.A. Resnick. "Effects of a Rape Experience: A Longitudinal Study." *Journal of Social Issues* 37 (1981): 105-122.

8. March, J.C., A. Geist, and N. Caplan. *Rape and the Limits of Law Reform.* Boston, Massachusetts: Auburn House Publishing Co., 1982.

9. McIntyre, J. "Final Report Summary: Victim Response to Rape." Rockville, Maryland: National Center for the Prevention and Control of Rape, 1980.

10. National Institute of Mental Health. "Research Support Programs." Rockville, Maryland, 1981.

11. Sanday, P. "The Sociocultural Context of Rape: A Cross-Cultural Study." *Journal of Social Issues* 37 (1981): 5-27.

12. Straus, M., R. Gelles, and S. Steinmetz. *Behind Closed Doors: Violence in the American Family.* New York: Doubleday, 1980.

PART II

VICTIMS

Victims of rape and sexual assault represent a large population in the United States. As these crimes of violence have increased in communities, there has been heightened awareness of many of the issues involved. This section presents research findings and raises questions for further study on the impact of victimization.

CHAPTER 3

THE MENTAL HEALTH NEEDS OF VICTIMS

An Introduction to the Literature

C. Richard Tsegaye-Spates

Victimization has been defined differently by different authors to emphasize unique consequences for the various classes of victims (Rich and Stenzel 1980; Salasin 1980; Ochberg 1980). Throughout all descriptions of victimization, however, there seems to exist a core concept. This core concept involves an interaction between two individuals where one is stronger or better armed than the other, and who proceeds to assault and damage the other. As a consequence, the victim is rendered less powerful, more fearful, and—in a social psychological sense—is knocked down a level or more on a dominance hierarchy. The victim responds with resignation or rage, or sometimes with both. The last half decade has seen increasing attention paid to the plight of the victim, although this attention has been long in coming. For many years, what was known about victims was derived mainly from anecdotal information, a few case studies, and very few follow-up studies from specific victim episodes. Our knowledge in the area is now supported by several clinical models of traumatic and protracted stress reactions, and by specific studies of selected classes of victims. This chapter will review illustrative samples of the research and clinical literature on victimization, with emphasis on the mental health needs of victims of personal violence.

From the outset it should be pointed out that not all individuals exposed to victimizing situations suffer in the ways portrayed in this chapter. As best as can be determined at this time, the outcomes for the universe of victims falls into three categories: those who as a result of the experience show no apparent psychological disturbance; those who in fact show substantial positive personality change following the experience, although this change is not attributed directly

to the experience so much as it is to the opportunity it provided for
self-examination and change; and finally, those who suffer mild to
severe disturbance in the wake of victimizing episode (Ochberg and
Spates 1980; Dohrenwend 1978). This chapter will focus on the clinical consequences for those persons falling into the last category, in
hopes of improving the reader's understanding of their mental health
needs.

Although different theorists outline slightly varying probable
reactions for victimized individuals, there seems to be general agreement that the victim will encounter several stages of emotional reaction. Symonds (1980) documents a sequence of characteristic responses
on the part of the victim, which includes paralysis, and denial of
sensory impressions. During the second phase, the victim enters a
period of terror-induced "frozen fright" and pseudo-calm detachment
from others; in addition, patterns of early childhood behavior predominate. In the third stage, the victim experiences circular bouts
of anger, resignation, resentment, constipated rage, insomnia, and
startle reactions, and relives the traumatic events through dreams,
fantasies, and nightmares. In the fourth stage, the individual, if
successful, resolves the trauma and integrates it into her or his
life style and behavior. There will be further development of more
efficient defensive-alert patterns and profound revision of values
and attitudes concerning possessions, and sometimes concerning individuals (Symonds 1980).

Bard (1982) described three stages of victim response, including
an initial stage of disorganization which he calls the "impact stage."
This stage may last from a few hours to a few days. It is here that
the individual feels a loss of personal intactness; the feeling is
often described, according to Bard, as being "numb," or disoriented
with behavior being automatic. He suggests that some people engage
in denial, which he views as a temporary strategy to minimize disorganization and "buy time." Others may express disbelief. Not infrequently, feelings of vulnerability and helplessness are experienced;
dependency needs increase, so that a formerly independent individual
may begin to behave with child-like dependency. While some victims
will feel and express anger, more often there will be a show of depression, isolation, and loneliness. The second stage, according to
Bard, is the "recoil stage" and it is central to the process of repair. "This period is marked by alarming shifts and contradictory
feelings: fear, anger, well-being, sadness, elation, self-pity, and
guilt." It is here that the victim may acknowledge and begin to deal
with the painful emotions aroused by the experience, and at the same
time actively deny that pain. The final stage in Bard's analysis is
called the "reorganization stage." "Fear and anger diminish and become more memory than reality. Attacks of anxiety and nightmares no
longer plague the victim. Levels of activity become more even and
balanced; energy shifts from the emphasis on the work of repair to
other constructive pursuits" (p. 12). Bard points out, however, that
the crime is never really forgotten. He suggests that the victim's
view of self and of the world will be permanently altered in some way.

As can be observed from the foregoing analyses, victims can be
expected to encounter a great deal of stress in the aftermath of the
assault. Stress is in fact central to most theory-based accounts of
the victimization experience, and therefore a brief review of several
theoretical models will follow.

THEORETICAL MODELS

Ochberg and Spates (1981) suggest that one productive model for understanding victimization is by analogy to Lindemann's formula of grief (1944). Grief is the psychological reaction to loss of a loved one or loss of a very cherished goal or ambition for oneself. Typically, a spouse, parent, or child dies, or is no longer present. Clinically, the human reaction is one of sadness, which looks very much like depression but is more limited and does not usually involve a lowering of self-image. Lindemann observed that this reaction is expected to last from four to eight weeks. The specific symptoms involve: sensations of somatic stress; preoccupation with the event (e.g., images of the deceased); self-blame or guilt at one's own personal behavior in relation to the deceased; hostility toward the caregivers or authorities; and a noticeable change in conduct, entailing restlessness, inability to organize activities or to perform common pleasantries. When, as a result of suffering such a loss, the individual's normal level of coping becomes defective, the syndrome of pathological grief reaction can occur. Here the individual displays an extended reaction, with an exaggerated symptom picture including: hyperactivity without a sense of loss; acquisition of symptoms held by the deceased; marked hostility without any signs of sadness; apathy and other depression-like symptoms; uncalled-for generosity, to the point of self-destructiveness; and substance abuse.

In suggesting this analogy, Ochberg recognizes that, like grief, victimization has a "normal" and a "pathological" variation, determined mainly by the intensity of the assault and the strength of the individual's coping behavior. The symptom picture of grief and pathological grief parallel in many significant ways the symptom picture of victimization. Based on this model, Ochberg (1981) proposes that victim services should assure access to a full range of services that include counseling, education, involvement of people who have gone through victimization and coped well, and, when necessary, psychological and psychiatric services. While it would not be advisable to press every personality for a psychiatric encounter, it is suggested that some level of reflection and honest discussion in a sympathetic environment could prove beneficial. In recent years, more and more of this kind of self and event examination has been taking place through self-help support groups, aided only marginally, if at all, by professional intervention. Although the evaluation of this self-help technique has only begun, and widespread outcome assessments have not been seriously attempted, there is limited support for the utility of this approach in meeting the mental health needs of victims (Vachon, M.L.S. et al., 1980)

A second model for understanding victimization is described by Horowitz (1976). It is called the "stress response syndrome" and it suggests that as a result of an assault there follows 1) an outcry; 2) denial of the event's occurrence; 3) intrusive ideation and disturbed cognitive processing; 4) "working through" via repetitive consideration of the event in a supportive environment; and 5) "completion," which restores the victim's ability to respond freely to her or his environment in an emotionally appropriate way. This sequence of reactions is viewed as relatively normal and is encountered by most trauma victims.

In a pathological variation of the stress response syndrome, the intensity of the event is stronger and 1) overwhelms the individual;

2) the outcry turns to panic, and if the event is prolonged still
more, leads to exhaustion; 3) the denial phase, which was initially
an adaptive maneuver, now leads to avoidance or escape behavior, that
is, phobias, drug dependence, running away, or suicide; 4) the intrusive ideas may lead to cognitive flooding where the individual responds mainly to internal cues regarding the event, if she or he responds at all; 5) when "working through" is blocked, the individual
enters a frozen emotional state and displays psychosomatic reactions;
and 6) when completion does not occur, the individual has difficulty
expressing feelings and displays character distortions.

Krupnick and Horowitz (1980) suggest that "although an assault
can be a traumatic and devastating experience, it also offers opportunities for growth and change" (p. 46). The victimizing experience
may highlight previous problems and conflicts which serve only to delay or impede recovery. In the context of a supportive environment,
it is possible to assess the victim's general coping style and level
of psychological development, and to discover the personal meaning of
the assault. Through this discovery, the victim will be able to differentiate between real and fantasized aspects of the assault, leading to effective control and a more positive sense of mastery. This
model suggests that brief therapy focusing on understanding the individual's response to the attack has proven effective in helping victims integrate the trauma and thereby stimulating psychological growth.

These recommendations for mental health intervention are similar
to those recommended by Ochberg (1981) above. One area of research
that would have practical value would address the question of whether
it makes a difference if this supportive environment is provided by
conventional therapy or by the self-help support group. If a difference is observed, then which approach is more effective with the pathological and which with the "normal" variation of victimization?
Current theory and practice would suggest that enlightened informal
helping networks might be as effective and, in many instances, more
effective than the professional encounter when dealing with the mental
health needs of a substantial portion of the victim population.

A third model for understanding victimization, developed by
Selye (1946) is called the "general adaptive syndrome." It represents
the psychological parallel to the stress response syndrome described
above. This model consists of three stages of response on the part of
an individual who is attempting to readjust or re-equilibriate following a stressful event. The first stage is the alarm reaction, which
occurs, in terms of victimization, in the earliest moments of the
assault. It involves a plethora of autonomic nervous system reactions:
reactions which have biological significance in assisting the organism
to reduce the apparent threat by either fighting or fleeing. When
sympathetic arousal occurs as in the first stage of the adaptive syndrome, the rate and force of heart contractions increase; blood supply
to the heart, large muscles, and brain increases with a concomitant
constriction of blood vessels to the stomach, intestines and colon;
blood pressure rises and salivation decreases, producing dry mouth
sensation; the bronchial passages dilate, permitting the lungs to con-
sume a greater amount of oxygen, thereby increasing the body's rate of
metabolism; dilation of the pupils occurs; portions of the endocrine
system are stimulated, releasing greater amounts of the hormones ad-
renalin and noradrenalin into the bloodstream; the liver, which normally stores glycogen, is stimulated to produce the simple sugar glucose

from glycogen to provide an additional fuel supply for the body's enhanced metabolic rate; transmission of neural impulses is facilitated by the production of noradrenalin at the synapse, which is required to innervate the smooth muscles of the viscera and blood vessels.

In the second stage of the general adaption syndrome, termed the "resistance stage," the individual attempts to adapt to the stressful situation. Concommitant with sympathetic arousal is the release by the posterior hypothalmamus (an area of the brain which mediates physiological changes associated with fear, anger, hunger, thirst, sex, and pleasure) of a hormone which stimulates the pituitary-adrenal system to produce adreno-corticotrophic hormone. Schwartz (1973) suggests that "stress results in abnormal amounts of adrenal secretion, and animal experiments show that the adrenals (glands) are enlarged. Variation in adrenal output in the three stages of the adaption syndrome (excess secretion in the resistance stage and deficient secretion in the exhaustion stage) have differential consequences. Cardiac and hypertensive disorders are exacerbated by excess adrenal output, and arthritic and rheumatic disorders are aggravated by decreased output" (p. 211).

If the attempt at adaption in the resistance stage proves unsuccessful and the stress-provoking situation continues, the third stage of the adaptive syndrome ensues. This is the "exhaustion stage" where efforts to adapt break down and, if the stress is prolonged, the individual will die.

Selye (1970) suggests that as a result of the physiological reactions produced in the adaptive syndrome, certain maladies occur to the body. Called diseases of adaption, they often do not manifest during exposure to stress but will occur long after the stressful episode has discontinued. This observation becomes particularly relevant in light of reports of increased physical ailments following certain episodes of victimization (Spates 1981).

The final model of stress to be reviewed here which assists an understanding of victimization is termed the "psychosocial model of stress" (Dohrenwend 1978). This model describes how situations in the environment and the psychological characteristics of the individual combine to produce a stressful life event. These situational and psychological characteristics are causally related to political action and/or general education and socialization of the individual, respectively. The stressful life event (for these purposes, victimization) leads typically to at least a transient stress reaction. The event may lead to further consequences depending on the availability of two kinds of mediators: situational mediators, or psychological mediators. The situational mediators involve the material and social supports, or handicapping conditions, brought to bear on the transient stress reaction. These are causally related to the level of community organization and development--the assumption being that relatively well organized and developed communities will have the necessary services available in sufficient quantity to assist a victim, whereas a less well developed community may not. The psychological mediators involve a number of personal factors, including the person's aspirations, values, and coping abilities or disabilities. These factors are causally related to the individual's prior development and experience. In addition to situational and psychological mediators, crisis intervention is identified as influencing the victim's transient stress reaction and leading to differential outcome.

This psychosocial model of stress identifies three possible outcomes for the victim, including a) psychological growth; b) no substantial, permanent change; and c) psychopathology, which may require corrective therapy. When applied to the context of crime victimization, this model can provide guidance to the would-be helper as to appropriate times and types of intervention. The model may have heuristic value in suggesting important research possibilities. For the most part, however, the wisdom of the model is implicit and reflects years of thinking on the part of those most involved with traumatic and other kinds of stress reactions.

Recent years have seen a great deal of research which either supports the above models or extends them to the victimization area (e.g., Salasin 1980, 1981; Stein 1980; Greacon 1975; Horowitz 1976, 1979, 1980; Burgess et al. 1976, 1978). Increasingly, the psychological reactions of victims are being better articulated and should ultimately lead to more responsive treatment and other services to facilitate victim recovery. The next section will examine suggested approaches to intervening on behalf of the victims' mental health needs.

INTERVENING ON BEHALF OF VICTIMS

Naturally, not all victim reactions follow the well-ordered sequence of stages described earlier in this chapter. No single description can capture the experiences of all victims. However, it is important that the clinician, the researcher, the policy maker, and the victim come to understand what is likely to occur, so that the necessary intervention can be developed and responsively implemented.

Recent experience suggests that any of several types of individuals may become involved in providing assistance to assault victims. Some of these "providers" comprise recognized formal helpers, while others are informal helpers. Formal helpers include professional medical or mental health interveners, as well as hospitals. Informal helpers include family, friends, self-help support groups, and bystanders. In addition, there is a plethora of paraprofessionals who would fall within the formal helping group—e.g., paramedics. Rather than discuss how these various providers can better integrate their assistance into a coordinated pattern of services (Ochberg and Spates 1980), this section will address what the individual helpers should consider in responding to the psychological needs of victims.

Many writers have acknowledged that the immediate needs of victims may have more to do with protection and material aid than with psychological or mental health care per se (Brody 1969; Eitinger 1964). Baluss (1980) indicates that victim services can provide access to emergency assistance, medicaid or medicare, and arrange for vocational rehabilitation if an injury dictates a job change. Victim programs can deal with the problems of housing security and offer counseling to reduce the chances of repeat victimization. The protective function of potential services was ranked highest by service providers in research conducted by Rich and colleagues (1982). Among other service providers, prevention of pregnancy and venereal disease have been identified as high priorities in working with rape victims (Burgess and Holmstrom 1974; Hilberman 1976). Obviously, emergency and primary medical care are necessary as a first measure of assistance for victims who require it. In addition, however, it is recognized that what is or is not done in the early stages of assistance to the victim can affect her successful psychological recovery. Symonds (1980) therefore invokes the concept of "psychological first-aid" to stress the importance of these early actions.

Bard (1982) suggested that the actions of others who come into contact with the victim in the aftermath of the crime are critically important to the psychological outcome. It is important that others express the proper mix of sensitivity and discipline; Bard stresses that the victim needs tolerance, stability, and reassurance as a demonstration of the essential "goodness" of others. Because the victim has been hurt by the willful act of another person, the intentionally compassionate and helpful acts of others are the most effective antidotes to the poisoned social existence that follow.

Symonds (1980) provides another basis for assuring the proper course of intervention during the early stages after victimization. He describes "the second wound" which many victims develop as a consequence of the way in which service providers intervene with that individual--who is prone to view the world, particularly authority figures, with distrust. The second wound is the victim's perceived rejection by and lack of expected support from the community, agencies, and society in general as well as from family and friends. It contributes to the delayed and persistent negative response of the victim after the assault. This second wound is predicated upon a clinical profile often displayed by victims, consisting of feelings of guilt, loss of self-esteem, shame, loneliness and wanting to be alone, feelings of defenselessness, and hopelessness (Rich and Stenzel 1980). Symonds refers to this pattern of response as "retroflexive rage," whereby victims avoid friends and family and become socially reclusive, even abrasive and unpleasant. Not infrequently the victim becomes phobic and develops hostile-dependent relationships. Given this tendency on the part of the victim, it becomes imperative that steps be taken by all would-be helpers to avoid aggravating this tendency through callous inattention.

No matter who offers the support or sympathy, there seems to be consensus among experts that crisis intervention is essential to assuring the maximum emotional recovery of the victim. Stein (1980) reports that many who initially appear to have survived the experience of crime intact may suffer acute distress days or even weeks later. Further, persons who experience victimization without adequate emotional support run a high risk of suffering long-term disability. Even those who weather the crisis well, according to Stein, may nonetheless suffer devastation in their family and social relationships. Crisis intervention therefore is a concrete service that alleviates one of the more deplorable consequences of criminal victimization; it restores the victim's coping skills which have been severely weakened by the shock.

For many victims, emergency and primary medical service providers will be among the first to intervene. Often only a bystander, the family, or friends will precede the paramedics in reaching the victim. Although their role is appropriately conceived as one of saving the victim's life by getting the injured party to competent medical care, it is nevertheless important that the victim be shown sensitivity and given choices about what happens to them, if they are conscious. Even though the victim may be experiencing shock, disbelief, temporary paralysis, and may not be generally processing information efficiently, it is critical that they be given power as one of the early antidotes to helplessness which accrues from the assault. Power in this instance can result from being a primary participant in decisions affecting one's care and treatment.

This principle should similarly guide the practices of hospital personnel, who are often next in line to see the victim. In some instances the victim may be entering the second stages of victimization at the hospital. (Again it must be emphasized that no one can predict which stage a victim will be in at a given time. These hypothetical transitions are used here to illustrate the fact that interveners need to be cognizant that the victim's state does change, and what to expect.) Active denial of the event may be taking place at this time; pseudo-calm detachment from others may be present; and patterns of early childhood behavior (immaturity) may predominate during this stage. This stage may outlast the emergency treatment for many victims. For others, the third stage will ensue, whereby the victim experiences circular bouts of anger, apathy, resentment, startle reactions, or resignation. It is here that it is especially crucial to note Symonds' observation about the second wound while caring for the victim. Equally important are Bard's observations about the need to extend compassion to an individual whose trust has just been shattered, and who perhaps justifiably may be less than eager to re-enter trusting relationships or allow themselves to become *objects* of more powerful people, even in the helping context. The tendency here is for the service provider to "revictimize" the victim by conducting business as usual. It should be clear that formal providers have no monopoly on revictimization. Symonds points out that it can be accomplished by family and friends as well, through their own tendencies to actively deny the victim's experience, or to fail to provide the supportive environment specified earlier by Ochberg and by Bard.

The third class of service providers likely to assist the victim is the ranking medical professional--e.g., a doctor or dentist. Every principle mentioned earlier deserves re-emphasis with this group; they are accustomed to exercising strong professional and personal prerogatives in how they treat patients. These prerogatives are often value-laden and can affect the victim's psychological recovery. Hilberman (1976) describes some of the pitfalls of medical personnel in treating rape victims--pitfalls that are equally applicable to other classes of victims. Among the suggestions to improve treatment are:

> --All hospital personnel who will have contact with the
> victim must be screened and educated so that (rape) victims
> are not exposed to additional insult.
> --All services offered to the victim must be based on informed
> consent. The victim has a right to information about all
> available options and thereby retains control throughout
> the hospital process.
> --All programs designed by medical facilities should be part
> of a community-oriented approach, since treatment of the
> (rape) victim involves both medical and legal issues. Such
> an approach would involve cooperative efforts by hospitals,
> citizen groups, law enforcement, and prosecutory agencies.

The formal mental health professional has received equal criticism over handling of victim treatment. Rape and incest victims have complained about Freudian concepts which serve to demean, degrade, or raise doubt about their motivations. Vietnam veterans have complained about therapists' refusal to acknowledge the contribution of the war's effect on current functioning, and the tendency of professionals to view them in standard psychopathological terms. These professionals must recognize the victim's need for psychological first aid (Symonds 1980). This means responding to the victim's silent expectation of nurturing and nonblaming behavior; it means reducing the victim's self-blame and restoring the feeling of power taken away by the criminal.

Finally, professionals (as well as all would-be interveners) must examine their own values regarding the status of victims as the proverbial "loser." Perhaps Bard describes this most clearly: " ... because we live in a competitive society, we tend to see the interaction between the criminal and the victim as a competitive one, with the victim as loser." Prevailing values dictate no gain in identifying with a loser. When coupled with the tendency for many people to blame the victim, the mindset of the victim (e.g., self-blame, loneliness, isolation) is highly reinforced. Much of this perception occurs at unconscious levels and are not easily addressed by conventional training, that is, in medical school or other clinical training. Understanding these values most effectively through self-examination and honest revealing in a supportive environment, much the same as for the victim in integrating her or his assault experience. The members of this supportive group should probably be other professionals or, ideally, victim-professionals capable of comprehending the dilemma of the service provider who at once is asked to be appropriately distant (to accomplish good treatment) yet sensitive in more than the usual degree.

Once these dispositional factors are addressed, medical and mental health professionals may be in a unique position to offer assistance to the victim, both directly and indirectly. First, there is the obvious need of some victims for corrective therapy, as outlined by Dohrenwend (1978). Second, the professional may be of assistance indirectly by consulting in the development and maintenance of self-help support groups. These groups have clearly become the primary locus of treatment for a majority of victims who refused to seek services through mainstream agencies (Rich 1982). Third, professionals can provide training opportunities for other indigenous helpers through community education. They can seek to develop programs in response to local assessed needs. And finally, the professional is uniquely prepared to conduct action and evaluation research on the needs for and effectiveness of victim services in a given locale. The Dohrenwend model suggests that such contributions can strengthen the situational and psychological mediators which assist the victim to cope well following the transient stress reaction, and in fact *may* reduce the need for corrective therapy, which has traditionally been identified as the primary locus of intervention for the professional.

REFERENCES

Baluss, M. "Services for Victims of Crimes: A Developing Opportunity." *Evaluation and Change*, 1980, 94-102. Minneapolis, MN: Minnesota Medical Research Foundation.

Bard, M. Testimony presented at a public hearing of the President's Task Force on Victims of Crime. Washington, D.C., September 14, 1982.

Brody, E., ed. *Behavior in New Environments*. Beverly Hills, California: Sage Publications, Inc., 1969.

Burgess, A., and L. Holmstrom. "Coping Behavior of the Rape Victim." *American Journal of Psychiatry* 134 (1976): 413-417.

Burgess, A., and L. Holmstrom. "Rape Trauma Syndrome." *American Journal of Psychiatry* 131 (1974): 981-985.

Burgess, A., and L. Holmstrom. "Recovery from Rape and Prior Life Stress." *Research in Nursing and Health* 1 (1978): 165-174.

Dohrenwend, B. "Social Stress and Community Psychology." *American Journal of Community Psychology* 6 (1978).

Eitinger, L. *Concentration Camp Survivors in Norway and Israel.* London: Allen and Unwin, 1964.

Greacon, J. "Arbitration: A Tool For Criminal Cases?" *Barrister Magazine* 2 (1975): 10-14.

Hilberman, E. *The Rape Victim*, Washington, D.C.: The American Psychiatric Association, 1976.

Horowitz, M. "Narcissistic Rage." Presented at the Pan American Forum for the Study of Adolescence. San Francisco, 1979.

Horowitz, M. *Stress Response Syndromes.* New York: Jason Aronson, 1976.

Horowitz, M., N. Wilner, N. Kaltreider and W. Alvarez. "Signs and Symptoms of Post-traumatic Stress Disorders." *Journal of Nervous and Mental Disease* 37 (1980).

Krupnick, J., and M. Horowitz. "Victims of Violence: Psychological Responses, Treatment Implications." In *Evaluation and Change* (Special Issue: Services to Survivors), Minnesota Medical Research Foundation, 1980.

Lindemann, E. "Symptomatology and Management of Acute Grief." *American Journal of Psychiatry* (1944), 101:141.

Ochberg, F. "Caring for Ex-Hostages." Unpublished manuscript, 1981.

Ochberg, F., and C. Spates. "Services Integration for Victims of Personal Violence." In *Evaluating Victim Services*, edited by S. Salasin. Beverly Hills, California: Sage Publications, 1981.

Rich, R., and D. Cohen. "Victims of Crime: Public Policy Perspectives and Models for Service." Paper presented at the Scientific Committee on the Mental Health Needs of Victims, World Federation for Mental Health. February 11, 1982, Washington, D.C.

Salasin, S. (ed.) *Evaluating Victim Services*, Beverly Hills, California: Sage Publications, 1981.

Salasin, S. "Evaluation as a Tool for Restoring the Mental Health of Victims: An Interview with Frank Ochberg." In *Evaluation and Change* (Special Issue: Services to Survivors), Minnesota Medical Research Foundation, 1980.

Schwartz, M. *Physiological Psychology.* New York: Appleton Century Croft, 1973.

Selye, H. "General Adaptation or Stress Syndrome." *Psychopathology Today*, edited by W. Sahakian. F.E. Peacock, 1970.

Selye, H. "The General Adaptation Syndrome and the Diseases of
  Adaptation." *Journal of Allergy* 17 (1946): 231-247.

Spates, C.R. "The Mental Health Needs of Victims: A Review of the
  Literature and Recommendations for Research," Monograph prepared
  for the National Institute of Mental Health, contract no. 379508166,
  1981.

Stein, J. "Better Services for Crime Victims: A Prescriptive
  Package." In *Evaluation and Change* (Special Issue: Services to
  Survivors), Minnesota Medical Research Foundation, 1980.

Symonds, M. "The Second Injury." In *Evaluation and Change*,
  (Special Issue: Services to Survivors), Minnesota Medical Research
  Foundation, 1980.

Vachon, M.L.S., W.A.L. Lyall, J. Rogers, K. Freedman-Letofsky and
  S.J.J. Freeman, "A Controlled Study of Self-Help Intervention for
  Widows," *American Journal of Psychiatry* 137, no. 11 (1980),
  1380-1384.

CHAPTER 4

RAPE TRAUMA SYNDROME AND POST TRAUMATIC STRESS RESPONSE

Ann Wolbert Burgess and Lynda Lytle Holmstrom

Rape affects the lives of thousands of people each year. The FBI Uniform Crime Reports indicate over a 100 percent increase in reported forcible rapes between 1970 (over 37,000 cases) and 1979 (over 75,000 cases). To truly grasp the enormity of the problem, those figures must be doubled since it is estimated that 50 percent of violent crimes go unreported (President's Task Force on Victims of Crime 1982) and criminal victimization surveys estimate between 40 and 50 percent of forcible rapes are not reported (Law Enforcement Assistance Administration 1975).

The legal definition of rape varies from state to state. However, the issues generally addressed include lack of consent, force or threat of force, and sexual penetration. The clinical definition of rape trauma--the focus of this paper--is the stress response pattern of the victim following forced, non-consenting sexual activity. This rape trauma syndrome of somatic, cognitive, psychological, and behavioral symptoms is an acute stress reaction to a life threatening situation.

Parallel with the increase in rape reporting has been the positive institutional response to rape victims through the establishment of sex crime units by law enforcement agencies, victim advocates in rape crisis centers, victim specialists in prosecutor's offices, and victim counselors in emergency departments of general hospitals. Rape rehabilitation services are also being covered by some insurance companies under its workers' compensation policies, thus placing a value on early intervention to expedite emotional and physical recovery of victims and assist in return to work.

Recognition of rape as a significant trauma and life event capable of disrupting normal life patterns is clearly being addressed by clinicians in the treatment setting. Concurrently, the admissibility of expert testimony on rape trauma syndrome is being tested both in criminal and civil litigation cases. This paper describes rape trauma syndrome within the new category of post-traumatic stress disorder of the Diagnostic and Statistical Manual, third edition (American Psychiatric Association 1980) whether both acute, chronic, or delayed, and discusses the use of rape trauma syndrome on court.

STRESS RESPONSE PATTERNS

The human purpose of achieving a stable yet evolving state of existence had been a topic of interest in the professional literature since the mid-nineteenth century (Engel 1953). Long before the concept of stress was formulated, Bernard (1945), a French physiologist, stated that the internal environment of all organisms must remain fairly constant despite changes in the external environment. Fifty years later Cannon (1932), an American physiologist wrote that the coordinated physiological processes might be called equilibria, although he favored the term homeostasis. Laboratory research on the physiological mechanisms of adaptation to the stresses of life was initiated in Canada by Selye in the 1930s and the general adaptation syndrome proposed by Selye (1974) states that the biophysiological process of adaptation to stressful situations develops in three stages. First, the alarm reaction which includes initial responses of surprise and anxiety and beginning mobilization of defenses both physiological and psychological; second, the stage of resistance in which use of all bodily resources are used to combat the problem; and third, the stage of exhaustion when all bodily resources have been depleted. (See Chapter 3 of this volume for a more complete description of this process.)

The psychological parallel to Selye's physiological model of stress response has been proposed by Horowitz (1976). This model draws on the early observations of Breuer and Freud (1895) in their study of hysterical neuroses, traumatic neuroses (Fenichel 1945), subsequent psychoanalytic studies summarized by Furst (1967), and clinical field studies of concentration camp survivors (Krystal 1968; Niederland 1968). Essentially, two main components of stress response are summarized as (1) an intrusive thought repetition tendency, and (2) a denial-numbing tendency. The persistence of the emotionally distressing trauma related to thoughts, according to Horowitz (1976), indicates that the event has been incompletely processed cognitively and thereby remains in active memory storage as a potential influence of behavior.

In another model of human response to severe stress, Symonds (1975) describes four phases of response in victims of violence in which phases I and II occur during the victimization and III and IV occur in the post-trauma phase. Phase I includes reactions of shock, disbelief, and denial to the occurring event with temporary paralysis of action and denial of sensory impression. Phase II--or when denial is overwhelmed by reality--is termed "frozen fright" and includes terror-induced, pseudo-calm, detached behavior. In Phase III after the criminal departs, the victim experiences circular bouts of apathy, resignation, anger, resentment, rage, insomnia, startle reactions, and a replay of the traumatic event through dreams and nightmares. Phase IV includes restoration, resolution, and integration of the experience into the victim's behavior and lifestyle.

Patterns of Victim Response to Rape

Rape, until the 1970s, thrived on prudery, misunderstanding, and silence. It is only in this past decade that the academic and scientific publications have multiplied on the topic. According to Chappell, Geis, and Fogarty (1974), studies performed prior to 1969 focused on the concern that individuals accused of rape should be protected and studies since 1969 have focused largely on protection and help for the victim. Midlarsky's (1977) review of articles on the psychological effects of rape, and intervention for rape victims in the post-traumatic period, located seventy-eight references between 1965 and 1976 with thirty-six on the effects of rape and forty-two on intervention.

The early materials on victims were personal observations, written primarily by feminists and carried common themes: the sense of personal outrage over intimate violation; a lack of clarity concerning how to characterize the event to oneself, and even how to characterize oneself following the event; the felt ineptness of systems that treat victims; the lack of consistent guidelines about the benefits of pursuing legal channels; and the lack of understanding of why the rape occurred and who the perpetrator was (Midlarsky 1980).

In the 1970s, several publications appeared in the psychiatric literature presenting a marked departure from the traditional view of rape as victim-provoked. Rather than discussing rape so exclusively in terms of intrapsychic concepts, the contemporary view began to portray rape as an event imposed upon the victim from the outside; that is, as an external event. Sutherland and Scherl (1970), early workers in rape counseling, observed a three-phase syndrome of reaction to rape by thirteen white, psychiatrically healthy young women, ages eighteen to twenty-four, whom they treated in a public health crisis service. They defined the immediate reaction as an acute phase, characterized by shock and disbelief followed by or alternating with fear and anxiety. The second phase, called "pseudo-adjustment," included such coping mechanisms as denial, suppression of affect, and rationalization used to regain equilibrium. The victim resumes normal activities, appears to be adjusting, and shows little interest in outside help. This reaction is believed to be a healthy response however temporary and superficial it may be. The final phase, integration, often begins with the victim feeling depressed and wanting to talk. A specific incident may trigger this phase--pregnancy, a court summons, seeing a man who looks like the assailant, flashbacks. During this phase, the victim must face and resolve feelings about herself and her assailant. Self-blame and a sense of defilement are common. Anger turned toward the assailant may be felt for the first time or be turned inward, intensifying the depression characteristic of early integration. Sutherland and Scherl observed that fear, anxiety, and depression are within normal limits if reactive, time-limited, and nonpsychotic.

Werner (1972) describes a psychotherapy case where the therapeutic process was interrupted by a rape. The patient, a graduate student in her twenties, was in the second year of therapy when the attack occurred. The situation was verified by witnesses and the police quickly caught the assailants. Werner conceptualized the attack as an external stress. He spoke of the subsequent therapy material as resulting from an "actual tragedy rather than a fantasy." He emphasized how the rape interrupted the therapy in several ways: (1) the pace and content changed in that it was no longer a leisurely exploration of relationships and fantasies, and (2) new symptoms of insomnia, appetite loss, frequent crying, and fears of being alone gave a clinical picture suggestive of a severe grief reaction.

In a 1973 hospital-based study using a sample of all (n=146) persons admitted to the emergency department with the complaint of rape, Burgess, a psychiatric nurse, and Holmstrom, a sociologist, describe three types of sexual victimization as rape trauma syndrome, accessory-to-sex, and sex stress situations. They analyze data from 109 child, adolescent, and adult victims, ages five to seventy-three, who had been subjected to forced sexual penetration. Discovering similarities in responses that seemed to qualify as a clinical entity, they term this acute traumatic reaction the rape trauma syndrome, in which the nucleus of the anxiety was a subjective state of terror and overwhelming fear of being killed. Rape trauma triggers intrapsychic disequilibrium with a resultant crisis state for the victim.

The rape trauma syndrome (Burgess and Holmstrom 1974) is divided into two phases which can disrupt the physical, psychological, social, and/or sexual aspects of a victim's life. The acute or disruptive phase can last from days to weeks and is characterized by general stress response symptoms. During the second phase--the long-term process of reorganization--the victim has the task of restoring order to her or his lifestyle and re-establishing a sense of control in the world. This phase is characterized by rape-related symptoms and can last from months to years.

RAPE-RELATED POST TRAUMATIC STRESS DISORDER

The early conceptualizations of the stress response patterns of rape victims are consistent with the diagnostic criteria of post-traumatic stress disorder (PTSD) of the DSM-III within the major category of anxiety disorders. The four cardinal criteria will be discussed with documentation from clinical research data.

Stressor of Significant Magnitude

The primary feature of PTSD is that the stressor be of significant magnitude as to evoke distinguishable symptoms in almost everyone. PTSD is defined by symptoms which have a temporal and presumably causal relationship to a stressor beyond usual human experience (Ochberg and Fojtik-Stroud 1982). The stressor under review is rape.

The contemporary view of rape sees it as an act of violence expressing power, aggression, conquest, degradation, anger, hatred, and contempt (Bart 1975; Brownmiller 1975; Burgess and Holmstrom 1974; Cohen et al. 1971; Davis 1968; Gelles 1977; Griffin 1971; Metzger 1976; Russell 1975; Schwendinger and Schwendinger 1974; Symonds 1976). Bard and Ellison (1974) have emphasized the significance of the personal violation for the rape victim. Hilberman (1976) characterizes rape as the "ultimate violation of the self, short of homicide, with the invasion of one's inner and most private space, as well as loss of autonomy and control." Hilberman argues that it is the person's self, not an orifice, that has been invaded and that the core meaning of rape is the same for the virgin, a housewife, a lesbian, and a prostitute.

Notman and Nadelson (1976) observe how a rape attack heightens a woman's sense of helplessness, intensifies conflicts about dependence and independence, generates self-criticism and guilt that devalue her as an individual, and interferes with partner relationships. Burgess and Holmstrom (1976) note that for almost all victims, the rape was something far out of the ordinary that seriously taxed their adaptive resources.

Rape is an interactional process involving at least two persons. In assessing the magnitude of the stressor, it is important to understand the behavior of rapists (Symonds 1976). Books have been written on psychosexual disorders starting in 1886 with von Krafft-Ebing's *Psychopathia Sexualis* (1965), the psychology of sex (Ellis 1942), and the study of the sex offender (Karpman 1954; Gebhard et al. 1965). Prior to 1970, the dominant view of offenders was derived from psychiatric theories which suggested that men raped because of mental illness (Leppman 1941; Karpman 1954), because of uncontrollable urges (Karpman 1954; Guttmacher and Weihofen 1952), or because alcohol reduced their social constraints (Leppman 1941; Guttmacher 1951). Criminology theory has attempted to explain the role of the rape victim in terms of victim precipitation and victim participation (von Hentig 1948; Mendelsohn 1963; Wolfgang 1966; Schafer 1968; Amir 1971).

Contemporary views of rapists include the feminist perspective, which sees rape as serving the function of social control (Brownmiller 1975; Griffin 1971; Reynolds 1974) by keeping women in their place

(Weis and Borges 1973; Russell 1975). The sociological perspective views rape as behavior learned socially through interactions with others (Scully and Marolla 1982). Sociologists also talk of ways in which certain social structures (Williams and Holmes 1981) and ideological systems (Burt 1980; Holmstrom and Burgess 1983) promote rape. The clinical perspective has classified the rapist by descriptive psychiatric categories (Rada 1978) and by psychological motivation (Cohen et al. 1971; Groth 1979). Of pragmatic assistance in assessing impact on the victim has been rape conceptualized as an act of violence and power rather than primarily a sexual act. On the basis of clinical data on 133 convicted rapists and 92 adult victims, Groth, Burgess, and Holmstrom (1978) viewed rape as complex, multidetermined, and addressing issues of hostility (anger) and control (power) more than passion (sexuality). Subdivisions of these categories include the power-assertive rapist who perceives rape as a means of expressing his virility and dominance; the power-reassurance rapist who uses the act of rape to resolve doubts about his sexual adequacy; the anger-retaliation rapist who seeks revenge by degrading and humiliating women; and the anger-excitation rapist who derives sexual excitement from inflicting pain and punishing his victim. In pair or group rape, the motive of seeking male camaraderie has been suggested (Holmstrom and Burgess 1980), and the motive of a sense of entitlement to sexual services has been observed in data on father-daughter incest (Herman and Hirschman 1981), wife rape (Russell 1982), and a comparison of avoiders and victims of rape (Bart and O'Brien, unpublished).

Analysis of the dynamics and method of operation of the rapist helps to explain what specific aspects terrorized or victimized the person. Style of attack has been classified as *blitz*, where the victim is quickly subdued and propelled into the assault, *con*, where the victim is approached verbally and then betrayed and assaulted, or *surprise*, where the rapist waits and targets a victim or sneaks up and surprises the victim (Burgess and Holmstrom, 1974; Hazelwood, forthcoming). Other factors to assess include site of attack (safe vs. unsafe territory), degree of prior acquaintance between assailant and victim, amount of physical force and subsequent injury, method of control used by assailant, use of weapon, resistance by victim and assailant response, conversation and language used by the assailant, sexual demands and sexual dysfunction of the assailant.

Intrusive Imagery

The second major diagnostic criterion of PTSD is re-experiencing of the trauma, most frequently evidenced by recurrent and intrusive recollection of the event ("It is the first thing I think of when I wake up in the morning"). Day images are common ("Something will trigger in my head and it all comes back"). The victim may feel as though the traumatic event were recurring ("I panicked at work when two people came into the store and acted suspicious"). Or the impact may be so intense that the victim will report not remembering anything initially and then being reminded constantly of the event. The victim may report seeing the assailant everywhere ("I see his face on every man") as well as searching him out ("I walk next to walls and look at every face and think: is he the one?").

Dreams and nightmares are common and very upsetting. Dreams include people chasing and reassaulting the victim. Dreams may be of three types: (1) replication of the state of victimization and helplessness ("I use my mace and it turns to water"); (2) symbolic dreams which include a theme from the rape, as in one case in which a victim pleaded unsuccessfully her fear of pregnancy and had recurrent dreams of eggs pouring out of her and babies rolling down the hill and dying; and (3) mastery dreams in which the victim is powerful in assuming control ("I took the knife and stabbed him over and over").

Non-mastery dreams dominate until the victim is recovered. An illustration of the wide range of non-mastery dreams is provided from the dream material of three victims of the same assault. A father, mother, and daughter, traveling on vacation, registered at a motel and were awakened around 1 a.m. by two armed men who broke into their room, bound the father and raped the mother and daughter. Nightmares averaged four to five times a week for the first year. The father's repetitive dream included faceless armed men chopping his wife and daughter into little bloody pieces. This dream would awaken the father with feelings of terror, cold, and sweat. He would get up, take his gun, walk downstairs to his den, light cigarette after cigarette and sit guarding the door until morning. The mother's repetitive dream included her seeing the men chase her. She buys three guns but in her dream is unable to kill them. The daughter dreams of the men coming after her. She takes a gun, shoots at them but is unsuccessful in killing them and they start chasing her. She starts running, gets to a tunnel which is all black inside and wakes up.

Numbing

The third major diagnostic criterion is a numbing of responsiveness to or reduced involvement with the environment. Victims talk of being in a "state of shock," or "feeling numb," or state "it doesn't feel real." They say they can't believe it happened. Sometimes this phenomenon is observed through the demeanor of the victim in an expressed style where the feelings are visible (e.g., anxiety, fear, shame, sobbing, relief, anger, paranoia), or in a controlled style where the victim appeared calm and controlled externally. This latter style is more common reflecting denial, shock, or exhaustion (Burgess and Holmstrom 1974; Horowitz 1976; Soules et al. 1978). This psychic numbing may be observed through the victim's reduced interests in former activities ("I used to enjoy sketching in the park but now am terrified of going out alone"). Victims will talk of now feeling constrained in their activities, of feeling isolated and estranged from others. Victims may be immobilized and refuse to venture out of their apartment except for work, or, if attacked inside the home, may feel less anxious at work or outside. Others may also comment on the sudden change in the victim's behavior, as one husband who said, "she used to be the spark plug in the family." Victims may become defensive and rigid in demeanor; may refuse to attend social functions; may stop work or school and withdraw from their family. Victims talk of how easily one can become a victim ("He was in the door in seconds"). One fifty-two year old woman became socially isolated from her friends, less patient with her grandchildren, and found it exceedingly difficult to attend to the health needs of her elderly parents.

Symptoms

The fourth criterion of PTSD states that there should be two of the following list of symptoms that were not present prior to the rape:

(1) Exaggerated startle response of hyper-alertness. Victims
report feeling moody, irritable, and experiencing crying
spells, often when crying was not a common behavior.
Victims report feeling paranoid ("I keep thinking I am
being followed"); search their house before feeling safe;
feel there are "eyes" everywhere; believe people can tell
by looking that they have been raped. They may act on
their hyper-alertness ("I scream when I hear footsteps
behind me") and may change residence and telephone number
in order to feel safely anonymous.

(2) Disturbance in sleep pattern. In the acute disruptive
phase there can be a wide range of somatic complaints
that frequently includes headaches as well as sleep pattern disturbances. Victims are either not able to fall
asleep or fall asleep only to wake and not be able to
return to sleep. Victims who have been suddenly awakened
from their sleep by the assailant may find themselves
waking each night at the same time the attack occurred.
Partners of victims report that the victim may cry or
scream out during sleep.

(3) Guilt about surviving or behavior employed during the
rape. Victims may express a self-blame reaction to the
rape because of their socialization to the attitude of
"blame the victim" (Ryan 1972). Or victims may feel
guilty about not reporting. In cases in which the same
assailant rapes a second person in the same work place or
apartment complex, the first victim may feel guilty for
not reporting initially. Or in cases in which a partner
or parent is present, there may be guilt for not being
able to prevent the rape of the partner or child.

(4) Impairment of memory and/or power of concentration. The
intrusive imagery, in part, is responsible for the victim
not being able to concentrate on work (Schuker 1979) or
usual activities. Victims may have memory lapses ("I
couldn't remember the names of my customers") or decreased
energy levels ("I found doing the laundry was too ex-
hausting"). Students have difficulty writing papers and
examinations ("I failed my final tests").

(5) Avoidance of activities that arouse recollection. Fears
and phobias develop as a defensive reaction to the circumstances of the rape. Rado (1948), in describing war
victims, used the term traumatophobia to define the phobic reaction to a traumatic situation. Some of the common phobic responses noted in rape victims include: fear
of indoors if the rape occurred inside; fear of outdoors
if the rape occurred outside the home; fear of being a-
lone ("I can't take a shower if my husband isn't home");
fear of crowds ("I panic when there are people are a-
round"); or fear of elevators or stairs or people behind
them ("I left my clothes in the dryer for four days because I was too scared to go to the cellar"). There are
a wide variety of activities that can trigger a flashback
("My stomach gets into a big knot when anything reminds
me of it"). Victims try to avoid memories by throwing
out clothes they were wearing during the rape or the fur-
niture from their room if attacked inside.

(6) Increased symptoms that symbolize or resemble the event. One of the more common rape-related symptoms that resemble the rape occurs when the victim is confronted with sexual activity. Many victims experienced disruption in their sexual life and developed a wide range of symptoms including change in sexual frequency (abstention, decreased activity as well as increased); flashbacks to the rape. Some women terminated primary relationships; there could be a change in gender preference for a sexual partner. Other symbolic events where linkage was noted between some idiosyncratic aspect of the rape included the following: difficulty swallowing, singing, or speaking after forced oral sexual penetration; repetition of symptoms from a prior victimization following the second victimization; and anniversary reaction due to the day or time of the month (e.g., full moon; during the victim's menstrual period; date of the month).

Subtypes of Rape Trauma

The DSM-III lists three types of PTSD: acute, chronic, and delayed response. Two additional subtypes have also been identified:

(1) Compounded reaction to rape trauma. Some victims may have a history of past or current physical, psychiatric, or social difficulties in addition to the acute rape trauma. This group may develop additional symptoms such as depression, psychotic behavior, psychosomatic disorders, suicidal behavior, or behavior associated with alcoholism, drug use, and marked change in sexual activity (Burgess and Holmstrom 1979).

(2) Unresolved sexual trauma. A delayed response to rape trauma--e.g., an unresolved sexual trauma--occurs in the victim who experienced the rape long before contact with with the clinician. This victim has not told anyone of the rape, has not settled or integrated her or his thoughts, feelings, or behaviors on the issue, and is carrying a tremendous psychological burden. Very often a second sexual trauma, crisis, or flashback will reactivate the person's reaction to the prior experience. The following example illustrates one of the longest sexual trauma secrets noted in the literature (Burgess and Holmstrom 1979)--a secret kept for 50 years. A 72-year-old woman was being seen in a neighborhood health clinic for treatment of a terminal illness. The patient developed a therapeutic alliance with the medical resident of the clinic. During one conversation in which the woman talked of her feelings about dying, she revealed an early sexual trauma. She reported a situation in which she was returning home from school and 4 teenagers grabbed her, pushed her into the bushes and raped her. She went home crying as well as terrified and told her mother. The mother instructed the daughter to "get down on your knees and beg forgiveness." The woman never told another person about the trauma. She reported living a non-sexual lifestyle, never married and remained in the home until she was the last living member of the family.

TREATMENT

The prototype of crisis response is the acute grief reaction (Notman and Nadelson 1976; Ochberg and Fojtik-Stroud 1982; Parad 1965; Rado 1948; Tyhurst 1951). Lindemann (1944) first described the grieving process after interviewing survivors and relatives of a community disaster involving fire. Response to loss was characterized by distorted, prolonged, or delayed reactions.

Crisis Intervention

Crisis intervention is clearly the best immediate treatment when a rape is disclosed (Burgess and Holmstrom 1974; Forman 1980; Fox and Scherl 1972; McCombie 1980). The basic assumptions underlying this type of intervention include: (1) the rape represents a crisis in that the victim's style of life is disrupted; (2) the victim is regarded as "normal" or functioning adequately prior to the external stressor; (3) crisis intervention aims to return the victim to her or his previous level of functioning as quickly as possible. The crisis model is issue-oriented treatment designed to ameliorate the symptoms of anxiety, fear, depression, loss of control, and decreased assertiveness. The most favorable prognosis for treatment of acute rape trauma occurs if the victim is seen immediately following the rape; the speed of the intervention is crucial. The use of the term "crisis intervention" provides a non-threatening term that avoids labeling the treatment in psychiatric terms. Other crisis services to offer the victim include advocacy services especially regarding legal matters, work with the victim's support system, and victim mutual support groups.

Within the acute period, issues unique to the crisis need to be resolved and integrated or the victim will fail to return to a pre-crisis level of functioning. Rape work--the term used by Bassuk (1980)--refers to the issues specific to rape which need to be addressed. The aim of rape work is to regain a sense of safety and a valued sense of self, and to reestablish sharing, altruistic, mutually satisfying partner relationships in a world where rape remains a threat to all women.

Treatment Models

The question of treatment models in general, as raised by Paul (1966), is not how one should best treat a patient, but which treatment model in the hands of which therapist is most appropriate for a particular type of patient as defined by a specific outcome measure. To apply this question to the rape victim, one needs to look at the assessment of efficacy of treatment. The clinician can assess whether the victim has come to terms psychologically and cognitively with the assault and whether the victim has returned to a pre-crisis level of functioning, especially with primary relationships as well as work, family, and social relationships. Working with the victim in therapy, the clinician can usually observe and evaluate the course of recovery, noting that victims follow their own pattern and proceed only with nonjudgmental support, concern, and guidance. Several clinicians (Burgess and Holmstrom 1979; Krupnick and Horowitz 1979; Schuker 1979) have observed that adaptive resolution of the rape trauma can lead to a higher level of psychological functioning for the victim.

There are several treatment models available for the rape victim. Cognitive-behavioral models (Kilpatrick et al. 1977) hypothesize that fear and anxiety responses are classically conditioned by a rape experience. Ochberg and Fojtik-Stroud (1982) propose a residential treatment setting for victims. Cognitive restructuring (Hepper and Hepper 1977) is especially useful in working on belief systems and thought patterns of victims. Sprung (1977) suggests some victims adjust by encapsulating the trauma into one area of functioning, enabling them to function adequately in others. Brief psychotherapy with hypnosis is described by Spiegel and Spiegel (1978). Other models include treating the family as a unit (Doyle and Dorlac 1978; Ellis 1978); helping husbands and boyfriends of victims share the crisis of rape (Silverman 1978); and providing public programs and services (Ochberg and Spates 1981).

It is not unusual for rape victims to resist seeking traditional psychotherapy services provided by mental health staff. Of a total number of 135 referrals of victims of sexual assault, Krupnick and Horowitz (1980) saw only 10 percent at their clinic. Of the 13 victims seen, 5 did not complete therapy. It was suggested by Krupnick and Horowitz that those who sought therapy did so because of intrusive imagery and symptoms that were disruptive to life functioning. Soules et al. (1978) report that with vigorous rehabilitation programs, the percentage of victims seeking services can increase.

The most common explanation for why victims do not seek psychological services is that, unless they have had psychotherapy prior to the rape, they are not inclined to define the rape as a psychological problem. Midlarsky (1980) even warns that providing psychotherapy for rape victims may be a way of actually encouraging the internalization of blame and a self-critical attitude.

Recovery

Longitudinal studies are beginning to address the process of recovery and the variables that exacerbate or reduce rape trauma. As noted by Ruch and Chandler (1983), rape trauma has been measured in diverse ways, including the nature of the stressor experienced by the victim, severity of the response, length of recovery time (Burgess and Holmstrom 1979; Williams and Holmes 1981), and adjustment problems (McCahill et al. 1979; Resnick et al. 1981). Ruch and Chandler (1980) found a curvilinear relationship between life change and rape trauma--victims experiencing moderate life changes during the year before the assault reported less trauma than victims with severe changes or no changes. Using a two week interval between initial interview and medical follow-up appointment to measure the trauma response, Ruch and Chandler (1983) suggest that, while rape trauma is a complex phenomenon, prior stresses operating on the victim at the time of the assault (e.g., life change, earlier rapes, and mental health problems) have an important and independent effect on the degree of rape trauma and on responses to that trauma. In their study of 166 victims, prior rape was the most significant in explaining delayed recovery. Other significant variables in the rate of recovery included low self-esteem, lack of social support, economic stress, and prior mental health problems (Burgess and Holmstrom 1979).

SUMMARY

The crisis that results when a person has been sexually assaulted is in the service of self-preservation. Victims generally cope with the choice that living is better than dying. The victims' reactions to the impending threat to their lives is the nucleus around which adaptive patterns may be noted.

   With the increasing statistics on rape and sexual assault, this is not a private syndrome. It is a public concern and its treatment, from hospital, police and criminal justice-level staff has been addressed in the President's 1983 Task Force on Victims of Violence as a public charge. Professionals are increasingly being called upon to assist rape victims and their families in the acute and long-term reorganization process as they attempt to repair and recover their lives.

REFERENCES

Amir, M. *Patterns in Forcible Rape*. Chicago, Illinois: University of Chicago Press, 1971.

American Psychiatric Association. *Diagnostic and Statistical Manual of Mental Disorders*, 3rd ed. Washington, D.C., 1980.

Bard, M., and K. Ellison. "Crisis Intervention and Investigation of Forcible Rape." *Police Chief* 16 (1974): 68-74.

Bart, P.B. "Rape Doesn't End With a Kiss." *Viva*, June, 1975.

Bart, P., and O'Brien. "Avoiders of Rape." (Manuscript in preparation.)

Bassuk, E. "A Crisis Theory Perspective on Rape." In *The Rape Crisis Intervention Handbook*, edited by S.L. McCombie. New York: Plenum, 1980.

Bernard, C. *Introduction à l'étude de la Medicine Expérimentale*. Paris: Editions Flammarion, 1945.

Borgida, E., and P. White. "Social Perception of Rape Victims: The Impact of Legal Reform." *Law and Human Behavior* 2 (1978): 339-351.

Breuer, J., and S. Freud. (1893-95) *Studies on Hysteria*, Standard Edition, 2. London: Hogarth Press, 1955.

Brownmiller, S. *Against Our Will: Men, Women and Rape*. New York: Simon and Schuster, 1975.

Burgess, A.W., and L.L. Holmstrom. "Coping Behavior of the Rape Victim." *American Journal of Psychiatry* 133 (1976): 413-418.

Burgess, A.W., and L.L. Holmstrom. *Rape: Crisis and Recovery*. Bowie, Maryland: Brady Co., 1979.

Burgess, A.W., and L.L. Holmstrom. "Rape Trauma Syndrome." *American Journal of Psychiatry* 131 (1974): 981-986.

Burt, M.R. "Cultural Myths and Supports for Rape," *Journal of Personality and Social Psychology* 38 (1980): 217.

Cannon, W.B. *The Wisdom of the Body*. New York: W.W. Norton, 1932.

Carrington, F. "Victims' Rights Litigation: A Wave of the Future?" In *Perspectives on Crime Victims*, edited by B. Galaway and J. Hudson. St. Louis, Missouri: C.V. Mosby Co., 1981.

Chappell, D., G. Geis, and F. Fogarty. "Forcible Rape: Bibliography." *Journal of Criminal Law and Criminology* 65 (1974): 248-263.

Cobb, K.A., and N.R. Schauer. "Michigan's Criminal Sexual Assault Law." In *Forcible Rape*, edited by D. Chappell, R. Geis and G. Geis. New York: Columbia University Press, 1977.

Cohen, M.L., R. Garofalo, R. Boucher, and T. Seghorn. "The Psychology of Rapists." *Seminars in Psychiatry* 3 (1971): 307-327.

Davis, A.J. "Sexual Assaults in the Philadelphia Prison System and Sheriff's Vans." *Trans-Action*, December, 1968: 8-16.

Doyle, A.M., and C. Dorlac. "Treating Chronic Crisis Bearers and Their Families." *Journal of Marriage and Family Counseling* 4 (1978): 37-42.

Dworkin, R.B. "The Resistance Standard in Rape Legislation." *Stanford Law Review* 18 (1966): 680-689.

Ellis, A. "Family Therapy: A Phenomenological and Active Directive Approach." *Journal of Marriage and Family Counseling* 4 (1978): 43-50.

Ellis, H. *Studies on the Psychology of Sex*, 2 vols. New York: Random House, 1942.

Engel, G.L. "Homeostasis, Behavioral Adjustment and the Concept of Health and Disease." In *Mid-Century Psychiatry*, edited by R.R. Grinker. Springfield, Illinois: C.C. Thomas, 1953.

Fenichel, O. *The Psychoanalytic Theory of Neurosis*. New York: Norton, 1945.

Forman, B.D. "Psychotherapy with Rape Victims." *Psychotherapy: Theory, Research and Practice* 17 (1980): 304-311.

Fox, S.S., and D.J. Scherl. "Crisis Intervention with Victims of Rape." *Social Work* 17 (1972): 37-42.

Furst, S.S. "Psychic Trauma: A Survey." In *Psychic Trauma*, edited by S.S. Furst. New York: Basic Books, 1967.

Gebhard, P.H., J.H. Gagnon, W.B. Pomeroy, and C.V. Christenson. *Sex Offenders*. New York: Harper & Row, 1965.

Gelles, R.J. "Power, Sex and Violence: The Case of Marital Rape." *Family Coordinator* 26 (1977): 339-347.

Griffin, S. "Rape: The All-American Crime." *Ramparts* 10 (1971): 26-35.

Groth, A.N. *Men Who Rape: The Psychology of the Offender*. New York: Plenum, 1979.

Groth, A.N., A.W. Burgess, and L.L. Holmstrom. "Rape: Power, Anger and Sexuality." *American Journal of Psychiatry* 134 (1977): 1239-1243.

Guttmacher, M.S. *Sex Offenses*. New York: Norton, 1951.

Guttmacher, M.S., and H. Weihofen. *Psychiatry and the Law*. New York: Norton, 1952.

Hazelwood, R.R. A behaviorally-oriented interview of rape victims. *F.B.I. Law Enforcement Bulletin* 52 (1983): 8-15.

Hentig, H. von. *The Criminal and His Victim*. New Haven: Yale University Press, 1948.

Hepper, P.P., and M. Hepper. "Rape: Counseling the Traumatized Victim." *Personnel and Guidance Journal* 56 (1977): 77-80.

Herman, J., and L. Hirschman. "Families at Risk for Father-Daughter Incest." *American Journal of Psychiatry* 138 (1981): 967-970.

Hilberman, E. *The Rape Victim.* Washington, D.C.: American Psychiatric Association, 1976.

Holmstrom, L.L., and A.W. Burgess. "Sexual Behavior of Assailants During Reported Rape." *Archives of Sexual Behavior* 9 (1980): 427-439.

Holmstrom, L.L., and A.W. Burgess. *The Victim of Rape: Institutional Reactions.* New York: Wiley, 1978; New Brunswick, N.J.: Transaction, 1983.

Horowitz, M.J. *Stress Response Syndromes.* New York: Jason Aronson Inc., 1976.

Karpman, B. *The Sexual Offender and His Offenses.* New York: Julian Press, 1954.

Kilpatrick, D.G., L.J. Veronen, and P.A. Resick. "The Aftermath of Rape: Recent Empirical Findings." *American Journal of Orthopsychiatry* 49 (1979): 658-669.

Krafft-Ebing, R. von. *Psychopathia Sexualis.* New York: Putnam's Sons, 1965.

Krupnick, J.L., and M.J. Horowitz. "Victims of Violence: Psychological Responses, Treatment Implications." *Evaluation and Change.* Minnesota: Minneapolis Medical Research Foundation, Inc., 1980.

Krystal, H., ed. *Massive Psychic Trauma.* New York: International Universities Press, 1968.

Law Enforcement Assistance Administration. *Criminal Victimization Surveys in 13 American Cities.* Washington, D.C.: U.S. Government Printing Office, 1975.

LeGrand, C.E. "Rape and Rape Laws: Sexism in Society and Law." *California Law Review* 61 (1973): 919-941.

Leppman, F. "Essential Differences Between Sex Offenders." *Journal of Criminal Law and Criminology* 32 (1941): 366-380.

Lindemann, E. "Symptomotology and Management of Acute Grief." *American Journal of Psychiatry* 101 (1944): 141-146.

McCahill, T.W., C. Meyer, and A.M. Fischman. *The Aftermath of Rape.* Lexington, Massachusetts: D.C. Heath Co., 1979.

McCombie, S.L., ed. *The Rape Crisis Intervention Handbook.* New York: Plenum, 1980.

Mendelsohn, B. "The Origin of the Doctrine of Victimology." *Excerpta Criminologica* 3 (1963).

Metzger, D. "It Is Always the Woman Who Is Raped." *American Journal of Psychiatry* 133 (1976): 405-408.

Midlarsky, E. Discussion of Schwartz Paper, in *Methodology in Sex Research.* Conference proceedings, U.S. Department of Health and Human Services, DHHS 80-766, 1980.

Midlarsky, E. "Women, Psychopathology, and Psychotherapy: A Partially Annotated Bibliography." *Journal Supplement Abstract Service*, manuscript 1472, American Psychological Association, 1977.

Niederland, W. "Clinical Observations On Survivor's Syndrome." *International Journal of Psychiatry* 49 (1968): 313-319.

Notman, M.T., and C.C. Nadelson. "The Rape Victim: Psychodynamic Considerations." *American Journal of Psychiatry* 133 (1976): 408-413.

Ochberg, F.M., and K.M. Fojtik-Stroud. "A Comprehensive Mental Health Clinical Service Program for Victims." Unpublished manuscript, 1982.

Ochberg, F.M., and C.R. Spates. "Services Integration for Victims of Personal Violence." In *Evaluating Victim Services*, edited by S. Salasin. Beverly Hills, California: Sage Publications, 1981.

Parad, H.J. *Crisis Intervention: Selected Readings*. New York: Family Service Association, 1965.

Paul, G.L. *Insight vs. Desensitization in Psychotherapy*. Stanford, California: Stanford University Press, 1966.

President's Task Force on Victims of Crime. Final Report, Washington, D.C., 1982.

Rabkin, J.G. "The Epidemiology of Forcible Rape." *American Journal of Orthopsychiatry* 49 (1979): 634-647.

Rada, R.T. *Clinical Aspects of the Rapists*. New York: Grune & Stratton, Inc., 1978.

Rado, S. "Pathodynamics and Treatment of Traumatic War Neurosis (Tramatophobia)." *Psychosomatic Medicine* 4 (1948): 362-368.

Resnik, P.A., K.S. Calhoun, B.M. Atkeson, and E.M. Ellis. "Social Adjustment in Victims of Sexual Assault." *Journal of Counseling and Clinical Psychology* 49 (1981): 705-712.

Reynolds, J.M. "Rape as Social Control." *Catalyst* 8 (1974).

Ruch, L.K., and S.M. Chandler. "Life Change and Rape Impact." *Journal of Health and Social Behavior* 21 (1980): 248-260.

Ruch, L.O., and S.M. Chandler. "Sexual Assault Trauma During the Acute Phase." *Journal of Health & Social Behavior* 24 (1983): 174-185.

Russell, D.E.H. *The Politics of Rape*. New York: Stein and Day, 1975.

Russell, D.E.H. *Rape in Marriage*. New York: Macmillan, 1982.

Ryan, W. *Blaming the Victim*. New York: Random House, 1972.

Schafer, S. *The Victim and his Criminal*. New York: Random House, 1968.

Schuker, E. "Psychodynamics and Treatment of Sexual Assault Victims." *Journal of American Academy of Psychoanalysis* 7 (1979): 553-573.

Schwendinger, J.R., and H. Schwendinger. "Rape Myths in Legal, Theoretical and Everyday Practice." *Crime and Social Justice* 1 (1974): 18-26.

Scully, D., and J. Marolla. "Convicted Rapists' Construction of Reality: The Denial of Rape." Paper presented at the annual meeting of the American Sociological Association. San Francisco, California, September, 1982.

Selye, H. *Stress without Distress*. New York: Lippincott, 1974.

Silverman, D.C. "Sharing the Crisis of Rape: Counseling the Mates and Families of Victims." *American Journal of Orthopsychiatry* 48 (1978): 166-173.

Soules, M., S.K. Stewart, K.M. Brown, and A.A. Pollard. "The Spectrum of Alleged Rape." *Journal of Reproductive Medicine* 20 (1978): 33-39.

Spiegel, H., and D. Spiegel. *Trance and Treatment*. New York: Basic Books, 1978.

Sprung, S. "Resolution of Rape Crisis: Six to Eighteen Month Follow-up." *Smith College Studies in Social Work* 48 (1977): 20-24.

Sutherland, S., and D. Scherl. "Patterns of Response Among Victims of Rape." *American Journal of Orthopsychiatry* 40 (1970): 503-511.

Symonds, M. "The Rape Victim: Psychological Patterns of Response." *American Journal of Psychoanalysis* 36 (1976): 27-34.

Symonds, M. "Victims of Violence." *American Journal of Psychoanalysis* 35 (1975): 19-25.

Tyhurst, J.S. "Individual Reaction to Community Disaster: The Habitual History of Psychic Phenomenon." *American Journal of Psychiatry* 107 (1951): 764-769.

Weis, K., and S.S. Borges. "Victimology and Rape: The Case of the Legitimate Victim." *Issues in Criminology* 8 (1973): 72.

Werner, A. "Rape: Interruption of the Therapeutic Process by External Stress." *Psychotherapy: Theory, Research and Practice* 9 (1972): 349-351.

Williams, J.E., and K.A. Holmes. *The Second Assault: Rape and Public Attitudes*. Westport, Connecticut: Greenwood Press, 1981.

Wolfgang, M.E. *Patterns in Criminal Homicide*. New York: Science Editions, 1966.

CHAPTER 5

VIOLENCE IN THE HOME: A PUBLIC PROBLEM

Mary Hanemann Lystad

Considerable research in this country has been focused in the
last fifteen years on the phenomenon of family violence. Most of the
research has dealt with physical abuse of children, but more recently
the focus has expanded to include wife battering and the sexual abuse
of children and wives. Evidence shows that violence in the family
occurs when neither the family nor other social support systems fulfill the needs and demands of the individual, when a violent mode of
expression is easily available, and when it is condoned, sometimes
rewarded, by cultural norms (Finkelhor 1979; Gelles and Straus 1979;
Lystad 1982; Steinmetz 1977; Straus 1980).
     This chapter reports on 1) the incidence of violence; 2) causal
studies concerned with the psychological needs of the violent individual, the social situation in which violence occurs, and the norms
and values which sanction the violence; 3) intervention measures that
have been employed; and 4) prevention strategies.

INCIDENCE STUDIES

     Incidence data on violence in the home is sparse. Few family
members admit to such behavior, and, except for homicide or severe
child abuse, the behavior is easy to hide.
     A number of studies have revealed, however, that a high propor-
tion of victim/offender pairs consists of relatives. At the extreme
end of the violence spectrum, studies of homicide indicate that between 30 and 70 percent of the involved persons are relatives (Boudouris 1971; Field and Field 1973; Voss and Hepburn 1968; Wolfgang
1969). Straus (1980) found in his study of 2,143 husbands and wives
that 16 percent had engaged in violent acts with their spouses during
the year studied. Research by Walker (1979) on 120 battered women
shows that 59 percent of the women interviewed felt they had been
raped by their battering partners. Marital rape is not defined as a
crime in most states, and many men feel that their marriage license
is a sexual license as well. Most of the women in Walker's sample,
however, defined the interaction as sexual assault.
     Zalba (1971) estimates that 200,000 to 250,000 children, 30,000
of them badly hurt, need protection against child abuse in the United
States each year. The National Center on Child Abuse and Neglect
(1981) conservatively estimates that 100,000 children are sexually
abused each year, and that a high proportion of the cases involve
parents or other persons familiar to the child. Gil (1970) asserts
that reported cases are only a fraction of the real number of abused
children, which they estimate at between 2.5 and 4.1 million per year.
Analysis of the limited statistics leads to the conclusion that underreporting is massive, due to the fear of family disruption and social
stigma that would result from disclosure (De Frances 1969; Kempe 1979).
According to Kempe, sexual abuse is as frequent and as damaging as

This chapter is reprinted with permission, Mary H. Lystad, "Violence
in the Home: A Major Public Problem," *Urban and Social Change Review*,
15 (1982): 21-25.

physical abuse to the long-term development of children.

Some investigators feel strongly that all incidence reports of family violence are too low. The frequencies of brother-sister, child-parent, close friend or lover-family member violence have seldom been examined. What is clear, however, is that the problems are significant enough to warrant immediate attention.

CAUSAL STUDIES OF FAMILY VIOLENCE

Studies of family violence have analyzed the phenomenon from psychological, social, and cultural perspectives. A review of the literature leads to the conclusion that a comprehensive study of violence at home must take into account factors at these several levels, placing individual functioning within the social group and within the cultural norms by which the group operates. Each perspective is addressed here.

Psychological Problems

The offender is usually a male aggressor against a female wife, child, or stepchild. Some studies indicate that the aggressor suffers from psychological disorders: personality disorders, maladaptive behaviors, and psychoses, including manic depressive and schizophrenic behavior (Bennie and Sclare 1969; Elmer 1971; Grumet 1970). Zalba (1966), in analyzing child battering by schizophrenic parents, states that parents act out or displace their anger over marital conflicts onto their children. Children become convenient targets of abuse and injury, with the adult denying interpsychic--emotional upset which occurs as a result of interactions of persons with one another--and other hostility and aggression.

Alcoholism and drug abuse frequently accompany male aggressive behavior. Spouses, in particular, tend to reject the offender because of their disgust at the alcoholism and its consequences. Alcohol also lessens the offender's inhibitions against committing violence. Many alcoholic offenders have records of previous criminal offenses and especially of other violent crimes (Awad 1976; Fontana 1971; McCord 1972).

Interpsychic stress is frequently reported in the literature on violent behavior in the home. Adult violence in the home is repeatedly cited as a cause for marital unhappiness, discord, and divorce (Cormier 1962; Snell 1974). In an anlysis of complaints of husbands and wives seeking divorce, Levinger (1966) reports that wives complain about neglect, physical or verbal abuse, lack of love, or other matters included under the catch-all term of "mental cruelty." Husbands are also disturbed by neglect, emotional cruelty, and lack of love, but they are more prone to express complaints in terms of in-law intervention or sexual mismatching.

Some studies relate the psychological problems between mother and father to child abuse (Holter and Friedman 1968; Johnson and Morse 1968; Terr 1970), where the husband or wife displaces hostility onto the child. Still other researchers have found child abuse to be related to the stress of mothering. Elmer (1971) and others point out that child abuse is usually the result of accumulated stresses within the family and that they occur most frequently in the lower socioeconomic classes. Among the stress-producing factors are the birth of several children close together, premature birth, and special physical or emotional problems incurred by children. With the increasing isolation of the nuclear family from relatives, and with the increasing number of one-parent families, parents--most often mothers--are on call twenty-four hours a day, seven days a week, fifty-two weeks of the year. When there is no relief from the pressures of this job, the result is often aggression of one sort or another.

Social Situations

Explanatory models which rely solely on the factors of psychopathological and personal stress are not sufficient to a full understanding of the problems. Certain social variables are also significantly correlated with the occurrence of violence. Among the significant social characteristics of the offender are his childhood socialization, his position in the family, and his position in society.

A number of studies of physical assaults in the family identify a generational pattern of abuse. The battered child tends to become a battering adult. This phenomenon can be described as an identification with the aggressive parent, an identification which occurs with the aggressive parent, an identification which occurs even though the offspring may strongly wish to be different (Jenkins 1970; Lascari 1972; Oliver 1971). In particular, being a victim of sexual abuse as a child appears to be a factor in whether or not one becomes a sexual abuser. Swift (1977) reports that a large proportion of males who abuse children have been sexually abused as children. She interprets the adult offenders as both sexually ignorant and socially immature. Groth (1982) has found that, whereas only 20 percent of a population of convicted drug offenders reported sexual abuse as children, 57 percent of a population of convicted sex offenders, rapists, and child molesters reported hands-on sexual abuse as children.

The power structure within the family is also a factor in offender behavior. Gelles and Straus (1979) and Steinmetz (1980) point to the traditionally superordinate-subordinate relationships of men and women and of adults and children, found both in the family and in other societal groups as well. These relationships allow for and condone the use of power by those of superior status. Men are expected to play hard, work hard, and treat others in a hard manner. Women and children are expected to react submissively and silently. Not only are women victimized, but they are also blamed for their victimization--because they have not learned to fight back and because they lack the socio-economic supports which would enable them to leave the abusive relationship. Bart (1978) acknowledges that a comparative study of victims and avoiders could be interpreted in such a way as to place blame on victims for acquiescing to the violence. She believes, however, that locating the source of the problem within the social structure rather than within the personality structure of those involved supplies a more valid interpretation. Children are even less able than adults to avoid abuse. Finkelhor (1979) argues that children do not know enough about psychosexual development or needs to define the situation as abusive. Because of their low power status, they are helpless to ward off the abuse.

Finally, the social position of the offender in the larger society appears to relate to violent behavior. Lower socio-economic status (using educational, income, and occupational indices) has been shown to be significantly correlated with family violence (Julian and Mohr 1979; Straus 1980; Zuckerman et al. 1972). Straus found further that the most intense violence occurs in households in which the husband is unemployed or employed part-time. In his national sample, unemployed men are twice as likely as fully employed men to use severe

violence on their wives. Men employed part-time had a rate of wife
beating three times the rate for men employed full-time. Further,
unemployed men and men employed part-time were three times more likely to be beaten by their wives. Children whose fathers were employed
part-time were nearly twice as likely to be victims of severe violence
as were children whose fathers held full-time jobs.

Cultural Factors
     Cultural factors in offender behavior, as reported by Mokran and
Kramer (1976) and Steinmetz (1977), relate to the historical roots of
male dominance and violence against women in American and other cultures. Perpetrators of violent acts are described as having personality traits of dominance and aggression; they feel it is acceptable
to be physically and sexually abusive, since they are males and leaders in the society. Further, young boys in general have been socialized to such roles and young girls have been socialized to be passive
and to accept such male behavior.
     Because of male dominance in society, some women acquiesce to
the notion that wife battering of a sexual or other nature is all
right because the wife belongs to the husband. According to Walker
(1979), such women feel powerless to make their wishes and needs
known. They may stay in the home because of economic, legal, and social dependence, and may feel that alternative living arrangements
are unacceptable. Many daughters similarly accept sexual abuse, because they do not feel they have any other rights or choices.
     Abrahamsen (1970) and Gil (1970) discuss the attitudes and values
of cultures which sanction violence as a way of life. Gil writes that
the reason for considerable child abuse in American society is that
the cultural norms of child rearing allow the use of a certain amount
of physical force towards children by adults caring for them. Use of
force is encouraged by the mass media and particularly by television,
which, in both adult- and child-centered shows, frequently and provocatively projects violent behavior.

                              INTERVENTION

     Violence in the family has been conceptualized in the mental
health literature as a symptom of family dysfunction, which may or
may not be accompanied by psychiatric disorder. During periods in
which abuse does occur, the family may be in general neurotic equilibrium, able to function well in areas such as household management
and economic support, but not in the area of interpersonal relationships. Family members--offenders, victims, and others surrounding
them--often fear disintegration of the family if the violence were to
be made known, and they make great efforts to hide the fact of abuse.
     The family requires, then, a range of professional and community-
based resources for early identification and treatment, including
legal, health, mental health, and social services. Paulson (1978)
states that the strategies for effecting such help must recognize the
needs of all those involved, including victims, offenders, and other
family members. The literature stresses the need for multidisciplinary intervention. Professional persons concerned include the primary
care physician, the emergency room physician and nurse, the social
worker, the volunteer counselor or companion, police, and other members of the law enforcement team (Community Council of Greater New
York 1979; Kempe 1979; Nadelson and Rosenfeld 1980).
     Some victims, primarily women and children, may need a totally

supportive temporary environment. Shelters or immediate hospitalization can provide immediate physical care and emotional support after a serious incident. These temporary environments further allow the victim, if an adult, and child welfare workers, if the victim is a child, time to plan interim treatment and living requirements. They can provide crucial social supports in time of crisis. The supports, however, are only temporary, makeshift measures. In most cases, women and children do go back to their family, although it is hoped they return with added psychic strength to a better functioning unit. Most victims want to go home, preferring their own family to the alternatives: for a woman, of living alone for a time; or for a child, of being separated from parents (Straus 1980; Walker 1979).

Treatment, several authors feel, should consist of both individual and family therapy in order to reach the underlying dynamics within the family (Bernstein 1979; Burgess 1977; Devine 1980). Although there have been numerous articles describing treatment, outcomes and prognosis, data from current treatment programs are scarce.

In addition to describing traditional voluntary treatment models, the literature also describes community treatment models. These models assume that effective intervention requires organized community control and the mobilization of many resources working cooperatively. Phases of treatment in a model reported by Anderson and Shafer (1979) include: the family broken into small units for treatments such as individual counseling; alcohol abuse intervention when appropriate; the family reunited in therapy but not in the household; and family therapy continued after the return home of the missing member from an institution. Still another community treatment model presented by Giarretto (1976) involves self-help groups, such as Parents United, in conjunction with professional community services. The thrust of this model is a sharing of experiences and ways of coping with them. Greater support services for families must be available in communities in order both to alleviate violence in the family and to provide an adequate atmosphere for child rearing.

Much of the literature on the treatment of families raises concerns about splitting up the family group for any length of time. Removal of victims or immediate incarceration of the perpetrator, some investigators argue, may cause more harm than good, if it results in the absence of therapeutic services. A more realistic conceptualization of the appropriate treatment of prolonged violence requires therapeutic planning and careful intervention, undertaken over a long period of time in a family which remains fully intact throughout the treatment period (Nadelson and Rosenfeld 1980).

PREVENTION

Intervention measures are needed to protect the physical and emotional well-being of victims and of other family members. Intervention measures, however, are not designed to substantially reduce or eliminate violence in the home. Achievement of the latter requires the American society to initiate significant educational and social action programs in its communities. Prevention measures which relate to what is known about the causes of violence are outlined below:

> --*Special help to families with mentally ill and substance-abusing members*. These families are more vulnerable to family violence, especially to child abuse, and it is crucial that the members be made aware of alternative ways of working out frustrations and anxieties.

--*Educational programs for teenagers and young adults, dealing with family functioning and child care.* Interpersonal stresses in the home, especially around child rearing, are related to violence. In addition to learning algebra and geometry, young persons should be informed about the needs of a family, about the problems that may arise in meeting the needs, and about age-appropriate behaviors of children. Classes currently offered in community mental health centers, YWCAs, and church groups often do address these needs.

--*Interpersonal networks for nuclear families.* The isolation of nuclear families, which leaves them alone to cope with daily pressures of child rearing and economic survival, is related to violence. Without the traditional supports of the extended family, small families and one-parent families need outreach--in the apartment building, on the block, or in the church. Support networks allow a spouse or parent time to get away from the family and to talk with someone about common family problems.

--*Parent education in the use of non-violent techniques for raising children and especially in the positive reinforcement of the child's strengths and capabilities.* Parents who abuse children produce children who abuse. They teach children by their own example to deal with life's stresses through violent behavior. They say, in effect, that the control of people through violent means is legitimate and effective. Parent discussion groups and other self-help groups could provide educational services that counterbalance the effects of violent role models.

--*Education of teachers in the rights and responsibilities of children in social and physical interactions.* Children are socialized in the school as well as in the home. They need role models of nonviolence, and they need to be told clearly what is acceptable behavior and what is not acceptable behavior towards their peers in the halls, classrooms, and on the playing field. Educators need awareness of this as part of their professional training.

--*Liberation of women and men to perform and enjoy family tasks as they are able.* Rigid sex roles in the family and sexual inequality at home and in society contribute to family violence. Women with children should not be expected to stay at home all the time and be denied stimulating activities outside of the home. Nor should the fathers of children be deprived of pleasures and rewarding responsibilities of child care. The Women's Movement, with help from concerned men, has had considerable impact nationally in changing sex role images, but more must be done.

--*Increase in employment of men and of those women who want to or must work.* Inequities in the social structure--unemployment, underemployment, and poverty--are related to violence between family members. American society places high value on the work ethic. A person's dignity and self-esteem is thought to be related to her or his position in the work-place, and every person needs such dignity and self-esteem in order to be an adequate husband, wife, and parent.

--*Sensitization of parents to the importance of all children having a positive self-image of themselves, including respect for others.* As long as girls and boys are treated differently from the time of birth in terms of the cultural artifacts given to stimulate them (guns for boys, rag dolls for girls) and in terms of the demands made on them (heavy competition in sports for boys, politeness for girls) there will be male offenders and female victims in and out of the home. Again, parent discussion groups, perhaps with some help from women's groups, would be most useful.

--*Reduction in the frequency and intensity of violence displayed in the mass media.* The American culture of violence--from television war stories and crime shows for adults (which children watch) and cartoon violence for children--has been discussed repeatedly, but little has changed. Crimes of violence are presented on television, in popular magazines, comic books, and elsewhere as legitimate and exciting ways of controlling people. Retribution through violence is also extolled. Public demand for a change is essential.

The prevention measures mentioned here are not all-inclusive; some are more far reaching than others. Could they be accomplished in this decade? Certainly not by a single federal program, nor even by the cooperative efforts of mental health professionals (who do play a crucial educational role). They can only be accomplished by an American public sufficiently incensed by the problems of family violence to act upon these feelings of outrage and fear. Many Americans esteem "the family" as a sacred and cherished institution. And most Americans do care--about their families, their children, and their children's children. It is this value and this sense of care that provide some hope for the future.

REFERENCES

Abrahamsen, D. *Our Violent Society.* New York: Funk and Wagnalls, 1970.

Anderson, L., and G. Shafer. "The Character-Disordered Family: A Community Treatment Model for Family Sexual Abuse." *American Journal of Orthopsychiatry* 49 (1979): 436-445.

Awad, G. "Father-Son Incest: A Case Report." *Journal of Nervous and Mental Disease* 162 (1976): 135-139.

Bart, P. "Victimization and Its Discontents." In *Continuing Medical Education: Syllabus and Proceedings in Summary Form.* Washington, D.C.: American Psychiatric Association, 1978.

Bennie, E., and A. Sclare. "The Battered Child Syndrome." *American Journal of Psychiatry* 125 (1969): 975-979.

Bernstein, G. "Physician Management of Incest Situations." *Human Sexuality* 13 (1979): 67, 71, 75, 79, 83, 87.

Boudouris, J. "Homicide and the Family." *Journal of Marriage and the Family* 33 (1971): 667-676.

Burgess, A., L. Holmstrom, and M. McCausland. "Child Sexual Assault by a Family Member: Decisions Following Disclosure." *Victimology* 2 (1977): 236-250.

Community Council of Greater New York. "Sexual Abuse of Children: Implications from the Sexual Trauma Treatment Program of Connecticut Community Council of Greater New York." New York: Community Council, 1979.

Cormier, B. "Psychodynamics of Homicide Committed in a Marital Relationship." *Corrective Psychiatry and Journal of Society Therapy* 8 (1962): 187-194.

De Frances, V. *Protecting the Child Victim of Sex Crimes Committed by Adults.* Denver, Colorado: The American Humane Society, 1969.

Devine, R. "A Review of the Literature." *Sexual Abuse of Children: Selected Readings.* Washington, D.C.: National Center on Child Abuse and Neglect, DHHS Publication No. (OHDS) 78-30161, 1980.

Elmer, E. "Child Abuse: A Symptom of Family Crisis." In *Crisis of Family Disorganization*, edited by E. Pavenstedt. New York: Behavioral Publications, 1971.

Field, M., and H. Field. "Marital Violence and the Criminal Process: Neither Justice nor Peace." *Social Service Review* 47 (1973): 221-240.

Finkelhor, D. *Sexually Victimized Children.* New York: Free Press, 1979.

Fontana, V. "Which Parents Abuse Children?" *Medical Insight* 3 (1971): 16-21.

Gelles, R., and M. Straus. "Determinants of Violence in the Family: Toward a Theoretical Integration." In *Contemporary Theories About the Family*, edited by W. Burr. New York: Free Press, 1979.

Giarretto, H. "The Treatment of Father-Daughter Incest: A Psychosocial Approach." *Children Today* 5 (1976): 2-5, 34-35.

Gil, D. *Violence Against Children: Physical Child Abuse in the United States.* Cambridge, Massachusetts: Harvard University Press, 1970.

Groth, N. "The Sexual Assault of Males: Victim and Offender Issues." Paper presented at the Fourth National Conference and Workshops on Sexual Aggression. Denver, Colorado, 1982.

Grumet, B. "The Plaintive Plaintiffs: Victims of the Battered Child Syndrome." *Family Law Quarterly* 4 (1970): 296-317.

Holter, J., and S. Friedman. "Principles of Management in Child Abuse Cases." *American Journal of Orthopsychiatry* 38 (1968): 127-136.

Jenkins, R. "Interrupting the Family Cycle of Violence." *Journal of the Iowa Medical Society* 60 (1970): 85-89.

Johnson, R., and H. Morse. "Injured Children and Their Parents." *Children* 15 (1968): 147-152.

Julian, V., and C. Mohr. "Father-Daughter Incest: Profile of the Offender." *Victimology* 4 (1979): 348-360.

Kempe, C.H. "Recent Developments in the Field of Child Abuse." *Child Abuse and Neglect* 3 (1979): ix-xv.

Lascari, A. "The Abused Child." *Journal of the Iowa Medical Society* 62 (1972): 229-232.

Levinger, G. "Sources of Marital Dissatisfaction Among Applications for Divorce." *American Journal of Orthopsychiatry* 36 (1966): 803-807.

Lystad, M. "Sexual Abuse in the Home: A Review of the Literature." *International Journal of Family Psychiatry.* 3 (1983): 3-31.

McCord, J. "Etiological Factors in Alcoholism: Family and Personal Characteristics." *Quarterly Journal of Studies on Alcohol* 33 (1972): 1020-1027.

Mokran, A., and R. Kramer. "Incest and Incestuous Behavior in Forensic Practice." *Ceskoslovenska Psychiatrie* Praha, 72: 320-323.

Nadelson, C., and A. Rosenfeld. "Sexual Misuse of Children." In *Child Psychiatry and the Law*, edited by D. Schetky. New York: Brunner Mazel, 1980.

National Center on Child Abuse and Neglect. *Child Sexual Abuse: Incest, Assault, and Sexual Exploitation.* Washington, D.C.: DHHS Publication No. (OHDS) 81-30166, 1981.

Oliver, J., and A. Taylor. "Five Generations of Ill-Treated Children in One Family Pedigree." *British Journal of Psychiatry* 119 (1971): 473-480.

Paulson, M. "Incest and Sexual Molestation: Clinical and Legal Issues." *Journal of Clinical Child Psychology* 7 (1978): 177-198.

Snell, J. "The Wifebeater's Wife: A Study of Family Interaction." *Archives of General Psychiatry* 11 (1974): 107-112.

Steinmetz, S. *The Cycle of Violence: Assertive, Aggressive, and Abusive Family Interaction.* New York: Praeger, 1977.

Steinmetz, S. "Women and Violence: Victims and Perpetrators." *American Journal of Psychotherapy* 34 (1980): 334-350.

Straus, M., R. Gelles, and S. Steinmetz. *Behind Closed Doors: Violence in the American Family.* New York: Doubleday, 1980.

Swift, C. "Sexual Victimization of Children: An Urban Mental Health Center Survey." *Victimology* 2 (1977): 322-327.

Terr, L. "A Family Study of Child Abuse." *American Journal of Psychiatry* 127 (1970): 665-671.

Voss, H., and J. Hepburn. "Patterns in Criminal Homicide in Chicago." *Journal of Criminal Law, Criminology and Police Science* 59 (1968): 499-508.

Walker, L. *The Battered Woman.* New York: Harper and Row, 1979.

Wolfgang, M. "Who Kills Whom." *Psychology Today* 3 (1969): 54-56, 72-75.

Zalba, S. "The Abused Child: I. A Survey of the Problem." *Social Work* 11 (1966): 3-16.

Zalba, S. "Battered Children." *Transaction* 8 (1971): 58-61.

Zuckerman, K., J. Ambuel, and R. Bandman. "Child Neglect and Abuse." *Ohio State Medical Journal*, 1972, 68 (7): 629-632.

CHAPTER 6

THE "NORMALITY" OF INCEST:

Father-Daughter Incest as a Form of Family Violence.
Evidence from Historical Case Records

Linda Gordon
and
Paul O'Keefe

In recent years, several clinical and survey studies of incest
have produced new evidence about the nature and etiology of that behavior, as well as hypotheses about the characteristics of its participants (Herman 1981; Finkelhor 1979). In the course of a study of
family violence and its social control, using case records from
Boston-area social-service agencies from 1880 to 1960,[1] we found our
random sample of 502 to include 50 incest cases. We decided to examine these incest cases separately in the light of recent scholarship, and what follows is a presentation of some of our findings.[2]
    Neither our study nor our analysis was designed to be value-free.
On the contrary, we included incest in our study of family violence
because we had been persuaded by several recent scholarly works arguing that, when incest appears to families and social welfare agencies
as a social problem, it is usually a form of abuse (Butler 1978;
Groth 1978; Herman 1981; Rush 1977; MSPCC, *Annual Reports*). Two
works were particularly influential. Finkelhor's (1979) survey of
796 college students regarding childhood sexual activity found that
10 percent reported a cross-generational incestuous experience; of
these experiences, 93 percent were among girls and older men. Herman
(1981) compared father-daughter incest with other cases in which
there was a seductive, but not sexual, relationship between father
and daughter. She found that the former families were characterized
by rigid conformity to traditional sexual roles, fathers who dominated families through use of force and expressed no contrition for
their behavior, and frequently disabled (physically or psychologically) mothers. The girls in most cases did not tell anyone about their
incestuous activity but often became stubborn and rebellious as they
reached adolescence.

DEFINITIONS

    We used a social, not a legal, definition of incest. Incest
laws in the United States define a degree of blood relationship within which marriage is not permitted; these vary by state, of course,
but their focus is almost always on marriage. Incestuous sex outside
of marriage may be prosecuted as a form of indecent assault or statu-

This research was funded in part by NIMH Grant No. 5 R01 MH 33264-03.
The authors wish to acknowledge also the help of Anne Doyle Kenney,
Jan Lambertz and Nancy McKerrow whose labor and insights were of in-
estimable value. We also benefited from critical comments by Lou
Ferleger, David Finkelhor, and Judith Herman. Another version of
this paper appears in *Journal of Marriage and the Family*, February
1984. Revised June 1983.

tory rape. We were concerned, however, neither with criminal nor with marriage law, but with family violence and the social relations within households and families. Thus, we considered sexual relations incestuous not only if the two people were kin, but also if they occupied kinship roles--for example, stepfather and daughter. Especially among the poor, who were over-represented in our case records, the absence of legal marriage was common; yet this absence did not necessarily alter fundamental domestic relationships. For example, the legal distinction between a stepfather and a mother's lover did not necessarily correspond to a social-rational difference.

RESEARCH DESIGN

In our overall sampling of case records of the family violence atudy, we used the files of three nonsectarian private Boston social-work agencies.[3] We chose a random sample of cases from 1880 and every census year thereafter through 1960, and from four additional twelve-month periods chosen because they were stressful due to war and/or economic depression (7/1/93-6/30/94; 7/1/33-6/30/34; 1917; 1944). Of the randomly chosen cases we read 1,534, out of which 502 were relevant--that is, containing confirmed allegations of child abuse, child neglect, marital violence, or incest. The "case," that is, our unit of analysis, was the case record as defined by the social work agency. For that reason, our cases varied greatly in size, complexity, duration, and quantity of information. Some consisted of a few typewritten sheets; the average was about twenty pages; others contained as much as one hundred pages of typed agency reports plus scores of pages of documentation, test results, correspondence, and legal papers. We were unable to get some information that we had hoped for because of the high incidence of missing data in the earlier and less detailed records. We were, however, able to get large quantities of information on matters such as income level, household composition, the presence of particular stress factors, and the intervention of various social control agencies. We found incest cases in two different ways. First, we separated out those of the 502 randomly chosen cases which contained incest; these we call Sample A in the description of findings below. Second, we read 30 case records chosen in a search for incest cases; the total of these plus Sample A we call Sample B, which is nonrandom. Nevertheless, the 30 additional incest cases were not selected for any particular features, but include every incest case in the order that we found it in examining all cases from the given year in numerical order; given the nature of the record-filing systems of the agencies, there is no reason to suspect that Sample B is less representative than Sample A. In this paper, all statistics cited refer to random Sample A unless otherwise noted.

Our data have certain crucial limitations. First, since they are all clinical--that is, they are produced by the record-keeping practices of social workers--they represent only those family violence cases which have come to the attention of social control forces. These cases bear an indeterminate relation to the overall incidence of family violence, and we can make no judgments about that problem in the population at large. Second, the people in our sample were significantly poorer than the average in Boston. Third, we have no control group. We made no attempt, nor would we have been able, to compare the people in our sample to non-violent people. Fourth, we pooled data from various agency records, and cannot distinguish pos-

sible biases that might have been created by differential recording
techniques and emphases. Fifth, we were unable to identify quanti-
fiable changes over time in the incest cases, because there were too
few of them.

We did compare different types of family violence, something
which has not to our knowledge been done before. We compared incestuous families to families with nonsexual child abuse or adult
violence with regard to several characteristics.

FINDINGS

Of the 502 randomly chosen cases, 50 (10 percent) had incestuous
episodes. It is worth noting that this incidence approximates that
found by Finkelhor in his survey.

We examined the sex and age differential between incest partners.
The relationships were predominantly heterosexual. Forty-nine out of
50 of the older partners were male; 93 out of 197 of the younger
partners were female; the four young males were incestuously involved
with female siblings (Sample B).[4]

The mean age of the 49 male incest perpetrators was 35.2, the
median 38.[5] This was approximately 25 years older than the mean age
of the child participants, which was 10.2. These figures almost certainly overestimate age, because they report ages at the time the
incest was discovered. As we shall see below, most incest relationships continued for several years; in most cases we had no information about their starting dates and could only use the age of participants when the agency case record was opened.

In evaluating the significance of the children's ages, it is
important to note that these figures include cases from as long ago
as 1880, when puberty occurred later than it does today. One estimate places the mean age of female puberty at 15.1 years in the peri-
of 1850-1899, and 14.4 years during 1900-1949 (Shorter 1975, p. 294n).
Thus, most girls became incestuous partners of older men at least
four years prior to puberty. This finding becomes important for considering hypotheses that girls' developing bodies and sexual interests were causal in stimulating incestuous relations.

We also quantified the duration of these relationships. Sixty-
seven percent continued for at least several years--38 percent continued for three or more years, and 29 percent for one to three years.
Five percent continued for months; 17 percent occurred "several
times"; and 10 percent just once (Sample B). In our cases, the incest relations were terminated either by the girl's moving away from
the household, by discovery by some outside authority, or, least frequently, as a result of discovery by another family member.

In every family-violence case (not only the incest), we asked
whether a child's developing adolescent sexual interest was labelled
a causal factor by any family member or agency worker. The incest
cases had the highest association with adolescent sexuality: 21.9
percent as compared to 8.8 percent in child abuse and 6.1 percent in
child neglect.[6] That the girl's sexuality was labelled a factor in
one out of five incest cases is a low association for a form of abuse
that is sexual.

In an effort to look at the girls' willingness in the incestuous
relationships, we coded their responses.

TABLE 1   TYPE OF VICTIM RESISTANCE BY TYPE OF ABUSE

Type of Resistance	Type of Abuse		
	Incest	Child Abuse	Child Neglect
Attempts to Flee* (n = 557)	38.9	53.5	25.3
Any Resistance (n = 542)	85.2	71.4	46.0
Fought Back (n = 542)	22.2	6.6	3.6
Told Police (n = 542)	25.9	16.3	6.5
Told Others (n = 542)	74.1	65.1	43.9

Note. Figures given are percents for each type of abuse.

* N sizes refer to number of episodes for which information on the particular type of resistance was available.

As Table 1 indicates, we measured resistance in all types of family violence cases in a variety of ways, and in only one area was the resistance of child incest perpetrators less than that of children in other types of family violence. Indeed, some forms of resistance of child incest perpetrators less than that of children in other types of family violence. Indeed, some forms of resistance occurred more frequently among incest victims. One likely explanation is that victims of nonsexual abuse may themselves view their treatment as deserved punishment, or at least as an extension of inevitable parental authority, while sexual molestation is not usually presented to the child as punishment, and the secrecy surrounding it undermines its legitimacy as punishment.

We also looked at children's resistance to family violence by using the agencies' category, "complainant," that is, who first brought the problem to the attention of social workers or other extrafamily authorities. Girl incest participants were as likely to be listed as complainants as the victims of other forms of family violence. The agency identifications of complainant were not very accurate, however, as they frequently listed police, school, or other agencies as complainants; this merely pushes the question back, and does not identify who complained to that previous agency. In the incest cases we made a more thorough search for the complainant, tracing the matter through other agency records where necessary and possible. We found that the incestuous girls were themselves the complainants in 50% of the cases (n = 45).

Since the incest taboo is usually understood in terms of a barrier between biological relatives (Fox 1967; Renvoize 1982), in looking at how such a taboo operates in actual family life, we expected to find a disproportionate number of nonbiological fathers among the assailants. This was the case, but it was also true that

the proportion of biological fathers was substantial--48 percent.
The overall proportion of close blood relatives was 71 percent. The
remaining 29 percent was composed of step-fathers.

The accompanying Tables illustrate the kinship position of the
incest assailants[7] in two ways: Table 2 compares incest to child a-
buse considering all assailants; Table 3 compares incest to other
family violence for male assailants.

TABLE 2   RELATIONSHIP OF ASSAILANT TO VICTIM BY TYPE OF ABUSE

	Type of Abuse	
Assailant	Incest[a] (n = 63)	Child Abuse (n = 198)
Biological Fathers	47.6	41.4
Step-, Foster-, and Adoptive Fathers	28.6	7.1
Other Adult Male Relatives	22.2	7.1

Note. Figures given are percents for each type of abuse.
a.   Incest assailants include one mother

TABLE 3   RELATIONSHIP OF ASSAILANT TO VICTIM BY TYPE OF ABUSE
                --ADULT MALE RELATIVES ONLY

	Type of Abuse		
Relationship	Incest (n = 62)	Child Abuse (n = 110)	Other Violence (n = 478)
Biological Fathers	48.4	74.5	83.5
Step-, Foster-, and Adoptive Fathers	29.0	12.7	11.1
Other Adult Male Relatives	22.6	12.7	5.4

Note. Figures given are percents for each type of abuse.

Biological fathers represented slightly less than half of all
incest assailants (of whom all but one were male). When considering
all assailants, biological fathers were slightly more often represented in incest than in nonsexual child abuse, while "social fathers"
were four times more often involved, and other male relatives three
times more. These proportions reflect, first, the fact that over
half the nonsexual assailants were women, whereas by contrast women

virtually never sexually abused children.[7] Second, these proportions
also show that nonbiological (social) fathers were indeed over-represented in incest, in comparison to their presence in households in
our study. These patterns are corroborated when one considers male
assailants only: biological fathers were more likely to be the nonsexual than the sexual assailants; they were even more likely to be
the assailants in other types of abuse because marital violence figures importantly in this category; and biological fathers were represented at least in proportion to their numbers as the assailants of
their wives. Among men who were not biological fathers, this pattern
is reversed: they were more likely to be the sexual than the nonsexual assailants of family members. Their role may well reflect the
fact that nonsexual child abuse frequently results from punishment
conceived as legitimate and even required of a child's caretaker.

In searching for explanations for the lower proportion of biological fathers who were incestuous, we considered the degree of involvement of the father in the upbringing of the child. This factor
was called to our attention by our qualitative analysis of cases, in
which one of the striking characteristics of the incest assailants
was their lack of empathy with the distress they caused their victims.
(This finding corroborates that of Herman 1981.) We could not measure fathers' participation in child-raising directly from our data;
in most of our cases, as in society in general, most of that work was
done by women. Still we found one indirect way to measure father-
child involvement: the actual presence of fathers in their children's
household, which would make it at least possible for father to have
continuous child-care responsibilities. We found that male incest
assailants were less likely to live with their child victims than in
other types of child abuse. Ninety-five percent of male nonsexual
child abuse assailants were in the household with their children, as
compared with 68 percent of incest assailants. This is the more
striking considering that sharing a house often provided more opportunity for an illicit sexual relationship.

Male presence in the child's household did seem to provide
greater opportunity for incest in cases where there was no mother
present. Twenty-two percent of incest episodes took place in households with no adult woman playing a mother role (Sample B). Thus,
male-headed single parent households were over-represented among incest cases; they were only 3.6 percent of our total family violence
sample.

The absence of the mother might have other meanings than simply
creation of opportunity. For example, Herman's and Finkelhor's works
both found the absence or weakness of a mother to make a girl psychologically as well as physically more vulnerable to sexual assault.
In houses that did have a mother figure, we asked about various factors that contibute to maternal weakness. We found that 78 percent
of these mothers had one or more of these indicators (Sample B). The
most common such indicator was that the woman herself was the object
of her husband's or lover's violence--44 percent were or had been
victims of abuse themselves, usually at the hands of the man who was
also the incest assailant. (In the whole study, 34 percent of cases
had wife-beating.) Thirty-six percent of the mothers were ill or
had some disability. Thirty-four percent had weaknesses such as alcoholism, rejection by their own relatives, recent migration to the
United States and unability to speak English well (Sample B). Many

were, of course, in several of these categories.

It is difficult to determine whether the mothers knew of the incest in many cases, because our source of information is usually only the case notes of social workers. Many pressures led people to dishonesty in talking to these workers--for example, fear of losing their children, shame, or fear of prosecution. Still, in our analysis of the incest cases the inaction of mothers was noticeable. Fifty-two percent of the resident mothers appeared, to social workers and victims, to know about the incest; 32 percent of them admitted this knowledge; and 28 percent intervened (Sample B). The subtlety needed in interpreting this finding, and evaluating its reliability, may be indicated by comparing it with another finding: mothers of incest victims were as likely to be the complainants, bringing social work or police intervention into their families, as were the mothers of any other type of family violence victims.[8]

An association between drunkenness and/or alcoholism and incest has been noted not only by Herman's recent clinical study but also by most of the earlier clinical literature (e.g., Rhinehart 1961; Gebhard 1965; Browning and Boatman 1977; Brandt and Tisza 1977). By contrast we found a relatively low association between alcohol abuse and incest, in comparison with other types of family violence. Drunkenness was a contributing factor twice as often in child neglect (70 percent of episodes) and adult violence (75 percent) as in incest (28 percent), considering male assailants only. Drunkenness was also more associated with child abuse (50 percent) than with incest, also considering male assailants only.

To refine our view of the role of drinking further, we separated incest cases into two groups--those in which nonsexual child abuse also occurred, and those in which it did not. For simplicity we call the former group the "incest-and-abuse" cases and the latter the "pure-incest" cases. The distinction allowed us to examine what is characteristic of incest itself, abstracted from its surrounding behaviors. In incest-and-abuse cases, 63 percent of the male assailants were alcohol abusers, as compared to 41 percent of pure-incest assailants.

Although alcohol is the most notorious, many stress factors may contribute to the behavior of the family violence assailant. Indeed, the most current sociological research about family violence emphasizes stress as a leading cause of family violence (Straus 1968; Straus 1980; Farrington 1980). We were able to identify and codify the presence of ten such factors in creating stress for the assailant.

Six of these ten factors were mentioned less for incest assailants than for any other form of family violence. Two of the remaining four were more common almost by definition in incest cases--accusations of provocative adolescent sexuality on the part of the victim (the most common single defense offered by the alleged assailant), and the single parent family which results in less protection for girls. A third stress factor--stress caused by the death or illness of another close family member--is related to single parent status, as many incestuous fathers turn to their daughters for sex when their wives or lovers die or withdraw due to illness. We did not find any evidence that incest, often conceived as a uniquely heinous deviance, is a product of greater stress than other forms of family violence.

In addition to these single stress factors, we also looked at measures of household cohesion and kinship-network cohesion created

by combining several specific data. Both households and kinship networks in pure-incest families were more cohesive than in incest-and-
abuse households.

TABLE 4   CONTRIBUTION OF STRESS FACTORS BY TYPE OF ABUSE

	Type of Abuse		
Type of Stress	Incest	Child Abuse	Child Neglect
Drunkenness (n = 1514)*	31.3	42.8	66.2
Mental Illness (n = 1030)	29.4	34.3	30.7
Unemployment (n = 1460)	24.3	21.2	35.2
Poverty (n = 1462)	36.7	41.4	65.5
Physical Illness (n = 1282)	6.5	16.2	29.5
Death/Illness of Other Family Member (n = 1331)	20.6	17.9	33.3
Desertion (n = 1713)	6.7	7.7	23.5
Adolescent Sexuality of Victim (n = 1678)	21.9	8.8	5.1
Single Parenthood (n = 1901)	25.0	19.1	48.9
Unusually Many or Closely Spaced Children (n = 1368)	0.0	13.6	18.6

*N sized refer to number of episodes of violence for which informa-
tion on the particular stress factor in question was available.

Figures given are percents for each type of abuse.

DISCUSSION

In several respects our study of incest cases from 1880 to 1960
corroborate findings and arguments in recent studies; in other respects our finding diverge. First, we argue that incest becomes a
social problem in large part because it is coercive, a form of sexual
abuse of girls. Second, we question the accuracy of considering incest a "tabooed" behavior, much more rare than behavior which is merely "prohibited" such as wife-beating or murder. Third, we question
the view that incest is provoked by severe external stress.

We found that to the extent incest appeared to social service
agencies and family members as a problem, it was almost always a

sexual relationship between an older man and a younger girl, and a form of assault. We group our evidence for this interpretation in several categories.

First, we would cite (a) the young age of the girls; (b) the age differential between the girls and the men; and (c) the heterosexual nature of the cases, in which the older partners also had more power because they were men. For example, while there was some brother-sister incest which appeared as problematic in the case records (see Table 2), the brothers were usually much older than the girls, and never younger.

A second sort of evidence for the coerciveness of incest was the relatively low association of the beginning of the relationships with any sign of the girl's developed sexual interest as a result of adolescence. In only one of five cases was this alleged.

A third sort of evidence was that pertaining to the girls' attempts at resistance. Our findings about resistance diverge from those of previous scholarship and interpretation (Herman 1981; Burgess et al, 1978; Armstrong 1978; Butler 1978; Forward and Buck 1978). These previous works share the opinion that the shame and guilt felt by incest victims make it difficult for them to tell or to seek help, and that most victims comply passively. The pressure placed on incest victims to keep secrecy is substantial, and for many there is the further disincentive that to complain or resist might cost them their family. In fact, we found that only in attempts to flee were the incest victims less resistant than victims of other forms of family violence. This reluctance to leave is understandable, since incest victims are precisely characterized by their relative domestic "imprisonment," often playing the roles of surrogate mothers (Herman 1981; Gordon 1982). In seeking outside help and attempting to resist sexual overtures, incest victims were relatively aggressive. They took these actions despite heavy costs to themselves: in the outcome of most incest cases, the assailants were at most embarrassed, while the children were usually sent to foster care, reformatories, or other institutions. Given these penalties, we found the girls' activity in seeking escape from the incestuous relationships evidence for their dislike of those relationships.

We also believe that our findings shed some light on the questions of the incest "taboo," and on the role of stress. These are related. Prior to the last several decades of research, most studies of incest considered it to be extremely rare, and the taboo against it so strong that those involved in it were pathological and/or driven to the relaxation of inhibition as a result of high levels of stress. The more recent scholarship has revised estimates of incidence upwards (Lukianowicz 1972; Finkelhor 1979) but retained, on the whole, the view that unusual stress and/or psychological pathology were key causal factors (Straus 1968). Our findings do not justify a view of incest as extremely rare. We would not argue that incest is common, nor that our 10 percent incidence among family violence cases represented the incidence in the general population. Nevertheless, enough is known now about family violence that one cannot argue that the families in these case records are necessarily pathological or even atypical. To consider a behavior with this level of frequency "taboo" is to drain that concept of meaning. What has been tabooed is the formation of new families based on incestuous mating; it may be that nonreproductive incestuous sex, particularly between older males and younger females, has been socially prohibited, as murder has been prohibited, but with plenty of violations (Breines and Gordon 1983). It is sometimes argued that the taboo on incest is evolutionary, or sociobiological (Fox 1967), which hypothesis would explain the disproportionate number of assailants who are "social fathers." The hypothesis does not however explain the substantial number of assailants who are biological relatives, even fathers. Furthermore, these proportions are at least equally well explained with the hypothesis that men who have not internalized a need to protect the interests of their children, whether biological or social, are more likely to abuse them sexually.

Further stimulating our doubts about whether incest is tabooed more deeply than other crimes of assault was our evidence that it did not seem to require unusually great stress to induce an assailant to overcome the social prohibition. We did not find stress levels higher for incest than for other crimes. The assailants were not poorer, nor more often unemployed, nor sicker. They did not appear to need alcohol as much as other types of assailants to lose whatever controls might be operating against the abuse. Furthermore, other evidence suggests that incest more than any other type of family violence is calculated and premeditated, not a result of a sudden loss of control. We have pointed out that the typical incestuous relationships continued for years. In no case did the older participant (the male) break off the sexual relationship, as one might expect if one supposed them to feel guilt. Our qualitative evidence shows that the process of obtaining privacy for the sexual activity in most cases also required premeditation.

The pattern that we found most consistently associated with incest was extreme male domination of the family. We found this quantitatively in the various indicators of the "weakness" of mothers—her death, her illness or disability, or her own victimization from wife-beating. We found it qualitatively in the victims' and wives' expressions of submission and fear towards the male incest assailants. This pattern of male domination cannot be considered a "stress" because it is the fundamental structure of the families in question, and because it is a pattern defined as within the normal range and reinforced by prevalent social norms.

Our findings thus lead us to the suggestion that further research about incest should include inquiry into internal family dynamics and power relations.

NOTES

1. This time period and place were chosen for several reasons. First, child abuse was first "discovered" as a social problem in the 1870s and the first Boston agency devoted to its control established in 1878. Second, by stopping in 1960 we were able to use only closed records, thereby limiting the degree to which we were intruding on clients' privacy. Third, Boston has the richest collection of historical case records of any city in the United States.

2. In this paper we do not mean to imply that incest patterns have not changed historically. In a chapter of her book, "Cruelty, Love, and Dependence: Family Violence and its Social Control, Boston 1880-1960," forthcoming, 1986, Pantheon, Linda Gordon will examine these historical changes.

3. We used records from the Massachusetts Society for the Prevention of Cruelty to Children (MSPCC), the Boston Children's Service Association, and the Judge Baker Guidance Center. From each year we took a random sample, coding at least 3 percent and when possible 5 percent of the relevant cases (that is, those containing confirmed incidents of sexual and nonsexual violence). The records themselves consist primarily of social workers' notes, although they often also include correspondence, records of medical and psychological examinations, notes on ongoing therapy, and legal papers. Each case record usually continues for a period ranging from a few weeks to several decades, averaging several years; many records are also inter-generational, that is, they contain material on different related households.

4. This gender distribution is true not only of incest but of all sexual abuse: sexual abuse of children is almost by definition a male crime. See for example, MacFarlane 1978.

5. The under-representation of younger men or boys does not necessarily mean that they were not involved in incestuous relations, but that these did not appear as problems.

6. The victim's sexuality could become a causal factor in a child-abuse case, for example, when a girl is severely punished by a parent for her sexual conduct.

7. The coding system adopted in this study, because we were looking at several types of family violence, required that in all cases the chief perpetrator be called "assailant"; use of this term does not in itself imply any particular degree or type of violence.

8. Mothers were complainants in incest cases at a rate ranging from 11 percent to 19.6 percent. These rates cannot be combined because they come from incompatible sources. The low rate represents the agency's definition of complainant, which does not inquire who complained to a previous agency, but will merely list that agency, or police, or school, as the complainant. The high rate comes from our detailed study of complainants in incest cases in which we inquired, who was the first person to bring the problem to the attention of any agency. A few similar studies of complainants from small groups of cases for all types of violence, between 1880 and 1900, produced a mean of 19.5 percent.

REFERENCES

Armstrong, L. *Kiss Daddy Goodnight: A Speak-Out on Incest.* New York: Hawthorn Books, 1978.

Boszormenyi-Nagy, I., and G.M. Spark. *Invisible Loyalties.* Hagerstown, Maryland: Harper and Row, 1973.

Brandt, R.S., and V.B. Tisza. "The Sexually Misused Child." *American Journal of Orthopsychiatry* 47 (1977): 80-90.

Breines, W., and L. Gordon. "The New Scholarship on Family Violence." *Signs* 8 (1983): 490-531.

Browning, D., and B. Boatman. "Incest: Children at Risk." *American Journal of Psychiatry* 134 (1977): 72-79.

Burgess, A.W., A.N. Groth, L.L. Holmstrom, and S.M. Sgroi. *Sexual Assault of Children and Adolescents.* Lexington, Massachusetts: Lexington Books, 1978.

Butler, S. *Conspiracy of Silence: The Trauma of Incest.* San Francisco, California: New Glide Publications, 1978.

Farrington, K. "Stress and Family Violence." In *Social Causes of Husband-Wife Violence*, edited by M. Straus and G. Hotaling. Minneapolis: University of Minnesota Press, 1980.

Finkelhor, D. *Sexually Victimized Children.* New York: The Free Press, 1979.

Forward, S., and C. Buck. *Betrayal of Innocence: Incest and Its Devastation.* New York: Penguin, 1978.

Fox, R. *Kinship and Marriage.* London: Pelican, 1967.

Gebhard, P. *Sex Offenders, An Analysis of Types.* London: Heinemann, 1965.

Gordon, L. "Two Types of Father-Daughter Incest." Unpublished. Boston: University of Massachusetts, 1982.

Groth, A.N. "Patterns of Sexual Assault Against Children and Adolescents." In *Sexual Assault of Children and Adolescents*, A.W. Burgess et al. Lexington, Massachusetts: Lexington Books, 1978.

Henderson, D.J. "Incest. A. Freedman, H. Kaplan, and B. Sadock. *Comprehensive Textbook of Psychiatry*, 2nd ed. Baltimore, Maryland: Williams and Wilkins, 1975.

Herman, J.L. *Father-Daughter Incest.* Cambridge, Massachusetts: Harvard University Press, 1981.

Kugel, B.C. *Sibling Incest: A Clinical Profile.* Northampton, Massachusetts: Smith College School for Social Work. M.S.W. Thesis, 1978.

Lukianowicz, N. "Incest." *British Journal of Psychiatry* 120 (1972): 301-313.

MacFarlane, K. "Sexual abuse of children." In *The Victimization of Women*, edited by J.R. Chapman and M. Gates. Volume 3 of Sage Yearbooks in Women's Policy Studies. Beverly Hills, California: Sage Publications, 1978.

Maisch, H. *Incest.* Translated by C. Bearne. London: Andre Deutsch, 1973.

Massachusetts Society for the Prevention of Cruelty to Children (MSPCC). *Annual Reports.* Boston, Massachusetts, 1881 ff.

Renvoize, J. *Incest, A Family Pattern.* London: Routledge & Kegan Paul Publishers, 1982.

Rhinehart, J. "Genesis of Overt Incest." *Comprehensive Psychiatry* 2 (1961): 338-349.

Rush, F. "Freud and the sexual abuse of children." *Chrysalis* 1 (1977): 31-45.

Shorter, E. *The Making of the Modern Family.* New York: Basic Books, 1975.

Straus, M. "Stress and Child Abuse." In *The Battered Child*, edited by R. Helfer and C.H. Kempe. Chicago, Illinois: University of Chicago Press, 1968.

Straus, M.   "Social Stress and Marital Violence in a National Sample
    of American Families."   In *Forensic Psychology and Psychiatry,
    Annals, New York Academy of Sciences*, edited by F. Wright et al.
    347 (1980): 229-50.

Weinberg, S.   *Incest Behavior*.   New York: Citadel Press, 1955.

CHAPTER 7

FATHER-DAUGHTER INCEST

Judith Herman

The incest taboo is universal in human culture. It is generally
considered by anthropologists to be the foundation of all kinship
structures and the basis of human social order. Though no single
definition of the taboo applies among all peoples, virtually every
known culture restricts sexual contact within the nuclear family,
that is, between parents and children, brothers and sisters. All
cultures, including our own, regard violations of the taboo with horror and dread. Breaches of the taboo are viewed not merely as crimes,
but as desecrations of the primordial law establishing the place of
human beings in the natural and supernatural world. The mythology of
many cultures associates violations of the incest taboo with bestiality, cannibalism, and witchcraft (Levi-Strauss 1949/1969).

Because the incest taboo has been surrounded by secrecy and awe,
it is generally assumed that violations of the taboo are extremely
rare. In our own culture, this assumption has been tenaciously held
until very recently. However, an increasing body of research data,
accumulated over the past thirty years, indicates that certain forms
of sexual relations between family members are a common occurrence.

Prevalence

In the early 1950s, Kinsey and his associates conducted extensive
interviews with over 4,000 women regarding their sexual experiences.
Included in the questionnaire was a section on childhood sexual contacts with adults. The results, largely ignored at the time, indicated that female children are regularly subjected to sexual approaches by adult males who are part of their intimate social world. Twenty-five percent of the women in the Kinsey study reported a sexual
encounter with an adult male before age twelve. Six percent reported
a sexual experience with an adult male relative, and 1 percent reported an incestuous relationship with a father or stepfather (Kinsey et
al. 1953). These findings have since been replicated by other investigators in two large-scale questionnaire surveys of college students
(Finkelhor 1979; Landis 1956).

There is reason to believe that these prevalence estimates may
actually be low when applied to the entire population, since they are
based almost entirely on the reports of white, urban, college educated
women. Preliminary data from interviews with a random sample of over
900 women in California indicate that 38 percent have had a childhood
sexual contact with an adult, 16 percent with a relative, and 4.6 percent have been involved in father-daughter incest (Russell 1983).

Less information is available on the early sexual experiences of
boys. Kinsey and his colleagues did not gather systematic data on
sexual contacts between boys and adults, believing that such contacts
occurred infrequently, but they did indicate that most such contacts
were homosexual (Kinsey et al. 1948). Landis (1956) and Finkelhor (1979)
surveyed male as well as female college students and reported somewhat discrepant results. In Finkelhor's study, 8.6 percent of the men
reported a childhood sexual encounter with an adult; in Landis's sur-

vey, the corresponding figure was 30 percent. However, both surveys
indicated that in cases where boys were abused by adults, the majority of perpetrators (85 percent) were male. Family members were rarely implicated, and no cases of father-son or mother-son incest were
identified.

Thus, the data available from general surveys indicate that incest follows the general pattern of sex offenses, in which the majority of victims are female and the overwhelming majority of perpetrators
are male. This pattern emerges even more clearly from studies of reported cases of incest. In several large-scale studies conducted
over the past thirty years, the vast majority (94 percent) of cases
of parent-child incest that came to the attention of mental health
centers, child protective services, or police involved fathers and
daughters (Justice and Justice 1979; Lukianowicz 1972; Maisch 1972;
Meiselman 1978; Weinberg 1955).

It should be noted that only a minute percentage of sexual encounters between children and adults are ever reported to any agency
at the time of occurrence, and the more intimate the relationship between perpetrator and victim, the less likely it is that the sexual
contact will be disclosed. Thus, for example, in Russell's (1983)
survey, only 2 percent of the women who gave a history of sexual a-
buse by a family member indicated that the incidents had been reported to the police. Reported incest cases, therefore, represent a very
small and probably skewed sample of the total. It is conceivable
that cases involving male children or female adults are under-repre-
sented in both case reports and general survey data. Nevertheless,
the considerable evidence available to date indicates that the incest
taboo is quite commonly breached by fathers and very rarely by mothers,
and that daughters are victims far more often than sons.

There are no data associating a particularly high or low prevalence of incest with any social class, racial, or ethnic group. Poor
and disorganized families are heavily over-represented among cases
reported to public agencies, probably because they lack the resources
to preserve secrecy.

The Family Constellation

Descriptions of incestuous families derive from two sources:
clinical reports of families in which incest was detected, and retrospective accounts given by daughters in later life, usually of families in which secrecy was preserved. Clinical descriptions of incestuous families are usually based on direct observation of child victims and their mothers; direct studies of incestuous fathers are under-
standably rare. Both victim and clinician sources repeatedly identify
certain common features, on the basis of which it is possible to construct the outlines of a "family portrait."

The theme most commonly repeated, and which contradicts popular
belief, is the apparent normality and conventional appearance of incestuous families. In most cases, the family structure represents a
pathological exaggeration of generally accepted patriarchal norms.
Because paternal dominance is socially accepted, the abuse of paternal
authority often goes unrecognized. Incestuous fathers are often well-
respected in their communities. For example, in a study of six military men convicted of incest, one clinician described the fathers as
"strongly motivated to maintain a facade of role competence as the
family patriarch in the eyes of society" (Lustig et al. 1966). The

fathers are frequently described as "good providers," and their wives
are often completely dependent upon them for economic survival. Incestuous fathers often attempt to isolate their families, restricting
both the mobility and the social contacts of their wives and daughters.
It is not unusual for the daughters to report that their mothers cannot drive a car, that the family never has visitors, or that they are
not allowed to participate in normal peer activities because of their
fathers' jealousy and suspiciousness. Finally, incestuous fathers
often enforce their dominance in the family through violence. In a
survey of forty women with an incest history, over half reported
having witnessed their fathers beating their mothers or other children (Herman and Hirschman 1981). The daughter singled out for the
sexual relationship is usually spared the beatings; however, she
understands clearly what might happen to her if she incurs her father's displeasure.

For these reasons, incestuous fathers are often described as
"family tyrants" (Cormier et al. 1962; Maisch 1972; Weinberg 1955).
However, once the incest has been detected, they are unlikely to
present themselves in this manner in a clinical interview. On the
contrary, they commonly appear as pathetic, meek, bewildered, and in-
gratiating (Walters 1975). Because they are exquisitely sensitive to
the realities of power, they rarely attempt to intimidate anyone who
has equal or greater social status, such as an adult professional.
Rather, they will attempt to gain the professional's sympathy and
seek to deny, minimize, or rationalize their abusive behavior. Inexperienced professionals may incorrectly conclude that the father is
a relatively powerless figure in the family and may even describe the
family system as mother-dominated.

Most mothers in incestuous families, however, are not in any
position to dominate their husbands; often they can barely take care
of themselves and their children. One of the most consistent findings
in the literature is the unusually high rate of serious illness or
disability in mothers of sexually abused daughters (Browning and Boatman 1977; Finkelhor 1979; Herman and Hirschman 1981; Maisch 1972).
Undiagnosed major mental illness--such as schizophrenia, depression,
or alcoholism--is frequently observed in the mothers.

It should be noted also that one of the most common causes of
maternal "disability" in the incestuous family is the mother's inability to take control of her reproductive life. Numerous surveys
have documented the fact that incestuous families have more children
than the prevailing norms (Herman and Hirschman 1981; Kaufman et al.
1954; Lukianowicz 1972; Miasch 1972; Tormes 1968).

Economically dependent, socially isolated, battered, ill, or
encumbered with the care of many small children, mothers in incestuous
families are generally not in a position to consider independent survival, and must therefore preserve their marriage at all costs, even
if the cost includes the conscious or unconscious sacrifice of a
daughter.

Incestuous fathers do not assume maternal caretaking functions
when their wives are disabled; rather, they expect to continue to receive female nurturance. The oldest daughter is usually deputized to
take on a "little mother" role, often assuming major responsibility
for housework and child care (Herman and Hirschman 1981; Justice and
Justice 1979; Kaufman et al. 1954; Lustig et al. 1966). The daughter's sexual relationship with the father often evolves as an extension of her other duties.

Sexual estrangement of the marital couple is frequently cited as a factor in the genesis of incest. However, careful interviewing of offenders and their wives indicates that most incestuous fathers continue to have sex on demand with their wives as well as with their daughters; those fathers who confine their sexual activities to their children do so by choice (Groth 1979). Furthermore, in many cases, fulfillment of the father's aggressive rather than sexual wishes may be the primary motivation for the incest. Like other sex crimes, incest may be seen as the expression of a wish for power and dominance. Cavallin (1966), who administered psychological tests to convicted incest offenders, concluded that the incest was an expression of hostility to all women, and that the daughter was selected as the victim because she was perceived as the woman least capable of retaliation. Similarly, alcoholism, though frequently observed in the fathers, does not seem to play a determining role in the development of overt incest; problem drinking is reported as frequently in fathers who are seductive but not overtly incestuous, and in the general population (Herman and Hirschman 1981). To be sure, many fathers attempt to excuse their behavior by attributing it to "demon alcohol"; however, careful interviewing again reveals that the compelling sexual fantasy is present when the father is sober. He may drink in order to provide a "time out" during which he can disclaim responsibility for his actions (Groth 1979). The actions, however, are not impulsive but carefully planned.

The description of the incestuous father has been remarkably stable over time. For example, Gordon (1981) studied case reports from child protective agencies in the late nineteenth and early twentieth centuries, including seventy-three documented incest cases. Incestuous fathers were often described as violent, but in contrast to those fathers reported for physical child abuse, they were not under particularly severe social stress, did not see the sexual abuse as a loss of control, and usually expressed little contrition or nurturant concern for their daughters. Gordon remarks further: "Often the incest assailant did not even experience the coercive aspects of his behavior as wrong because he was accustomed to the use of force in having his way sexually. Incest was often coincident with coercive, brutal, or other non-mutual sexual relations with wives or adult lovers."

Diagnostically, it has been difficult to characterize incestuous fathers, other than to note that most of those fathers who have been directly observed are not psychotic and are of normal or above-average intelligence (Carmen et al. in press; Gebhard et al. 1965; Maisch 1972; Weiner 1962). The fathers' attitude of entitlement to female service, and their willingness to use coercion to obtain it from their wives and daughters, indicate a kind of circumscribed sociopathy, limited to the family and not ordinarily displayed in other social situations. Because paternal domination of the family is accepted and condoned, we lack a diagnostic category which recognizes this extreme paternal dominance as a form of psychopathology. About the best we can do is locate the fathers somewhere in the ill-defined range of personality disorders. In addition, the incestuous behavior, once established, has repetitive and compulsive aspects which liken it to an addiction.

The Incest History

Incestuous abuse usually begins when the child is between the ages of six and twelve though cases involving younger children, including infants, have been reported (Herman 1981; Kaufman et al. 1954; Lukianowicz 1972). The sexual contact typically begins with fondling and gradually proceeds to masturbation and oral-genital contact. Vaginal intercourse is not usually attempted, at least until the child reaches puberty. Physical violence is not often employed, since the overwhelming authority of the parent is usually sufficient to gain the child's compliance. The sexual contact becomes a compulsive behavior for the father, whose need to preserve sexual access to his daughter becomes the organizing principle of family life. The sexual contact is usually repeated in secrecy for years, ending only when the child finds the resources to escape. The child victim keeps the secret, fearing that if she tells she will not be believed, she will be punished, or she will destroy the family (Herman 1981; Summit 1982). The consequences of breaking secrecy are often represented to the child as loss of a parent ("Your mother will have a nervous breakdown"; "I'll be put in jail") or expulsion from the family ("You'll be sent away"). These prospects are terrifying to any child. In addition, positive inducements are sometimes offered to the child for continuation of the incestuous relationship. The daughter may be singled out for special attention, privileges, or gifts, and may in the process be alienated from mother and siblings, who are jealous of the "special" father-daughter relationship but unaware of the overt sexual involvement.

Clinicians frequently assert the belief that the mother is aware of and "complicit" in the sexual relationship (Kempe and Kempe 1978), and cases have been documented in which this is undeniably true (Tormes 1968). However, in retrospective reports, the majority of daughters indicate that they never told their mothers (Herman 1981; Lukianowicz 1972). Rather, they gave vague and indirect indications of distress, and felt betrayed and disappointed when their mothers failed to recognize the nature of the problem.

Distress symptoms frequently displayed by incestuously abused children include insomnia, nightmares, bedwetting, fearfulness, social withdrawal or misbehavior, and somatic complaints, particularly lower abdominal or pelvic pain (Adams-Tucker 1982; Burgess and Holmstrom 1978; De Francis 1969; Sgroi 1978). A few children may attempt to re-eneact the sexual encounters with younger playmates.

As the child reaches adolescence, distress symptoms may heighten for several reasons. First, the father may increase his sexual demands, attempting intercourse for the first time. This added intrusion, as well as the risk of pregnancy, makes continuation of the incestuous relationship increasingly intolerable for the child. In addition, the normal course of the girl's maturation, which at this stage of life includes increased awareness of sexual norms and increased social involvement with peers, inevitably represents a threat to the maintenance of the incest secret. The father frequently responds to this threat with jealousy verging upon paranoia, and may attempt to place severe restrictions upon his daughter's social contacts. The result is an increase in family conflict and escalating symptoms of distress. Runaway attempts, suicide attempts, drug and alcohol use, hysterical seizures, indiscriminate sexual activity, and early pregnancy are frequently seen in teenage incest victims (Benward and Densen-Gerber 1976; Goodwin 1982; Herman 1981).

As the oldest daughter becomes more resistant and threatens to escape entirely from the incestuous relationship, the father may turn his attention sequentially to younger daughters. Repetition of the incest with more than one daughter or with other available children (nieces, stepchildren, grandchildren) has been a common finding of numerous clinical reports (Cavallin 1966; Herman 1981; Lukianowicz 1972). On the other hand, there are virtually no clinical reports of cases in which an incestuous relationship was spontaneously ended by the father's initiative and choice. It seems reasonable to conclude that once an incestuous relationship has begun, the father will seek to perpetuate it, either with the first victim or with another, as long as he can.

The present state of knowledge of the incestuous family constellation and the course of the usual incest history permits a tentative identification of high risk situations. Father-daughter incest should be suspected in any family which includes a violent or domineering and suspicious father, a battered, chronically ill, or disabled mother, or a daughter who appears to have assumed major adult household responsibilities. Though the oldest daughter is particularly vulnerable, once incest has been reported with one child, all other children to whom the father has intimate access should be considered at risk. Incest should also be suspected as a precipitant in the behavior of adolescent girls who present to an agency as runaways, "sex delinquents," drug abusers or make suicide attempts (Herman and Hirschman 1981).

Long-Term Sequelae

Data on long-term sequelae of father-daughter incest are derived almost entirely from clinical reports, that is, from studies of women who identified themselves as patients in need of mental health services. There is no current basis on which to estimate what percentage of incest victims complain of long-lasting harm. One survey of women recruited by radio advertisement indicates that at least some women with a history of childhood sexual abuse perceive themselves as relatively well-adjusted in adult life. These women's self-assessments correlated well with clinical evaluations based on interviews and psychological testing. While acknowledging the sexual abuse as a trauma, these women believed they had recovered from it. Many of the women who had escaped without permanent harm attributed their recovery to helpful intervention from other people; most frequently cited were supportive friends and family members, who assured these women that they were not at fault, and patient lovers, who helped them rediscover and reclaim their sexuality (Tsai 1979).

Thus, it would be an exaggeration to claim that incestuous abuse inevitably leads to lasting emotional distress. Nevertheless, the preponderance of clinical evidence indicates that many, and perhaps most, incest victims suffer significant and persistent psychological impairment in adult life. Problems most frequently reported include severely impaired self-esteem, negative identity formation, difficulty in forming intimate relationships, and sexual dysfunction Herman 1981; Meiselman 1978). "Flashbacks"--vivid, emotion-laden memories of the incestuous contacts--may be stimulated during adult sexual relations or in other situations associatively linked to the incest. Incest victims in outpatient psychiatric treatment have been described as more symptomatic and significantly more disturbed than ordinary patients (Meiselman 1978), and significantly more disturbed than a comparison group of women patients who reported that their fathers were seductive but not overtly incestuous (Herman 1981). An unusually high prevalence of incest has been reported in the histories of female psychiatric patients (Carmen et al. in press), women with multiple personality disorder (Putnam and Post 1982), and prostitutes (James and Meyerding 1977).

Finally, a history of incestuous abuse appears to be linked to unusually high risk of repeated victimization in later life, both rape and battering (Miller 1978; CWPS 1979). Russell (1982), in her survey of over 900 women in California, found that women who were sexually abused by their relatives were significantly more likely to report being raped at some time in their lives, being sexually coerced by their husbands, being beaten by their husbands, and being asked to pose for pornographic pictures or perform sexual acts that their partners had seen in pornographic movies, pictures, or books. The more serious the history of sexual abuse, the stronger was the association with adult experiences of repeated victimization.

Given the incest victim's apparent difficulty with self-esteem and self-protection, she may be at unusually high risk for marriage to an abusive spouse. For this reason, the potential for repetition of the incest in the next generation must be considered. The phenomenon of "generational transmission" has frequently been reported anecdotally (Meiselman 1978; Raphling et al. 1967; Tormes 1968; Weiner 1962). Goodwin (1982), in the only controlled study to address this issue, documented a significantly higher prevalence of incest history in mothers of abused children compared to a roughly matched group of "normal" mothers. Among the mothers from families involved in child abuse, 24 percent reported an incest history, compared to 3 percent of the control group. It should be noted, however, that in this study, three quarters of the mothers of abused children did *not* have a history of sexual abuse in their own childhood, a finding that should lead to caution in the facile application of the "generational transmission" hypothesis. A second potential mechanism of "generational transmission" may be traced through the sons of incestuous fathers, who may develop abusive behavior in identification with their fathers. Anecdotal reports of such behavior are increasingly prevalent, but no controlled studies have as yet been done to document this phenomenon.

Identification of Incestuous Families

Effective intervention in incestuous families begins with identification of the problem. Given the prevalence of incest and other forms of child sexual abuse and the evidence of psychiatric morbidity, a strong case can be made for including questions about sexual contacts between adults and children routinely in all clinical evaluations. The main obstacle to obtaining a history of incest is the clinician's reluctance to ask about it. Incest provokes strong emotional reactions even among seasoned professionals. Denial, avoidance, and distancing are universal responses. Clinicians may have particular difficulty considering the possibility of incest in families of similar racial, ethnic, religious, or class backgrounds to their own, while families that are comfortably different may be more easily suspected.

For a clinician who has mastered these counter-transference reactions, obtaining a history does not present unusual difficulties. Calm, direct questioning is often sufficient. For children, some

specialized interviewing techniques have been developed; these include the use of drawings and anatomically correct dolls (Adams-
Tucker 1982; Burgess and Holmstrom 1978). Using these materials,
even very young children are able to describe what has happened to
them and to distinguish fantasy from reality. False complaints of
sexual abuse are rare; on the other hand, it is common for a child
to retract a true allegation under pressure from the family (Goodwin
1982).

Crisis Intervention

The discovery of incest represents a major family crisis, requiring rapid and decisive intervention. Usually by the time of disclosure, the incest has been going on for several years, and the
family's defenses have been organized around preservation of the incest secret. Disclosure represents a serious disruption to established patterns of functioning and a threat to the survival of the
family. The father faces loss of the sexual activity which has become an addiction. He also faces possible loss of his wife and family, social stigmatization, and even criminal sanctions, though in
practice these are virtually never applied. The mother faces possible
loss of her husband, social stigma, and the terrifying prospect of
raising her family alone, a task for which she is ill prepared.

In this situation, the father usually reacts by maintaining
steadfast denial. He insists that the child is lying and directs his
efforts to persuading his wife and outsiders that he is innocent.
The mother finds herself torn between her husband and her daughter.
Though she may initially believe the child and attempt to take protective action, unless she receives rapid and effective support she
will usually rally to her husband's side within a short time. If
she persists in believing her child, she has a great deal to lose
and very little to gain. The daughter, therefore, may find herself
discredited, shamed, punished for bringing trouble on the family,
and still unprotected from continued sexual abuse. Suicide and runaway attempts are particularly likely at this time. Without effective intervention, the child may be scapegoated and driven out of
the family.

Unfortunately, most therapists are not well prepared to intervene in this crisis, because they fail to recognize incest either as
criminal or as addictive behavior. This can be seen most commonly
in the resistance to the use of criminal terms—"offender" and "victim"—and in the failure to report incest to child protective agencies, even though such reporting is mandated by law. Naive therapists may tend to accept the offender's denial or his assurances
that the sexual abuse has stopped. Therapists may also be seduced
by the offender's rationalizations, all of which are widely supported
in popular and professional culture. The most common rationalizations
are, first, that incest is harmless, or would be if not for prudish
social condemnation; second, that incest is consensual, and that
children are willing participants; and third, that incest is simply
a response to deprivation of adult sexual expression and can be
treated as such.

Failing to recognize the criminal and addictive nature of the
abusive behavior, the therapist may approach the family as though
incest were merely a symptom of family dysfunction. He may attempt
to treat the underlying dynamics, using a traditional individual or
family therapy model in which the therapy contract is freely chosen,

one therapist assumes full treatment responsibility, and the rule of confidentiality is observed. This model, which is useful and appropriate for neurotic and some psychotic patients, is ineffective for addicts and for character-disordered patients who commit crimes. Successful crisis intervention with incestuous families requires an active, directive, even coercive approach, and it requires ongoing cooperation between the therapist and agencies of the state (i.e., law enforcement and child protective services). No therapist can treat incest alone (Summit 1981).

Because the problem of incest has only recently claimed the serious attention of mental health professionals, principles and techniques of therapeutic intervention are still in early stages of development. Successful intervention with the incestuous family clearly requires a high degree of institutional coordination, clinical sophistication, and plain hard work. Well documented treatment outcome studies do not as yet exist, and even published program descriptions are rare. The following treatment guidelines are derived from site visits to five of the most fully developed treatment programs in different areas of the country, and from verbal reports of clinicians working in forty to fifty other programs. They represent an attempt to define points of consensus and of controversy among experienced clinicians in the field. A fuller elaboration of these guidelines may be found in Herman (1981).

The initial focus of crisis intervention should be on stopping the sexual abuse and establishing a safe environment in the family. Reporting to the mandated authorities should be done promptly, preferably in the presence of the family, and should be explained as a protective, non-punitive measure. The therapist must assume that the child's complaint of sexual abuse is valid and should not be confused by initial denial on the part of parents.

Once the incest has been reported, debate often revolves around whether or not the child should be temporarily removed from the home. In some cases this appears to be the only practical means of ensuring the child's safety. However, this intervention is destructive to the child for several reasons. First, it makes her feel that she has done something wrong and is being punished by banishment from her family; second, it reinforces the tendency of the parental couple to bond against the child; and third, it is difficult to find an appropriate placement for the child. If safety can not be guaranteed at home, it is much preferable to have the father leave during the crisis period. Unfortunately, child protective agencies do not have the legal authority to remove a parent from the home; however, this result can often be accomplished either by persuasion or in some states through the use of civil protection laws. A court order may be obtained requiring the father to vacate the home and to provide for mandated treatment may also be established by the court. Clinicians working with incestuous families should become familiar with these legal procedures.

During the crisis period, all family members are in need of intensive support. The child needs to be assured that there are protective adults outside her family who believe her story and will not allow her to be further exploited. She should be praised for her courage in revealing the incest secret, assured that she is not to blame for the incest, and told that she is helping, not hurting, her family by seeking outside help. She should also be told explicitly

that many children retract their initial complaints and that she will
not be abandoned should this happen in her case. The mother needs
help believing her daughter and resisting the tendency to bond with
her husband against the child. If the couple separates, the mother
also needs help with issues of practical survival. Previously untreated health problems should also receive prompt attention. The
father needs help facing the fact that secrecy has been irrevocably
broken, and that he must now admit and give up the sexual relationship with his daughter before the family can be restored.

The crisis initiated by the revelation of the incest secret is
resolved at the point that the family is under the supervision of
the mandated agency and a coordinated treatment plan is in place.
Cooperation between all professionals working with the family facilitates quick and effective crisis intervention and greatly improves
the prospects for treatment.

Treatment in the Post-Crisis Period

Following the crisis of disclosure, the incestuous family is
generally so divided and fragmented that family treatment is not the
modality of choice. Experienced practitioners who have begun programs with a family therapy orientation have almost uniformly abandoned this method except in late stages of treatment (Giarretto et
al. 1978). Group treatment for mothers, fathers, and child victims
appears to be a far more promising approach; in some cases, individual, couple, or family therapy may also be recommended. For all
family members, the issues of stigma, isolation, and poor self-esteem
are especially amenable to group treatment. For fathers, group treatment is effective also in breaking through denial and rationalization
of the criminal behavior. Many group programs for offenders follow a
highly structured model similar to programs for the treatment of alcoholism and other addictions. In early stages of treatment, the
offender acknowledges that he has lost control of his behavior and
must submit to external control. Progression through the program
involves increasing acceptance of responsibility for present behavior
and restitution to others for past abuses (Brecher 1978; Silver 1976).

Opinion is divided on whether incest offenders can be motivated
to remain in treatment without a credible threat of criminal sanctions for failure to comply. To date, the most highly developed
treatment programs for incest have been those which rely on a court
mandate (Berliner 1981; Giarretto et al. 1978). No program has yet
demonstrated an ability to engage offenders in sustained treatment
without legal sanctions.

In addition to group and individual treatment, many programs
incorporate a partial self-help component, most frequently called
Parents United and Daughters and Sons United. Self-help activities
supplement more formal therapeutic work in a number of ways. During
the crisis period, the family's intense need for support may be met
by frequent peer contact. The father in particular may be more easily
persuaded to admit the incest and cooperate with a treatment program
if he is rapidly put in contact with other offenders who have successfully participated in treatment. In the post-crisis period, families
beginning treatment may benefit from the experience of those further
along, while "advanced" group members may gain self-esteem from being
in a helping role. Finally, after formal treatment in terminated,
self-help groups provide a continued source of support and community.

Criteria for Terminating Treatment

Restoration of the incestuous family centers on the mother-daughter relationship. On this point there seems to be wide consensus among experienced practitioners, even those most committed to reuniting the parental couple (Giarretto et al. 1978). Safety for the child is not established simply by improving the sexual or marital relationship of the parents; it is established only when the mother feels strong enough to protect herself and her children, and when the daughter feels sure that she can turn to her mother for protection.

The father may be judged ready to return to his family when he has admitted and taken full responsibility for the incest, apologized to his daughters in the presence of all family members, and promised never to abuse his children again. When the father is ready to return to the family, the family may or may not be ready and willing to receive him. This choice properly rests with the mother, once the mother-daughter bond has been restored, and once neither mother nor daughter feels intimidated. A decision for divorce may be as valid as a decision to rebuild the marriage; certainly the preservation of the parents' marriage should not be considered the criterion of therapeutic success. Probably the best gauge of successful treatment is the child victim's subjective feeling of safety and well-being, the disappearance of her distress symptoms, and the resumption of her interrupted normal development.

Given the present state of therapeutic knowledge, no one can claim to "cure" incest; rather, the behavior may be brought under control, first by outside intervention, then by empowering the mother as a protective agent within the family system, and finally to a limited degree by developing the father's inner controls. The father's internal controls should never be considered sufficient to ensure safety for the child; if the family decides to reunite, mother and daughter should be explicitly prepared for an attempt to resume the incestuous relationship (Groth 1979). Some degree of outside supervision should probably be maintained as long as children remain in the home.

Further investigation is needed in order to continue the development of effective treatment for all family members. Direct clinical studies of incestuous fathers are still quite rare and largely confined to convicted offenders, who comprise a very small and skewed sample. Long-term follow-up studies of treated and untreated families, and comparative studies of differing treatment approaches, are needed in order to document what is at present part of the oral culture of recent clinical experience.

REFERENCES

Adams-Tucker, C. "Early Treatment of Child Incest Victims." Paper presented at the Annual Meeting of the American Psychiatric Association. Toronto, Canada, 1982.

Benward, J., and Densen-Gerber, J. *Incest as a Causative Factor in Anti-Social Behavior: An Exploratory Study.* New York: Odyssey Institute, 1976.

Berliner, L. "King's County Approach to Child Sexual Abuse." In *Innovations in the Prosecution of Child Sexual Abuse Cases*, edited by J. Bulkley. Washington, D.C.: American Bar Association, 1981.

Brecher, E. *Treatment Programs for Sex Offenders.* Washington, D.C.: U.S. Government Printing Office, 1978.

Browning, D., and B. Boatman. "Incest: Children at Risk." *American Journal of Psychiatry* 134 (1977): 69-72.

Burgess, A., and L. Holmstrom. "Accessory-to-Sex: Pressure, Sex, and Secrecy." In *Sexual Assault of Children and Adolescents,* A. Burgess et al. Lexington, Massachusetts: D.C. Heath, 1978.

Burgess, A., and L. Holmstrom. "Interviewing Young Victims. In *Sexual Assault of Children and Adolescents,* A. Burgess et al. Lexington, Massachusetts: D.C. Heath, 1978.

Carmen, E., P. Rieker, and T. Mills. "Victims of Violence and Psychiatric Illness." *American Journal of Psychiatry* 141 (1984): 378-383

Cavallin, H. "Incestuous Fathers: A Clinical Report." *American Journal of Psychiatry* 122 (1966): 1132-1138.

Center for Women Policy Studies. *Response to violence and sexual abuse in the family.* January, 1979.

Cormier, B., M. Kennedy, and J. Sangowicz. "Psychodynamics of Father-Daughter Incest." *Canadian Psychiatric Association Journal* 7 (1962): 203-215.

De Francis, V. *Protecting the Child Victim of Sex Crimes Committed by Adults.* Denver, Colorado: American Humane Association, 1969.

Finkelhor, D. *Sexually Victimized Children.* New York: Free Press, 1979.

Gebhard, P., J.H. Gagnon, W.B. Pomeroy, and C.V. Christenson. *Sex Offenders: An Analysis of Types.* New York: Harper & Row, 1965.

Giarretto, H., A. Giarretto, and S. Sgroi. "Coordinated Community Treatment of Incest." In *Sexual Assault of Children and Adolescents,* A. Burgess et al. Lexington, Massachusetts: D.C. Heath, 1978.

Goodwin, J. *Sexual Abuse: Incest Victims and Their Families.* Boston, Massachusetts: John Wright, 1982.

Gordon, L. "The "Normality" of Incest: Preliminary Findings of an Historical Study." Unpublished manuscript. Boston: University of Massachusetts, 1981.

Groth, N. *Men Who Rape: The Psychology of the Offender.* New York: Plenum, 1979.

Herman, J. *Father-Daughter Incest.* Cambridge, Massachusetts. Harvard University Press, 1981.

Herman, J., and L. Hirschman. "Families at Risk for Father-Daughter Incest." *American Journal of Psychiatry* 138 (1981): 967-970.

James, J., and J. Meyerding. "Early Sexual Experience and Prostitution." *American Journal of Psychiatry* 134 (1977): 1381-1385.

Justice, B., and R. Justice. *The Broken Taboo.* New York: Human Sciences Press, 1979.

Kaufman, I., A. Peck, and C. Tagiuri. "The Family Constellation and Overt Incestuous Relations Between Father and Daughter." *American Journal of Orthopsychiatry,* 24 (1954): 266-279.

Kempe, R., and C. Kempe. *Child Abuse*. Cambridge, Massachusetts: Harvard University Press, 1978.

Kinsey, A.C., W.B. Pomeroy, C.E. Martin, and P.H. Gebhard. *Sexual Behavior in the Human Female*. Philadelphia, Pennsylvania: Saunders, 1953.

Kinsey, A.C., W.B. Pomeroy, and C.E. Martin. *Sexual Behavior in the Human Male*. Philadelphia, Pennsylvania: Saunders, 1948.

Landis, J. "Experiences of 500 Children with Adult Sexual Deviation." *Psychiatric Quarterly Supplement* 30 (1956): 91-109.

Levi-Strauss, C. *The Elementary Structures of Kinship*. Boston, Massachusetts: Beacon Press, 1949/1969.

Lukianowicz, N. "Incest." *British Journal of Psychiatry* 120 (1972): 301-313.

Lustig, N., J. Dresser, T. Murray, and S. Spellman. "Incest." *Archives of General Psychiatry*, 14 (1966): 31-40.

Maisch, H. *Incest*. New York: Stein & Day, 1972.

Meiselman, K. *Incest*. San Francisco: Jossey-Bass, 1978.

Miller, J., D. Moeller, A. Kaufman, T. Di Vasto, D. Pathak, and J. Christy. "Recidivism Among Sex Assault Victims." *American Journal of Psychiatry* 135 (1978): 1103-1104.

Putnam, F., and R. Post. "Multiple Personality Disorder: An Analysis and Review of the Syndrome." Unpublished manuscript. Washington, D.C.: National Institute of Mental Health, 1982.

Raphling, D., B. Carpenter, and A. Davis. "Incest, a Genealogical Study." *Archives of General Psychiatry* 16 (1967): 505-511.

Russell, D. "The Incidence and Prevalence of Intrafamiliar and Extrafamilial Sexual Abuse of Female Children." *Child Abuse and Neglect: The International Journal* (May 1983). 133-146.

Russell, D. "Preliminary Report on Some Findings Relating to the Trauma and Long-Term Effects of Intra-Family Childhood Sexual Abuse." Unpublished manuscript. Berkeley, California: Mills College, 1982.

Sgroi, S. "Child Sexual Assault: Some Guidelines for Intervention and Assessment." In *Sexual Assault of Children and Adolescents*, edited by A. Burgess et al. Lexington, Massachusetts: D.C. Heath, 1978.

Silver, S. "Outpatient Treatment for Sexual Offenders." *Social Work* (1976): 134-140.

Summit, R. "Sexual Child Abuse, the Psychotherapist, and the Team Concept." In *Dealing with Child Sexual Abuse*. Chicago, Illinois: National Committee for Prevention of Child Abuse, 1981.

Summit, R. "Beyond Belief: The Reluctant Discovery of Incest." In *Women's Sexual Experience*, edited by M. Kirkpatrick. New York: Plenum, 1982.

Summit, R., and J. Kryso. "Sexual Abuse of Children: A Clinical Spectrum." *American Journal of Orthopsychiatry* 48 (1978): 237-250.

Tormes, Y. *Child Victims of Incest*. Denver, Colorado: American Humane Association, 1968.

Tsai, M., S. Feldman-Summers, and M. Edgar. "Childhood Molestations: Psychological functioning in Adult Women." *Journal of Abnormal Psychology* 88 (1979): 407-417.

Walters, D. *Physical and Sexual Abuse of Children*. Bloomington, Indiana: Indiana University Press, 1975.

Weinberg, S. *Incest behavior*. New York: Citadel, 1955.

Weiner, I. "Father-Daughter Incest: A Clinical Report." *Psychiatric Quarterly* 36 (1962): 607-632.

CHAPTER 8

SEXUAL ABUSE OF BOYS

David Finkelhor

Interest in the sexual abuse of boys has been limited for a variety of reasons. Perhaps most important is that, until recently, clinicians saw fairly few such cases, and those they did see appeared to be anomalies in the general tide of cases involving girls. But the sexual abuse of boys has been overlooked for two other reasons, as well. First, much of the attention which has been paid to the problem of sexual abuse has resulted from the sponsorship this problem has received from the women's movement. It was only after the women's movement had raised the general public consciousness about the problem of rape that professionals began to take increasing interest in the problem of sexually abused children. But the rape paradigm primarily sensitized people to inquire about the victimization of girls at the hands of men.

Second, the clinical information about the problem of sexual abuse quickly coalesced around one particular model which appeared to typify and explain it: the incestuous family. In this model, fathers become sexually involved with their daughters when their marital relationship has broken down and an eldest daughter replaces the mother in certain maternal and domestic responsibilities. This quickly became the "classic" model for sexual abuse cases; however, it is clearly a model that applies predominantly, if not exclusively, to girls. In the absence of any other obvious model, the sexual abuse of boys appeared to be an anomaly.

Now, however, questions about the sexual abuse of boys are increasing. This has resulted primarily from the fact that reports of such cases have mounted rapidly. Whereas five years ago many treatment programs saw only a few cases of abused boys, today some programs report that as many as a quarter or a third of their cases are of that sort (Gentry 1979; Rogers 1979; Swift 1979).

This increasing number of reported cases has prompted interest in understanding more about the sexual abuse of boys. The literature which has appeared on the subject up to now has consisted almost entirely of a few case histories (Awad 1976; Dixon et al. 1978; Langsley et al. 1968). Clinicians, administrators, and policy planners

The author's work is supported by grant MH34109 from the National Institute of Mental Health and grant 90CA840/01 from the National Center for Child Abuse and Neglect. The author wished to express appreciation to Pat Schene and John Fluke of the American Humane Association who made data available to him for purposes of this research. He also wishes to thank Dennis Redfield for help in analyzing the data and Ruth Miller for help in preparing the manuscript. Nicholas Groth made very valuable comments and criticisms to a draft of this paper. The Family Violence Research Program has a series of publications on sexual abuse and other forms of family violence; a complete list can be obtained by writing the Program Assistant, F.V.R.P., University of New Hampshire, Durham, N.H. 03824.

have begun to seek more information about the nature and scope of
the problem.

The purpose of this chapter is to try to draw together available
data on the sexual abuse of boys. It will try to answer some questions about how widespread the problem is, and how the sexual abuse
may compare in character to the sexual abuse of girls.

DEFINING SEXUAL ABUSE OF BOYS

Quite naturally, many of the questions being asked concern how
the sexual abuse of boys compares to the sexual abuse of girls. Is
it as widespread? Does it occur at the same age? Does it involve
the same types of offenders? Are the effects of the experience similar?

Yet, there is also some uneasiness about defining the sexual
abuse of boys in the way one might define the sexual abuse of girls.
This uneasiness, when articulated, usually stems from two presumptions: one is that sexual activities between boys and older persons
is more often initiated by the boys themselves; the second is that
boys are less negatively affected by what sexual contacts they may
have with older persons.

Not a great deal of evidence exists concerning either of these
presumptions. In a 1978 survey (Finkelhor 1979a), 796 college students were asked about childhood sexual experiences with much older
persons--defined as five or more years older for a child under thirteen and ten or more years older for a child under seventeen. The
prevalence figures for such experiences are discussed below. In
terms of frequency of initiation, the boys reported that the older
persons had initiated the contact in 91 percent of the encounters,
only slightly less than in the case of girls, where 98 percent of
the experiences had been initiated by the older person. In terms
of the negative effect, the findings from the college survey were
less straightforward. The boys did indeed rate their experiences as
being less negative than did the girls; only 38 percent of the boys--
as opposed to 66 percent of the girls--said the sexual encounters
were negative. Moreover, boys were more likely than girls to cite
interest and pleasure as reactions they had to the experiences at
the time. However, when considering long-term effects of the experience as measured by impact on sexual self-esteem, the boys seem to
have been affected as much if not more than the girls.

Thus, we need to be careful about these two presumptions concerning the sexual abuse of boys. For one thing, the male ethic itself has tended to portray youthful male sexuality in very positive,
adventuresome terms. As we point out below, it may be this very
ethic that is in part responsible for the serious underreporting of
sexual victimization experiences involving boys. This ethic may
have painted boys' experiences with older persons and adults as much
less victimizing than it actually is.

In addition, a body of opinion and research has emerged in recent years which appears to have as its intention the vindication of
pedophilia (O'Carroll 1980; Sandfort 1982). These reports have
given accounts of seductions initiated by boys as seen through the
eyes of pedophiles or as told by boys recruited through pedophile
networks. Undoubtedly such boy-initiated sex does occur, but there
is no evidence that the major proportion of boy-adult sexual encounters are of this sort. Available evidence suggests that most are
not.

Still, the possibility that some such encounters may be child-
initiated and may be positive raises the question of how sexual abuse
should be defined. As argued elsewhere (Finkelhor 1979b), a good
case can be made for calling encounters between children and much
older persons abuse, no matter who initiates them and no matter what
effect they have. These encounters involve older persons who have a
great disparity of power and knowledge about sex as compared to the
children; a high risk exists, therefore, of psychological damage to
the child. Probably the best argument for calling them abuse is that,
under current law and social mores, sexual activities with children
are considered illegal and taboo, and most older persons engaged in
such encounters know this.

An analogy is possible with child labor. Society has decided
that, for the welfare of children, they should not be employed under
a certain age. This does not mean that an individual child might not
solicit a job and benefit greatly from it. However, as a result of
social and historical experience, society has determined that such
employment is highly vulnerable to exploitation and abuse. Any employed child under a certain age would be considered in violation of
the law and would be counted in statistics on abuse of child labor.

Thus, we have favored an approach to defining child sexual abuse
as that which involves a significant age difference, although what
that age difference should be is a matter of some dispute. For the
purposes of this chapter, sexual abuse of boys is defined as encounters between prepubertal males and adults.

PREVALENCE OF SEXUAL ABUSE AMONG BOYS

Estimating the true prevalence of any kind of sexual abuse is
difficult at best, but estimating the prevalence for boys is riskier
still. Few prevalence studies exist, and those that do generally
suffer from methodological limitations including the problem of defining what is and what is not sexual abuse. But the abuse of boys
suffers under the additional burden of a lack of attention. Some of
the better studies of the prevalence of sexual abuse have limited
themselves to females (Russell 1983; Kinsey 1954), or have had quite
small samples of men (Bell and Weinberg 1978; Finkelhor 1979a).

Bell and Weinberg Survey
One methodologically plausible estimate comes from a study that
was not about sexual abuse at all: Bell and Weinberg's widely cited
study of homosexuality in San Francisco. These researchers needed a
control group of heterosexuals to compare with their large homosexual
sample, so they commissioned an area probability survey of heterosexual men in San Francisco. This was a classical "random" sample
obtained by field interviewers knocking on doors. Its main limitations were that it specifically excluded homosexuals and that it was
relatively small for a study of this sort. Nonetheless, of this
group of 284 men who were interviewed in person about a wide variety
of sexual matters, 2.5 percent said that they had a "pre-pubertal
sexual experience with a male adult involving physical contact" (See
Table 1).[1]

Bell and Weinberg give a somewhat higher figure for sexual abuse
of boys in their homosexual sample. The homosexual sample, however,
was not a random one, but was collected from volunteers found by paid
recruiters. The fact that the figure for abuse is almost twice as
high for the homosexual than for the heterosexual men (4.9 percent vs.

Table 1   Estimates of Prevalence of Sexual Abuse Among Boys

Estimate	% of all boys	N
Bell and Weinberg (1978) Prepubertal sexual experi- ence with male adult in- volving physical contact		
a. Heterosexual sample	2.5	(284)
b. Homosexual sample	4.9	(275)
Finkelhor (1979a) Child under 13 with adult	4.1	(266)
Finkelhor (1984) Prepubertal experiences with person 5 yrs. older involving physical contact	3.2	(185)
Fritz et al. (1981) Prepubertal sexual contact with post adolescent in- volving physical contact	4.8	(410)

Sample:	Bell and Weinberg	Heterosexual	Probability Sample (San Fran)
	" " "	Homosexual	Convenience Sample (San Fran)
	Finkelhor	(1979)	Whole classes of college students
	Finkelhor	(1982)	Probability Sample (Boston)
	Fritz et al.		Psychology students

2.5 percent) may have to do with the fact that the homosexual sample was composed of volunteers more willing to confide; whereas the hetero- sexual was composed of respondents selected randomly. But it also may reflect the fact that more homosexual men have had such experiences.

Finkelhor Boston Survey
This survey (1984) also includes data on sexual abuse of boys from a random community sample. The figures cited there, based on 185 fathers of children ages six to fourteen in the Boston area, showed that 6 percent of the men said they had an experience involving physical contact with a person five or more years older prior to age seventeen that they would term "abuse." However, this has been recalculated for Table 1 with a definition of abuse more consistent with that of Bell and Weinberg, for purposes of comparison: an experi- ence before the age of thirteen with a partner at least five years older

involving physical contact and labeled by the respondent as "abuse."
In line with Bell and Weinberg's findings, 3.2 percent of the men in
the Boston survey reported having such an experience.

Finkelhor Student Survey

This survey on sexual abuse among college students (1979) is
based on questionnaires administered by the author to whole classes
of students at seven New England colleges and universities. The main
figure reported in the student survey was that 8.7 percent of the
boys had had either an experience under the age of thirteen with a
partner five or more years older or an experience between the age of
thirteen and sixteen with a partner at least ten years older. Once
again, for comparison with Bell and Weinberg, Table 1 includes only
the experiences of boys under thirteen with partners who were actual
adults. This figure is 4.1 percent.

Fritz Student Study

Another group, this one at the University of Washington, also
conducted a survey of sexual abuse among a student population. Fritz
and his colleagues (1981) gave questionnaires to subjects enrolled in
psychology courses and collected results from a total of 410 males.
Of these, 4.8 percent described at least one sexual encounter involving physical contact with an adult before the subject had reached puberty.

ESTIMATING PREVALENCE

Even though none of the surveys in Table 1 are national samples
and two are not even random samples, the consistency of their figures
is intriguing and does suggest that the true prevalence figure for
abuse experiences to boys *under 13 or before puberty* might be between
2.5 and 5 percent. Just as an exercise in relative magnitudes, it is
interesting to see what those figures might show when extrapolated to
a national level. Suppose, for example, 2.5 to 5 percent of boys are
still being victimized by the time they reach thirteen. (This assumes
that the rate for boys who are now children will be the same as the
rate found among boys who are now adults.) This would mean that a
total of 550,000 to 1,100,000 of the 22 million boys under thirteen
in 1979 would eventually be victimized. Now, suppose also that the
rate of victimization remains relatively constant from year to year.
To produce that many victims, approximately 46,000 to 92,000 new
victimizations would have to occur each year. That gives us an idea
of what the annual incidence might be in the population of boys under
thirteen.

COMPARING ABUSE OF BOYS AND GIRLS

Another way of approaching the problem of the scope of abuse
among boys is to compare the amount of sexual victimization of boys
and girls that has been reported in different studies. All of the
studies shown in Table 2 recruited their male and female groups,
whether clinical or non-clinical, from the same sources.

The studies are quite diverse. They include statistics drawn
primarily from child protective sources, studies done at three hospitals, two studies based on police reports, and four studies based on
some non-clinical population. Altogether, the findings in Table 2 do
show some interesting regularities. First, sexually victimized boys
are reported by *all* sources. In some cases they make up a fairly
small proportion of the cases seen, but they are present nonetheless.

Second, some studies show quite a few more abused boys compared to girls than other studies. Larger numbers of boys tend to occur especially in general surveys and in the police based studies.

The fact that general surveys tend to show higher rates of male sexual abuse than the clinical studies suggests strongly that the sexual abuse of boys is not coming to public attention to the same extent as the sexual abuse of girls. Agencies may not be seeing the boys who are being abused.

Table 2   Ratio of Boy to Girl Victims in Child Sexual Abuse Cases
           According to Various Studies

Study	Year	Number of Boys per 100 Girls	N
Child Protective Agencies			
De Francis	1969	11	250
National Reporting	1978	15	6096
Hospitals			
Jaffe et al.	1975	13	291
Rogers	1979	33	114
Ellerstein & Canavan	1980	12	145
Griffith et al.	1981	21	1256
Police			
Queen's Bench	1976	47	131
Swift	1979	43	176
Mixed Agency			
Burgdorf	1981	20	3124
General Surveys			
Bell & Weinberg			
Heterosexual	1978	32	385*
Homosexual	1978	47	804*
Finkelhor	1979a	48	796*

*N's of whole survey, not N's of victims.

Underreporting of Abuse of Boys

There are several factors which singly and in combination would help explain why fewer abused boys than girls ever receive public attention.[2]

>   (1) Boys grow up with the male ethic of self-reliance. When they are hurt, when they are victimized, it is generally harder for them to seek help. The masculine ethic says, "Don't let others fight your battles"; "Don't complain"; "Keep your injuries to youself." It is not surprising then, that fewer boys than girls told anyone about their victimization experiences in Finkelhor's 1979 student study (25% vs. 33%).

(2) Boys have to grapple with the stigma of homosexuality surrounding so much sexual abuse. The preponderance of abuse boys suffer is at the hands of men (see *Identity of Abuser*, below), and for many boys this may create serious qualms about their masculinity. Homosexuality is one of the more fearsome stigmas among many male peer groups, and boys may be concerned about earning the label "queer" as a result of people finding out about a sexual abuse experience. Parents, too, when they find out about abuse of their sons, may be concerned about the stigma of homosexuality, and this may deter them from taking the report any further. One result of the whole society-wide anxiety about homosexuality may be that a large number of victimized boys fails to ever talk about their experiences and therefore they never get the information and reassurances that might save them years of silent suffering.

(3) Boys may have more to lose than do girls from reporting their victimization experiences. Boys in general are allowed more independence and unsupervised activity than are girls of a similar age. Boys may be justifiably afraid that, if parents were to find out about instances of sexual molestation, it would mean some curtailment of their freedom and independence. Rather than risk that curtailment, they let the incident go by unmentioned.

All these factors may help explain findings shown in Table 2, which confirm the generally held clinical opinion, that sexually abused boys are less likely to come to agency attention than the frequency of such abuse would lead one to expect.

RATIO AFFECTED BY SERVICE PROVIDED

Another interesting finding in Table 2 is that hospital and child protective agencies see proportionately fewer boys compared to girls than do the police. In fact, the police show a ratio that just about duplicates the ratio found in the general surveys.

The different ratios of boys to girls indicated in Table 2 is probably best explained by variations in the type of population each agency sees. The child protective agencies, for example, are primarily receiving reports about intrafamilial sexual abuse. It is likely (see *Boys and Non-Family Abuse*) that intrafamilial sexual abuse occurs less frequently to boys. Since the child protective agencies deal more exclusively with the intrafamilial cases, they tend to see more girls.

The disproportion of girls in studies limited to intrafamilial cases also shows up in the National Incidence study (Burgdorf 1981). Its cases of sexual abuse were based on reports to many kinds of agencies: child protective, hospital, police, schools, courts. It is interesting that the boy-girl ratios of the National Incidence study are closer to the child protective agencies and hospitals than to the police. This probably stems from the focus in the National Incidence study on abuse committed by caretakers and parents. When studies focus on intrafamilial abuse alone, it appears that they are likely to show a lower proportion of boys than when they focus on abuse both within and outside the family.

In contrast to child protective agencies, hospitals for their part are not limited to seeing only intrafamilial sexual abuse.

Hospitals also see many stranger rape cases where the victim is a child and other types of non-family child molesting. Nonetheless, there is probably bias in hospital-based programs toward seeing children who require a medical exam or some medical intervention. Because they have been forced to have intercourse, girls may be more likely to end up at a medical facility, whether to take evidence, to test for pregnancy, or to repair damage caused by penetration. Boys probably less often suffer medical conditions as a result of sexual abuse and therefore are not so often seen by hospitals.

Police seem to receive the most reports about what would be characterized as the stereotypical extrafamilial "child molester" experience. These involve the stranger in the school yard, the exposer in the park, or the neighbor who lures the children into his house with offers of money or favors. Such events are not seen as cause for social work intervention but rather as the province of the police. Boys may well be exposed to proportionately more of these kinds of abuse situations and therefore show up in larger proportions in police statistics.

IDENTITY OF THE ABUSER

Perhaps the major popular misconception about the sexual abuse of boys is that, since girls are primarily victimized by men, boys must be primarily victimized by women. However, there is little evidence to this effect. Rather, the great bulk of evidence, and it increases all the time, is that *boys like girls are primarily abused by men*.

This conclusion would appear to hold whether one considers data from agency reports or data from non-clinical surveys. In either case, males report that most of their victimization experiences occurred at the hands of other males. At times rumors have circulated among workers in the field of sexual abuse about large numbers of mother-son sexual encounters that had yet to be discovered. But the preponderance of research has failed to demonstrate a large quantity of abuse by women, inside or outside the family (Herman 1981).

In both of my studies on sexually abused boys (Finkelhor 1979a, 1984), for example, the offenders were primarily males. In the Boston (1984) study, the figure was 83 percent male; in the student study, 84 percent. Moreover, this preponderance of male offenders reported by boys cannot be explained by the claim that cases involving women partners do not get defined by the boys as abuse. The males in these studies were not asked to record only sexual *abuse* experiences. They were asked to record any childhood experience with an older person. So, positive experiences they had with women should have been recorded too. Few cases of male children involved with older and adult women came to light.

The data from the National Reporting study (1978) bear out the conclusion that most offenders are male, although certain reporting practices make the conclusion a bit fuzzier. When child protective workers fill out the reporting forms for their caseloads, they are asked on the form to report all caretakers involved in child abuse *and* neglect. In situations where a child has been sexually abused, the workers frequently feel that acts of neglect by a parent, particularly mothers, contribute to the situation where the sexual abuse occurred. For example, the mother might have known about the abuse but refused to take steps to stop it. Or the mother may have left the child alone for long periods with her boyfriend. In these kinds of

cases, mothers are often listed on the forms as co-perpetrators. But
it is not because they molested the child themselves, rather it is
because they were involved in the circumstances that permitted the
abuse.

Table 3A   Women as Perpetrators of Sexual Abuse

	Male Victims N = 757	Female Victims N = 5052
Female involved	41%	31%
Female alone	14%	6%
Mother involved	36%	27%
Mother alone	12%	5%

Data Source: National Reporting Study of Child Abuse and Neglect, 1978.

Table 3B   Boy and Girl Victims by Identity of Abusers

Identity of Abuser	Boys (N = 757)	Girls (N = 5052)
Male Abusers		
Parent	57%	71%
Relative	5%	9%
Other	23%	14%
Female Abusers		
Parent	12%	5%
Relative	–	–
Other	2%	1%

Data Source: National Reporting Study of Child Abuse and Neglect, 1978.

   This reporting practice shows up in the National Reporting
Study (1978) as a high percentage of cases where a woman (usually a
mother) is involved as a perpetrator in sexual abuse. In Table 3A,
we see that a female was listed as involved in 41 percent of the cases
where males were victimized and even 31 percent of cases where females
were victimized.
   However, in most of these cases where a female is listed as involved, a male was also involved, and he was the one doing the actual
molesting (Burgdorf 1981). A more accurate picture of the number of
children who were actually molested by women comes from looking at
the number of cases where a woman was the perpetrator alone, without
a male also being listed. These constitute a much smaller proportion
of the cases: 14 percent in the case of boys and 6 percent in the
case of girls (Table 3A). These percentages jibe with the findings

of our own data based on primarily nonreported cases, and confirm
that the actual use of children for purposes of direct sexual gratification is primarily the province of men.

Other studies of abused boys based on clinical samples show a
similarly high preponderance of male offenders--for example, Ellerstein and Canavan (1980), 100 percent males; and Griffith et al.
(1981), 94 percent males. But one isolated study does report conflicting results. Fritz et al. (1981) found that their psychology
students reported that 60 percent of their molestation was at the
hands of females--in most cases adolescent girls. The details on the
nature of this sample are not readily available, and until other studies confirm such results, we would be inclined to treat this study as
an anomaly among a preponderance of results that generally point in
the opposite direction.

BOYS AND NON-FAMILY ABUSE

Another important finding is that the sexual abuse of boys appears more likely than in the case of girls to come from outside the
family. Among reported cases in the National Reporting study, boys
were victimized by a male non-family member 23 percent of the time,
as compared to 14 percent for girls. Since this sample still deals
primarily with *caretakers*, these non-family members were not strangers.
Most of these offenders were individuals like teachers, institutional
staff, coaches, mother's boyfriends, babysitters, and others who had
some caretaking responsibility for the children.

These results are confirmed by the earlier findings in the
Finkelhor (1979a) student survey. There, because the offenders were
not limited to caretakers, the difference was even greater. About
83 percent of the persons who victimized boys in that sample were
non-family members. In the case of girls, only 56 percent were non-
family. The boys said they knew their offenders--they were not primarily strangers--but they were men who were not directly related.

Burgess and some of her colleagues in their current work (1981)
are uncovering a large amount of victimization that occurs to children in the form of "sex rings." These are groups of children who
become involved with the same adult usually through some recreational
or neighborhood activity, and the adult trades favors with many of
the children for sexual activities. It may be that boys are more
likely to be abused in this way, and this may be one of the common
sites where boys are victimized outside the family by people who know
them.

Groth (1981) suggests that this pattern of boys being more commonly molested outside the family is explained to some extent by the
characteristics of the sex offenders. He divides sex offenders a-
gainst children into groups labeled "fixated" and "regressed" (Groth
1979). Fixated offenders are men who have a relatively stable and
long-standing sexual preference for children. Regressed offenders
are men who have a primary preference for adults but who, in crisis
or under pressure, will turn to children as substitute partners.

Regressed offenders are often married. When they experience
crises in their marriages, they may turn to their daughter or other
close female family members in an attempt to substitute for their
marital relationship. Fixated offenders, by contrast, tend to prefer
boys as partners, are usually not married, and thus choose victims
from boys who are not related. Thus, in Groth's terms, offenders

against boys are more likely to be fixated-type men who are not members of their family. Offenders against females are more likely to be regressed types who select child substitutes within their own family.

SUMMARY

This article has reviewed available data for information about sexually victimized boys. The most important findings about sexually abused boys that can be gleaned are:

(1) Estimates drawn from surveys of men in the general population would indicate that perhaps 2.5 to 5.0 percent of men are sexually victimized before 13. Comparison with similar studies of girls would suggest that two to three girls are victimized for every boy.

(2) Boys, like girls, are most commonly victimized by men.

(3) Boys are more likely than girls to be victimized by someone outside the family.

(4) The abuse of boys is more likely to be reported to the police than to a hospital or child protective agency.

NOTES

1. The magnitude of the potential underestimate in Bell and Weinberg's survey is conveyed by comparing it with another survey of the San Francisco area. Russell (1983) conducted a survey in 1978 of 930 San Francisco women only, where the focus of the interview was on sexual assault experiences. Russell found 28 percent of the women had some sexual abuse experience with a family or non-family member before the age of fourteen. Bell and Weinberg's smaller sample of women for the same geographical area (N=101) found only 7.9 percent who had a pre-pubertal sexual experience with a male adult involving physical contact.

The definitions used in the two studies were not exactly the same: Russell's figures count some experiences with offenders who were not adults and also some experiences where the offenders were women. But aside from this, their definitions are roughly equivalent. The additional non-adult and women offenders in Russell's tabulation are not enough to account for the large 20 percent difference between her findings and those of Bell and Weinberg. The difference more likely stems from the fact that Russell gave her interviewers meticulous training in how to talk specifically about sexual abuse with respondents. She also embedded the question in a questionnaire whose whole intent was to bring up recollections of victimization experiences.

If Bell and Weinberg's figures do underestimate the number of abused girls, as comparison to Russell would suggest, then their figures on the number of abused boys may be underestimates, too. It is hard to say by how much.

2. I am indebted to Nicholas Groth for elaborating on much of the following section.

REFERENCES

Awad, G. "Father-Son Incest: A Case Report." *Journal of Mental and Nervous Diseases* 162 (1976): 135-139.

Bell, A., and M. Weinberg. *Homosexualities*. New York: Simon and Schuster, 1978.

Bell, A., and M. Weinberg. *Sexual Preference: Its Development Among Men and Women*. Bloomington, Indiana: Indiana University Press, 1981.

Benward, J., and J. Densen-Gerber. "Incest as a Causative Factor in Anti-Social Behavior: An Exploratory Study." Paper presented at the American Academy of Forensic Sciences. New York, 1975.

Brown, L., and W. Holder. "The Nature and Extent of Sexual Abuse in Contemporary American Society." In *Sexual Abuse of Children*, edited by W. Holder. Englewood, Colorado: American Humane Society, 1980.

Burgdorf, K. *Recognition and Reporting of Child Maltreatment: Findings from the National Study of the Incidence and Severity of Child Abuse and Neglect*, Washington, D.C.: National Center on Child Abuse and Neglect, 1981.

Burgess, A., N. Groth, and M. McCausland. "Child Sex Initiation Rings." *American Journal of Orthopsychiatry* 51 (1981): 110-118.

De Francis, V. *Protecting the Child Victim of Sex Crimes Committed by Adults*. Denver, Colorado: American Humane Association, 1969.

Dixon, K.N., E. Arnold, and K. Calestro. "Father-Son Incest: Unreported Psychiatric Problem?" *American Journal of Psychiatry* 135 (1978): 835-838.

Ellerstein, N., and W. Canavan. "Sexual Abuse of Boys," *American Journal of Diseases of Children* 134 (1980): 255-7.

Finkelhor, D. "Child Sexual Abuse in a Sample of Boston Families." Paper presented to the Symposium on Family and Sexuality, Minneapolis, Minnesota, 1982.

Finkelhor, D. *Sexually Victimized Children*. New York: Free Press, 1979a.

Finkelhor, D. "What's Wrong with Sex between Adults and Children?" *American Journal of Orthopsychiatry* 40 (1979b); 692-697.

Finkelhor, D. *Child Sexual Abuse: New Theory and Research*, New York: Free Press, 1984.

Fritz, G., K. Stoll, and N. Wagner. "A Comparison of Males and Females Who Were Sexually Molested as Children." *Journal of Sex and Marital Therapy* 7 (1981): 54-59.

Gentry, C. Personal communication to author. 1979.

Griffith, S., S. Anderson, C. Bach, and D. Paperny. "Intrafamilial Sexual Abuse of Male Children: An Underreported Problem." Paper presented at the Third International Congress of Child Abuse and Neglect. Amsterdam, 1981.

Groth, N. *Men Who Rape*. New York: Plenum, 1979.

Groth, N. Personal communication to author, 1981.

Herman, J. *Father-Daughter Incest*. Cambridge, Massachusetts: Harvard University Press, 1981.

Jaffe, A.C., L. Dynneson, and R. Ten Bensel. "Sexual Abuse: An Epidemiological Study." *American Journal of Diseases of Children* 129 (1975): 689-692.

Kaufman, A., P. DiVasto, R. Jackson, D. Voorhees, and J. Christy. "Male Rape Victims: Noninstitutionalized Assault." *American Journal of Psychiatry* 137 (1980): 221-223.

Kinsey, A., W. Pomeroy, C. Martin, and P. Gebhard. *Sexual Behavior in the Human Female*. Philadelphia, Pennsylvania: Saunders, 1954.

Langsley, D.G., M.N. Schwartz, and R.H. Fairbairn. "Father-Son Incest." *Comprehensive Psychiatry* 9 (1968): 218-226.

Meiselman, K. *Incest: A Psychiatric Study of Causes and Effects with Treatment Recommendations*. San Francisco, California: Jossey-Bass, 1978.

National Reporting Study of Child Abuse and Neglect. Unpublished data made available to author, 1978.

O'Carroll, T. *Paedophilia: The Radical Case*. Boston: Alyson Publications, 1980.

Queen's Bench Foundation. *Sexual Abuse of Children*. San Francisco, California, 1976.

Rogers, C. "Findings from a Hospital-Based Sexual Abuse Treatment Program." Paper presented at Children's Hospital Medical Center Conference on Sexual Victimization of Children. Washington, D.C., 1979.

Russell, D. "Incidence and Prevalence of Intrafamilial and Extrafamilial Sexual Abuse of Female Children." *Child Abuse and Neglect*. 7 (1983): 133-146.

Sandfort, T. *The Sexual Aspect of Pedophile Relations*. Amsterdam: Pan-Spartacus, 1982.

Swift, C. "Prevention of Sexual Child Abuse: Focus on the Perpetrator." *Journal of Clinical Child Psychology* 8 (1979): 133-136.

Weber, E. "Sexual Abuse Begins at Home." *Ms.* (April 1977): 64-67.

CHAPTER 9

INVESTIGATION OF SEX CRIMES AGAINST CHILDREN
A Survey of Ten States

Ralph B. D'Agostino, Ann Wolbert Burgess, Albert J. Belanger,
Michael V. Guio, Jean J. Guio, Renee Gould, and Caroline Montan

The past decade has witnessed increased public, legal, investigative, clinical, and legislative concern about the problem of child
abuse and neglect in our society, specifically with the passage by
the United States Congress of the Child Abuse Prevention and Treatment Act of 1974 (P.L. 93-247). In 1975 the National Incidence Study
was initiated, directed by the National Center on Child Abuse and
Neglect, to examine the scope of child maltreatment in the United
States. The research group collected data between May, 1979, and
April, 1980, on suspected incidents of child abuse and neglect occurring in a sample of 26 urban, suburban, and rural counties located
across the nation in 10 states from close to 600 agencies. Two major
conclusions drawn from the study include the following:
> (1) Child abuse and neglect in the United States is a problem
> of major proportions, estimating that at least 652,000
> children are demonstrably harmed by child maltreatment
> annually, with the actual figure estimated at 1 million
> or more. Of the estimated 351,000 abused children,
> 44, 700 (12.7 percent) were sexually exploited.
> (2) Only one fifth of the children recognized as maltreated
> by professionals in community institutions (e.g., schools
> or hospitals) are officially reported to local child
> protective agencies.

In the mid-1970s another problem regarding children became visi-
ble--that of the use of children in pornography and prostitution.
Congressional response to the testimony presented was to pass the
1977 Protection of Children Against Sexual Exploitation Act (P.L.
95-225). In 1978 the National Center on Child Abuse and Neglect,
while noting there was no reliable data on the magnitude of the problem of the use of children in pornography, found it clear from anecdotal evidence and surveys of pornographic periodic literature and
films that the problem was significant in its dimensions, especially
in certain metropolitan areas of the country. As a way of responding
to the problem, research proposals were solicited to study the issue
and two proposals were funded, one in Washington, D.C., and one in
Boston.

The Boston-based research group was especially concerned with
the question of whether or not the legislation had significantly
altered the commercial use of child pornography in particular and
sexual crimes against children in general. A team of consultants

The authors' work was supported by grant #90-CA-810 from the National
Center on Child Abuse and Neglect. This chapter is reprinted with
permission from The Police Chief volume Ll (2) Feb. 1984: 37-41.

(including law enforcement, federal agents from the FBI, customs and postal services, and clinicians) prepared a questionnaire to survey law enforcement agencies regarding the problem of child sex crimes. The questionnaire was developed to measure the extent, interrelation, and involvement of children in pornography, prostitution, and sexual assaults, and also to measure the attitudes of law enforcement agents regarding the seriousness of these crimes and appropriate treatment of adult criminals involved in them.

A letter was sent to the police chiefs in fifty states describing the intent of the study and inviting participation. Ten states responded indicating interest, and a total of 2,383 questionnaires were mailed to law enforcement agencies in these states. Overall, 832 agencies (34.9 percent) returned the questionnaires (see Table 1). In order to produce adequate sample sizes for analysis and also display differences and similarities across geographical regions, the states were aggregated into five regions or groups. The Northeast included the states of Maine, Massachusetts, New Hampshire, Rhode Island, and Vermont. The mid-Atlantic group contained the states of Maryland and South Carolina. Illinois, Iowa, and Indiana were kept separate due to their large individual response rates. The response rates varied from 21 percent for the Northeast to 59.5 percent for Indiana

Table 1

Number of Law Enforcement Agencies Receiving and Responding to
"Sex Crimes Against Children" Questionnaire
Given by Individual States

States	Number of Agencies Receiving Questionnaire	Number of Agencies Responding	Percent Response
Illinois	275	163	59.3
Indiana	400	238	59.5
Iowa	350	137	39.1
Maine	155	33	21.3
Massachusetts	382	77	20.2
New Hampshire	266	53	19.9
Rhode Island	47	8	17.0
Vermont	59	20	33.9
Maryland	126	45	35.7
South Carolina	323	58	18.0
	2383	832	34.9

Incidence of Use, Sale or Possession of Child Pornography
It has been difficult to obtain statistics on the use, sale, or possession of child pornography since the dynamics of child sexual exploitation include secrecy and pressure by the adult to insure the loyalty of the child. Thus, the behavior of the adult is frequently discovered by accident through investigation of another crime or through a specially designed undercover operation. In order to gather

some statistics on incidence, three questions were designed to measure
investigation by agencies of the *use* of children or adolescents for
pornography manufactured in their state; the *sale* of child pornography; and the *possession* of child pornography.

Analysis of data indicates that the percentage of agencies that
investigated the *use* of children in pornography ranged from 1.9 percent in the mid-Atlantic region to 16.8 percent for both the Northeast
and Indiana. The percentage of agencies that investigated the *sale* of
child pornography ranged from 3.7 percent for Illinois to 8.9 percent
for the Northeast. The percentage of agencies that investigated the
possession of child pornography ranged from 11.7 percent for Iowa to
21.5 percent for the Northeast (see Table 2). While there were differences among regions with regard to investigation of specific aspects of child pornography, these data indicate that all regions have
approximately 20 percent of agencies which have investigated at least
one aspect of child pornography (i.e., use, sale, or possession).

One important result displayed in Table 2 related to the "typical-
ness" of Illinois and Indiana. It was believed that the non-responders would consist of a higher-than-average proportion of agencies that
had no experience with child pornography. If this were true, given
the high response rates of Illinois and Indiana, one would expect them
to have lower-than-average experience with child pornography cases.
To the contrary, both these states are close to the average. One reasonable implication of this is that the non-responders from the other
regions are not substantially different in their investigation experience from those that responded.

Table 2

Number of Agencies with Investigations in
Aspects of Child Pornography*

Aspect of Investigation	IL	IN	IA	Mid-Atlantic	North-east	Total	Chi-Square	P level
Use of children in manu-facturing pornography	25 (15.3)	40 (16.8)	21 (15.3)	2 (1.9)	32 (16.8)	120 (14.4)	15.14	0.0044
Sale of pornography	6 (3.7)	14 (5.9)	6 (4.4)	7 (6.8)	17 (8.9)	50 (6.0)	5.16	0.2718
Possession of pornog-raphy	23 (14.1)	29 (12.2)	16 (11.7)	14 (13.6)	41 (21.5)	123 (14.8)	9.27	0.0547
Use of children *or* sale *or* possession	33 (20.2)	49 (20.6)	23 (16.8)	16 (15.5)	48 (25.1)	169 (20.3)	5.26	0.2621
Number of agencies re-sponding to questionnaire	163	238	137	103	191	832		

*Values in parentheses are percentages of reporting agencies with
investigation experience.

Commercial vs. Personal Use of Child Pornography

The Child Protection Act speaks to the commercial sale of child pornography; however, it was still unknown how child pornography was being used, whether for personal use or for both commercial and personal use. Analysis of the data indicates that there was no statistically significant difference regarding commercial or personal use among the regions on this variable (p = .34). While 62.4 percent of the agencies reported that the pornography was solely for personal use of the adult, 35 percent reported that it was for both personal use and commercial sales. The remaining 2.6 percent--or a total of only three agencies in Indiana--was reported as being solely for commercial sale. As can be seen in Table 3, these latter numbers represent a small proportion with respect to the number of agencies with investigation experience in child pornography.

In order to estimate the types of materials used in child pornography and the frequency, each agency was asked to state the kind of child pornography the agency had in custody. The materials included photographs, movies, videotapes, and magazines. The data indicate that the major item of major kind of pornography involves photographs of boys and/or girls. Items such as movies or videotapes have a low percentage of discovery. Since the data previously reported show that much of the child pornography is related to personal use, the high frequency of photographs is not surprising.

Table 3

Purpose of Child Pornography*
(Personal Use or Commercial Sale)
All Agencies Which Investigated Use of Children

Purpose	Regions					
	Illinois	Indiana	Iowa	mid-Atlantic	Northeast	Total
Personal use only	13 (54.2)	26 (66.7)	14 (70.0)	1 (50.6)	19 (59.4)	73 (62.4)
Commercial sale only	0 (0.0)	3 (7.7)	0 (0.0)	0 (0.0)	0 (0.0)	3 (2.6)
Commercial sale and personal use	11 (45.8)	10 (25.6)	6 (30.0)	1 (50.0)	13 (40.6)	41 (35.04)
Total	24++	39++	20++	2	32	117

Table Chi Square Value = 8.99, p = 0.3428

*Table contains counts, the numbers in parenthesis are percentages within regions.

++For Illinois, Indiana and Iowa there was one missing value each region.

Child and Adolescent Prostitution

The media linkage of child pornography to prostitution prompted
one section of the questionnaire to deal with this problem. Table 4
contains results of analyses of that section. Of the 832 agencies
responding, 19.7 percent reported having one or more investigations
involving child or adolescent prostitution between 1976 and 1980.
The percentages by region ranged from 15.5 percent for Indiana to
24.1 percent for the Northeast. These differences are marginally
significant.

Of the 164 agencies that investigated child prostitution cases,
only 6 had more than twenty cases from 1978 to 1980. Two of these 6
were agencies in Illinois and 4 were in the Northeast. These agencies
were in large Metropolitan areas and it was expected that they would
have a large volume.

The sex of the child prostitutes does vary significantly over
the country. Where the data relates to the sex of the child prostitutes, it is interesting to note that the agencies in the mid-Western
states of Illinois, Indiana, and Iowa investigated many cases that
did *not* involve males, while the agencies of the mid-Atlantic and
Northeast regions investigated many cases which did *not* involve females. The differences among regions on these variables are highly
significant.

Each agency that investigated at least one prostitution case
from 1976 to 1980 was also asked to supply the age of the youngest
boy prostitute and the age of the youngest girl prostitute. Except
for a five year old boy in Iowa and a one year old girl in Indiana,
these data are relatively homogeneous. The mean age of the youngest
boy and the youngest girl per agency is approximately thirteen to
fourteen years old. With the exception of the cases mentioned above,
the youngest boy or girl per region is usually eight to nine years
old. The only other exception is Illinois where the youngest girl
was twelve years old.

The number of adults arrested in connection with child and adolescent prostitution cases from 1976 to 1980 was also obtained from
the 164 agencies that had at least one prostitution case (see Table
5). The most interesting feature of this data is the high percentage
of agencies that reported no adult arrests; these range from 43.8
percent in the mid-Atlantic area to 63.0 percent in Iowa. The average
percentage of agencies that reported no adult arrests was 54.3 percent. Thus, over 50 percent of the agencies that have had child or
adolescent prostitution cases have made *no* adult arrests.

Child Sexual Assault

Another section of the questionnaire asked the agencies to
supply the number of arrests made in 1980 for various sexual assault
categories, such as indecent assault on a child under twelve, indecent
assault on a child under sixteen, indecent assault and battery on a
child under twelve, indecent assault and battery on a child under
sixteen, rape of a child under twelve, and rape of a child under sixteen.

An examination of the data generated by this section of the questionnaire clearly reveals differences across regions (see Table 6).
Iowa had the lowest percentage rate of agencies with arrests for all
forms of assault--except for indecent assault on a child under 12--and
there the difference between its rate and the lowest rate is only

Table 4

Summary Data for Child and Adolescent
Prostitution, 1976 to 1980

	Regions					
	Illinois	Indiana	Iowa	mid-Atlantic	Northeast	Total
Number of agencies responding to questionnaire	163	238	137	103	191	832
Number of agencies that investigated prostitution cases	39	36	27	16	46	164
(%)+	(23.9)	(15.1)	(19.7)	(15.5)	(24.1)	(19.7)

Chi Square Value = 8.435, p = 0.0769

	Illinois	Indiana	Iowa	mid-Atlantic	Northeast	Total
Number of agencies reporting *no boy* prostitutes	29	21	17	3	6	76
(%)++	(74.4)	(58.3)	(63.0)	(18.8)	(13.0)	(46.3)
Number of agencies reporting *no female* prostitutes	6	7	7	12	31	63
(%)++	(15.4)	(19.4)	(25.9)	(75.0)	(67.4)	(38.4)
Age youngest boy prostitutes by agencies						
Mean	13.7	13.1	10.0	13.8	13.0	
Range	(9-16)	(8-19)	(5-13)	(9-16)	(9-16)	
Age youngest girl prostitutes by agencies						
Mean	14.3	12.6	13.8	12.6	12.8	
Range	(12-17)	(1-16)	(8-17)	(9-15)	(9-17)	

+ Bases for these percents are number of agencies responding to
  questionnaire.
++ Bases for these percents are number of agencies that investigated
   prostitution cases.

0.3 percent (11.0 percent for Iowa and 10.7 percent for the mid-
Atlantic region). Only 16.8 percent of the reporting agencies in
Iowa had at least one assault arrest in 1980. Indiana, the next lowest region, had 29.4 percent--a difference of 12.6 percent. This difference is statistically significant for the variable of at least one
assault. While there is variation within each form of assault, overall Illinois and the Northeast have the largest number of agencies reporting assault arrests (38.0 percent and 37.7 percent respectively).
The mid-Atlantic , Indiana, and Iowa are next in magnitude with arrest
rates of 35.9, 29.4, and 16.8 percent respectively. The differences
among regions are highly significant.

Table 5

Frequency Distributions of Number of Adults Arrested Per Agency
Involved in Child or Adolescent Prostitution Cases, 1976 to 1980
(All Agencies Reported at Least One Prostitution Case)

	Regions				
	Illinois	Indiana	Iowa	mid-Atlantic	Northeast
Number of adult arrests					
0	24(61.5)*	17(47.2)	17(63.0)	7(43.8)	24(52.2) 89(54.2)
1	6	9	6	3	6
2	2	7	4	4	5
3	0	0	–	0	1
4	3	1	–	0	2
5	0	2	–	1	4
6 – 10	0	–	–	1	2
11 – 20	1	–	–	–	1
21 – 30	1	–	–	–	1
31 – 50	0	–	–	–	–
> 50	1	–	–	–	–
	39	36	27	16	46
Q^+_1	0	0	0	0	0
Median	0	1	0	1	0
Q^{++}_3	1	2	1	2	2.25
Mean	3.28	1.03	0.52	1.44	2.28
Standard Deviation	11.17	1.36	0.75	2.00	5.07
Maximum	65	5	2	7	30
Ratio of number of adult arrests to number of child prostitution	0.47	0.26	0.15	0.15	0.13
Ratio of number of adult arrests to number of prostitution cases	0.49	0.32	0.18	0.24	0.28

* Numbers in parenthesis are percents.

$+Q_1$ = 25th percentile

$++Q_3$ = 75th percentile

Within the separate forms of sexual assaults, the low rates for
Iowa are the major contributing factors accounting for the significant differences across regions. For indecent assaults on children
under twelve, Iowa and the mid-Atlantic have similar rates which are
different from the other regions' rates. For the variable indecent
assault on a child under sixteen, another explanation for the significant differences is that Illinois and the Northeast have much higher rates than the other three regions. A similar explanation holds
for the significant differences on the variable indecent assault and
battery of a child under sixteen. For the two rape variables, the
highly significant differences can be attributed to Iowa's low rates
and the high rates of the mid-Atlantic and Northeast regions.

An examination of the data on arrests in 1980 for the agencies
responding to the questionnaire shows that for any particular form of
sexual assault most agencies had twelve or thirteen arrests. At most,
only 1 percent of the agencies in any region had more than twelve
arrests for any particular form of sexual assault. In fact, at most
only 4.3 percent of the agencies in any region had more than five
arrests for any given form of sexual assault. Still, some agencies
did have a heavy volume; one agency in the Northeast, for example,
has fifty-one arrests for rape of a child under twelve, and one agency
in Indiana had thirty-seven arrests in 1980 for indecent assault on
an adolescent. Most agencies, therefore, had low volume of arrests
in 1980 for any of the types of sexual assaults described above.

The questionnaire also asked questions directed at quantifying
the relation between pornography and other forms of sexual crimes.
Of those agencies that investigated at least one child prostitution
case, the mean percentage of agencies that reported they investigated
prostitution cases that also involved child pornography was 26.2 percent. Of those agencies that reported at least one arrest for a
sexual assault against children, the percentage of those responding
yes as to whether the assault had involved the use of a camera for
photographs, movies, or videotapes varied from 8.9 percent in Illinois
to 20.3 percent in the Northeast, with a mean over the five regions
of 15.1 percent.

Agencies were classified in the regions according to whether the
agency had investigated a child pornography case from 1978 to 1980.
There were four categories, as follows: (1) only an arrest for sexual
assault in 1980 (no pornography investigation); (2) a sexual assault
arrest in 1980 and a pornography investigation from 1978 to 1980; (3)
only pornography investigation (no arrest for assault in 1980); (4)
neither an arrest for sexual assault in 1980 nor a pornography investigation from 1978 to 1980. It should be stressed that the percentage
of agencies that fall into category 2 are probably over-estimates of
the cases that involve simultaneous pornography and assault, since
the number of assaults are only for 1980, while the pornography investigations are for any time between 1978 and 1980. The percentage of
agencies falling into category 2 range from 7.8 percent for the mid-
Atlantic to 14.1 percent for the Northeast. The mean is 11.2 percent.

Law Enforcement Attitudes

The law enforcement agencies were also asked to state their
attitudes concerning the appropriate *sentences* for first offender
convicted sexual criminals, the *seriousness* of sexual crimes, and the
use of *drug therapy* on sexual criminals. In particular, there were

Table 6

Number of Agencies with Arrests in 1980
for Sexual Assaults Against Children+

Type of Sexual Assault			Regions				Chi Square	P Level
	IL	IN	IA	mid-Atlantic	North-east	Total		
indecent assault on child <12 yrs.	37 (22.7)	44 (18.5)	15 (11.0)	11 (10.7)	34 (17.8)	141 (17.0)	10.71	0.0300
indecent assault on child <16 yrs. (adolescent assault)	36 (22.1)	31 (13.0)	12 (8.8)	13 (12.6)	40 (20.9)	132 (15.9)	15.85	0.0032
indecent assault and battery on child <12 yrs.	10 (6.1)	17 (7.1)	4 (2.9)	4 (3.9)	18 (9.4)	53 (6.4)	7.04	0.1337
indecent assault and battery on child <16 yrs. (adolescent assault and battery)	18 (11.0)	13 (5.5)	4 (2.9)	7 (6.8)	20 (10.5)	62 (7.4)	11.08	0.0256
rape of child <12 yrs.	7 (4.3)	12 (5.0)	4 (2.9)	13 (12.6)	20 (10.5)	56 (6.7)	15.74	0.0034
rape of child <16 yrs. (rape on adolescent)	16 (9.8)	23 (9.7)	3 (2.2)	16 (15.5)	32 (16.8)	90 (10.8)	20.42	0.0004
Agencies with at least one sexual assault arrest in 1980	62 (38.0)	70 (29.4)	23 (16.8)	37 (35.9)	72 (37.7)	264 (31.7)	21.68	0.0002
Number of reporting agencies	163	238	137	103	191	832		

+ Values in parenthesis are percentages of reporting agencies

nine questions concerned with appropriate sentence. All of these
questions had the following form: "What do you personally think the
sentence should be for an adult male, first offender convicted of
_____." The blank in the above quote was: (1) possession of
child pornography; (2) sale of child pornography; (3) paying money
to a fourteen year old girl for sexual relations; (5) enticing chil-

dren with favors and money to pose for pornographic pictures, without any violence or sexual assault involved; (6) forcible rape of a
fourteen year old girl; (7) forcible rape of a fourteen year old boy;
(8) forcible rape of a six year old girl; and (9) forcible rape of a
six year old boy. The law enforcement agent completing the questionnaire had twelve possible responses to each of the above questions.
For analysis purposes these were reduced to the following eight responses: (1) no sentence; (2) probation only; (3) mental hospital;
(4) three to twelve months in jail; (5) one to five years in jail;
(6) five to twenty years in jail; (7) life imprisonment; or (8) death
penalty.

There were also five questions concerning the seriousness of
various sexual crimes, as follows: (1) How serious is the possession
of child pornography?; (2) how serious is the sale of child pornography?; (3) how serious is it to pay a fourteen year old girl for
sex?; (4) how serious is it to pay a fourteen year old boy for sex?;
and (5) how serious is the manufacturing of child pornography? For
each question the response requested was in the form of a five point
ordered scale where "1" corresponded to "making an obscene phone
call" and "5" corresponded to "forcible rape of a child."

The analysis of the attitudes concerning appropriate sentences
proceeded in two phases. First there was concern that the attitudes
of those agencies with experience in investigating pornography might
be different from those that had none. A comparison of the attitudes
of those agencies with experience and those without showed no significant difference (using chi-square tests). Therefore, all agencies
within a region were combined for further analysis. The second phase
of the analysis consisted of comparisons of the regions for these
data. The following presents the results of the comparisons.

First, as would be expected, for each region the sentence considered appropriate increased in severity as one moves from considering conviction for possession of pornography to conviction for rape
of a six year old child.

Second, except for the mid-Atlantic region--where there was a
significant difference between the appropriate sentence for a forcible rape of a fourteen year old girl and the sentence for a forcible
rape of a fourteen year old boy--there were no differences on the
average within regions between the appropriate sentence for the same
crime against a boy or against a girl. That is, the sentence is a
function of the crime, and not of the sex of the child involved.

Third, with regard to appropriate sentences, there were significant differences across regions. In general, the Northeast agencies tended to be less severe in their opinions of appropriate sentences than the other four regions and, while not as pronounced, the
mid-Atlantic region agencies tended to be the most severe. There
were only slight differences among the other three regions.

Finally, while there are differences across the regions, in
general the "average" appropriate sentence for the different crimes
are as follows: (1) possession of child pornography--no sentence,
probation, or mental hospital; (2) sale of child pornography--three
to twelve months in jail; (3) paying a fourteen year old child for
sexual relations--three to twelve months in jail; (4) enticing children to pose for pornographic pictures--one to five years in jail;
(5) forcible rape of a fourteen year old child--five or more years
in jail; and (6) forcible rape of a six year old child--five to
twenty years in jail.

As with the attitudes concerning appropriate sentences, the analysis of the seriousness of the crimes proceeded in two phases. A comparison was made between the attitudes of those agencies with experience of investigating pornography and those without. Two were significant, both in the mid-Atlantic region. However, two significant outcomes are well within chance fluctuations and it was accepted that there were no differences in the attitude of those agencies with investigation experience and those without. These agencies were then combined for further analysis.

As with the attitudes towards sentences, possession of child pornography is considered the least severe crime and enticement of children into posing for pornographic materials is the most severe. (The seriousness of rape was used as the upper measure of seriousness and so there were no questions inquiring about the seriousness of rape). Also, as with the sentencing questions, the agencies of the Northeast region tended to be, on the average, the least severe in their opinion when compared to the other four regions. However, two interesting points are that the mid-Atlantic region was clearly not the most severe in its opinion and Illinois had the highest ratings on the last three questions (see above for wording of the questions).

Three questions were also asked concerning the use and study of drug therapy for those who are sex offenders against children (see Table 7). The first question stated that drugs were available that might lower the sex drive of men who are stimulated by children and asked: "Do you personally think that the government should sponsor research on such drugs?" Analysis of data reveals statistically significant differences among regions. The mid-Atlantic and Northeast regions responded with the smallest yes rate (50.0 and 55.2 percent respectively); Iowa responded with the largest percentages of positive responses (72.2 percent). The average yes rate across the five regions was 61.0 percent.

Second, it was asked: "Do you personally feel it would be acceptable to offer convicted child molesters experimental drug treatment instead of prison sentences?" Analysis of data reveals that the possibility of replacing a prison sentence with drug treatment did not receive majority opinion in any region. The Northeast region had a yes rate of 34.4 percent, all other regions were below 23 percent. The significant differences among the regions were due mainly to the difference between the Northeast region and the other four regions.

The third question asked was: "Do you personally feel that the government should provide free treatment with experimental drugs to men who would like to be helped before being caught for a sex offense against a child?" There were no significant differences among the regions with regard to this question. The percentage of agencies saying yes ranged from 75 percent in the mid-Atlantic region to 84.6 percent in the Northeast. The average percentage was 78.2 percent.

Conclusions to be drawn from these drug questions are that, while law enforcement agencies believe these drugs should be made available and research should be undertaken, drug treatment should not be used to replace a prison sentence. The percentage of agencies against replacing prison sentences with drug treatment ranged from 65.6 percent in the Northeast to 85.3 percent in Indiana.

Table 7

Frequencies of Agencies Responding to
Drug Therapy Questions

				Regions					
Questions	Responses+	IL	IN	IA	mid-At- lantic	North east	Total	Chi Square	P Level
Sponsor re- search on drugs to lower sex drive	# respond- ing	161	228	133	98	181	801		
	# yes	105	139	96	49	100	489	15.70	0.0034
	(% yes)	(65.2)	(61.0)	(72.2)	(50.0)	(55.2)	(61.0)		
Offer ex- perimental drugs in- stead of prison sentences	# respond- ing	160	231	135	97	180	803		
	# yes	29	34	21	22	62	168	28.56	0.0001
	(% yes)	(18.1)	(14.7)	(15.6)	(22.7)	(34.4)	(20.9)		
Provide free drug treatment	# respond- ing	162	226	135	84	136	743	4.61	0.3300
	# yes	126	171	106	63	115	581		
	(% yes)	(77.8)	(75.7)	(78.5)	(75.0)	(84.6)	(78.2)		
Number of agencies respond- ing to question- naire		163	238	137	103	191	832		

+# responding = number of agencies answering either with a yes or no
  on the question.
yes = number of agencies answering with a yes on the question.

Summary

Sex crimes against children--sexual assault, sexual exploitation,
child pornography, and prostitution--are a major social problem in
the United States. Approximately 20 percent of 832 responding law
enforcement agencies from ten states have investigated either the use,
sale, or possession of child pornography (Table 2) and 19.7 percent
have investigated child prostitution cases from 1978 to 1980 (Table
4). These are revealing statistics, since sexual assaults against
children received even higher percentages (31.7 percent in Table 6).
Knowing that many crimes against children go undetected, unreported,
and unattended, the actual percentages may be higher. Furthermore,
the regional differences noted in the study could indicate even
greater under-reporting by regions.

This study raises additional research questions. Are the gender
differences in cases of boys in the Northeast region and girls in
other regions due to reporting discrepancies, attitudes, or cultural
aspects? Is the low volume of adult arrests due to lack of witnesses,

evidence, or bias? Is the endorsement given by law enforcement officers strong enough to encourage the government to sponsor research on anti-androgen drugs for the treatment of the child molester?

The questionnaire did not survey whether the victimized children were reported to child protective agencies or if the children and their families received services following disclosure of the sexual abuse. It is recommended that all agencies whose work brings them into contact with child victims of sexual crimes develop strong cooperative relationships in order that clinical services be forthcoming for the child and family for the prevention of long-term after-effects of the victimization.

CHAPTER 10

SEXUAL VICTIMIZATION OF ADOLESCENTS

Ann Wolbert Burgess

The past decade has seen advances in the way people think
about sexual victimization. The adult victim is less likely to be
viewed as "provocative" or "asking for it," and rape is more likely
to be understood as a crisis-inducing situation resulting from an act
of aggression. More recently, attention has been focused on the
sexual exploitation of children; slowly the myths of the seductive or
fantasizing child are eroding and children are being believed when
they report a victimization.

However, a neglected age-population that still remains is the
young person who has graduated from childhood yet remains uninitiated
into the rites and responsibilities of adulthood. The study of the
adolescent is a relative newcomer to the research arena. Lerner
(1981), in addressing the Conference on Research Directions for Understanding Stress Reactions in Adolescence, observed that a decade ago,
courses in adolescent psychology and adolescent development were not
available in his graduate program and that adolescence was viewed as
a relatively unimportant period in life. Thus, it is not surprising
that there is a dearth of research on the sexual victimization of the
adolescent. Given the limitations in knowledge, there have been some
strides made in the empirical and clinical literature on victims. The
adolescent or pubescent teenager—the focus of the chapter—has been
noted to be at risk for sexual victimization by various predators including peers (Ageton 1981; Burgess and Holmstrom 1979); adult acquaintances (Finkelhor 1979; Geiser 1979; Schultz 1980); family members (Weinberg 1968; Giarretto 1976; Lystad 1982); and strangers (National Crime Survey 1981; Uniform Crime Reports 1980).

Definitions of Sexual Victimization

Legal definitions of rape have expanded in recent years. Before
the early 1970s, for instance, almost all jurisdictions defined rape
as "illicit carnal knowledge of a woman, forcibly and against her
will," with "carnal knowledge" customarily interpreted as vaginal
penetration by the penis. This meant that rape laws failed to protect either males or separated spouses and overlooked all forced sex
acts except vaginal intercourse.

Recognizing the limitations of existing definitions, anti-rape
groups began to lobby for reforms. The Michigan Criminal Sexual Code
was one of their first accomplishments. This Code, still among the
most comprehensive, includes four major revisions of the legal definition: (1) it restricts the use of a victim's sexual history as evidence for the defense; (2) it provides a degree of structure for assaultive sexual acts; (3) it eliminates resistance standards; and

---

This chapter is reprinted with permission of the National
Center for the Prevention and Control of Rape from *The Sexual
Victimization of Adolescents*, by Ann Wolbert Burgess, 1984.

(4) it extends protection to males and separated spouses. By 1976, thirty-six other states had substantially revised their rape statutes, clearing the way for reforms within law enforcement and court sectors, and thirteen others had proposed new laws.

In the establishment of the National Center for the Prevention and Control of Rape, the federal government itself adopted a broader definition of rape, including statutory and attempted rape as well as completed rape and any other criminal sexual assault, whether homosexual or heterosexual, that involves the use of force or the threat of force, including coercion and bribery of children.

Aware of the damage that may result from all forms of sexual victimization (e.g., anal and oral as well as vaginal penetration), clinicians have long supported such a comprehensive definition of rape. Now certain clinical researchers have expanded the concept of sexual assault still further by defining coercion to include more subtle forms of sexual pressuring. Pressured sexual situations involve persons of unequal power and status in which sex is used by the person with the higher status to take advantage of the person with less power. These situations usually involve offenders known to the young person as in incidents of incest and activities such as prostitution and pornography. These situations may be termed sexual exploitation, that is, situations in which a person is used primarily for another's gratification, profit, or selfish purpose.

Relationship Between Victim and Offender

Sexual assault, by definition, is an interactional process; that is, at least two persons are involved. In adolescent assault, the relationship of offender to victim is especially noteworthy.

Three patterns of relationships between victim and offender emerge from the research on sexual assault: 1) stranger; 2) non-stranger; and 3) incest. Although all three patterns of relationship may have serious and long-term effects, they are presumed to be different in a number of important ways: in the nature of the dominant behavioral, psychological, and cognitive reactions they provoke; in the issues they raise for service providers and other potential helpers; and in the techniques that may be helpful for treating existing cases and presenting new ones. The ensuing sections briefly describe adolescent experience in victimization in these categories.

Stranger Relationship

The prevailing belief that rape usually occurs between strangers and that victims are targeted at random is generally not true (Rabkin 1979). Studies vary markedly in reporting victim-offender relationship, with ranges between 36 percent to 91 percent for stranger relationships. Amir (1971) found the offender to be a stranger in 42 percent of all rape cases (N=646) reported to Philadelphia police from 1958 to 1960. Holmstrom and Burgess (1979) noted 38 percent, or 41 out of 109 rape victims (5 of the victims sixteen years or younger, and 36 of the victims seventeen years or older), whose victimization was reported to Boston police in 1972 and 1973 were unable to identify their assailants. Rabkin (1979) believes that underreporting of offenses by victims is a function of degree of acquaintance with the offender, and suggests that the stranger rapes probably account for 50 percent of all rapes reported to the police. Amir, using the term "ecologically bound," describes rape occuring predominantly between residents of the same neighborhood, members of the same race, and at certain times of the day and week as key variables in relationship.

Non-Stranger Relationship
   Children and adolescents are particularly vulnerable to assault
by a person known to them, that is, the non-stranger category. The
known adult offender may be someone who lives within close proximity
to the adolescent, such as a neighbor, or who has contact with the
adolescent such as through recreational activities or sports, or by
someone in an official association with the teenager, such as a
teacher.
   The known offender may be someone within the same age, such as
a peer specifically in a dating situation. In adolescence especially,
dating is the cultural ritual that allows young persons to test their
developing sexuality and social skills in interpersonal and intimate
relationships. How smoothly these encounters go depends on the attitudes and expectation about sexual behavior couples bring to the situation. However, it is important to acknowledge, as early theorists
hypothesized, that the majority of children are socialized in a rape-
supportive society and thus absorb gender-specific behaviors that
legitimize rape. Dating within this context may become an arena for
sexual victimization.
   Recent studies of the causative factors of rape confirm the rape-
supportive nature of sex-role learning, traditional dating patterns,
and adherence to rape myths (Burt 1980; Koss and Oros 1982; Zellman
et al. 1979; Weis and Borges 1973). The research reveals, for instance,
that females associate femininity with softness, non-assertiveness,
and dependence on men; are socialized to be alluring yet sexually unavailable; and are assigned the role of pace-setter in sexual situations. Males, on the other hand, are conditioned to be strong, powerful, and aggressive. They are acculturated to be aggressors in sexual
situations and to view a woman's resistance to sexual overtures as
mere face-saving gestures.
   How clearly these attitudes are adopted by adolescents and how
strongly they influence their perceptions of male-female interactions
was demonstrated by a study of 432 Los Angeles area adolescents conducted by Zellman and colleagues (1979). Despite the liberalization
that has occurred in recent years, these adolescents (ages fourteen
through eighteen) still had traditional views of sex roles. Further,
male respondents viewed the world as "sexier" than females, that is,
they were more likely to differentiate between love and sex. On the
issue of force to achieve sexual intercourse, the findings are quite
revealing. Some 82 percent of the males and the females initially indicated that force was generally never acceptable. Yet, when offered
specific sets of circumstances involving force, the proportion of
those saying "never" decreased to 34 percent. Male and female respondents were consistent in the belief that force is "all right"
under certain conditions and is more acceptable when a girl leads a
boy on or gets him sexually excited.
   This common acceptance of forced intercourse serves only to perpetuate the aggressive tendencies of young males. Under these circumstances it is not surprising that adolescents concerned about their
sexuality are vulnerable to date or acquaintance rape, especially if
they adhere to common "sexual scripts."
   In studying adolescents and their offenders (Burgess and Holmstrom 1979), it becomes clear that teenagers are not only at risk for
rape by a peer but they may also face multiple assailants. In the
Burgess and Holmstrom study, over half of the seventeen adolescent
rape victims were attacked by multiple assailants, either a pair of

adolescent males or a group of young males, and often the adolescent offender was from the same community as the victim. Several variations of teenage peer rape may operate: 1) multiple assailants and a single victim; 2) multiple assailants and multiple victims; 3) multiple assailants and multiple serial victims; and 4) peer rape in tandem (e.g., offenders who group together specifically to rape). In our rape-supportive culture, the myth supportive of gang rape is that they are "just young boys sowing their wild oats."

Incest

Incest, like rape, is a legal term. Incest is proscribed in every state. Although statutes vary from state to state, incest usually refers to sexual intercourse between two persons so closely related that they are forbidden by law to marry. However, we can see the ambivalence in our societal attitudes just over the controversy about whether or not to involve some incest offenders in the criminal justice system. As social scientists have observed, women and children have been considered property and that has usually meant the adult male family members could and perhaps still can do whatever they want to members of their own family.

Clinical definitions are helpful to consider when dealing with the problem of incest. Herman and Hirschman (1981) differentiated incest—as any physical contact between parent and child that had to be kept secret—from seductive behaviors (e.g., peeping, exhibitionism, leaving pornographic materials within sight for the child, demanding detailed descriptions of the child's real or imagined sexual activities) that were clearly sexually motivated but did not include secrecy and physical contact.

Incest is now known to occur much more frequently than previously imagined. In 1968, Weinberg reported annual incidence at an estimated 1.9 cases per million population in this country; by 1976, Giarretto estimated annual incidence at the much expanded rate of 200 cases per million. Experts suspect that even current estimates greatly understate the problem, which is not only underreported to legal authorities but also shrouded in intense secrecy.

The most commonly reported adult-child sexual activity occurs between daughter and male in a caretaking role (e.g., father, stepfather, mother's paramour), and the least reported between mother and son. Although female victims outnumber reported male victims, clinical studies reveal that male children are not exempt from the problem. According to Giarretto (1976), ten years is the average age of onset for an incestuous on-going relationship involving an eldest daughter. Typically, the victim's participation is gained through the application of authority, subtle pressure, persuasion, or misrepresentation of moral standards (Burgess and Holmstrom 1975). Trust of parents and obedience appear to be key factors placing children at high risk of sexual abuse. As children approach puberty, even the very trusting and obedient children may begin to question their parents' authority; at this time, those who have been victims in incest may begin to see their situation through new eyes, looking for ways out. Also, one of the most consistent findings in the incest literature reviewed by Herman in Chapter 7 of this Handbook is the unusually high rate of serious illness or disability of mothers of sexually abused daughters.

INCIDENCE OF SEXUAL ASSAULT AMONG ADOLESCENTS

It is difficult to obtain a true grasp on the scope of the problem of adolescent sexual victimization. Statistics on the incidence
of adolescent victimization vary considerably for several reasons.
First, there is no centralized national or state recording system or
index for sexual offenses against youths (Schultz 1980). Second, a
true measure of this problem is almost impossible to obtain because
children and adolescents typically are extremely reluctant to report
sexual assault to parents or significant others (Landis 1956; Peters
1973). Third, the agencies may report child and adult sexual assault
figures with the adolescent range included in both, e.g., sixteen or
under for child and age seventeen to nineteen for adult victims.
There is confusion over what ages to include in defining a "minor,"
"adolescent," and "juvenile" (Schultz 1980). The data on the age of
victims depends to some extent on the definition of the crime and the
age used for reporting statistics either via an agency or by researchers. Adolescents usually come to the attention of an official reporting agency by an adult (e.g., parent or teacher) who finds out
about the rape or injuries. This lack of reliable incidence and frequency data, argues Schultz, makes it difficult to present the problem to the public, to influence policy makers, law enforcement and
budget bureaus, and human service agencies in providing resources.

The above concerns notwithstanding, there are several strata of
incidence reporting that we may examine to provide some preliminary
understanding of the numbers of sexually victimized adolescents by
the typology of the perpetrator.

Stranger Rapes
Through the FBI national crime reporting statistics (1981) the
victims of reported forcible rape did not include males, but did provide summary statistics on females of all ages (N-82,090). In 1980,
an estimated 34.4. out of every 100,000 females in the country were
reported rape victims, a 94.2 percent rate increase over 1971. Since
older adolescent girls are at particular risk for rape, it is safe to
assume that the reported rape for adolescents is considerably higher
than this. Also, these data consist primarily of cases of stranger
rape.

Non-Stranger Assault
Another source of incidence data is the National Crime Survey.
This survey is a household survey, the point of which is to identify
crimes which are not reported to official agencies and which, therefore, do not appear in the FBI national crime statistics. These data
include non-stranger and acquaintance rape. The 1979 National Crime
Survey provides the following profile on reported cases of sexual
victimization:

> Victimization occurs at the rate of 2.5 cases per 1,000
> females age 12 to 15. This rate climbs precipitously to 5.7
> cases per 1,000 females age 15 to 19. The next age group,
> females 20 to 24 reports a somewhat lower rate of 4.7 per
> 1,000. Protection then comes with age: females between 25
> and 34 reporting a rate of 2.1 per 1,000; those between 35
> and 49 at a rate of 1.00 per 1,000; and those 50 and over at
> a statistically unreliable level of 0.1 per 1,000.

The sexual abuse of boys is a seriously neglected area of victimization, both from an understanding of incidence and for the provision of services. Although statistically reliable estimates could not be developed for males using the NCS, the figures that NCS do report create the same profile as for females, sexual victimization starting at a rate of 0.2 per 1 thousand males in the 12 to 15 age range, quickly reaching a zenith of 0.7 in the 16 to 19 age group, then dropping to 0.5 for males age 20 to 24, to 0.4 for those age 25 to 34, and to 0.1 for those between 35 and 64.

Incest Assaults

Another source of incidence reporting is the National Incidence Study (Burgdorf 1981) which surveyed cases reported to various kinds of agencies: hospitals, child protective agencies, police and courts. This study found .7 per 1,000 cases of sexual exploitation, defined as sexual assault or abuse of a child by a parent or other adult caretakers whose acts included genital penetration, genital or breast contact as well as unspecified behaviors. Thus, the focus of this survey was on abuse committed by caretakers and parents (e.g., incest) rather than stranger or non-stranger.

A fourth population to study for incidence are young persons living in residential facilities. No statistics are available on the incidence of child maltreatment, especially sexual victimization in these settings. Harrell and Orem (1980) report that over 400,000 children live in child-caring institutions annually such as treatment centers, temporary and long-term shelters, detention homes, youth correctional facilities, centers for the mentally retarded and developmentally disabled and group homes with an additional 400,000 children living in foster homes. The sexual victimization of juveniles in institutions other than correctional has been virtually neglected in the literature (Shore 1982). The sexually abused youths residing in child-care homes are only now beginning to receive attention. These children are viewed by Shore as one of the most invisible and oppressed of all underserved populations--a population which is "at home" and behind closed doors. The literature is beginning to cite and suggest parallels and differences between maltreatment occurring within a residential institution charged with the care of the child and that occurring within a child's own family.

Gender of the Victim

The incidence reports can be examined in terms of gender of the victim. The studies comparing sexual abuse of girls and boys are diverse and in clinical populations and general surveys, girl victims outnumber boy victims three to one. Finkelhor (1979), conducting a large study surveyed 796 college-aged students, demonstrated what has been reported through the clinical literature: 1) children are at high risk for sexual assault and 2) they will not report it. In his sample, 19.2 percent of the women students surveyed had been in a sexual encounter with an adult (the mean age of these women at the time of exposure was 10.2 years and 63 percent of them did not tell anyone of the experience). In the sample, of the 8.6 percent male students who had a sexual encounter with an older person (mean age of 11.2) 73 percent did not tell at the time.

Swift (1977) in a survey of mental health professionals in an urban mental health center found that young males made up one-third of the child case load in treatment reporting sexual exploitation;

one-fifth of the adult case load reporting sexual exploitation as children; and one-sixth of the victims of self-confessed exploiters seen in treatment. However, police and law enforcement agencies report seeing twice as many boy victims as are found in general surveys or clinical settings (Finkelhor 1979); and clinicians and law enforcement seeing child and adolescent victims of sex ring crimes finds males more frequently victimized than females (Burgess 1984).

In comparing incidence data for stranger, non-stranger and incest, it is apparent that stranger rape is under-reported and non-stranger and incest sexual exploitation and abuse is even less often reported.

Fresh evidence to this effect is beginning to surface from a multi-year, national survey of adolescent vulnerability to sexual assault conducted by Suzanne Ageton. As defined in this survey, "sexual assault" encompasses a range of sexual pressuring, from familiar and somewhat expected verbal ploys to unbidden violence. Ageton's preliminary findings strongly support two clinical impressions: 1) that the vast majority of adolescent victims are assaulted by someone they know; and 2) that very few of these cases ever come to the attention of parents, police, or any other responsible adults:

> An overwhelming 92 percent of identified female victims of sexual assault (N=64) were acquainted with their assailant(s): 56 percent of these nonstranger victims had been attacked by a date, 30 percent by a friend, and 11 percent by a boyfriend. The majority (78 percent) of victims did not relate the incident to their parents but most (71 percent) did tell one or more friends. A mere 6 percent of the victim sample contacted the police, the absence of injury and prior acquaintance with the assailant being the most common reasons for not reporting.

Finally, a minimal number sought professional assistance or advice. Above all, Ageton's research underlines the peer orientation common among adolescents and their typical reluctance to communicate openly with adults; therefore, it suggests that adults who work with youth are themselves unlikely to be approached by adolescent victims of nonstranger rape and that indirect methods will be required to deal with most individual incidents of this kind.

The incidence data, difficult as it is to obtain, reveals that there are sexually victimized adolescents, a minimum of 32.9 for every 100,000 adolecents in the general population. This estimate is for incest primarily and extrapolated from figures from the National Incidence Study (Bergdorf 1981). Their figures state 38 percent of the general population in the United States fall between the ages 12-17. However, their "in scope" population (i.e., maltreated children) is 47 percent for the 12-17 age range, suggesting that young adolescents (21 percent in the age range 12-14 and 26 percent in the age range 15-17) have a higher probability of having a sexual victimization reported than necessarily younger persons, at least in incest situations.

Indications are strong that there are actually many more sexually victimized adolescents, with estimates ranging from a conservative double to even triple the numbers reported when including stranger and nonstranger sexual assaults. The rates are even higher in the vulnerable populations where there is family disorganization, absent or incapacitated parent, the psychiatrically ill or retarded group,

the runaway and the adolescent in institutional or foster homes.
Thus, adults whose work brings them into contact with adolescents
might expect about 20 percent of the general population to have experienced sexual victimization, up to 50 percent to have experienced
victimization without having disclosed this fact to a responsible
adult. Those adults who have contact with high risk vulnerable adolescent populations can expect to find even higher percentages of the
adolescents victimized in either or both childhood and adolescence.

DEVELOPMENTAL TASKS OF ADOLESCENCE
IN RELATION TO THE TRAUMA OF SEXUAL ASSAULT

Adolescence has long been recognized as a period in development
fraught with its stressful aspects. It is a period of extraordinary
change, multiple conflicts, and marked societal demands upon the individual for the successful completion of significant developmental
tasks (Garmezy 1981).

In terms of change, there are the hormonal, physiological, and
somatic changes that are reflected in pubertal development. Over an
average span of four brief years, the child is transformed, at least
in terms of physical characteristics, into an adult (Peterson and
Taylor 1980). But equally important psychological demands induced by
puberty are a heightened sexuality, the growth of peer attachments,
a striving to achieve autonomy from and to reduce dependency upon
parents, the assumption of specific gender roles, and a heightened
search for personal identity (Garmezy 1981).

The search for identity is facilitated in adolescence by the
cognitive changes that occur during this period. The acquisition of
formal logic accounts for some but not all of the shifts that take
place. Identity is an abstraction, as are concepts such as justice,
friendship, loyalty, morality; to comprehend these abstract concepts,
a child can no longer be bound by concrete thinking. In addition,
the ability to problem solve, inhibit impulses, and delay gratification accompany cognitive growth and maturation (Keating 1981).

As for conflict, this tends to be focused on parents as the
most significant adults in the life of the adolescent. The roots of
such stressful experiences are often to be found in the disparity between the values of the adolescent peer culture and familial values.
Although such parent-adolescent disagreements are commonplace, their
frequency does not necessarily moderate their intensity (Garmezy 1981).

As for societal demands, one need only consider the many developmental tasks required of adolescents to complete their transition to adulthood. Garmezy outlines these requirements as follows:
1) to achieve the gender-appropriate social role; 2) to accept one's
body image; 3) to achieve independence from parents; 4) to find a
responsible sexuality; 5) to complete requisite academic goals; 6) to
prepare for an occupation; 7) to develop a set of values necessary
for filling later roles as spouse and parent; and 8) to evolve a set
of values and a philosophy of life that will be compatible with successful passage into adulthood.

These multitudinous changes can be viewed as stressors in the
sense that they entail significant adaptation to restore a sense of
inner harmony and homeostasis to the individual. The assumptions of
roles related to sexuality and academic, occupational, interpersonal,
and social responsibility are major transitions that can bring dis-

comfort and emotional distress in their wake. Thus, it is not surprising that any form of sexual victimization can easily disrupt the
adolescent's developmental tasks, producing serious effects in both
the short and long term.

To appreciate the possible profundity of these effects, it is
necessary to comprehend development as a cumulative process and to
understand stress response patterns. Erik Erikson's (1950) "Eight
Stages of Development in the Human Life Cycle" provides a useful
framework for development as a cumulative process. In this conceptualization, each life stage involves certain developmental themes and
tasks, to which there are negative alternatives. Moreover, each
stage is an integral part of the developmental process; success in
completing one set of developmental tasks prepares the individual to
advance to the next phase and also contributes greatly to the resolution of the crisis issues that are then encountered. As a corollary,
disruption at any point can compromise the individual's ability to
accomplish the tasks required at succeeding phases and can also im-
peril the accomplishments of earlier phases.

The crisis that the rape victim faces can be analyzed by looking
at the interaction between the developmental phase the person is in
and the externally imposed event of the rape. The sexual assault
takes on specific meaning to victims according to their stage of development in the life cycle. The helper needs to look at the developmental point of the victim and try to understand what the attack
means to the victim at that stage.

The major developmental task during adolescence is gaining a
sense of identity. The adolescent's previous trust in her or his
body is somewhat shaken by rapid body growth and this new image must
be gradually reevaluated. Thus, for the adolescent, whose primary
task is self-definition, sexual assault tends to produce feelings and
behaviors of a different sort. The assaulted adolescent female, for
instance, may be worried about pregnancy in particular and may be
acutely aware of her continuing vulnerability. The assaulted adolescent male may feel conflict about his gender identity and have
fears of homosexuality when raped by another male. For both, the
assault may constitute a frightening, ego-shattering experience, en-
gendering feelings of extreme helplessness, particularly if forcibly
raped. The issue of sexuality may be more pronounced in incidents
involving peers and/or acquaintances. In either case, how well the
adolescent recovers from the assault will depend largely on his or
her previous psychosocial functioning, the coping and personality
style, the level of maturity, and the type of support received from
those close to him or her. When adolescents conceal their feelings
and experiences from others, they have the difficult task of using
their own inner resources to heal and integrate the incident adaptively.

A second important consideration in evaluating the impact of a
sexual assault on an adolescent is the stress response pattern of
the victim. Clearly, the same phenotypic experience causes different
reactions in different people and requires distinct coping mechanisms and internal processes from each individual (Moss 1981). In arguing for a taxonomy of stress, Moss suggests that the following distinctions be made:

      --Normal developmental stress: individuals in different
        stages of life have to master developmental challenges

inherent in that stage of life; dealing with and mastering these challenges could constitute stress for the individual.

--Chronic stressful conditions: this classification might include serious illness, a handicap, extreme poverty, or feelings of "second class citizenship" because of minority status; response could be different from that elicited by normal developmental stress.

--Severe unexpected stress: individuals experience turbulence of some sort in all stages of life; all adolescents feel some stress for their future.

Although very little research has been directed to the study of stress response in adolescence, Maddi (1981) speculates on the implications of stress resistance in adolescence from his work on the phenomenon in adulthood. Stressful events are seen as increasing organismic arousal or strain. Strain, continued long enough, can result in various signs of breakdown, or illness of a physical and mental nature. But several other mediating variables need to be taken into account. Constitutional, personality, and social support factors can influence the stressfulness of events through the coping process and can modulate the magnitude of stress reactions through health practices.

To Maddi, coping has components of both cognition and action. He differentiates between "transformational coping" and "avoidance coping." Transformational coping decreases the stressfulness of events that have occurred both through cognitive appraisal, in which an event recognized as stressful is not so terrible after all when put in perspective, and through decisive actions, which are aimed at altering the event to decrease its stressfulness. Coping by avoidance, however, involves pessimistic cognitive appraisal, in which the event may really be "as bad as it seems," and evasive actions, which are designed to distract or remove the person from interaction with the event. Since it does not change the event, avoidance coping must be continued as protection against the stress. Maddi and his colleagues believe that transformational coping is more advantageous in the long run. They believe that particular characteristics of personality and social supports increase the likelihood of transformational as opposed to avoidance coping, and lead to positive health practices that can decrease strain reactions. Thus, personality and social supports can maintain health by decreasing both stress and strain. In applying the coping responses to adolescent victims, the pattern of avoidance is often observed and needs serious attention, especially since the majority of victims do not report their victimization.

Although the crisis reactions outlined above have been associated mainly with persons victimized by strangers, victims of known assailants may experience similar symptoms, prompted by the sense of shock and disbelief they can feel in the aftermath of less violent forms of sexual assault.

Incidents included under the rubric "nonstranger assault" often vary from study to study. For instance, one particular sample may be heavily weighted with incest cases, whereas another may exclude incest entirely; or one sample may be comprised of incidents perpetrated by assailants who were mere passing acquaintances of their victims,

whereas another may involve a high proportion of date rapes. Thus
it is not surprising that findings about reactions to "nonstranger
rape" do not have a high level of consistency. And for this reason,
any comparisons and observations should be considered suggestive, not
definitive.

The relationship between victim and offender has received attention in victimization studies. Our concern here is the psychosocial
impact to the victim when the offender is known to her.

One-third of the victims in the follow-up study by Burgess and
Holmstrom of their original study (1979) reported knowing their assailant. The term "known" is used to refer to even the slightest
prior relationship, including partner or boyfriend, acquaintance,
neighbor, fellow employee, or fellow student. In talking with victims at the time of crisis counseling as well as on follow-up, it is
clear that when the victim knows the assailant there are different
issues to cope with that are not involved in victim-stranger relationships. First, the psychological issue that someone the victim
knows raped her and what that means; second, the social component
which implies that the victim has to deal with a group to which she
is already connected; and third, the legal issue that involves the
victim making a decision regarding loyalty ties and whether to press
charges.

First, consider the psychological issue. When the rapist is a
stranger, one response by victims is to increase environmental security and psychological defenses against all "unknowns." This process is not dissimilar to the way many people regularly live their
lives; that is, they act on the assumption that the world is a dangerous place and people need to be tested until proved trustworthy. In
contrast, when victims are raped by someone they know, the situation
is different. They cannot compartmentalize people into "good" and
"possibly dangerous" merely by whether they are strangers or not.
Victims, therefore, have the psychological task of either 1) learning
a new way of predicting dangerous human situations, or 2) remaining
in a chronic fearful state of existence in relating to people, especially to men.

The second psychological point is that the victim must try to
"explain" why this happened. Part of the psychological rape recovery
work is to make some sense out of the event that has happened. This
step is more complicated when the rapist is known and may be quite
difficult depending on the degree of relationship with the offender.

There are two components to the social issue when the victim
knows the offender, neither of which she has much control over.
First, when the rapist is known, he can talk to a group with which
the victim has interpersonal ties. Second, the victim is more apt to
have more interpersonal contact with the assailant and his social network.

The third issue, the legal issue, affects the prosecution of
rape cases when the assailant is known. There were no convictions
in the Burgess and Holmstrom (1979) sample for offenders of rape victims who knew their assailant; in contrast, there were seven pleas
for convictions for cases of victims of strangers.

Particular pressures are brought to bear on the victim when the
assailant is known. The pressure from social network or family loyalties, as well as interpersonal factors, play a part when the assailant is known.

Ageton's (1981) findings on reactions to non-stranger assault
are similar in kind but different in degree, moderated perhaps by the
low level of violence involved in the incidents she analyzed or by
the success that most of her respondents had in resisting their assailants. It is instructive to contrast the reactions of victims
identified in Ageton's survey (92 percent of them victims of non-
stranger assault) to the reactions of a victim sample assessed by
Williams and Holmes (1981) which included primarily cases of
stranger assault. The initial emotional response of the non-stranger
assault sample was more likely to include feelings of guilt, embarrass-
ment and depression than the stranger rape sample who exhibited feelings
of fear, anxiety, apprehension and confusion.

Reactions to non-stranger assault tend to be more variable and
less clear-cut than reactions to stranger rape, probably because the
concept "non-stranger rape" itself covers such a diverse multitude of
incidents, from a neighbor's attempted assault on the girl next door
to a young man's rape of a person he met that evening in a bar.

Adolescent Reaction to Incest

There is considerable historical data on the stress reactions of
children and adolescents to incest. Goodwin et al. (1979), in reviewing folk beliefs connecting seizures with incest, writes that the
second-century Greek physician Galen believed seizures were the result of premature intercourse in childhood, and that the Navajo Indi-
ans have recognized for centuries a tripart syndrome of incest, seizures, and witchcraft--for example, when a Navajo has a seizure it
is often assumed she has experienced incest and may be a witch (Temkin 1971).

Ferenczi (1949), in a paper published ten years after it was presented at a Viennese Psychoanalytic Society meeting, documented the
following outcomes of incest and early childhood sexual trauma as 1)
the undeveloped or perverted nature of the child's sexual life; 2) a
traumatic progression of a precocious maturity; 3) the terrorism of
suffering; and 4) the introjection of guilt feelings as an adult.

Lystad (1982), in reviewing the professional literature on consequences of rape on victims, noted reports of medical hazards, disease, biological consequences, symptoms of severe anxiety attacks,
depression, hostility, anger, self-blame, self-mutilation, and hysterical seizures. Problems in sexual identity and sexual development
can also occur. A fragmented body image can result, as well as problems in establishing a further relationship with the opposite sex,
including promiscuity and an inability to form lasting heterosexual
relationships.

Among children and adolescents, gradual social and psychological
withdrawal are characteristic reactions to incest, and may be particularly pronounced when the victim has been pledged to secrecy and
has kept this pledge through an extended period of repeated sexual
encounters. The incest secret becomes a symbol of profound difference
from other people. Interpersonal relationships are impeded by fears
of exposing the secret. However, social isolation interferes with
important latency age tasks. Specifically, there is inhibited mutual
sharing of secrets, fantasies, and significant experiences with
friends of the same sex which, in turn, provide a variety of self-
validation functions.

Older adolescents frequently react with profound hostility, anxiety, guilt, and depression which may be masked by somatic symptoms and behavioral problems--for example, learning disabilities, delinquency, promiscuity, drug or alcohol abuse, and, in extreme cases, attempted suicide. Quite often, the adolescent will try to remove her or himself from incestuous situations by running away. But once on the streets, they only become vulnerable to further sexual exploitation in the form of pornography and prostitution. The developmental task of self-identity is markedly impeded.

In this chapter, a framework has been presented in which to view the relationship between the developmental tasks of adolescence and the reactions of adolescents to sexual assault, including short and long-term effects. This perspective can be used when considering the implications of empirical findings on both victims and offenders which follow in this volume.

REFERENCES

Ageton, S.S. "Sexual Assault Among Adolescents: A National Survey." National Institute of Mental Health: research project RO1 MH31751, 1981.

Amir, M. *Patterns in Forcible Rape.* Chicago, Illinois: University of Chicago Press, 1971.

Bart, P.B., and P.H. O'Brien. "Stopping Rape: Women Who Did." Manuscript in preparation.

Bassuk, E., R. Savitz, and S. McCombie. "Organizing a Rape Crisis Program in a General Hospital." *Journal of the American Women's Association* 1975: 486-490.

Browning, D., and B. Boatman. "Incest: Children at Risk." *American Journal of Psychiatry* 134 (1977): 69-72.

Brownmiller, S. *Against Our Will: Men, Women and Rape.* New York: Simon & Schuster, 1975.

Burgdorf, K. "Recognition and Reporting of Child Maltreatment: Findings from the National Study of the Incidence and Severity of Child Abuse and Neglect." Washington, D.C.: National Center on Child Abuse and Neglect, 1981.

Burgess, A.W. *Child Pornography and Sex Ring Crimes.* Lexington, Massachusetts: D.C. Heath, 1984.

Burgess, A.W., and L.L. Holmstrom. *Rape: Crisis and Recovery.* Bowie, Maryland: Brady, 1979.

Burgess, A.W., and L.L. Holmstrom. "Rape Trauma Syndrome." *American Journal of Psychiatry* 131 (1974): 981-986.

Burgess, A.W., and L.L. Holmstrom. "Sexual Trauma of Children and Adolescents: Pressure, Sex and Secrecy." *Nursing Clinics of North America* 10 (1975): 551-563.

Burgess, A.W., A.N. Groth, L.L. Holmstrom, and S.M. Sgroi, eds. *Sexual Assault of Children and Adolescents.* Lexington, Massachusetts: D.C. Heath, 1978.

Burgess, A.W., A.N. Groth, and M.P. McCausland. "Child Sex Initiation Rings." *American Journal of Orthopsychiatry* 51 (1981): 110-119.

Burgess, A.W., L.L. Holmstrom, and M.P. McCausland. "Child Sexual Assault by a Family Member: Decisions Following Disclosure." *Victimology* 2 (1977): 236-250.

Burt, M.R. "Cultural Myths and Supports for Rape." *Journal of Personality and Social Psychology* 38 (1980): 215-220.

Cohen, M.L., R. Garofalo, R.B. Boucher, and T. Seghorn. "The Psychology of Rapists." *Seminars in Psychiatry* 3 (1971): 307-327.

Erikson, E. *Childhood and Society.* New York: Norton, 1950.

Farberow, N.L., and N.S. Gordon. *Manual for Child Health Workers in Major Disasters.* National Institute of Mental Health: DHHS Publication no. (ADM) 81-1070, 1981.

Ferenczi, S. "Confusion of Tongues Between Adult and Child." *International Journal of Psychoanalysis* 30 (1949): 220-230.

Finkelhor, D. *Sexually Victimized Children.* New York: Free Press, 1979.

Foley, T., and M. Davis. *Nursing Care of the Rape Victim.* Philadelphia, Pennsylvania: Lippincott, 1983.

Garmezy, N. "Overview." In *Adolescence and Stress.* National Institute of Mental Health Conference Report. DHHS Publication No. (ADM) 81-1098, 1981.

Gebhard, P., P.B. Johnson, G. Zellman, and R. Giarrusso. *Child Molestation in Problems of Sex Behavior.* New York: Crowell, 1968.

Geiser, R. *Hidden Victims: The Sexual Abuse of Children.* Boston, Massachusetts: Beacon Press, 1979.

Giarretto, H. "The Treatment of Father-Daughter Incest: A Psychosocial Approach." *Children Today* 5 (1976): 2-5, 34-35.

Goodchilds, J.D., P.B. Johnson, G. Zellman, and R. Giarrusso. "Adolescent Perceptions of Responsibility for 'Dating' Outcomes." Paper presented at the Eastern Psychological Association Meetings. Philadelphia, Pennsylvania, April, 1979.

Goodwin, J., M. Simms, and R. Bergman. "Hysterical Seizures: A Sequel to Incest." *American Journal of Orthopsychiatry* 49 (1979): 698-703.

Groth, A.N. *Men Who Rape.* New York: Plenum, 1979.

Groth, A.N. "The Sexual Assault of Males: Victim and Offender Issues." Paper presented at Fourth National Conferences and Workshops on Sexual Aggression. Denver, Colorado, 1982.

Groth, A.N., A.W. Burgess, and L.L. Holmstrom. "Rape: Power, Anger and Sexuality." *American Journal of Psychiatry* 134 (1977): 1239-1243.

Harrell, S., and R. Orem. *Preventing Child Abuse and Neglect: A Guide for Staff in Residential Institutions.* Washington, D.C.: Health and Human Services, 1980.

Herman, J., and L. Hirschman. "Families at Risk for Father-Daughter Incest." *American Journal of Psychiatry* 138 (1981): 967-970.

Holmstrom, L.L., and A.W. Burgess. "Rape and Everyday Life," *Society* 20 (1983): 33-40.

Hummer, K.E. "Leadership Training Workshops for North Carolina Rape Crisis Centers." Final Report, National Center for the Prevention and Control of Rape. Grant No. J 31 MH15664, 1980.

Keating, D. "Cognitive Development." In *Adolescence and Stress*. National Institute of Mental Health Report. DHHS Publication No. (ADM) 81-1098, 1981.

Koss, M.P., and C.J. Oros. "Sexual Experience Survey: A Research Instrument Investigating Sexual Aggression and Victimization." *Journal of Consulting and Clinical Psychology* 50 (1982): 455-457.

Landis, J. "Experiences of 500 Children with Adult Sexual Deviation." *Psychiatric Quarterly, Supplement* 30 (1956): 91-109.

Lerner, R. "Keynote Address." In *Adolescence and Stress*. National Institute of Mental Health Conference Report. DHHS Publication No. (ADM) 81-1098, 1981.

Luther, S., and J. Price. "Child Sexual Abuse: A Review." *Journal of School Health* 60 (1980): 161-165.

Lystad, M. "Child Sexual Abuse: When It Happens in the Home." *Response* 5 (1982): 5-7.

Lystad, M. "Violence at Home: A Review of the Literature." *American Journal of Orthopsychiatry* 45 (1975): 328-345.

Maddi, S. "Personality development." In *Adolescence and Stress*. National Institute of Mental Health Conference Report. DHHS Publication No. (ADM) 81-1098, 1981.

Montgomery County Sexual Offenses Committee. "Sexual Assault: The Role of Education in Prevention and Attitude Change." In *Report of the Montgomery County Sexual Offenses Committee*. Rockville, Maryland, 1975.

Moss, H. "Individual Development." In *Adolescence and Stress*. National Institute of Mental Health Conference Report. DHHS Publication No. (ADM) 81-1098, 1981.

National Crime Survey. "Criminal Victimization in the United States, 1979." Report issued by the U.S. Department of Justice, 1981.

National Incidence Study. Project conducted by Westat, Inc. under Contract No. HEW 105-76-1137. National Center for Child Abuse and Neglect, 1981.

Peters, J. "Child Rape: Defusing the Time Bomb." *Hospital Physician* 9 (1973): 46-47.

Peterson, A.C., and B. Taylor. "The Biological Approach to Adolescence." In *Handbook of Adolescent Psychology*, edited by J. Adelson. New York: Wiley, 1980.

Prendergast, R. New Jersey Sex Offenders Program. Workshop conference, 1974.

Rabkin, J.G. "The Epidemiology of Forcible Rape." *American Journal of Orthopsychiatry* 49 (1979): 634-647.

Rada, R.T. *Clinical Aspects of the Rapist*. New York: Grune &
   Stratton, 1978.

Ruch, L.O., and S.M. Chandler. *The Sex Abuse Treatment Center Program Evaluation Report*. Honolulu, Hawaii, 1978.

Sanday, P.R. *Female Power and Male Dominance: On the Origins of
   Sexual Inequality*. New York: Cambridge University Press, 1981.

Schultz, L.G. *The Sexual Victimology of Youth*. Springfield, Illinois: Charles C. Thomas, 1980.

Scully, D., and J. Marolla. "Convicted Rapists' Construction of
   Reality: The Denial of Rape." Paper presented at the American
   Sociological Association Meetings. San Francisco, California,
   September, 1982.

Sgroi, S.M. *Handbook of Clinical Intervention in Child Sexual Abuse*.
   Lexington, Massachusetts: D.C. Heath, 1982.

Sgroi, S.M. "Sexual Molestation of Children: The Last Frontier in
   Child Abuse." *Children Today* 4 (1975): 18-21.

Shore, D.A. "Sexual Abuse and Sexual Education in Child-Caring
   Institutions." *Social Work and Child Sexual Abuse* 1 (1982):
   171-184.

Summit, R. "Recognition and Treatment of Child Sexual Abuse." In
   Providing for the Emotional Health of the Pediatric Patient,
   edited by C.E. Hollingsworth. New York: Spectrum, 1981.

Sutherland, S., and D. Scherl. "Patterns of Response Among Victims
   of Rape." *American Journal of Orthopsychiatry* 40 (1970): 503-511.

Swift, C. "Sexual Victimization of Children: An Urban Mental Health
   Center Survey." *Victimology* 2 (1977): 322-327.

Symounds, M. "Victims of Violence." *American Journal of Psychoanalysis* 35 (1975): 19-26.

Uniform Crime Reports. Federal Bureau of Investigation, U.S.
   Department of Justice, 1980 + 1981.

Temkin, O. *The Falling Sickness*. Baltimore, Maryland: Johns
   Hopkins Press, 1971.

Weinberg, K. *Incest in Problems of Sex Behavior*. New York: Thomas
   Y. Crowell, 1968.

Weis, K., and S.S. Borges. "Victimology and Rape: The Case of the
   Legitimate Victim." *Issues in Criminology* 8 (1973): 71-115.

Williams, J.E., and K.A. Holmes. *The Second Assault: Rape and Public
   Attitudes*. Westport, Connecticut: Greenwood Press, 1981.

Zellman, G.L., P.B. Johnson, R. Giarrusso, and J.D. Goodchild.
   "Adolescent expectations for Dating Relationships: Consensus and
   Conflict Between the Sexes." Paper presented at the American
   Psychological Association meetings, New York, September, 1979.

CHAPTER 11

SEXUAL ASSAULT AND THE HANDICAPPED VICTIM

Eileen E. Rinear

Statistics on rape, child molestation, and incest clearly reveal that these problems are reaching alarming proportions in the United States, and that they are on the increase (Longo and Gochenour 1981). The FBI Uniform Crime Reports statistics (1980) indicate the steady increase of rape, and it is estimated at present that a woman is raped in the United States every seven minutes (Magnuson 1981). The incidence data on child sexual assault has estimated that one in four females will be sexually molested or assaulted by the time she reaches twenty years of age, and/or she will be at risk for sexual victimization by a family member (Kinsey 1953); however, more contemporary surveys are indicating an even higher number (Russell 1983). The numbers for male victimization are more hidden; however, clinical data is increasingly suggesting that boys may be at equal risk for sexual victimization since they are the preferred targets of habitual pedophiles and victims of child sex rings (Lanning and Burgess 1984).

Rape research focusing on both the victims and the perpetrators of this crime has been extensively conducted. Epidemiologic, attitudinal, and coping patterns have been examined in an effort to gain more data on the incidence, consequences, and prevention of sexual assault. Paradoxically, those individuals who are perhaps the most vulnerable to sexual assault and the least able to resist their offenders, that is, those who are physically or emotionally handicapped, have received almost no attention from researchers on victimology. This chapter, in addition to providing some information on these special interest groups and on the unique problems encountered by them in relation to sexual assault, has as its major goal to draw attention to this badly neglected research area.

VULNERABILITY OF HANDICAPPED PERSONS

Shulker (1980) states that rapists often select particular types of victims because of some "special vulnerability such as youth, old age, physical deformity or handicap." Handicapped individuals not only suffer from an increased vulnerability to sexual assault, but they also face a number of unique problems after victimization occurs. It seems reasonable to infer that these unique factors, a summary of which follows, serve to compound the trauma reaction that handicapped victims of sexual assault typically experience.

First, emotionally handicapped individuals may find that others fail to believe that they were actually victimized, but rather, view their accounts as either manifestations of their emotional illnesses or contrived stories aimed at gaining attention. (Longo and Gochenour 1981). From a psychodynamic standpoint, the person handicapped by a psychotic disorder with its associated problems of trust, ego boundary diffusion, and social isolation clearly faces a complex recovery process as a consequence of sexual victimization.

Second, individuals with physical and perceptual handicaps may also be targeted as victims of sexual offenders because of their re-

stricted abilities to detect approaching danger, as well as their
limitations in providing descriptive information on their assailants
to law enforcement personnel. Again, the danger of a compounded
trauma reaction occurring as a consequence of the rape exists in
cases in which the victims are in the process of recovering from the
disabling event in their lives at the time that the assault occurs
(Longo and Gochenour 1981; Burgess et al. 1978).

Third, handicapped persons are limited, albeit in varying degrees, in the type and amount of resistance that they are able to
mount against their assailants. Groth et al. (1977) have categorized
rapes as either "anger" or "power" in nature, based upon an examination of the motivational intent of the perpetrator. Clearly, the
handicapped individual represents an "ideal" victim for either type
of offender.

Finally, handicapped individuals who are dependent upon others
for assistance may be exploited by offenders who manipulate or distort the victim's dependence, in order to satisfy their own unful-
filled desires. Longo and Gochenour (1981) state that, "since the
victim often views the offender as a helper, there appears to be a
lack of awareness that the assault is inappropriate."

COPING BEHAVIORS OF RAPE VICTIMS

Burgess and Holmstrom (1976) have analyzed the coping behaviors
used by rape victims and have found that these can be viewed as comprising three distinct phases: (1) the threat of attack; (2) the attack itself; and (3) the period immediately thereafter. In the next
section of this chapter, these three phases will be discussed and
potential linkages or inferences to handicapped victims will be addressed.

In their study of rape victims interviewed at Boston City Hospital's Emergency Department over a one-year period, investigators Burgess and Holmstrom noted that the majority of these victims perceived
the rape as a life-threatening experience, and those in the minority
that did not experience it this way still agreed that it was an a-
cutely stressful, frightening, and degrading experience. They state
that, "for almost all victims, the attack was something far out of
the ordinary that seriously taxed their adaptive resources."

These investigators further note that "appraisal of the degree
of danger, threat, or harm is a psychological process that intervenes
between a stressful event and coping behavior. This early awareness
may be cognitive, perceptual, or affective--often, the victim describes it as a 'sixth sense' or a feeling of impending danger."
They note the coping task during this phase is to react quickly
to this warning. It is easy to understand how a variety of handicapped individuals, especially those with serious perceptual or psychiatric disorders, might easily have been unable to recognize that
a danger to their safety or well-being existed.

Threat of Attack

Burgess and Holmstrom (1976) describe this first phase as constituting the point at which the victim realizes that there is a
definite danger to her or his life; the individual realizes that
something critical is going to happen, although she or he may not
realize that rape is the imminent danger. The investigators describe

the coping task in this phase as constituting avoidance of or escape
from this situation. They further note that, while coping behaviors
were analyzed from the standpoint of the victim's ability to react to
this confrontation with danger, this ability was often dependent upon
the following factors: (1) the amount of time between the threat of
attack and the attack itself; (2) the type of attack; and (3) the
type of force or violence used. Clearly, the cognitive, verbal, or
physical strategies available for use by handicapped individuals will
vary with the nature and extent of their disability, and, accordingly,
may render avoidance or escape from such a situation impossible.

During the Attack
     Burgess and Holmstrom (1976) note that "at the moment of the
actual attack it becomes clear to the victim that forced sexual attack is inescapable. The coping task during this phase is to survive
the rape despite the many demands forced upon the victim, such as
oral, vaginal, and anal penetration." They also add that some victims
may be forced to engage in conversation with their assailants during
the rape attack. Again, available cognitive, verbal, and physical
strategies will vary with the nature and extent of the victim's disability. It seems plausible to speculate that individuals with ac-
quired physical or perceptual handicaps might be even more effective
in coping during this phase of a rape attack than their non-disabled
counterparts, due to the development of coping behaviors necessitated
by the crisis of the previous disabling event.

After the Attack
     Burgess and Holmstrom remind us that the stressful situation does
not end when the actual rape is over, since the victim must still
escape from her assailant and from the place where she has been left,
as well as alert others to her distress. For the physically or perceptually handicapped, the coping task of this phase--namely, to be
free or to escape from the assailant--poses serious problems. Bargaining seems to be the most feasible strategy for handicapped persons
who can successfully negotiate with their assailants, since physical
limitations may severely restrict the handicapped victim's ability to
alert others to her situation, or to free herself physically either
from any restraints or from the location of the assault.
     The investigators add that, once free from the assailant, the
victim is still faced with the task of coping with the aftermath of
rape, and that often they are immediately faced with the task of trying to cope with the institutions that are set up to deal with rape.
Again, the handicapped victim faces unique problems at this point in
the assault experience, some of which will be elaborated upon in the
following section of this chapter.
     A handicapped psychologist who herself was raped, stated in an
interview with the *Minneapolis Star* that "the problems and frustrations that a handicapped person faces after an assault are enormous."
She elaborates on some of these problems, stating that "first of all,
it's very hard to talk about the sexual issues involved ... there is
a myth that people wouldn't be violent with a handicapped person,
that a person wouldn't rape her or beat her because she is handicapped. People don't want to believe it or deal with it, but it
happens" (Dawson 1979).
     Accessibility to victim services and treatment facilities is
just one of a myriad of problems that a handicapped victim faces

after she has been sexually assaulted. Many crisis facilities and
neighborhood support groups are located in buildings that are old and
inaccessible to handicapped persons, and thus render it difficult for
such individuals to utilize these services. Some facilities do provide for home visits to handicapped rape victims, but even when such
services are offered they typically limit availability to immediate
crisis care. Getting legal help, much less a conviction, is another
one of the obstacles faced by the handicapped victim. For example,
some severely handicapped or mentally disabled individuals may know
nothing about sex and, consequently, may not even be aware that their
rights have been violated. The courtroom process is physically ex-
hausting for the "healthy victim," but can be torture to the victim
with a physical handicap. Another problem that exists in prosecuting
such cases is that of jury prejudice. Hennapin County Assistant
District Attorney Ann Alton has commented on this problem, drawing
from an actual case involving a handicapped rape victim. She states
that "[the jury] distanced themselves from her. There was a 'there
but for the grace of God go I' feeling. We [able-bodied] are scared
of the handicapped. The jury thought she was sweet, but she wasn't
a real human being to them" (Dawson 1979).

    Both law enforcement personnel and attorneys agree that it is
easy to understand why handicapped victims, who have such dismal results with the judicial system, are reluctant to report rape assaults.

SEXUAL VICTIMIZATION OF HANDICAPPED CHILDREN

    As with adult handicapped victims, disabled or handicapped chil-
dren represent easy prey for adults, who because of their own inadequate personalities, turn to children to satisfy their needs for control, affiliation, or--less frequently--sadism. Handicapped children,
like their non-disabled counterparts, are most likely to be sexually
victimized by an adult who is known to the child and her or his parents; who stands in a position of power or authority in relation to
the child; and who uses this position, or his relationship with the
family, to gain access to the child. Handicapped children who have
recently suffered a disabling event, and who are unable to participate in age level activities with their peers, are especially vulnerable to the acceptance, attention, and affection that are so skillful-
ly provided her or him by the pedophile.

PREVENTION OF VICTIMIZATION OF HANDICAPPED PERSONS

    While it is clear that we cannot completely protect our handi-
capped citizens from sexual assault, it is equally clear that we have
remained essentially ignorant of the unique problems they face as potential or actual victims. In addition to the need for research in
this area so that a data base can be established from which thoughtful actions may emerge, the following recommendations might prove to
be a fruitful beginning and one that can be realistically implemented:
        --Vigorous efforts on the prevention of victimization should
        be implemented and focused on those handicapped individuals
        who seem to be most vulnerable to attack. While not geared
        primarily toward sexual assault, a good beginning aimed at
        crime prevention for deaf individuals has emerged out of
        Galludet College (1981) in the form of captioned public

service announcements. Similar adaptations in educational
efforts should be made to target other groups of handicapped individuals so that dissemination of preventive information can be facilitated.

--Self-defense classes tailored to meet the individual needs
of handicapped persons should be made readily available to
a broader segment of the handicapped population. Such a
course is not only useful in providing the handicapped person with a repertoire of coping skills to use in an attack
situation, but also seems valuable in minimizing the psychological handicaps of fear and vulnerability experienced
by these individuals.

One handicapped individual states it this way: "Last November I had my purse snatched while I was sitting in my car
at a stoplight ... I screamed in a high voice, honked my
horn, struggled, but let go of the purse for fear of being
hurt. The incident made me feel how vulnerable I was. I
took self-defense more to rebuild my emotional security
than to be proficient in karate.... Now, I feel that if my
purse were snatched, I'd have a different reaction. Instead
of letting out a high feminine shriek, I would be able to
Ki [a cry of attack pronounced kee-eye] and convey the attitude, 'Don't mess with me'" (Lewis 1981).

--Crisis centers and support groups should strive to be cen-
trally located and to make the physical modifications needed to render facilities accessible to handicapped individuals. Ideally, transportation to these facilities and
to courtroom appearances should be provided to handicapped
sexual assault victims. Crisis counseling through home
visits, until such time as the needed structural changes
can be accomplished, should be immediately instituted for
handicapped rape victims. It would be beneficial to develop a list of resources familiar with the unique problems
faced by handicapped victims (e.g., recovering handicapped
victims, legal counsel, behavioral scientists, etc.) and to
provide handicapped victims with this information at the
time of the initial crisis evaluation.

--Educational efforts directed toward prosecutors, and also
toward the general public, should be implemented in an effort to sensitize these individuals to the plight of the
handicapped victim. In addition, jury selection efforts
should address the issue of bias toward handicapped victims
and should control selection for this factor, whenever
possible.

--Handicapped persons should be encouraged, through educational interventions, to report cases of sexual victimization
and to collectively lobby for greater visibility of their
needs.

--Institutions committed to the care of handicapped persons
should provide educational programs (e.g., via formal conferences, institutional closed circuit TV, patient/family
educational groups, etc.) focusing on the problems of both
adult and childhood sexual victimization.

INTERVENTION

It is essential that individuals who deal with sexually victimized individuals develop a working knowledge of the needs and problems of handicapped victims. In addition, those individuals providing victim services should also familiarize themselves with the
psychological reaction to sexual assault commonly experienced by victims and termed by Burgess and Holmstrom (1974) as the "rape trauma
syndrome," as well as with the compounded trauma responses which may
be seen in handicapped victims.

Clients with psychological handicaps must be aided in understanding when their rights have been violated sexually; perceptually
handicapped individuals or children may require procedural modifications in order to be able to express what has actually happened to
them; and child victims need mobilization of both professional and
family support systems so that their feelings of guilt, inadequacy,
or lowered self esteem can be resolved.

Finally, the guidelines and strategies suggested by Burgess et
al. (1978) for dealing with handicapped persons who have been sexually assaulted should be implemented by professionals who encounter
these victims. Such strategies and guidelines include: (1) identification of the nature and extent of the victim's handicap; (2) evaluation of whether or not this handicap will interfere with the interview process; (3) assessment of the impact of the rape on the victim's
behavior; (4) completion of the customary protocol for evaluation and
examination of sexual assault victims, with adaptations as necessary
to accommodate the victim's physical or perceptual limitations, her
or his stress level, and the victim's and family's need for additional staff time; (5) the avoidance of the projection of stereotyped
conceptualizations or labels onto handicapped victims, the use of
careful observation and assessment, and discussion of the rape assault
with the victim and family in a manner that is respectful and that
fully acknowledges the impact of this experience on them; and (6) recording of interview data in terms that demonstrate not only respect
for the handicapped victim and her or his family, but that objectively reflect the clinician's finding.

Victims who have handicaps affecting their capacity to communicate are especially prone to social and psychological problems, as
well as frustration related to their type of disability. These types
of victims pose especially difficult problems for prosecutors and
they are likely to experience a great deal of shame, difficulty, and
insecurity in just trying to describe their assault experience.
Thus, these victims need specialized attention from those whom they
encounter (i.e., police, medical personnel, etc.) after an assault.

Sexual assault is a traumatic experience for any individual, but
for the handicapped individual the problems posed by such an experience are especially complex, and as such, may serve to intensify or
prolong the victim's trauma response. One hopes that as the base of
empirical data on handicapped victims expands, these individuals will
encounter professionals whose treatment and services are designed to
accommodate their unique needs and concerns.

REFERENCES

Burgess, A.W., A.N. Groth, L.L. Holmstrom, and S.M. Sgroi, eds.
   Sexual Assault of Children and Adolescents. Lexington, Massachusetts: D.C. Heath, 1978.

Burgess, A.W., and L.L. Holmstrom. "Coping Behavior of the Rape
   Victim." *American Journal of Psychiatry* 133 (1976): 413-418.

Burgess, A.W., and L.L. Holmstrom. "Rape Trauma Syndrome." *American
   Journal of Psychiatry* 131 (1974): 981-986.

Burgess, A.W., and K.V. Lanning. "Child Pornography and Youth
   Prostitution Rings." Paper presented at the Western Conference of
   the American Society for Adolescent Psychiatry. Seattle, Washington, September 25, 1982.

Dawson, J. "Disabled Fall Easy Prey to Violence." *The Minneapolis
   Star* (July 9, 1979).

Federal Bureau of Investigation. *Crime in the United States: Uniform
   Crime Reports*. Washington, D.C.: U.S. Government Printing Office,
   1980.

Galludet College. "Crime Prevention Public Service Announcements."
   Press Release (March 30, 1981).

Groth, A.N., A.W. Burgess, and L.L. Holmstrom. "Rape: Power, Anger
   and Sexuality." *American Journal of Psychiatry* 134 (1977): 1239-
   1243.

Kinsey, A.C., et al. *Sexual Behavior in the Human Female*. Philadelphia, Pennsylvania: Saunders, 1953.

Lanning, K.V., and A.W. Burgess, "Child Pornography and Sex Rings,"
   FBI Bulletin 53 (1) January 1984: 10-16.

Lewis, Vicki. "Fight Back." *Blind Services* (1981): 10-11.

Longo, R.E., and C. Gochenour. "Sexual Assault of Handicapped
   Individuals." *Journal of Rehabilitation* (July/August/September
   1981): 24-27.

Magnuson, E. "The Curse of Violent Crime." *Time* 117 (1981): 16-21.

Russell, D. "The Incidence and Prevalence of Intrafamilial and
   Extrafamilial Sexual Abuse of Female Children." *Child Abuse and
   Neglect: The International Journal* 7 (May 1983): 133-146.

Schulker, P.C. "Degrading and Unpredictable: Rape Can Happen to
   Anybody." *New York Times*, October 26, 1980.

CHAPTER 12

MARITAL RAPE

Kersti Yllö and David Finkelhor

The burgeoning literature on sexual assault and family violence attests to the growing recognition of the problem of sexual and physical abuse. Rape, wife-beating, and incest are crimes that we are beginning to better understand as years of research begin to accumulate. Marital rape has much in common with these other forms of assault. Yet, it is different in a crucial way: it is legal in most of the United States. It is the one form of sexual abuse and family violence which we, as a society, formally and explicitly condone. Moreover, it is a form of abuse which is generally not taken very seriously.

Only very recently has marital rape become a public issue, and, state by state, it is gradually being criminalized. Despite the controversy surrounding the Rideout case in Oregon in 1978, that trial proved to be a turning point. For the first time, marital rape was brought into public consciousness. For millions, the problem of marital rape was finally named.

Although lagging far behind the research on rape in general and on wife-beating, studies of marital rape are now forthcoming and a tentative picture of this type of wife abuse is beginning to take form. The purpose of this chapter is to overview this research, which five years ago was non-existent, and to sketch out this picture. The first question addressed is, what is marital rape? Second, how widespread a problem are we discussing? Third, how does it happen and why? Fourth, what are the effects on the women? And finally, why is this form of sexual violence still legal in the United States?

WHAT IS MARITAL RAPE?

Legally, "marital rape" is a contradiction in terms. Most sexual assault statutes define rape as involving intercourse through force or threat of force, without the consent of the woman, *other than one's wife*. It is this "spousal exemption" which makes marital rape legally non-existent.

Rape, marital or otherwise, has been defined in a number of other ways, however. Besides rejecting the spousal exemption, many feminists have argued for a broader definition which is not limited to vaginal penetration. Brownmiller (1975), for example, defines rape as any sexual intimacies forced on one person by another. Yet marital rape researchers have not been completely consistent in their definitions, nor for that matter in their terminology.

In her landmark work, *Rape in Marriage* (1982), Russell uses the term "wife rape" rather than marital or spousal rape because she wants to make explicit that this is not a gender-neutral issue; it is wives who are the victims of marital rape. However, Russell's definition of rape remains fairly close to traditional legal definitions (excluding, of course, the spousal exemption). While she includes forced oral, anal, and digital penetration, she does not go as far as Brownmiller to include other forced intimacies, such as forced fondling of genitalia.

Finkelhor and Yllö (1983) consider the forms of sexual coercion which may be involved in marriages. They share Russell's view that there is a continuum of sexual relations, not just a rape/not rape dichotomy. They identify four basic types of coercion. Some women submit to sex in the absence of desire because of social pressure-- because they believe it is their wifely duty. This can be considered "social coercion." Other wives comply because they fear their husbands will leave them if they do not, or because their husbands have threatened to cut off their source of money or humiliate them in some way. In these cases husbands use their resource and power advantage to force their wives. This second type of coercion, "interpersonal coercion," refers to threats by husbands that are not violent in nature. The third type involves the "threat of physical force." Threatened force can range from an implied threat that a woman could get hurt if she doesn't give in, to an explicit threat that she will be killed if she doesn't comply. For many women, the memory of previous beatings is enough to ensure cooperation. The fourth kind of coercion, "physical coercion," requires little explanation. Instances of physical coercion range from physically holding a woman down to striking her, choking her, tying her up, or knocking her out to force sex on her.

While Finkelhor and Yllö recognize that, in some cases, interpersonal coercion might constitute rape, they limit their research to sex coerced through force or threat of force. Like Russell, they include other forms of sex besides vaginal intercourse. Unlike Russell, they use the term "marital rape" in discussing the rape of wives.

Frieze (1983), who also writes in terms of "marital rape," defines it as "forced sexual activity demanded of a wife by her husband." In her empirical work, Frieze actually uses several different "rape" questions ranging from "husband has pressured you to have sex" to "husband has raped you." Other researchers have relied on a single question--i.e., has your husband physically forced you to have sex?--as the indicator for marital rape (Shields and Hanneke 1983).

Despite some variations in definitions and interview questions used by different researchers, it appears that marital rape can be defined the same way as any rape. Rape occurs when a person has sex with another by force and without her or his consent. A rape is "marital" simply when the attacker is the husband of the women being attacked.

PREVALENCE OF MARITAL RAPE

The notion that, if marital rape does exist then it must be a rare phenomenon, is being dispelled by the latest research. Studies of rape in general, wife-beating, and incest have challenged the myth that such assaults are perpetrated by a very small number of crazed individuals. These types of assaults are not uncommon, and neither is rape within marriage.

The best data on the prevalence of wife rape currently available come from Russell's (1982) survey of women in San Francisco. Russell and her staff interviewed over 900 women (age eighteen or older) who had been scientifically selected to be representative of all the women living in that city. The women were asked about sexual assault experiences involving strangers, dates, family members, and husbands or ex-husbands. Twelve percent of the ever-married women reported that their husbands had committed acts that would qualify under the legal definition of rape in California--"forced intercourse or intercourse obtained by physical threat or intercourse completed when the woman was drugged, unconscious, asleep, or otherwise totally helpless and unable to consent." Another 2 percent reported an experience of being forced to engage in some other sexual activity, such as oral sex or anal sex. A total of 14 percent of the wives had been sexually assaulted in some manner by their husbands.

Finkelhor and Yllö (1983) also have data from a representative sample of Boston area women, all mothers of children ages six to fourteen, who were questioned at length about sexual abuse of children. Within this context, the women were asked whether their spouses or live-in sexual partners had ever used physical force or threat of force to try to have sex with them. Altogether, 323 women were asked these questions, and, of them, *10 percent* reported that their husbands had used force or threat of force to try to have sex with them.

Although precautions were taken to preserve candor in both the San Francisco and Boston surveys, it is still very likely that both counts of sexual assault experiences in marriage are low. In all probability, some women did not feel comfortable enough to reveal what had happened to them. Moreover, some women may have forgotten about sexual assaults, since they were asked about assaults over the course of a whole marriage, or, they may have repressed unpleasant memories. Thus, although between 10 and 14 percent of married women surveyed acknowledged a sexual assault by a husband, the real incidence is probably higher, but it is difficult to estimate by how much.

Perhaps the most remarkable finding of both Russell's and Finkelhor and Yllö's studies is that sexual assault by husbands is the most common kind of sexual assault. When most people think of rape, they tend to think of "stranger rape," that is, rape by someone unknown to the victim. This is the kind of rape most likely to be reported to police, and hence most likely to be reported in crime surveys. Yet in Russell's study, more than twice as many women had been raped by a husband as had been raped by a stranger. And in the Finkelhor and Yllö study, 10 percent of the women had been sexually assaulted by a husband while only 3 percent had been similarly assaulted by a stranger since the age of sixteen.

Additional data from other studies bolster the findings of the San Francisco and Boston surveys that rape in marriage is widespread. A newspaper survey in New Jersey found that 8 percent of the women readers who responded indicated that their partner or lover had used violence or threat of it to force them to have sexual intercourse (Doron 1980). Although not based on a representative sample, this figure is fairly consistent with the other studies.

Prevalence data focused on battered wives have also been provided by other research. For example, Frieze's (1983) Pittsburgh-area study was based on a sample of 137 battered women who volunteered for a study of violence in marriage as well as a matched comparison sample of women from the same neighborhoods. Of the battered women, 73 percent indicated that their husbands pressured them to have sex, in contrast with 45 percent of the comparison group. When asked directly if their husbands had raped them, 34 percent of the battered group and 3 percent of the comparison group answered affirmatively. While the 3 percent rate is much lower than that reported in other studies, it is important to note that this question asked specifically about "rape" rather than forced sex. Clearly, many wives share the common stereotype that rape is an act committed by strangers, and are thus less likely to label their own experience of forced sex with their husbands as "rape."

Additional research on battered women confirms their high vulnerability to marital rape. Spektor (1980) surveyed 304 battered women in ten shelters in the state of Minnesota and found that 36 percent said they had been raped by their husbands or cohabiting partner. Giles-Sims (1982) found a similar proportion of women in shelters reporting a forced sex experience, and Pagelow (1981) reported a figure of 37 percent based on a sample of 119 women in California. Forced sex is clearly a common element in the battering situation.

The slowly accumulating evidence is that marital rape is widespread. With prevalence estimates ranging between 3 percent and 14 percent of married women, with much higher rates among battered women, it is clear that millions of women in the United States have been raped by their husbands. It appears that marital rape is, in fact, the most common form of rape. Yet, it remains the least recognized and its victims remain the most silenced.

THE NATURE OF MARITAL RAPE

The first social science article on marital rape was not published until 1977. In introducing the problem to the scholarly community, Gelles wrote that "the research carried out to date allows no direct insights into the incidence or nature of the phenomenon" of marital rape. As the previous section indicated, we now do have data which enable us to estimate how widespread a problem rape is in marriage. While these rates are important, they are limited, for they tell us nothing about "the nature of the phenomenon." Fortunately, the recent research allows us to go beyond percentage figures and offers real insights into the nature of marital rape. The picture of rape in marriage which is beginning to come into focus is perhaps better described as a collage. Marital rape is complex, and there is no one "type" of woman who gets raped. Nevertheless, the various dimensions of marital rape are becoming clearer.

Marital Rape and Wife-Beating

One of the more controversial issues to emerge in the descriptive research on marital rape is the relationship between wife rape and wife-beating. Based on data cited earlier, Frieze (1983) suggests that marital rape is rare in nonviolent marriages. Other researchers concur that marital rape is almost always associated with other forms of domestic violence (Shields and Henneke 1983; Doron 1980).

The image that rape always occurs in the context of a beating suggests that wife rape is just an additional dimension of wife-battering and that they can be understood as two aspects of one phenomenon. This notion is challenged by other research which offers evidence that rape and battering in marriage are often separate phenomena. The best data available on this issue are from Russell's (1982) survey:

> The question of overlap between wife rape and wife-beating can be dealt with in different ways. With regard to our

study, one can simply focus on the 644 women who had ever been married, and report the numbers and percentages of these women who experienced both wife rape *and* beating (63 women or 10 percent), as compared with those who experienced wife rape only (24 women or 4 percent), or wife beating only (75 women or 12 percent).

Russell goes on to point out that this approach ignores the fact that a women may be a victim of wife rape and wife-beating, but by two different husbands. She then examines marriages in which there was either rape, beating, or both. Of such marriages, 37 percent of wives were both raped and beaten; 14 percent were raped only; and 49 percent were beaten only. Moreover, of the marriages in which both rape and battering occurred, these assaults occurred at different times in 56 percent of the cases.

Although their Boston survey did not include questions on both rape and battering, Finkelhor and Yllö (1983) have data on this issue based on fifty in-depth interviews with victims of marital rape. Of these fifty women (who were clients of family planning clinics or battered women's shelters), 60 percent were married to men who could be classified as chronic batterers. Physical violence was an ongoing part of their marriages and the rapes tended to be an additional form of violence perpetrated by their husbands. For a small minority the physical violence was an element of their husband's sexual sadism. For the other 40 percent of their sample, however, the rapes were not associated with beatings. While many of these marriages were not entirely violence-free, the incidents of physical abuse were quite minor compared to the rapes.

So, it appears that while rape in marriage is associated with battering in the majority of cases, wife rape does occur separately for a sizeable minority. Russell suggests that the combination or separation of rape and beatings need to be examined more closely. She outlines five types of marriages within which violence toward wives occurs, ranging from "wife rape only" to "wife rape and wife beating of approximately equal significance" and "wife beating only." An important function of this typology is that it illuminates the fact that there is more than just one type of marriage in which wife abuse occurs.

Types of Marital Rape

In presenting the range of marital rape experiences of the interviewees, Finkelhor and Yllö (1983) develop a different typology from that of Russell. They outline three ideal types, recognizing that the actual experiences of some victims may not fall neatly into only one category. The first type of forced sex experience is labelled "battering rape" and describes the rape experiences of battered wives. These women were subject to extensive physical and verbal abuse, much of which was unrelated to sex. Their husbands were frequently angry and belligerent to them and often had alcohol and drug problems. The sexual violence in these relationships appeared to be just another aspect of the general abuse. Along with the other kinds of anger and physical pain which these men heaped on their wives, they also used violent sex.

They quote briefly from a case study of one of these "battering rapes":

The interviewee was a 24-year-old woman from an affluent
background. Her husband was a big man, over six feet tall,
compared to her 5'2". He drank heavily and often attacked
her physically. The most frequent beatings occurred at
night after they had had a fight and she had gone to bed.

Their sexual activities had violent aspects, too. Although
they shared the initiative for sex and had no disagreements
about its timing or frequency, she often felt that he was
brutal in his lovemaking. She said, "I would often end up
crying during intercourse, but it never seemed to bother
him."

The most violent sexual episode occurred at the very end of
their relationship. Things had been getting worse between
them for some time. They hadn't talked to each other in two
weeks. One afternoon she came home from school, changed into
a housecoat and started toward the bathroom. He got up from
the couch where he had been lying, grabbed her, and pushed
her down on the floor. With her face pressed into a pillow
and his hand clamped over her mouth, he proceeded to have
anal intercourse with her. She screamed and struggled to no
avail. Afterward she was hateful and furious. "It was very
violent ...," she said, "... if I had had a gun there, I
would have killed him."

Her injuries were painful and extensive. She had a torn
muscle in her rectum so that for three months she had to go
to the bathroom standing up. The assault left her with
hemorrhoids and a susceptibility to aneurisms that took five
years to heal.

The second group of women have somewhat different relationships
with their husbands. These relationships are by no means conflict-
free, but on the whole there is little physical violence. In this
group, the forced sex grew out of more specifically sexual conflicts.
There were long-standing disagreements over some sexual issue, such
as how often to have sex or what were appropriate sexual activities.
The following is an excerpt from a case study of a "force-only
rape":

The interviewee was a 33-year-old woman with a young son.
Both she and her husband of ten years are college graduates
and professionals. She is a teacher and he is a guidance
counselor. Their marriage, from her report, seems to be of
a modern sort in most respects. There have been one or two
violent episodes in their relationship, but in those instances, the violence appears to have been mutual.

There is a long-standing tension in the relationship about
sex. She prefers sex about three times a week, but feels
under considerable pressure to have more. She says she is
afraid that if she refuses him that he will leave her or
that he will force her.

He did force her about two years ago. Their lovemaking on
this occasion started out pleasantly enough, but he tried to
get her to have anal intercourse with him. She refused. He

persisted. They ended up having vaginal intercourse. The
force he used was mostly that of his weight on top of her.
At 220 pounds, he weighs twice as much as she.

"It was horrible," she said. She was sick to her stomach
afterward. She cried and felt angry and disgusted. He
showed little guilt. "He felt like he'd won something."

In addition to the sexual assaults classified as battering and
force-only, there were a handful that defied such categorization.
These rapes were sometimes connected to battering and sometimes not.
All, however, involved bizarre sexual obsessions in the husbands that
were not evident in the other cases. Husbands who made up this group
were heavily involved in pornography. They tried to get their wives
to participate in making or imitating it. They sometimes had a history of sexual problems, such as difficulty in getting aroused, or
guilt about earlier homosexual experiences. Sometimes these men
needed force or highly structured rituals of sexual behavior in order
to become aroused. A case study of one of these "obsessive rapes" is
illustrative:

The interviewee was a 31-year-old marketing analyst for a
large corporation. She met her husband in high school and
was attracted to his intelligence. They were married right
after graduation because she was pregnant.

After the baby was born, he grew more and more demanding
sexually. "I was really just his masturbating machine," she
recalls. He was very rough sexually and would hold a pillow
over her face to stifle her screams. He would also tie her
up and insert objects into her vagina and take pictures
which he shared with his friends.

There were also brutal "blitz" attacks. One night, for
example, they were in bed having sex when they heard a commo-
tion outside. They went out in their bathrobes to investigate to discover it was just a cat fight. She began to head
back to the house when her husband stopped her and told her
to wait. She was standing in the darkness wondering what he
was up to when, suddenly he attacked her from behind. "He
grabbed my arms behind me and tied them together. He pushed
me over the log pile and raped me," she said. As in similar
previous assaults, he penetrated her anally.

The interviewee later discovered a file card in her husband's
desk which sickened her. On the card, he had written a list
of dates, dates that corresponded to the forced sex episodes
of the past months. Next to each date was a complicated
coding system which seemed to indicate the type of sex act
and a ranking of how much he enjoyed it.

In developing this typology of marital rape, Finkelhor and Yllö
(1983) go beyond a description of the abuse and begin to consider the
husbands' motivation in committing these assaults. They find Groth's
work on *Men Who Rape* (1979) very helpful for understanding the husbands. Based on the incarcerated rapists he has interviewed, Groth
has developed what he believes are some distinctions among the motives
that impel men to rape. One important distinction he makes is between

anger rapes and *power* rapes. Although all rapes have elements of anger and power, anger rapes`are assaults committed primarily to express hostility toward women, to retaliate against them and humiliate them. Power rapes, in contrast, are assaults committed primarily to assert dominance and control over women.

These two types of rape seem to distinguish between two types of marital rapes: battering rapes and force-only rapes. The battered women appear to be victims primarily of anger rapes. The non-battered women are primarily victims of power rapes.

Here is how Groth (1979) describes the two types:

> [In anger rape] the assault is characterized by physical brutality. Far more actual force is used in the commission of the offense than would be necessary if the intent were simply to overpower the victim and achieve sexual penetration. Instead, this type of offender *attacks* his victim, grabbing her, striking her, knocking her to the ground, beating her, tearing her clothes, and raping her. His aim is to hurt and debase his victim, and he expresses contempt for her through abusive and profane language --- Often this type of offender forces his victim to submit to or to perform additional sexual acts that he may regard as particularly degrading, such as sodomy or fellatio.

In contrast, Groth describes the power rape:

> In another pattern of rape, power appears to be the dominant factor motivating the offender. In these assaults, it is not the offender's desire to harm his victim but to possess her sexually. Sexuality becomes a means of compensating for underlying feelings of inadequacy and serves to express issues of mastery, strength, control, authority, identity, and capability. His goal is sexual conquest, and he uses only the amount of force necessary to accomplish this objective.

Groth identifies a third category of rapist as well, "sadists," which seems to describe the perpetrators of the "obsessive rapes":

> In the third pattern ... both sexuality and aggression become fused into a single psychological experience known as sadism. There is a sexual transformation of anger and power so that aggression itself becomes eroticized. This offender finds the intentional maltreatment of his victim intensely gratifying.

In using the Groth categories, it is important to understand the difference between anger rapists and sadistic rapists, both of whom inflict pain in a sexual situation. The anger rapists presumably use sex as a way of hurting their victims. They are angry and want to punish their wives. For sadistic rapists, by contrast, the goal is not so much to punish as to get aroused, which they can only do through anger and hurt. Although perhaps a subtle distinction on paper, one distinguishing feature of the sadistic rapists is the ritualistic and preoccupied quality they bring to their brutality.

The overlap between Groth's three categories of rapists and Finkelhor and Yllö's three types of marital rape suggests that these may be important dimensions of rape in marriage, as well as of other forms of rape. Certainly, though, the data are not conclusive and

further research into these types and how they are related to other
rape typologies is needed.

One such typology is that developed by Russell (1982) regarding
husbands in relation to wife rape. She outlines a five point continuum: (1) Husbands who prefer raping their wives to consensual sex with
them; (2) Husbands who are able to enjoy both rape and consensual sex
with their wives or who are indifferent to which it is; (3) Husbands
who prefer consensual sex with their wives, but who are willing to
rape (or try to rape) them when their sexual advances are refused;
(4) Husbands who might like to rape their wives, but who do not act
out these desires; (5) Husbands who have no desire to rape their
wives.

While there is some overlap between these categories and the
distinctions made by Finkelhor and Yllö and Groth, Russell's typology
has a different focus. She includes all husbands and ranks them regarding their attitudes and behavior. An intriguing direction for
research would be to study husbands and test the validity of these
typologies, none of which is based on data from the general population of men.

THE TRAUMA OF MARITAL RAPE

Many people fail to get alarmed about the problem of marital
rape because they think it is a rather less traumatic form of rape.
Being jumped by a stranger in the street, they imagine, must be so
much more damaging than having sex with someone you have had sex with
several times before. This misconception is based on a failure to
understand the real violation involved in rape and seeing rape primarily in sexual terms. What is most salient for rape victims is
most often the violence, the loss of control, and the betrayal of
trust.

Women raped by strangers often go through a long period of being
afraid, especially about their physical safety. They become very
cautious about being alone, where they go, and who they go with (Burgess and Holmstrom 1974). Women raped by husbands, however, are often traumatized at an even more basic level: in their ability to
trust. The kind of violation they have experienced is much harder to
guard against, short of a refusal to trust any man. It touches a
woman's basic confidence in forming relationships and trusting inti-
mates. It can leave a woman feeling much more powerless and isolated
than if she were raped by a stranger. Moreover, a woman raped by her
husband has to live with her rapist, not just a frightening memory of
a stranger's attack. Being trapped in an abusive marriage leaves
many women vulnerable to repeated sexual assaults by their husbands.

The research bears out the traumatic impact of marital rape.
Shields and Hanneke (1983) conducted a quantitative study designed to
assess the extent to which marital rape has an impact on the victim,
separate from the impact of non-sexual battering. Based on data
from ninety-two wives of violent men (referred to the study by public
and private social service agencies and self-help groups), these researchers statistically assessed the relative impact of rape in marriage. They found that the women who had been raped by their husbands
(41 percent of their sample), had also experienced more severe forms
of non-sexual violence and had more negative reactions overall. When
the severity of non-sexual violence was controlled, it was found that

marital rape is significantly related to low self-esteem; negative attitudes toward men; having husband arrested for violence; not wanting sexual relations; and withholding sex. Furthermore, it appears that the more often the victim experiences marital rape, the more serious are her reactions (e.g., a greater number of psychosomatic reactions and attempted suicide).

The Shields and Hanneke data lend support to the contention that victims of wife rape do indeed feel the impact of their assaults. Frieze's (1983) work provides further statistical evidence in this regard. She investigates both emotional and behavioral reactions to marital rape. The majority of the raped wives felt anger or other negative emotions toward their husbands. The frequency of rapes had a clear impact, however. The more frequent the rapes, the more often the women blamed themselves. Six percent of those who were raped once blamed themselves as compared to 20 percent who were raped often.

In terms of behavioral reactions, Frieze found that the battered women in her sample who had also been raped were more likely to seek help for marital problems and were more likely to call the police and press charges. Unfortunately, attempts to get help were not usually successful. For example, only 36 percent of these women reported positive consequences as a result of calling the police. Sixteen percent felt that the blame was placed on them and 12 percent experienced retaliation from their husbands. No effect or other effects were reported by 41 percent.

In addition to seeking outside help, the raped women in this sample were the most likely to want to leave their husbands, and almost half of them were divorced or separated at the time of their interview. Frieze concludes that "It was ... clear that rape by one's husband leads to even worse consequences than 'only' being battered. In every comparison done, the raped and battered women demonstrated more extreme reactions than other battered women who had not been raped." A major limitation of the Shields and Hanneke and Frieze studies is that their analyses compared raped and battered wives with "only" battered wives. The entwined impact of these two forms of abuse are difficult to untangle, although Shields and Hanneke do take steps in this direction by introducing statistical controls.

Russell's (1982) study offers additional information about the trauma of marital rape, and has the advantage of including all forms of wife rape, reflecting her representative sample. The most common negative long-term effects on wives she uncovers are some of the same ones mentioned in the studies above. Increased negative feelings and behavior toward men in general was reported by 37 percent of the victims of wife rape. Thirty-two percent indicated negative feelings/behavior toward their husbands, and 27 percent reported a deterioration in the marriage, including divorce.

More importantly, with regard to the stereotype that marital rape is not serious, Russell shows that wife rape has the greatest long-term effect on the victim of all types of rape. "Fifty-two percent of the women raped by a husband and 52 percent of women raped by a relative ... report that the rape(s) had a great effect on their lives, as compared with 39 percent of women raped by a stranger, 33 percent of women raped by an authority figure, 25 percent by an acquaintance, and 22 percent by a friend, date, or lover."

These quantitative data go far in demonstrating the impact of marital rape. Yet, the words of one victim serve to give real meaning to the numbers:

> The physical abuse was horrible, but that was something I could get over. It was like a sore that heals. When he forced me to have sex, that was more than just physical. It went all the way down to my soul ... He just raped me ... my whole being was abused ... I feel if I'd been raped by a stranger, I could have dealt with it a lot better ... When a stranger does it he doesn't know me, I don't know him. He's not doing it to me as a person, personally. With your husband, it becomes personal. You say, this man knows me. He knows my feelings. He knows me intimately and then to do this to me. It's such a personal abuse (Finkelhor and Yllö, forthcoming).

MARITAL RAPE AND THE LAW

In the United States, the marriage license is, in effect, a raping license. While research cited earlier has highlighted the high prevalence of forced marital sex and has documented some of its human cost, the criminal justice system is locked in an anachronistic view of the subject. As of January 1982, approximately thirty-six of the fifty states and the District of Columbia exempt a husband from prosecution for the rape of wife with whom he is currently living. (An excellent review of the laws on a state-by-state basis is available from the National Center on Women and Family Law; see Schulman 1980). Most states have a so-called spousal exemption in their rape laws, and thirteen states extend this exemption not just to husbands but also to cohabiting lovers (Schulman 1980). Such laws effectively deny the possibility of charging a husband with rape, no matter how brutal or violent he may be in pursuit of sex. They also contain the implicit assumption that upon marrying a woman gives permanent and irrevocable (short of divorce) consent to any and all sexual approaches a husband wishes to make.

This spousal exemption in the rape laws is an historical remnant which reflects the original purpose of rape laws. The criminalization of rape was not designed to protect women, but rather to protect male property (Brownmiller 1975). Thus, the rape of a man's virgin daughter or fertile wife by an outsider is regarded as a serious crime. The lingering notion of wife as property to be used as the husband wishes is only thinly veiled in current rape statutes.

Changing the laws has been vehemently opposed in some quarters. "But if you can't rape your wife, who can you rape?" lamented California Senator Bob Wilson when faced with the prospect of eliminating the spousal exemption (Russell 1982). Those who oppose criminalization are generally reluctant to advocate the issue of rape in marriage. Rather, they claim that allowing prosecution would result in a rash of fabricated complaints or that marital rape is already adequately prohibited under existing assault laws. However, evidence from countries and states where marital rape is a crime shows that few frivolous complaints are being brought (Geis 1978). Moreover, the research on rape shows that sexual assault is a crime different from other assaults. Marital rape, just like other rape, deserves special classification within the legal codes (New York University Law Review 1977).

CONCLUSION

Marital rape victims endure intimate violation and experience trauma, much as victims of other sorts of sexual assault. Yet their suffering remains the most silenced because the crime against them is not regarded as a crime at all. As long as marital rape remains legal, it is clear that we, as a society, condone it. As Russell (1982) puts it, "to continue to see rape in marriage as a husband's privilege is not only an insult, but a danger to all women." While our understanding of other forms of abuse, such as wife-beating, makes it clear that criminalization of abuse is by no means a solution, it must be regarded as an important first step, if only in a symbolic sense.

This review of the research on rape in marriage demonstrates what enormous progress can be made in a few short years. We are starting to grasp the magnitude of the problem and are beginning to understand the nature of marital rape. At this stage, the studies are largely descriptive. Percentage rates, case studies and typologies have revealed much. Yet there is much still to be discovered. More theoretical work, causal explanations, and a greater focus on rapists are needed. By developing a better understanding of rape in marriage, we can better work to end it.

REFERENCES

Brownmiller, S. *Against Our Will: Men, Women and Rape*. New York: Simon & Schuster, 1975.

Burgess, A.W., and L.L. Holmstrom. *Rape: Victims of Crisis*. New York: Prentice-Hall, 1974.

Doron, J. "Conflict and Violence in Intimate Relationships: Focus on Marital Rape." Paper presented to the American Sociological Association. New York, August, 1980.

Finkelhor, D., and K. Yllö. *License to Rape: Sexual Abuse of Wives*. New York: Holt, Rinehart & Winston, forthcoming.

Finkelhor, D., and K. Yllö. "Rape in Marriage: A Sociological View." In *The Dark Side of Families: Current Family Violence Research*, edited by D. Finkelhor, R. Gelles, G. Hotaling, and M. Straus. Beverly Hills, California: Sage Publications, 1983.

Frieze, I. "Investigating the Causes and Consequences of Marital Rape." *Signs* 8 (1983): 532-553.

Geis, G. "Rape-in-Marriage: Law and Law Reform in England, the U.S. and Sweden." *Adelaide Law Review* 6 (1978): 284-347.

Gelles, R. "Power, Sex and Violence: The Case of Marital Rape." *The Family Coordinator* 26 (1977): 339-347.

Giles-Sims, J. *Wife-Battering: A Systems Theory Approach*. New York: Guilford Publishers, 1982.

Groth, N. *Men Who Rape: The Psychology of the Offender.* New York: Plenum Press, 1979.

New York University Law Review. "Marital Rape Exemption." Volume 52 (1977): 306-323.

Pagelow, M. *Woman-Battering: Victims and Their Experiences.* Beverly Hills, California: Sage Publications, 1981.

Russell, D. *Rape in Marriage.* New York: Macmillan, 1982.

Schulman, J. "The Marital Rape Exemption." *National Center on Women and Family Law Newsletter* 1 (1980): 6-8.

Shields, N., and C. Hanneke. "Battered Wives' Reaction to Marital Rape." In *The Dark Side of Families: Current Family Violence Research*, edited by D. Finkelhor, R. Gelles, G. Hotaling and M. Straus. Beverly Hills, California: Sage Publications, 1983.

Spektor, P. Testimony delivered to the Law Enforcement Subcommittee of the Minnesota House of Representatives, February 29, 1980.

PART THREE

FAMILY AND LEGAL RESPONSE TO THE VICTIM

The increased attention and awareness of rape as a traumatic
event has surfaced the impact that rape and sexual assault has on
the family and community. This section reviews the family response
to a victimized family member and the manner in which the legal
system--criminal justice and civil--has responded over the decade.

CHAPTER 13

FAMILY RESPONSE TO RAPE AND SEXUAL ASSAULT

Theresa S. Foley

A perspective on the current research in family response to rape
and sexual assault is essential for readers new to this area of inquiry. Family response to sexual assault is a fairly new field of
investigation beset with many limitations that accompany early exploration about the nature of the problem and treatment interventions.
The following chapter examines the following areas: (1) background
and research on the problem of sexual assault; (2) partner response;
(3) family response; and (4) counseling families of sexual assault
victims.

BACKGROUND

During the 1960s, the feminist movement became actively involved
with difficulties faced by sexual assault victims within treatment
settings and with the roots of the crime. As awareness expanded a-
bout the problems victims encounter, research and services emerged
which focused on victims' responses and ways of meeting their needs.
This initial step largely ignored the crisis and adaptation of the
family to the stress of a sexual assault. In the last two decades,
the majority of literature and research has focused on the psychology
of the offender; on sociological variables that substantiated claims

Sections of this chapter are modified and reprinted with the
courtesy of P. McCullogh, ed. *Proceedings of the 5th Pittsburgh
Family Systems Symposium*. The University of Pittsburgh: Western
Psychiatric Clinic, June 1982.

made by the feminists about the crime, its roots, and perpetuation
within western society; and on descriptive studies specifying victim
response patterns to the assault. While such inquiry has been a necessary starting point, there remains, by comparison, a substantial
gap in knowledge about the impact of sexual assault on family interaction patterns, on specific needs of these families, and on effective interventions. This gap in knowledge is a serious problem in
that the victim usually turns to those emotionally close to her or
him* for support and, from what is known, the response of family members are often more harmful than helpful (Foley 1982; Foley and Davies
1983; Frank 1979b; Silverman 1978).
        Current literature (Etherington 1979; Schmidt 1981) speculates
that up to 3 to 4 family members may seek services for every victim
receiving crisis counseling within community or institutional settings.
Thus, supportive help from crisis counselors and/or therapists is indicated.
        As a traumatic event, sexual assault not only precipitates a
crisis for the victim, but it also assaults the psychological equilibrium of the family. The assault stresses vulnerable areas in any relationship (Silverman and McCombie 1980). Even when chronic difficulties have not been present in a relationship prior to the assault,
the victim's family members may find it difficult to be empathetic
and supportive for a variety of reasons. The response of these persons to the assault and to the victim are influenced by multiple factors such as beliefs in rape myths which defame the victim's character
and hold her responsible for the assault; a criminal justice system
which deliberates the victim's innocence; and their own and others'
definition of what constitutes rape and who is to blame. These elements influence the victim and family members' decision to inform
others of the assault, report the crime, and/or seek treatment. Pivotal in restoring a family's equilibrium post-assault is the response
of significant others, both within and external to the family. However, the victim and family members are often in self-imposed isolation or feel shamed into silence (Metzger 1976; Foley 1982; Foley and
Davies 1983).
        Since there are relatively few studies which focus solely on
family response to sexual assault, it was necessary to conduct a
global search of the literature to locate articles which made *any*
references to families of sexual assault victims. Thus, facets which
related to family response were reviewed--such as the victim's social
adjustment within the extended family (Frank 1979b, 1981), factors
aiding or delaying victim recovery (Burgess 1979d) and counseling of
victims to facilitate their disclosure to or coping with family members (Davenport 1980; Etherington 1979; Schmidt 1981; Foley and Davies
1983). Hence, the discussion which follows must be read with caution,
since some of the results are drawn by inference. Further, many of
the sub-topics apply to more than one topic heading. For example,
while victims report trust disturbances and difficulties in sexual

---

*The author acknowledges that males are victims of sexual assault.
However, to facilitate writing style, hereafter victims are referred
to as women, and persons emotionally close to the victim (such as
boyfriends or partners, spouses, and family members) are referred to
as family.

adjustment post-assault with partners or husbands, concerns about sexual adjustment and trusting men also arise for families of adolescent victims.

PARTNER RESPONSE TO SEXUAL ASSAULT

The literature indicates that sexual assault sets in motion multiple factors which disrupt and have a long-term impact on the relationship of victims with their partners. Partner response is influenced by socialization within western society, a rape-prone society (Sanday 1982) where belief in rape myths and factors such as "appropriate" sex-role behaviors affect one's response to the assault. Dimensions of a relationship which may be disrupted by the sexual assault include trust disturbances, problems with communication and disclosure patterns, and sexual adjustment.

Male Response to Sexual Assault

The personal impact of sexual assault on a loved one can be seen in the emotional distress of men who report intense feelings of anger, frustration, and a desire for revenge or violent retribution (Foley and Davies 1983; Holmstrom and Burgess 1979; Mehren 1983; Rodkin et al. 1982; Rosenblatt 1983). Men express feelings such as wanting to "kill the bastard" to "surgically castrate the S.O.B.," or to "get the guy" by legal means. Holmstrom and Burgess (1979) report that the desire for revenge is not specific to whether the man held a traditional view of rape--i.e., as a sexually motivated act where the woman is diminished as a person due to the assault--or a more modern view of rape as a violent crime.

Jealousy and a sense of loss are also common responses in male partners (Foley and Davies 1983; Rodkin et al. 1982; Silverman 1978). These feelings are apparent when men say, "I'm afraid she liked it," reveal feeling cheated because "something has been taken away from me," or view the victim as "damaged goods and tainted property." Jealousy is often associated with views of the woman as the man's exclusive personal property and misperceptions of rape as a sexually motivated act (Foley and Davies 1983; Holmstrom and Burgess 1979; Silverman 1978). In such instances, the man may insist upon sexual relations with the victim on the day of the assault to explore how he feels about his own prowess or adequacy as a sexual partner, may avoid sexual relations with the victim, and/or may find her physically revolting or no longer arousing his interest.

A sense of guilt or self-blame for the assault is often associated with the man's view of the victim as his "property" and of the male role as protector of the woman's virginity and safety from harm (Foley and Davies 1983; Holmstrom and Burgess 1979; Rodkin 1982). These feelings are noted by statements such as, "If only I had not let her go down there or had gone with her," or "If only I had been home this could have been prevented."

It is not surprising that many men believe in rape myths and blame or deliberate the legitimacy of the woman's victimization. Krulewitz (1982) investigated the reactions of 107 males and 98 female undergraduates to different rape circumstances (i.e., home-blitz, outside-blitz, or acquaintance rape) in terms of the perceived effect of these variables on the victim's psychological recovery. The subjects were asked to evaluate the degree of a victim's emotional response to assault, according to the circumstances of the rape. Men

in the study more often judged the home-blitz and outside-blitz style
of assault as more upsetting than rape by an acquaintance in the victim's home, while the women perceived all the situations as very upsetting to the victim.   In fact, research reports on victims' response to sexual assault indicate that victims assaulted by acquaintances experience interpersonal difficulties and psychological problems of a longer duration and greater severity than those assaulted
by strangers, particularly in terms of severe trust disturbances with
men (Burgess and Holmstrom 1975; Brothers 1982; Mehren 1983).

Further, in the Krulewitz study, the men perceived the calm
emotional response of a victim as indicative of a future good sexual
adjustment.   This perception differs from that of Burgess and Holmstrom (1974) and others who note that the calm and emotionally controlled victim is just as likely, if not more at risk, to experience
protracted psychological distress and an unresolved sexual trauma
(Burgess et al. 1978; Holmstrom and Burgess 1978), whereas victims
who express guilt and self-blame may be more likely to recover quickly (Janoff-Bulman 1979).   Finally, consistent gender differences were
noted in that the men were less sympathetic and less willing to talk
with the victim than were the women.

Krulewitz's findings are supported by Ashton (1982) who investigated twenty-six college students' views of rape.   Ashton found that
males had a higher mean acceptance score on rape myths which positively correlated to dogmatism scores.   Dogmatism refers to an inability
to receive, evaluate, or act on relevant information on its own in-
trinsic merits (Rokeach 1960; Troldahl and Powell 1965).   Ashton's
and Krulewitz's research confirms previous gender differences in adherence to rape beliefs (Barnett and Feild 1977) as well as data from
other sources on attitudes of the general population and professionals
toward victims as being causally responsible for their victimization
(Feild 1978; Holmstrom and Burgess 1978; Krulewitz 1982; Krulewitz
and Nash 1979; Krulewitz and Payne 1978).

These studies and other literature reviewed indicate the need
for preventive education with males, particularly since victims of a
sexual assault often initially contact a friend or relative, and
young adult men are thus likely to come in early contact with a victim (Krulewitz 1982).   Further, the subjects in these studies were in
a young adult age group--the target population at high risk for a
sexual assault crisis--and, as boyfriends, friends or spouses, are
also likely to have to resolve the impact of the crime as a personal
event in their own lives.   Since the nature of support received from
friends and relatives facilitates or impedes the victim's recovery,
it is imperative that active efforts be made to inform more men about
the nature of rape and its impact on victims (Egidio 1981; Rodkin et
al. 1982).

Marital Adjustment

A number of researchers and clinicians report that sexual assault
places a great burden on the partner-victim relationship.   One of the
most damaging consequences is a disruption in the communication process, as noted by a frequent lack of accurate understanding of each
other's psychological state and response to the assault (Burgess and
Holmstrom 1979; Foley and Davies 1983; Frank 1979b; Miller 1979a,b;
Rodkin et al. 1982).   The intensity of the emotional distress evoked
by sexual assault often precludes the partners' ability to respond

empathetically to each other's feelings or even to talk about the assault and its impact on them. The victim's post-assault responses of physical symptoms, depression and apathy, worry and fears, and phobias are more problematic if the assault was two or more years past and are often associated with excessive dependency which, as a cumulative effect, places a high degree of stress on the relationship; the partner finds it difficult to cope with the victim's responses both initially and on a longer-term basis (Heil 1981; Holmstrom and Burgess 1979c; Miller et al. 1982). In addition, the partners are usually out of sequence in their emotional response to the assault. For example, while the victim's fear and anxiety continue the partner's anger and rage may emerge, and when the partner is ready to resume sexual relations the victim may not be ready to do so or responds with generalized fears to sexual behaviors (Feldman-Summers 1979; Miller et al.; Rodkin et al. 1982; Veronen and Kilpatrick 1980). In an effort to be supportive of the victim, the partner often tries not to burden her with his feelings. However, the lack of communication can result in mutual distrust, avoidance behaviors, and resentment. The net effect of the crisis is the development or perpetuation of a dysfunctional relationship that requires crisis intervention for many couples, long-term counseling for other couples, and, in some cases, separation or divorce.

The severity of the assault on the partner relationship is noted by Halpern (1978), who indicates that between 50 and 80 percent of women who are raped suffer the loss of their boyfriends or husbands as a result of the assault. Miller, Williams, and Bernstein (1982) note that psychiatrically impaired victims evidenced relationship difficulties of a comparable intensity to those experienced by nonpsychiatrically impaired victims, but after a longer period of time following the rape. This finding is consistent with other reports on the long-term impact of sexual assault on victims (Burgess and Holmstrom 1979).

A number of researchers indicate that the reactions of the "support" network may do more harm than good to facilitate the victim's recovery (Burgess and Holmstrom 1979c; Frank 1979b; Miller et al. 1982; Silverman 1978). Frank reports that the complex reactions of significant others interfered with their ability to be empathetic with the victim. These reactions included: (1) anger directed at the assailant or victim; (2) guilt over neglect in protecting the partner; (3) sexual overtones attributed to the rape which aroused feelings of insecurity in the partner about the victim's "real" feelings; (4) difficulty in understanding the victim's behavioral response to the rape; and (5) questions about the victim's compliance, all of which compounded the resolution process. Frank reports that a vicious negative interaction cycle was established when the victim counter-reacted to a lack of understanding from her immediate significant others. She psychologically distanced herself from others, concluding that persons once trusted did not meet her expectations. The consensual validation sought by the victim was further removed by her self-isolation and was often accompanied by elevated levels of fear, anxiety, and depression which created further problems in social adjustment at work or school. The victim's significant others compounded these difficulties by blaming her for the assault, being angry at her, and/or focusing on their own self-doubts and concerns. The end result was a series of increasingly negative interactions among individuals who were feeling hurt, angry, irritable, frightened, and rejected.

Miller, Williams, and Bernstein (1979a, b, 1982) investigated the long-term impact of rape on the victim, her male partner, and the marital relationship. Assessment measures included the clinicians' ratings and observations and the couple's self-report in a sample of eighteen couples seen in marital therapy and twenty-five couples interviewed in their homes. The victim's response pattern followed that generally reported in the literature, including generalized fears, a changed response to men, and obsessional reactions. The predominant male response was rage, typically directed toward the rapist. The couple's response to the rape included problems in understanding and commitment, communication disturbances, and sexual concerns and dysfunction.

Rodkin, Hunt, and Cowan (1982) report on clinical work with fifteen male significant others (husbands, boyfriends, and fathers) of rape victims in a support group. The clinicians noted that the men experienced three developmental phases in resolving the effect of the rape on their relationship with the victim. The initial phase was characterized by a search for quick-cure solutions and an externalized focus; the second phase by glossing over feelings through coping mechanisms such as denial, suppression, and rationalization. In the third phase, the men began to "own" their feelings and confront their own conflicts about the rape incident. The clinicians cited four major themes they believe reflect male stereotyped role prescription based on the socialization of men in western society: (1) guilt or self-blame; (2) desire for revenge and deep frustration; (3) jealousy, anger, and a sense of loss; and (4) the need to protect or confine the victim.

Sexual Adjustment

A review of current literature indicates clearly that sexual assault negatively affects the sexual relationship of a couple. This fact is not surprising in light of the preceding discussion about the impact of an assault on the couple's marital adjustment.

Feldman-Summers, Gordon, and Meagher (1979) studied quantitative assessment of changes in the sexual behavior of fifteen women who were sexually active prior to a rape experience and who remained with the same partner no less than two months following the assault. Time lapse since the sexual assault ranged from two months to seven years, with a median of twelve months. Included in the study was a comparison group of fifteen non-victimized women who were similar to the victimized sample on demographic variables. In evaluating the victim's pre- and post-rape sexual satisfaction, the researchers found that the assault significantly affected the victim's retrospective recollection of satisfaction with most sexual behaviors at one week and two months post-assault as compared to pre-assault satisfaction. While victims reported increased satisfaction at two months post-assault, the satisfaction level did not reach the same point as pre-assault level. Sexual behaviors that were *not* affected as a function of time from the assault were behaviors rarely forced on victims. These included autoerotic behaviors (e.g., orgasms with clitoral manipulation by oneself), and primary affectional behaviors (e.g., holding hands), and the absolute frequency of other sexual behaviors. In contrast, sexual behaviors that were most affected were directly linked to behaviors usually forced on victims during a sexual assault.

These behaviors included sexual intercourse, touching of genitals, and visual exposure to male genitals. The researchers indicate that these sexual behaviors could be expected to acquire fear and pain-related associations and thus affect decreased satisfaction levels post-rape. This finding is consistent with Veronen and Kilpatrick (1980), who note that the fears of rape victims generalize in accord with classical conditioning theories.

In evaluating the victim's satisfaction with current sexual behaviors, Feldman-Summers and colleagues found no statistical difference between the victim and non-victim group in the reported frequency of oral sex, sexual intercourse, anal intercourse, masturbation, or orgasm. However, the victimized group reported significantly less satisfaction with current sexual relations. The researchers conclude that treatment of rape victims should include sexual counseling designed to ameliorate these impacts.

Veronen and Kilpatrick (1980) conducted a study with twenty rape victims and twelve non-victims to test the hypothesis that rape victims' fears are classically conditioned (i.e., that fears present during the assault will also arise subsequent to it). The researchers conclude that items and situations rated as most disturbing for rape victims support the hypothesis that victims are significantly disturbed by rape-related situation variables and associations, that these have a propensity to generalize post-rape, and that the violent rather than the sexual aspects of the assaults are fear-provoking. Further, they conclude that the stimuli and situations which elicit fear responses in victims, as well as the time of onset of these responses, support classical conditioning as an explanatory theory for the acquisition of such responses.

Burgess and Holmstrom (1979c) interviewed eighty-one adult female rape victims four to six years after the rape on subsequent sexual functioning. Four dependent variables included: (1) sex life prior to rape; (2) changes in frequency of sexual relations; (3) symptoms; and (4) partner's reaction. Most victims who were sexually active reported changes in frequency of sexual activity and in sexual responses. The researchers' data indicated that prior level of sexual activity did not affect the length of the victim's recovery from an assault, and that virgins or sexually inexperienced victims did not experience a protracted recovery period. In resuming sexual relations with their partners, the most common pattern was abstinence of sexual activity (38 percent, 24/63), followed by a decrease in the frequency of sexual activity or a delay in resuming sexual relations (33 percent, 21/63), followed by no change in the frequency of sexual relations (92 percent, 11/12), followed by increased frequency in sexual relations (.1 percent, 6/63) which victims sometimes reported as a means of countering the negative experience of the assault.

Sexual responsiveness with partners was affected by the victim's subjective reactions, physiological response, and the partner's reaction. Subjective reactions included reports of sexual activity as physically and mentally aversive; enjoying sexual relations as an "exception rather than the rule"; global aversion to all sex as unpleasant; and affectively as "boring." Victim responsiveness was affected by the psychosocial climate in which sexual relations transpired and by flashbacks to the sexual assault in which the present partner was felt by the victim to be the rapist. The researchers did not report the frequency of these latter subjective response

patterns. Physiological responses which precluded enjoying the
sexual relationship included experiencing pain and discomfort, difficulty with orgasm, arousal dysfunction, vaginismus, and difficulty
experiencing any sexual feelings (41 percent, n=26).

Satisfaction with sexual relations was also affected by the victim's worries and concerns about her partner's reactions, and the
helpful behaviors of partners which facilitated the victim's recovery.
Worries and concerns about the partner's reaction included being
blamed for the assault, not being believed, being accused of enjoying
the assault (sex), having had "sex" with another man, being accused
of having wanted it, being made to feel degraded and soiled, and
being undesirable. Victims were equally divided on the frequency of
worries and concerns about the partners' reactions post-assault. It
is noteworthy that, while some victims reported no worries about
partners' reactions, they did report informing subsequent sexual
partners of the rape to see if the partner had an aversion, was liberal, or was prejudiced. Helpful partner reactions were reported by
over half of the victims, but in twelve of the sixty-three subjects
it was with a new partner. The victims were divided on the strategy
of talking about the rape with their partners as a measure which
would aid recovery (twenty-one said yes, eleven no). The most helpful partner style victims described as non-pressuring, a gentle approach, and putting the victim in control of the couple's sex life.

In investigating the responses of ten out of sixteen couples,
Holmstrom and Burgess (1979c) found that all couples reported some
problems in resuming sexual relations. None of the subjects were
able to continue having sex as if nothing had happened. The common
pattern was to wait several days to several weeks post-assault before resuming sexual relations. The main concerns for the woman included temporary aversion to physical contact, experience of flashbacks of the rape, physical discomfort during sex, changes in the
physical response to sexual stimulation, worry over her partner's
reaction, and concerns over whose child it would be in event of
pregnancy, if sexual relations were resumed prior to the woman's
menstrual period. The male partner's typical response was to want
to have sex with the victim quite soon after the rape. In some cases
the man focused exclusively on his own sexual needs and wanted sexual
relations quickly post-assault to "either (a) test himself to see if
he would be able to do it, or (b) to prove to himself that things
would remain as they had always been, that the rape would not interfere." In other cases, the man attempted to balance his own sexual
needs with his partner's need for time to recover from the assault.
These men reported being afraid of touching the victim for fear of
upsetting her and waited several weeks before resuming sexual relations. These results are consistent with the findings of other researchers (Miller, Williams and Bernstein, 1979a,b; 1982; Rodkin et
al. 1982).

Becker, Skinner, Abel, and Treacy (1982) investigated the impact
of sexual assault on the sexual lives of eighty-three nonpsychotic
victims of rape and incest. The sample ranged in age from 18 to 60
with a mean of 29.5 years. Of this sample, twenty-two subjects were
victims of rape and twelve were victims of incest. Despite the fact
that the majority of the victims (85 percent) were seen at least one
year post-rape, significant chronic sexual dysfunctions persisted for
years, a finding consistent with the results of Veronen and Kilpatrick

(1980), and other researchers as noted previously. The authors emphasized that the subjects' sexual functioning was disrupted as a result of their tendency to perceive sexual stimuli as anxiety-provoking or to negatively re-label sexual feelings. Victims who did *not* report sexual dysfunctions were subjected to assaults characterized by minimal verbal coercion and more or excessive physical coercion by the assailant. The authors suggest that the absence of sexual dysfunction in these cases is related to their tendency to label the sexual assault as clearly an offender-initiated attack in which there is less opportunity to feel guilt and, according to Frank (1979b), more support from their social network due to the brutality of the assault and views by persons in the victim's network as less culpable for the incident. The researchers emphasized the importance of counselors recognizing the chronicity of sexual dysfunctions following sexual assaults and of providing service to ameliorate these effects.

In a follow-up study of forty-one victims without a history of mental or emotional disturbance one to two and a half years post-rape, Nadelson, Notman, and Zackman (1982) found the subjects experiencing post-rape sexual difficulties in their partner relationships. Over one third of the subjects reported changes in sexual attitudes and/or relationships including new suspiciousness of men. Husbands and boyfriends were described by the victims as evidencing changed behavior including rape-related separations.

The researchers note that their findings are consistent with McCahill and associates (1979), who followed 213 rape victims for one year and found that at least one third of the sample reported worsened sexual relations with their partners. Nadelson and associates found that many of the subjects in their sample did not spontaneously volunteer information about their sexual difficulties; however, the information was easily elicited by direct questioning, a finding which speaks to the importance of professionals and other crisis counselors asking victims about the sexual relationship difficulties they experience post-assault.

In summary, sexual assault clearly precipitates a crisis and long-term disruption in the partner-victim relationship. Problematic areas which partners are forced to cope with include (1) the male response to rape as a socially conditioned phenomenon; (2) disruption in the relationship of partners due to the mutual interaction of intense psychologic distress and communications problems; and (3) sexual dysfunctions in the relationship by one or both partners. The importance of providing counseling to rape victims and their partners was stressed throughout the literature reviewed. Table 1 summarizes the long-term impact of a sexual assault on the victim-partner relationship.

FAMILY RESPONSE TO SEXUAL ASSAULT

The following section addresses literature specific to the response of parents and significant others of sexual assault victims, hereafter referred to as family members. Persons in this category are coping with the sexual assault of (a) an adolescent, (b) a family member that is living with parents, who may or may not be emotionally and/or economically dependent on them regardless of age, (c) the nuclear and extended family of victims, or (d) persons emotionally close to the victim who are affected by the incident. The literature in this field is far more limited than that previously

Table 1 Impact of Sexual Assault on the
Partner-Victim Relationship System*+

Phase of Response to Rape	Victim Response	Partner Response to Victim	Relationship Dimensions
Acute Response	Guilt (for failure to prevent assault=socially conditioned response to rape)	Guilt (for not having been protective enough)	Mutual Complementarity
	Anxiety & Shock	Anxiety & Shock	
	Fear (longer duration than partner due to "near-death" trauma)	Fear (shorter duration than victim; subsides with victim's physical well being assured).	
	Dependency on partner	Need to protect partner: *knows her pain *believes he should not burden her with his feelings Anger and rage emerge --desire for revenge	
	Trust disrupted	Trust disrupted	
	Avoids discussing the rape: clearly signals does not want to talk or think about the rape; worries over partner reaction	Avoids discussing the rape: tries to guess what partner is feeling & needs.	
	Rape trauma syndrome	Sleeping/eating disturbances	
Longer-term response	Fear & Anxiety continue at high levels *partner's rage her anxiety state *reminds her of violence of the rape *fears partner will get into trouble	Anger & Rage continue *less able to meet partner's dependency needs *sense of threat & loss	Emotional Distance
	Dependency on partner related to: *High levels of anxiety & fear *Depression	Attempts to provide desired support but is undermined by:	

*Phobic anxiety & behaviors *Somatization *Obsessive-compulsive symptoms *Impaired social adjustment	*own emotional trauma *pressure of external commitments *duration & intensity of victim's response to rape Resents victim's dependency Aggression sublimated (e.g. workaholic)	
Perceives partner behavior and feels partner: *unresponsive to her needs *not understanding or supportive	Appears understanding & supportive to partner	
Mutual Poor Communication *Feelings not communicated *Fail to perceive or understand partner's changing needs *Protects partner from her intense feelings	Mutual Poor Communication & Lack of Empathy: *Feelings not communicated *Fail to perceive or understand partner's changing needs & desires	
Mutual Resentment due to: *unmet dependency needs *lack of open communication	Mutual Resentment due to: *partner's dependency needs *lack of open communication	Mutual Avoidance and/or Conflict
Sexual relationship disrupted/dysfunctional by 1 or more of the following: *fears rejection *feels undesirable or unwanted *abstains, avoids, or is hesitant to initiate sexual relations *flashbacks *feels used, rape repeated & autonomy lost	Sexual relationship disrupted/dysfunctional: *fears rejection *abstains, avoids or is hesitant to initiate sexual relations *forces sexual relations	

*anorgasmic &/or vaginismus
*1 or both partners unresponsive
*sex devoid of tenderness & affection
 	
Net Effect--
Family/marital system:
  *in crisis/con-flict
  *separation
  *divorce
	*premature ejaculation
	*1 or both partners unresponsive
	*sex devoid of tenderness & affection
	
	Net Effect--
	Family/marital system:
	  *in crisis/con-flict
	  *separation
	  *divorce	

Counseling--Work through the experi-ence to:
1)Resolve the rape
 	
2)Maintain or re-establish func-tional relation-ship with partner
3)Grief resolution
	Counseling--Work through the experi-ence to:
	1)confront & resolve own conflict about the rape including feelings of:
	  *guilt or self-blame
	  *revenge/frustra-tion
	  *jealousy/anger/ sense of loss
	  *the need to pro-tect or confine
	
	2)tolerance for others' values and behaviors
	
	3)learn how to be supportive and confirming to the victim
	
	4)Maintain or re-establish func-tional relation-ship with partner
	5)Grief resolution
		Equilibrium Re-estab-lished
		
		or
		
		Relationship Dissolved

+ Key: = conflict   = increased

                = interaction   = decreased
                leads to

---

* Based on: Becker, J.V., et al. "Incidence and types of sexual
    dysfunctions in rape and incest victims," *J. of Sex and Marital
    Therapy*, 8(1): 65-74, 1982; Brothers, D., et al. "Trust dis-

turbances among victims of rape and incest," *J. of Adolescent and Health Care*, 3(2): 150, 1982; Burgess, A.W. and Holmstrom, L.L. "Adaptive strategies and recovery from rape," *Amer. J. of Psych.*, 136 (1979): 1278-1282; Burgess, A.W. and Holmstrom, L.L. "Sexual disruption and recovery," *Amer. J. of Orthopsych.*, 49 (1979): 648-657; Feldman-Summers, S., et al. "The impact of rape on sexual satisfaction," *J. of Abnormal Psychol.*, 88 (1): 101-05, 1979; Frank, E. "Psychologic response to rape: An analysis of response patterns," The University of Pittsburgh, Ph.D. Dissertation, 1979; Frank, E., et al. "Depressive symptoms in rape victims," *J. of Affective Disorders*, 1 (4): 269-77, 1979; Heil, D.A. "Victims of sexual aggression: Longterm aftereffects," *Dissertation Abstracts International*, 42 (4): 1607, 1981; Holmstrom, L.L., et al. "Rape: The husband's and boyfriend's initial reactions," *Family Coordinator*, 28 (3): 321-30, 1979; Miller, W.R., et al. "The effects of rape on marital and sexual adjustment," *Amer. J. of Family Therapy*, 10 (1): 51-58, 1982; Rodkin, L.I., et al. "A men's support group for significant others of rape victims," *J. of Marital and Family Therapy*, 8 (1): 91-97, 1982; Silverman, D. "Sharing the crisis of rape: Counseling the mates and families of victims," *Amer. J. of Orthopsych.*, 48 (1): 166-173, 1978.

---

discussed, partially due to the difficulty of conducting well-designed family systems research. The following discussion addresses: (1) disclosure patterns about the rape; (2) adolescent concerns in the nuclear family and peer relationship system in response to the assault; (3) parental response to the rape; and (4) prior and/or current responses to stressful life events including prior psychiatric history.

Disclosure Patterns About Rape

Shore (1979), in a retrospective exploratory study of 127 victims, reported that in the immediate aftermath of the assault the victim initially contacted family or friends, usually a female, and the disclosure decision was based on the degree of emotional closeness or physical proximity to that person. Most subjects described close-knit families, particularly closeness with their mother and informing her of the rape. The father was not informed of the rape by most victims in the immediate post-rape period but was usually informed by another sibling or relative; he was often more supportive than the mother when he found out. Generally, the initial conflictual relationships with mothers were resolved; the least supportive and most conflictual relationships over time occurred with husbands and boyfriends. In the post-rape period, subjects reported the social network to diminish and be less supportive with a notable degree of marital and family conflict.

Burgess and Holmstrom (1979b), in a follow-up study of eighty-one rape victims, analyzed the decisions of sixty-two available subjects to tell or not tell parental family members of the rape and subsequent satisfaction with their initial decision. Four major issues in the disclosure process were reported: (1) making the decision of whether the victim could tell the news of the rape; (2)

trying to find the right words or language to inform others of the rape; (3) the timing of disclosing the rape to parents; and (4) having to cope with the initial response of the person told.

Foley (1982) found that, in terms of the content level of disclosure, the three families interviewed had a high degree of shared information that agreed with the victim's account of the rape. Families accurately reported their daughters as being victims of completed forcible rapes through a "confidence" style of attack. The families were aware of their daughters having been raped by a casual acquaintance or stranger; the number of assailants involved; the degree of threat used; and the perceived safety of the assault location.

In Foley's study, families were asked about their decision to disclose or keep the rape and details about the rape a secret, and who in the family stipulated such a position. The parents did not widely or openly discuss the rape within the nuclear or extended family, or with others in the community. Concerns regarding not informing others about the rape included not upsetting the family, protecting elderly family members from the traumatic event, protecting the victim and family from stigma due to anticipated negative responses of neighbors or peers of the victim, emotional instability of nuclear and extended family members, and fear of over-reaction by family members. When asked what concerns the victim had regarding others being informed about the rape, all of the families reported the victim as expressing concerns about fear over being blamed for the rape or not being believed, anger and rejection from others, shame and stigma, fear of peers talking at school or work, fear of boyfriends or men, and a desire for privacy. This finding is consistent with research results in the literature as discussed previously. The results of disclosure data in this study suggest that Gilbert's (1976) curvilinear principle applies with respect to patterns of family functioning, and that high levels of disclosure about the details of a rape to family members may be indicative of more dysfunctional family systems, particularly where the victim is working through separation-individuation issues (as was the case for the victims in this study).

In summary, the issue of disclosure about the rape is a problematic area for both the family and the victim. Disclosure is also a concern for adolescents within nuclear and extended families, and in coping with the reactions of their peers, as discussed below.

Adolescents: Special Consideration

In a report of clinical work with 468 adolescent rape victims over the course of three years, Schmidt (1981) reports that the victim's main concern is the family's perception of the event and whether she will be believed. The victim's anticipated lack of credibility was often associated with acting-out and regressive coping styles, psychologic defenses already within the adolescent's approach to resolving tasks of this developmental life-cycle. Such behaviors, however, tended to reinforce others' notions of the victim's lack of credibility. Belligerence, defensiveness, and/or aloofness was particularly noted when the victim was questioned as to aspects of the assault. False assumptions tend to be prevalent and particularly problematic for adolescent victims of a date or acquaintance rape. Concerns reported by the family included: (1) confronting the fact that their child is a sexual person; (2) whether to encourage her to talk about the assault; (3) whether to encourage her to return to work or school; and (4) whether to treat the victim differently.

In a clinical report of follow-up counseling of adolescent rape victims, Felice (1980) indicated the importance of offering support to these victims in working with the family and larger community. The author notes that adolescents are often made to feel guilty about the rape, particularly if they are attractive. Blaming the victim was noted as more of a problem if the assailant was a family friend, neighbor, or acquaintance. In these cases, the family sometimes attempts to protect the assailant rather than the victim. Additional problems are faced by the adolescent in coping with the reactions of others when news of the rape is spread throughout the neighborhood. Wide disclosure about the rape can result in changed response to her by boys and men including leers, lewd jokes, other comments and, in this writer's clinical work, ostracism from the peer group.

Mann (1981), investigating the self-reported stresses of 122 adolescent rape victims over an eighteen month period, reported a consistent difference in the concerns of victims which were *not* shared with the same frequency by their parents. While victims primarily feared for their life or bodily harm (e.g., irrational fears such as undetected internal injuries or slowly rotting organs, abnormal genital appearance, inability to have children), these concerns were shared by only 50 percent of the parents—almost exclusively (90 percent) by parents whose children were physically injured. Anger was expressed more commonly by the parents (69 percent) than by the adolescents (45 percent). In cases where the adolescent disagreed with the parents' demand for retaliative action or immediate prosecution, the parental anger was directed against the victim for not listening to or for disregarding the parental distress over the rape. Blaming the victim for the rape was a frequent response.

A discrepancy between the concerns of adolescent victims and their parents is consistently reported in this study as well as by other researchers. In the Mann (1981) study, parents were concerned about the victim's emotional well-being and future sexual disturbances and venereal disease. The victims were most concerned about peer reactions and communication difficulties with their parents. While families in this study reported concerns both similar to and different from problems confronted by victims and families not in this age range, Mann notes that unresolved discrepancies may delay the victim's recovery from the assault.

Parental Response to Rape

A review of the literature in the area of parental response to sexual assault reveals two relevant studies, Foley (1982) and Frank (1979b). In a pilot study of three families of rape victims, including three mothers and one father, Foley investigated the patterns of family functioning following sexual assault and whether different victim patterns of disclosure were associated with the patterns of family functioning.

The families interviewed by Foley tended to be restructive in their support network both within nuclear and extended families as well as within the larger community. In adapting to past stressful life events, the mothers more actively reached out to others and continued to do so in response to the rape. The support people for mo-

thers were crisis counselors rather than nuclear or extended family.
The pattern of the fathers was observed to be one of withdrawal and
emotional distance from the family, a pattern previously used and
exacerbated in response to the rape. Emotional cut-offs in nuclear
and extended families was the most prevalent pattern of functioning
in these families both pre- and post-assault. The intensity of emotional distance varied with the degree of anxiety about the rape, but
even during relatively calm periods, relationships were not open to
communication. Other patterns of family functioning which evidenced
a frequency included marital conflict, projection processes, multigenerational transmission of family issues, and a low level of differentiation.

        Frank found that victims reported family members to evidence
greater empathy and less blaming behavior if the victims were more
brutalized physically during the assault and if a weapon was used.
The stronger support by family members appeared related to their
ability to view the victim as not culpable for the assault. This
finding was substantiated by low scores on the "threat index" which
were associated with a disruption in immediate family relationships.
Frank suggests this result indicates that family members respond to
the stereotypic myth that a "legitimate" victim endures high levels
of suffering.

        The importance of pre-rape patterns of family functioning and
support of the social network to the victim post-rape adjustment is
clear from these two studies. Another facet affecting the adaptation
of families to a sexual assault is their history of prior and/or continuing stressful life events and psychiatric intervention.

Stressful Life Events and Psychiatric History
        In an attempt to clarify variables beyond the rape that affected
adaptation of families to a sexual assault, a history of prior stressful events was examined. Foley (1982) found that two of three families completing a stressful life event scale (Holmes and Rahe 1967)
experienced a high degree of stress with scores over 340. When asked
to indicate the severity of these events in their lives on a 4 point
scale (4=severest, 1-minimal), two of the three families reported
total scores over 6350 (event x degree of impact). Completing an
assessment of prior stressful life events put the families' current
stress response to the rape in a perspective distinct from pre-existing
stressful life events. Research has shown that persons experiencing
high levels of prior stressful life events within a two-year period
have more difficulty in adaptation and are more prone to physical and/
or emotional difficulties, as was the case for families in this
study (Williams and Holmes 1978; Selye 1976; Norbeck 1982b). The
findings of this study are thus consistent with the research literature on stress and adaptation. Some researchers indicate that negative stressful life events are more significant in affecting adaptation and have thus modified earlier scales to take this fact into
account (Saranson et al. 1978), as well as a history of events important in victimology research such as history of abuse (Norbeck 1982b),
stressful life events specific to younger rape victims and their
families, and post-rape factors such as prosecution of or continued
harassment by an assailant (Hughes and Frank 1982). It is important
in future research on families resolving a sexual assault to utilize
instruments that take these factors into account.

Finally, literature was reviewed to examine the adaptation of families to a sexual assault in terms of the history of psychiatric difficulties reported by families and a history of such events as reported by victims. In cases where victims reported prior and/or current psychiatric difficulties, dysfunction was found in their social adjustment with extended family members, impaired functioning in work or school, and high levels of psychologic distress. The victim's psychologic distress has been noted in this chapter as a concern stressing both the partner-victim relationship and the families of victims.

Frank (1979b, 1980) found rape victims (n=50) to be functioning less well than non-victims in all areas of social adjustment, including their relationships with immediate and external family members, personal social relationships, work and school functioning, use of leisure time, and global functioning. Women who reported prior rape assaults, incest, or child molesting evidenced more disruption in their immediate household and poorer global adjustment socially. Prior psychiatric history, suicide ideation, and alcohol abuse were also related to poorer social adjustment, and 31 percent of the victims reported first and second degree relatives to have experienced a clear-cut history of psychiatric problems. Victims who had received psychiatric intervention in the past (37 percent of the sample) evidenced poor adjustment in relations with extended families postrape. Similarly, Katz and Mazur (1979) found the incidence of *reported* rape among psychiatrically ill women to be notably higher than among "normal" women, and that these women had more difficulty resolving the rape experience.

Foley (1982) found a similar pattern of prior multigenerational and/or continuing psychiatric history among three families of sexual assault victims. These difficulties included a history of domestic violence and child physical abuse in one mother's extended family, psychiatric or emotional illness among siblings in the extended family, and past or current use of prescribed psychotropic medications. Further, one of the victims in this study was currently in private therapy, and one family had previously obtained individual counseling for the victim due to their concerns over her "deviant" behavior as well as marital therapy and family therapy to cope with the problematic behavior. In addition, varying degrees of marital conflict were reported by all parents or spouses. Thus, the history of prior and current emotional and/or psychiatric difficulties was associated with the impaired effectiveness and functioning of these families in adapting to the crisis precipitated by the rape. The studies of Frank (1979b, 1980, 1981) and Foley (1982) indicate the importance of further research with respect to family generational patterns that explore a relationship between a history of psychiatric illnesses in a family and the incidence of sexual assault in such families, difficulty in resolving sexual assault, the need for prevention programs, and subsequent strategic interventions with vulnerable populations.

Similar results regarding maladaptiveness in the social network post-assault can be cautiously drawn by inference from a number of studies. Burgess and Holmstrom (1979a, 1978) found that a report by victims (n=18) of a sense of not being recovered from the rape four to six years post-rape was positively associated with an absence of strong social network ties, with social drifting, with conditions other than the rape (e.g., auditory hallucinations) as particularly

problematic; and with distress over a life-style in which they had
not been successful in gaining any personal achievements. In another
study, Ellis, Atkeson, and Calhoun (1982) found multiple-incident or
repeat rape victims to be less well adjusted in their functioning
prior to the current rape in a number of areas. Included in the reported difficulties were problems with social and sexual relationships, more suspiciousness of others with a frequent preference to
keep to themselves, and more problems with depression and a history
of suicide attempts as compared to single-incident rape victims.
The only report in which this writer found an absence of overt mental
illness or even mental health contacts was the study conducted on a
sample of forty-one rape victims one to two and a half years post-
assault by Nadelson, Notman, and Zackman (1982). In this study, victims were excluded if a history of psychiatric or emotional difficulties were present. Overall, the majority of researchers reviewed
were in agreement that the rape had a negative impact on the adjustment of persons in the victims's social network, as well as on the
victim herself. These findings are summarized in Table 2.

In conclusion, sexual assault results in a high degree of stress
in families of these victims which persists over a long period and,
in some cases, for years. The literature notes that most of the
families experience a history of pre-assault psychiatric or emotional
difficulties and a high level of prior stressful life events. These
variables affect the severity of the impact of the assault on the
families of victims in terms of the suffering experienced by them,
and negatively affects their effectiveness in coping with the incident and the victim's response to the assault. While rape situation
variables have not been associated with the victim's response to the
assault (Frank 1980), the literature reviewed here indicates that
the families of the victims are negatively affected by these variables in their response to and supportiveness of the victim. Finally,
it must be said that the mere fact these families sought crisis intervention is in itself a healthy, adaptive behavior. One could speculate that there are also many families of sexual assault victims in
the general population who are dysfunctional pre- and post-rape, and
who do not seek crisis intervention or treatment, and that these
families are more dysfunctional when compared to the families who
sought help and/or participated in research studies. The response of
families to sexual assault clearly needs further well-designed research investigation.

Table 2

Key: * = Not statistically significant
      ** = Objective measures not used, based on clinical reports
       x = Statistically significant higher levels of social adjust-
           ment dysfunction and psychological distress as compared to
           non-victims on objective measures (See Frank et al. 1981).
       V = Victim
       F = Family
+ Based on Burgess and Holmstrom 1979; Burgess et al. 1979b, 1979c,
Ellis et al. 1982; Feldman-Summers et al. 1979; Foley 1982; Foley and
Davies 1983; Frank et al. 1981; Holmstrom et al. 1979; Kilpatrick 1979;
Miller 1982; Nadelson et al. 1982; Resick et al. 1981; Rodkin et al.
1982; Ruch et al. 1980.

Table 2 Post-Rape Social Adjustment as Related to Selected Psychiatric History Characteristics +

| Variable | Social Adjustment Dysfunction | | | | | | | | | | Psychological Distress | | | | | | | |
| | Immediate Family Relations | | Extended Family Relations | | Work or School Setting | | Social Relations & Use of Leisure Time | | Global Functioning | | Depression | | Fear | | Anxiety State | | Anxiety Trait | |
	V	F	V	F	V	F	V	F	V	F	V	F	V	F	V	F	V	F
Some form of prior or current psychiatric treatment			X	**	X	**						**		**		**		
Having been in or currently receiving psychotherapy			X	**	X	**	X	**				**		**		**		
Having been given or currently receiving psychotropic medication			X	**	X	**			X		X		X		X			
Alcohol abuse				**	X	**					**		X					
Stimulant abuse			X		X													
Marijuana abuse*							X											
Suicidal ideation			X	**	X	**	X	**	X		X	**		**	X	**	X	
Prior suicide attempts	**		X	**			X	**			X				X		X	
Prior victimization	X			**							**	**	**	**		**		

COUNSELING FAMILIES OF SEXUAL ASSAULT VICTIMS

All of the reports reviewed address the importance of providing counseling services to families of sexual assault victims, and many offered intervention approaches for specific problematic response patterns. For example, counselors were advised to encourage these families to express their sense of hurt, loss, and rage in individual and/or conjoint sessions with the counselor, facilitating families to view the rape as a shared life crisis (Foley and Davies 1983; Silverman 1978; Silverman and McCombie 1980). While counseling sexual assault families is clearly a critical intervention which affects both the family and the victim's resolution of the rape, this writer found no reports of *research* on the effectiveness of varying treatment interventions with this population. This fact is not entirely surprising in view of two points which need to be taken into consideration. First, research on the healthy functioning of families is at this time only in its infancy, while reports on dysfunctional families are numerous. Thus, there are a limited number of research reports on "healthy" families from which researchers could make comparisons or use as control groups. Second, it would be premature to begin investigating the effectiveness of varying treatment interventions without sound descriptive data on the functioning of families of sexual assault victims, including the comparison of results with treatment decliners and families that do not seek or feel the need of crisis and counseling services. With this perspective on the problems of conducting research on the counseling of families of sexual assault victims, what can be reported at this time are suggestions offered by researchers and clinicians for counseling these persons.

Assessment and Crisis Intervention

Foley and Davies (1983) compiled a list of adaptive and maladaptive responses of families to a sexual assault based on clinical reports and research in the field (see Table 3). The authors suggest that this list can be used as a tool to assess the family's response to an assault by identifying problematic areas in need of intervention. In addition, the authors report characteristics of optimal healthy family functioning which serve as an additional guideline in identifying dysfunctional families. According to the literature reviewed here, families at high risk for difficulties in resolving a sexual assault/rape include those with: (1) a high number of early pre-assault traumatic life events, and poor early relationships (Brothers, Hilton, and Kunker 1982); (2) a history of emotional and psychiatric difficulties; (3) low levels of functioning in the nuclear and extended family; (4) a history of early sexual trauma (Burgess and Holmstrom 1975; Nadelson et al. 1982); (5) expressed beliefs in rape myths; (6) a pre-assault history of chronic relationship difficulties including disturbed communication patterns, a lack of empathy for and understanding of family members' needs and concerns; (7) social and sexual adjustment dysfunctions both pre- and post-assault; and (8) discrepancies in concerns between victims and family members or parents post-assault.

Foley and Davies (1983) discuss specific nursing interventions in counseling families during an acute reaction period in relation to psychologic distress, problematic areas of response to the assault, and suggested interventions to help families cope with these. In

Table 3 Adaptive and maladaptive family stress reactions to rape *

Adaptive stress reactions	Maladaptive stress reactions
Care and concern for the victim	Concern primarily about how others will think of the family
Support of the victim	Contested feelings over who was raped, hurt most, or victimized
Feelings of shock, disbelief, dismay	Minimizing the victim's feelings or response
Feelings of helplessness and disequilibrium	Feeling guilty or responsible for not having protected the victim
Physical revulsion which may parallel the victim's affective responses	Rape trauma syndrome
Distraction tactics to keep the victim and themselves occupied	Patronizing or overprotecting the victim
Reacting to rape as a violent act	Viewing rape as a sexually motivated acts and the victim as "damaged goods"
Anger and rage directed at the rapist or society	Direct or indirect anger and resentment as seen in communication difficulties
Blame directed at the rapist	Blame directed at the victim or family members
Thoughts about violent retribution or active retaliation	Act out violent retribution toward assailant or victim
Reaching out to extended family/ significant others for support	Emotional cut-offs with extended family/significant others
Empathic with each other	Absence of empathic responses with each other; emotional isolation or withdrawal
Use of crisis counseling as needed	Failure to seek professional counseling when needed
Supportive of victim's medical or gynecological care needs and follow-up care	Failure to seek medical or gynecological care and follow-up care
Cooperation with criminal justice system to prosecute rapist	Inability to cooperate with criminal justice system
Participation in rape prevention programs	Belief in rape myths
Supporting the victim's decisions and wishes	Action pressured against victim's wishes, such as forced or pressured sexual relations with victim, informing others, dropping charges, or insisting that prosecution be carried out
Reevaluating previous relationship with the victim	Divorce/separation
Unit stays intact	

Based on Burgess, A.W., and Holmstrom, L.L.: *Rape Victims of Crisis*, Bowie, Md., 1974, Robert J. Brady, Co.; Halpern, S.: *Rape: Helping the Victim.* Oradell, N.J., 1978, Medical Economics Company Book Division; Silverman, D.: "Sharing the crisis of rape: counseling the mates and families of victims," *American J. Orthopsychiatry* 48: 166, 1978.
* Foley, T., and M. Davies. *Rape: Nursing Care of Victims.* St. Louis, Missouri: C.V. Mosby Co., 1983. Reprinted with permission.

addition, Foley (1982) found that families requested assistance with a variety of tasks that correspond to needs experienced by the victim as well, such as information, validation, and crisis intervention. Interventions suggested by the authors have also been reported by Burgess and Holmstrom (1974b), Silverman (1978), and Silverman and McCombie (1980). Further, a number of clinicians have identified interventions that are helpful in crisis counseling with families of rape victims; see Table 4.

Table 4 Goals of Crisis Intervention For Families of Rape Victims *

--Assigning a primary nurse to spend time talking with the family in the emergency department waiting room while the victim receives medical care;

--Asking if the nurse can check back with the family the next day to see how they are getting along and answer any questions they may have;

--Helping the family to openly express their immediate feelings in response to a rape--as a shared life crisis;

--Helping the family to be supportive of and reassuring to the victim;

--Helping the family work through immediate practical matters and initiate problem-solving techniques;

--Helping the family develop cognitive understanding of what the rape experience actually means to the victim and to the family;

--Explaining the possibility of future psychologic and somatic symptoms that characterize a rape trauma syndrome and what the family can do to minimize these symptoms;

--Activating qualities characteristic of healthy family functioning during the impact and resolution phases of the shared crisis;

--Educating the family about rape as a *violent crime*, not a sexually motivated act, and eliminating focus on the victim's guilt or responsibility;

--Eliminating the family's sense of guilt for not protecting the victim by assuring them that they could not have anticipated or prevented the rape;

--Discouraging violent, destructive, or irrational retribution toward the rapist (under the guise of being on the victim's behalf) by encouraging a sharing of feelings of helplessness, sadness, hurt, and anger;

--Encouraging discussion of the sexual relationship between partners; suggesting that the man let the victim know (a) that his feelings have not changed (when this is true) and that he still sexually desires her, (b) that he will wait for her to approach him, and (c) that sex therapy is available if they have difficulties that persist and want assistance in reestablishing normal sexual relations;

--Explaining the possibility of venereal disease and pregnancy that may result from a rape, the preventive care necessary for the victim and spouse or boyfriend, and the follow-up care indicated;

--Explaining that early crisis intervention often prevents long-term problems in resolving the crisis and that to seek counseling at this time does not imply mental illness (the nurse specifies that crisis intervention usually lasts for three to six hours during the first few weeks post-rape);

--Giving families, lovers, and friends a copy of "A Note to Those Closest to Rape Victims" [Available from Washington, D.C. Rape Crisis Center]

--Referring the family for direct counseling when members' shared
responses to the crisis interfere with their ability to cope
adaptively;
--Providing factual data, resource lists for counseling, and follow-
up care *in writing* (Because highly stressed persons do not hear or
recall information verbally communicated);
--Letting families know that some decisions, such as whether to prosecute the rapist or move to a safer residence, can be postponed
while more immediate needs, such as medical care, are taken care
of (this action helps the family (1) set priorities and organize
decisions about what has to be done now, and (2) gain emotional
distance from the urgency and confusion felt during a crisis state
to permit sound decision making later);
--Identifying how the family has handled crises in the past and encouraging members to use adaptive coping mechanisms for this crisis;
--Encouraging contact with persons identified as supportive to the
family and offering to contact such persons;
--Allowing time for thoughts and feelings in a decision-making process;
--Using empathic listening to convey understanding of the family's
feelings and concerns.

Sources: Burgess, A.W., and Holmstrom, L.L.: "Rape: sexual disruption
and recovery," *Am. J. Orthopsychiatry*, 49:648, 1979; Burgess, A.W.,
and Holmstrom, L.L.: *Rape: Victims of Crisis*, Bowie, Md., 1974, Robert
J. Brady Co., pp. 59-63; Halpern, S., editor: *Rape: Helping the Victim*,
Oradell, N.J., 1978, Medical Economics Company Book Division, pp. 51-54;
Kliman, A.: *Crisis: Psychological First Aid for Recovery and Growth*,
New York, 1978, Holt, Rinehart & Winston; Lewis, J.M., Beavers, W.R.,
Gossett, J.T., and Phillips, V.A.: *No Single Thread: Psychological
Health in Family Systems*, New York, 1976, Brunner/Mazel Publishers.

* Foley, T., and M. Davies. *Rape: Nursing Care of Victims*. St.
Louis, Missouri: C.V. Mosby Co., 1983. Reprinted with permission.

Other clinicians and researchers reported counseling interventions related to the specific topic under discussion. These specific
counseling suggestions related to three areas: (1) interventions with
men and male partners; (2) sexual dysfunction in partner-victim relationship; and (3) the specific needs of adolescents and their families.

Interventions With Men and Male Partners
Rodkin, Hunt, and Cowan (1982) identified five goals for a support group with male significant others of rape victims: (1) to incorporate a philosophy of rape as a violent and aggressive crime as
opposed to a sexually motivated act; (2) to facilitate the constructive release of feelings; (3) to solidify the man's self-esteem,
which was threatened by the event; (4) to encourage the man to confront and attempt to resolve both intrapsychic and intrafamilial difficulties that were precipitated by the assault; and (5) to develop
self-awareness and self-honesty with the hope of promoting caring,
sensitivity, and understanding of the victim's rape experience.
Egidio and Robertson (1981) developed a rape awareness program
for men which was pilot tested with fraternity students on a college

campus and later adopted on a national basis. The program included:
(1) an introduction setting the stage for the program and background
information; (2) viewing and discussion of the film *The Reality of
Rape*; (3) the legal definition of rape and statistics on the crime
were cited; (4) viewing and discussing of the film *Rape Culture*; (5)
a discussion of the sociology of rape; (6) viewing the film *Rape--A
New Perspective*; and (7) small discussion groups which focused on
rape prevention and citizenship responsibility as well as concerns
expressed by the participants. Such educational programs have been
developed by others and cited as a necessity (Foley 1979), particularly given the male response to rape as discussed earlier.

Sexual Counseling

Becker and associates (1982) emphasize the importance of counselors being aware of treating persons with sexual dysfunctions post-
assault, especially since these problems tend to be rape related,
generalize to current partner relationships, and are long-lasting if
not chronic. Nadelson and associates (1982) indicate that short-term,
issue-oriented therapy is crucial for victims who experience sexual
dysfunctions post-rape. Counseling couples with sexual dysfunctions
is a specialty field and family members evidencing these difficulties
need to be referred to such experts. At the very least, counselors
without such expertise need to be comfortable in exploring sexual issues in their work with families and Latham (1981) describes a program
developed to achieve this objective. Support for *routinely* providing
sexual counseling designed to ameliorate sexual dysfunctions was noted
by Feldman-Summers, Gordon, and Meagher (1979), Kilpatrick, Veronen,
and Resick (1979), Veronen and Kilpatrick (1980), and Burgess and
Holmstrom (1979c).

Etherington (1979) reports encouraging victims to discuss only
those details of the assault that she is comfortable in sharing, a
principle consistent with Gilbert's (1976) discussion about the curvilinear nature of disclosure patterns directly affecting the quality
of satisfaction in a relationship. Further, Etherington reports explaining to the husband that (1) his partner's limited disclosure a-
bout the rape does not imply that she is rejecting him, and (2) the
victim's decision to not share all the details of the rape with him
is affected by being required to re-tell the rape episode to innumer-
able medical and legal persons. Etherington supported the finding of
Holmstrom and Burgess (1978) that the manner in which the victim is
responded to is more important than the gender of that person.

Marital Therapy

Miller, Williams, and Bernstein (1982) were the only researchers
to indicate that conjoint marital therapy led to significant improve-
ments in both marital and sexual adjustments both in pre- and post-
assault states, and this adjustment was maintained at six months follow-up. In contrast, couples who received no therapy showed no change
in their adjustment patterns over a comparable period of time. Unfortunately, the researchers did not specify the nature of the marital
therapy interventions for others to attempt replication of the results, a limitation common to many of the clinical reports. The researchers support the use of couples' counseling for families who
have experienced a sexual assault and find the absence of victims
seeking such counseling a troubling fact. This writer noted that the
situation is further alarming in that many counseling centers do not

routinely offer such services as part of their protocol in providing services to victims, nor actively explore with families the need and helpfulness of such counseling. This fact is partially due to the lack of awareness by many counselors about the need for such services.

Families of Adolescent Victims

The special needs of adolescents and their families were reported by a number of researchers and clinicians. Burgess and Holmstrom (1975) have provided a comprehensive discussion of intervention measures for the treatment of child and adolescent victims of sexual assault. Davenport and Davenport (1978, 1980) describe the use of role-playing as an effective intervention in helping adolescents explore how to disclose the sexual assault to their family members and peers, and for learning how to cope with reactions from these persons. The role-play intervention was also described as helpful in preparing victims for the trial in prosecuting the assailant, a finding illustrated in detail by Foley and Davies (1983). Felice (1980) discusses five guidelines for use in follow-up counseling of adolescent rape victims: (1) offer all adolescent victims the opportunity for counseling immediately or in the future; (2) avoid unnecessary repeated descriptions of the details surrounding the rape incident; (3) assess the victim for signs of a suicidal tendency; (4) recognize signs of the "teenage rape syndrome" characterized by a phobic phase, followed by a denial phase, followed by a psychosomatic phase; and (5) offer support to the victim in dealing with family, community, and police.

Mann (1981) has developed counseling guidelines for implementation in crisis counseling with adolescents as a result of preliminary research findings that parents and professionals differ from victims with respect to what their main concerns are. Schmidt (1981) addressed the importance of helping the victim view the family as a resource that could support her through the crisis post-assault. When adolescent victims are reluctant to disclose the rape to parents, Schmidt stresses the importance of facilitating the victim's efforts to identify other supportive persons in her network. It is noted that the nurse could often function as a mediator between the adolescent and her parents in working through their separate and mutual concerns. Schmidt stresses the importance of being aware that different age groups of sexual assault victims and their families have different developmental needs that must be taken into consideration in counseling these persons, a position discussed in detail by Foley and Davies (1983). Burgess and Holmstrom (1979d) identify guidelines to help victims with the disclosure dilemma with their parents.

In summary, the reviewed literature suggests clinical interventions with families of sexual assault victims. Some of these areas relate to the clinician's responsibilities (e.g., assessment), while other reports address specific problematic areas of response to a sexual assault. The entire field of counseling these families needs to be researched for the effectiveness of varying treatment approaches.

REFERENCES

Ashton, N.K. "Validation of Rape Myth Acceptance Scale." *Psychological Reports* 50 (1982): 22.

Atkeson, B.M. "Victims of Rape: Repeated Assessment of Depressive Symptoms." *Journal of Consulting and Clinical Psychology* 50 (1982): 96-102.

Barnett, N., and H.S. Feild. "Sex Differences in Attitudes Toward Rape." *Journal of College Student Personnel* 18 (1977): 93-96.

Becker, J.V., L. Skinner, G. Abel, and E. Treacy. "Incidence and Types of Sexual Dysfunctions in Rape and Incest Victims." *Journal of Sex and Marital Therapy* 8 (1982): 65-74.

Bowen, M. *Family Therapy in Clinical Practice.* New York: Jason and Aronson, 1978.

Brodsky, S.L., and S.H. Klemmack. "Blame Models and Assailant Research." Unpublished paper. University of Alabama, Department of Psychology, 1977.

Brodsky, S.L., and M. Walker, eds. *Sexual Assault.* Lexington, Massachusetts: D.C. Heath, 1976.

Brothers, D., I. Hilton, and C. Kunkes. "Trust Disturbances Among Victims of Rape and Incest." *Journal of Adolescent Health Care* 3 (1982): 150.

Burgess, A.W., and L.L. Holmstrom. "Adaptive Strategies and Recovery from Rape." *American Journal of Psychiatry* 136 (1979a): 1278-1282.

Burgess, A.W., and L.L. Holmstrom. "Rape: Disclosure to Parental Members." *Women and Health* 4 (1979b): 255-268.

Burgess, A.W., and L.L. Holmstrom. "Rape Trauma Syndrome." *American Journal of Psychiatry* 131 (1974a): 981-986

Burgess, A.W., and L.L. Holmstrom. *Rape: Victims of Crisis.* Bowie, Maryland: Robert J. Brady Company, 1974b.

Burgess, A.W., and L.L. Holmstrom. "Recovery from Rape and Prior Life Stress." *Research in Nursing and Health* 1 (1978): 1665-1679.

Burgess, A.W., and L.L. Holmstrom. "Rape: Sexual Disruption and Recovery." *American Journal of Orthopsychiatry* 49 (1979c): 648-657.

Burgess, A.W., and L.L. Holmstrom. "Sexual Trauma of Children and Adolescents." *Nursing Clinics of North America* 10 (1975): 551-563.

Burgess, A.W., and L.L. Holmstrom. "Victims of Sexual Assault." In *Out-Patient Psychiatry: Diagnosis and Treatment*, edited by A. Lazare, Baltimore, Maryland: Williams and Wilkins, 1979d.

Burgess, A.W., L.L. Holmstrom, A.N. Groth, and S.M. Sgroi. *Sexual Assault of Adolescents and Children.* Lexington, Massachusetts: D.C. Heath, 1978.

Calhoun, L.G., A. Cann, J. Selby, and D. Magee. "Victim Emotional Response: Effects on Social Reaction to Victims of Rape." *British Journal of Social Psychology* 20 (1981): 17-21.

Carter, E., and McGoldrick. *The Family Life Cycle: A Framework for Family Therapy.* New York: Gardner Press, Inc., 1980.

Davenport, J., and J. Davenport. "Role-Playing Helps Rape Victims Prepare for the Next Ordeal." *Innovations* 5 (1978): 35.

Davenport, J., and J. Davenport. "Role-Playing in a Rape Crisis Center." *Health and Social Work* 5 (1980): 65-68.

Egidio, R.K., and D. Robertson. "Rape Awareness for Men." *Journal of College Student Personnel* 22 (1981): 455-456.

Ellis, E.M., et al. "An Assessment of Long-Term Reaction to Rape." *Journal of Abnormal Psychology* 90 (1981): 263-266.

Ellis, E.M., B. Atkeson, and K. Calhoun. "An Examination of Differences Between Multiple- and Single-Incident Victims of Sexual Assaults." *Journal of Abnormal Psychology* 90 (1982): 221-224.

Ellis, E.M. "Sexual Dysfunction in Victims of Rape--Victims May Experience a Loss of Sexual...." *Women and Health* 5 (1980): 39-47.

Etherington, C. "Nurse on Metro Police Squad Counsels Rape Victims, Families." *American Nurses* 11 (1979): 5, 12.

Federal Bureau of Investigation. Uniform Crime Index. Washington, D.C.: U.S. Government Printing Office, 1979.

Feild, H.S. "Attitudes Toward Rape: A Comparative Analysis of Police, Rapists, Crisis Counselors, and Citizens." *Journal of Personality and Social Psychology* 35 (1978): 156-179.

Feldman-Summers, S., P. Gordon, and J. Meagher. "The Impact of Rape on Sexual Satisfaction." *Journal of Abnormal Psychology* 88 (1979): 101-105.

Feldman-Summers, S., and K. Lindner. "Perceptions of Victims and Defendants in Criminal Assault Cases." *Criminal Justice Behavior* 4 (1976): 135-150.

Felice, M. "Follow-up Counseling of Adolescent Rape Victims." *Medical Aspects of Human Sexuality* 14 (1980): 67-68.

Foley, T.S. "The Client Who Has Been Raped." In *Lippincott Manual of the American Handbook of Psychiatric Nursing*, edited by S. Lego. Philadelphia, Pennsylvania: J.B. Lippincott Co., 1983a.

Foley, T.S. "Counseling the Victims of Rape." In *Principles and Practices of Psychiatric Nursing*, edited by F. Stuart and S. Sundeen. St. Louis, Missouri: C.V. Mosby Co., 1983b.

Foley, T.S. "Family Response to Rape: A Pilot Study." In *Proceedings of the Fifth Pittsburgh Family Systems Symposium*. The University of Pittsburgh: Western Psychiatric Institute and Clinic, June, 1982.

Foley, T.S., and M.A. Davies. "Family Response to Rape." In *Rape: Nursing Care of Victims*, edited by T.S. Foley and M.A. Davies. St. Louis, Missouri: C.V. Mosby Co., 1983.

Frank, E., et al. "Depressive Symptoms in Rape Victims." *Journal of Affective Disorders* 1 (1979a): 269-277.

Frank, E., S. Turner, and B. Stewart. "Initial Response to Rape: The Impact of Factors Within the Rape Situation." *Journal of Behavioral Assessment* 2 (1980): 39-53.

Frank, E. "Past Psychiatric Symptoms and the Response to Sexual Assault." *Comprehensive Psychiatry* 22 (1981): 479-487.

Frank, E. "Psychological Response to Rape: An Analysis of Response Patterns." University of Pittsburgh: Ph.D. Dissertation, 1979b.

Gilbert, S.J. "Self-Disclosure: Intimacy and Communication in Families." *The Family Coordinator* 5 (1976): 221-231.

Halpern, S. *Rape: Helping the Victim--A Treatment Manual.* Oradell, New Jersey: Medical Economics Company Book Division, 1978.

Heil, D.A. "Victims of Sexual Aggression: Long-Term After-effects." *Dissertation Abstracts International* 42 (1981): 1607.

Holmes, T.H., and R.H. Rahe. "The Social Readjustment Rating Scale." *Journal of Psychosomatic Research* 11 (1967): 213.

Holmstrom, L.L., and A.W. Burgess. "Rape: The Husband's and Boy-friend's Initial Reactions." *The Family Coordinator* 28 (1979): 321-330.

Holmstrom, L.L., and A.W. Burgess. *The Victim of Rape: Institutional Reactions.* New York: John Wiley and Sons, 1978.

Hughes, C., and E. Frank. "Life Event Schedule." *The Rape Victim: Her Response and Treatment.* University of Pittsburgh: School of Medicine, Department of Psychiatry, National Institute of Mental Health Grant #201-34-5715, 1982.

Ipema, D.K. "Rape: The Process of Recovery." *Nursing Research* 28 (1979): 272-275.

Janoff-Bulman, R. "Characterological Versus Behavior Self-Blame: Inquiries into Depression and Rape." *Journal of Personality and Social Psychology* 37 (1979): 1798-1809.

Jones, C., and E. Aronson. "Attribution of Fault to a Rape Victim as Function of Respectability of the Victim." *Journal of Personality and Social Psychology* 26 (1973): 415-419.

Kanin, E.J., and S.R. Racell. "Sexual Aggression: A Second Look at the Offended Female." *Archives of Sexual Behavior* 6 (1977): 67-76.

Katz, S., and M.A. Mazur. *Understanding the Rape Victim: A Synthesis of Research Findings.* New York: John Wiley and Sons, 1979.

Kilpatrick, D.G., L.J. Veronen, and P. Resick. "The Aftermath of Rape: Recent Empirical Findings." *American Journal of Orthopsychiatry* 49 (1979): 658-659.

Kilpatrick, D.G., P. Resick, and L.J. Veronen. "Effects of a Rape Experience." *Journal of Social Issues* 37 (1981): 105-122.

Klemmeck, S.H., and D.L. Klemmack. "The Social Definition of Rape." In *Sexual Assault*, edited by S. Brodsky and M. Walker. Lexington, Massachusetts: D.C. Heath, 1976.

Kliman, A. *Crisis: Psychological First Aid for Recovery and Growth.* New York: Holt, Rinehart and Winston, 1978.

Krulewitz, J.E. "Reactions to Rape Victims--Effects of Rape Circum-stances, Victims' Emotional Response...." *Journal of Counseling Psychology* 29 (1982): 645-654.

Krulewitz, J.E. "Sex Differences in Evaluation of Female and Male Victims' Responses to Assault." *Journal of Applied Social Psychology* 11 (1978): 460-474.

Krulewitz, J.E., and J.E. Nash. "Effects of Rape Victims' Resistance, Assault Outcome, and Sex of Observer on Attributions About Rape." *Journal of Personality* 47 (1979): 557-574.

Krulewitz, J.E., and E.J. Payne. "Attributions about Rape: Effects of Rapist Force, Observer Sex, and Sex Role Attitudes." *Journal of Applied Social Psychology* 8 (1978): 291-305.

LaFree, G.D. "Review of *The Other Side of Rape and Understanding the Rape Victim.*" *Journal of Marriage and the Family* 42 (1980): 452-454.

Latham, T. "Facing Sexual Issues with the Family." *Journal of Family Therapy* 3 (1981): 153-165.

Leckie, M., and E. Thompson. "Symptoms of Stress Inventory: A Self Assessment." Seattle, Washington: University of Washington, Department of Psychosocial Nursing SC-76, 1978.

Lewis, J., W. Beavers, J. Gossett, and V. Phillips. *No Single Thread: Psychological Health in Family Systems.* New York: Brunner/Mazel Publishers, 1976.

McCahill, T.W., L.C. Meyer, and A.M. Fischman. *The Aftermath of Rape.* Lexington, Massachusetts: Lexington Books, 1979.

Mann, E.M. "Self-Reported Stresses of Adolescent Rape Victims." *Journal of Adolescent Health Care* 2 (1981): 29-33.

Mehren, E. "A Case of Attempted Rape." *Newsweek* (March 14, 1983): 11.

Metzger, D. "It Is Always the Woman Who Is Raped." *American Journal of Psychiatry* 133 (1976): 405-408.

Miller, W.R., A.M. Williams, and M.H. Bernstein. "The Effects of Rape on Marital and Sexual Adjustment." *The American Journal of Family Therapy* 10 (1982): 51-58.

Miller, W.R., A.M. Williams, and M.H. Bernstein. "The Effects of Rape on Marital and Sexual Adjustment." Paper presented at the meeting of the Eastern Association for Sex Therapy. Philadelphia, Pennsylvania, March, 1979a, b.

Miller, W.R., A.M. Williams, and M.H. Bernstein. "The Effects of Rape on Marital and Sexual Adjustment." Unpublished paper. Research Report, National Institute for Mental Health Grant RO1-MH-28975, 1979b.

Nadelson, C., M.T. Notman, and H. Zackson. "A Follow-up Study of Rape Victims." *American Journal of Psychiatry* 139 (1982): 1266-1270.

Norbeck, J. "Psychological and Social Factors in Complications of Pregnancy, A Prospective Multivariate Approach." Paper presented at the Ninth Annual Nursing Research Symposium. The University of Michigan, School of Nursing, April 30, 1982a.

Norbeck, J. "Modification of Life Event Questionnaires for Use with Female Subjects." *Research in Nursing and Health* 7 (1984): 61-71.

Norris, J., and S. Feldman-Summers. "Factors Related to the Psychological Impacts of Rape on the Victim." *Journal of Abnormal Psychology* 90 (1981): 562-567.

Peters, J. The Philadelphia Center for Rape Concerns. Philadelphia, Pennsylvania, 1979.

Resick, P.A., K. Calhoun, B. Atkeson, and E. Ellis. "Social Adjustment in Victims of Sexual Assault." *Journal of Consulting and Clinical Psychology* 49 (1981): 705-712.

Rodkin, L.I., E. Hunt, and S. Cowan. "A Men's Support Group for Significant Others of Rape Victims." *Journal of Marital and Family Therapy* 8 (1982): 91-97.

Rokeach, M. *The Open and Closed Mind.* New York: Basic Books, 1960.

Rosenblatt, R. "The Male Response to Rape." *Time* (April 18, 1983): 98.

Ruch, L.O., S. Chandler, and R. Harter. "Life Change and Rape Impact." *Journal of Health and Social Behavior* 21 (1980): 248-260.

Sanday, P.R. "The Social Context of Rape." *New Society* (Sept. 30, 1982): 540-542.

Saranson, I.G., J.H. Johnson, and J.M. Siegel. "Assessing the Impact of Change; Development of the Life Experience Survey." *Journal of Counseling and Clinical Psychology* 46 (1978): 932-946.

Schmidt, A.M. "Adolescent Female Rape Victims: Special Considerations." *Journal of Psychosocial Nursing and Mental Health Services* 19 (1981): 17-19.

Selye, H. *The Stress of Life.* New York: McGraw-Hill Book Co., 1976.

Shore, B. "An Examination of Critical Process and Outcome Factors in Rape." National Institute for Mental Health Grant #171-14-8194. Report to the Public, December 1979; Final Report, January 1980.

Silverman, D. "Sharing the Crisis of Rape: Counseling the Mates and Families of Victims." *American Journal of Orthopsychiatry* 48 (1978): 166-173.

Silverman, D., and S. McCombie. "Counseling the Mates and Families of Victims." In *The Rape Crisis Intervention Handbook: A Guide for Victim Care*, edited by S. McCombie. New York: Plenum Press, 1980.

Smith, R.E., J. Keating, R. Hester, and H. Mitchell. "Role and Justice Considerations in the Attribution of Responsibility to a Rape Victim." *Journal of Research in Personality* 10 (1976): 346-357.

Troldahl, V.C., and F.A. Powell. "A Short Form Dogmatism Scale for Use in Field Studies." *Social Forces* 44 (1965): 211-214.

Veronen, L., and D. Kilpatrick. "Self-Reported Fears of Rape Victims--A Preliminary Investigation." *Behavior Modification* 4 (1980): 383-396.

Weis, K., and S.A. Borgess. "Victimology and Rape: The Case of the Legitimate Victim." *Issues in Criminology* 8 (1973): 71-115.

West, D. "Social Support as Related to Outcome in Rape Victim Response." University of Pittsburgh: School of Medicine, Department of Psychiatry. National Institute for Mental Health Grant #201-340-5715. Personal Communication of research in progress.

White, P.N., and J. Rollins. "Rape: A Family Crisis." *Family Relations* 39 (1981): 103-109.

Williams, C., and T. Holmes. "Life Change, Human Adaptation, and Onset of Illness." In *Clinical Practice in Psychosocial Nursing: Assessment and Intervention*, edited by D. Longo and R. Williams, New York: Appleton-Century-Crofts, 1978.

CHAPTER 14

THE CRIMINAL JUSTICE SYSTEM'S RESPONSE TO THE RAPE VICTIM

Lynda Lytle Holmstrom

The criminal justice system's reaction to the rape victim is important on several counts: for its effect on those victims who report or may report, for its effect on the accused rapists brought before it, and for the general statement it makes about the community's stance on this crime. This chapter will look at the criminal justice system and rape, especially in relation to the victim.

Both feminist and research interest in this subject started in the early 1970s. When I, with my co-researcher Burgess, began to study the topic in 1972, not much was known about the victims of rape and few services existed for them. Feminist groups, however, had begun to talk openly about the crime. The 1971 New York Speak Out on Rape may be thought of as a turning point. Through feminist speeches and publications, women brought a taboo topic out into the open and called for change. Academic publications on rape mushroomed and numerous practical reforms occurred. This chapter looks at some highlights of this research, and then makes a few comments about the practical implications of this body of knowledge.

In our own research, as well as some of the other early work, there was an interest in getting an overview of the system. In our project beginning in 1972, we met victims at the emergency ward of Boston City Hospital when they were first admitted. We collected both sociological and clinical data, as well as providing counseling. We followed victims from the time of the rape through the time of sentencing and beyond (Holmstrom and Burgess 1978). Another early study started by a psychiatrist, the late Joseph J. Peters, contacted victims soon after they reported a rape to Philadelphia General Hospital. In that study, a notification form from the hospital was sent to the Center for Rape Concern. The Center's policy was that the social worker should try to reach the victim within forty-eight hours of the case being assigned. That study also was interested in how cases fared in the criminal justice system, and they followed cases through sentencing (McCahill, Meyer, Fischman 1979). A Canadian study (Clark and Lewis 1977), using police records as data, studied the several stages of the criminal justice system. In the Canadian scene also, the researchers found that "the progress of a rape case through the criminal justice system reflects a highly selective process of elimination."

All three studies mentioned above show the attrition of cases and the many stages at which rape cases may drop out. More recently a number of studies have focused on certain specific steps in the process--for example, on the victim's decision whether to report, on police investigations, or on jurors.

THE DECISION TO REPORT A RAPE

It is well established that many rapes go unreported. A number of studies have looked at why victims report, and several have compared those who do and do not. Studies have looked at what victims want if they report, the influence of the victim's social network, and differences between the rapes of reporters and nonreporters.

Why Victims Report

The victim's main emotional response during a rape is fear
(Burgess and Holmstrom 1974) and many experience the event as life
threatening. Furthermore, the body has been physically assaulted.
McCahill, Meyer and Fischman (1979) state that 38 percent of the victims (for whom there are data) reported the rape "because of a desire
for help or comfort, whether physical, emotional, or medical." In
the Dukes and Mattley study (1977), the idea of a "haven" emerges.
"The findings of this research support a model which suggests that
for crimes in which victim fear is a characteristic, if police are
perceived as providing a haven for an extremely frightened victim,
she is likely to report the crime to them."

A similar theme emerges in the Feldman-Summers and Ashworth
(1981) research. They asked hypothetical questions to a sample of
fifty women, inquiring as to what they would do if raped. "Of all
the perceived outcomes [of reporting], one was by far the most important for women of all ethnic groups--namely: feeling calm and safe."
The authors suggest that individuals or agencies who want to increase
the probability of a victim reporting to them, should develop procedures to help the victim regain her feeling of well-being, and
should make sure that potential victims know of the availability of
this support.

The Victim's Social Network

To understand reporting patterns, one has to look at the interaction between the victim and her social network. In our study (Holmstrom and Burgess 1978), we found it was common for someone other
than the victim to be involved in notifying the police. Among ninety-
four reports to authorities of the rape of an adult, there were fifty-
seven cases in which someone other than the victim made the decision
to contact the police, acted as an intermediary, or gave advice that
led to reporting. In only twenty-two cases did the adult victim herself contact the police on her own initiative. Among twenty-three
pre-adult victims, only two contacted the police on their own initiative. McCahill, Meyer, and Fischman (1979) found that among 761
cases reported to the police, only 175 victims (23 percent) contacted
the police themselves.

The Feldman-Summers and Ashworth (1981) study emphasizes once
again the importance of the social network. The victim's perceived
outcomes of reporting are important; it is also important to the victim that reporting is a decision that is supported by people, especially males, in her social network. "It seems clear that efforts to
increase rape reporting must include steps to strengthen social norms
that support intentions to report."

Differences between Reported and Nonreported Rapes

Studies have shown differences between the rapes of reporters
and nonreporters. A very recent study by Williams (in press) has
analyzed this phenomenon. The general idea guiding this inquiry is
that there is a "classic" type of rape and that women who have been
assaulted in this way are more likely to report the assaults. The
study analyzed 1980-1981 file data from the Seattle Rape Relief, and
compared 146 victims who reported to the police and 100 nonreporters.
She found that women were more apt to report if the assailant broke
into their home, attacked them in their cars, or attacked them in
(or abducted them from) public places; in contrast, those raped in a

social situation, such as a date, were the least apt to report.
Women whose assailants were strangers or acquaintances were more apt
to report than those whose assailants were friends or relatives.
Women threatened with a weapon were very likely to report, as well as
women seriously injured.

Currently there is an increase in studies in which the samples
include types of cases previously overlooked. Russell's study of
rape in marriage (1982) is a case in point. Russell approximated a
statistically random sample, and then inquired whether the women had
been victimized through rape or attempted rape by their husbands (or
ex-husbands); 87 of the 644 ever-married women in the sample had been
so victimized. The nonreporting pattern of these victims is striking.
Of the women who were raped by their husbands, only 9 reported the
incidents to the police. The few who did go to the authorities reported being beaten instead of being raped--a finding that is not
surprising since wife rape was not a crime at the time. Data from
samples such as these can help us rethink the meaning of rape and
appropriate policy responses.

POLICE AS GATEKEEPERS

When a victim, or someone on her behalf, reports a rape to an
authority, typically the first person to whom it is reported is a
police officer. Thus the police occupy a pivotal position in the
criminal justice system. Studies of the police have looked at their
attitudes, the way they make decisions, and contrasts between police
work and prosecutorial work.

Attitudes of the Police

Feild (1978) studied the attitudes of four groups: police,
rapists, crisis counselors, and citizens. Among a total of 1,448
subjects, the police subsample consisted of 254 patrol officers from
two urban and two rural communities. The rapist subsample consisted
of 20 offenders committed to a state mental hospital. The findings
regarding how rapists differed from rape crisis counselors are of
interest:

> In comparison to the counselors, the rapists were *more*
> likely to endorse the following views: Rape prevention
> is primarily woman's responsibility (p<.001); rape is
> motivated by a desire for sex (p<.001); punishment for
> rape should not be severe (p<.001); victims are likely
> to precipitate rape through their appearance or be-
> havior (p<.01); rapists are not mentally normal (p<.01);
> rape is not motivated by a need for power (p<.05); a
> raped woman is a less desirable woman (p.<.01); and
> women should not resist during rape (p<.01). [Emphasis
> in the original.]

Of particular interest are similarities between police and assailants.
"The patrol police officers were more similar to the rapists than
they were to the counselors in their views of rape." There were no
differences between the police officers and the rapists on the issues
of what motivates rapists, whether rapists are normal, and the effect
of rape on the attractiveness of a victim.

Feldman-Summers and Palmer (1980) studied attitudes of criminal
justice personnel--police officers, prosecutors, and judges--and compared them to rape center workers. They found differences between
members of the criminal justice system and rape center workers on a

variety of issues, including ideas about causes of rape and how to
reduce rape. "[Criminal justice system personnel's] beliefs about
the causes of rape and how rape can be prevented tend to place a substantial degree of the blame and responsibility on the victim as well
as on sexually frustrated and mentally ill men." But, the groups did
not differ regarding the criteria they used to distinguish true and
false reports. People looked for such factors as injuries, a consistent story, prompt reporting, absence of premarital and extramarital
relations, and lack of social contact between victim and assailant.
As the authors point out, "given what information is currently available about rape complaints, most women who report being raped will
not fare well under these criteria."

Decision-Making

It is important to look not only at attitudes, but also at the
organizational context of police work. McCahill, Meyer, and Fischman
(1979) review studies showing that there are various motives for police to label a case as rape or nonrape, including: (1) deliberate
statistical manipulation (for example, to improve the clearance rate);
(2) idiosyncratic rules of a department (departments in different
cities label cases differently); and (3) the labeling strategies of
detectives.

Given both the police attitudes described and the organizational
structure, how do the decisions actually turn out? In our own research (Holmstrom and Burgess 1978), we found that police officers
saw rape cases as "strong" or "weak," and that their enthusiasm for
pursuing a case varied accordingly. Their criteria included the
quality of the information they could get about the event, the victim's behavior and moral character, the relationship between victim
and offender, and characteristics of the alleged rapist. A number
of items went into how they categorized cases, and the victim was a
significant part of that equation.

Other researchers have also found the victim to be a significant
factor. McCahill, Meyer, and Fischman have taken the approach of
seeing what variables distinguish between founded and unfounded rape
cases in Philadelphia. Regarding who the police believe, they analyze a number of factors. They note that if a female police officer
is present--even if only doing secretarial tasks--cases are less apt
to disappear or to be given non-offense labels, and are more likely
to be categorized as founded. Analysis of other variables indicated
that "Police tend to doubt the credibility of extremely obese women,
women who have seen psychiatrists, women who are 12 years old or more,
women who allege penile-vaginal intercourse [was completed], and women
who receive welfare."

While the above findings suggest that aspects of the organizational setting (e.g., whether a policewoman is present) and of the
assault (e.g., whether the act is completed) are relevant, it is
clear that the victim's characteristics and behavior are very important in judgments of a case. The Rose and Randall (1982) fieldwork
study of a police department in still another geographic region,
Texas, confirms the importance of the victim. One finding about the
investigative stage was that "the major clues (accurate or otherwise)
contained in the OIRs [Offense Incident Reports] which lead to investigator designations of cases as 'legitimate' or as 'deals' involve
characteristics or actions of the *victim*" [emphasis in the original].

Contrasts between Police and Prosecutorial Work

For a rape case to wend its way through the justice system, there has to be some measure of cooperation between police and prosecutor. On a very abstract level, they may share certain goals. However, several authors have commented on their differences. Stanko (1981) presents the two occupations as being in "antagonistic cooperation." She notes that the occupational environment differs for the two--it is the street for the police and the court for the prosecutor. In general, the police goal is constabulatory or "maintaining the peace" (Banton 1964; Bittner 1967). The district attorney's concern, in contrast, is the prosecution of the felony case. Although prosecutors are dependent on police officers to bring them cases and data, Stanko often witnessed strained relations between the two.

The disjunction between the two types of work is perhaps even more important than whether they have strained relations. A study of the police done by researchers at the Rand Corporation (Greenwood and Petersilia 1975) found that very few departments "'consistently and thoroughly document the key evidentiary facts that reasonably assure that the prosecutor can obtain a conviction on the most serious applicable charges.'"

McCahill, Meyer, and Fischman (1979), observed a similar pattern. They found that the Philadelphia police focused more on solving cases than on laying the groundwork for solid prosecution. The police tended to spend more time and energy on cases they did not solve than on cases they solved. For example, searching for crime-scene clues, contacting a crime laboratory, utilizing various identification procedures, and talking to witnesses were more commonly done in the unsolved cases. To understand this disjunction between police and prosecutorial work, one has to look not only at the environment (street vs. court) in which the actors work, but also at the differential reward structure: i.e., what activities are police rewarded for, and what lines of activities hold rewards for the prosecutor.

The Prosecutor: Winning Cases Is the Goal

The district attorney wants to win cases. Part of the district attorney's job is behind-the-scenes (e.g., preparing a case), but a considerable portion of the job takes place in a highly visible arena, the public courtroom. In our research on rape (Holmstrom and Burgess 1978), we found that district attorneys felt their professional competence was tested as they entered the courtroom, and their worst fear was of looking bad in court. In this connection, they focused on the victim as a witness and on possible problems in the case. The courtroom places a premium on verbal skills, and a trial is, in large measure, a battle fought with linguistic weapons. District attorneys thus wanted a rape victim who was articulate and would give consistent testimony. They worried about the effect her appearance and demeanor would have on the jury. They also worried about evidence of force and penetration, the behavior and reputation of the victim, and whether there was a prior relationship between the victim and the accused.

The prosecutor's perception of the victim was found by Stanko (1981-82) to be a key factor in screening decisions. In her fieldwork study of a New York prosecutor's office, she observed the screening of a variety of types of cases, noting especially those of robbery, rape, and assault. She concluded that "the character and credibility of the victim is a key factor in determining prosecutorial

strategies, one at least as important as 'objective' evidence about
the crime or characteristics of the defendant." The following quote
is illustrative of the enthusiasm prosecutors express when they find
a good victim. An elderly woman who had her purse snatched by a
teenage male, then chased the defendant through a park. The district
attorney spoke with excitement, saying, "'These are the cases that
try themselves. Any case that has a stand-up complainant should be
indicted. You put her on the stand--the judge loves her, the jury
loves her--dynamite complainant!'" In a contrasting robbery case,
of two prostitutes, the district attorney reduced the charges, com-
menting that he would be in court with two complainants who worked
the streets.

Prosecutors' views of rape victims and of how they will affect
a case are quite resistant to change. Two recent studies have shown
the continued use of traditional criteria despite the reform of rape
laws (Loh 1981; Marsh, Geist, and Caplan 1982). The Loh study evaluated the impact of legal reform in the State of Washington. The reforms included a shift regarding non-consent to focusing less on resistance by the victim and more on the assailant's use or threat of
force. Nevertheless, both before and after reform, the prosecutors
focused on force, prior assailant-victim social interaction, corroboration, the credibility of the victim, and race. Loh looked at convictability and at charging, and found a significant positive relationship under both the old and the new statutes. Looking at linear
trends in both the before and after data, he states, "the inference
is that prosecutors employ the same convictability standard irrespective of the substantive law. As a practical matter, certain factors
must be present in order to win at trial, and these remain unchanged
despite reforms in the legal elements of the crime." Legal reforms,
discussed below, do have an impact on certain other aspects of the
outcome of cases.

The Legal Outcome

In our research on rape (Holmstrom and Burgess 1978), we collected detailed fieldwork data on hearings and trials. We found that
court outcome was associated with a number of variables, some legal
and some extra-legal, some related to the victim and some related to
other aspects of the case. In most cases, the defense attorney's
strategy was to blame the victim; in a minority of cases, the defense
attorney claimed misidentification.

Other research also shows that the victim is one key factor in
the court outcome. In the McCahill, Meyer, and Fischman (1979) study,
the research social worker made a judgment as to whether the concept
"victim precipitation" (defined as naivete, indiscretion, or compli-
city) could be applied to the case. The research team then looked to
see if that designation correlated with court outcome. Aspects of
the victim's behavior just prior to the incident were more strongly
associated with the outcome of the trial than were the other variables
that the authors tested. There was a guilty verdict in 71.4 percent
of the 91 cases with no suggestion of victim precipitation; in contrast, there was conviction in only 44.7 percent of the 76 cases which
could be said to display some elements of victim precipitation. One
paradoxical finding is that cases with brutal beatings were most apt
to lead to the jury acquitting the defendant. The authors speculate
that this result may occur because, in this type of case, the defense

is likely to claim mistaken identity rather than consent, and that juries fear convicting the wrong person in a brutal (and therefore "serious") case. Victims' characteristics, as well as characteristics of the victim-offender dyad, correlate with sentencing.

More recently, LaFree (1980a, 1980b; LaFree et al. 1982), has written a set of papers looking at the outcome of rape cases using midwestern data. Perhaps most interesting methodologically is the paper by LaFree, Reskin, and Visher based on interviews with members of the jury. The analysis is based on post-trial interviews with 331 jurors who deliberated on forcible sexual assault cases between 1978 and 1980.

These authors make an important research point, namely, that in analyzing rape cases, it is crucial to categorize cases by type of defense strategy. In their research, they found that jurors responded differently in cases where the legal issues at hand were unique to rape, compared to cases where the legal issues were the same as in other crimes. They divided their cases into two broad groups. First, there were cases where the defense was either that a) the victim consented or b) there was no sexual contact. Second, there were cases where the defense was either a) misidentification or b) diminished responsibility (e.g., insanity). In *consent* cases, jurors were more apt to see the defendant as innocent when the victim engaged in behavior defined as inappropriate for women, when the victim was black, or when the woman held a blue-collar job. They were also influenced by the character, life style, and criminal record of the defendant; in contrast, the jurors were not influenced by the types of evidence examined by the authors (e.g., weapon). In *identification/diminished responsibilty* cases, the jurors were more apt to see the defendant as innocent if the woman was employed, was not at her own home when assaulted, or was said to have had extramarital sex. They were more apt to see the defendants as guilty if they lacked stable social ties.

Another important methodological point made in the LaFree, Reskin, and Visher (1982) paper is that there may be a difference between doing research on actual jury behavior and on simulations. Actual jury work differs from simulation in important ways, one of them being the existence in the former of the jury selection process. In the authors' opinion, it should not be surprising if one finds differences between the results of the two types of research.

Other research has focused on comparisons. Some research has compared rape and nonrape cases. Other research has compared rape cases before and after reform legislation. Space limitations preclude a review here of this literature (see Holmstrom and Burgess 1983). Suffice it to say that Loh's (1981) evaluation of the Washington State reform emphasizes the increase in the accuracy of labelling cases (e.g., calling a rapist a rapist); Marsh, Geist, and Caplan's (1982) evaluation of the Michigan State reform emphasizes the increase in convictions.

RECOMMENDATIONS

The research reviewed above leads to some suggestions for reform. If one's goals are to encourage rape victims to cooperate with the criminal justice system and to increase the conviction rate of rapists, then these practices would seem useful to consider. In some jurisdictions, numerous reforms have already been instituted, and hence a major need is for evaluation of what has been tried.

Other jurisdictions may have changed a little, and there the need
is for initial reform.

Audit Trail: Studies show the multiplicity of steps at which
rape cases drop out of the system. Some way is needed to keep
track of cases. McCahill, Meyer, and Fischman (1979) suggest the
development and use of an "audit trail" that follows a case through
the system from initial complaint through final disposition. They
note that such a system would let one trace cases, pull sets of cases
out for analysis (e.g., to look at all unfounded cases), and would
promote the idea that the responsibility of the police officer continues until the ultimate disposition.

Policewomen: It appears that cases are less apt to be unfounded
when a policewoman is present. Thus, to encourage cases being given
a careful evaluation and to not be dropped before such an evaluation,
the presence and utilization of policewomen should be encouraged.

Victim as an Ally: Our own research has shown how the quality
of information that criminal justice personnel can obtain is crucial.
They need consistent, explicit, and accurate data. In the past, the
victim often was seen as an adversary. Although it is the officer's
and prosecutor's duty to be suspicious, there is nevertheless a
great deal to be gained from taking the approach, when interviewing,
that the victim is an ally. The victim in most rape cases is the
most knowledgeable witness to the crime.

Reward Structure for Police: Part of the reason police tend to
focus on solving cases rather than documenting evidence for use at
court, is that they are rewarded for the former. If performance
measures and rewards tend to emphasize clearance rates, it is not
surprising that officers focus on this. To encourage officers to
follow through with documentation of evidence, further thought needs
to be given to how to better evaluate and reward that aspect of their
performance.

Legal Reforms: Admittedly, it is difficult to tell if changes
after law reform are due to the reform or to other simultaneously
occurring events. Nevertheless, the evaluation of legal reforms,
as noted above, suggests that there are changes after reform. Particularly encouraging, given the findings of other studies on attitudes toward rape, is that changes can occur even though attitudes
remain the same. As Marsh, Geist, and Caplan (1982) state, "two
threads--specific procedural changes and overall attitudinal stabili-
ty--run throughout our examination of the changes that the law has
produced." In conclusion they note, "participants implement most
provisions while maintaining attitudes essentially inconsistent with
the law's intent." The point--which in some respects is encouraging--
is that one can bring about certain concrete positive changes even if
one cannot change attitudes.

Advice for Victims: Studies show that the rape victim is one
important factor in the outcome of the case in court. One cannot
change facts about the victim--who she is, her race, whether she is
employed, whether she had extramarital sex. But, one can give the
victim advice and counsel about how to approach the courtroom experience and how best to field the questions that she will be asked. Numerous victim-witness programs now exist, often connected to district
attorneys' offices or rape crisis centers. Information is available
about them through the National Center for Prevention and Control of
Rape (NCPCR, Washington, D.C.) and the National Organization of Victim Assistance (NOVA, Washington, D.C.).

REFERENCES

Banton, M. *The Policeman in the Community*. New York: Basic Books, 1964.

Bittner, E. "The Police on Skid Row: A Study of Peace Keeping." *American Sociological Review* 32 (1967): 699-715.

Burgess, A.W., and L.L. Holmstrom. "Rape Trauma Syndrome." *American Journal of Psychiatry* 131 (1974): 983.

Clark, L.M.G., and D.J. Lewis. *Rape: The Price of Coercive Sexuality*. Toronto, Ontario: The Women's Press, 1977: 57.

Dukes, R.L., with the assistance of C.L. Mattley. "Predicting Rape Victim Reportage." *Sociology and Social Research* 62 (1977): 63.

Feild, H.S. "Attitudes Toward Rape: A Comparative Analysis of Police, Rapists, Crisis Counselors, and Citizens." *Journal of Personality and Social Psychology* 36 (1978): 169.

Feldman-Summers, S. and G.C. Palmer. "Rape as Viewed by Judges, Prosecutors and Police Officers," *Criminal Justice and Behavior*, 7 (1980) 34-36.

Greenwood, P.W., and J. Petersilia. *The Criminal Investigation Process, Vol. A: Summary and Policy Implications*. Santa Monica, California: The Rand Corporation, 1975, viii (quoted in McCahill, Meyer, and Fischman).

Holmstrom, L.L., and A.W. Burgess. *The Victim of Rape: Institutional Reactions*. New York: Wiley, 1978. New edition 1983 by Transaction, New Brunswick, New Jersey.

LaFree, G.D. "The Effect of Sexual Stratification by Race on Official Reactions to Rape." *American Sociological Review* 45 (1980a): 842-854.

LaFree, G.D. "Variables Affecting Guilty Pleas and Convictions in Rape Cases: Toward a Social Theory of Rape Processing." *Social Forces* 58 (1980b): 833-850.

LaFree, G.D., B.F. Reskin, and C.A. Visher. "The Effects of Rape Victims' Characteristics and Jurors' Attitudes on Jurors' Reactions to Defendants." Paper presented at the American Sociological Association meeting. San Francisco, California, September, 1982.

Loh, W.D. "Q: What Has Reform of Rape Legislation Wrought? A: Truth in Criminal Labelling." *Journal of Social Issues* 37 (1981): 43.

McCahill, T.W., L.C. Meyer, and A.M. Fischman. *The Aftermath of Rape*. Lexington, Masschusetts: D.C. Heath, 1979.

Marsh, J.C., A. Geist, and N. Caplan. *Rape and the Limits of Law Reform*. Boston, Massachusetts: Auburn House, 1982.

Rose, V.M., and S.C. Randall. "The Impact of Investigator Perceptions of Victim Legitimacy on the Processing of Rape/Sexual Assault Cases." *Symbolic Interaction* 5 (1982): 33.

Russell, D.E.H. *Rape in Marriage*. New York: Macmillan, 1982.

Stanko, E.A. "The Arrest Versus the Case: Some Observations on
    Police/District Attorney Interaction." *Urban Life* 9 (1981):
    401, 411.

Stanko, E.A. "The Impact of Victim Assessment on Prosecutors'
    Screening Decisions: The Case of the New York County District
    Attorney's Office." *Law and Society Review* 16 (1981-82): 226, 231.

Williams, L.S. "The 'Classic' Rape: When Do Victims Report?" Un-
    published paper. University of Washington: Department of Sociol-
    ogy, (In press.)

CHAPTER 15

THE CHILD AND THE CRIMINAL JUSTICE SYSTEM

Lucy Berliner

Until the early 1970s, cases of sexual assault of children rarely came to the attention of the criminal justice system. Although there has been a dramatic rise in the prosecution of cases, it is still nowhere near comparable to the incidence of these crimes in the population. Retrospective incidence studies have shown since the early 1950s that a significant portion of adults say they were victims of some form of sexual assault in their childhood (Kinsey et al. 1953; Landis 1956; Russell 1982). They also overwhelmingly respond that they did not report it to anyone, and in one reliable study only 6 percent said that there had been police involvement in their situation (Finkelhor 1979).

Part of the discrepancy between high rates of these offenses and the low rate of criminal prosecution can be attributed to lack of reporting. Clearly, the criminal justice system cannot pursue cases which are not reported. Yet, when cases are known it does not necessarily mean that involvement of the criminal justice system follows. Some of the reasons that cases are not reported in the first place are due to the way the criminal justice works or is perceived to work.

It is not only sexual assault cases where there are issues of low reporting, and reluctance to cooperate with the criminal justice system. Law Enforcement Assistance Administration (LEAA) victimization studies suggest that less than one-half of all victims of crime report to law enforcement agencies.

Numerous reports and stories in the popular press have pointed to a decreasing faith in the criminal justice system among citizens. All crime victims, including sexual assault victims, share concerns about how the legal system operates and its effects on victims.

The issues facing sexual assault victims are particularly complex. There is no societal agreement about what constitutes criminal sexual behavior or about the proper institutional response. The reasons for this are many and reflect long-held beliefs about the roles and rights of men and women, both in general and in terms of sexual behavior. Although there is now more discussion and demonstrable change in the prevailing attitudes about sexual assault, there is still significant ambiguity about where society stands, and this is reflected in the low numbers of sexual assault cases that are prosecuted.

Child victims are confronted with some of the same problems as adult sexual assault victims. Like women, children are also perceived as likely to make false reports. In addition, children's statements about sexual abuse are sometimes attributed to fantasy or the programming of another adult (e.g., mother in divorce situation). The child's lack of knowledge may be blamed for causing a misinterpretation of innocent behavior or the parent may be seen as overreacting. The different capabilities of children to recall and describe events, especially sexual ones, is used to discredit their statements. This attitude of not believing child victims of sex offenses is reflected in legal writing and decisions (Bienen, 1983).

The credibility and the competence of the witness in a sexual assault case is the central issue. For child victims, simply the fact of being a child renders them less credible. The characteristic patterns of child sexual assault contribute to the problem of belief as well. It is usually a situation where a known or related adult involves children in sexual activity by nonviolent means. They use existing relationships for access to and control over the child victims and will usually commit repeated acts against the children by convincing them that reporting will have worse consequences than passively acquiescing to the abusive behavior (Conte and Berliner 1981). So there is no physical evidence, and no immediate reporting of the crimes. The offenders are often people who are otherwise apparently normal and law-abiding; they will usually deny the accusation and the situation is reduced to an unsupported accusation by a child against an ostensibly responsible adult.

Even when there is acknowledgement that illegal sexual behavior took place, it does not always mean prosecution. Victims and their families and the personnel of the criminal justice system share concerns about whether or to what extent the law should be involved in these cases. This is for reasons related to both the type of crime and the nature of the adversary system itself.

Criminal sexual behavior is considered in many cases to be the product of a psychological disorder in the offender. It is distinguished from other types of criminal behavior and the offender is often described as "sick" and requiring treatment. Although a crime has been committed, the perpetrator is not perceived to be a criminal.

Both the legal and medical/mental health professions may consider this behavior to be in their purview. Yet each system has an entirely different way of defining and responding to human behavior. The goal of the criminal justice system is to identify and punish lawbreakers; the goal of the medical/mental health professionals is to treat disorders. Punishment and treatment are considered to be the two opposing perspectives. The general community as well as the professionals are ambivalent about criminal justice system involvement in situations involving behavior which is seen as resulting from psychological problems. The response to crimes commited while under the influence of alcohol illustrates similar ambiguity and raises similar questions. Even victims and families often see the offenders as needing help and do not seek punishment as the goal of intervention.

There is no consensus about the proper role of the criminal justice system in child sexual abuse and there are schools of thought representing the full spectrum of degrees of support for involvement with the legal system. The closer the relationship of the offender to the family, the more likely it is that the family will be compassionate toward the offender and reluctant to bring criminal charges. Since about 90 percent of reported cases involve an offender who is known to the victim, there is some degree of ambivalence in almost all cases (Burgess et al. 1978). There have been many constraints against the intrusion of the legal system in family life. Mandatory child abuse reporting laws have only existed for about fifteen years (National Center on Child Abuse and Neglect 1980). There has been a long history of toleration of criminal behavior between family members, both by statute and by practice. In reported sexual abuse cases, only about half of the offenders are related to the victim.

That is not to say that there aren't cases where there is agreement. No matter how disturbed an eighteen-year-old who violently rapes an eighty-year-old woman might be, it is necessary to prosecute and incarcerate the youth for the protection of society. But there are times when even law enforcement would agree that the criminal justice system is not the best way to handle a situation. For example, a single nonviolent sexual episode between a twelve-year-old and a seven-year-old might be a sign of serious psychological problems. Although it is technically a crime, the better approach may be to try counseling rather than prosecution initially.

The adversary process itself, even in cases which are properly in the criminal justice purview, presents difficulties for both the system and the victims and families. The family fears that the process will be more traumatic to the child victim than the assault experience. They worry that the child might encounter insensitive or untrained personnel, and be subjected to unnecessary interrogations, delays, and costs. It may seem to be opposite of what would lead to the child's recovery from the effects of assault.

The police and prosecutors also have misgivings about the ability of children to cooperate with the legal process. The nature of the adversary system means that the credibility of the victim witness will be challenged at every point by the opposing counsel. There are legal requirements for competency, which must be met when the victim is a child. Since the child's testimony is generally the only evidence, the case rests on the capacity of the victim to communicate clearly and convincingly about what happened. There are obvious barriers inherent in the subject matter as well as in the public and formal setting of court. In a system which limits and structures the type and amount of information presented in court, these cases are extremely difficult to prove. Prosecutors therefore often use their discretion about not filing charges in cases where, although they believe a crime was committed, it does not seem possible to achieve a conviction. It is not worth putting the victim through testifying, nor committing the necessary resources, when the inevitable outcome is acquittal.

It is clear that there are many reasons why so few cases of child sexual assault are prosecuted. There has not been a widespread awareness that child sexual abuse was a common occurrence and that children in general are telling the truth about such matters. There is also no agreement about what should actually be done once the sexual abuse is discovered. The particular quality of sexual assault as a crime and as a behavior disorder causes conflicting responses in the community at large, in victims and families, among mental health professionals and in the legal system. Beyond that, actual participation in the justice response may be painful and exacerbate the effects of abuse on the victim. From the point of view of the system personnel, these cases are time-consuming and emotionally draining and hard to win.

Many questions remain unanswered, but much has happened in the past ten years. It has been the first decade of a concerted effort to make society aware of the shocking reality that a significant percentage of all children in the United States were sexually abused and that almost nothing was being done about it. The women's movement and the rape crisis centers, the child abuse and child advocacy movements, and the victim/witness movement all began in the 1970s. The increase in reporting of cases to both social and legal agencies can be directly linked to the awareness created by these advocacy groups.

Education about how to talk to children about sexual abuse, and how to recognize symptoms which might be indicators of abuse, has become widespread. For example, many communities provide information for parents and students; professionals receive in-service education; and there are professional conferences and seminars. There has been an outpouring of literature and the beginnings of research. The issue has been raised in the media, national and local, print and electronic. And sexual abuse of children has become an acceptable subject for prime time TV. This has meant many more cases coming to the attention of the criminal justice system.

The criminal justice process in many communities has changed over the past decade. This has happened in response to community activism and because of recognition by the system that the traditional approach to these crimes is not effective with child sexual abuse. The concept of using the legal system as a leverage to get offenders in treatment programs and supervise their progress has become widespread. The Child Sexual Abuse Treatment Program in Santa Clara County, California, was the first major treatment program to operate successfully within the legal structure (Kroth 1979). This idea has gradually gained acceptance by both the therapeutic community and the legal justice personnel. Combining the sanctions of the legal system with the possibility of court ordered treatment has been a critical factor in changing perceptions and involvement with the criminal justice system. This approach gives victims and families, as well as the therapists, the sense that there is hope for a constructive outcome of the legal intervention. Except in rare cases, a strictly punitive response is not the goal of the mental health professionals. For the legal personnel, there is the acknowledgement of the need to hold people responsible for breaking the law and have offenders formally identified as lawbreakers, even if counseling is the outcome of the legal process. There is also the practical advantage that defendants are more likely to plead guilty if treatment is a part of the consequence.

This is not to say that there is complete agreement. Many law enforcement officers continue to see counseling as ineffective and counselors as more committed to explaining behavior than changing it. There is also significant disagreement in the mental health community about whether the basic values of a therapeutic relationship are compromised by the very idea of coerced treatment and lack of confidentiality. But increasingly, forensic practitioners exist who can comfortably provide mental health services within a legal framework.

Treatment under the auspices of the correctional system can be provided by contracting or referring to mental health professionals, or programs may be actually operated by the state. In general, evaluation and outpatient treatment is done in the community by mental health professionals who specialize in forensic psychiatry or psychology and practice in the community, while inpatient programs exist in correctional institutions. Different levels of legal intervention may occur, depending both on the type of crime committed and on treatment options available. There are pre-prosecution diversion programs which may require completion of the treatment program as an alternative to prosecution. There are suspended or deferred sentences for the convicted offender where treatment is a condition of the probation, or there may be commitment to an inpatient program within the correctional system. Many states have programs to which convicted offenders may be sentenced (Brecher 1978); some are in hospitals and others are special programs within prisons. Community-based treatment programs are most often reserved for incest offenders, while secure facilities are used for non-family child molesters and rapists (Kirkwood 1979).

Another major development has been the recognition that the nature of this crime and of children as witnesses mandates a different kind of response by the criminal justice system. Training for police officers on the characteristics of child sexual abuse, interviewing child witnesses, and interrogating suspects has become common. The need for specialized investigative personnel is reflected by the fact that many police departments have sex crimes units, child abuse detectives, or childrens' bureaus in which the assigned investigators usually have special training. The same holds true with the prosecuting attorneys' offices; many jurisdictions have created specialized units where designated attorneys handle sexual assault or child abuse cases.

In addition to specialization, there is the need for coordination with the other involved community agencies. In incest cases, the Child Protective Service will almost always also be involved in the case. There may be parallel proceedings in juvenile or family court relating to custody. The growth of the victim advocacy movement means that in most urban areas there are rape crisis centers, sexual assault programs, and victim witness units. Child abuse intervention teams and networking groups are solutions which have been tried in many communities. Sometimes they have a formal structure and hold regular meetings; in other areas they may be more ad hoc and informal. In some cases even social gatherings may be a part of the networking process. Innovative approaches to prosecuting child sexual assault have developed in many communities where legal and other professionals work together (Legal Resource Center for Child Advocacy and Protection 1981).

The child protection teams may develop protocols for case handling where criteria for referral to different agencies are agreed upon and the procedures for intervention are specified. These kinds of guidelines help avoid the problems inherent in coordinating intervention by legal and social service systems. The responsibilities for case management can be divided appropriately or conducted conjointly, depending on the local preference. For example, in one area it might be decided that Child Protective Service interviews the victims and the police interview the suspects, while another possibility is a joint investigation.

In addition to the reforms mentioned above, there have been procedural changes in case handling to accommodate the natural limitations of child witnesses and to minimize additional trauma to the children (Libai 1977). The changes have been generally oriented toward reducing unnecessary interviews and delays, and decreasing the number of personnel in contact with the victim. For criminal justice system personnel there is a practical advantage to these changes because children do not tolerate the normal difficulties of participation in the criminal justice system well and may become less and less effective witnesses without special considerations. Innovations have taken various forms, but many include eliminating the uniformed officer interview except in emergency cases and substituting the detective interview, or combining interviews such as the detective-prosecutor or

detective-CPS worker conducting the only interview. In some areas
the interview is videotaped for subsequent viewing by other personnel
such as prosecutors, grand jury members, or defense counsel. Occasionally the videotape may be used in court and several states have
legislation allowing this. In one case the judge agreed to grant a
defense-requested delay for trial, but insisted that the child's
testimony be taken on videotape because of the significant impact
the delay could have on a young child's memory.

The importance of the investigative interview has been well
established. The facts of the case are usually gotten from the child
and there is rarely any physical evidence--for example, injury, in-
fection, or witnesses. The competency of the child as a witness is
also evaluated during the interview. Eliciting the most complete
history from children requires sensitivity, and expertise. The interview must be done in a way that the children understand the questions (content and manner of asking), and are comfortable enough to
respond. There are many programs which provide interviewers with
special training in communicating with children in appropriate language, talking about sexual matters, anticipating and allaying the
child's fears, and explaining the purpose and the process of the criminal justice system. Interviewing guidelines have been developed
and aids to successful interviewing are commonly used, such as special interviewing rooms, with or without a one-way mirror, having
toys and drawing materials, and the presence of a support person
(Berliner and Stevens 1980). Anatomically correct dolls are commercially available to assist children in describing sexual activities.

The prosecuting attorney makes the decision on whether to file
charges, what charges to file, how many counts, during what time
period, and in what jurisdiction. Depending on the jurisdiction
there will be different laws and different proceedings governing the
discretionary powers of the prosecuting attorney. There are also requirements for establishing the competency of child witnesses. During the past ten years there has been increasing willingness to file
charges based simply on the child's statement, except in jurisdictions
where corroboration is statutorily required.

In communities with highly developed networks of services and
agencies there is a strong likelihood that the offender will plead
guilty and a trial avoided (Conte and Berliner 1983). The filing
standards may be tailored to the particular nature of the crimes
committed over a period of time prior to reporting and, since children are not able to really recall dates and times like adults, the
charging practices are usually modified. For example, one or two
counts of a crime may be charges to cover a period of time and a
plea to one count may be accepted. District attorneys are encouraged
to file cases with the objective of seeking a plea in exchange for
some kind of recommendation for treatment instead of or in addition
to punishment. Some of the procedural changes include formation of
special units to handle the cases so that the same deputy prosecutor
handles the case throughout. In jurisdictions which require a grand
jury investigation or a preliminary hearing, videotape or depositions
are sometimes allowed to substitute for actual testimony.

There is always a percentage of cases that actually go to trial
and where children must usually testify. Special approaches have
been developed for handling cases involving children as witnesses
in trial. Preparation for testifying will often include a trip to

visit a courtroom, a practice session on the witness stand, and an explanation of what is going to happen. An advocate is recommended for the child and family either from a community agency or within the prosecutor's office. In communities with operating victim witness programs there may be assistance with child care, transportation, and parking. Secluded waiting areas and information pamphlets or movies are sometimes provided. Whenever possible, the witnesses are notified in a timely way and unnecessary trips to the courthouse are avoided.

Prosecuting attorneys have learned effective strategies for successfully prosecuting these cases. At every opportunity the issue of the inherent credibility of children is promoted, because the case will usually rest primarily on the victim's testimony. The voir dire process of selecting jurors will explore whether a child's testimony will be taken seriously and there is a search for prejudicial beliefs about children or sexual abuse. In most states the prosecutor must establish competency of child victims before they can testify; there are certain legal standards which must be met relating to the child's memory at the time of the event, the ability to retain independent recollection, and the ability to understand and answer simple questions and to demonstrate knowing the difference between telling the truth and telling a lie. The type and manner of questioning for competency can also greatly enhance the credibility of the child. A good prosecutor has learned a series of sensible and effective questions which show that children can distinguish events accurately. Courts seem to have increasingly taken a broader interpretation of competence requirements and allowed young children to testify. Judges are usually willing to intervene to block inappropriate or deliberately confusing interrogation by defense counsel. Prosecutors are more likely to request and receive latitude in questioning, with more leading questions allowed. Most judges are very solicitous of young witnesses and may allow some testimony to be taken in chambers, or have the courtroom cleared while young victims testify. The children may be permitted to sit next to the judge or prosecutors or on a parent's lap, and taken frequent breaks. Demonstrations by the child with dolls or drawings may be allowed and there may be limitations on the length and kind of direct and cross-examination.

While corroboration in a traditional sense is not common, the prosecuting attorney may try to introduce witnesses or testimony which will enhance or support childrens' testimony. This may include testimony by others the child has told, which may be brought into evidence through an exception to the hearsay rule, such as excited utterance or statements made for the purposes of the medical examination. Many prosecutors have tried to expand the definition of the exception to encompass the particular characteristics of child sexual abuse and several states are attempting to create through statute a new exception for these cases. Sometimes testimony by relatives or teachers about a change in the child's behavior or attitude toward the defendant can be introduced. Expert testimony has been allowed in several jurisdictions to describe what is know about the characteristics and dynamics of child sexual abuse, for example, delay in reporting, or mixed feelings toward the offender. This kind of information gives the jurors an appropriate context in which to deliberate on the evidence so that apparent inconsistencies can be better explained and understood (Bulkley 1981).

Once a conviction is obtained, either through a plea or trial
and conviction, the dispositional phase occurs. Generally the judge
will receive formal recommendations from the prosecutor, the defense
counsel, and the probation department. There may be direct or indirect imput from the victim and family, offender and family, and
other interested community members. The judge will be constrained
by statutory sentencing options and ranges, and the judge's decision
is often modified by the parole board, which sets minimum and maximum
sentences. The outcome of cases is influenced by the climate of the
professional and law community and the level of cooperation with the
criminal justice system in a given community. In communities with
supportive professionals with a range of treatment programs, there
will be a greater number of people sentenced to community-based treatment in addition to punishment.

There have been significant changes in the laws relating to
sexual assault in the past ten years. Major reform legislation has
passed in most states, making changes in definition, corroboration
requirements, and prohibiting information about the victim's past experiences into court. These efforts have been directed primarily at
forcible rape, but often include the laws on child molesting and incest (Bienen 1980). Some states, such as Washington and California,
have passed specific legislation about child sexual assault and hearsay exceptions to extend the statute of limitations to closed court-
rooms for childrens' testimony. Victim witness legislation has also
benefited child victims through laws which allow an advocate to be
present, require notification of court appearances, restitution and
victims compensation.

Experience in the last ten years has shown that child sexual
assault cases can be successfully prosecuted when the criminal justice
system responds to the concerns about the system-induced trauma and
punishment, the possibility of rehabilitation is addressed, as well
as promoting the safety of the community. The mental health and medical community has become more cooperative with the legal system and
more involved in developing treatment programs and working with the
justice system personnel. Almost every community is now acknowledging
that the problem exists and is seeking to develop some kind of coordinated response.

There has been a great deal of change in the awareness and response to child sexual assault. There is much still to be learned
and new questions and barriers which were not known or anticipated
are now apparent. Doing a better job and knowing more will not be
enough to reduce the incidence of this crime. Some of the issues to
be further addressed concern what to do about those cases which simply
cannot or should not become involved in the criminal justice system,
as when the victim is an infant or nonverbal. No matter how likely
it is that the crime has been committed, some children are too young
to be truly competent as witnesses. With more education, children
may report sexual abuse situations earlier, perhaps before an actual
criminal act has been committed and no charges can be filed. Those
cases cannot be ignored, but no one is designated the responsibility
to intervene.

The criminal justice system itself is in the midst of a swing
against rehabilitation and towards determinant punishment and presumptive sentences. Sexual psychopath laws and indeterminate sentences are going out of favor (Prager 1982). Community supervision and

parole are being eliminated. Programs which have been built around diversion or probation requirements for treatment may be in jeopardy unless there is an active community organization to continue sentencing options in these cases.

One area yet to be explored is a questioning of the values and structure of the adversary system of legal justice. Changes in attitude, procedures, and policy have been made without directly challenging the basic premise of the legal system in this country. It is an inescapable fact that individuals break the laws against sexual contact with children with shocking frequency and with almost complete impunity. In the few cases when they are caught, the legal system has seemed to operate in a way which benefits the accused and discounts and traumatizes the victim. The law is a social institution and can and should be open to change when it is not serving its basic function in society.

REFERENCES

Berliner, L., and D. Stevens. "Advocating for Sexually Abused Children in the Criminal Justice System." *Sexual Abuse of Children: Selected Readings*. U.S. Department of Health and Human Services, Washington, D.C.: National Center on Child Abuse and Neglect, 1980.

Bienen, L. "Rape III: National Developments in Rape Reform Legislation." *Women's Rights Law Reporter* 6 (1980): 177–213.

Bienen, L. "A Question of Credibility: John Henry Wigmore's Use of Scientific Authority in Section 924a of the Treatise on Evidence," 19 Cal. W.L. Rev. 235 (1983).

Brecher, E. *Treatment Programs for Sex Offenders*. Washington, D.C.: Law Enforcement Assistance Administration, 1978.

Bulkley, J. *Child Sexual Abuse and the Law*. American Bar Association, Washington, D.C.: National Legal Resource Center for Child Advocacy and Protection, 1981.

Burgess, A.W., A.N. Groth, L.L. Holmstrom, and S.M. Sgroi. *Sexual Assault of Children and Adolescents*. Lexington, Massachusetts: D.C. Heath, 1978.

Conte, J.R., and L. Berliner. "Prosecution of the Offender in Cases of Sexual Assault Against Children." *Victimology* 8 (1983):

Conte, J.R., and L. Berliner. "Sexual Abuse of Children: Implications for Practice." *Social Casework: The Journal of Contemporary Social Work* December (1981): 601–606.

DeFrancis, V. "Protecting the Child Victim of Sex Crimes Committed by Adults." *Federal Probation* 35 (1971): 15–20.

Finkelhor, D. *Sexually Victimized Children*. New York: Free Press, 1979.

Kinsey, A.C., W. Pomeroy, C. Martin and P. Gebhard. *Sexual Behavior in the Human Female*. Philadelphia, Pennsylvania: Saunders, 1953.

Kirkwood, L. "Incest and the Legal System: Inadequacies and Alternatives." *University of California, Davis Law Review* 12 (1979).

Kroth, J.A. *Child Sexual Abuse: Analysis of a Family Therapy Approach*. Springfield, Illinois: Charles C. Thomas, 1979.

Landis, J.T. "Experiences of 500 Children with Adult Sexual Devia-
    tion." *Psychiatric Quarterly* 30 (1956): 91-109.

Libai, D. "The Protection of the Child Victim of a Sexual Offense
    in the Criminal Justice System." *Wayne Law Review* 15 (1969):
    979-1032.

National Center on Child Abuse and Neglect. *Child Abuse and Neglect
    State Reporting Laws*. U.S. Department of Health and Human Services,
    Washington, D.C., 1980.

National Legal Resource Center for Child Advocacy and Protection.
    Innovations in the Prosecution of Child Sexual Abuse Cases. Ameri-
    can Bar Association, Washington, D.C., 1981.

Prager, I. "Sexual Psychopathy and Child Molesters: The Experiment
    Fails." *Journal of Juvenile Law* 6 (1982):

Russell, D. "The Incidence and Prevalence of Intrafamilial and
    Extrafamilial Sexual Abuse of Female Children." *Child Abuse and
    Neglect: The International Journal* (1983): 133-146.

PART IV

THE AGGRESSOR

The dynamics of human aggression have been an area of study through the ages. The past decade has renewed interest in the motivation of the aggressor and in rape behavior. Part IV presents a wide range of research expertise not only in viewing the aggressor from many perspectives, but also in studying the treatment approaches and new investigative techniques for the apprehension of suspects.

CHAPTER 16

RAPE AND RAPE-MURDER: ONE OFFENDER AND TWELVE VICTIMS

Robert K. Ressler, Ann Wolbert Burgess and John E. Douglas

Rape-murder is a crime of increasing concern in our society. It is difficult to gather dependable statistics on the number of people who die this way for several reasons: (1) the victim is officially reported as a homicide statistic and not as a rape assault; (2) evidence is inconclusive or lacking to determine that the victim has been sexually assaulted;[3] and (3) there is failure to recognize the underlying sexual dynamics of an "ordinary" murder.[4,5]

Taken separately, the crimes of rape and murder are increasing. The 1980 FBI Uniform Crime Reports indicate a 13.2% increase in the number of rape offenses between the years 1978 and 1979[6] and a 9.7% increase in the number of murders in the same time frame.[7] However, the incidence of rape-murder is difficult to estimate. Hayman et al.[8] reported that a total of 7 victims (N = 1223) were brought to D.C. General Hospital dead on arrival. Of the 7 victims, four were reported definitely raped and three were probably raped. In examining 444 homicide cases from records maintained by a court-based diagnostic and evaluation clinic on a 50% sample between 1955-1973, only 5 cases were said to qualify as sexual homicide.[9] Extrapolating from national statistics in 1973, Brownmiller estimated 400 rape-murders per year.[2]

Research on rape-murder stands to be compartmentalized according to type of crime and by the parties involved.[10] And although the literature is replete with reports on the murderer, it is relatively silent on the victims. This omission from the professional literature

---

Reprinted with permission, *American Journal of Psychiatry* 140:1, January 1983, pp. 36-40. Supported in part by National Institute of Justice grant CX-0065. Copyright 1983 American Psychiatric Association.

significantly impedes our understanding of the possible parameters
of a rape assault and handicaps our progress in victimology. To
contribute to the study of rape-murder, this paper analyzes 13 rape-
motivated crimes by one teenage offender over a four-year period.

METHOD

In the spring of 1978 the Training Division of the Federal
Bureau of Investigation issued a mandate to its staff to conduct
original, in-depth research in order to advance the state of
knowledge in areas relevant to the law enforcement community.
Sexual homicide cases were selected as the initial area of focus and
concentration, given that it is a lethal type of crime which attracts
a great deal of public attention. An interview guide was developed
for accumulating data through interviews and law enforcement records,[11]
and the criteria for the sample population were derived as follows:

Convicted murderers of three or more victims
Access to retrospective crime scene evidence for corroboration
Available prison and court evaluation records
Consent of subject and prison staff for participation in the
study

This article reports one case from the larger study that will
address such issues as crime scene investigation, typology of sex-
related murder, and murder prevention.

Sample

Offender Profile. The offender, born in 1958 in the mid-west,
was the youngest of three children with an older adopted brother and
natural sister. The parents separated and divorced when the offender
was 7, and both parents remarried shortly thereafter. The offender
continued to live with his mother even though the second marriage
dissolved in 1970. The offender completed age-level work until his
senior year in high school when he was involuntarily withdrawn from
school due to excessive absenteeism and lack of progress. The
offender was of average intelligence and had aspired to attend
college. He was athletically inclined and played league baseball.
He was outgoing, often attended social events, had a close circle
of firends, both male as well as female. He saw himself as a leader,
not a follower. At birth, it is reported that he was an RH baby
and required a complete blood transfusion. He had reportedly suffered
no major health problems.

The offender was sent out-of-state to a psychiatric residential
facility following his first felony of rape and burglary at age 14.
During his nineteen-month stay he received regular individual insight
psychotherapy, and the discharge recommendation was that he live at
home, attend public school, and continue psychotherapy on a weekly
outpatient basis with his mother actively involved in his treatment.
The offender readily admitted to the use of alcohol and drugs of
all types from his early teen years. He worked sporadically throughout his high school years in a program where he attended school in
the morning and worked in the afternoon. The offender's anti-social
behavior was first recorded at 9 when he and three other boys were
caught by the school principal writing "cuss" words in the sidewalk.
The boys were required to wash the sidewalks until the words were
removed. Starting at 12, his criminal behavior record begins with

assaultive and disruptive behavior--he broke into an apartment--and
stealing property valued at $100. At 13 he was charged with driving
without an operator's license; at 14 he was charged with burglary and
rape and committed two other minor acts of petty larceny and stealing
a car before being sent to the residential facility. Three weeks
after returning home from the residential facility, he was charged
with attempted armed robbery--an act intended to be rape. This
charge took one year to come before the judge for sentencing, and
in that time the first rape and murder had been committed but not
charged to the offender. This disposition on the attempted armed
robbery was probation and out-patient psychotherapy from September
1976 until his apprehension for the 5 murders in May 1977. His
psychiatric diagnoses have included: adolescent adjustment reaction,
character disorder without psychosis, and multiple personality. At
the time of his arrest for the murders the young man was 19 years
old, weighed 144 pounds and was 5'7" tall. He was given five life
sentences for the five rape-murders. After two years of incarceration,
he admitted to 6 additional rapes for which he was never charged.

    Victim Profiles. Of the 13 victims, 8 were white, 4 were black
and 1 was Cuban. All were female with an age range of 17-34, and all
were older than the offender by as much as 9 years. Several victims
were taller and heavier. Ten victims were total strangers; three
unknown by sight. Two of the ten stranger-victims recognized him
after capture. All of the victims were of middle-income status,
and the majority lived in the apartment complex where the offender
also lived with his mother. All of the victims except one high
school student were employed full-time, working such positions as
teacher, postal supervisor, store buyer, airline stewardess, administrative assistant. Some victims, in addition, carried part-time
jobs as well or were continuing their college education. The majority
of victims were not married; several were divorced. Two victims were
known to have children. Five of the women were raped and murdered;
five were raped; two were gang-raped; and one escaped from the
offender prior to the completion of a criminal act. Most of the
victims were approached at knifepoint as they entered the elevator
to their apartment building. All rape-murder victims were abducted
from the same location, killed in different areas, and found fully
clothed. The time difference in locating their bodies ranged from
one day to six weeks.

Data Collection

    Data collection was achieved in two ways: (1) interviews with
the offender and completion of an interview guide;[11] and (2) use of
police reports, court evaluation records, photographs of crime scene
investigations, and medical examiner's reports. An obvious limitation
to the interviews is having to rely on the offender's retrospective
memory and reconstruction of the crime. This bias has been countered
with documentation from prison and court records. On the other hand,
the offender's admission of 6 additional rapes adds to the data not
available in official channels. Another methodological drawback is
that the information on what victims say and do comes from the
offender. The data are secondhand. There does not seem to be any
way to solve this problem. Rape-murder is not something that
researchers can observe firsthand. And only a small percentage of
rape-murders are available to researchers.

FINDINGS

The analysis of data suggest that the offender's criminal

TABLE 1

ESCALATION OF CRIMINAL BEHAVIOR

Date	Offender's Age	Offense	Victim's Age/Race	Disposition
9/1971	12	Petty Larceny		Probation: 11/71-6/72
9/1971	12	Disrupting School		Probation: 11/71-6/72
10/1972	13	No Operator's License		Continued till 18th birthday
4/1973	14	Burglary & Rape	25/white	State Dept. Welfare Inst. (Psychiatr. Ctr. 2/74-8/75)
6/1973	14	Petty Larceny		SDWI
7/1973	14	Breaking & Entering		SDWI
12/1974	16	Rape	25/black	Never charged
2/1975	16	Rape	25/Cuban	Never charged
3/1975	16	Burglary & Rape (co-defendant)	17/white	Never charged
6/1975	16	Rape (co-defendant)	25/white	Never charged
9/1975	17	Attempted Armed Robbery	22/white	Probation & Out-Psych. Under probation 9/14/76-5/30/77
4/1976	18	Rape	25/white	Never charged
8/1976	18	Rape & Murder	24/white	Life
3/1977	19	Rape & Murder	22/white	Life
4/1977	19	Rape & Murder	34/black	Life
4/1977	19	Rape	25/white	Never charged
4/1977	19	Rape & Murder	27/black	Life
5/1977	19	Rape & Murder	24/white	Life

behavior changed in two major ways: (1) the sexual aggression escalated
from rape to rape & murder, and (2) the offenses increased in frequency
as noted by the decrease in time between offenses (see Table 1).
Of special note are the facts that (1) all rape & murder offenses
except the first were committed while the offender was under
psychiatric supervision and probationary regulation; (2) the six
rapes that were not charged to the offender were also commited
while he was under psychiatric supervision and probationary regulation;
and (3) the five homicides were neither linked to one offender nor
indicated to include rape until the offender was apprehended and
described the offenses.

Rape: The First Seven Offenses

The first charged rape, in 1973 when the offender was 14,
occurred in the next apartment to where the offender lived with
his mother. The offender had returned home from a party, went to
bed, woke up fantasizing about the 25-year-old divorced neighbor
woman who often employed him for small errands. He got up, went
outside wearing a ski mask, scaled the apartment wall as a "cat
burglar," entered the woman's third floor apartment through her
patio door. He raped the woman several times, left through her
front door, returned to his own apartment and went to sleep. He
was apprehended three weeks later and eventually convicted on
evidence found in the apartment (i.e., fingerprints, clothing) and,
not on the victim's identification of him. A woman judge sentenced
him to an out-of-state psychiatric residential facility.
The second rape (first never-charged rape) occurred in 1974
when he was home for Christmas vacation. The evening prior to his
returning to the residential facility, he approached a black woman
in the elevator to the apartment complex and at knife point took
her to another location and raped her. The second never-charged
rape (third in sequence) occurred three months later when he approached
a Cuban woman in the school parking lot where he was attending a local
school for the residential facility. He forced the woman at kinfe-
point to drive to her apartment where he raped her. The third and
fourth never-charged rapes included co-defendents. While on a weekend
pass, the offender and two patients stole a car, traveled out of state,
broke into a house, stole two guns and money and each raped a white
17-year-old girl who was in the house. The offender did return home,
however, his mother immediately sent him back to the residential
facility and he was counseled on his runaway behavior. Three months
after returning to the facility the offender and another patient went
to a local swimming pool. They broke into a women's locker room and
raped a young woman, covering her head with a towel.
The fifth offense was three weeks after his release from the
residential treatment facility when he was arrested for attempted
armed robbery. He had targeted a woman entering the elevator of
the apartment complex, wore a ski mask and held a knife to the victim.
She was successful in escaping as follows:

> She broke. . .pushed me out of the way and
> started going to the front of the elevator,
> pushed the button to open the door and started
> to run and she stumbled. I'd started to run
> after her and stumbled over her and at that
> point the knife fell and she was on the ground
> hollering and I was on the ground next to her,

>   scared to death. My mind went blank. I ran
>   out of the building

     The sixth rape (5th never-charged rape) was prior to his first
rape and murder and was a woman he had seen in his own apartment
building. He obtained an air pistol, captured her in the apartment
elevator, took her to a storage room and raped her twice, covering
her face with her jacket.
     During all the rapes, the offender was very concerned about
being identified. During the rapes, he either covered the victim's
face, wore a mask, or left town immediately following. However,
in the 7 offenses, he was caught twice and both times he had worn
the mask. Although the first rape victim was not able to positively
identify him, the 6th victim did make a positive identification.

Murder: The Last Six Offenses

     The last six victims were selected at random as the offender
watched cars drive into the apartment complex where he lived. Once
targeted, the offender would then walk behind the victim, follow her
into the apartment elevator, pull his knife and tell her it was a
stick-up. Then they would leave the building, either for the
victim's car or for an area near the apartment complex. In one
case the pattern was reversed. The offender was hitchhiking, given
a ride by a woman who was going to a party in his apartment complex.
She let him off at his building; he then watched her park her car and
then ran across the complex, entered the elevator with her and captured
her there. All abductions and murders occurred within his own territory.
Thus, known territory was a distinct advantage for the offender ("Going
somewhere that I didn't know or where the cops patrolled might get
me caught. I knew what time the cops came by in the morning because
I'd be sitting there.") Indeed he was right. One of the reasons
he was not caught until after the 5th murder was the police were
looking for strangers and suspicious characters--not a teenager
living in the area.
     The offender's use of either verbal and/or physical strategies
to assert control over the victim depended on the initial response
of the victim. The victim who was compliant with the show of a weapon
received no additional threats or orders. Victims who screamed
received verbal threats and those who refused to cooperate were
physically struck as in the following example.

>   She faints and falls down on the floor. I pat
>   her face. She wakes up, has a real frightened
>   look on her face and she starts to scream. I
>   put my hand over her mouth and stick the gun to
>   her head and tell her if she screams I'm going to
>   blow her head off. She asks what I want and I
>   tell her I want money and to rape her. She balked
>   on that and said, "No white man fucking me no time."
>   I'm thinking she's one of these prejudiced types.
>   I said, "I'm gonna do what I want" and I backhanded
>   her. First time I hit one. She started whimpering
>   and crying a bit. . .We go to the basement. I tell
>   her to take off her clothes. She says, "I'm not
>   doing a damn thing." I cocked the trigger back and
>   she started hurrying up, taking off her shirt. And
>   this time I'm feeling good because I'm domineering

> over her and forcing her to do something and
> I'm thinking this prejudice bitch is going to
> do what I want when I want her to do it.

Interaction Between Offender and Victim. Reconstruction of the victims' talk and actions as viewed from the offender's perspective reveals that conversation and behavior serve to either neutralize or escalate the affective state of the offender.

Murder victim 1, rape victim 8: The victim's talk raises the offender's suspicion of her lifestyle.

> She asked, "Which way do you want it?" I
> wondered what kind of woman is this. . .told
> her to lay down. She said, "I'm going to do
> what you say. Just don't hurt me." It was
> her asking if it felt good and telling me that
> it felt good to her and that maybe we could
> work something. . .that maybe I could come
> and see her once a week or something like
> that. . .made me suspicious.

After the rape and both were dressing, the offender describes that he had not decided what to do with the victim and that her attempt to escape angers him.

> I had thought about killing her. . .saying what am
> I going to do when this is over? Am I going to
> let her go so she can call the cops and get me
> busted again? So when she took off running--
> that decided it in my mind that killing her was
> what I was going to do. I was thinking, why did
> she run? It made me mad. I was angry and
> frustrated.

The anger triggers the feeling of frustration that results in an increase in aggression and the offender states:

> She took off running down the ravine. That's
> when I grabbed her. I had her in an arm lock--
> she was bigger than me. I started choking her
> and she started spitting up on my arm. She
> started stumbling; lost consciousness. We
> rolled down the hill into the water. I banged
> her head against the side of a rock and held
> her head under water.

Death in this case was determined to be strangulation.

Murder victim 2, rape victim 9: The victim's talk consisted of many questions which served to annoy the offender:

> She asked all kinds of questions: why I wanted
> to do this; why did I pick her; didn't I have a
> girl friend; what was my problem? I am resenting
> this all the time, telling her to shut up.

As the offender and victim were driving after the rape, the offender describes that he was uncertain as to his actions. The victim questions his next move and then acts to counter his control of the car:

> She asked what I was going to do--kill her or tie
> her up and leave her. I told her I hadn't decided.
> I felt I had decided to let her go but would knock
> her out and tie her up or shoot her--not killing her--
> but hurt her to where she would know that if she
> did say anything that someone would be after her
> to scare the hell out of her. I told her all of
> this. So she started going down the road, stomps
> on the gas and says, "If you don't throw that gun
> out of the car right now I'm going to run into this
> tree down here." She's going about 70mph. I turned
> the ignition off and stepped my foot on the brakes
> and the car slides sideways. Then she gets out and
> runs across the road to the barbed wire fence. She
> sees some houses and she's screaming and trying to
> get someone's attention. It's just starting to get
> light out. I get the knife. She's run into the
> woods. I go into the woods after her. From then
> on I knew I had to kill her. She trips and falls
> over a log and that's when I catch up to her and I
> just start stabbing her.

The victim was stabbed 14 times in the chest.

   Murder victim 3, rape victim 10: The offender claimed he had
not decided whether he would kill this victim. He would not
let her talk as they drove in the car because "the more I got to
know about the woman the softer I got." He ordered the victim to be
quiet and to turn the car radio on. In this case the offender said
he decided to kill her when he heard her moving from the place where
he left her.

> I was thinking. . .I've killed two. I might as well
> kill this one too. After I killed the first two,
> I knew if I raped anybody else or robbed that I
> was going to kill them because something in me
> was wanting to kill. After the sex was over, we
> walked up the hill and then I said, "I'm going to
> have to tie you up so I can leave." Then I decided
> to kill her. I'd decided when we were driving, but
> I didn't want her getting scared and running rabbit
> on me. So I tied her up. She took off her stockings.
> I tied her feet and the back of her hands. And I
> don't know what possessed me to do it, but I started
> to walk away after I tied her up, cuz I figured
> I'd take the car and just go back and I don't know
> if she'd say anything or not. . .than I heard her
> through the woods kind of rolling around and making
> muffled sounds. And I turned back and said, "No,
> I've got to kill her. I've got to do this to
> preserve myself and protect myself." I picked up
> a rock about this size, went back there and hit her
> on the side of the head with it.

The offender also stabbed the victim and cause of death was from 21
stab wounds to the left thorax and upper abdomen.

Rape victim 11: The offender had decided to kill this victim but her talking saved her life. She told the offender that her father was dying of cancer and that she was very depressed over that fact. This talk evidently neutralized the offender's aggression ("She had it bad already.") and he decided to let her live.

> I was going to kill her, but something she said hit me and I thought of my own brother who had cancer. I couldn't kill her. She had it bad enough already. I took the car keys and threw them out in the woods and told her not to move for 10 minutes, that I was going to be up in the woods watching, but during that time I was running.

Murder victim 4, rape victim 12: The offender had decided to kill this victim. Her resistance and attempt to escape triggered his violence.

> She put back on her clothes. We took a short cut and I decided to kill her then. It was in my mind from the beginning that I would end up having to kill her. Had to go up an embankment. I helped her and as I started to climb up, she had a hold of hand like she's trying to help. She let go of my hand and swings down with her other hand and she scratched me across the side of the face. She had long nails. And I got mad, then she started to run. I got up from falling down, chased after her. As soon as she turned around and ran about two steps, she ran into a tree. I caught her. I grabbed her, we wrestled, rolled over the embankment into the water. I landed with my face in the water. She was struggling with me and my head was kind of underneath and that's where the idea just came into my head to drown her. She was fighting and she was strong. But I put her head underneath the water and I just sat there with my hands on her neck. I was spreadeagle on top of her and my knees were on both sides of her. I saw the bubbles start coming up and then the bubbles stopped. I sat there maybe a good 45 minutes before I got up out of the water.

The cause of death for this victim was by forced drowning.

Murder 5, rape victim 13: The victim's talk led the offender to realize that she knew him. This knowledge escalated the fear of disclosure and, in turn, led to the offender confessing the four previous murders.

> I realized I had known her younger brother until he was killed in an accident. I'd met her at a funeral and she had been really broken up about it. So she knew me and I knew I had to kill her. I told her I was the one that did the four murders in that area.

The decision to kill was made quickly.

> We were walking along, through the culverts,
> underneath the highway. That's when I pulled the
> knife out and without even saying, I stabbed her.
> I had the gun in this hand and the knife came from
> my back pocket and I just came around like this and
> hit her like this. She fell right there and she
> screamed as she was falling. I kept stabbing. She
> fell down and landed just on the ground. I kept
> stabbing--maybe 50-100 times.

The offender buried this victim's body in a shallow grave by moving
rocks ("Just wanted to cover her up so that if anybody would be
walking by, at first sight, unless they were really looking for a
body they wouldn't notice it.")

   Behavior Following the Murders. Following the murders, the
offender would usually (1) take some item of jewelry from the
victim's body for a souvenir, (2) go back to the victim's car and
search through her purse for money, (3) drive the victim's car
for an extended time period, (4) park the victim's car several
blocks from his apartment, (5) return to his apartment and go to
bed, and (6) watch the television and newspapers for discovery of
the body.

DISCUSSION

   Although one case does not permit generalization, an instructive
feature of this case study is that it provides additional insights
into the psychodynamics of rape and murder.

Psychodynamics of Rape-Murder

   Two concepts important in an analysis of sexual homicide are
intent (essential to criminal law) and motive (essential to the
psychology of the offender). Avison[12] defines intent to mean the
degree of intention on the part of the offender to cause the death
of his victim--ranging from clear intent to kill to no intent to
kill. Motive, in contrast, is defined to mean the reason for the
social interaction between the offender and his victim as seen from
the offender's point of view. Avison[12] further presents a division
of types of sexual homicide as (1) those with problem-solving actions,
and (2) those having a more complicated interaction between victim
and offender. Some studies suggest that rapists rarely murder[13] but
when they do, the motives are social rather than personal; that is,
to prevent detection and silence the victim.[14] This motive differs
from lust-murder whereby sexuality and aggression fuse into a single
psychological experience known as sadism.[15] Rada[16] argues, and we
agree, that rapists are capable of murder but for different reasons
than the lust murderer. One reason, Rada suggests, is that in some
rapists there appears to be a progressive increase in aggressive
fantasies toward women which over time may eventually lead to murder.[16]
   This case suggests that for some rapists there is a progression
in the offender's *intent* or decision-making toward killing. In the
first three murders the decision is made during the interaction period
between victim and offender, but in the last two murders, according
to the offender, the decision to kill had already been made. The

case also suggests an additional dimension to *motive* in rape-murder.
The contemporary view of rape sees it as an act of violence expressing
power as one motive.[17] We suggest that the psychological motive for
power expands for the rapist who murders from a need for power over
one person ("It was a real turn-on to realize the victims weren't
reporting or identifying me.") to a need for power over a collective
group ("I'm too slick for them.") that included law enforcement,
judges, psychiatrists and psychologists. As the offender put it:

> I'd been listening to the news and the fact that
> the police were baffled and then it became a contest
> more or less between me and them and how many I
> could get away with before they caught me. I thought,
> "No, they can't catch me. I'm too slick for them."
> I kept going. I'd been through the whole thing with
> psychiatrists and psychologists. Nothing was going
> to stop me from doing what I was doing until they
> caught me and I felt when they caught me they were
> going to have to kill me.

This case illustrated the influence of the affective state
when combined with various degrees of intent for lethal behavior.
A review of the offender's last 6 offenses suggest that two affective
states may influence the decision to kill: (1) escalating the anger
motive[17] in the rapist may trigger the aggression in the service of
dominance and authority, and (2) stimulating fear and decreasing the
power motive in the rapist may trigger the aggression in the service
of self-preservation.

Conclusions

The fact that the offender was under psychiatric supervision
when the majority of his criminal acts were committed suggests close
attention be paid to interviewing techniques. We offer two suggestions
on interviewing patients with criminal charges.

1. When interviewing a patient with a criminal conduct charge,
pay careful and consistent attention to the deviant behavior and
focus on all dimensions of the interactional aspects of the crime.
If possible and if within agency policy, gather supplementary data
regarding crime scene, victim statements, police interviews, official
reports, and talk with staff who have worked with the patient. This
corroborating data will provide a perspective other than the patient's
for assessment and challenge to the patient. Maintain a high index
of suspicion when patients deny or refuse to talk about their charged
crimes or deviant behavior and consider the possibility that they
are maintaining other secretive and dangerous behavior. A parallel
to the dynamics of sex and secrecy[18] can be made to incest research
and treatment.

2. Rape and attempted rape behavior should be viewed as serious,
chronic and thus repetitive. Do not assume a patient with a history
of sexual assault has only committed it the number of times for which
he or she is charged. When the patient has been under stress and
especially at times when other criminal acts have been charged to him
or her (i.e., breaking & entering, stealing cars, larceny), interview
for concurrent assaultive behavior or rape fantasies. This case

supports the findings from a study by Groth, Longo & McFadin[19] of
convicted felons and sex·offenders recommended for treatment who
report an average of 5 sexual assaults were committed by each offender
for which he was never apprehended.
The fact that a psychiatric profile was written by a psychiatrist
for this case suggests further work in this area. Psychological
profiling is an important technique in law enforcement in working
with unsolved crimes. In comparing the accuracy of the profile
when the facts of the case were known, those correct included:
gender, familiarity with the geography of the area, mode of transportation, residence, mood state, current stress, body build, and
mental state. Two inaccurate areas need to be addressed. First,
no one speculated that the victims had been raped. The fact that
all murdered victims were found fully clothed and without clinical
evidence of sexual intercourse made the cases seem non-sexually
related. The offender admitted to usually raping the victims several
times. The possibility that the offender had a sexual dysfunction--
retarded ejaculation--was never considered.[3] And second, the profile
report stated that because the offender was targeting women and using
their underwear to bind them indicated a hostility toward his mother.
While the offender talked of his mother and his father, he did say
that his mother was "ineffective in supervising him during his
formative years." However, he suggested other authority figures to
whom he was hostile:

> That woman judge sent me to a diagnostic center.
> That's what started me off resenting authority
> and bucking authority. Nobody could tell me
> what do do when to do it or how to do it.

In summary, gaps do exist in fully understanding a criminal
act in general and sexual homicide in particular because each of
the various disciplines involved work only with one part of the
picture. Cooperation through sharing of information and collaborating on cases is not practiced in the work setting. To address
this gap in the transfer and sharing of criminal data, this study
was undertaken. The research step of developing descriptive
patterns of murder as human action is encouraged by Frazier[20] with
the caution to avoid simple reductionistic conclusions about the
cause(s) of murder. We agree with this research position and
encourage studies across disciplines.

REFERENCES

1. MacDonald, J.M. *Rape Offenders and Their Victims*. Springfield,
   Ill., Charles C. Thomas, 1971:173.

2. Brownmiller, S. *Against Our Will: Men, Women and Rape*. New York,
   Simon and Schuster, 1975:215.

3. Groth, A.N., Burgess, A.W. "Sexual Dysfunction during Rape,"
   New England Journal of Medicine 297:764-766 (Oct. 6, 1977).

4. Revitch, E. "Sex Murder and the Potential Sex Murderer,"
   Diseases of the Nervous System 26:640-648, 1965.

5. Cormier, B.M., Simons, S.P. "The Problem of the Dangerous Sexual
   Offender," *Canadian Psychiatric Association Journal* 14:329-334,
   1969.

6. Federal Bureau of Investigation. "Crime in the United States," *Uniform Crime Reports, 1978-1979*, Washington, D.C.: U.S. Government Printing Office, p. 13

7. Federal Bureau of Investigation, "Crime in the United States," *Uniform Crime Reports, 1978-1979*, Washington, D.C.: U.S. Government Printing Office, p. 6

8. Haymen, C.R., Lanza C., Fuentes, R., Algor, K. "Rape in the District of Columbia," *American Journal of Obstetrics and Gynecology*, 111 (1) 91-97, May, 1972.

9. Swigert, V.L., Rarrel, R.A., Yoles, W.C. "Sexual homicide: Social, Psychological and Legal Aspects," *Archives of Sexual Behavior* 5 (5) 391-401, Sept. 1976.

10. Katz, S., Mazur, M.A. *Understanding the Rape Victim: A Synthesis of Research Findings*, New York, Wiley, 1979.

11. Ressler, R.K., Douglas, J.E., Groth, A.N., Burgess, A.W. "Offender Profiles: A Multidisciplinary Approach," *FBI Law Enforcement Bulletin* 49(9) 16-20, 1980.

12. Avison, N.H. "Victims of Homicide," in *Victimology: A New Focus*, Vol. IV, *Violence and Its Victims*, edited by Drapkin I., Viano E., Lexington, Mass., D.C. Heath Co., 1973, pp. 55-68.

13. Selkin, J. "Rape," *Psychology Today* 8:70-72, 74, 76, January 1975.

14. Podolsky, E. "Sexual Violence." *Medical Digest* 34:60-63, 1966.

15. Groth, A.N. with Birnbaum, H.J. *Men Who Rape*, New York, Plenum, 1979, p. 44.

16. Rada, R.T. "Psychological Factors in Rapist Behavior," In *Clinical Aspects of the Rapist*, edited by Rada, R.T., New York, Grune & Stratton, 1978, pp. 51-52

17. Groth, A.N., Burgess, A.W., Holmstrom, L.L. "Rape: Power, Anger and Sexuality," *American Journal of Psychiatry* 134:11, November 1977, pp. 1239-1243.

18. Burgess, A.W., Holmstrom, L.L. "Sexual Trauma of Children and Adolescents: Pressure, Sex and Secrecy," *Nursing Clinics of North America* 10:3 Sept. 1975, 551-563.

19. Groth, A.N., Longo, R., McFadin, B. "Undetected Recidivism among Rapists and Child Molesters," *Crime and Delinquency* (forthcoming).

20. Frazier, S.H. "Murder--Single and Multiple," *Aggression* 52:304-312, 1974.

CHAPTER 17

CLASSIFICATION OF SEXUAL OFFENDERS;
PERSPECTIVES, METHODS, AND VALIDATION

Raymond A. Knight, Ruth Rosenberg,
and Beth A. Schneider

There is growing concern in society over the frequency of sexual offenses and the seriousness of both the physical and psychological harm to the victims (Burgess and Holmstrom 1974; Burgess and Lazare 1976; Finkelhor 1979; Geiser 1979; Jaffe et al. 1975; Jones et al. 1980; Norris and Feldman-Summers 1981; Peters 1976). Society's recognition of this damage is reflected in the special legislation many states have passed to deal specifically with such offenders (Bowman and Engel 1965; Kozol et al. 1972; Sullivan 1976). The evidence that has provoked such concern, however, is only the tip of the iceberg. It is estimated that only one in five rapes comes to the attention of the police (Brownmiller 1975), and that only one in ten leads to arrest (Peterson et al. 1980). Pedophilic offenses are even less frequently reported because of the insufficient resources and low status of children.

Despite the gravity of the problem, the amount of systematic empirical research directed at understanding the perpetrators of rape and child molestation has been minimal. The bulk of the data thus far accumulated has been predominantly descriptive, portraying sex offenders sampled from diverse correctional and psychiatric facilities (Abrahamsen 1950; Apfelberg et al. 1944; Brancale et al. 1965; Ellis and Brancale 1956; Frosch and Bromberg 1939; Gebhard et al. 1965; Glueck 1956; Henn et al. 1976; McCaldron 1967; Mohr et al. 1964; Pacht and Cowden 1974; Pacht et al. 1962; Rada 1975, 1976; Revitch and Weiss 1962; Shaskan 1939; Swenson and Grimes 1958). Although an adequate description of offender characteristics is an essential primary step for scientific investigation (Hempel 1965), the quality of these data has been so compromised by definitional and

[1] Research conducted at the Massachusetts Treatment Center described in this chapter is supported by grants from the National Institute of Mental Health (MH 32309) and the National Institute of Justice (82-IJ-CX-0058. Our collaborators in this research have included Leonard Bard, Richard Boucher, Daniel Carter, David Cerce, Murray Cohen, Ralph Garofalo, Alison Martino, Denise Marvinney, Robert Prentky, and Theoharis Seghorn.

sampling limitations that they have provided at best only a weak
basis for developing scientific theories of sexual aggression. Definitions of what constitutes a "sexual offense" have varied from state
to state, resulting in marked differences in the reported frequencies
of offense and behavior categories in different samples. Such definitional problems have been compounded both by the highly vague specification of legal charges (Karpman 1954) and by the unpredictable
consequences of plea bargaining on the specification of charges
(Glueck 1956). Earlier studies were especially problematic because
"sexual offender" samples were inflated by the inclusion of groups who
are now no longer considered sexual offenders. For instance, consenting homosexuals constituted 20 to 25 percent of some early studies (e.g., Apfelberg et al. 1944; Brancale et al. 1965). Biased
sampling procedures have added further complications. Many studies
have examined offenders referred for pre-sentencing psychiatric assessment (Pacht and Cowden 1974; Swenson and Grimes 1958), thereby
overestimating the prevalence of certain psychopathological conditions among offenders. It is not surprising that descriptions of
the "typical" sexual offender or sexual offense differed widely, depending on such factors as time, place, and the sample under investigation.

One unassailable conclusion can nevertheless be drawn from these
descriptive studies. The class of "sexual offender," however it has
been defined, masks a manifest heterogeneity of offenders and crimes.
Offenders with widely varying degrees and kinds of criminal activity,
who differ in age, background, personality, psychiatric diagnosis,
race, and religion, have all been lumped together simply by the presence of aberrant sexual activity in their criminal histories. Their
sexual offenses have also varied markedly with respect to numerous
features, such as the location and time, the sex and age of the victim, the degree of planning, and the amount of violence. Despite
this manifest diversity, sexual offenders have frequently been viewed
as a homogeneous class of individuals. The discrepancy between the
myth of their homogeneity and the reality of their heterogeneity led
inevitably to a great deal of inconsistency and confusion in the
early literature regarding this group. This confusion in turn prompted the earliest efforts at classification.

Classification of entities into homogeneous groups is a fundamental process in all sciences. Without such a grounding in cohesive
constructs, the development of a scientific understanding of a domain
is impossible (Hempel 1952). Construction of an adequate typology of
offenders would not only provide a touchstone to assess the problematic cross-sample differences we have noted, but it is also an essential preliminary step to research on etiology and prognosis. If, as
the data suggest, sexual offenders do constitute a heterogeneous
group, correlational analyses between prodromal variables and current
clinical and criminal status and between current status and outcome
would be weakened. Relations among variables that might emerge if
cohesive subgroups were examined could be masked or cancelled out in
analyses of larger samples with great intra-group differences. Thus,
to the degree that subgroups within this population are heterogeneous
with respect to relevant variables, progress in important research is
blocked.

All attempts to create taxonomies must be initiated within some
conceptual framework. The very selection of what data to gather,

what behaviors to observe and ignore, necessarily requires the application of some theory, however vague or ineffable (Popper 1972).
Even statistical cluster techniques, which might seem at first glance
to epitomize an inductivist approach to taxonomy construction, pre-
suppose specific theoretical models and are unsuccessful when naive
empiricism guides the selection of their input variables (Blashfield
1980). The demands of a theoretical orientation have significant implications both for how we should approach the literature on sexual
offenders and for how we should make use of the data described there.
First, both the descriptive and clinical literatures, in spite of
their manifold methodological failings, are important sources for
discovering those behaviors, traits, and symptoms that are relevant
to any typological investigation. To the degree that we are successful in selecting the crucial discriminating variables and rejecting
irrelevant variables, we increase the probability that our typological schemes will be useful. Conversely, to the degree that we fail
to choose only theoretically important variables, we will be grouping
offenders on irrelevancies. Second, the developed typologies in this
literature are the products of active clinical practices and provide
us with the best guesses for structuring offender types.

The major intent of the present chapter is to review the data,
methods, and perspectives that provide the basis for a systematic
investigation of typologies of sexual offenders. First, we will summarize and synthesize the relevant empirical and clinical findings
from the sociological legal and psychiatric, psychometric, and phy-
siological/behavioral literatures. In keeping with a theoretical
orientation we will focus on culling out from these descriptive,
empirical literatures the crucial discriminating variables that
should form the database for either rational or empirical classification systems. Second, we will review the extant clinical typologies,
emphasizing both the key variables that form the cornerstones of
these systems and the way these systems are structured. We will also
examine the commonalities across systems to determine both whether
consistent types emerge and whether any single system sufficiently
captures the majority of these consistent types so that it can serve
as a good *a priori* system against which the incremental validity of
any new system can be judged. Finally, after integrating the empirical
and clinical literatures and summarizing the current state of typological research, we will briefly sketch the strategies necessary to advance
the field.

DESCRIPTIVE STUDIES OF SEXUAL OFFENDERS

The descriptive characteristics of rapists and child molesters
have been investigated from several different perspectives. Sociological descriptive methods have examined the sequence of events of
a sexual offense (e.g., offender-victim interactions) in an attempt
to understand these events within their sociocultural context. Studies from the legal and psychiatric perspectives have aimed at determining whether the application of descriptive categorization systems
derived to determine legal disposition or to differentiate other deviant populations can enhance the understanding of differences among
sex offender subgroups. Psychometric methods have been well-repre-
sented in the attempts to describe sexual offenders, with a wide
variety of self-report and projective techniques being administered.
Finally, physiological/behavioral measures of sexual arousal have
been made of various sex offender subgroups under a variety of stim-

ulus conditions. We will review in turn the descriptive data gathered within each of these five perspectives, attempting to abstract
from each the discriminating variables essential for the development
of a typology. It should be noted that these perspectives are by no
means mutually exclusive. Since a study may reflect more than one
perspective, it may be considered in more than one section.

Sociological Approach

The sociological perspective on sexual offenses is distinguished
by its attention to the cultural context and societal values and attitudes surrounding such acts. It emphasizes the understanding of
sexual assault within its sociocultural context. The value of such
a perspective is illustrated in studies (e.g., Chappell 1976) that
have documented radically different cross-cultural incidence rates
of various sexual offenses and have, therefore, highlighted possible
cultural influences on such behavior.

Research from the sociological perspective has typically been
descriptive in nature and the unit of study has been the rape or
child molestation "situation." Thus, victim and environmental variables like the physical setting or time of the event have been as
much a focus of this research as the offender. Indeed, the major
goal of this research has been the specification and clarification
of the relations among offender, victim, physical situation, and
socio-cultural context variables.

Unlike the psychiatric and psychometric perspectives we will
discuss below, this approach has not been concerned with how offender
pathology or internal motivation contribute to offense behavior.
When the individual offender has been studied from this perspective,
it has been his social role, as expressed in demographics like age,
religion, and socioeconomic or marital status that has been examined.
Moreover, what is important in this approach is not the offender's
social role *per se*, but rather how this role interfaces with the
social role of the victim and the situational factors in the offense.
It is the interaction of the various components, not any single factor, that constitutes the crime's sociological meaning.

Despite this interactionist basis, research from the sociological perspective has yielded insights highly relevant for the development of typologies based on offender attributes. Ironically, for
example, in delineating the network of relations among offender, victim, situation, and cultural context variables, sociological studies
have contributed to taxonomic research by demonstrating that certain
victim and situational variables may be highly correlated with important offender characteristics. Similarly, sociological research does
not simply help elucidate specific cultural or subcultural conditions
that act in general to encourage or restrain rape-related behavior;
it can also shed light on particular subgroups for whom such cultural
influences play either a greater or lesser role in leading to the
commission of a sexual offense. In this regard, Amir's (1971) distinction between rapists whose offenses are role-supportive or role-
expressive and rapists whose offenses are more idiosyncratic in nature or in function exemplifies the typological implications of the
data gathered by researchers with a sociological perspective.

Such explicit reference to offender "types" within the sociological literature is rare, however. When "syndromes" are specified in
such sociological research, the type of offender is often defined by
characteristics of the offense pattern and not by specific offender
attributes. For example, Amir's (1971) pair-rapist is distinguished

by the consistent presence of a partner in crime. When certain offender attributes (often demographics) are used to discriminate particular groups (e.g., Mohr, Turner, & Jerry's (1964) senescent pedophiles), there is often little assurance that such groups share any more in common that a demographic label, and such isolated groups are never part of a structured taxonomy of offenders (Megargee, 1982).

The most detailed and exemplary sociological analysis of sexual offending is Amir's (1971) study of rape in Philadelphia. His intent was to determine whether particular patterns of rape could be discerned. To accomplish this goal he collected data on 646 cases that occurred during two separate year-long time periods (1/58-12/58 and 1/60-12/60). The unit of analysis was the entire interactional sequence between the victim and offender(s) from their initial encounter to post-rape separation. Amir gathered information on both the victim's and offender's race, age, marital status, employment level, and previous arrest record. He collected data assessing the time of day, season, and location of both the initial encounter and the actual offense. Finally, he examined characteristics of the offense itself, including the degree of planning involved, methods used to subdue the victim, degree of violence, actual acts in the offense, degree and form of victim resistance, whether or not the offense occurred during the commission of another felony, and the presence of alcohol in both the victim and offender.

Such a detailed database enabled him to determine empirically the validity of several speculations about patterns of rape and to dispel certain myths. He discovered, for example, that 1,292 offenders were involved in the 646 rape events with 370 cases involving lone perpetrators, 105 cases involving pairs of perpetrators, and 171 cases involving groups of three or more perpetrators. Clearly, rape was not exclusively a one-on-one encounter. In fact, lone perpetrators accounted for only 57 percent of the rapes in his sample. Also, 75 percent of the rapes involved some degree of planning. This seriously challenged the commonly held myth that rape is primarily an impulsive, explosive event and suggests that because there are marked individual differences on this dimension, it is important to determine whether there is covariance with offender characteristics. The large number of rapes found to occur in either the victim's or offender's residence also challenged the assumption that rape is a dark-alley or parking-garage event. Finally, related to the location data, he found that in over one-third of his cases the rapes occurred between victims and offenders who knew each other as close neighbors or acquaintances. Rape in his sample was not an event occurring exclusively or even primarily between strangers, a finding which suggests that exploring various aspects of offender/victim relationships might provide important discriminating information about offenders.

It is important to emphasize that if Amir had studied offender characteristics alone, many of the patterns he outlined would never have been uncovered. Equally important for those concerned with the development of taxonomies is the potential contribution of victim and offense characteristics to the delineation of offender types. A partial incorporation of this perspective is in fact reflected in some offender typologies that use either characteristic offense styles (e.g., Cohen et al. 1971; Groth and Burgess 1977; Groth et al. 1977; Karpman 1954) or consistent victim characteristics (Gebhard et al. 1965; Mohr et al. 1964) to specify types.

Mohr et al.'s (1964) analysis of victim and offense characteristics reinforces the importance of these variables. As part of a larger investigation of several different kinds of sexual offenders, they studied all court-referred child molesters seen at the Forensic Clinic of the Toronto Psychiatric Hospital from April, 1956 to July, 1959. Their aim was "to learn everything (they) could about the act, the agent (offender), the object (victim), and the history and consequences of the phenomenon" (p. 5). Spurred in part by the real desence of empirical data on these subjects, the authors collected detailed information that included demographic characteristics of both victims and offenders, offense characteristics (both acts involved and contextual variables), and historical data on offenders' families, social adaptation, and deviant behavior.

Mohr et al.'s results, like Amir's (1971), suggested interesting patterns and contradicted some myths. For example, these researchers identified a clear tri-modal age distribution of child molesters that formed the basis of a subsequent sample breakdown into adolescent, middle-aged, and senescent subgroups. This finding (especially in conjunction with other findings regarding the sex of the victim) suggested that the offenses have very different meanings or motivations for the three different age groups. Moreover, it shattered the stereotype that child molesters are typically older and that many manifest signs of senility.

Both Amir's and Mohr et al.'s studies illustrate the importance of attending to demographics, to victim characteristics, and to offense characteristics. Amir's results document large variances in offense styles (number of perpetrators, degree of planning, amount of violence, etc.) and in offender/victim prior relationships, and thus highlight these variables as possible typological discriminators. Mohr et al.'s data suggest further that the age and sex of a child victim as well as the child's relationship to the offender might not simply be important because of the public policy implications; these same variables may also contribute to our understanding of the psychological meanings of the offense for the offender and cue typological distinctions. Thus, the sociological perspective not only contributes to a more comprehensive theoretical understanding of the phenomenon of sexual offending (e.g., Brownmiller 1975), but it also suggests specific variables that might be important in the development of a useful taxonomy of offenders. By examining such variables from a sociological perspective, clear differences have been revealed across different sexual offending events. Such variables might in part reflect important individual differences of the offenders involved.

Legal and Psychiatric Approaches

In contrast to the sociological approach, the emphasis in legal and psychiatric studies has always rested squarely on the offender. Such a focus was inevitable given the mandate of the legal and psychiatric professions to work with individual offenders. Faced with the heterogeneity of individuals who were grouped solely on the basis of legal dispositions and who showed marked diversity in offense aims and behavior, as well as in general life history and functioning (Megargee 1982), clinicians, administrators, and researchers inevitably sought to divide offender samples into more cohesive subgroups. Both the legal and psychiatric attempts at such classification involve

the application to sex offenders of systems designed for purposes
that were not directly related either to the understanding of sexual
violence or to the discrimination of homogeneous sex offender types.
The former was created to fulfill society's need of equitably meting
out punishment for transgressions, and the latter was constructed on
other populations to discriminate various types of mental illness.
It is understandable that such legal processing and psychiatric treatment distinctions, which are so intricately involved in society's response to sexual offenders, should constitute a major focus of early
research.

  Legal, Offense-Focusing Categorization. Naturally enough, the
first sub-groups explored were defined on the basis of the events
that led to the subject's legal classification as a sexual offender
in the first place--his sexual offenses. The use of offense type to
categorize sexual offenders has been used frequently with samples of
varying size and heterogeneity. Apfelberg et al. (1944) delineated
six global classes for their sample of 250 offenders: 1) incest cases;
2) sex relations associated with force against a female "capable of
the act"; 3) statutory rape (involving consenting females "capable of
the act"; 4) homosexuality; 5) pedophilia, including all cases involving children under the age of fourteen; and 6) indecent exposure/
exhibitionism. Later studies examined subsamples of offenders distinguished on the basis of more refined descriptions and groupings of
offense types. Essentially, the question asked was whether analyzing
offender groups created by specifying various aspects of criminal
acts could reveal any consistencies in offender type. In many of
these investigations relatively large, highly mixed samples of offenders were studied. For example, Ellis and Brancale's (1956) delineation of some fifty distinct categories describing the "mechanisms" of the offenses of their sample of 1,206 offenders illustrates
this approach. They distinguished, for example, noncoital sexual assault against females over sixteen from forcible rape against females
of any age, and differentiated both of these from noncoital sexual
abuse of females less than sixteen and from homosexuality, under
whose general rubric the abuse of male children was included. Other
studies using this approach began with more restricted samples and
used offense features to arrive at even more homogeneous subgroups.
Glueck (1956), for example, gathered data only on sexual offenders
whose crimes involved sexual contact. He then differentiated his
sample into seven groups based on choice of victim--child, minor, and
adult males and females, with incestuous victims of any kind treated
as a separate group. Mohr et al. (1964), as we have seen. focused on
child molesters and exhibitionists and used a variety of criteria, including both offense and offender variables, to establish subgroups.

  Such differentiation of larger samples into more homogeneous
subgroups on the basis of offense type had obvious advantages. First,
these studies provided more specific descriptions than had been available previously. Second, since the criteria used to separate groups
were the same as those used to define the acts as illegal and the
perpetrators as "offender," the classifications has substantial face
validity. Third, categorization by offense type had the added advantage of accounting for most, if not all, of the subjects in the
sample. Thus, with the exception of the very earliest studies, such
as that of Shaskan (1939), who assigned 26% of his 100 subjects to a
category labelled "miscellaneous," most of these studies had good
"coverage" (Blashfield & Draguns, 1976; Skinner, 1981).

While these classifications improved the descriptive specificity
of sex offender studies, five methodological difficulties make the
use of the data in these studies problematic. First, as is obvious
from the examples given above, many of these studies divided their
samples into such different offense groups that cross-sample comparisons are often impossible. The same offender would be assigned to
radically different groups in different systems. For example, a violent, sadistic child molester would fall into the pedophile group of
Apfelberg et al. (1944), and thus most likely be grouped with more
passive and less aggressive individuals. This same offender could
have been classified by Ellis and Brancale (1956) as forcible rape
(if coitus had occurred), as noncoital sexual abuse (if the victim
were female and the acts excluded intercourse), or as homosexual (if
the victim had been male).

Second, even within the same study certain group comparisons may
be difficult, since many of the offense-related criteria for group
assignment were neither hierarchically organized nor consistently applied across groups. In the most common strategy, membership in one
group was determined by the presence or absence of a particular offense characteristic and in another group by a different criterion
variable. Such a procedure may result in the serious confounding of
important variables. For example, in Apfelberg et al.'s (1944) scheme,
an offender was identified as a pedophile solely as a function of victim
age, while assignment to the sexual-relations-with-force group was
determined by the amount of force used to subdue to victim. Thus,
in the former grouping differences in force or violence would be
masked, and there would be no way to compare rapists of adult women
to rapists of female minors or children.

Gebhard et al.'s (1965) system is a notable exception to this
problem of confounded dimensions. They arrived at seventeen possible
sexual offender categories by crossing and combining distinctions
that they defended as the most basic to describing a sexual offense:
1) the absence/presence of sexual contact (to separate out indecent
exposers and voyeurs); 2) the absence/presence of an immediate family
tie to the victim (to allow for a separate consideration of incest
cases); 3) the absence/presence of force or violence (correlating
with the presence/absence of consent); 4) the sex of the victim; and
5) the age of the victim--child, minor, or adult. By using such consistent organizing principles, they could empirically test multiple
group comparisons to determine the validity of the discriminators
they employed. For example, their data suggest that specific group
delimiters covaried with different offender characteristics. Juvenile
criminal history covaried with victim age. Such histories appeared
more frequently in the records of those with adult and minor victims
than of those with child victims. When, however, nonsexual criminal
history was examined, nonaggressive child molesters were distinguished
from their aggressive counterparts, who more closely resembled agres-
sors against adults and minors. Thus, differences between subgroups
were found as a function of both victim age and offense violence; the
specific nature of the differences depended on which aspect of criminal
history was analyzed. Such results confirm the importance of considering multiple dimensions simultaneously and of defining groups on
the basis of more than a single dimension. Gebhard et al.'s (1965)
work is noteworthy for its avoidance of dimension confounding, but it
is problematic for other reasons detailed below.

The third major problem of the offense classification studies
has been their handling of multiple offenses. Some studies make the
implicit and untested assumption that the particular offense coded
is typical of all the offender's sexual crimes. Such an assumption

minimizes the contribution of many nonoffender variables in the commission of any single crime like victim availability, victim resistance, precipitating stressors, etc., and ignores as well as possible
patterns or progressions in offense histories. Other researchers like
Gebhard et al. (1965) and Glueck (1956), have unfortunately resolved
this problem by multiply classifying any offenders eligible for more
than one group. Thus, in Gebhard et al.'s study, although 1,356 offenders were sampled, 1,685 offender categories were coded. Such a solution
destroys group independence and with it the possibility of comparative
analyses.

The fourth difficulty in all but the most recent studies has
been the complete failure to assess reliability for both group assignments and ratings of dimensional variables. The fact that a
primary data source for these studies has been criminal or clinical
records, which may provide only partial or contradictory information,
increases the need for such assessments, even for the simplest ratings.

The fifth problem with these studies has been the frequent failure to employ significance tests, leaving the reader to determine
which differences might be important. In those studies (e.g., Gebhard et al. 1965; Glueck 1956) in which group independence has been
destroyed, even the presentation of detailed tables does not allow
the reader to calculate statistical analyses.

Since the legal classification literature, especially the earlier studies, has been so flawed methodologically, and since replication of even such straightforward results as IQ differences has been
the exception rather than the rule (e.g., Christie et al. 1979;
Glueck 1956), conclusions about these studies must remain tentative.
We will attempt therefore to summarize the results of only those legal categories that have had adequate cross-sample representation and
have received somewhat consistent definitions across studies. The
global distinction of rapist versus child molester meets these criteria, as well as some subdivisions within each of these groups.

Among the rapist/child molester comparisons perhaps the most
surprising results, in light of early clinical writings that described
these groups very differently, are the number of similarities between
these two groups that are also typical of any general prison population. Among such commonalities are a relatively low socioeconomic
status, a high rate of high school failure or drop-out, and subsequent unstable employment of an unskilled nature (Gebhard et al. 1965;
Glueck 1956; Christie et al. 1979). Though Gebhard et al. saw some
evidence for a downward mobility from parental occupational status,
other authors (e.g., Christie et al. 1979) have emphasized a continuity from an equally poor family of origin in which the father, when
present, tended to be an unskilled laborer. Moreover, Christie et al.
(1979) reported that the alcoholism rates in the parents of both rapists
and child molesters were as high as 50 percent. Rapists and child molesters also show similarity in the percent of each group with outpatient
mental health experience and previous convictions for nonsexual offenses. It should be noted, however, that studies of defendants referred for evaluation have typically found less extensive criminal
histories in child molesters (e.g., Henn et al. 1976; Barclay and
Fjordback 1979).

The data on aggressive behavior and offenses are more contradictory. It was commonly thought that child molesters were less
likely than rapists to manifest aggression in both offense and non-
offense contexts (e.g., Kopp 1962; Revitch and Weiss 1962). Christie
et al. (1979), however, found comparable histories of nonsexual assault convictions in the two groups, and Rada's (1976) data indicated
that both groups had a similar incidence of fighting when drunk.

Marshall and Christie (1981), in reviewing the criminal records of their sample of convicted child molesters, pointed to the unexpectedly high degree of violence evident in their family backgrounds, offenses, and non-offense interpersonal behavior. These authors strongly suggest that popular conceptions of child molesters as less physically violent than rapists have overlooked important data. They cite in this regard a personal communication from Abel about a group of child molesters who showed higher levels of sexual arousal to depictions of sexual aggression than did a group of rapists. This finding appeared particularly noteworthy, since it was based on sexual offenders being treated on an outpatient basis.

The controversy over relative levels of aggression in the two groups will no doubt continue until a valid classification system exists to compare sample composition across studies. Perhaps the most that can safely be stated at present is that both child molesters and rapists show wide intragroup variability in offense aggression. This variability may be greater within the group of child molesters, since members of this group can be convicted for offenses involving little or no force, while there is an inherent element of force and aggression, by definition, in all offenses of rape. Thus, summary measures of offense aggression among child molesters may differ widely across studies as a function of the relative proportions of aggressive and nonaggressive molesters sampled, complicating interpretation of differences between rapists and child molesters.

In less controversial areas, a number of important differences between rapists and child molesters have been reported in age, achieved education, and intelligence that attest to greater heterogeneity in the latter group. Most studies have found rapists to be predominantly younger (i.e., under age thirty), while child molesters have been found to be more evenly distributed throughout the age span (Christie et al. 1979; Henn et al. 1976). This is in line with Mohr et al.'s (1964) previously mentioned finding of a tri-modal age distribution for pedophiles--adolescent, middle-aged, and senescent. Although differences in mean grade level completed have not always been obtained, Christie et al. found that significantly fewer child molesters (57 percent) had progressed beyond the eighth grade level than had rapists (74 percent). Similarly, while data on intellectual functioning as measured by IQ have been inconsistent, there is evidence from some studies for a higher incidence of mental retardation and organic brain syndrome in child molesters referred for evaluation (Henn et al. 1976; Swanson 1968). These very basic contrasts have clear implications for possible differences in other areas of functioning. Methodologically, they point to the necessity of going beyond simple comparisons of means in evaluating group differences, suggesting that one of the most important differences between the two groups may be their variability in such domains as age, education, and intellectual functioning.

Other studies have reported differences of potentially even greater psychological import. The area of social competence has constituted a major focus of such studies. Although both groups have been described as deficient in their social skills and accomplishments (e.g., Becker and Abel 1978; Glueck 1956), rapists have been found more likely to show behavioral excesses and to err by being over-assertive or explosive, while child molesters have shown more normative levels of assertion or under-assertion (Marshall et al. 1979). Rapists, not surprisingly, seem to have had greater adult heterosexual experience--they are more likely to have married (Glueck 1956) or to have cohabited for at least one year (Christie et al. 1979). Despite child molesters' self reports that they had lower self esteem and social confidence (Marshall et al. 1979), they nonetheless also reported in the same study *less* anxiety and fear around social/sexual interactions than did the rapists. The authors interpreted this finding as possibly a function of a lifetime of isolation and withdrawal which reduced the number of situations that elicited social anxiety. Such an interpretation is supported by data suggesting that child molesters do in fact show greater isolation in their formative years (Glueck 1956) and are more frequently diagnosed schizoid as adults (Apfelberg et al. 1944; Law 1979). No easy generalizations are possible, however, since the same study (Christie et al. 1979) that found child molesters less likely to maintain heterosexual relationships also found them more likely to report satisfactory relationships with their wives than did rapists. This may be attributable not only to the complex nature of interpersonal skills and attitudes (i.e., perhaps the happily married pedophiles had lower expectations than did the rapists), but also to the previously emphasized heterogeneity within the child molester group. It is possible that the child molester group studied contained a mix of offenders who either had never developed mature relationships with adult females or alternatively had turned to children only after a failure of previously successful adult adaptation. These and other intra-group differences must be accounted for in any attempt to derive cohesive subgroups.

While the rapist/child molester dichotomy is the most frequently used global division of aggressive sex offenders, it is important to note that it is not the only victim-age subgrouping possible. Gebhard et al. (1965) also studied offenders against minors ("hebephiles") and presented data suggesting that heterosexual hebephilic aggressors may be even more psychopathic than aggressors against adult women or female children. Whereas the heterosexual aggressors against children were described as "dull, alcoholic, and asocial," the heterosexual aggressors against minors were characterized as "amoral" or "subcultural" delinquents. These heterosexual, aggressive hebephiles showed the highest degree of juvenile delinquency, the earliest sexual offenses, the greatest extent of drug use, and the most unstable marriages of any of Gebhard et al.'s groups (though it must be remembered that statistical comparisons were lacking). These findings may in part be related to this group's comparatively young age. Even so, these data suggest that finer breakdowns by victim age may be beneficial for creating more homogeneous subgroups.

In addition to the age of the victim, two other offense-related variables have shown some promise for differentiating subgroups. As we suggested above, the amount of violence in the offense has discriminating power among rapists and child molester samples. The data relevant to the rapist distinctions will be discussed in the section on physiological measures. Gebhard et al. (1965) have presented data comparing violent and nonviolent child molesters. In a number of the areas assessed, the violent child molesters were more like rapists than their nonviolent counterparts. Compared to the nonviolent child molesters, they manifested higher levels of social interaction and social skills and also had a higher incidence of antisocial characteristics (e.g., frequent, brief marriages; alcoholism; etc.). It might be that the unexpectedly high incidence of antisocial behavior and antisocial personality disorder found in some child molester samples (e.g., Marshall and Christie 1981; Virkkunen 1976) is due to a large representation of either these violent offenders or the aggressive hebephiles described above. Virkkunen found that antisocial child molesters were significantly younger at their first offense and at the time of their first sexual experience, were reported to have been more hyperactive as children, and were more often married. The non-antisocial child molesters, in contrast, fit the more traditional conception of the "true" pedophile--they were described significantly more often as childish, shy and timid, and happier with children.

A second potentially discriminating offense variable is the sex of the victim. This variable has of course been explored more in relation to child molesters, since the rape of an adult male rarely comes to official attention. Mohr et al. (1964) examined preferred sex of victim--male, female, or either--in their sample of pedophiles and found corresponding differences in offending patterns. The heterosexual pedophiles tended to choose victims in the eight to eleven age range and were more likely to be acquainted with these victims. The homosexual offenders, in contrast, preferred minors with whom they were unacquainted, used alcohol less, and were more orgasm-oriented in their sexual activity. Similar findings were reported by Fisher (1969), Fisher and Howell (1970), and Glueck (1956). Mohr et al. (1964) also found that offenders who were indiscriminate in their choice of victim sex had the youngest victims and tended to be the most psychiatrically disturbed. The overrepresentation in child molester samples of offenders with such indiscriminate patterns of victim sex (e.g., Marshall et al. 1979), and the underrepresentation of homosexual pedophiles (e.g., Law 1979), particularly aggressive homosexual pedophiles (Gebhard et al. 1965), have made comparisons between the homosexual and heterosexual subgroups difficult. Not surprisingly, the majority of differences found between these groups have related to sexual experience. For example, homosexual offenders marry less frequently (Fisher and Howell 1970; Glueck 1956; Mohr et al. 1964). When differences in nonsexual spheres have emerged, it is often difficult to determine the degree to which they may simply be correlates of preferred victim age or of level of offense aggression. For example, Gebhard et al. (1965), who collected extensive data on both heterosexual and homosexual offenders against children, found a number of similarities between the two groups, including comparable patterns of alcohol use in offense and nonoffense contexts, similar incidences of psychosis or neurosis, and similar proportions of mental defectives. The homosexual child molesters, however, showed an earlier age of onset of criminal activity and a slightly greater degree of planning in their sexual offenses, both of which may be related to the fact that pedophilic child molesters (i.e., those with an exclusive or long-standing preference for children) accounted for one-half of the homosexual sample but only one-quarter to one-third of the heterosexual group. Similarly, the homosexual child molesters were found to have a more extensive nonsexual criminal history (particularly for such offenses as disorderly conduct, drunkenness, and vagrancy) and to rely somewhat more on force or threats in their sexual offenses. Since, however, the heterosexual child molesters who used force in their offenses were classified in a separate group, it is difficult to interpret these results. Thus, while victim sex might reflect the general sexual adaptation of child molesters, its role as a subtype discriminator might be limited and of secondary value to victim age and offense aggression.

In sum, several variables that may prove important in discriminating offender subgroups have emerged from studies of these individuals from a legal or offense-focusing perspective. Considerable evidence suggests that differences in victim age and offense violence tap important subgroup differences. Dichotomizing on victim age produces rapist and child molester subgroups that differ on a number of both offense and nonoffense dimensions, but this global differentiation still leaves groups that are markedly heterogeneous. The introduction of a third category, the hebephile, might reduce some of the heterogeneity within the child molester group, suggesting that it is important for us to remain flexible in the divisions we create. The data suggest that the amount of violence in the offense might either provide finer discriminations within rapist and child molester subgroups or help to isolate subtypes for whom victim age is irrelevant. Finally, the victim sex variable needs further consideration to specify its role in differentiating child molesters.

Psychiatric Perspective. In discussing the psychiatric approach we are referring specifically to studies that have diagnosed sex offenders according to established psychiatric systems (e.g., DSM I, II, or III), and not to the broader "medical model" methodology that underlies the creation of such taxonomies and constitutes a more general approach to classification. These psychiatric studies have specified the incidence and prevalence of various psychiatric disorders among sex offenders. They have consistently shown that while all diagnoses are represented in sexual offender samples, psychoses and major mental illnesses are rare (Barclay and Fjordbak 1979; Brancale et al. 1952; Frosch and Bromberg 1939; Henn et al. 1976; Groth and Birnbaum 1979; Groth and Burgess 1977; Karpman 1954). The data clearly offer little support for the notion that "insanity" causes sexual offending (Barclay and Fjordbak 1979).

A small but significant subsample of sexual offenders, ranging from 7.7 to 31 percent has been diagnosed either entirely free of psychopathology or as sexually deviant in the absence of any other disorder (Apfelberg et al. 1944; Brancale et al. 1952, 1965; Frosch and Bromberg 1939). The variation in these rates can be accounted for by sample differences (those referred for psychiatric evaluation would be expected to show a higher incidence of psychopathology) and by variability in the diagnostic systems and criteria employed. A larger proportion of sex offenders (43 percent to 77 percent) have been diagnosed as having one of the neurotic or personality disorders (Apfelberg et al. 1944; Barclay and Fjordbak 1979; Brancale et al. 1952, 1965; Frosch and Bromberg 1939; Groth and Birnbaum 1979; Groth and Burgess 1977; Guttmacher 1951; Karpman 1954; Virkkunen 1976). While differences in diagnostic criteria make cross-study comparisons difficult, the most frequently reported personality disorder for rapists has been some version of the antisocial personality disorder (e.g., Henn et al. 1976). This coincides with several rational typologies of rapists in which the defining characteristic of one type is an antisocial lifestyle with rape as only one of a large variety of antisocial behaviors (e.g., Gebhard et al. 1965; Guttmacher and Weihofen 1952; Kopp 1962; Seghorn and Cohen 1980). Although somewhat less prevalent among child molesters, antisocial personality is still the most frequently diagnosed personality disorder (e.g., Virkkunen 1976), followed by schizoid personality (e.g., Apfelberg et al. 1944).

Although alcoholism has not often been seen as a primary diagnosis in sex offender samples, it frequently appears as a problem. When rapists have been considered as one group, the incidence rate of problem drinking/alcoholism ranged from approximately one-third to a little over one-half of several samples studied (Apfelberg et al. 1944; Christie et al. 1979; Frosch and Bromberg 1939; Henn et al. 1976; Rada 1975; Rada et al. 1979). Similarly, 25 to 33 percent of several samples of child molesters have been found to have heavy drinking problems or alcoholism (Apfelberg et al. 1944; Frosch and Bromberg 1939; Henn et al. 1976; Rada 1976; Rada et al. 1979; Swanson 1968). Although the range is considerable, even at the low end (25 percent) alcohol has been found to be problematic for a substantial number of sex offenders.

Three conclusions can be drawn from these studies. First, in assessments of psychopathology in general and personality disorders in particular, sex offenders have been found quite heterogeneous. Indeed, Rosenberg (1981) and Schneider (1981) reported that in their sample of rapists and child molesters every DSM-III personality disorder was represented. These data, especially when coupled with the hypotheses from the clinical literature that personality style may be an important discriminator of types in this population (e.g., Cohen et al. 1971; Groth and Birnbaum 1979; Kopp 1962), suggest that assessments of such styles should be considered in creating typologies of such offenders. Indeed, the antisocial personality might constitute by itself a cohesive type (e.g., Virkkunen 1976). Second, although only a small proportion of sex offenders have been diagnosed as psychotic or mentally retarded, such atypical offenders might add considerable noise to any typological analysis. Some investigators (e.g., Gebhard et al. 1965; Rada 1978) have dealt with this problem by separating out those offenders. They have essentially determined the offense behavior to be of secondary diagnostic importance to a primary disorder of psychosis or severe retardation. The validity of such a solution needs to be studied. Third, alcoholism seems to be a substantial problem in both rapists and child molester groups, and more research on the significance of such abuse for sex offender typologies is important (Amir 1971; Gebhard et al. 1965).

Psychometric Approach

There is a large body of research reporting the results of psychological tests and inventories administered to sexual offenders. The instruments employed have included: (a) a variety of projective tests--the Draw-A-Person Test (e.g., Jensen et al. 1971; Wysocki and Wysocki 1977), the House-Tree-Person Test (e.g., Hammer 1954a, 1954b, 1955), the Blacky Pictures Test (e.g., Lindner 1953; Stricker 1967), and the Rorschach (e.g., Blanchard 1959; Hammer and Jacks 1955; Piotrowski and Abrahamsen 1952; Perdue and Lester 1972); (b) several self-report inventories--the Minnesota Multiphasic Personality Inventory (MMPI) (e.g., Armentrout and Hauer 1978; Cabeen and Coleman 1961; Carroll and Fuller 1971; McCreary 1975; Panton 1958, 1978, 1979; Rader 1977), the Edwards Personality Preference Schedule (EPPS) (Fisher and Howell 1970; Fisher and Rivlin 1981), and the Sex Inventory (SI) (Allen and Haupt 1966; Cowden and Pacht 1969; Haupt and Allen 1966; Thorne 1966a, 1966b; Thorne and Haupt 1966); and (c) the Wechsler Adult Intelligence Scale (WAIS) (e.g., Ruff et al. 1976; Wiens et al. 1959).

The projective studies of sex offenders exhibit many of the methodological flaws that have plagued much of the projective literature in general, including inadequate standardization of instructions, problems with interrater and retest reliability, poor internal consistency, spurious or illusory convergent validity (Chapman and Chapman 1967), lack of discriminant validity, and absence of cross-validation (Anastasi 1982; Jensen 1965; Kinslinger 1966). This particular literature is, unfortunately, replete with sweeping post hoc generalizations. Interpretations have frequently been made on the basis of fortuitous differences of questionable practical value. For example, Hammer's (1955) conclusion that homosexual pedophiles evidenced more serious psychopathology than rapists because they drew more "dead" trees is typical of many results and interpretations in these studies. Given the unsystematic approach of much of this research, it is not surprising that results have frequently failed to replicate (e.g., Fisher 1968; Jensen et al. 1971). Indeed, at times even contradictory results have emerged. For instance, Prandoni et al. (1973) found that sex offenders had significantly longer response latencies to Card VI of the Rorschach, while in contrast Guertin and Trembath (1953) had found earlier that they responded faster than controls to Card VI (although not significantly). Although recently there have been attempts to provide a psychometrically sound basis for certain projective instruments (e.g., Exner 1974, 1978; Wiener-Levy and Exner 1981), such measurement advances have not yet been applied to sex offenders. Since the projective studies of sex offenders have not produced a body of replicable, externally validated data about the differences among them that might contribute to typology construction, we will forgo any extensive discussion of their results.

Although the research employing self-report inventories to study sex offenders has avoided many of the pitfalls of the projective tests, it still has some serious methodological problems of its own. The MMPI is not only the self-report inventory most extensively used for the assessment of general criminal populations (Gearing 1979), but, as we shall see, it is also the most frequently used in sex offender research. We will therefore limit our methodological comments to this inventory, but our criticisms would apply to any self-report inventory. The problems Gearing highlighted as the most commonly encountered in the MMPI studies on general criminal samples also apply to the subset of studies of sex offenders. These include: no cross-study consistency of time of administration; poor sampling procedures; failure to control major sources of subject variance like race, IQ level, and age; inadequate assurance of profile validity; and insufficient analysis of profile data.

The time of administration is especially crucial in sex offender samples because of the differences in legal status, length of institutionalization, and treatment status that covary with it and could affect either a subject's response set (Dahlstrom et al. 1972) or his psychological state. Since it has been shown that sociopaths (Lawton and Kleban 1965) and prisoners (Gendreau et al. 1973) can "fake good," it is quite possible that different response sets associated with different legal statuses (whether the offender is a self-referred outpatient, a defendant awaiting trial, an observation case, a sentenced criminal, or a committed patient) could bias the results obtained. In addition, Pierce (1972) found significant differences in several MMPI scales when prisoners were tested at admission to prison and retested six weeks later. Thus, institutional adjustment or associated attitude changes might affect responding. Finally, the effects of treatment, when available, could considerably change results. Since these contextual conditions of testing vary widely across studies of sex offenders, the cross-study comparability of results is questionable.

In dealing with Gearing's (1979) four other methodological points, the sex offender research has fared rather poorly. These studies have often simply chosen samples of convenience, have made no attempt to consider the major sources of subject variance that have been demonstrated to bias results, have frequently neglected any assessment of profile validity, and have neither exhaustively analyzed their profile data nor clearly specified their criteria in determining code types. Gearing concluded that the MMPI studies of general criminal samples have limited generalizability and must be interpreted cautiously. This same conclusion is appropriate for the sex offender studies.

A final concern about using standardized self-report tests to study sex offenders has been that most of these instruments were not designed specifically to test sex offenders, and thus they might not adequately sample the variables crucial for discriminating within this population (Dietrich and Berger 1979). Group equivalence cannot therefore be inferred when significant differences are not found.

In our review of the self-report literature we will focus on the most widely used inventory, the MMPI, and on the SI, which was designed specifically to discriminate sex offenders. The only other inventory with published reports on sex offenders, the EPPS, employs *ipsative* scores that do not provide an adequate psychometric base for normative analyses (Anastasi 1982). Thus, we will not consider the three EPPS studies.

The earliest MMPI assessments of sex offenders focused on ill-fated attempts to create empirically keyed scales to detect sexual offenders (e.g., Marsh et al. 1955; Peek and Storms 1956; Wattron 1958). These were followed by a number of studies in which heterogeneous sex offender groups were compared to various controls. Little or no differentiation was found either between such heterogeneous groups and normals (Carroll and Fuller 1971; Panton 1958) or between those groups and other violent offenders (Carroll and Fuller 1971; Hartman 1967; Panton 1958; Persons and Marks 1971).

Recent, more rigorous studies have found positive results by tightly defining their sex offender subgroups. Rader (1977) found that rapists manifested greater disturbance than either nonsexual assaulters or exposers, with no differences between the latter two groups. The finding of 4-3 (Pd-Hy) and 4-8 (Pd-Sc) profiles as common among rapists was in line with expectations based on previous research with violent offenders (Persons and Marks 1971). Armentrout and Hauer (1978) confirmed these results, finding a modal 4-8 profile for rapists of adults and a modal 8-4 profile for rapists of children in contrast to the single peak on scale 4 evident for non-rapist sex offenders. Similar modal profiles were obtained by Panton (1978), who found in addition that rapists of adults and of children both differed from nonviolent child molesters in scoring higher on scales 6, 8, and 9 (Pa, Sc, and Ma) and lower on scales 3 (Hy) and L.

Finer breakdowns of sex offender subgroups have also been assessed using the MMPI. In another study by Panton (1979), incestuous

and non-incestuous child molesters were compared. Both groups showed
the elevated scale 4 (Pd) and secondary peak on scale 2 (D) a scale
that had characterized nonviolent child molesters in the earlier
study. Interestingly, however, the incest offenders scored higher
on the Social Introversion (SI) scale. A study by McCreary (1975)
compared repetitive as opposed to first-time child molesters. The
group with one or more prior arrests was found to show greater disturbance, with higher scores on scales 1, 3, 4, and 8 (Hs, Hy, Pd,
and Sc).

Anderson et al. (1979) argued that previous MMPI research had
suggested a heterogeneity rather than a homogeneity of profile types
for sexual offenders. They therefore did a Q-type factor analysis
of sex offender MMPI profiles, identified three profile types, and
validated these types by comparing the groups on various social and
personality variables. Their first type, which they described as a
"bad judgment" or "low social intelligence" group, had notable peaks
on F and scale 8 (Sc) with elevations on scales 2, 4, 6, and 7 (D,
Pd, Pa, and Pt). This group had poorer military and work histories
than the other types and showed the most serious behavior disturbances on the ward. They were more likely to have degraded their victims, and they blamed their victims for the sexual assault. The
second type had peaks on scales 4 and 9 (Pd and Ma). They were seen
as primarily character disorders and showed the best pre-rape adjustment and ward behavior. The third type, who had peaks on scales 2
and 4 (D and Pd), were older and less educated and showed chronic
borderline social adjustment with more histories of alcohol abuse and
more frequent serious crimes. Thus, Anderson et al.'s results both
supported their hypothesis that consistent families of profile types
characterized sex offenders and suggested several variables that
might be important candidates in clustering these offenders.

The MMPI data give us three kinds of information relevant to
creating typologies. First, if the particular sex offender subgroups
chosen for comparison by researchers are shown to differ in important
and consistent ways on the MMPI, some *prima-facie* evidence for the
validity of the distinction(s) has been provided and the group delimiters become candidates for further typological analysis. Thus,
the MMPI studies indicate that the degree of offense violence might
be important in contrasting subgroups, even across victim age (Panton
1978), that the frequency of offenses has discriminatory power
(McCreary 1975), that relationship to the victim might identify differences among child molesters (Panton 1979) and that the age of the
victim carries substantial typological information (Armentrout and
Hauer 1978).

Second, if types generated by cluster analyses of MMPI profiles
show consistent discriminating patterns on validating variables, the
variables on which they differ might have typological importance.
Thus, Anderson et al.'s (1979) cluster study suggests that offender
age, education, pre-offense social and occupational adjustment, alcohol abuse, frequency of crimes, and institutional behavior might distinguish offender subgroups.

Third, the traits associated with the various MMPI profile configurations commonly found in sex offender samples may suggest additional group discriminators. Traits correlated with profile types
are a sounder source of discriminators than individual clinical scales.
The clinical scales were derived by an empirical keying technique that

selected items that differentiated criterion groups from controls. Since these groups differed on multiple traits, the resultant scales are multidimensional (Dahlstrom et al. 1975). Thus, sex offenders may obtain high scores on these scales for different reasons. Interpreting profile patterns reduces this difficulty (Anastasi 1982), even though it does not completely solve the problem (Gynther et al. 1973a).

As we have seen, several two-point codes have been found prevalent in sex offender samples: 4-2 (Pd-D) (Anderson et al. 1979; Panton 1979); 4-3 (Pd-Hy) (Rader 1977); 4-8 (Pd-Sc) (Armentrout and Hauer 1978; Rader 1977); and 4-9 (Pd-Ma) (Anderson et al. 1979). It is not surprising that these are also the profiles seen most frequently in general prison samples (e.g., Persons and Marks 1971), since Scale 4 (Pd) was originally developed to identify psychopathic individuals. An examination of the extensive literature on the behavioral and personality correlates of these high-point codes might be helpful in pointing to potentially important discriminators of sex offender subgroups. Some caution must be exercised, however, in interpreting the reports of such empirical correlates, since attempts at cross-sample replication have not always been successful (e.g., Buck and Graham 1978; Gynther et al. 1973a, 1973b; Lewandowski and Graham 1972). The difficulties in establishing robust, stable differences across studies have been attributed to the diversity of the samples assessed (which vary widely in age and in mental and criminal status), to the lack of standardized procedures for defining profile types, and to the small sample sizes that result when the subsamples with discrete code types have been identified (e.g., Lewandowski and Graham 1972; Walters et al. 1982). In our search for possible typology discriminators we will focus somewhat conservatively on only those descriptors for which there is some evidence of cross-study replication.

Over the years support has emerged from diverse populations (e.g., Davis and Sines 1971; Kelley and King 1979; Persons and Marks 1971; Walters et al 1982a, 1982b) for the earlier description of individuals with 4-3 profile types as hostile and angry, generally inhibited (possibly overcontrolled) but prone to episodic aggressive outbursts (Dahlstrom and Welsh 1960). This pattern may be indicative of a potential for particularly assaultive and violent crimes (Davis and Sines 1971; Gearing 1979; Persons and Marks 1971; Walters et al. 1982b), though this may be limited in discriminatory power to prison samples of comparatively young age (Buck and Graham 1978; Gynther et al. 1973b). A considerable body of research (e.g., Butcher 1965; Gilberstadt and Duker 1965; Marks and Seeman 1963) also supports the pattern of attributes linked to the 4-9 code type, originally described as "extroverted, talkative, ambitious, and energetic, frequently irritable, and occasionally violent" (Dahlstrom and Welsh 1960, p. 192). Although many of the specific correlates of this code type have not survived subsequent attempts at replication, the general picture remains an antisocial character without major mental illness (Gynther et al. 1973a) likely to be irritable and easily annoyed (Lewandowski and Graham 1972). Unfortunately, less attention has been devoted to the 4-8 code pattern, which because of its association with sexual preoccupations (Graham 1977) and crimes that are extremely brutal, often bizarre, and poorly planned (Pothast 1956) may have important implications for the study of sexual offenders. The data available from replications (e.g., Lewandowski and Graham 1972) do not contradict the depiction of individuals with 4-8 codes as displaying antisocial behavior in the context of a schizoid adaptation that is characterized by unusual thoughts and behaviors and marginal social competence (Dahlstrom and Welsh 1960). Similarly, the 4-2 code type, which was found in samples of child molesters (Panton 1978, 1979), has been infrequently studied. One recent description of such individuals in an outpatient college sample (Kelley and King 1979) concurs with Dahlstrom and Welsh's (1960) portrayal of psychopathic features (e.g., impulsivity, criminal acts, and aggression) accompanied by depressive features and substance abuse.

These data would tentatively support speculations that various personality styles (intermittent explosive (overcontrolled), antisocial, avoidant, and possibly dependent) are important in this population. The differentiating offender characteristics among these types might include the amount of anger or hostility and its manner of expression, social competence, the nature and quality of interpersonal relations (e.g., detached versus dependent/ambivalent/independent) and the activity level of the individual in the pursuit of goals (Millon 1969, 1981), and the use of alcohol and drugs. The profile differences also suggest that certain offense variables might discriminate among subtypes, such as the degree of planning and the amount of anger and violence in the assault.

Although recent MMPI studies have been more successful than earlier studies in suggesting variables for the typological study of sex offenders, the MMPI's contribution to such subgroup discrimination is limited by its failure to sample several domains important for understanding sex offenders (e.g., level and quality of psychosexual adaptation, preferred sexual orientation, and sexual practices and attitudes). It was the limitations in the assessment of sexual issues in this and other standardized inventories that led Thorne and his colleagues (Thorne 1966b; Thorne and Haupt 1966) to develop the Sex Inventory.

This instrument, the final version of which was composed of 200 true-false items, was based on the assumption that directly questioning the sexual offender about aspects of his sexual activity and attitudes may more readily yield relevant information than indirect or projective techniques. The Sex Inventory was subjected to extensive studies of the test-retest reliability of its scales (Allen and Haupt 1966), their factorial structure (Thorne 1966a), and their validity in distinguishing sex offenders from various control groups (Haupt and Allen 1966). Additionally, the Sex Inventory's usefulness in discriminating subgroups of sexual offenders was tested in a study comparing sex offenders determined under Wisconsin law to be sexually deviant to those sex offenders found not sexually deviant (Cowden and Pacht 1969). The sexually deviant group scored higher on a number of scales: Sex Drive and Interests, Sexual Frustration and Maladjustment, Loss of Sex Controls, Homosexuality, and Promiscuity. They scored significantly lower on Repression of Sexuality. An attempt was made to arrive at cutting scores to yield accurate classifications using those scales (Sexual Maladjustment and Loss of Sex Controls) that had shown significant levels of discrimination in the original construction samples. The authors concluded that this attempt at classification achieved sufficiently low levels of false positives and false negatives to warrant further investigation of the Sex Inventory as an initial screening device for sexual deviates. Cowden and Morse (1970) subsequently attempted to add a "defensiveness correction" to the SI, but this did not improve the discriminatory accuracy of the test. Howells and Wright (1978) confirmed the discriminatory power of the Sexual Maladjustment and Loss of Control scales, finding significant differences between sexual and nonsexual offenders.

In sum, the data thus far gathered support the instrument's ability to distinguish subgroups of offenders that differ markedly in their degree of sexual deviation, maladjustment, and loss of control. The SI has not, however, received sufficient empirical validation to support its use as a solitary screening device. Indeed, Thorne (1966b) repeatedly stressed that the most appropriate use of the SI was as an adjunct to other methods of clinical assessment. Unfortunately, there has not been enough research to determine whether the SI can contribute to finer typological distinctions among sex offenders.

The final area of psychometric assessment, WAIS studies, have yielded somewhat inconsistent results. Several studies have found no IQ differences between sex offenders and controls (Cabeen and Coleman 1961; Carroll and Fuller 1971; Marsh et al. 1955). Ruff et al. (1976) found that rapists had lower IQs than both nonviolent and violent nonrapists. All studies found substantial IQ variances and ranges within their heterogeneous sex offender groups, leaving unanswered the question of subgroup differences.

Physiological/Behavioral Approach

Recently, behaviorally oriented experimental psychopathologists have carried out a series of physiological and behavioral studies aimed at isolating the factors that contribute to the rapist's and child molester's sexual arousal. It was reasoned that if such components could be detected, specific behavioral measurement techniques might have both diagnostic and treatment evaluation applications (Abel et al. 1978a). Toward these ends, researchers developed a psyphysiological method that employed a penile plethysmograph to quantify precisely erotic preferences (Abel and Blanchard 1976).

A number of studies demonstrated consistent differences between the plethysmographic penile circumference responses (PRs) of men with histories of forcible sexual assault and of various controls, including nonsexual offenders and men with histories of other unconventional sexual behavior, like homosexuality, pedophilia, and exhibitionism (Abel 1976; Abel et al. 1977, 1974, 1975, 1978b; Barbaree et al. 1979; Quinsey et al. 1981). In these studies erotic audiotapes have served as stimuli. In one, mutually enjoyable intercourse with a consenting loving, involved partner is depicted. In the second, intercourse with the same partner is described, but here the woman is resisting and showing substantial physical and emotional pain. Rapists were equally aroused by both tapes, but normals and nonrapists were aroused more by the scenes of conventional loving intercourse. In one study (Abel et al. 1977), nonrapists' subjective reports closely paralleled their physiological responses, but rapists systematically downgraded their subjective report of sexual arousal to rape. This finding documented the limited value for this population of self reports of sexual arousal and preference. The PRs are not, however, completely immune to faking. Although early studies had difficulty in voluntarily controlling their PRs, later studies (Laws and Holmen 1978; Quinsey and Carrigan 1979) have demonstrated that PRs can be faked. While this does not invalidate the positive findings, it sug-

gests that researchers should take precautions to minimize these effects in future research (Laws and Holmen 1978).

The attempt to differentiate among rapists' responses to aggression generated important typological data. Abel et al. (1977) introduced a third tape to their repertoire--one depicting a man slapping,
hitting, and holding a woman down against her will, but not sexually
abusing her. Across all rapists, the nonsexual aggression tape elicited only 40 percent of the sexual arousal of the rape scene. The
most interesting results came from a comparative analysis between
rapists' case histories and PRs. Rapists with a history of preference for conventional intercourse, who resorted to rape when the victim was unwilling, showed small erections to the aggression story,
greater response to the rape tape, but the largest response to conventional intercourse. Rapists with histories of repeated sadistic
assaults on women showed minimal arousal to conventional intercourse
and a marked increase when the aggressive component was added. Moreover, the nonsexual aggression tape elicited large levels of arousal
from this group. This relation between the sexual arousal to non-
sexual-violent audiotapes and the increased probability of physically
harming victims has since been confirmed in an independent laboratory
(Quinsey and Chaplin 1982). Thus, one type of rapist seems behaviorally more responsive to the sexual component of the crime, while another
seems to require violence to achieve sexual arousal.

Abel and his colleagues further refined the relation between
rapists' differential arousal to sex and aggression in the laboratory
and in their criminal behavior by developing a "rape index"--the ratio
of arousal to rape descriptions to arousal to scenes depicting mutually consenting intercourse. This index correlated with the number of
rapes the patient had committed and the amount of violence he had
used. The researchers hypothesized that this cluster of related
variables defined a sadistic rapist. Subsequent research (Abel et al.
1978a) has continued to support the use of this index both for treatment evaluation and diagnostic purposes, even under conditions where
subjects were instructed to suppress their arousal. Also, Quinsey et
al. (1981) demonstrated that this index discriminated rapists from
normals whose instructional set gave them more freedom to respond to
deviant stimuli. One study (Quinsey and Chaplin 1982) has, however,
failed to replicate the correlation between the rape index and offense
severity.

Psychological measures have also been found sensitive to victim
age preferences (Abel et al. 1977; Freund 1967; Quinsey et al. 1975),
suggesting, as did the legal descriptive, psychiatric, and psychometric data reviewed earlier, that this age variable might have important implications for typing. Moreover, in a 29-month follow-up
study of thirty child molesters discharged or transferred from a psychiatric institution, Quinsey et al. (1980) found that a post-behavior-
al-treatment ratio of PRs to pictures of adults divided by PRs to pictures of children significantly differentiated recidivists from non-
recidivists. Since neither the pretreatment ratios nor the treatment
change scores were analyzed, it is not clear whether the absolute
level of this ratio or the ability to learn to control such responses
was able to predict outcome. The data do suggest, however, that some
aspect of PRs has predictive validity.

In addition to measuring sexual arousal, behaviorally oriented
researchers (Becker and Abel 1978; Becker et al. 1978; Whitman and
Quinsey 1981) have also contributed to the assessment and training of
social skills in sexual aggressives. Working under the hypothesis

that inadequate social skills may contribute to deviant sexual behavior of some sexual aggressives (Becker et al. 1978; Quinsey 1977),
researchers have developed and validated a heterosocial skills scale
(Barlow et al. 1977) and have begun social skills training programs
for sex offenders (Abel et al. 1978; Whitman and Quinsey 1981).
Since a subgroup of rapists have been observed to be deficient in
assertiveness (Becker and Abel 1978), it has been speculated that
such a social skills deficit in communicating needs and feelings to
significant others might lead these rapists to "displace" pent-up
frustrations on an unsuspecting and inappropriate victim. Thus, assertiveness training has been integrated into treatment programs
(Abel et al. 1978). Finally, since empathy for the feelings of others
has been found lacking in some rapists, techniques for training such
skills have been initiated (Becker et al. 1978).

The physiological-behavioral literature thus suggests several
variables that tap important components of sexual aggressives' behavior, and could serve as a basis for differentiating distinct subgroups within this population. The arousal to aggression, the target
of sexual aggression, and various aspects of the social skills deficits of the aggressor seem to constitute differentially important components of the behavior and motivation of these offenders.

Summary of the Descriptive Literature

The descriptive studies of the sex offender suggest a number of
variables as viable candidates for differentiating more homogenous
types within this population. Table 1 lists the most important variables in the descriptive research and attempts to assess the strength
of the various convergent lines of empirical support for each potential discriminator. The strength of support within each perspective
is indicated by the number of asterisks assigned to a variable. A
blank indicates that, for those studies we reviewed within a particular perspective, we found no empirical evidence supporting the potential discriminating power of a variable. One asterisk means that minimal, tentative, or inconsistent evidence was found within that perspective. A two-asterisk rating corresponds to reasonably strong
support in a single study that was not contradicted by the results
of another study in that perspective. A three-asterisk rating was assigned to those variables that showed a consistent cross-study ability
to differentiate among sex offenders. The overall potential discriminating power of a variable can thus be globally assessed by considering
both its within-perspective and across-perspective empirical support
Several caveats are necessary before examining this table.
First, the table is meant solely to provide a global estimate of the
current empirical support for the variables researchers have chosen
to consider. The absence of a variable from the list does not necessarily mean that it is useless. It might simply not have been considered in these studies. Second, although the focus of each perspective is reflected to some degree in the differential emphasis given
certain item groups (e.g., the psychiatric approach looked exclusively
at offender characteristics), this table is not intended to validate
our particular structuring of perspectives. As we indicated earlier,
these perspectives are not mutually exclusive. Although they do
serve as a convenient backdrop for organizing the descriptive research
of sex offenders, they do not deserve reification. The sole function
of the table is to summarize the network of support for the variables
specified.

It is clear from Table 1 that certain variables have had solid
empirical support (three asterisks) within several perspectives--vic-

Table 1
Empirical Support for Potential Typological Variables
Within Each Perspective

	Socio-Logical	Legal	Psychiatric	Psychometric	Physiological/Behavioral
Cultural Influences	***				
Offense Variables					
Degree of planning	**	**		*	
Time	**				
Location	**	**			
Number of offenders	**	**			
Degree of violence	**	***		**	***
Sexual acts in offense	**	***		**	
Coincidence with nonsexual offense	**				
Alcohol in offense	**	**			
Victim Characteristics					
Age	**	***		***	***
Sex	**	***			
Relation to offender	**	***		**	
Offender Characteristics					
Age	**	***		**	
Nonsexual criminal history	**	***		***	
Sexual criminal history		**		**	**
Occupational status/stability	**	**		**	
Education	*	*		**	
Social skills/adjustment		***		***	***
Assertion skills		**			*
Social anxiety		**			
Empathy					*
Heterosexual adaptation	**	***		**	
Alcohol use/abuse		***	***	***	
Intelligence	*	*	***	*	
Sexual arousal/motivation				*	***
Level of psychopathology		*	***	***	
Antisocial personality		*	***	*	
Personality styles			***	***	
Hostility/aggressiveness		*		*	
Activity level				*	
Compensatory motivation				*	

tim age, social skills, and alcohol abuse. Several additional characteristics have shown substantial discriminating power (three asterisks) within two perspectives--degree of violence, nonsexual criminal
history, level of psychopathology, and personality styles. Finally,
there are those variables that have shown cross-study validity within
a single perspective (three asterisks), but have only single-study or
inconsistent support in other perspectives--e.g., sexual acts in the
offense, victim sex and relation to offender, and offender age, heterosexual adaptation, intelligence, sexual arousal, and antisocial
personality. This last set of variables, though having a somewhat
limited network of validating evidence, is nonetheless important.
The lack of cross-perspective validation seems due to their neglect
within certain perspectives, rather than a failure of cross-perspective support.

CLASSIFICATION SCHEMES OF SEXUAL OFFENDERS

In the preceding sections we examined a number of perspectives
taken in studying sexual offenders and attempted to identify those
variables that have shown some potential for discriminating subtypes
among them. We encountered numerous studies that investigated differences among sex offender subgroups. A common research strategy
in these studies was to divide offenders into groups by creating cut-
offs on hypothetically important dimensions (e.g., victim age, offense frequency, etc.) with the intent of demonstrating the discriminatory power of these dimensions. As we have seen, such a strategy
has helped to identify relevant variables. It has, however, neither
adequately addressed the crucial problem of the multidimensional nature of such divisions, nor led to a specification of the theoretical
models that might underlie such divisions. For hypotheses about
these important issues we must turn to the typological schemes of
sexual offenders generated from specific theoretical models.

We will not attempt to provide an exhaustive review of all classification schemes proposed for sexual offenders. First, our presentation will be restricted to taxonomies of rapists and child molesters. Second, we will focus only on well-documented, clearly articulated schemes that either have been derived from well specified
theoretical models or that have been generated inductively but are
multidimensional in nature. As we will see, these two approaches
differ not only in how types are created but also in how those types
are related to one another. For those schemes that are more inductively based, the term "classification" applies only loosely, since
"a strict classification is composed of a set of variables or attributes which are linked to form a number of logically possible combi-
nations" (Clinnard and Quinney 1967, p. 2). Moreover, few of the extant offender schemes, even those that have been theoretically de-
reived, are true typologies, since "typologies are classifications
which, in addition, attempt to specify the ways in which attributes
or variables are empirically connected" (*ibid.*). We will use the
terms classification and typology interchangeably in our review, and
at the conclusion, assess the appropriateness of each term for the
systems described.

Despite differences in their manner of deriving and structuring
subtypes, the various types proposed by different investigators evidence sufficient conceptual similarity that comparisons across schemes
are possible. Tables 2 and 3 present the schemes to be reviewed,
along with the central dimensions that are consistently applied in

SEXUAL OFFENDING

TABLE 2
Rapist Classification Schemes

Secondary Diagnostic Consideration	Primary Diagnostic Consideration

Primary Diagnostic Consideration

MOTIVATION

Aggression as End/Expressive	Aggression Means/Instrumental

PSYCHOPATHIC PERSONALITY/LIFESTYLE

Present	Absent	Present and Primary Diagnosis	Absent

SADISM

Present	Absent

	Guttmacher & Weihofen (1952)	Kopp (1962)	Gebhard et al. (1965)	Groth et al. (1977)	Cohen et al. (1971); Seghorn & Cohen (1980)
	Sadistic Rapists		Assaultive-Sadistic	Anger-Excitation	Sex-Aggression Defusion/Sadistic
	Aggressive Offender	Type II Aggressive Psychopaths	Explosive	Anger-Retaliation	Aggressive Aim/Displaced anger
			Amoral Delinquents		Impulsive
	True Sex Offenders	Type I Compliant	Double Standard	Power-Reassurance	Sexual Aim/Compensatory
				Power-Assertive	

Secondary Diagnostic Consideration:

Drunken
Miscellaneous

differentiating these subgroups. These tables have been arranged so that comparable types across schemes are placed in the same rows. We considered types to be comparable if they shared many descriptive features. Our discussion will be aimed at highlighting a scheme's central features and pointing out its relation to other schemes, rather than describing each scheme exhaustively.

Rapist Classification Schemes

Guttmacher and Weihofen (1952) proposed one of the earliest rapist typologies. Psychoanalytic in its roots, this scheme differentiated three rapist subtypes on the basis of motivational components in the offense. One group was defined by the predominantly sexual aims of its offenses that were hypothesized either to release "pent-up sexual impulse(s)" or to stem from latent homosexual tendencies. Rapists in this group were considered True Sex Offenders. A second type, identified as Sadistic Rapists, included those individuals for whom aggressive motivations are at least as important, if not more important, than the sexual motivation. This group was depicted as particularly hostile to women. The third group, labelled Aggressive Offenders, was composed of individuals for whom rape is just one of a variety of acts of plunder. Specific sexual and/or aggressive motives were seen as contributing little to the understanding of this type, whose clinical picture resembles that of more generally criminal (i.e., nonsexual) offenders.

Kopp (1962) divided rapists into two types on the basis of whether the offense behavior could be seen as ego-syntonic or ego-dystonic, that is, as consonant or dissonant with the offender's characteristic style. The offenses of the Type I rapist were conceptualized as a break in the individual's character defense. As described by Kopp, this rapist is likely to feel guilty after the offense and may demonstrate some after-the-fact concern for the victim (similar to types described by Groth et al. (1977) and by Cohen et al. (1971) that are reviewed below). The Type I rapist was described as a compliant person who devotes considerable time and effort to pleasing others in an attempt to gain their appreciation and affection. Kopp reported that this type of rapist is often highly motivated to begin therapy.

Kopp described the Type II rapist as an antisocial, psychopathic individual who lacks empathy and is unconcerned with the consequences of his behavior. He was seen as cold and unfeeling and as showing no guilt for his offenses. Rape for this type is just one of many instances of aggressive exploitation. Like Guttmacher and Weihofen's Aggressive Offender, his offenses are consistent with his general style and he manifests disturbances of a characterological nature. In contrast to Kopp's Type I rapist, the Type II rapist is uninterested in therapy except as a means of gaining release from prison. Kopp considered the treatment of such offenders to be as difficult as the treatment of psychopaths who have committed nonsexual offenses.

Gebhard et al. (1965) distinguished two basic types of rapists: 1) those for whom offense aggression is a means to an end (by far the more frequent type), and 2) those for whom violence is an end in itself (whether primary or secondary). Like Guttmacher and Weihofen (1952), Gebhard and his colleagues therefore viewed the quality of aggression in the offense as a fundamental distinction between rapist subgroups, and one far-reaching in its clinical implications.

In describing their empirical findings, based on extensive interviews and archival data collection Gebhard et al. (1965), however, abandoned this simple dichotomy and reported on seven varieties of "heterosexual aggressors against adults." Although connections between these seven types and the two broader categories of aggression as means versus aggression as end can be inferred in most cases (see Table 2), Gebhard et al. did not explicitly relate the seven observed types back to the more theoretical model based on motivational themes. Since the Gebhard subtypes appear to have been derived more on the basis of salient features of observed cases than on organizing principles of a rational model, the system is less formally structured than the other taxonomies and consequently includes types that diverge somewhat from those in the other systems.

The most common of the seven types described by Gebhard et al. was the Assaultive Offender, who comprised 25 to 33 percent of the samples they studied. The offenses of this rapist were characterized by the presence of unnecessary violence, such that sexual activity alone appeared insufficient to gratify his needs. This group therefore clearly belongs in the more general category of offenders for whom aggression is an aim in itself. Gebhard et al. found that the rapists in this group were generally unacquainted with the victim prior to the offense. They usually committed their offenses alone and rarely made any preliminary attempts at seduction. Use of weapons was common, and the Assaultive Offender typically had a past history of violent behavior. His sexual offenses tended to include bizarre or idiosyncratic acts of some kind, such as an inexplicable theft of a trivial item. Gebhard et al. noted that this subtype had more cases of erectile dysfunction during the offense than other subtypes, an interesting finding in light of Groth and Burgess' (1977) report of erectile problems in 16 percent of their rapist sample. Such a dysfunction, if indeed it is disproportionately found in a particular subtype, could serve as an important diagnostic marker.

The second Gebhard et al. subtype was labelled the Amoral Delinquent and accounted for 12 to 17 percent of the sampled rapists. This group was distinguished by a general failure or unwillingness to heed social controls, and therefore corresponds to Gutmacher and Weihofen's (1952) Aggressive Offender. According to Gebhard and his colleagues, this rapist holds a particularly callous disregard for the rights of others, especially women, and believes that it is legitimate for a man to force a reluctant or refusing female to participate in sexual intercourse.

A somewhat similar set of beliefs is espoused by the third of Gebhard et al.'s types, the Double Standard rapist. This group included 10 percent of the sample. Though less antisocial than the Amoral Delinquents, these individuals were also seen as ascribing to the view that moderate force or threats are a justifiable means of achieving sexual intercourse. Since, however, these rapists apply this belief only to women they consider sexually lax or promiscuous and exempt other women from this attitude, the Double Standard label is quite appropriate.

The fourth Gebhard et al. subgroup, observed in 10 to 15 percent of the cases, was labelled the Explosive subtype because the offenses of these individuals appeared as unexpected, atypical departures from generally nonaggressive lifestyles. These offenders' earlier lives provided no indication of potential assaultiveness, and the offense violence appeared suddenly and inexplicably. Apart from their sex offenses, these rapists were typically law-abiding.

Drunken Offenders constituted Gebhard et al.'s fifth group and represented between 12 and 17 percent of the samples under study. Offense aggression in this group, which might be explained by the effects of intoxication, ranged from "uncoordinated grabbing and pawing" to extremely brutal assaults. Gebhard et al. did not offer a lengthy description of this subtype, although the examples cited suggest a great deal of heterogeneity with respect to background characteristics, degree and aim of aggression in the offense, and response to victim resistance.

The last of Gebhard et al.'s groups included a small number of individuals whose sexual offenses appeared secondary to mental deficiency or psychosis, and a larger seventh group that appeared to be comprised of blends of the varieties described above. This miscellaneous group accounted for up to one-third of all cases studied. The incidence of mixed cases in Gebhard et al.'s system may be somewhat inflated because of the lack of clear differentiating characteristics. In particular since, as we have seen, the incidence of alcohol use during rapes has been reported to be as high as 50 percent (Rada 1975), it is apparent that many rapists could be categorized both as Drunken Offenders and as members of some other group.

Gebhard et al.'s seven-fold classification, though less theoretically grounded than the other schemes reviewed here, and though less consistent and systematic in the dimensions used to differentiate subtypes, was an important contribution to the literature because of the large empirical database on which it was based. The availability of this extensive database enabled Gebhard et al. to provide frequency estimates for the various types they observed, an achievement not possible in earlier clinical investigations and theoretical writings. The early typological literature generally included only the roughest estimates of type frequency, and did not permit any estimates of the coverage provided by any particular scheme.

Further work on the subtyping of rapists did not appear in the literature until the 1970s, when two separate but related systems were developed by Cohen and his colleagues (1969, 1971) and Groth and his colleagues (Groth et al. 1977; Groth and Birnbaum 1979). Both of these classification systems had roots in the earlier typologies and both incorporated underlying motivations and personality styles in their formulations. Both were also developed out of early collaborative investigations. Although they were based on somewhat similar distinctions and on the same or similar samples, the Cohen et al. and Groth et al. schemes were independently refined and these authors described their subtypes somewhat differently. In particular, although the types derived have many parallels, as is evident in Table 2, the systems differ in the emphases given to the various motivations hypothesized to underlie sexual offending.

The Groth et al. (1977) scheme resembles those already discussed in its emphasis on analyzing the interrelations among the various motivations and aims presumed to underlie the act of rape. It differs in its introduction of a more sociocultural interpretation of rape its focus on the role of masculine issues of power, dominance, and aggression in motivating rape in our society. Since rape was conceptualized by these authors as a "pseudo-sexual" act, in which sex serves as a vehicle for the expression of power and/or aggression, two broad categories of rape were postulated--Power rape and Anger rape.

In Power rape, the offender is seeking to establish power and control over his victim, and physical aggression, threats, and intimidation are directed toward obtaining submission. Achieving sexual intercourse is for this rapist evidence of a conquest. This type of rapist is seen as having few skills for negotiating interpersonal relationships and as basically feeling inadequate in both sexual and nonsexual life spheres. Groth et al. conceptualize rape for this offender as a test of his competency. His offense is frequently premeditated and there is frequently the fantasy that the victim, although initially resistant, will in the end be grateful and appreciative of his advances. Although the amount of force in the offenses may vary, it is always in the service of achieving control and submission, and this offender is not characterized as using violence for its own sake. The offender often asks the victim questions about her own sexual life and seeks her reaction to his performance. Rape is this offender's way of asserting "his identity, potency, mastery, strength, and dominance and (denying) his feelings of worthlessness, rejection, helplessness, inadequacy, and vulnerability" (Groth et al. 1977, p. 1240).

Two subtypes are further differentiated within the group of Power rapists on the basis of whether the primary goal of the offense is reassurance or assertion. The Power-reassurance rapist is hypothesized to use rape to alleviate specifically his felt sexual inadequacies and to seek from his victims a confirmation of his masculinity that he cannot attain elsewhere. The Power-assertive rapist, in contrast, rapes to express potency, mastery, and dominance. Such rapes are committed by individuals whose doubts about their adequacy and effectiveness are more general and pervasive.

In Anger rape, the sexual assault is frequently accompanied by unnecessary violence and by sexual acts that are particularly degrading or humiliating. The offense serves to vent rage, and sex is a weapon for the expression of this anger. Groth et al. characterize this offender as displaying a great deal of anger and contempt for women generally. He may in fact be physically abusive in what are characteristically conflictual relationships with women. Often his offenses are precipitated by conflict with a significant female and represent a displacement of his anger. Although his victims may be any age, Groth et al. noted that older or elderly women may be particular targets of this offender's violence. Physical injury to the victim is often extreme and extensive.

Groth et al. differentiated the group of Anger rapists into two subtypes on the basis of whether the aggression and degradation are experienced as rage or pleasure by the offender. For the Anger-retaliation rapist, the offense serves to vent his rage towards women. He is seeking revenge and his goals are to degrade and humiliate the victim as much as possible. The Anger-excitation rapist, in contrast, obtains sexual gratification from the aggression. Violence is eroticized and his offenses are not only brutal but sadistic.

Groth et al. are quite clear in stating that rape is never primarily sexually motivated, but that, rather, sex is used to express other needs and motives. As can be seen in Table 2, however, their types share many features with the types proposed by investigators who have hypothesized underlying sexual motivations. Thus the differences in the systems seem to lie more at the level of hypothesized underlying motivational mechanisms than at the phenotypic, descriptive level. Based on their work with both offenders and victims, Groth et al. have reported that Power rapes outnumber Anger rapes by approximately a 2:1 margin, and that the Anger-excitation offender appears to be the least common.

A focus of our own taxonomic investigations has been the rapist classification scheme originally developed by Cohen, Seghorn, and their colleagues at the Massachusetts Treatment Center (Cohen et al. 1968, 1971; Seghorn and Cohen 1980). As noted above, this scheme has some conceptual similarities to the Groth et al. (1977) system, especially in the emphasis it has accorded motivational components. Moreover, the resulting phenotypic descriptions of the subtypes are comparable. The schemes differ in their hypotheses about the underlying motivations. Whereas Groth et al. concentrated on the motives of power and anger, Cohen et al. followed the lead of Guttmacher and Weihofen (1952) and of Gebhard et al. (1965) in focusing on the relative contributions of sexual and aggressive motivations. Cohen and his colleagues distinguished four types of rapists, derived by considering the interplay of sexual and aggressive aims: 1) a group for whom sexual aims predominate, with aggression employed in the service of accomplishing the sexual act; 2) a group for whom the aggressive aim is primary, with sexual acts serving as a vehicle for the expression of anger; 3) a group for whom the sexual and aggressive aims are synergistically related, in whose sadistic assaults violence increases sexual arousal and vice-versa; and 4) a group whose offenses are not readily understood in terms of either sexual or aggressive drives, but rather appear to be simply one facet of a pervasive predatory outlook and lifestyle. For the first and fourth types, aggression does not exceed the minimum level necessary to subdue the victim and achieve the sexual aim (i.e., it remains *instrumental*), but for the second and third types the aggression is *expressive* and constitutes an end in itself (Seghorn 1981).

These subtypes were proposed as ideal types, and Cohen et al. (1971) emphasized that rapists might in fact be distributed more continuously along the discriminating dimensions, rather than neatly divided into discrete classes. Yet, the Cohen et al. (1971) and Seghorn and Cohen (1980) descriptions of prototypic cases of their initial four rapists might be classified in groups that are homogeneous on a wide range of offense behaviors and life history variables.

In their scheme the first rapist subtype, for whom the offense aim was described to be primarily sexual as opposed to aggressive, was labelled the Compensatory rapist. His offenses appeared to represent a "compensatory" defense against low self-esteem and feelings of inadequacy. While Cohen et al. (1971) did not refer to power motives, as did Groth et al. (1977), nonetheless the portrait of the Compensatory rapist resembles in many details that of the Power-reassurance rapist depicted by Groth. The offenses of the Compensatory rapist appear compulsive; they are usually repetitive and often routinized. His rapes are often described as the culmination of long-standing fantasies in which the victim, though initially resistant, yields to the offender's power to control and even please. Thus, in addition to a high level of sexual arousal and an accompanying likelihood of premature ejaculation, key features of the Compensatory rapist include a tendency to distort the experience of the victim, misguided attempts to impress or even satisfy the victim through foreplay, and explicit requests for verbal confirmation by the victim of the offender's prowess. Aggression in the offense is limited to securing the victim's cooperation. If sufficient resistance is encountered, the offender's fantasy may be dispelled and he may flee. If, on the other hand, he should succeed in engaging the victim, his judgment may be so distorted by the fulfillment of his fantasy that he may seek further contact with the victim, thereby increasing the probability of his subsequent apprehension.

According to Cohen et al. (1971), the sexual preoccupations of the Compensatory rapist may be quite extensive and may be evident in a variety of perversions frequently beginning in early adolescence. The Compensatory rapist is described as the least socially competent of the rapist groups, with a lifestyle marked by passivity, withdrawal or isolation, and minimal educational and occupational achievements.

The Displaced Aggressive subtype, in contrast, commits explosive and quite often violent offenses that may at first appear inconsistent with his character. This individual frequently attains adequate or even high levels of social and occupational achievements and maintains a very active interpersonal life. Upon closer inspection, however, difficulties relating to women are evident, particularly in the appropriate assertion of his feelings in these relationships. As described by Cohen et al. (1971), these offenders "are capable ... of finding socially acceptable outlets for (this) aggression under normal circumstances and similarly capable of aim-inhibited feelings of warmth, kindness, and love. The characteristic mode of relating, however, is in a cool, detached, overcontrolled manner. They are active, assertive, excessively counterdependent, and intolerant of the passive aspects required to true mutuality in relationships" (p. 314).

These offenders' difficulties in assuming passive roles, when coupled with their split image of women—overidealization of maternal roles and devaluation of all other roles—are hypothesized by Cohen et al. to create the conflicts that produce their anger and lead ultimately to rape. The offenses of these individuals are hypothesized to represent a displacement of anger, initially experienced toward a significant female, onto the victim, who is almost always a stranger. As does Groth et al.'s Anger-retaliation rapist, the Displaced Aggressive rapist seeks to hurt, humiliate, and degrade his victim. The offender's affective state during the attack is one of anger and rage, and he may verbally express his contempt for women through derogatory statements to the victim. Like Kopp's (1962) Type I rapist, however, this offender is likely to feel some concern for the victim after the offense and may attempt restitution. He is often considered a good candidate for treatment and a good risk for eventual release.

While the offenses of the Displaced Aggressive rapist may be quite brutal, the aggression is not eroticized, as it is for Cohen et al.'s Sex-Aggression-Defusion type. For this rapist, who resembles Groth's Anger-excitation offender, violence and aggression lead to and may be necessary for sexual arousal. Although the degree of violence is often extreme and its manifestation sadistic and bizarre, anger may be absent and the aggression may be focused on the "sexual" areas of the body. This rapist shares some features of the aggressive and psychopathic types of other schemes, e.g., manipulative and impulsive behavior, unstable interpersonal relations, lack of empathy, history of nonsexual offense, etc. Typically, however, a very early onset of cruel and malicious behavior is noted, and his later aggression may be discriminated from that of other antisocial personalities by its primitive nature. Offenders in this subtype are often further distinguished by their severe psychiatric disturbance, particularly their paranoid symptoms.

The fourth and final rapist type in this scheme is the Impulsive rapist who was introduced in the 1969 paper and described in more detail in Seghorn and Cohen (1980). He is set apart by the exploitative nature of his offenses and his general antisocial lifestyle. For the Impulsive rapist, sexual assault is a predatory act that may not be seen by him as much different from his thefts of property. It is often the case, in fact, that the Impulsive rapist may attack a victim in the course of another felony. Thus, his offenses are impulsive, prompted by contextual factors and opportunity. This offender might not even be particularly sexually aroused at the outset of the assault, although situational factors may trigger arousal. While not disposed to show empathy for the victim, he also does not set out specifically to harm her. The Impulsive offender corresponds most closely to the Amoral Delinquent of Gebhard et al. (1965), and the Aggressive types of Guttmacher and Weihofen (1952) and of Kopp (1962).

In summary, our review of the most elaborate and comprehensive taxonomies of rapists reveals a remarkable consistency in the theoretically-derived types, with at least four well-distinguished groupings evident. There appears to be one type, with possibly two variants, for whom aggression in the offense either serves to enhance the offender's sense of power, masculinity, or self-esteem, or enables him to express feelings of mastery and conquest. Another type specified in various schemes commits rape out of anger toward women and seeks in the offense to hurt, humiliate, and degrade his victim. A sadistic type of rapist is easily identified by his sexual arousal in response to violence and the very brutal, and possibly bizarre, nature of his assaults. A final type described in several systems is the rapist whose sexual offenses are only one component of an impulsive, antisocial lifestyle and an extensive criminal history.

That different investigators working with different samples at different times observed and described similar types is testimony to the potential validity and stability of these types. We will discuss in greater detail the conceptual and structural similarities of the different rapist schemes and consider what empirical support they have received after we examine the systems developed for the classification of child molesters.

Child Molester Classification Schemes

Table 3 presents the child molester schemes we will review. One of the earliest systems was proposed by Fitch (1962), who distinguished five subtypes. His first two types were defined on the basis of whether the child molestation was seen as a preferred and long-standing form of sexual behavior (Immature type), or as a reaction to some sexual or emotional frustration at the adult level (Frustrated type). A third type, simply labelled Sociopathic and resembling the antisocial, aggressive rapist types, included offenders whose sexual crimes were part of a generalized social nonconformity. Child molesters whose sexually assaultive behavior was seen as secondary to psychosis, mental defect, or some organic condition constituted Fitch's

SEXUAL OFFENDING

Secondary Diagnostic Consideration | **Primary Diagnostic Consideration**

ACHIEVED LEVEL OF RELATIONS: Regressed   Nonregressed

ANTISOCIAL PERSONALITY LIFESTYLE: Present   Absent

Table 3
Child Molester Classification Schemes

Diagnostic framework	Fitch (1962)	Kopp (1962)	Gebhard et al. (1965)	McCaghy (1967)	Swanson (1971)	Groth (1978)	Cohen et al. (1979)
Nonregressed	Immature	Type I (Timid, passive, immature)	Sociosexually Underdeveloped	High Inter-action Molester	Classic Pedo-philiac	Sex-Pressure Offender	Fixated-Passive Offender
Regressed / Antisocial Absent	Frustrated		Pedophile; Situational	Asocial Molester	Situational Violator	Sex-Force Exploitative Offender (No)	Regressed; Exploitative
Regressed / Antisocial Present	Sociopathic	Type II (Self-righteous, self-important, man of the world)	Amoral Delinquent	Spontaneous-Aggressive Molester	Inadequate Sociopathic Violator	Sex-Force Sadistic Offender (Yes)	Aggressive Pedophile
Pathological	Pathological		Mentally Defective; Senile Deteriorate; Psychotic	Senile Molester; Incestuous Molester	Brain-damaged		
Secondary: Miscellaneous			Drunken	Career Molester			

SADISTIC (Groth, 1978): Yes / No

fourth type, which he labelled Pathological. Fitch allowed a fifth, Miscellaneous category for offenders who could not be classified by the previous criteria. Child molesters in this group typically had offenses that were isolated, impulsive, and appeared unrelated to any obvious pattern of emotional or sexual difficulty.

Kopp (1962) subdivided child molesters into two classes. His Type I appears similar to Fitch's Immature type--an individual seen as timid, passive, and somewhat withdrawn in his relationships with peers. This offender was described as feeling more comfortable a-round children, and as not viewing his preference for their company as inappropriate. This contrasts with Kopp's Type II who, like Fitch's Frustrated type, appeared much more assertive and self-impor-tant. This offender may marry one or more times, and he actively participates in the adult community. His sexual offenses were there-fore seen as incongruous with his typical level and quality of psycho-sexual adaptation.

Gebhard et al.'s (1965) classification of sexual offenders a-gainst nonadults stands in stark contrast to the schemes that both preceded and followed it. Unlike these other schemes, their typology lacks an underlying theoretical framework to organize the distinc-tions among types. As a result, the types they proposed appear much more descriptive in nature: each is characterized by a singular, ma-jor theme, as opposed to a systematic integration of multiple dimen-sions. This scheme also differs from the others reviewed here be-cause of its explicit attention to separate subclasses of offenders against nonadults. As was detailed above in the review of the de-scriptive literature, Gebhard et al. subdivided their sample at the outset on the basis of several variables, including victim sex and presence of aggression in the offense. Additionally, they employed a tripartite breakdown of victim age, considering offenders against minors as a group separate from either offenders against children or against adults. Their discussion of types therefore focuses in turn on each of six relatively discrete subclasses: 1) heterosexual, non-aggressive offenders against children; 2) homosexual nonaggressive offenders against children; 3) heterosexual, nonaggressive offenders against minors; 4) homosexual, nonaggressive offenders against minors; 5) heterosexual, aggressive offenders against children; and 6) hetero-sexual, aggressive offenders against minors (note that aggressors were too infrequent in the homosexual group to merit separate consid-eration). Since neither these offense-type subclasses, nor the themes that characterized the subtypes within each subclass, were mutually exclusive, considerable overlap among types both within and across these subgroupings was evident. Our review of the Gebhard et al. types will focus on the most distinctive types in each subgroup of offenders.

Among nonaggressive offenders against children, eight types were presented that differed in incidences in the heterosexual and homo-sexual subgroups. The most frequent type was the Pedophile, who ac-counted for 25-33 percent of the heterosexuals and 50 percent of the homosexuals. This type appears to be distinguished primarily by the extent of the offender's sexual activity with children and the ease with which he accepts children as sexual partners. In contrast to the other systems, an exclusive preference for children and the de-velopment of affectionate relationships with them are not necessary for inclusion in the Pedophile group of Gebhard et al.'s scheme. A

second type, accounting for 10 percent of the heterosexual group, was
labelled Sociosexually Underdeveloped. This type, who was characterized by his comparatively young age (generally under thirty) and his
failure to establish mature heterosexual relations, seems to overlap
with both Fitch's (1962) Frustrated and Immature types, since his offenses may appear either as "continuations of prepubertal sex play"
or as a response to unsuccessful attempts to develop relationships
with women. Immaturity was clearly implicated in the offenses of a
Third type, the Mentally Defective, observed for 20 percent of the
heterosexual molesters and 10 percent of the homosexuals. A fourth
type, the Amoral Delinquent, is, like its counterpart rapist type,
distinguished by offenses that are impulsive, opportunistic, and part
of a pervasive antisocial makeup and criminal history. The remaining
Gebhard et al. child molester types were relatively infrequent. Two
were defined on the basis of a single offender characteristic, the
Senile Deteriorates and the Psychotics, each of which accounted for
one in twenty heterosexual offenders. Two others, the Drunken and
Situational offenders, were specified on the basis of offense features only and included a diversity of individuals.

Many of these same types were observed in the group of nonaggressive heterosexual offenders against minors, 20 percent of whom could
be classified into one of the child molester types described above
and 8 percent of whom had committed offenses against both children
and minors. Two unique types were, however, proposed for this group:
1) the Subcultural offender, who belongs to a social milieu in which
young adolescent girls are considered acceptable sexual partners; and
2) the Near-Peer offender, whose proximity in age or maturity to his
victim makes the sexual relationship "psychologically and socially
appropriate, although illegal." Two types were also posited for the
nonaggressive homosexual offenders against minors. The first, accounting for one-third to one-half of the sample, was labelled the
Hebephile and defined as an individual who turns from adult homosexual
relations to relationships with minors because of the greater availability and lesser demands of younger partners. The second, in contrast, remains sexually active with adult males but has some encounters with boys as a result of either periodic "lapses of normal control and judgment" or a general lack of concern for the age of partners.

Finally, Gebhard et al. also hypothesized types for the aggressive child offenders against children and minors. The majority of
aggressive child molesters, though difficult to classify, seemed to
be differentiated by a cluster of attributes that included alcoholism
or problem drinking, mental impairment or illness, and very low socio-
economic status. The heterosexual aggressors against minors seemed
to fall in the gap between the rapists of adult women and the non-
aggressive offenders against minors, so that the two most prevalent
types in this offense class had counterparts in each of these other
classifications. The first of these is the Amoral Delinquent, representing one-third of the observed cases. The second displays features
of the Amoral Delinquent, but also resembles the Subcultural offender
against minors and the Double Standard rapist, and shares the name of
the latter. These individuals, although less antisocial than the
Amoral Delinquents and unlikely to assault strangers or use extreme
violence, employ force to achieve sexual relations with young girls
who are construed to have behaved in an inviting manner.

McCaghy (1967) proposed a six-fold classification for child molesters, based in part on an empirical study of the relation between characteristics of the offender and of the offense. His classification was not only founded on clinical observations; it also, like Gebhard's, incorporated findings from an empirical investigation. He obtained data on 181 molesters from both interviews and official record sources and, unlike many studies, included molesters on probation (one-third of his sample) in addition to incarcerated offenders. McCaghy went beyond simply describing salient features of this sample and tested several theoretically based hypotheses. The one most relevant for classification concerned the child's meaning for the offender. He hypothesized that individual differences in the child's meaning for the offender would be manifested in offense behavior. McCaghy operationally defined this meaning in terms of the extent of non-offense interactions with children and subdivided his total sample into the following three groups: 1) high interaction molesters, consisting of 18 offenders with numerous contacts with children not from their home or neighborhood; 2) limited interaction molesters, 103 offenders who interacted with children either in their own home, in their extended family, or in their neighborhood; and 3) minimal interaction molesters, 60 offenders with little or no contact with children apart from their offenses.

These groups were compared on four aspects of offense behavior--the familiarity of the victim, the amount of coercion, the context of the encounter immediately preceding the offense, and the nature of the sexual behavior. Consistent differences were found in the anticipated direction (all significant at least at $p<.05$), most of which clearly distinguish the high interaction molester from the other two groups. This high interaction offender rarely molested strangers, did not employ overt coercion, was usually engaged in some nonsexual interaction with the child prior to the offense (not simply for the purpose of enticement), and was more likely to fondle or caress the child than to seek genital contacts.

Since the minimal and limited interaction offenders did not show such clearcut patterns of behavior, McCaghy concluded that the only type to receive strong empirical support from his study was the high interaction molester. This type, though relatively infrequent, is similar to the various pedophilic types described by other investigators. McCaghy tentatively suggested five other types, two of which, the Career Molester and the Spontaneous-Aggressive Molester, were described in too little detail to allow for comparisons to other schemes (although he noted that the latter is characterized by features directly contrasting with those of the High Interaction Molester). Two others, the Senile Molester and the Asocial Molester, have counterparts in other systems. McCaghy allotted a separate category for the Incestuous Molester. Interestingly, he found that almost half of the offenders characterized as having limited interactions with children lived with children to whom they were usually related, but these offenders rarely had contact with children outside the home. He contrasted this pattern with that of the High Interaction offenders who, although well-acquainted with their eventual victims, did not offend against children over whom they had some authority (e.g., as teachers or parents).

Swanson (1971) outlined four groups of child molesters. His Classic Pedophiliac is similar to Fitch's (1962) Immature type, Kopp's (1962) Type I, and McCaghy's (1967) High Interaction Molester, and was described as an individual with a consistent, often exclusive interest in children. He may in fact at the outset simply want to play with and care for them. In contrast, the Inadequate Sociopathic Violator does not show a specific sexual attraction to children, and will exploit an older female child if she is either a convenient or available source of gratification. The Situational Violator was described as one for whom environmental circumstances are particularly important. He most closely resembles Fitch's Frustrated type and Kopp's Type II. This child molester may have a marital relationship, and his offenses tend to be impulsive and later regretted. He differs from the Inadequate Sociopathic Violator in that he is typically more stable in other areas of functioning, such as employment stability, and is descriptively shyer and more schizoid-like. Swanson's Brain-damaged type is similar to Fitch's Pathological type and refers to an individual whose molesting is a function of (or of secondary importance to) some other clinical condition, such as senility or mental retardation.

Groth (1978) also distinguished between the offender who manifests a persistent pattern of child molestation reflecting fixation at a psychosexually immature stage and the offender whose molestation represents a regression from a more mature level of psychosexual adaptation. In the first group, Sex-pressure type, the offender entices or bribes the child and may desist if the victim actively refuses or resists. This offender is seen as caring for the child on some level, as in Fitch's (1962) Immature type, Kopp's (1962) Type I, McCaghy's (1967) High Interaction molester, and Swanson's (1971) Classic Pedophiliac. Within Groth's second group of Sex-force child molesters there are two identified subtypes. The first, labelled Exploitative, uses threats or force to overcome the victim and shows little regard for the child's feelings. This type corresponds to the Inadequate Sociopathic Violator described by Swanson. The second of the Sex-force types, the Sadistic child molester, has no specified counterpart in any other scheme except that developed by Cohen and his colleagues (1979). This group is comprised of offenders for whom force and aggression have become eroticized, and thus is similar to Groth's group of Anger-excitation rapists: both are likely to be quite brutal in their offenses.

In the scheme developed by Cohen et al. (1979), three descriptive dimensions were used to derive subtypes of child molesters: 1) the motivation of the act (including the quality of the offender's perception of the child as a sexual object); 2) the degree to which the offense reflects a life-long fixation on the child as a preferred object (vs. a regression from a more mature level of psychosexual relationships with adults); and 3) the quality and role of aggression in the offense. From these dimensions four basic subtypes were derived.

The Fixated type has had counterparts in every scheme described so far. This is the offender with a long-standing, exclusive preference for children as both sexual and general social companions. Few of these offenders have married and there is a negligible history of dating or peer interaction in adolescence or adulthood. Frequently the child is known to the offender in the context of some platonic relationship before any sexual behavior occurs. Offense behavior typically involves minimal if any force or aggression, and the sexual acts pursued are typically non-genital in nature, i.e., fondling, caressing, kissing, or sucking. This offender usually has average or near average intelligence, and his social skills are adequate for day to day management, although he is described as shy, timid, and passive. His work history may be steady although it may be at a level below his apparent capabilities. Cohen et al. noted the difficulty in treating this individual who is not anxious about or disturbed by his behavior or his exclusive preference for children. In addition, the Fixated offenders were reported to settle easily into an institutional setting, where they typically create no management problems. Although the least dangerous of the child molester types in terms of physical damage done to any victims, this group was noted to be the most recidivistic.

The Regressed type is similar to the Fixated in that aggression in the offense, if present, is instrumental and the child is seen as a love object. There is a higher likelihood with this group, however, of offense behavior including attempts at more genital sex. The most distinctive features of this group are the typically high levels of social and sexual adaptation achieved. This offender has usually established adult relationships and is likely to have married and to have made a satisfactory work adjustment. These adaptations may be quite tenuous, however, and in the face of severe stress in which the offender's sense of competence and adequacy is questioned, he may regress and turn to an inappropriate object. This behavior is frequently dystonic for the offender, and he may experience guilt, remorse, or disbelief afterwards. There is typically no sexual fixation on the child so that recidivism depends on the offender's subsequent ability to cope appropriately with adult stressors.

The Exploitative child molester is quite different. This offender exploits the weakness of the child and uses him or her specifically to gratify his own sexual needs. Genital sexual acts are commonly attempted, and aggression, while typically instrumental, will decidedly be used if the offender feels it will ensure compliance. He does not care about the emotional or physical well-being of the child, who is typically unknown to him. This offender is descriptively similar to Fitch's (1962) Sociopathic and Swanson's (1971) Inadequate Sociopathic Violator types. He frequently shows many features of the antisocial personality disorder, including a history of anti-social and possibly criminal acts, a chaotic childhood, pervasively poor impulse control, and unstable relationships with peers. Cohen et al. noted that these Exploitative child molesters tend to be less socially facile than many individuals labelled psychopathic; they lack the charm or glibness frequently associated with that disorder. Cohen and his colleagues hypothesize that the markedly defective interpersonal skills of this group may in fact contribute substantially to their choice of children for their offenses.

The final group of child molesters in this scheme is comprised of Aggressive offenders. Their crimes always contain both sexual and aggressive features, and like the sadistic rapists, there is a tendency for their aggression and violence to be focused on sexual areas. Victims are more likely to be male, which Cohen et al. interpreted as symbolizing "a complex sexualized identification with a punitive parent and with the punished bad child" (p. 9). There is typically a long history of poor adult adaptation in both sexual and non-sexual areas, as a result these offenders are considered very difficult to treat. Because of the fused aggressive and sexual components, they are also considered quite dangerous. Fortunately, as Groth (1978)

noted in discussing his comparable Sadistic child molester, they are
the least common type.

It is noteworthy that every child molester scheme included a
type with an exclusive and long-standing sexual and social preference for children and contrasted this type with a second whose offenses were seen as a regression from an adult level of psychosexual
adaptation in response to stress. Most systems also posited a third
type comprised of psychopaths with very poor social skills who turned
to children largely because they are easy to exploit, not because
they are preferred or desired partners. These three types, therefore,
seem quite salient and appear to present clinically meaningful and
distinct profiles.

CLASSIFICATION SCHEMES OF SEX OFFENDERS: AN ASSESSMENT

The preceding sketch of rapist and child molester rational typological schemes suggests that there is substantial agreement among
clinical theoreticians on the variables that seem important for differentiating subtypes of sexual offenders. Moreover, a specific subset of types has repeatedly emerged across the various schemes. Such
consistencies suggest that a comparative analysis of the schemes reviewed might yield important theoretical information. The general
aim of the present section is therefore to evaluate the consistencies
across these schemes in an attempt to abstract and integrate those
elements of the various systems that might contribute to the formation of a theoretical framework to guide future research. Toward
that end we intend a) to highlight the consistencies in the content
domain across schemes and compare the best-represented variables to
those dimensions found to have discriminatory power in the descriptive literature, b) to examine the structural underpinnings of the
various models for consistencies in specifying the linkages among
types, and c) to assess the current empirical status of the proposed
schemes.

Content Domain
The determination of which variables to select for distinguishing subtypes is crucial. Both the success of subgroup differentiation and the ultimate utility of any typological scheme depend on
which variables are used to discriminate types. It has frequently
been pointed out that different typologies on the same population
might be useful for different purposes (Blashfield and Draguns 1976;
Brennan 1980; Skinner 1981). For example, one typology might better
facilitate the investigation of etiology, while a second could be
more successfully applied to management and therapy decisions. Such
systems might differ radically in the domains they tap. Thus in considering the content of our typologies we must be cognizant of their
intended purposes.

All of the typologies reviewed above are esentially descriptive,
focusing primarily on patterns of offense behavior and on the traits
and attitudes that characterize the offender's general adaptation.
Since the explicit aim of those proposing typologies has been explanatory and often predictive, there is the implicit assumption that the
descriptive variables on which their typologies are based capture
consistent root elements of the offender's sexual behavior and general adjustment. Although some authors have hypothesized etiological
factors for specific types (e.g., Cohen et al. 1971), such variables
have not been central to definition or discrimination of their types.

Given the emphasis on current adaptation and offense behavior, it is
not surprising that the content domains of the typological schemes
and the descriptive empirical studies overlap substantially.

Those variables that have served repeatedly as basic type discriminators are summarized in Tables 2 and 3. In both Tables an initial determination must be made about whether the sexual offense history is the primary diagnostic problem or whether the sexual assault
is secondary to a diagnosis of psychosis, mental retardation, or alcoholism. In some schemes such decisions are made explicit and result in an assignment to a particular type (Fitch 1962; Gebhard et
al. 1965; Rada et al. 1979; Swanson 1971). In other schemes there
is either an implicit exclusion of such severely impaired offenders
from the classification system or the issue is not addressed. The
problem of how or whether to classify these individuals as sex offenders is, as we stated earlier, too important to be ignored. Our
review of the psychiatric literature indicated that, although their
numbers are small, such seriously impaired offenders do constitute a
consistent subsample of sex offenders (e.g., Barclay and Fjordbak
1979; Henn et al. 1976). Since the motivational factors proposed by
the various schemes might be obscured by psychosis or intellectual
impairment, failure to exclude this subsample or to provide a separate type for them might add distorting error variance to any attempts to validate a scheme. Attempts to create new schemes might
include level of psychopathology and intelligence as discriminating
typological variables, since some tentative evidence suggests specific types might evolve around these variables (Anderson et al. 1979;
McCreary 1975). The strategy of simply excluding such severely disturbed offenders from sex offender typologies seems somewhat less
defensible for child molesters than rapists, since child molesters
have been reported to have a higher incidence of such disorders
(Bard et al. 1984; Henn et al. 1976), and the hypothesis that such
mental impairment might contribute to the choice of a child as an
acceptable sexual partner has some face validity. It is interesting
in this regard that separate subtypes of pathological offenders were
more frequent in child molester schemes than in rapist schemes.

While there was variability on whether to consider and how to
handle the domains of psychosis and retardation, other content domains were consistently represented in most schemes. One distinction
repeatedly used in both the rapist and child molester schemes is the
quality or role of aggression in the offense. As we saw in our review of the descriptive literature, there is substantial cross-study,
cross-perspective support for the discriminating power of the degree
of violence in the offense for both rapist and child molester groups.
Unfortunately, the studies that have examined violence empirically
have typically focused exclusively on the amount of damage done to
the victim or the frequency of the offender's violent acts and not on
the finer motivational nuances that characterize the distinctions
made in the typological schemes. Even the physiological studies,
which have attempted to examine the interaction of sexual arousal and
aggression, have operationalized violence in terms of the amount of
damage or the frequency of brutal assault (e.g., Abel et al. 1977;
Quinsey and Chaplin 1982). Only two published studies have attempted
to distinguish offenders on the basis of the quality or motivational
component of their violence. Cohen et al.'s (1969) assignment of sex
offenders to their typology required such a discrimination, but they

provided no specific criteria for their judgments and did not present any reliability data on their diagnoses. Quinsey et al. (1981) reported that they failed in their attempt to reliably differentiate between sadistic and nonsadistic rapist groups, but they omitted the details of their procedures. Thus, while the discriminatory power of the amount of violence has firm empirical support, the motivational aspects of violence, so important to the typological schemes we reviewed, have virtually escaped empirical scrutiny.

The major similarity in the use of aggression as a discriminator in both rapist and child molester typologies is the identification in several schemes of a sadistic offender type whose characteristic brutality manifests a fusion of sexual and aggressive aims. The role of aggression in discriminating among the remaining types is, however, radically different for the two victim-age schemes, with the nature of aggression having a more significant role in the rapist classification systems. As seen in Table 2, two broad groupings of rapists tend to be distinguished on the basis of whether the aggression is, in Seghorn's (1981) terminology, instrumental or expressive. According to Seghorn, when aggression is instrumental, the offender's aim is primarily sexual and only enough force is used to achieve the compliance of the victim. When the aggression is expressive, the primary aim is to harm the victim physically or psychologically. The Sadistic rapist's expressive aggression is eroticized, while the Displaced Anger type's aggression is not. In the child molester schemes only the Sadist type displays expressive aggression. Although other types vary in the nature of their relationship with the child, and thus by implication in the amount of instrumental force they would be willing or required to use to attain submission, aggression is clearly secondary to other more important discriminations for these types.

The Sadistic child molester can be discriminated from the other child molesters by the amount of violence in the assault. Such a simple quantitative measure would not distinguish the Sadistic rapist from the Displaced Anger type, since this discrimination requires the additional judgment of the meaning of the sexual aggression for the offender. Moreover, adult women are typically more capable of resisting rape than children, and the amount of instrumental aggression needed to subdue a woman might be substantial. Thus, a straightforward assessment of the amount of violence may at times even be a poor discriminator between instrumental and expressive aggression among rapists, and once again some judgment of the offender's motivation is required. Given these assessment problems, it is not surprising that there have been more empirical studies examining the degree of violence in child molester samples, where the variance of aggression is greater and the discrimination among types is easier than among rapist types.

Despite the absence of studies in the empirical, descriptive literature directly examining the subtleties of rapists' offense aggression, the importance of such distinctions has been indirectly supported by studies of related variables. In particular, research within various perspectives, including the legal (Marshall et al. 1979), the psychometric (4-3 type: Rader 1977), and the behavioral (Becker and Abel 1978) concurs in suggesting that some rapists have extreme difficulties with appropriate assertion and expression of anger that culminates in explosive outbursts. These attributes are precisely those described as characteristic of the rapist type variously labelled Explosive (Gebhard et al. 1965), Anger-Retaliation (Groth et al. 1977), and Displaced Anger (Cohen et al. 1971; Seghorn and Cohen 1980). Thus, although the difficulties in establishing reliable criteria to distinguish the motivational components of aggression seem considerable (Quinsey and Chaplin 1982), there is some indirect evidence that suggests that the effort might have a sizable payoff.

A second omnipresent typological discriminator that emerges in many guises is social competence. It is most clearly evident in the child molester typologies where the "regressed/nonregressed" distinction constitutes a major discriminator in several systems (Fitch 1962; Kopp 1962; Gebhard et al. 1965; Groth 1978; Cohen et al. 1979). This distinction is essentially a variant of achieved level of social competence. The regressed offenders are distinguished from the nonregressed by the higher level of interpersonal relations they have achieved. They are more likely to have been married and to have developed age-appropriate heterosexual relationships prior to their "regressive" sexual offense(s). Related to this dimension is the offender's relationship with the child. In most systems the Immature (Fitch 1962), Type I, passive (Kopp 1962), Classic (Swanson 1971), Sex-Pressure (Groth 1978), Fixated (Cohen et al. 1979) child molester is hypothesized like McCaghy's (1967) High Interaction Molester to have a considerable number of relationships with children, while the regressed and sociopathic types have relatively fewer relationships with children and choose them as sexual objects either as a compensation--e.g., the Frustrated (Fitch 1962) or Regressed (Cohen et al. 1979) type--or as a convenience--e.g., Sociopathic (Fitch 1962) type. Although this relationship component reflects to some degree the offender's social skills with adults, it is also confounded with other variables like impulsivity (distinguishing both the Fixated and Regressed from the Sociopathic) and possibly the presence or absence of other precipitating life stressors (which may play a more important role in the Regressed type's behavior).

In contrast with its role in discriminating among child molester types, social competence has typically played a secondary role in the rapist typologies. Nonetheless, the various rapist types have been described as widely different in their levels of social competence. This is most clear in the Groth et al. and Cohen et al. schemes where social competence covaries with the motivational and personality style components that define their types. For example, in both systems the Power or Compensatory types are hypothesized to be distinguished by their social incompetence and their inadequate interpersonal skills, and in the Cohen et al. system the Displaced Anger type is hypothesized to have achieved the highest level of social competence.

In spite of the crucial role that social competence plays in typological schemes of child molesters and its importance as a type correlate in more recent rapist schemes, few empirical studies have directly compared different subgroups. In a number of studies child molesters have been found to differ from rapists in marital status, heterosexual experience, and peer interaction (Bard et al. 1984; Christie et al. 1979; Glueck 1956). Other investigators have noted the deficient social skills and social confidence of child molesters (Becker and Abel 1978; Becker et al. 1978; Glueck 1956; Marshall et al. 1979; Quinsey 1977) and the assertion problem in some rapists (Becker and Abel 1978; Marshall et al. 1979). Only one study (Cohen et al. 1969), which we will discuss in detail below, actually compared offender subgroups and found some supporting evidence for the typological significance of one aspect of social competence, especially among rapists. Thus, while the empirical literature strongly suggests that the offender's level of social competence and his interpersonal skills, especially his assertiveness, might have considerable typological import, we have little data about whether for this population it is a homogeneous construct, how types differ on it or its components, or how it correlates in this population with important discriminators like aggression.

The third and final set of variables that have contributed in diverse ways to the typological schemes reviewed are those that have been associated in the psychiatric literature with the various personality disorders. The personality construct most frequently used to discriminate a type in the rapist and child molester schemes has been the antisocial personality. Many schemes for both victim-age groups have isolated an impulsive, exploitative type whose sexual offenses are simply one part of an extensive criminal history and antisocial lifestyle.

With the exception of the antisocial disorder the traditional personality disorders have not served as type markers. The sex offender types, while generated from different criteria than the personality disorders, do, however, in some instances share descriptive similarities with the personality disorders. For instance, we have mentioned in our discussion of the types similarities between the Displaced Anger type (Cohen et al. 197.) and the intermittent explosive or "overcontrolled" personality (Megargee 1966) and between the Compensatory type (e.g., Cohen et al. 1971; Kopp 1962) and the DSM-III avoidant or dependent/compliant personalities.

The psychiatric descriptive research we have reviewed supports those schemes that have posited an antisocial type. Although they by no means account for a majority of sex offenders, antisocial offenders are still common in this population. Their prevalence has been found to range from 6 percent to 47 percent (Henn et al. 1976; Schneider 1981). The available empirical data suggest, however, that this diagnosis, when present, may be associated with a wide range of behavioral patterns (e.g., Armentrout and Hauer 1978; McCreary 1975; Virkkunen 1976), so the possibility that this group could be subdivided into more homogeneous groups within the sex offender population cannot be dismissed without further evidence. As we indicated in our review of the MMPI research, there is some evidence that antisocial (4-9), intermittent explosive (4-3), avoidant (4-8), and possibly dependent (4-2) personality profiles are well represented in sex offender samples. Moreover, our summary of the psychiatric literature also suggested that a wide range of personality disorders were found in sex offender samples. The relation of these personality types and their characteristics to the sex offender types still needs exploration. Our own research (e.g., Schneider 1981) suggests that while there is some relation between the offender and personality schemes, they are by no means isomorphic and might better be considered alternative methods of typing this population.

Several other features, which play lesser roles in a few schemes, such as attitudes toward women, alcoholism, relation to the victim, and recidivism (e.g., Cohen et al. 1971; Gebhard et al. 1965; McCaghy 1967), have also been found in the descriptive literature to have discriminatory potential. The issues of how these auxiliary variables

relate to the core discriminators, or indeed of how core discriminators relate to each other, though addressed in several theoretical
schemes, are lacking in empirical support. As we have seen, it is
not even evident that the core discriminators that have been used as
the cornerstones of various typologies are homogeneous constructs.
Thus, while there is substantial support in the descriptive literature that the proposed theoretical models have focused on a domain
of variables that have discriminatory potential, the structure of
the variables they use, the subtleties of the distinctions they make,
and the covariation of these variables that they propose all await
empirical justification.

Structural Models
     In reviewing the different schemes proposed for the classifica-
tion of sex offenders, we contrasted two general approaches to the
specification of types. One strategy gives more emphasis to induc-
tion and is most clearly exemplified in the Gebhard et al. (1965) typologies. A second, more theoretically based strategy, characterizes
the majority of the remaining schemes.
     The relative merits of grounding classifications in descriptive
data as opposed to relying on theoretical constructs that require
more inferences have been a subject of much debate (Hempel 1965).
These approaches are not, however, mutually exclusive or opposing
(Skinner 1981). Even the most inductively derived scheme cannot be
produced in a conceptual vacuum (Popper 1972). The very selection
of what to observe necessarily implies the application of some theory.
For example, in the development of Gebhard et al.'s system, theoretical considerations guided the initial breakdown of the sample into
relevant subgroups, the selection of criterion variables, and the
manner of designating and describing each type in terms of its central features (e.g., "sociosexual underdevelopment," "double standard," etc.). Similarly, the theoretically-oriented schemes require
some empirical base for the generation of their hypothetical types.
The two approaches differ, therefore, not in the presence of theoretical structures or in the ultimate reliance on an empirical data base,
but rather in how these elements are used. Those investigators employing a more inductive strategy hope that gathering valid individual bits of discriminating, descriptive data will ultimately provide
a basis for a more theoretical formulation of the disorder. The more
theoretically oriented researchers proceed by generating reasonable
hypotheses and empirically eliminating those that are false. To be
scientifically respectable, their theories must be severely tested
and withstand disconfirmation. Thus, they create and test theoretical structures that are highly falsifiable (i.e., that are precise
and have high explanatory power) so that a large range of specific
states can be deduced from them (Popper 1959).
     One important component of the theoretically oriented taxonomist's
precision is the careful elaboration of the structural relations a-
mong types. This refines what constitutes a "type" and thus increases
falsifiability. Several kinds of structural models can be distinguished (Skinner 1981). We will focus on the three most common, two
of which, the categorical and hierarchical, can be clearly discerned
in the rationally-derived sex offender schemes and a third, the dimensional, is exemplified in the only published clustering study of sex
offenders (Anderson et al. 1979).
     Systems based on a categorical model define types as discrete
(i.e., mutually exclusive) and internally consistent classes (Skinner

1981). Most of the schemes reviewed above employed categorical
models. In Kopp's (1962) schemes, for example, individuals are assigned to one of two contrasting types. Given the assumption of
qualitative differences among types, the categorical model is frequently adopted by investigators working from observations of the
distinctive features that appear to characterize cohesive subgroups
in the population. Thus, Gebhard et al.'s (1965) system falls within the general rubric of a categorical model as well. The efficacy
of systems based on categorical models depends on whether the derived
types can indeed be shown to be homogeneous and distinct from all
other types. A high degree of overlap between types, as evident in
the Gebhard et al. types as originally described, therefore reduces
a system's potential validity and utility.

Hierarchical models were also present in the schemes reviewed
above, most notably those of Cohen et al. (1971) and Groth and his
colleagues (Groth et al. 1977; Groth 1978). Such models posit hierarchical relations among types at different levels of the system,
with successive breakdowns of classes at higher levels into finer
subgroups at lower levels. In their rapist schemes, for example,
Groth et al. and Cohen et al. first distinguished two broad groupings
of offenders (power or anger-oriented, instrumentally or expressively
aggressive) as a function of offense motivations, and then proceeded
to distinguish within each of these fairly global groups two more refined subgroups on the basis of specific offense styles. The specification of hierarchical models can be seen as a natural development
in the refinement of systems that begin by defining types as a function of their extreme positions along some theoretically important
dimension. Once two initial groups have been determined, evidence
that substantial within-group heterogeneity remains leads to consideration of a second theoretical construct, which in turn yields more
cohesive subgroups that are opposed on this dimension. These resulting subgroups are nested in the groups defined at the higher level,
and a hierarchical, tree-like structure is obtained.

A third strategy for structuring relations among types--the dimensional model--has seen frequent application to diverse psychiatric
and criminal populations, but was not explicitly represented among
the rationally-derived sex offender schemes reviewed above. The dimensional model assumes that differences among types are continuous
and quantitative in nature. While all attempts at classification require a means of assessing differences among types and rules for comparing an individual case to a prototypic, class exemplar (Skinner
1977), the quantitative assumptions of the dimensional model are more
difficult to fulfill with rationally-derived schemes that lack objective measures of the constructs involved. Thus, dimensional models
are more frequently adopted in classifications based on psychological
test or inventory data, in which scale scores serve as measures of
the theoretical constructs and procedures for case assignment are defined on the basis of some aspect of profile similarity. For example,
the Differential Personality Inventory (Jackson and Messick 1971) has
been used in attempts to delineate personality types among alcoholic
(e.g., Skinner et al. 1974, 1976) and general criminal (e.g., Carlson
1972) populations. The closest approximation to a dimensional approach to classification in the literature on sex offenders was the
MMPI study by Anderson et al. (1979). Having specified three representative profile configurations that had some initial descriptive

validity, these authors could proceed to classify new cases by establishing some definition of profile similarity to these prototypic
configurations.

Although no dimensional models have been explicitly proposed in
any of the sex offender schemes, the issue of whether type differences may be more quantitative than qualitative has been considered.
In the presentation of their rapist classification, for example,
Cohen et al. (1971) refrained from referring to their system as a
typology because they did not wish to exclude the possibility that
the differences between types may indeed fall along a continuous dimension and be a matter of degree rather than a question of clearly
discrete categories. It is therefore possible that one strategy for
developing their system could involve some combination of models with
dimensional differences characterizing groups at the same level and
hierarchical relations existing between groups at different levels.
Such complex models are becoming more frequent in the general classification literature, as exemplified by the adoption in DSM-III of a
categorical, and at times hierarchical, structuring of symptom and
personality disorders along Axes I and II in conjunction with quantitative assessments of the severity of psychosocial stressors (Axis IV)
and of the level of adaptation (Axis V) (Skinner 1981).

While there appears to be a movement toward more hierarchical
and dimensional models in the classification of sex offenders, the
issue of which kinds of models will ultimately prove most appropriate
and useful remains unresolved. Before outlining possible avenues of
research that could explore the issue of structural models in more
detail, we need to consider the empirical support that has been provided for the existing schemes.

Empirical Status of the Extant Schemes

Ideally, the development of a classification is a process involving continual shifting between theoretical formulation and empirical assessment (Skinner 1981). An initial framework is specified and
tested, leading to refinement of the original model and further testing, and so on. Since for the majority of the sex offender classification schemes we have reviewed, little information is available on
this process, we can only evaluate the end product. Most of these
schemes, though they may have been based on years of clinical and/or
research experience with sex offenders, appear in the literature as
single attempts to differentiate important subgroups and have never
been practically applied. While in a few cases the theoretical constructs proposed were subsequently followed up by other investigators
(e.g., Cohen et al. (1971) made use of Gebhard et al.'s (1965) distinction between aggression as means and aggression as an end), attempts to replicate or refine earlier systems have been the exception
rather than the rule.

Unfortunately, there are few data available for evaluating the
validity of the classification schemes as *systems*. There is a relatively high degree of overlap between those variables suggested to
have discriminatory potential in the descriptive/empirical studies
and those variables accorded central status in the typological schemes.
As we have stressed, however, such support for these variables in isolation cannot be taken as evidence for the validity of the systems
that employ them, since these systems posit complex interrelations
among the component variables, and these interrelations remain largely

untested. For example, a central assumption underlying the Cohen et al. (1971) rapist scheme is that differences in offense motivations will be reflected in clusters of specific offense behaviors that co-vary for each of the four rapist types (e.g., initial approach to the victim and response to resistance on her part). It has not been empirically established, however, whether these behaviors co-occur to the degree or in the manner detailed in the prototypic descriptions of their types. Thus, the homogeneity of the types on their central, defining characteristics has not yet been demonstrated.

A further hypothesis implicit in the schemes of Cohen, Seghorn, and their colleagues is that the relatively discrete offense styles will in turn distinguish subgroups differing in their non-offense functioning and adaptation. This hypothesis has been tested in one of the few systematic attempts to apply and validate a sex offender classification scheme (Cohen et al. 1969). Cohen and colleagues sought to determine whether, as hypothesized, the various subtypes would differ in their levels of social functioning. Subtype assignment was made by clinicians familiar with the system using offense and life history information available from official record sources. Their judgments were global and unstructured, assignment being determined by the similarity of the observed case to a prototype. Their dependent measures were derived from sociometric peer ratings. Fellow patients judged which subjects they would most or least prefer as associates in a variety of activities or as patient government representatives. While no group differences were found between rapists and child molesters, a variety of significant differences among the subtypes emerged, most of which were in anticipated directions. Specifically, the Displaced Anger rapists and the Regressed child molesters were consistently ranked highest in social efficacy, while the Sex-aggression rapists repeatedly evidenced the lowest level of social skills. The Compensatory rapists were found, as expected, to be fairly isolated and deficient in social understanding, but, in line with hypotheses that they are interpersonally passive and submissive, they were seen as least offensive by their peers. In contrast, results for two of the subtypes diverged somewhat from expectations. The Impulsive rapists did not appear as socially insensitive, nor did the Fixated child molesters seem as socially isolated, as had been anticipated. In general, therefore, this study provided initial support for some hypothesized differences among particular subtypes in social competence, but also failed to corroborate other hypotheses.

Several methodological weaknesses of this and related studies (e.g., Seghorn 1970) limit the conclusions that can be drawn about the validity of the scheme. These included: the absence of any assessment of the interrater reliability of group assignment; small cell sizes employed; the failure to specify the representativeness of the sample of offenders studied; and the inability to relate certain hypotheses to particular subgroups. Even more problematic was the failure to specify the criteria used in classifying subjects. Since the clinicians involved in the subtyping were not blind to the hypotheses of the study, and may have incorporated into their classifications social competence data specified in the files, their judgments may have been biased.

In summary, although some initial support for the descriptive validity of at least one of the classification systems reviewed has been established, this support has covered only a very narrow range of the variables presumed to characterize types and has emerged from studies with inadequate methodologies. Moreover, none of the extant typologies have been assessed for their predictive validity or gener- alization, both of which need to be demonstrated before these schemes could be considered for clinical applications.

STRATEGIES FOR REFINING AND DEVELOPING SEX OFFENDER CLASSIFICATION SCHEMES

Among the factors that have hindered the research necessary to develop more reliable and valid sex offender classification schemes, the absence of operational definitions of typal constructs, the lim- ited specification and testing of the relations among these constructs and among the resulting types, and the relatively unsystematic methods that have been employed in classifying empirical cases have most im- peded progress. In this section, we will address these and other as- pects of taxonomic development in outlining two approaches to advanc- ing the classification of this population. One strategy is to refine one or more of the extant rational schemes, while the second involves empirically generating new systems through the application of cluster analytic techniques. Although we will discuss each of these strate- gies separately and in so doing touch briefly on their comparative advantages, it is important to recognize their complementary nature. We will argue that the greatest benefits will accrue from integrated programs of research in which both approaches are applied and the re- sults from one approach are used to help clarify and refine the other.

To illustrate this presentation, we will focus on research con- ducted as part of an ongoing investigation at the Massachusetts Treat- ment Center. We will first describe efforts to refine and validate the rapist and child molester schemes of Cohen, Seghorn, and their colleagues (Cohen et al. 1971; Cohen et al. 1979; Seghorn and Cohen 1980) and then, in a following section, report on preliminary at- tempts to develop empirical classification schemes on the sample--ap- proximately 200 convicted sex offenders determined under Massachusetts state law to be "Sexually Dangerous Persons."[1] In describing this research with our collaborators, our intent is not to prescribe our chosen methodology as most appropriate or promising, but rather to exemplify one attempt to implement the general principles of theoreti- cal formulation and internal and external validation (cf. Skinner 1981). Clearly, various other ways of structuring, operationalizing, and testing rational schemes and numerous other cluster analytic pro- cedures are possible, but our aim is to convey the principles that would apply in general.

Rationally-Derived Schemes

Even though there is meager evidence that the extant rationally- derived schemes can in their present forms provide reliable and valid means of classifying sex offenders, they should not be abandoned. These schemes represent the best current guesses as to how this popu-

---

[1] Chapter 123A of the Massachusetts General Laws defines the "Sexual- ly Dangerous Person" as an individual "whose misconduct in sexual mat- ters indicates a general lack of power to control his sexual impulses, as evidenced by repetitive or compulsive behavior and either violence or aggression by an adult against a victim under the age of sixteen years, and who as a result is likely to attack or otherwise inflict injury on the objects of his uncontrollable desires" (St. 1958, C. 646).

lation might be subdivided into cohesive, clinically meaningful subtypes. If improved so that they become empirically applicable, they
could constitute an important basis of evaluating any new schemes
that may be developed. In particular, as we will describe below in
more detail, the rational schemes could serve as *a priori* models a-
gainst which the incremental validity of other approaches (e.g.,
cluster analyses) may be assessed. Furthermore, since schemes can
differ in the degree to which they achieve various goals (e.g. etiological clarification versus prediction), there are obvious benefits
to be gained from the simultaneous investigation of diverse schemes.
Because the rationally-based schemes are therefore vital to future
research in this area, this section is devoted to the tasks faced by
investigators seeking to develop or refine such systems.

The first step in elaborating the conceptual framework of any of
the extant classification systems, or any new systems in which the
rudiments of a classification are present (i.e., the content domain
has been specified and a limited number of types have been defined by
this content) is the explication of the structural model (Skinner
1981). Are the types hypothesized to differ qualitatively or quantitatively? Is some degree of overlap anticipated, or are the types
presumed to represent fairly discrete entities? Consideration of
structural issues at an early stage of taxonomic development is critical, since the answers to these questions will guide the operationalization of constructs and the selection of a method for classifying
subjects.

Our attempts to refine the Cohen et al. rapist and child molester schemes began with a pilot study that addressed such structural
issues, the results of which led us to conceptualize these schemes
as fully hierarchical and to operationalize the case assignment process as a series of steps in a decision tree (Seghorn 1981; refer to
Figures 1 and 2). The adoption of a hierarchical model was consistent with the emphasis in Cohen et al. (1971, 1979) on the instrumen-
tal/expressive aggression distinction as providing a primary, superordinate subdivision of both rapist and child molester groups, subsequent to which other, finer distinctions can be drawn. Two findings
from the pilot research were important in confirming the appropriateness of a hierarchical structure for these schemes.

The first of these concerned the degree of overlap observed a-
mong types when pairs of clinical raters independently assigned a
sample of research subjects to one of the existing four rapist or
four child molester subtypes. Although the level of interrater agreement in this study was rather poor (roughly 40 percent), the majority
of disagreements were confined to cases that fell, among rapists, between the Compensatory and Impulsive types, and among child molesters,
between the Fixated and Exploitative types. Detailed examination of
these two major sources of discrepancies suggested that these mixed
or borderline groups might constitute distinct, cohesive types in
themselves, such that revisions in the schemes to accommodate at
least two new types appeared necessary. Attempts to specify the
variables distinguishing these hybrid cases from the related types
in the original schemes led to a renewed focus on each scheme's underlying constructs. The decision tree structure evolved in part from
these efforts to systematically reduce within-group heterogeneity
and interrater disagreements through successive applications of finer
distinctions. In the rapist tree, for example, the third and final

Figure 1

DECISION TREE FOR SUBTYPING RAPISTS

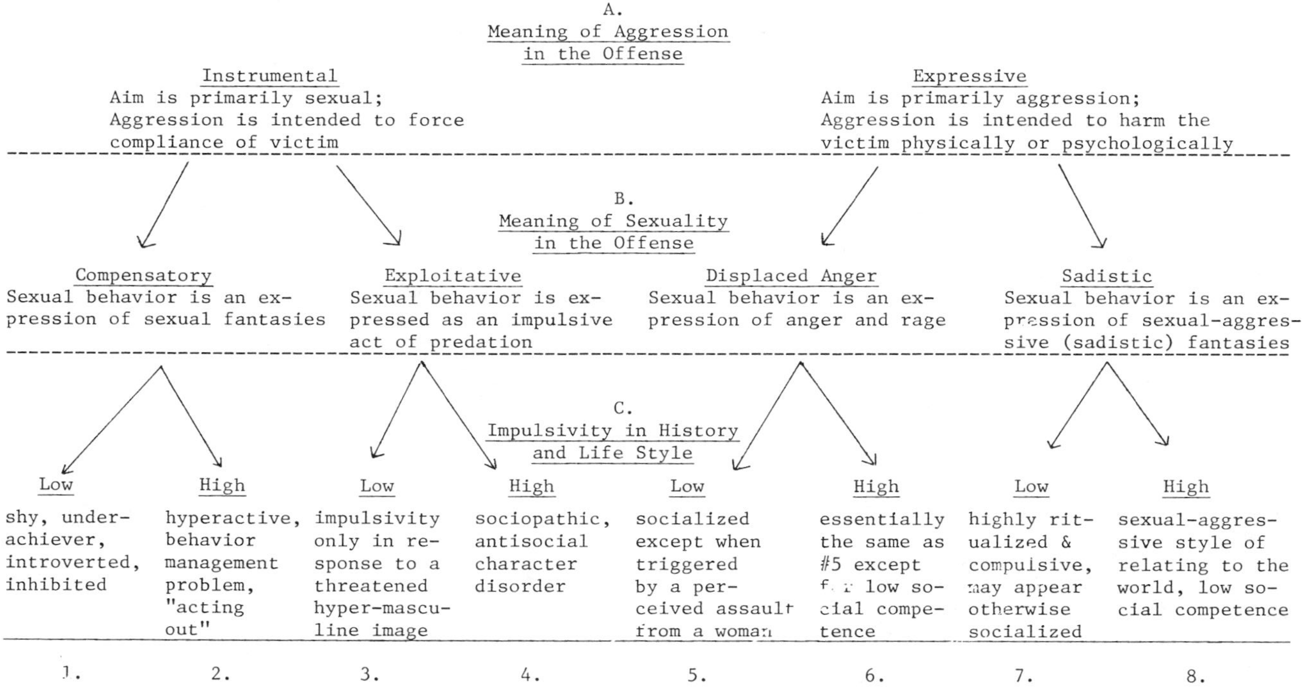

A. Meaning of Aggression in the Offense

Instrumental
Aim is primarily sexual;
Aggression is intended to force compliance of victim

Expressive
Aim is primarily aggression;
Aggression is intended to harm the victim physically or psychologically

B. Meaning of Sexuality in the Offense

Compensatory
Sexual behavior is an expression of sexual fantasies

Exploitative
Sexual behavior is expressed as an impulsive act of predation

Displaced Anger
Sexual behavior is an expression of anger and rage

Sadistic
Sexual behavior is an expression of sexual-aggressive (sadistic) fantasies

C. Impulsivity in History and Life Style

	Compensatory		Exploitative		Displaced Anger		Sadistic	
	Low	High	Low	High	Low	High	Low	High
	shy, under-achiever, introverted, inhibited	hyperactive, behavior management problem, "acting out"	impulsivity only in response to a threatened hyper-masculine image	sociopathic, antisocial character disorder	socialized except when triggered by a perceived assault from a woman	essentially the same as #5 except for low social competence	highly ritualized & compulsive, may appear otherwise socialized	sexual-aggressive style of relating to the world, low social competence
	1.	2.	3.	4.	5.	6.	7.	8.

Figure 2

DECISION TREE FOR SUBTYPING CHILD MOLESTERS

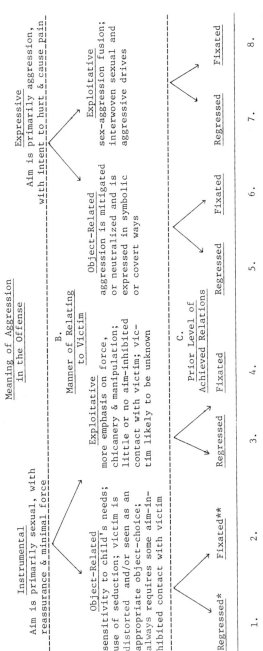

A.
Meaning of Aggression
in the Offense

Instrumental
Aim is primarily sexual, with
reassurance & minimal force

Expressive
Aim is primarily aggression,
with intent to hurt & cause pain

B.
Manner of Relating
to Victim

Object-Related
sensitivity to child's needs;
use of seduction; victim is
distorted and/or seen as an
appropriate object-choice;
always requires some aim-inhibited contact with victim

Exploitative
more emphasis on force,
chicanery & manipulation;
little or no aim-inhibited
contact with victim; vic-
tim likely to be unknown

Object-Related
aggression is mitigated
or neutralized and is
expressed in symbolic
or covert ways

Exploitative
sex-aggression fusion;
interwoven sexual and
aggressive drives

C.
Prior Level of
Achieved Relations

Regressed*	Fixated**	Regressed	Fixated	Regressed	Fixated	Regressed	Fixated
1.	2.	3.	4.	5.	6.	7.	8.

* Regressed: higher level than Fixated; more likely to have been married and have age-appropriate heterosexual relationships prior to Regression; more likely to have mastery in other areas; likely to show Regression as a decompensation

** Fixated: low level of social competence except in relationships with children; distortion of age of victim; offenses are often ego syntonic

decision assessed for all four offense styles pertains to the level of impulsivity in the offender's general lifestyle. Inclusion of this variable allows for specification of a type whose offenses are Compensatory, but who is impulsive in non-offense contexts (the type observed in the pilot study), and also for other types not previously considered but logically possible (e.g., offenders manifesting displaced aggression in their offenses but who show higher levels of general impulsivity than previously hypothesized for this type).

Not only did the hierarchical model appear best-suited for mapping hypothesized and observed relations among types, but other results from the pilot study also suggested that it might better mirror the clinical judgment method of case assignment than other approaches. Specifically, an attempt in the pilot study to validate an additive-criterion approach modeled on the Research Diagnostic Criteria of Spitzer, Endicott, and Robins (1975) proved unsuccessful.[2] Subtype assignments using this approach were determined by a subject's cumulative score on sets of presence/absence items devised to represent inclusion or exclusion criteria essential for type definition. The objective of this study was to establish the optimum number and type of characteristics necessary to make the additive-criterion type assignments match clinical judgments of type membership. Classifications made using the two methods were found, however, to differ radically. In contrast to the emphasis in the additive-criterion approach on type-specific, categorical criteria, it appeared that the global, clinical judgments involved continual comparisons of the case under consideration to various subtypes in an attempt to locate that subject's position on the series of relevant dimensions that form consistent threads through the types (e.g., instrumental versus expressive aggression). As opposed to the linear, additive methodology of the criterion approach, the classification process as conducted by the clinical subtypers was more sequential and conditional in nature: hypotheses developed early in the reading of a case determined not only the emphasis to assign subsequent material but the very kind of further information to be sought. This process was made explicit in the decision tree in which, for example, classification of a rapist begins with an initial dichotomous decision about the quality of the aggression in the offense, then proceeds to an assessment of the meaning of sexual aggression for that offender, and finally concludes with a judgment of the degree of impulsivity evident in his daily functioning (cf. Figure 1).

In addition to facilitating the consideration of new types and establishing a standard sequence of specific judgments to be employed in case assignment, the adoption of the decision tree structure as a preliminary working model had several advantages. First, specification of the component variables to be applied at the different stages of the classification process allows for multiple measures that can be separately examined for their reliability. Second, the decision tree format provides a theoretically cohesive model for collapsing subtypes to obtain better interrater agreement and/or increased cell sizes for the analysis of more global types. Third, because it more

---

[2] The additive-criterion scales were created by Gail Birnbaum, Ruth Rosenberg, and Raymond Knight as part of Birnbaum's Honors Thesis at Brandeis University.

precisely delineates and specifies those constructs essential to the definition of the types, the decision tree model lends itself to more highly-focused attempts at validation. For example, since the fixated/regressed distinction, which pertains to the offender's general level of psychosexual functioning and possibly to his social competence, is separated in the revised child molester scheme from consideration of his style of relating to the victim, more adequate assessment of the empirical interrelations of these two variables is possible.

The revised, operationalized schemes were tested on a sample of 184 offenders in residence at the Massachusetts Treatment Center. This first classification attempt yielded important information about the internal properties (i.e., reliability and coverage) of these systems (which we will hereafter refer to as the MTC schemes to distinguish the refined schemes from the original versions). With regard to reliability, it had been hoped that the revisions in the schemes, particularly the increased systematization of the decision process, would increase the level of interrater agreement over that obtained in the pilot study. Some improvement was clearly evident-- whereas previously the raters had agreed on 40 percent of the cases in assigning one of four types, in the more recent application agreements were present for 58 percent and 59 percent in assigning one of eight rapist or child molester types, respectively. These levels, though slightly improved, however, are far from adequate, confirming that one of the major problems in investigations of rationally-derived schemes will involve determining how to tighten the decision criteria to produce reliable judgments. The observed reliabilities of the MTC schemes are equivalent to the reliabilities of many psychiatric diagnoses reported prior to the advent of DSM-III (e.g., Spitzer and Fleiss 1974), and they compare favorably with the reliabilities of diagnoses of personality disorder using DSM-III (Spitzer et al. 1979). Thus, they represent an encouraging initial step, but require further refinement and tightening.

The revised schemes, by incorporating a series of component variables that are separately measured, have facilitated the analysis of where in the classification process interrater discrepancies are most likely to occur. For example, in the classification of rapists, the instrumental versus expressive aggression distinction was the most highly reliable decision, whereas the ratings of offense style (e.g., compensatory versus exploitative, displaced anger versus sadistic) were more frequently sources of disagreement (Prentky et al. 1984). Thus, those areas in need of more concrete operational definitions were pinpointed and can be revised in future studies.

The coverage of classification is its "applicability ... for the domain of patients for which it was intended" (Blashfield and Draguns 1976, p. 144). According to these authors, the issue of coverage has been relatively neglected in classification research, perhaps because the most widely-applied systems (e.g., DSM-III) for very practical reasons provide near-total coverage through the inclusion of various "wastebasket" categories. When coverage was assessed at all in the literature on sex offender typologies, it varied greatly across systems. For example, Gebhard et al. (1965), even though they proposed numerous types, were unable to classify close to 33 percent of their rapist sample. In contrast, Groth et al. (1977), in rating their four rapist types based on data from both offender records and victim reports, were apparently able to apply their classification to all cases. In the Prentky et al. (1984) application of the MTC rapist and child molester schemes, 95 percent of the subjects were accounted for by one of the sixteen types (eight for each scheme). It is noteworthy that Prentky et al. did not exclude psychotic or retarded offenders from their classification study. Indeed, they argued that the MTC scheme was designed as a system that theoretically should account for all sex offenders. Since there is often an inverse relation between coverage and reliability (Blashfield and Draguns 1976), such a high goal for coverage, attempting to include all sex offenders, might have reduced reliability. That is, to the degree that the criteria are loosened or blurred to permit greater inclusion of subjects, reliability will suffer. Conversely, the more precise (and therefore reliable) are the criteria for classification, the more difficult it would be to fit all subjects into a category, and hence coverage would be poorer. Blashfield (1973) has pointed out that the seemingly paradoxical inverse relation between coverage and reliability applies only to classifications that lack descriptive validity. Thus, decisions about what balance of coverage and reliability to seek can only be made in a context of the examination of the descriptive validity of a system.

Establishing the descriptive validity of a classification involves demonstrating both its convergent and discriminant properties (Campbell and Fiske 1959; Skinner 1981). That is, across a variety of measures, will individuals be assigned to the same subgroups, and will consistent differences among these subgroups be obtained? The variables used to assess the descriptive validity of a classification system may either measure specific aspects of the characteristics that define types, or reference a diversity of other relevant content domains (Blashfield and Draguns 1976; Skinner 1981).

To evaluate the descriptive validity of the MTC schemes, for example, we have relied on data gathered on various aspects of the offender's life history and adaptation, including information on sexual offenses, general criminal history, personality traits and psychiatric symptoms, educational, occupational, and interpersonal functioning, family background, and child and adolescent development. In keeping with our attempt to achieve a multitrait-multimethod approach, these data have been collected from multiple sources. including official record sources, standardized tests, computer-programmed questionnaires, and clinical interviews. In addition, a group of clinical raters (separate from those involved in the subtyping procedure) diagnosed subjects according to Axes I and II of DSM-III (where appropriate) and also rated and classified subjects on the dimensions and types of Millon's (1969) system of disordered personality patterns. The rationale for including these diagnostic assessments was to determine the degree to which the MTC subtypes might overlap with categories that have had more general clinical application.

In summary, our analyses of the MTC schemes to date have focused on their internal structure, interrater reliability, coverage, and descriptive validity (e.g., Schneider 1981; Schneider and Knight 1982).

Cluster Analytic Schemes

A second approach to deriving subtypes of sexual offenders is more inductive in its process. In this approach, an attempt is made to find naturally occurring groups of individuals on the basis of their similarities and differences on a specified set of attributes.

The statistical technique for accomplishing this goal is cluster analysis.

This strategy has shown promise in other areas of psychopathology (Everitt et al. 1971; Magaro and Smith 1981; Paykel and Rassaby 1978) and represents a significantly different approach to elucidating naturally occurring groups. Over the past several years the marked increase in the number of clustering techniques developed (Blashfield and Aldenferfer 1978) has given researchers a powerful set of tools for creating classification schemes that may be more reliable, objective, and predictive than those determined by other methods. The application of such techniques, virtually untried in classifying sexual offenders, could prove to be an important method of objectively defining and refining types already described in the clinical literature. Further, to the extent that a rational-deductive and an empirical-inductive approach arrive at similar types, we have a form of convergent validity for those types.

Although various clustering techniques differ from one another, they all share in common an identity as a set of procedures that separate a group of N individuals into subgroups based on a set of p variable scores on each individual. The intent is to separate the individuals so as to create groups in which members are similar to one another and dissimilar to members of other groups. Since the clusters are based on similarities between individuals on scores on a set of variables, the meaningfulness of the clusters is a function of the relevancy of the input variables to the classification problem. In this respect, and others discussed in the following paragraphs, it is similar to the rational-deductive approach. Like the rational method, cluster analysis is a tool that is most appropriately and effectively used when an investigator is guided by theory and models.

The use of theory to select the most relevant subgrouping variables has been discussed at length earlier in this chapter and will not be belabored here. It is sufficient to reiterate that to the extent that the variables chosen are theoretically important, the resulting groups will be meaningful and interpretable within a defined framework. The use of theory as a guide is particularly helpful when, for very practical reasons, it is important to select only a small subset of relevant variables.

The use of an hypothesized model that organizes the subtypes into, for example, discrete classes, or hierarchically related groups, is particularly germane in the selection of one's clustering technique. There should be some hypothesized structure to the data to guide the selection of one's cluster analysis technique, as different techniques reflect very different models (Blashfield 1980). Each of these techniques also, to a certain extent, imposes a specific structure on the data (Chignell and Stacey 1980). The choice of a clustering technique is not arbitrary and should not be determined by convenience. If appropriately used, these techniques can have substantial advantages (Blashfield and Aldenderfer 1978; Skinner and Blashfield 1982).

First, cluster analysis forces a more precise operationalization and quantification of one's subgrouping variables. Since input variables must be clearly specified, they are easily examined and reevaluated to determine their meaningfulness and relevance. While, as we have seen, quantification of one's subgrouping variables can be problematic, it is an essential component of any classification effort, however informally done. Even though in the rational schemes one does not have to assign a number to a subject's degree of aggression (e.g., in the Groth et al. (1977) or Cohen et al. (1971) schemes), one must judge that certain types (and individuals) are "more" aggressive and others "less" so. The greater specificity of quantification required for cluster analysis allows us to determine more precisely the interaction of variables in defining a subtype.

Second, the precision of cluster analysis enhances reliability. As a computer-performed statistical procedure, it has the advantage, given the same data base, of always typing the same individual in the same way. Rater reliability is inherent.

Finally, cluster analysis taps the vast potential of computer technology to store and simultaneously consider numerous variables, providing a distinct advantage over the human mind. Thus, complex interactions between variables that may only be speculated upon by a human mind can be clearly illuminated with the aid of a computer. This advantage related to one of the principal purposes of this method: to clarify relations between variables and individuals. Meehl (1979) notes that a technique like cluster analysis will not "discover" any type not previously clinically observed. But, it may aid in defining already noted types, and it can certainly aid in understanding various types' relations to one another. As an exploratory tool, cluster analysis has great potential for highlighting and abstracting the underlying structure of a given data set and in generating new hypotheses about how these variables relate.

Our own work in this area may once again serve as an illustration of these points. In addition to restructuring and tightening a rational scheme, we have also started to develop empirical, cluster-analytic-based schemes. As the first step in developing such schemes, we combed the previous empirical and clinical literature on sexual offenders to ascertain the most relevant and potentially discriminating variables for defining subtypes of this group. A set of thirty-three variables was selected that included aspects of achievement in education and employment, drug and alcohol use, impulsivity, aggression, childhood maladjustment, peer interactions, and social relations. Rationally constructed scales were generated to measure these variables with careful attention to achieving adequate interrater reliability on all scales and internal consistency where appropriate. We then rated 125 rapists and child molesters on these scales.

Before clustering subjects, we clustered the variables using a principal components analysis. This procedure was used to reduce the variable set to a more manageable number of meaningful constructs for several reasons. First, the analysis itself was inherently interesting and important, since it answered several questions we have raised in this chapter about how various measures covary in this population. Second, if the variables naturally clustered into a smaller group of meaningful dimensions with good internal consistency, such dimensions would be more stable, richer, and more reliable measures than the individual variables comprising them. Third, if the variable set could be reduced with minimal loss of information, the relations between items being considered simultaneously in the clustering of the offenders would be easier to comprehend. Fourth, as Meehl (1979) has pointed out, a common problem with many cluster analytic studies has been the use of many variables in a given subgrouping problem, some highly relevant and others less so. This results in potentially obscuring the more important defining characteristics among an array of less important factors.

Four dimensions were suggested by the principal component analysis. *Substance Use* tapped the degree and kind of involvement a subject had with drugs and alcohol. *Social Incompetence* tapped aspects of a subject's social and life management skills including employment and educational achievements as well as levels and kinds of social relationships achieved. *Antisocial Behavior* tapped aggressive, problematic, and impulsive behaviors over the subject's lifetime, and *Offense Impulsivity* assessed the degree of impulsivity manifested in the subject's sexual offenses alone. These four dimensions were then converted to scales by retaining and summing for each dimension the items that loaded at a $\geq$ .40 level. An additional scale, *Sexualized Aggression*, remained unique through the principal component analysis but was retained for the purposes of the cluster analysis of subjects, since several investigators in this area (e.g., Cohen et al. 1971; Groth and Burgess 1977) had hypothesized that this variable is theoretically important for typologies, and it had consistently shown discriminatory power within this population in a number of empirical studies. This scale measured the degree of aggression manifested in the offender's sexual behavior alone. All five scales were then standardized prior to their use in the cluster analysis of subjects.

For the clustering of the subjects, we specifically selected a hierarchical cluster analysis technique for our initial analyses to approximate the model reflected in the MTC schemes (Prentky et al. 1984; Seghorn 1981). It should be noted that in this initial study (Rosenberg 1981), no attempt was made *a priori* to separate or divide the sample in any way. As we have seen, victim age has frequently been used as a primary determinant of sexual offender subtypes. We decided, however, to examine certain noted similarities between subtypes across victim-age classifications. Thus, rapist and child molesters were analyzed together and victim age was not included as a clustering variable. This allowed us to see whether the rapist/child molester distinction would emerge spontaneously as a function of the other important determinants of the subtypes.

An eleven cluster solution that provided complete coverage was selected for interpretation. Each cluster had 5 to 18 members and a distinct clinical picture. Space considerations preclude a separate description of each cluster. Interestingly, several of the types that emerged in the cluster analysis were descriptively similar to the rationally derived types in the MTC schemes, and in fact when a sample (n = 109) of sexual offenders was typed using both systems, a high degree of concordance (Table 4) was found between some of the clusters and some of the MTC types. For example, one small cluster (#2) emerged that appeared non-aggressive, not antisocial, not impulsive, and relatively dependent. Remarkably, this cluster was composed exclusively of Fixated Pedophiles (according to the MTC subtyping scheme). Two other purely rapist clusters (#3 and #4) emerged that on clinical description appeared similar to MTC Displaced Anger, Low-impulse and Displaced Anger, High-impulse types. Thus, the typological importance of victim age was manifested despite its absence from the typing criteria. Another group (#9), comprised of both rapists and child molesters, could be characterized as relatively socially incompetent, moderately impulsive in their offenses, and show-

Table 4
Concordance of Clinical and Empirical Types

		Empirical Clusters										
		1	2	3	4	5	6	7	8	9	10	11
Rapist Types*	Compensatory--Lo-Impulse	7	-	1	-	-	1	-	-	-	1	1
	Compensatory--Hi-Impulse	5	-	-	-	6	1	4	-	2	1	1
	Exploitative--Lo-Impulse	-	-	-	-	-	-	-	-	-	2	-
	Exploitative--Hi-Impulse	1	-	-	1	6	1	-	-	5	4	1
	Displaced Anger--Lo-Impulse	-	-	-	1	-	1	-	-	-	-	-
	Displaced Anger--Hi-Impulse	-	-	2	2	2	2	-	-	-	1	1
	Sadistic--Lo-Impulse	-	-	1	-	-	-	-	2	-	-	-
	Sadistic--Hi-Impluse	-	-	-	1	-	-	1	2	-	2	1
Child Molester Types**	Pedophile--Regressed	1	-	-	-	-	-	-	-	-	1	-
	Pedophile--Fixated	1	4	-	-	-	-	-	-	-	-	1
	Child Molester--Exploitative Regressed	2	-	-	-	-	-	-	-	-	-	-
	Child Molester--Exploitative Fixated	1	-	-	-	-	1	7	-	6	1	3
	Child Molester--Aggressive Regressed	-	-	-	-	1	-	-	-	-	-	-
	Child Molester--Aggressive Fixated	-	-	-	-	1	2	1	-	-	1	-

*   After Seghorn and Cohen 1980

** After Seghorn 1981

ing a history of antisocial behavior and substance use. Consistent with this description, a number of these offenders emerged as Exploitative Fixated child molesters or Exploitative rapists. Without detailing the entire empirically-derived scheme (see Rosenberg 1981), these examples serve to illustrate the promising results gained from the technique of statistical cluster analysis. Importantly, this overlap of types derived through two radically different approaches provides a certain degree of confirmation for both systems and allows us to have additional confidence in their validity.

Additionally, the value of cluster analysis as an heuristic was illustrated in the emergence (in our preliminary analysis) of a type (Table 4, #11) not found in the MTC schemes, but cited in Gebhard et al.--sexual offenders whose primary defining feature seemed to be problems with alcohol, to a degree exceeding that found in other sexual offenders. This finding leads us to reconsider the possible role and importance of alcohol in defining clinically meaningful groups and to begin a more detailed investigation of this area (Morris et al. 1983).

Cluster analysis is also an exploratory tool. We are in the process of using it to help us "break set" and explore other possible structural models for organizing offender types. Thus, we are applying widely different algorithms to the same data set in an effort to see which groups remain cohesive across analyses, and to determine whether another organization (besides an hierarchic one) produces a scheme that makes more clinical sense.

The utility of the various schemes we are comparing rests not on the kinds of concurrent validity that we have been describing, but on demonstrations of their predictive validity--establishing that types differ in theoretically consistent ways in their causes, courses, responses to intervention, and outcomes. It is conceivable that the most homogeneous and reliable types could have no practical significance. Most of the sex offender schemes we reviewed were proposed with the clear intent of eventually enhancing differential treatment and management decisions. For example, many types in various schemes were hypothesized to differ in their appropriateness for and likelihood of benefitting from psychotherapy (e.g., Kopp 1962), or their likelihood of recidivating upon release (e.g., Cohen et al. 1971). To date, however, these hypotheses have not been empirically tested.

Our research group has recently undertaken an extensive followup study aimed at assessing the predictive validity of our MTC and empirical schemes. The subjects of this study are a large group of offenders (n = 260) who at one time were committed to the Treatment Center as "Sexually Dangerous Persons," but who have subsequently been released. A broad range of criminal record sources will be accessed in an attempt to predict, not individual acts of violence, but rather patterns of post-release adaptation and criminal offenses. In seeking to minimize problems inherent in trying to predict behaviors that have a low base-rate (Meehl and Rosen 1955), we have adopted outcome measures that are multidimensional (e.g., social adjustment as well as criminal convictions) and multileveled (reflecting gradations of contact with the law as opposed to dichotomous measures of recidivism). The follow-up data will provide a basis for examining several different issues related to the validation of the typologies. First, and most basic, they will allow a crude assessment of the cross-situational consistency and prognostic utility of our dimensions and types. In accord with the theoretical underpinnings of the MTC schemes and on the basis of preliminary empirical investigation of patterns of adjustment and criminal behavior in our population prior to incarceration (Knight et al. 1983), we hypothesize that the types will be found to differ in consistent, predictable ways in their post-release adaptation and contacts with the law. Second, in attempting to identify characteristic outcomes for the different types, we will try to cull from the follow-up data aspects of person type-situation interactions (Repucci and Clingempeel 1978) to achieve a finer understanding of how the release environment and the offender's response to it (or structuring of it) mediates outcome. Such assessments have rarely been attempted in studies of criminal populations (Monahan 1981; Shah 1978), but are critical to any eventual applications of the typologies for treatment and management decisions. Finally, the follow-up data will not only serve to test the predictive validity of the types, but also provide a means for clarifying and unconfounding types. This approach, which has elsewhere been referred to as a bidirectional strategy (Knight and Roff 1983), involves refining the various schemes (both rational and empirical) as a function of their predictive validity. For example, types from one scheme found to be similar in outcome could be collapsed for the purposes of prediction, or evidence of great within-type heterogeneity in outcome could lead to subdivision of the types involved. Moreover, we will be able to compare the MTC and empirical typologies to determine whether one more consistently relates to post-release adaptation and adjustment, or whether they differentially relate to the various outcome measures employed.

The importance of using multiple methods to derive schemes and of having a number of schemes to compare should be obvious. Each method has its inherent strengths and weaknesses (Meehl 1979; Skinner and Blashfield 1982). The two strategies we have employed, the rational and the empirical, should be viewed as complementary methods that provide reciprocal benefits when used concurrently in any research program. The results of each can enrich the interpretation of the other and generate new research questions. Differences, where they occur, can lead to important advances in our knowledge. Indeed, it is important to emphasize that the comparison of multiple schemes that are reliable and precisely delineated enhances falsifiability. A central difficulty in experimental psychopathology has been the role played by "saving" or auxiliary theories that can be postulated as explanations for the failure of any particular study to corroborate the theory that is being tested (Lakatos 1970). More specifically, if a predicted behavior derived from a particular typological scheme is disconfirmed, it is often difficult to determine whether the scheme itself, the auxiliary theories that link it to the measured observables, or some experimental particular was responsible for the negative result (Meehl 1978). Multiple schemes often share many auxiliary theories and experimental particulars. When one investigates multiple schemes and can demonstrate that one scheme has predictive validity in an area in which another scheme is unsuccessful, one is less likely to attribute the failure of one scheme to such auxiliary theory problems or experimental particulars. Thus, the simultaneous examination of multiple schemes increases the potential to demonstrate convincingly the inadequacies of the schemes we are studying. Since falsifiability is essential to scientific progress (Popper 1972), this is an important advantage indeed.

SUMMARY

This chapter has attempted to summarize and integrate the existing empirical and theoretical literature relevant to creating and evaluating typologies for rapists and child molesters. The review indicated that the descriptive literature has specified dimensions and constructs that have empirically been shown to have discriminatory potential with this offender population. This domain of variables has essentially served as the set of building blocks for the typological schemes that have been proposed in the theoretical literature on such offenders. Lacking, however, are empirical data on the homogeneity and reliability of these variables, greater specification of certain variables so that subtleties of the theoretical literature can be assessed empirically, and data on the covariation within this population of both core and auxiliary constructs. Furthermore, little empirical data exist on the reliability or validity of the various typologies proposed. We have, therefore, also attempted to outline strategies and methods that might be used to improve and refine the extant typologies. Many of these we have incorporated into our own research, which we have used to illustrate the process of typology construction and validation, cognizant always of our program's limits. In particular, we discussed the value of having multiple schemes available for comparative analyses so that the relative value of different schemes can be evaluated. It should be apparent that the task of developing good classifications is enormous and complex, requiring not only multiple approaches and methods, but the integration of the contributions of many investigators.

REFERENCES

Abel, G.G. "Assessment of Sexual Deviation in the Male." In *Behavioral Assessment: A Practical Handbook*, edited by M. Herson and A.S. Bellack. New York: Pergamon, 1976.

Abel, G.G., D.H. Barlow, E.B. Blanchard, and D. Guild. "The Components of Rapists' Sexual Arousal." *Archives of General Psychology* 34 (1977): 895-908.

Abel, G.G., D.H. Barlow, E.B. Blanchard, and M. Mavissakalian. *The Relationship of Aggressive Cues to the Sexual Arousal of Rapists.* Paper presented at the meeting of the American Psychological Association. New Orleans, Louisiana, August, 1974.

Abel, G.G., J.V. Becker, E.B. Blanchard, and A. Djenderedjian. "Differentiating Sexual Aggressives with Penile Measures." *Criminal Justice and Behavior* 5 (1978a): 315-332.

Abel, G.G. and E.B. Blanchard. "The Measurement and Generation of Sexual Arousal." In *Progress in Behavior Modification* (Vol. II), edited by M. Herson, R. Eisler, and P.M. Miller. New York: Academic Press, 1976.

Abel, G.G., E. Blanchard, D. Barlow, and M. Mavissakalian. "Identifying Specific Erotic Cues in Sexual Deviations by Audio Taped Descriptions." *Journal of Applied Behavior Analysis* 8 (1975): 247-260.

Abel, G.G., E.B. Blanchard, and J.V. Becker. "An Integrated Treatment Program for Rapists." In *Clinical Aspects of the Rapist*, edited by R. Rada. New York: Grune & Stratton, 1978b.

Abrahamsen, D. *Report on Study of 102 Sex Offenders at Sing Sing Prison.* Utica, New York: State Hospitals Press, March, 1950.

Allen, R.M., and T.D. Haupt. "The Sex Inventory: Test-Retest Reliabilities of Scale Scores and Items." *Journal of Clinical Psychology* 22 (1966): 375-378.

American Psychiatric Association. *Diagnostic and Statistical Manual of Mental Disorders. DSM-III.* Washington, D.C.: Author, 1980.

Amir, M. *Patterns in Forcible Rape.* Chicago, Illinois: University of Chicago Press, 1971.

Anastasi, A. *Psychological Testing.* New York: Macmillan Publishing Company, 1982.

Anderson, W.P., J.T. Kunce, and B. Rich. "Sex Offenders: Three Personality Types." *Journal of Clinical Psychology* 35 (1979): 671-676.

Apfelberg, B., C. Sugar, and A.Z. Pfeffer. "A Psychiatric Study of 250 Sex Offenders." *American Journal of Psychiatry* 100 (1944): 762-769.

Armentrout, J.A., and A.L. Hauer. "MMPI's of Rapists of Children, and Non-Rapist Sex Offenders." *Journal of Clinical Psychology* 34 (1978): 330-332.

Barbaree, H.E., W.L. Marshall, and R.D. Lanthier. "Deviant Sexual Arousal in Rapists." *Behavior Research Therapy* 17 (1979): 215-222.

Barclay, R.L., and T. Fjordbak. *Characteristics of Sex Offenders Raising the Insanity Defense.* Paper presented at the meeting of the American Psychological Association. New York, September, 1979.

Bard, L.A., D.L. Carter, D.D. Cerce, R.A. Knight, R. Rosenberg, and B. Schneider. *A Descriptive Study of Rapists and Child Molesters: Developmental, Clinical and Criminal Characteristics.* Manuscript submitted for publication, 1984.

Barlow, D.H., G.G. Abel, E.B. Blanchard, A.R. Bristow, and L.D. Young. "A Heterosocial Skills Behavior Checklist for Males." *Behavior Therapy* 8 (1977): 229-239.

Becker, J.V., and G.G. Abel. "Men and the Victimization of Women." In *Victimization of Women*, edited by J.R. Chapman and M.R. Gates. Beverly Hills, California: Sage Publications, 1978.

Becker, J.V., G.G. Abel, E.B. Blanchard, W.D. Murphy, and E. Coleman. "Evaluating Social Skills of Sexual Aggressives." *Criminal Justice and Behavior* 5 (1978): 357-367.

Blanchard, W.H. "The Group Process in Gang Rape." *Journal of Social Psychology* 49 (1959): 259-266.

Blashfield, R.K. "Evaluation of the DSM-II Classification of Schizophrenia as a Nomenclature." *Journal of Abnormal Psychology* 82 (1973): 382-389.

Blashfield, R.K. "Propositions Regarding the Use of Cluster Analysis in Clinical Research." *Journal of Consulting and Clinical Psychology* 48 (1980): 456-459.

Blashfield, R.K., and M.L. Aldenderfer. "The Literature on Cluster Analysis." *Multivariate Behavioral Research* 13 (1978): 271-295.

Blashfield, R.K., and J.G. Draguns. "Evaluative Criteria for Psychiatric Classification." *Journal of Abnormal Psychology* 85 (1976): 140-150.

Bowman, K.M., and B. Engel. "Sexual Psychopath Laws." In *Sexual Behavior and the Law*, edited by R. Slovenko. Springfield, Illinois: Charles C. Thomas, 1965.

Brancale, R., A. Ellis, and R.R. Doorbar. "Psychiatric and Psychological Investigations of Convicted Sex Offenders: A Summary Report." *American Journal of Psychiatry* 109 (1952): 17-21.

Brancale, R., D. MacNeil, and A. Vuocolo. "Profile of the New Jersey Sex Offender: A Statistical Study of 1,206 Male Sex Offenders." *The Welfare Research Report* 16 (1965): 3-9.

Brennan, T. "Multivariate Taxonomic Classification for Criminal Justice Research." Unpublished manuscript, 1980. (Available from the National Institute of Justice, Office of Research and Evaluation Methods, Department of Justice, Washington, D.C. 20531).

Brownmiller, S. *Against Our Will*. New York: Bantam Books, Inc., 1975.

Buck, J.A., and J.R. Graham. "The 4-3 MMPI Profile Type: A Failure to Replicate." *Journal of Consulting and Clinical Psychology* 46 (1978): 344.

Burgess, A.W., and L.L. Holmstrom. *Rape: Victims of crisis*. Bowie, Maryland: Prentice-Hall, 1974.

Burgess, A.W., and A. Lazare. "The Sexually Abused." In *Community Mental Health: Target Populations*, edited by A.W. Burgess and A. Lazare. New Jersey: Prentice-Hall, 1976.

Butcher, J.N. "Manifest Aggression: MMPI Correlates in Normal Boys." *Journal of Consulting Psychology* 29 (1965): 446-454. (Also in *Dissertation Abstracts* 25 (1965): 6755-6756.)

Cabeen, C.W., and J.C. Coleman. "Group Therapy with Sex Offenders: Description and Evaluation of Group Therapy Programs in an Institutional Setting." *Journal of Clinical Psychology* 17 (1961): 122-129.

Campbell, D.T., and D.W. Fiske. "Convergent and Discriminant Validation by the Multitrait-Multimethod Matrix." *Psychological Bulletin* 56 (1959): 81-105.

Carlson, K.A. "Classification of Adult Offenders: A Multivariate Approach." *Journal of Abnormal Psychology* 79 (1972): 84-93.

Carroll, J.L., and G.B. Fuller. "An MMPI Comparison of Three Groups of Criminals." *Journal of Clinical Psychology* 27 (1971): 240-242.

Chapman, L.J., and J.P. Chapman. "Genesis of Popular but Erroneous Psychodiagnostic Observations." *Journal of Abnormal Psychology* 72 (1967): 193-204.

Chappell, D. "Cross-cultural Research on Forcible Rape." *International Journal of Criminology and Penology* 4 (1976): 295-303.

Chignell, M., and B.G. Stacey. "Practical Problems Associated with the Use of Cluster Analysis." *Psychological Reports* 46 (1980): 131-134.

Christie, M.M., W.L. Marshall, and R.D. Lanthier. *A Descriptive Study of Incarcerated Rapists and Pedophiles*. Report to the Solicitor General of Canada, 1979.

Clinnard, M.B., and R. Quinney. "Types of Crime." In *Criminal Behavior Systems: A Typology*, edited by M.B. Clinnard and R. Quinney. New York: Holt, Reinhart, & Winston, 1967.

Cohen, M.L., R.J. Boucher, T.K. Seghorn, and J. Mehegan. *The Sexual Offender Against Children*. Presented at a meeting of the Association for Professional Treatment of Offenders, Boston, Massachusetts, 1979.

Cohen, M.L., R.F. Garafalo, R. Boucher, and T. Seghorn. "The Psychology of Rapists," *Seminars in Psychiatry* 3 (1971): 307-327.

Cohen, M.L., T. Seghorn, and W. Calmas. "Sociometric Study of the Sex Offender," *Journal of Abnormal Psychology* 74 (1969): 249-255.

Cowden, J.E., and E.L. Morse. "The Relationship of Defensiveness to Responses on the Sex Inventory." *Journal of Clinical Psychology* 26 (1970): 505-509.

Cowden, J.E., and A.R. Pacht. "The Sex Inventory as a Classification Instrument for Sex Offenders." *Journal of Clinical Psychology* 25 (1969): 53-57.

Dahlstrom, W.G., and G.S. Welsh. *An MMPI Handbook: A Guide to Use in Clinical Practice and Research.* Minneapolis: University of Minnesota Press, 1960.

Dahlstrom, W.G., G.S. Welsh, and L.E. Dahlstrom. *An MMPI Handbook, Volume I: Clinical Interpretation.* Minneapolis: University of Minnesota Press, 1972.

Dahlstrom, W.G., G.S. Welsh, and L.E. Dahlstrom. *An MMPI Handbook, Volume II: Research Applications.* Minneapolis: University of Minnesota Press, 1975.

Davids, A., and H. Pildner, Jr. "Comparison of Direct and Projective Methods of Personality Assessment Under Different Conditions of Motivation." *Psychological Monographs* 72 (1958): (11, Whole No. 464).

Davis, K.R., and J.O. Sines. "An Antisocial Behavior Pattern Associated with a Specific MMPI Profile." *Journal of Consulting and Clinical Psychology* 36 (1971): 229-234.

Dietrich, S.G., and L.S. Berger. "The MMPI in Criminology: Abuses of Application." *The Journal of Psychiatry and Law* 6 (1979): 453-479.

Ellis, A., and R. Brancale. *The Psychology of Sex Offenders.* Springfield, Illinois: Charles C. Thomas, 1956.

Exner, J.E. *The Rorschach: A Comprehensive System.* New York: John Wiley & Sons, 1974.

Exner, J.E. *The Rorschach: A Comprehensive System, Volume 2: Current Research and Advanced Interpretations.* New York: John Wiley & Sons, 1978.

Everitt, B.S., A.J. Gourlay, and R.E. Kendell. "An Attempt at Validation of Traditional Psychiatric Syndromes by Cluster Analysis." *British Journal of Psychiatry* 119 (1971): 399-412.

Finkelhor, D. *Sexually Victimized Children.* New York: Free Press, 1979.

Fisher, G. "Human Figure Drawings Indices of Sexual Maladjustment in Male Felons." *Journal of Projective Techniques and Personality Assessment* 32 (1968): 81.

Fisher, G. "Psychological Needs of Heterosexual Pedophiles." *Diseases of the Nervous System* 30 (1969): 419-421.

Fisher, G., and L.M. Howell. "Psychological Needs of Homosexual Pedophiles." *Diseases of the Nervous System* 31 (1970): 623-625.

Fisher, G., and E. Rivlin. "Psychological Needs of Rapists." *British Journal of Criminology* 11 (1971): 182-185.

Fitch, J.H. "Men Convicted of Sexual Offenses Against Children: A Descriptive Follow-Up Study." *British Journal of Criminology* 3 (1962): 18-37.

Freund, K. "Erotic Preference in Pedophilia." *Behavior Research and Therapy* 5 (1967): 339-348.

Frosch, J., and W. Bromberg. "The Sex Offender: A Psychiatric Study." *American Journal of Orthopsychiatry* 9 (1939): 761-776.

Gearing, M.L. "MMPI as a Primary Differentiator and Predictor of Behavior in Prison: A Methodological Critique and Review of the Recent Literature." *Psychological Bulletin* 86 (1979): 929-963.

Gebhard, P.H., J.H. Gagnon, W.B. Pomeroy, and C.V. Christenson. *Sex Offenders: An Analysis of Types.* New York: Harper & Row, 1965.

Geiser, R.L. *Hidden Victims: The Sexual Abuse of Children.* Boston, Massachusetts: Beacon Press, 1979.

Gendreau, P., M. Irvine, and S. Knight. "Evaluating Response Set Styles on the MMPI with Prisoners: Faking Good Adjustment and Maladjustment." *Canadian Journal of Behavioral Science* 5 (1973): 183-194.

Gilberstadt, H., and J. Duker. *A Handbook for Clinical and Actuarial MMPI Interpretation.* Philadelphia, Pennsylvania: W.B. Saunders Co., 1965.

Glueck, B.C. *Final Report, Research Project for the Study and Treatment of Persons Convicted of Crimes Involving Sexual Aberrations, June 1952 to June 1955.* New York: State Department of Hygiene, 1956.

Graham, J.R. *The MMPI: A Practical Guide.* New York: Oxford University Press, 1977.

Groth, A.N. "Patterns of Sexual Assault Against Children and Adolescents." In *Sexual Assault of Children and Adolescents*, edited by A.W. Burgess, A.N. Groth, L.L. Holmstrom, and S.M. Sgroi. Lexington, Massachusetts: D.C. Heath, 1978.

Groth, A.N., and H.J. Birnbaum. "Adult Sexual Orientation and Attraction to Underage Persons." *Archives of Sexual Behavior* 7 (1978): 175-181.

Groth, A.N., and H.J. Birnbaum. *Men Who Rape.* New York: Plenum Press, 1979.

Groth, A.N., and A.W. Burgess. "Rape: A Sexual Deviation." *American Journal of Orthopsychiatry* 47 (1977): 400-406.

Groth, A.N., A.W. Burgess, and L.L. Holmstrom. "Rape: Power, Anger, and Sexuality." *American Journal of Psychiatry* 134 (1977): 1239-1243.

Guertin, W.H., and W.E. Trembath. "Card VI Disturbance on the Rorschachs of Sex Offenders." *The Journal of General Psychology* 49 (1953): 221-227.

Guttmacher, M.S. *Sex Offenses: The Problem, Causes, and Prevention.* New York: W.W. Norton & Company, 1951.

Guttmacher, M.S., and H. Weihofen. *Psychiatry and the Law.* New York: W.W. Norton & Company, 1952,

Gynther, M.D., H. Altman, and R.W. Warbin. "A New Actuarial-Empirical Automated MMPI Interpretation Program: The 4-3/3-4 Code Type." *Journal of Clinical Psychology* 29 (1973a): 229-231.

Gynther, M.D., H. Altman, and R.W. Warbin. "Behavioral Correlates for Minnesota Multiphasic Personality Inventory 4-9, 9-4 Code Types: A Case of the Emperor's New Clothes?" *Journal of Consulting and Clinical Psychology* 40 (1973b): 259-263.

Hammer, E.F. "A Comparison of H-T-P's of Rapists and Pedophiles." *Journal of Projective Techniques* 18 (1954a): 346-355.

Hammer, E.F. "A Comparison of H-T-P's of Rapists and Pedophiles: III. The 'Dead' Tree as an Index of Psychopathology." *Journal of Clinical Psychology* 11 (1955): 67-69.

Hammer, E.F. "Relationship between Diagnosis of Psychosexual Pathology and the Sex of the First Drawn Person." *Journal of Clinical Psychology* 19 (1954b): 167-170.

Hammer, E.F., and I.A. Jacks. "A Study of Rorschach Flexor and Extensor Human Movement Responses." *Journal of Clinical Psychology* 11 (1955): 63-67.

Hartman, B.J. "Comparison of Selected Experimental M.M.P.I. Profiles of Sexual Deviates and Sociopaths Without Sexual Deviation." *Psychological Reports* 20 (1967): 234.

Haupt, T.D., and R.M. Allen. "A Multivariate Analysis of Variance of Social Scores on the Sex Inventory, Male Form." *Journal of Clinical Psychology* 22 (1966): 387-395.

Hempel, C.G. *Aspects of Scientific Explanation.* New York: Free Press, 1965.

Hempel, C.G. *Symposium: Problems of Concept and Theory Formation in the Social Sciences, Language and Human Rights.* Philadelphia: University of Pennsylvania Press, 1952.

Henn, R.A., M. Herjanic, and R.H. Vanderpearl. "Forensic Psychiatry: Profiles of Two Types of Sex Offenders." *American Journal of Psychiatry* 133 (1976): 694-696.

Howells, D., and E. Wright. "The Sexual Attitudes of Aggressive Sexual Offenders." *British Journal of Criminology* 18 (1978): 170-174.

Jackson, D.N., and S. Messick. *Differential Personality Inventory.* London, Ontario: Authors, 1971.

Jaffe, A.C., L. Dynneson, and R.W. ten Bensel. "Sexual Abuse of Children: An Epidemiologic Study." *American Journal of Diseases of Children* 129 (1975): 689-692.

Jensen, A.R. "Review of the Rorschach." In *The Sixth Mental Measurements Yearbook*, edited by O.I. Buros. Highland Park, New Jersey: Gryphon Press, 1965.

Jensen, D.E., J.R. Prandoni, and N.H. Abudabbeh. "Figure Drawings by Sex Offenders and a Random Sample of Offenders." *Perceptual and Motor Skills* 32 (1971): 295-300.

Jones, B. Mc., L.L. Jenstrom, and K. MacFarlane. *Sexual Abuse of Children: Selected Readings.* Washington, D.C.: U.S. Department of Health and Human Services (Pub. No. OHDS 78-30161), 1980.

Karpman, B. *The Sexual Offender and His Offenses, Etiology, Patholo-gy, Psychodynamics and Treatment*. New York: Julian, 1954.

Kelley, C.K., and G.D. King. "Behavioral Correlates of Infrequent Two-Point MMPI Code Types at a University Mental Health Center." *Journal of Clinical Psychology* 35 (1979): 576-585.

Kinslinger, H.J. "Application of Projective Techniques in Personnel Psychology Since 1940." *Psychological Bulletin* 66 (1966): 134-149.

Knight, R.A., R. Prentky, B. Schneider, and R. Rosenberg. "Line-ar Causal Modeling of Adaptation and Criminal History in Sexual Of-fenders." In *Prospective Studies of Antisocial Behavior*, edited by K. Van Dusen and S. Mednick. Boston, Massachusetts: Kluwer-Nijhoff Publishing Company, 1983.

Kinght, R.A., and J.D. Roff. "Childhood and Young Adult Predictors of Schizophrenic Outcome." In *Origins of Psychopathology: Research and Public Policy*, edited by D. Ricks and B. Dohrenwend. Cambridge: Cambridge University Press, 1983.

Kopp, S.B. "The Character Structure of Sex Offenders." *American Journal of Psychotherapy* 16 (1962): 64-70.

Kozol, H., R. Boucher, and R. Garofalo. "The Diagnosis and Treatment of Dangerousness." *Crime and Delinquency* 18 (1972): 371-392.

Lakatos, I. "Falsification and the Methodology of Scientific Research Programs." In *Criticism and the Growth of Knowledge*, edited by I. Lakatos and A. Musgrave. Cambridge: Cambridge University Press, 1970.

Law, S.K. "Child Molestation: A Comparison of Hong Kong and Western Findings." *Medical Science Law* 19 (1979): 55-60.

Laws, D.R., and M. Holmen. "Sexual Response Faking in Pedophiles." *Criminal Justice and Behavior* 5 (1978): 343-356.

Lawton, M.P., and M.Y. Kleban. "Prisoners' Faking on the MMPI." *Journal of Clinical Psychology* 21 (1965): 269-271.

Lewandowski, D., and J.R. Graham. "Empirical Correlates of Frequently Occurring Two-Point MMPI Code Types: A Replicated Study." *Journal of Consulting and Clinical Psychology* 39 (1972): 467-472.

Lindner, H. "The Blacky Picture Test: A Study of Sexual and Non-Sexu-al Offenders." *Journal of Projective Techniques* 17 (1953): 79-84.

Magaro, P.A., and P. Smith. "The Personality of Clinical Types: An Empirically Derived Taxonomy." *Journal of Clinical Psychology* 37 (1981): 160-167.

Marks, P.A., and W. Seeman. *The Actuarial Description of Personality: An Atlas for Use with the MMPI*. Baltimore, Maryland: Williams and Wilkins, 1963.

Marsh, J.T., J. Hilliard, and R. Liechti. "A Sexual Deviation Scale for the M.M.P.I." *Journal of Consulting Psychology* 19 (1955): 55-59.

Marshall, W.L., and M.M. Christie. "Pedophilia and Aggression." *Criminal Justice and Behavior* 8 (1981): 145-158.

Marshall, W.L., M.M. Christie, and R.D. Lanthier. *Social Competence, Sexual Experience and Attitudes to Sex in Incarcerated Rapists and Pedophiles*. Report to the Solicitor General of Canada, 1979.

McCaghy, C.H. "Child Molesters: A Study of Their Careers as Deviants." In *Criminal Behavior Systems: A Typology*, edited by M.B. Clinnard and R. Quinney. New York: Holt, Rinehart, & Winston, 1967.

McCaldron, R.J. "Rape." *The Canadian Journal of Corrections* 9 (1967): 37-59.

McCreary, C.P. "Personality Differences Among Child Molesters." *Journal of Personality Assessment* 39 (1975): 591-593.

Meehl, P.E. "A Funny Thing Happened to Us on the Way to Latent Entities." *Journal of Personality Assessment* 43 (1979): 564-580.

Meehl, P.E. Prefatory comment. In *Readings in Personality Assessment*, edited by L.D. Goodstein & R.I. Lanyon. New York: Wiley, 1972.

Meehl, P.E. "Theoretical Risks and Tabular Asterisks: Sir Karl, Sir Ronald, and the Slow Progress of Soft Psychology." *Journal of Consulting and Clinical Psychology* 46 (1978): 806-834.

Meehl, P.E., and A. Rosen. "Antecedent Probability and the Efficacy of Psychometric Signs, Patterns, or Cutting Scores." *Psychological Bulletin* 52 (1955): 194-216.

Megargee, E.I. "Psychological Determinants and Correlates of Criminal Violence." In *Criminal Violence*, edited by M.E. Wolfgang and N.A. Weiner. Beverly Hills, California: Sage Publications, 1982.

Megargee, E.I. "Undercontrolled and Overcontrolled Personality Types in Extreme Antisocial Aggression." *Psychological Monographs* 80 (1966): (No. 611), 1-29.

Millon, T. *Disorders of Personality: DSM-III Axis II*. New York: John Wiley & Sons, 1981.

Millon, T. *Modern Psychopathology*. Philadelphia, Pennsylvania: Saunders, 1969.

Mohr, J.W., R.E. Turner, and M.B. Jerry. *Pedophilia and Exhibitionism*. Toronto, Ontario: University of Toronto Press, 1964.

Monahan, J. *The Clinical Prediction of Violent Behavior*. NIMH Crime and Delinquency Issues Monograph, U.S. Department of Health and Human Services Publication No. ADM81-921. Washington, D.C.: U.S. Government Printing Office, 1981.

Morris, K., B. Schneider, and R. A. Knight. *Patterns of Alcohol Abuse in Sexual Offenses*. Paper presented at the meeting of the Eastern Psychological Association. Philadelphia, Pennsylvania, April, 1983.

Norris, J., and S. Feldman-Summers. "Factors Related to the Psychological Impacts of Rape on the Victim." *Journal of Abnormal Psychology* 90 (1981): 562-567.

Pacht, A.R., and J.E. Cowden. "An Exploratory Study of Five Hundred Sex Offenders." *Criminal Justice and Behavior* 1 (1974): 13-20.

Pacht, A.R., S.L. Halleck, and J.C. Ehrmann. "Diagnosis and Treatment of the Sexual Offender: A Nine Year Study." *American Journal of Psychiatry* 118 (1962): 802-808.

Panton, J.H. "M.M.P.I. Profile Configurations Among Crime Classification Groups." *Journal of Clinical Psychology* 14 (1958): 305-308.

Panton, J.H. "M.M.P.I. Profile Configurations Associated With Incestuous and Non-Incestuous Child Molesting." *Psychological Reports* 45 (1979): 335-338.

Panton, J.H. "Personality Differences Appearing Between Rapists of Adults, Rapists of Children, and Non-Violent Sexual Molesters of Female Children." *Research Communications in Psychology, Psychiatry, and Behavior* 3 (1978): 385-393.

Paykel, E.S., and E. Rassaby. "Classification of Suicide Attempters by Cluster Analysis." *British Journal of Psychiatry* 133 (1978): 45-52.

Peek, R.M., and L.H. Storms. "Validity of the Marsh-Hilliard-Liechti M.M.P.I. Sexual Deviation Scale in a State Hospital Population." *Journal of Consulting Psychology* 20 (1956): 133-136.

Perdue, W.C., and D. Lester. "Personality Characteristics of Rapists." *Perceptual and Motor Skills* 35 (1972): 314.

Persons, R.W., and P.A. Marks. "The Violent 4-3 M.M.P.I. Personality Type." *Journal of Consulting and Clinical Psychology* 36 (1971): 189-196.

Peters, J.J. "Children Who Are Victims of Sexual Assault and the Psychology of Offenders." *American Journal of Psychotherapy* 30 (1976): 398-421.

Peterson, M.A., H.B. Braiker, and S.M. Polich. *Doing Crime: A Survey of California Prison Inmates*. Santa Monica, California: Rand Corporation, 1980.

Pierce, D.M. "MMPI Correlates of Adaptation to Prison." *Correctional Psychologist* 5 (1972): 43-47.

Piotrowski, Z.A., and D. Abrahamsen. "Sexual Crime, Alcohol, and the Rorschach Test." *Psychiatric Quarterly Supplement* 26 (1952): 248-260.

Popper, K.R. *The Logic of Scientific Discovery*. New York: Basic Books, 1959.

Pothast, M.D. "A Personality Study of Two Types of Murderers." Ph.D. dissertation, Michigan State University, 1956. (Also in *Dissertation Abstracts* 17 (1957): 898-899.)

Prandoni, J.R., D.E. Jensen, J.T. Matranga, and M.O. Waison. "Selected Rorschach Response Characteristics of Sex Offenders." *Journal of Personality Assessment* 37 (1973): 334-336.

Prentky, R., M. Cohen, and T. Seghorn. "Development of a Rational Taxonomy for the Classification of Sexual Offenders: Rapists." *American Academy of Psychiatry and The Law*, 1984.

Quinsey, V.L. "The Assessment and Treatment of Child Molesters: A Review." *Canadian Psychological Review* 18 (1977): 204-220.

Quinsey, V.L., and W.F. Carrigan. "Penile Responses to Visual Stimuli: Instructional Control with and without Auditory Sexual Fantasy Correlates." *Criminal Justice and Behavior* 5 (1978): 333-342.

Quinsey, V.L., and T.C. Chaplin. "Penile Responses to Nonsexual Violence among Rapists." *Criminal Justice and Behavior* 9 (1982): 372-381.

Quinsey, V.L., T. Chaplin, and W. Carrigan. "Biofeedback and Signaled Punishment in the Modification of Inappropriate Sexual Age Preferences." *Behavior Therapy* 11 (1980): 567-576.

Quinsey, V.L., T.C. Chaplin, and G. Varney. "A Comparison of Rapists' and Non-Sex Offenders' Sexual Preferences for Mutually Consenting Sex, Rape, and Physical Abuse of Women." *Behavioral Assessment* 3 (1981): 127-135.

Quinsey, V.L., C.M. Steinman, S.G. Bergersen, and T.F. Holmes. "Penile Circumference, Skin Conductance, and Ranking Responses of Child Molesters and "Normals" to Sexual and Nonsexual Visual Stimuli." *Behavior Therapy* 6 (1975): 213-219.

Rada, R.T. "Alcoholism and the Child Molester." *Annals of the New York Academy of Sciences* 273 (1976): 492-496.

Rada, R.T. "Alcoholism and Forcible Rape." *American Journal of Psychiatry* 132 (1975): 444-446.

Rada, R.T. *Clinical Aspects of the Rapist*. New York: Grune & Stratton, 1978.

Rada, R.T., R. Kellner, D.R. Laws, and W.W. Winslow. "Drinking, Alcoholism, and the Mentally Disordered Sex Offender." *The Bulletin of the American Academy of Psychiatry and the Law* 6 (1979): 296-300.

Rader, C.M. "MMPI Profile Types of Exposers, Rapists, and Assaulters in a Court Service Population." *Journal of Consulting and Clinical Psychology* 45 (1977): 61-69.

Repucci, N.D., and W.G. Clingempeel. "Methodological Issues in Research with Correctional Populations." *Journal of Consulting and Clinical Psychology* 46 (1978): 727-746.

Revitch, E., and R.G. Weiss. "The Pedophilic Offender." *Diseases of the Nervous System* 23 (1962): 73-78.

Rosen, R.C. "Suppression of Penile Tumescence by Instrumental Conditioning." *Psychosomatic Medicine* 35 (1973): 509-513.

Rosenberg, R. "An Empirical Determination of Sex Offender Subtypes." Unpublished Masters Thesis, University of Rhode Island, 1981.

Ruff, C.F., D.I. Templer, and J.L. Ayers. "The Intelligence of Rapists." *Archives of Sexual Behavior* 5 (1976): 327-329.

Schneider, B. "Validation of Sex Offender Subtypes Through Personality Assessment." In *Assessment of Subtypes of Rapists and Pedophiles: Implications for Treatment*, chaired by R.A. Prentky. Symposium presented at the meeting of the American Psychological Association. Los Angeles, California, August, 1981.

Schneider, B., and R.A. Knight. "The Millon Clinical Multiaxial Inventory in the Validation of a Sex Offender Taxonomy." Paper

presented at the meeting of the Eastern Psychological Association.
Baltimore, Md., April 1982.

Seghorn, T.K. "Adequacy of Ego Functioning in Rapists and Pedophiles."
Ph.D. dissertation, Boston University Graduate School, 1970. See
also *Dissertation Abstracts International* 31 (1971): 7613A-7614A.
University Microfilms No. 70-22, 413).

Seghorn, T.K. "The Decision Tree: Factors in the Clinical Subtyping
of Sexually Dangerous Persons." In *Assessment of Subtypes of
Rapists and Pedophiles: Implications for Treatment*, chaired by R.A.
Prentky. Symposium presented at the meeting of the American Psychological Association. Los Angeles, California, August, 1981.

Seghorn, T., and M. Cohen. "The Psychology of the Rape Assailant."
In *Modern Legal Medicine, Psychiatry, and Forensic Science*, edited
by W. Cerran, A.L. McGarry, and C. Petty. Philadelphia, Pennsylvania: F.A. Davis Company, 1980.

Shah, S. "Dangerousness: A Paradigm for Exploring Some Issues in Law
and Psychology." *American Psychologist* 33 (1978): 224-238.

Shaskan, D. "One Hundred Sex Offenders." *American Journal of Orthopsychiatry* 9 (1939): 565-569.

Skinner, H.A. "'The Eyes That Fix You': A Model for Classification
Research." *Canadian Psychological Review* 18 (1977): 142-151.

Skinner, H.A. "Toward the Integration of Classification Theory and
Methods." *Journal of Abnormal Psychology* 90 (1981): 68-87.

Skinner, H.A., and R.K. Blashfield. "Increasing the Impact of Cluster
Analysis Research: The Case of Psychiatric Classification." *Journal
of Consulting and Clinical Psychology* 50 (1982): 727-735.

Skinner, H.A., D.N. Jackson, and H. Hoffman. "Alcoholic Personality
Types: Identification and Correlates." *Journal of Abnormal Psychology* 83 (1974): 658-666.

Skinner, H.A., P.L. Reed, and D.N. Jackson. "Toward the Objective
Diagnosis of Psychopathology: Generalizability of Modal Personality
Profiles." *Journal of Consulting and Clinical Psychology* 44 (1976):
111-117.

Spitzer, R., J. Endicott, and J. Robins. *Research Diagnostic Criteria*.
Unpublished manuscript, 1975. (Available from: Biometrics Research,
New York State Psychiatric Institute, 722 West 168th St., New York,
10032).

Spitzer, R.L., and J.L. Fleiss. "A Reanalysis of the Reliability of
Psychiatric Diagnosis." *British Journal of Psychiatry* 125 (1974):
341-347.

Spitzer, R.L., J.B.W. Forman, and J. Nee. "DSM-III Field Trials: I.
Initial Interrater Diagnostic Reliability." *American Journal of
Psychiatry* 136 (1979): 815-817.

Stricker, G. "Stimulus Properties of the Blacky to a Sample of Pedophiles." *The Journal of General Psychology* 77 (1967): 35-39.

Sullivan, P. "Commitment of Sexual Psychopaths and the Requirements
of Procedural Due Process." *Fordham Law Review* 44 (1967): 923-949.

Swanson, D.W. "Adult Sexual Abuse of Children: The Man and Circumstances." *Diseases of the Nervous System* 29 (1968): 677-683.

Swanson, D.W. "Who Violates Children Sexually?" *Medical Aspects of
Human Sexuality* 5 (1971): 184-197.

Swenson, W.M., and B.P. Grimes. "Characteristics of Sex Offenders Admitted to a Minnesota State Hospital for Pre-Sentence Psychiatric Investigation." *Psychiatric Quarterly Supplement* Part 1 (1958): 1-14.

Thorne, F.C. "A Factorial Study of Sexuality in Adult Males." *Journal of Clinical Psychology* 22 (1966a): 378-386.

Thorne, F.C. "The Sex Inventory." *Journal of Clinical Psychology* 22 (1966b): 367-374.

Thorne, F.C., and T.D. Haupt. "The Objective Measurement of Sex Attitudes and Behavior in Adult Males." *Journal of Clinical Psychology* 22 (1966): 395-403.

Virkkunen, M. "The Pedophilic Offender with Antisocial Character." *Acta Psychiatrica Scandinavica* 53 (1976): 401-405.

Walters, G.D., R.L. Greene, and G.S. Solomon. "Empirical Correlates of the Overcontrolled Hostility Scale and the MMPI 4-3 High-Point Pair." *Journal of Consulting and Clinical Psychology* 50 (1982a): 213-218.

Walters, G.D., G.S. Solomon, and R.L. Greene. "The Relationship Between the Overcontrolled Hostility Scale and the MMPI 4-3 High-Point Pair." *Journal of Clinical Psychology* 38 (1982b): 613-615.

Wattron, J.B. "Validity of the Marsh-Hilliard-Liechti M.M.P.I. Sexual Deviation Scale in a State Prison Population." *Journal of Consulting Psychology* 22 (1958): 16.

Whitman, W.P., and V.L. Quinsey. "Heterosocial Skills Training for Institutionalized Rapists and Child Molesters." *Canadian Journal of Behavioral Science* 13 (1981): 105-114.

Wiener-Levy, D., and J.E. Exner, Jr. "The Rorschach Comprehensive System: An Overview." In *Advances in Psychological Assessment* (Vol. 5), edited by P. McReynolds. San Francisco, California: Jossey-Bass, 1981.

Wiens, A.N., J.D. Matarazzo, and K.D. Gaver. "Performance and Verbal IQ in a Group of Sociopaths." *Journal of Clinical Psychology* 15 (1959): 191-193.

Wysocki, A.C., and B.A. Wysocki. "Human Figure Drawings of Sex Offenders." *Journal of Clinical Psychology* 33 (1977): 278-284.

CHAPTER 18

RAPE AND VOCABULARIES OF MOTIVE:
ALTERNATIVE PERSPECTIVES

Diana Scully and
Joseph Marolla

For the past fifty years, the field of psychiatry has dominated
the literature on rape and especially the literature on rapists. Not
only have psychiatrists defined the problem from their particular perspective, but they have also defined what constitutes "proper" treatment. The psychiatric-psychopathological model, like all models of
human behavior, is not a description of what exists, but rather an
interpretation of behavior based upon a set of logically-related concepts. It is, then, an imposition in the sense that all theories or
models impose an order on things that may or may not be real. Psychiatrists have imposed such an order on the study of rape and the
elements that they have chosen to emphasize have become the generally
accepted explanations for the behavior. This chapter will present a
critical analysis of the psychopathological model and conclude by
suggesting an alternative model in which rape can be examined as a
form of extreme, yet normative, male role behavior. This analysis
should demonstrate the critical importance of understanding the inherent biases in any perspective that is allowed to dominate thought
on a social problem.

VOCABULARY OF MOTIVE

The psychiatric rape literature can be most fruitfully interpreted from a sociology of knowledge framework, the analytic tool that
can be used to demonstrate the relationship between interest, ideology, and ideas. Confronted with a theory or explanation, this approach
asks the basic question of whose interests are being served. That is,
"In whose interest is this theory?"

"Vocabulary of motive," the concept developed by Mills (1940),
further informs this discussion. According to Mills, "Rather than
fixed elements 'in' an individual, motives are the terms with which
interpretation of conduct by social actors proceeds" (p. 904). Appropriate vocabularies of motive--or "reasons"--exist within all cultures for individuals who have broken a norm or set of norms. The
appropriateness of the motive depends upon the reference group. That
is, there is no universal answer to the question "Why did you do that?"
The answer depends upon what a particular group or society will accept
as appropriate. These reasons or motive statements, then, not only
justify the past actions of the actor but, equally important, they
justify present and future behaviors of others.

In the literature influenced by the psychoanalytic approach,
there are primarily four types of motive statements attributed to

---

Parts of this chapter were adapted from Marolla, J. and D. Scully.
"Rape and Psychiatric Vocabularies of Motive." In *Gender and Disordered Behavior: Sex Differences in Psychopathology*, E.S. Gomberg
and V. Franks, eds. New York: Brunner/Mazel, 1979.

rapists. Although they are often found combined, for analytic purposes each will be treated as a separate category. They are (1) uncontrollable impulse; (2) mental illness or disease; (3) momentary
loss of control precipitated by unusual circumstances; and (4) victim
precipitation. Each of these explanations serves the similar function of providing a very insular view of rape. First, each is an individualistic explanation, thus negating the necessity to study the
problem of rape beyond the individual offender. Next, each one assumes that the behavior is strange or abnormal (with the exception of
victim precipitation). Thus, rape is removed from the realm of the
everyday or "normal" world and is seemingly less threatening, especially to males. Additionally, each explanation absolves everyone,
except the victim, from responsibility. And finally, as Szasz (1963)
points out in his discussion of the insanity plea, the effect is to
avoid the study of society and/or social injustices. The psychiatric
view of rapists has had the same consequence. It removes the necessity of investigating the elements within a society which precipitate
violent aggression against women.

In the remainder of this paper, the logic behind each category
and the consequences of each will be examined in greater detail before
presenting an alternative view. Consistent with a sociology of knowledge perspective, we assume that the intellectual products of a group
in power ultimately function in the interest of that group. In the
case of rape, the psychiatric vocabulary of motive is the intellectual
product of a male-dominated profession and a patriarchal society. It
will become apparent that by labeling rape the product of individual
pathology, the rapist is placed outside the parameters of normal
group membership and, thus, the connection between "normal" men and
rape can be avoided. When an individual case cannot be made to fit
the pathological model, other explanations, such as alcohol or victim
precipitation, can be substituted. In the end, attention is forced
away from the possibility that sexual aggression may be consistent
with normative male sexual behavior.

IRRESISTIBLE IMPULSE

In 1925, Glueck presented the argument that irresistible impulse
and insanity affected an individual in similar ways. He argued that
self control involves the power to attend to distant motives and general principles of conduct. Disease of the brain weakens control and
an uncontrollable impulse can result. The individual will not know
that his behavior is wrong because he will not relate the particular
act to the general rules forbidding it. Therefore, the behavior is
not voluntary and the individual is not accountable. Glueck suggested
expert (i.e., psychiatric) examination of these people because "the
external symptoms are but indicative of a much deeper disturbance,
the relation of which to the criminal act can only be ascertained by
mental analysis" (Glueck 1925:323).

Since Glueck's writing, psychiatric literature has been filled
with the assertion that irresistible impulse is at the root of rape.
For example:

> Whether it is comparatively mild as in the case
> of simple assault, or whether it is severely ag-
> gravated assault, it is, as a rule, an expression
> of an uncontrollable urge, committed without
> logic or rationale, under the influence of a
> strong, overpowering drive (Karpman 1951:185).

> It is not intended to suggest that all re-
> cidivous sex offenders are physically danger-
> ous, but experience shows that some of them
> are compulsively so, and that most of them
> are driven by uncontrollable impulsions that
> do not respond to customary procedures (Rein-
> hardt and Fisher 1949:734).

And Guttmacher and Weihofen (1952) list "explosive expression of pent-
up impulse" as a primary motivation for rape.

It is important to note the consequences of this particular vocabulary of motive. Not only does it abdicate responsiblity for the
act, but it also removes the behavior from legal jurisdiction. "There
is little doubt that the reactions that are attributed to sexual psychopaths are beyond the sphere of conscious control and appear as irresistible impulses, which explains why, in practice, these cases do
not profit by punishment; uncontrollable instinct is beyond punishment" (Karpman 1951:191).

In order for a crime to be prosecuted, the element of volition
or criminal intent is often critical. When an act is attributed to
irresistible impulse, the volitional element and, thus, responsibility, is removed. Spirer (1942) noted that most things that are called
impulses can be resisted up to a point and, therefore, irresistible
is a relative, not absolute, term. Further, from a strict behaviorist
view, almost all behavior might be considered irresistible. "But, as
we well know, not every person who is thus emotionally stimulated
finds a release in an aggressive act for, if this were so, the incidence of violent crimes would be tremendously greater than is now the
case" (Spirer 1942:459). He argued that criminal habituation need
not to be viewed as deep-seated pathology but, rather, arises in the sam
manner as non-criminal habituation. The psychological processes involved in learning are the same whether the outcome is a criminal act
or a legal one.

The impulse theory lacks empirical support. Of critical importance is Amir's (1971) finding that 71 percent of the rapes he studied were premeditated. If the act were impulsive, by definition the
offender should not have been able to delay his response. Finally,
since impulse theory could hypothetically be applied to any behavior,
it is interesting to question why it has been used as an appropriate
motive for crimes against women and not for other types of criminal
behavior. The motive doesn't necessarily explain rape, but it does
fit psychiatric assumptions about male and female sexuality (Albin
1977). In more recent literature, irresistible impulse is often replaced by mental illness, a more sophisticated vocabulary of motive.

THE DISEASE MODEL

Irresistible impulse theory differs from the disease model in
at least one significant way. Irresistible impulse does not necessarily imply a character disorder and is often associated, in the
literature, with special circumstances. Sexual deprivation, for example, is believed to remove the normal social constraints which usually prevent aggressive sexual attacks. In contrast, when psychoanalysts employ the disease model, one or more of the following assumptions are usually made: rape is directly or indirectly sexual in
nature; it is perpetrated by a perverted or sick individual who often
has latent homosexual tendencies; he has experienced an abnormal

childhood which has resulted in a sadistic personality; and, finally, rape is often an attack on a mother figure and should be considered as symptomatic of inner conflicts which are the real problem. While it is tempting to place all writers who have employed the disease model into one category, such an approach would obscure the broader implications of the particular psychoanalytic models used. Consequently, an examination of each assumption is warranted.

A Sexual Act

M.L. Cohen stated in 1977, "I have never studied a rapist where there was not present together with many other problems, a rather severe sexual disorder...." (Albin 1977:431). Cohen's statement derives from Freud's dual instinct theory in which sexual and aggressive drives are combined. "A sexual act becomes dynamically an act of aggression towards the partner, while aggression may readily have a disguised sexual meaning" (Fine 1965:149). In psychoanalytic theory, the act of sexual intercourse is intricately tied to aggression. Fine interpreted Freud's sexual stages of development in terms of hostility "in the oedipal situation as rivalry towards the parent of the opposite sex; in the anal phase as the anal-sadistic wish; in all infantile sexuality as the partial instinct of sadism; and as a result of frustration" (p. 149). East (1946) hinted at the element of power in rape but only within a sexual context. "Psychoneurotic persons sometimes show their sexual inferiority and striving for superiority by committing a sexual murder or other sexual crime" (p. 540). He related this to Freud's stages of sexual pleasure and early childhood sexual traumas.

Karpman (1951), firmly committed to a sexual interpretation of rape, took issue with the legal definition. "Rape, clearly a sexual crime, is regarded by law as an assault on a person" (p. 185). In Karpman's view, incest and homosexuality were the real problems and rape was merely symbolic of these "greater crimes." Guttmacher and Weihofen (1952) were in partial agreement. They maintained that the "true" sex offender was motivated by "an explosive expression of a pent-up impulse" (p. 116) and a strong latent homosexual component.

By 1965, the influence of psychiatry was evident as thirty states and the District of Columbia had sexual psychopath laws in which the offender was defined in sexual terms. "The sexual psychopath is usually defined as a person unable to control his sexual impulses or having to commit sex crimes" (Bowman and Engle 1965:758). The psychiatric profession had successfully claimed a new territory. Psychiatrists became the expert consultants in cases of suspected sexual psychopathy. This encroachment on the legal profession was undoubtedly facilitated by the desire of some judges to be relieved of the responsibility of making difficult decisions.

The major research efforts on sexual psychopathy in the 1960s consisted primarily of elaborate discussions of early childhood sexual behavior and later adult sexual habits (Ellis and Brancale 1956; Gebhard et al. 1956; Abrahamsen 1960). Research also concentrated on individual characteristics of rapists and seldom moved beyond a discussion of sexual practices.

When rape is viewed as a sexual disorder, it implies the presence of impulsive or uncontrollable drives. The rapist's responsibility for the behavior is, therefore, abated. This presumes a belief about the uncontrollable nature of male sexuality which is as

outdated as the Victorian belief in universal female frigidity. This
is not to argue that rape is never the result of a sexual disorder.
It is, however, to question why the atypical, rather than the more
usual, has been so emphasized in psychiatric literature.

Rape is, of course, in part a sexual act.[1] Indeed, it is the
sexual aspect of rape that distinguishes it from other forms of assault. This fact, however, does not necessarily make rape sexually
pathological behavior.

Recent studies of rapists, both in and outside of prison, indicate that sex is implicated in rape in several ways. First, some
rapists use sex as a vehicle to express anger and the desire to dominate, control, and humiliate women (Groth 1979). The attitude that
sex is a male entitlement is another factor in rape, especially in
what is popularly called "date rape." Scully and Marolla (1984)
found that this belief also allowed some convicted rapists to justify their forced sexual behvior and deny it was rape when the victim
had withheld their expected sexual compensation. Finally, rape provides men with sexual access to women who are otherwise either unwilling or, because of age, class or race differences, unavailable
(Smithyman 1978; Scully and Marolla 1983). When the victim is
attainable and sex is viewed as a form of conquest, the function
of rape is to seize what isn't offered. Indeed, Smithyman (1978)
found that sexual access was the prime energizer for the self-reported, undetected rapists he studied. It is interesting to note that
while theft and robbery can be thought of as similar behavior--taking
unavailable desirable objects--neither is typically attributed to
disease nor to impulsive and uncontrollable drives.

Disordered Individuals

Another assumption frequently made by psychoanalysts is that
rapists are sick and, therefore, their behavior is really symptomatic
of a mental disorder. Although research comparing convicted rapists
to other groups--including convicts, other sex offenders, and college
males--has been at best inclusive and at worst, from the disease-model
perspective, non-supportive of psychological differences, the belief
that rapists are or must be sick is amazingly persistent.

Research on convicted rapists indicates that fewer than 5 percent of the men were psychotic at the time of the rape (Abel et al.
1980). Other research indicates that some convicted rapists were experiencing problems of everyday living at the time of the rape
(Scully and Marolla 1984). They were under stress but they were not
mentally ill. And Smithyman (1978) concludes about undetected rapists:

> The rapist must solve all the problems of daily
> living like everyone else. In the case of the
> men participating in this investigation, they
> apparently do so to a degree somewhat better than
> expected.... Along almost every dimension ex-
> amined, these men seemed not to differ markedly
> from the majority of males in our culture. In-
> deed, there appears to be such a wide variety of
> backgrounds among males who rape that no sweep-
> ing generalizations about them should be made
> (p. 49).

Other research efforts have concentrated on distinguishing rapists from non-rapists on the basis of projective and other personality tests but results have been, at best, inconclusive. For example, although Hammer and Jacks (1955) found that the Rorschach Test distinguished between rapists, characterized by an aggressive behavioral orientation, and pedophiles characterized by a passive submissive behavioral orientation, attempts to use projective tests to distinguish between rapists and normals (Pascall and Herzberg 1952) and between rapists and men convicted of aggressive non-sexual crimes (Perdue and Lester 1972) have not revealed significant differences.

Rada (1978), summarizing several studies of rapists utilizing the Minnesota Multiphasic Personality Inventory (MMPI), states that MMPI composite profiles of rapists sometimes show elevation in the psychopathic deviate scale. However, he also cautions that individual rapists often show markedly different MMPI profiles from the composite profile. He suggests that the relative lack of clinical studies in the past ten years may be due to dissatisfaction with these techniques and the inability to correlate personality type with specific criminal behavior.

Early works on mental disorders and criminal behavior were simplistic and straightforward. Glueck (1925) described sexual aggression as the result of a "disease of the brain which so weakens the sufferer's powers as to prevent him from attending or referring to general principles of conduct" (p. 243). Disease was used in the literal sense to mean a physical problem which affects behavior. In the same tradition, Leppmann (1941), based on personal experience in prisons, arrived at three types of rape-related diseases: (1) twilight-state--offender is unaware of what he is doing; (2) general paresis--organic disease occurring mostly in middle-aged men; and (3) schizophrenia--delusions with sexual intonations.

Karpman (1951) presented a slightly different use of the disease model. Whereas Glueck, Leppmann, and others referred to mental illness as an organic disease of the brain, Karpman argued that most sex offenders were really suffering from a neurosis rather than a psychosis and separated "paraphilliac neurosis," defined as developmental, from sexual psychopathy, defined as organic.[2] Karpman reflected the beliefs of others (Reinhardt and Fisher 1949) when he stated that sex offenders were sick and, therefore, not responsible for their behavior. "Sexual psychopaths are, of course, a social menace, but they are not conscious agents deliberately and viciously perpetrating these acts; rather, they are victims of a disease from which many suffer more than their victims ..." (Karpman 1951:190). Thus, a direct consequence of placing rapists in the sick role is to alleviate them of responsibility for their behavior.

Following a set of categories developed in 1952 by Guttmacher and Weihofen, Cohen et al. (1971) used the descriptive features of the rape act to categorize rapists. Although the possibility that other factors may contribute to rape was considered, their approach was primarily psychoanalytic and "sex offenders" were treated as sick people who can be cured with psychotherapeutic techniques.

In 1973, the *Police Law Quarterly* referred to an article by analyst Ner Littner as "one of the finest psychological studies of the sex offender ever published." In the article Littner argued, "The single most important item we need to know about the sex offender is how sick he is emotionally. This is far more important than the nature of the crime that he has committed" (p. 7). He reasoned

that if the degree of illness was known, recovery could be predicted.
Yet, in the same article, he stated that there are no personality
characteristics common to all rapists and that the only universal was
the act itself. Furthermore, he noted that there was little difference in recidivism among treated and non-treated first offenders
and, with regard to repeat offenders, the prognosis was usually poor.
Consequently, his argument has no significance for first offenders
and usually fails when applied to repeat offenders.

The ability to predict recovery is undoubtedly linked to the
ability to diagnose sexual psychopathy. Relevant to this point, Bowman and Engle (1965) argued that sexual psychopathy "subsumes a long
broadly-descriptive list of personality traits and is not a specific
diagnostic label based on scientific data" (p. 766). They pointed
out that legal definitions mixed with psychiatric terms have proven
to be ineffective administratively and suggested that psychiatrists
should return to a consultant role. Supporting this position, Ellis
and Brancale (1956) demonstrated that individuals who would be defined as having more serious emotional disturbances quite often commit minor offenses and vice versa.

Wenger and Fletcher (1969) have demonstrated the effect of legal
counsel on psychiatric recommendations for commitment. They suggest
that if the decision to commit is based upon medical diagnosis, the
presence of legal counsel should not have an impact on the outcome.
However, in a study of eighty-one cases, they demonstrated that the
presence of legal counsel did affect the psychiatrist's recommendation and concluded that the use of psychiatric categories to determine legal responsibility is dangerous.

Further evidence for the view that categorizing of rapists has
traditionally been subject to social, class, and racial bias is the
fact that of all men executed for rape in the United States since
1930, 89 percent have been black. "Heavier sentences imposed on
blacks for raping white women is an incontestable historic fact"
(Brownmiller 1975:216). If the problem were purely a medical one,
it is strange that sentencing is distributed differently across
social classes.

The disease model has several obvious functions. It places the
behavior in a "special" category and, thus, protects the interest of
"normal" males. Behavior attributed to incapacity beyond the individual's control carries the obligation of admitting illness and
seeking professional help. Ultimately, the offender is returned to
psychiatry's domain.

Symptomatic Behavior
      Given the presumption of illness, many psychiatrists conclude
that rape is merely symptomatic of the real disorder or disease. Psychiatrists often read into behavior hidden motives such as latent
homosexuality or hostility toward a mother figure. This leads to an
investigation that has, for the most part, ignored an analysis of the
behavior itself. For example, Guttmacher and Weihofen believed that
"sex offenses are symptoms of mental disorders" (1952:116). They argued that the actual behavior cannot be taken seriously because very
often a sex offense is not really committed by a sexual deviate.
Rather, poorly-organized egos and "noxious circumstances can momen-
tarily break down defenses" (p. 112). To illustrate their point,
they discuss the case of a man who, while riding on a bus, became
very nervous and agitated. He resolved his problem by getting off

the bus and approaching a woman who he demanded have oral sex with him. The analysts explained that the man had a claustrophobic experience (noxious circumstance) on the bus and was merely trying to get his mind off his "self." This type of interpretation is frequently found in psychiatric literature. They do not explain why the man chose to free his psyche by assaulting a woman rather than a man.

Finally, Littner (1973) epitomized the application of the psychoanalytic model to sexual offenders and the current belief in rape as symptom. "Similarly, when we talk about rape, we are describing an act that is the symptom of a mental illness; we are not indicating what the mental disease is. We must study the rapist carefully in order to understand his underlying mental disease" (p. 6). The consequence of emphasizing the secondary nature of the behavior is clear in this passage. The act is attributed to a particular, individualistic disease and is not associated with the cultural context in which it occurs. However, Szasz (1961), among others, has argued that behavior always communicates a set of beliefs and values. Consequently, the origin and substance of these beliefs and values are relevant to understanding the behavior.

Homosexuality

The idea that rapists are often latent homosexuals frequently appears in psychiatric literature. For example, Guttmacher and Weihofen (1952) listed latent homosexuality as one of two sources of motivation for the "true" sex offender. Implicit in other psychoanalytic discussions of rape, even after homosexuality was redefined in the American Psychiatric Association Diagnostic and Statistical Manual, is the belief that homosexuality is the root of the "evil" (Karpman 1951; East 1946; Guttmacher 1951; Littner 1973).

The linkage between homosexuality and rape can be explained in the same way Szasz (1973) interpreted the use of homosexuality, in general, as "the model psychiatric scapegoat"--subhuman, defective and in need of repair. Obviously, this places rapists in a group that historically has been composed of outsiders and, therefore, assures minimal identification with "normal" men. Thus, using a homosexual "scapegoat" protects the interests of the dominant group in our society.

ALCOHOL AND UNUSUAL CIRCUMSTANCES

The use of alcohol by rapists prior to the act is mentioned throughout the literature. While alcohol is not claimed to cause rape, most writers maintain that it removes social constraints (disinhibition thesis) and leaves men at the mercy of their sexual drives. Overwhelmed by these drives, they attack a convenient victim.

This belief is based on very limited empirical research. Carpenter and Armenti (1972) noted that "the amount of experimental evidence for opinions about the actions of ethyl alcohol on either sexual behavior or aggression is extremely small" (p. 509). In an extensive review of the literature, they show that the relationship between alcohol and sexual desire has not been empirically established. Experiments with animals and with humans have failed to demonstrate a positive relationship. "Sexual desire may or may not be increased by alcohol. At present, there is no real evidence for or against such an idea" (p. 524). Only one study they reviewed suggested that disinhibition was a reasonable thesis. However, so many writers have reported a correlation between alcohol and rape that some type of association must exist (Leppmann 1941; East 1946; Guttmacher 1951; Amir 1971; and Rada 1975).

Rada (1975) presented an alternative explanation. Noting the widespread acceptance of disinhibition theory, he suggested that rapists may be using alcohol as an excuse for their behavior. In vocabulary of motive terms, alcohol has become an acceptable excuse for deviant behavior in our culture. Supporting his hypothesis, McCaghy (1968) found that child molesters used alcohol as a technique for neutralizing their deviant identity.

Equally interesting, while alcohol consumption is often used to the advantage of rapists, it has the opposite effect for victims. In fact, victim intoxication is a primary cause for declaring rape complaints unfounded. For example, LeGrand (1973) found that among the rape complaints filed by victims who had been drinking, 82 percent were classified unfounded. Although he does not feel drunkenness can be used as an excuse for rape, Judge Ploscowe (1968) stated, "when a woman drinks with a man to the point of intoxication, she practically invites him to take advantage of her person. She should not be permitted to yell when she is sober, 'I was raped'" (p. 215). Surely, attorneys as well as offenders are aware of the utility of a defense based on alcohol consumption and that it can be used to shift responsibility to the victim.

Whatever may be the true role of alcohol and drugs in sexual violence, research indicates that convicted rapists are aware of the utility of a defense based upon this vocabulary of motive. In their study of convicted rapists, Scully and Marolla (1984) found that admitters (men who admitted sexual contact with the victim which they defined as rape), and deniers (men who admitted sexual contact with the victim, but did not define it as rape) differently applied alcohol and drug use depending upon whether the object was to excuse or justify their own behavior. Admitters did not accuse their victims of being drunk or high, but they did attempt to remove some culpability for their own behavior by claiming to have been under the influence of alcohol and/or drugs at the time of the rape. In contrast, deniers attempted to construct a situational justification for their own actions and, at the same time, implicate their victim and cast doubt on her integrity. Thus, deniers claimed that they personally had not been affected by alcohol or drugs at the time of the rape but that their victim had been drunk and/or high. This use of alcohol and drugs is a classic example of the differential application of vocabularies of motive. In both rapists' accounts and psychiatric literature, females are discredited for the same act that males can use to justify and excuse their behavior.

VICTIM PRECIPITATION

Victim-precipitated rape is another major theme within psychiatric literature. Traditionally, support came from victimology, a subfield of criminology, in which the victim's contribution to the genesis of crime was the object of study. Recently victimology has also focused on crime from the victim's perspective.

Criminologist von Hentig was one of the first to articulate the victimologists' position. Writing in 1940, he argued that "the human victim in many instances seems to lead the evildoer actively into temptation. The predator is—by varying means—prevailed to advance against the prey" (p. 303). If there are born criminals, he argued,

there are born victims who are self-harming and self-destructive.
Central to his thesis is the question of why a particular victim was
chosen. In the case of incest and rape, seduction played a prominent
role, leading him to question whether rape may not be considered a
case of "the oversexed on the oversexed" (p. 209).

The work of sociologist Amir (1972) is a more contemporary example of the application of victimology to rape. Amir made a distinction between victim precipitative behaviors through acts of commission
and through acts of omission. Commissive behavior included "last moment retreating from sexual advancement" or "agreeing voluntarily to
drink or ride with a stranger" (p. 155). Omission referred to a lack
of preventive measures such as failing to react strongly enough to
sexual suggestions or "when her outside appearance arouses the offender's advances which are not staved off" (p. 155). Amir stated that
under these circumstances, "the victim becomes functionally responsible for the offense by entering upon and following a course that will
provoke some males to commit crimes" (p. 155). Thus, Amir argued
that attention should be focused upon the victim-offender relationship, the moral character of the victim, and "victim's personality
makeup which may orient her toward the offender and the offense" (p.
132). While the field of victimology can be accused of overidentify-
ing with offenders, in the case of rape, psychoanalytic theory has
provided the vocabulary of motive with which victims could be discredited.

In psychoanalytic terms, the core female personality consists of
three characteristics: narcissism, masochism, and passivity. The
masochistic element accounts for women's alleged unconscious desire
to be raped. In her summary and critique of the psychoanalytic view
of female personality, Horney (1973) stated:

> The specific satisfactions sought and found in
> female sex life and motherhood are of a maso-
> chistic nature. The content of the early sexual
> wishes and fantasies concerning the father is
> the desire to be mutilated, that is, castrated
> by him. Menstruation has the hidden connota-
> tion of a masochistic experience. What the
> woman secretly desires in intercourse is rape
> and violence, or in the mental sphere, humili-
> ation.... This swinging in the direction of
> masochism is 'part of the woman's anatomical
> destiny' (pp. 22-24).

While many analyses of the psychoanalytic view of women have been
made (see Chesler 1972; Miller 1973), with the exception of Albin
(1977), no one has noted how easily it can be translated into a rationalization for male sexual aggressive behavior.

Masochism and Seduction

In the psychiatric literature, victims are frequently sorted
into categories on the basis of personal or circumstantial characteristics. Littner (1973) distinguished between "true victims," those
who do not consciously or unconsciously wish to be raped and "professional victims," those who have an inner masochistic need to be raped.
According to Littner, "professional victims" have an inner need to be
sexually molested or attacked even though consciously they are totally
unaware of their motivation. Because of these unconscious desires,

they "unwittingly cooperate with the rapist in terms of covertly making themselves available to the rapist" (p. 28).

Likewise, similar assumptions are made about the masochistic needs of sex offenders' wives. Abrahamsen (1960), in his discussion of eight wives who had been subjected to sexual aggression by their rapist husbands, stated: "the offender needs an outlet for his sexual aggression and finds a submissive partner who unconsciously invites sexual abuse and whose masochistic needs are being fulfilled" (p. 163). The fact that these women divorced their rapist-husbands didn't alter Abrahamsen's belief in the psychoanalytic model. Instead, he argued that the wives were also latently aggressive and competitive. In Abrahamsen's scheme, the rapist was the innocent victim of his wife, his mother, and the women whom he raped. "There can be no doubt that the sexual frustration which the wives caused is one of the factors motivating the rape which might be tentatively described as a displaced attempt to force a seductive but rejecting mother into submission. The sex offender was not only exposed to his wife's masculine and competitive inclinations, but also, in a certain sense, was somehow 'seduced' into committing the crime" (p. 165).

Seduction by the victim frequently appears in psychiatric literature as an explanation for rape. Used in this way, a criminal attack takes on the appearance of a normal sexual encounter. For example, Hollander (1924) stated, "Considering the amount of illicit intercourse, rape of women is very rare indeed. Flirtation and provocative conduct, i.e., tacit if not actual consent, is generally the prelude to intercourse" (p. 130).

Since psychiatrists view rape as a sexual act and since women are supposed to be coy about their sexual attractions, a refusal has little meaning. The fact that violence and often a weapon are used to accomplish the act is not considered.

> The conscious or unconscious biological and
> psychological attraction between man and woman
> does not exist only on the part of the offender
> toward the woman but also on her part toward
> him, which in many instances may to some extent
> be the impetus for his sexual attack. Often a
> woman unconsciously wishes to be taken by force--
> consider the theft of the bride in Peer Gynt
> (Abrahamsen 1960:161).

Even more interesting than what psychiatrists say about women is what they say about female children who are the victims of rape and/or incest. Girls are alleged to have the same motive as their adult counterparts. For example, Abrahamsen presented the thesis that sexual trauma was often unconsciously desired by the child and that it represented a form of infantile sexual activity. "If there is an underlying unconscious wish for it, the experiencing of sexual trauma in childhood is a masochistic expression of the sexual impulse .... We can say that children belonging to this category show an abnormal desire for obtaining sexual pleasure and, in consequence of this, undergo sexual traumas" (Abrahamsen 1960:54).

A frequently-quoted psychiatric study of girls (Weiss et al. 1955) who were the victims of adult sex offenders distinguished between "accidental" victims and "participating" victims, "those who took part in initiating and maintaining the relationship." Half, or twenty-three out of the forty-four victims labeled "participating," were under age ten, and some were as young as four or five years of age. Furthermore, "participation" was determined on the basis of psychiatric evaluations of the victims' personality rather than on the objective facts of the case. The authors concluded that the girls had severe emotional problems which motivated the initiation and participation in their own victimization, but they never considered the possibility that these problems might be the result, not the cause, of the rape or incest. Elsewhere in the literature (Bender 1965), girl victims are described as very attractive, charming, appealing, submissive, and seductive.

Boys as well as girls are sexually victimized by adult men. However, discussions of males lack the suggestion that masochism, seduction, or promiscuity are causative factors. For example, Halleck (1965) stated "Most girl victims are familiar with the offender and many are willing or passive participants in the sexual act" (p. 681). About males, he stated that "A significant number of male victims may be considered as truly 'accidental' in the sense that they did not know the attacker and did not willingly participate in the act" (p. 680).

"Nice Girls Don't Get Raped"

Perception of fault in rape is also affected by the belief that "nice girls don't get raped." The victim's reputation as well as characteristics or behavior which violate normative sex role expectations are perceived as contributing to the commission of the act. For example, hitchhike rape is defined as a victim-precipitated offense (Nelson and Amir 1975). The inherent injustice of this position is compounded by the criteria which have been used to determine the victim's reputation. For example, one indication used by the President's Commission on Crime in Washington, D.C. was "substantiated statements by offenders that the victim was generally known to be a loose or easy object of sexual assault" (Curtis 1974:600). Reputation has been used to discredit the victim, to present her as the legitimate object of sexual attack, and it ultimately functions to deny women legal protection. Von Hentig (1940) obviously echoed the the opinion of others in the criminal justice system when he stated, "The victim could be held unworthy of being protected by the law, either not being a female of previous chaste character or succumbing to false pretenses which would not deceive a man of ordinary intelligence and caution" (p. 307).

The psychiatric assumptions which underscore allegations of victim-precipitated rape are a clear example of how vocabularies of motive can be constructed without empirical data and used to discredit the powerless--in this case, women and girls. Equally important, when this vocabulary is used, attention is focused on the behavior and motives of the victim rather than on the offender. Consequently, responsibility for the act is also shifted to the victim. The power and influence of this vocabulary extends beyond psychiatric journals. As numerous observers have noted, in court it is the rape victim who appears to be on trial. Perhaps feminist psychiatrists like Elaine Hilberman whose book, *The Rape Victim* (1976), was approved by the American Psychiatric Association, will begin to correct these damaging beliefs.

This review has also demonstrated the biases inherent in the motive statements generated by the psychiatric perspective. Each motive functions to emphasize the individual, idiosyncratic nature of the problem. When rapists are defined as sick and in need of help, individual responsibility is removed. When offenders are placed in the category of "outsider," the connection with "normal" men is eliminated. Finally, much of the blame can be placed on the victim. Each motive functions, as Mills (1940) pointed out, to justify or excuse the past behavior of the actor and, as a result, the social and cultural conditions within the society which might be the source of the problem are not examined.

AN ALTERNATIVE PERSPECTIVE

The psychiatric model, as we have seen, is premised on the assumption that rapists have somehow distorted the input that normal men receive throughout their lives. But it is equally relevant to ask if rather than distortion, rapists may not represent one end of a quasi-socially sanctioned continuum of male sexual aggression. In this view, rapists may be conforming to their perception of male sex role expectations. An investigation of rape predicated on a presumption of normalcy, rather than pathology, is a challenging alternative to the psychiatric model.

The theoretical approach primarily associated with Sutherland (1970) and Differential Association or Cultural Transmission Theory suggests a framework for understanding how deviant behavior, such as rape, becomes actualized. The fundamental premise is that deviant behavior is learned in the same way as conforming behavior, that is, socially through interaction with others. Learning includes not only the techniques of committing the crime, but also motives, drives, rationalizations, and attitudes that are compatible with the behavior.

Traub and Little (1975) note that the most important modification of Differential Association Theory is Glaser's (1956) introduction of the concept of differential identification. That is, individuals identify with real or imaginary persons or reference groups whose view of criminal activity is acceptable to them. Thus the concept suggests that criminality need not be learned exclusively through direct association with others but, rather, any number of indirect cultural influences can also affect behavior.

When this approach is applied to sexual assault, it suggests that rape may also be behavior that is learned. If behavior is learned socially in interaction with others and through cultural contact, it suggests there must be some degree of support for sexual aggression against women in this society. Therefore, it is not sufficient to look at personality traits alone for an explanation of rape. It is also necessary to investigate the social and cultural factors that influence learning and that encourage violent aggression against women.

Feminist literature provides insight on how the content of male sex role learning and socialization produces definitions favorable to sexual aggression against women. The feminist perspective views rape as an act of social control which functions to "keep women in their place" (Brownmiller 1975; Kasinsky 1975; Russell 1975). Rather than deviant behavior, rape is seen as normative behavior, the result of conformity or overconformity to the values and prerogatives which define the traditional male sex role (Russell 1975). Typical of this perspective, Griffin (1971) called rape "The All-American Crime."

Traditional socialization encourages males to associate power, dominance, strength, virility, and superiority with masculinity, and submissiveness, passivity, weakness, and inferiority with femininity (Rosenkrantz et al. 1968). Furthermore, males are taught to have expectations about their level of sexual needs and about correspond- ing female accessibility which functions to justify forcing sexual access. In a dating situation, this can result in a level of sexual aggression undesired by the female partner (Kanin 1971). Socializa- tion then prepares women to be "legitimate" victims and men to be po- tential offenders (Weis and Borges 1973). In one study of fifty- three college males, Malamuth, Haber, and Feshback (1980) found that 51 percent indicated a likelihood that they themselves would rape if assured of not being punished.

The justification for sexual access is further buttressed by legal, social, and religious definitions of women as male property and sex as an exchange of goods. Several feminists (LeGrand 1973; Brownmiller 1975; Griffin 1971) have argued that rape laws and the corresponding penalties are not intended to protect women as much as they are intended to protect man's property which, having been dam- aged, loses market value.

The feminist perspective, and the model which derives from it, views rape as an extension of normal male sexual aggression which can best be understood within the context of hostility toward women and male sex role expectations. Combining elements of cultural transmis- sion with the feminist perspective produces a framework for examining rape that stands in stark contrast to the psychopathological model. The concept of rape is expanded to include a number of factors that are ignored when the behavior is attributed to an individual disorder.

Starting with the observation that cultures can and do generate predispositions to behavior that are, at the same time, defined as deviant or dysfunctional, the presumption is that rape, at least in part, is the product of social learning. In this view, rapists are representative of a group of men who have learned the attitudes and actions consistent with rape. Integral to the learning is acquisi- tion of a vocabulary of motive that can be used to assuage responsi- bility and to justify and excuse sexual violence.[3] (Scully and Marolla 1984) An investigation of these relevant attitudes and motive vocabu- laries as articulated by rapists themselves, rather than filtered through a psychiatric perspective, is essential to a broader understanding of sexual violence. Such an examination sheds light on men's motives for rape. But equally important, this approach involves culture as a criti- cal and contributing factor to men's sexual aggression, an important omission in approaches that view rape as no more than an individual- istic and idiosyncratic problem.

NOTES

1. In a desperate effort to change public attitudes and to improve the plight of victims by reforming laws premised on the idea that women both ask for and enjoy rape, feminists have emphasized the violent and aggressive character of rape. Often these arguments have been accompanied by a denial that sex plays any part in the crime at all. Certainly, from the victim's perspective, rape is not a sexual act. It is a violent intrusion that invades a wom- an's most private experience. It is the ultimate violation by one human being of another's right to physical and bodily autono- my. Still, it is illogical to argue that rape is an extension of normal male sexual behavior and, at the same time, to deny

that sex plays any part in rape. For a discussion of victim
response to rape see Holmstrom and Burgess 1978; Burgess and
Holmstrom 1974; and Feldman-Summers et al. 1979.

2. Hollingshead and Redlich (1958) found that clinical diagnosis
varies by social class and that the middle class is more likely
to be labeled neurotic while the lower class is more likely to
be labeled psychotic. There is a similar potential for class
bias in the disposition of rape cases. Since sexual psychopathy
is believed to be deteriorating, sentencing is indeterminate;
but since neurosis is considered treatable, the offender has a
better chance for release.

3. For a complete discussion of neutralization techniques, see
Scott and Lyman 1968; Hall and Hewitt 1970; Hewitt and Hall
1973; Hewitt and Stokes 1975; Stokes and Hewitt 1976; and Sykes
and Matza 1957.

REFERENCES

Abel, G.G., J.V. Becker, and L.J. Skinner. "Aggressive Behavior and
Sex." *Psychiatric Clinics of North America* 3 (1980): 133-151.

Abrahamsen, D. *The Psychology of Crime*. New York: John Wiley &
Sons, 1960.

Albin, R. "Psychological Studies of Rape." *Signs* 3 (1977): 423-435.

Amir, M. *Patterns in Forcible Rape*. Chicago: University of Chicago
Press, 1971.

Amir, M. "The Role of the Victim in Sex Offenses." In *Sexual Behavior: Social, Clinical, and Legal Aspects*, edited by H. Resnik
and M. Wolfgang. Boston: Little, Brown, 1972.

Bender, L. "Offended and Offender Children." In *Sexual Behavior
and the Law*, edited by R. Slovenko. Springfield, Illinois: C.
Thomas, 1965.

Bowman, K., and B. Engle. "Sexual Psychopath Laws." In *Sexual Behavior and the Law*, edited by R. Slovenko. Springfield, Illinois:
C. Thomas, 1965.

Brownmiller, S. *Against Our Will*. New York: Simon & Schuster,
1975.

Burgess, A.W., and L.L. Holmstrom. "Rape: Sexual Disruption and Recovery." *American Journal of Orthopsychiatry* 49 (1979): 648-657.

Burgess, A.W., and L.L. Holmstrom. *Rape: Victims of Crisis*. Bowie,
Maryland: Robert J. Brady, 1974.

Carpenter, J., and N. Armenti. "Some Effects of Ethanol on Human
Sexual and Aggressive Behavior." In *The Biology of Alcoholism*,
Vol. 2, edited by B. Hessin and H. Begleiter. New York: Plenum
Press, 1972.

Chesler, P. *Women and Madness*. New York: Doubleday, 1972.

Cohen, M., R. Garofalo, R. Boucher, and T. Seghorn. "The Psychology
of Rapists." *Seminars in Psychiatry* 3 (1971): 307-327.

Curtis, L. "Victim Precipitation and Violent Crime." *Social Problems* 21 (1974): 594-605.

East, W. "Sexual Offenders--a British View." *Yale Law Review* 55 (1946): 527-557.

Ellis, A., and R. Brancale. *The Psychology of Sex Offenders.* Springfield, Illinois: C. Thomas, 1956.

Feldman-Summers, S., P.E. Gordon, and J.R. Meagher. "The Impact of Rape on Sexual Satisfaction." *Journal of Abnormal Psychology* 88 (1979): 101-105.

Fine, R. "Psychoanalytic Theory of Sexuality." In *Sexual Behavior and the Law*, edited by R. Slovenko. Springfield, Illinois: C. Thomas, 1965.

Gebhard, P., J. Gagnon, W. Pomeroy, and C. Christenten. *Sex Offenders: An Analysis of Types.* New York: Harper and Row, 1965.

Gibbens, T., C. Way, and K. Soothill. "Behavioral Types of Rape." *British Journal of Psychiatry* 130 (1977): 32-42.

Glaser, D. "Criminality Theories and Behavioral Images." *American Journal of Sociology* 61 (1956): 433-44.

Glueck, S.S. *Mental Disorders and the Criminal Law.* New York: Little, Brown, 1925.

Griffin, S. "Rape: The All-American Crime." *Ramparts* (September 1971): 26-35.

Groth, N.A. *Men Who Rape.* New York: Plenum Press, 1979.

Guttmacher, M. *Sex Offenses: The Problem, Causes, and Prevention.* New York: Norton, 1951.

Guttmacher, M., and H. Weihofen. *Psychiatry and the Law.* New York: Norton, 1952.

Hall, P.M., and J.P. Hewitt. "The Quasi-Theory of Communication and the Management of Dissent." *Social Problems* 18 (1970): 17-27.

Halleck, S. "Emotional Effects of Victimization." In *Sexual Behavior and the Law*, edited by R. Slovenko. Springfield, Illinois: C. Thomas, 1965.

Hammer, E. "A Comparison of H-T-P of Rapists and Pedophiles." *Journal of Projective Techniques* 18 (1954): 346-354.

Hammer, E., and I. Jacks. "A Study of Rorschach Flexor and Extensor Human Movements." *Journal of Clinical Psychology* 11 (1955): 63-67.

Hewitt, J.P., and P.M. Hall. "Social Problems, Problematic Situations and Quasi-Theories." *American Sociological Review* 38 (1973): 367-374.

Hewitt, J.P., and R. Stokes. "Disclaimers." *American Sociological Review* 40 (1975): 1-11.

Hilberman, E. *The Rape Victim.* New York: Basic Books, 1976.

Hollander, B. *Psychology of Misconduct, Vice and Crime.* New York: Macmillan, 1924.

Hollingshead, D., and F. Redlich. *Social Class and Mental Illness.* New York: John Wiley, 1958.

Holmstrom, L.L., and A.W. Burgess. "Sexual Behavior of Assailant and Victim During Rape." Paper presented at Annual Meetings of American Sociological Association, San Francisco, 1978.

Horney, K. "The Problem of Feminine Masochism." In *Psychoanalysis and Women*, edited by J. Miller. Baltimore, Maryland: Penguin Books, 1973.

Kanin, E. "Male Aggression in Dating-Courtship Relations." *American Journal of Sociology* 63 (1957): 197-204.

————. "Male Sex Aggression and Three Psychiatric Hypotheses." *Journal of Sex Research* 1 (1965): 227-229.

————. "Reference Groups and Sex Conduct Norm Violation." *Sociological Quarterly* 8 (1967): 495-504.

————. "Selected Dyadic Aspects of Male Sex Aggression." *Journal of Sex Research* 5 (1969): 12-28.

————. "Sexually Aggressive College Males." *The Journal of College Student Personnel* 1971, March, p. 107-110.

Karpman, B. "The Sexual Psychopath." *Journal of Criminal Law and Criminology* 42 (1951): 184-198.

Kasinsky, R. "Rape: A Normal Act?" *Canadian Forum* (September 1975): 18-22.

LeGrand, C. "Rape and Rape Laws: Sexism in Society and Law." *California Law Review* 61 (1973): 919-941.

Leppmann, F. "Essential Differences Between Sex Offenders." *Journal of Criminal Law and Criminology* 32 (1941): 366-380.

Littner, N. "Psychology of the Sex Offender: Causes, Treatment, Prognosis." *Police Law Quarterly* 3 (1973): 5-31.

Malamuth, N.M., S. Haber, and S. Feshbach. "Testing Hypothesis Regarding Rape: Exposure to Sexual Violence, Sex Differences, and the 'Normality' Rapists." *Journal of Research in Personality* 14 (1980): 121-137.

McCaghy, C. "Drinking and Deviance Disavowal: The Case of Child Molesters." *Journal of Social Problems* 16 (1968): 43-49.

Miller, J., ed. *Psychoanalysis and Women*. Baltimore, Maryland: Penguin Books, 1973.

Miller, W. "Lower Class Culture as a Generating Milieu of Gang Delinquency." In *Juvenile Delinquency: A Book of Readings*, edited by R. Giallombardo. New York: John Wiley, 1966.

Mills, C.W. "Situated Actions and Vocabularies of Motive." *American Sociological Review* 5 (1940): 904-913.

Nelson, S., and M. Amir. "The Hitchhike Victim of Rape." In *Victimology: A New Focus*, Vol. 5, edited by I. Drapkin and E. Viano. Massachusetts: Lexington Books, 1975.

Pascal, G., and F. Herzberg. "The Detection of Deviant Sexual Practices from Performance on Rorschach Test." *Journal of Projective Techniques* 16 (1952): 366-373.

Perdue, W., and D. Lester. "Personality Characteristics of Rapists." *Perception and Motor Skills* 35 (1972): 514.

Ploscowe, M. "Rape." In *Problems of Sexual Behavior*, edited by E. Sagarin and D. MacNamara. New York: Thomas Crowell, 1968.

Rada, R. "Alcoholism and Forcible Rape." *American Journal of Psychiatry* 132 (1975): 444-446.

Rada, R. *Clinical Aspects of the Rapist*. New York: Grune and Stratton, 1978.

Reinhardt, J., and E. Fisher. "The Sexual Psychopath and the Law." *Journal of Criminal Law and Criminology* 39 (1949): 734-742.

Rosenkrantz, P., S. Vogel, H. Bee, D. Broverman, and I. Broverman. "Sex Role Stereotypes and Self-Concepts in College Students." *Journal of Consulting and Clinical Psychology* 32 (1968): 287-295.

Russell, D. *The Politics of Rape*. New York: Stein and Day, 1975.

Scott, M., and S. Lyman. "Accounts." *American Sociological Review* 33 (1968): 46-62.

Scully, D., and J. Marolla. "Convicted Rapists' Vocabulary of Motive: Excuses and Justifications," *Social Problems* 31 (1984): 530-544.

Scully, D., and J. Marolla. "Incarcerated Rapists: Exploring a Sociological Model." Scully and Marolla report of findings on research funded by The National Rape Center, National Institute of Mental Health, 1983.

Smithyman, S.D. "The Undetected Rapist." Unpublished dissertation, Claremont Graduate School, 1978.

Spirer, J. "Psychology of Irresistible Impulse." *Journal of Criminal Law and Criminology* 33 (1942): 457-462.

Stokes, R., and J.P. Hewitt. "Aligning Actions." *American Sociological Review* 41 (1976): 838-849.

Sutherland, E. "Sexual Psychopathy Laws." *Journal of Criminal Law and Criminology* 40 (1950): 543-554.

Sutherland, E., and D. Cressey. "The Theory of Differential Association." In *Criminology*, edited by E. Sutherland and D. Cressey. New York: Lippincott, 1970.

Sykes, G., and D. Matza. "Techniques of Neutralization: A Theory of Deviance." *American Sociological Review* 22 (1957): 664-670.

Szasz, T.A. *Law, Liberty and Psychiatry*. New York: Macmillan, 1963.

Szasz, T.A. *The Manufacture of Madness*. Frogmore, St. Albans: Paladin, 1973.

Szasz, T.A. *The Myth of Mental Illness*. New York: Harper and Row, 1961.

Traub, S., and C. Little. *Theories of Deviance*. Itasca, Illinois: F.E. Peacock, 1975.

von Hentig, H. "Remarks on the Interaction of Perpetrator and Victim." *Journal of Criminal Law and Criminology* 31 (1940): 303-309.

Weis, K., and S. Borges. "Victimology and Rape: The Case of the
    Legitimate Victim." *Issues in Criminology* 8 (1973): 71-115.

Weiss, J., E. Rogers, M. Darwin, and C. Dutton. "A Study of Girl
    Sex Offenders." *Psychiatric Quarterly* 29 (1955): 1-29.

Wenger, D., and C. Fletcher. "The Effects of Legal Counsel on Ad-
    mission to a State Mental Hospital: A Confrontation of Professions."
    Journal of Health and Social Behavior 10 (1969): 66-72.

CHAPTER 19

PSYCHOLEGAL RESEARCH ON RAPE TRIALS

Eugene Borgida and Nancy Brekke

All too often for crime victims, the initial criminal event
marks only the beginning of the experience of being a victim. Insensitive treatment by police and prosecutors, court delays, and numerous inconveniences encountered in the justice system can produce
what psychiatrists who treat crime victims refer to as the "second
wound," a wound that may have even longer lasting effects than the
initial victimization. As recently publicized reports on victims of
crime and violence have documented, however, many state and local
governments since the 1970s have taken steps to make the law enforcement and justice systems more responsive to the needs of victims
(U.S. President's Task Force Final Report 1982). Various reforms,
for example, have incorporated victim rights into the plea-bargaining
process, bail hearings, trial scheduling, the trial itself, sentencing, and parole. Perhaps the most dramatic reforms have been introduced to reduce the likelihood that rape victims will be "on trial"
along with their accused assailants (Berger 1977; Borgida 1980; Tanford and Bocchino 1980).

The focus of this chapter is on perceived victim credibility
which is crucial to an understanding of how these evidentiary reforms
affect the prosecution of rape cases. Perceptions of credibility,
for example, may affect whether an assailant initially decides to
victimize someone and, in turn, whether the police decide to unfound
or prosecute the case. Perceptions of credibility affect the reactions of significant others to the victim and perhaps even the extent
of self-blame later experienced by the victim. Perceptions of credibility also play a key role in how the victim is treated throughout
the justice system and especially (should she get there) in courtroom
proceedings.

Some scholars who study courtroom dynamics, in fact, have argued
that testing witness credibility is at the heart of conceptualizing
the trial process (Miller and Boster 1977; Miller and Burgoon 1982).
Jurors' understanding of case facts, in this view, revolve around
their assessments of witness credibility. Perceptions of credibility,
in turn, are related to witness and juror characteristics and mediate
juror verdicts (Borgida 1981; Whobrey et al. 1981). This certainly
characterizes rape trials where eyewitnesses are rare and physical
evidence is often minimal or legally tainted. In most rape cases,
moreover, the basic issue is consent. Jurors therefore must determine whether the victim or the defendant is more credible. Ironically, social psychologists interested in the social perception of rape

Research conducted by Eugene Borgida and discussed in this chapter
was supported by NIMH Grant R01 MH30724-01 and by a faculty research
grant from the Graduate School of the University of Minnesota.
Nancy Brekke was supported by a National Science Foundation Graduate
Fellowship.

and psychologists of the law interested in the trial process, with
few exceptions, have neglected to study perceptions of credibility
(Elwork et al. 1981; Whobrey et al. 1981).

The purpose of this chapter, therefore, is to pursue the question of victim credibility in rape trials in greater depth than previous treatments of the topic. First, we examine social psychological research on the social perception of rape victims. While most
of these experimental studies were not designed to address legal
questions about rape in an externally valid manner, they nevertheless
suggest some of the factors that might impinge on perceptions of victim credibility in court. Once those factors and processes that may
attenuate victim credibility in social and quasi-legal settings have
been identified, the chapter reviews two approaches to preserving
victim rights that seem to affect victim credibility in the courtroom:
statutory reform and countering rape myths through the use of expert
testimony. The chapter concludes with a discussion of the controversial legal status of expert testimony on rape trauma syndrome.

SOCIAL PERCEPTION OF RAPE VICTIMS

Studies on the social perception of rape victims have typically
attempted to identify the determinants of victim evaluations, particularly attributions of responsibility. Because the focus of such
research has been the development and testing of social psychological
theories rather than legal questions, legally relevant outcomes have
either been neglected or included as attributional correlates. In
addition, few studies have attempted to simulate the adversarial nature of rape trials, and instead have presented brief narrative descriptions of hypothetical rape incidents. Consequently, victim
credibility has been of less interest to researchers in this domain
and has not, with few exceptions, been investigated directly.

In a trial setting, however, perceptions of victim credibility
take on considerable importance (Elwork et al. 1981), and most probably causally mediate *both* social perception and legal judgments.
In order to determine the extent of victim responsibility, for example, a juror must first decide whether to believe her account of the
incident. Hence, research which examines those factors affecting social perception of rape victims may contribute to the identification
of those factors that affect perceptions of victim credibility in
court. In the following sections, therefore, research that deals
with the impact of victim, defendant, subject, and contextual characteristics on the social perception of rape victims will be reviewed.

Victim Characteristics
One of the first experimental investigations of the impact of
victim characteristics on judgments about rape was conducted by Jones
and Aronson (1973), which then became the prototype for much subsequent research in the area. They hypothesized that a socially respectable victim would be seen as more at fault for a rape than would
a socially unrespectable victim. Although this prediction might seem
counterintuitive, it followed from Lerner's (1970) just world hypothesis. According to Lerner, people tend to believe in a world in
which individuals get what they deserve and deserve what they get.
If a woman is raped (or some other negative event befalls her), then
she is seen as deserving it either because she is an evil person or
because her behavior precipitated the event. When a socially unrespectable woman is raped, according to this line of reasoning, it is

easy to reason that "women like her deserve to be raped," thereby maintaining one's belief in a just world. The rape of a respectable woman, however, may be somewhat threatening. It is difficult to view such a rape as just, unless one can blame the victim for provoking the incident. Thus, the respectable woman may be seen as more directly at fault for a rape than an unrespectable woman.

On the other hand, Jones and Aronson (1973) expected that a man who raped a respectable woman would be punished more severely than a man who raped an unrespectable woman. Presumably, raping a respectable woman (e.g., a virgin) causes more "damage" than raping an unrespectable woman (e.g., a divorcee) and thus requires harsher punishment.

In order to test these hypotheses, the researchers had college students read a very short narrative account of a sexual assault, followed by brief "police descriptions" of the victim and the defendant. The victim was described as either a divorcee (low respectability), a married woman, or a virgin prior to the incident (high respectability). After reading the case account, subjects rated the extent to which the rape was the victim's fault, and indicated the length of the prison sentence they thought the defendant should receive.

In accordance with predictions, the virgin and the married victim were rated as significantly more at fault for the rape than the divorcee, yet a harsher sentence was recommended for the rape of a married woman than the rape of a divorcee. This suggests that although respectable victims may be held more responsible for their rapes, the presumed severity of victim suffering, rather than the extent to which she is blamed, may determine judgments regarding punishment for the crime.

Unfortunately, these findings have not been replicated. A number of studies (Kahn et al. 1977; Kanekar and Kolsawalla 1977; Kerr and Kurtz 1977) have failed to find any significant effects of victim respectability on attributions of responsibility and recommended sentence, despite the fact that they used stimulus materials that were identical or virtually identical to those used by Jones and Aronson (1973).

Other investigators have obtained evidence which appears to contradict directly the Jones and Aronson findings. Feldman-Summers and Lindner (1976), for example, found that as the respectability of the victim decreased, attributed responsibility to the victim *increased*, rather than decreased. Moreover, although their subjects believed that rape had less psychological impact on less respectable victims (as Jones and Aronson had suggested), recommendations regarding punishment of the rapist did not vary with the respectability of the victim.

Still other studies suggest that the impact of victim respectability may be far more complex than was previously assumed. Smith and colleagues (1976), for example, found that a less respectable victim was held more responsible than a more respectable victim only when the victim and her assailant were acquainted prior to the incident. Kanekar and Kolsawalla (1980), on the other hand, found that the effect of victim respectability on attributions of responsibility depended on how provocatively the victim was dressed and whether the person judging the victim was male or female.

Why have investigations of the impact of victim respectability on judgments about rape victims yielded such variable and inconsistent results? A number of explanations have been advanced. One possibility is that attitudes toward rape and rape victims have somehow changed. With the rise of the women's movement over the past decade, rape has become a major political and social issue, and there is evidence that perceptions of rape have been changing (Nagao and Davis 1980). It seems unlikely, however, that such trends could fully account for this body of discrepant findings. Most studies were conducted within a period of only a few years, using very similar subject populations (i.e., college students). More important, no trends are evident in the data which might reflect such attitudinal changes; there appear to be no systematic relationships between the time at which a study was conducted and the nature of the results that were obtained.

Luginbuhl and Mullin (1981) hypothesized that respectability, rather than influencing the *amount* of responsibility attributed to a victim, would influence the *type* of blame attributed to her. One might expect people to blame the unrespectable victim's character, while attributing more responsibility to behavior and to chance in the case of a respectable victim. The failure to distinguish between various types of blame may account for some of the negative and ambiguous results in this domain, but Luginbuhl and Mullin's hypothesis was not even completely successful in accounting for their own findings. The effects of respectability on attributions of blame to chance and the victim's character were as predicted, but attributions to the victim's behavior were not. Although the pattern was more pronounced for respectable victims, subjects always assigned the least blame to a victim's character, more to her behavior, and the most blame to chance.

Kahn et al. (1977) have suggested that the original Jones and Aronson findings were actually statistical artifacts, owing to capitalization on chance through the use of numerous selected *t*-tests, rather than the more appropriate analysis of variance. If so, then the failure of others to replicate is not surprising; perceived victim respectability may be irrelevant to attributions of responsibility for rape. But what about other studies that *have* obtained evidence for the impact of victim respectability? Upon close examination, studies which obtained significant victim respectability effects and those which did not may not actually be contradictory. Feldman-Summers and Lindner (1976), for example, found that a low respectability victim was held more responsible than a high respectability victim. It must be noted, however, that these investigators expanded the range of respectability in their study to include a non-virgin and a prostitute, as well as the married woman, virgin, and divorcee considered in most other research. Feldman-Summer and Lindner actually found no differences in attributions of responsibility to the married woman, virgin, and divorcee. The significant victim respectability effect that they obtained was entirely due to the fact that the prostitute was judged to be more responsible for the rape than were any of the other victims. Such a finding does not really contradict the null results obtained by others who investigated a more limited range of victim responsibility. Instead, it suggests that victim respectability may have little impact on judgments except in very extreme cases, such as the rape of a prostitute.

In a similar vein, it is readily apparent that research which demonstrated that the effects of victim respectability were moderated

by other variables is not necessarily inconsistent with research that
failed to obtain respectability effects without including these moder-
ator variables in their experimental designs. Of course, the existence of such interaction effects and the absence of main effects implies that the impact of victim respectability on attributions may be
quite complex and difficult to determine for any individual case.
Victim respectability may interact with a nearly infinite array of
variables, including characteristics of the victim and her assailant,
contextual variables, and characteristics of the person making the
judgments.

Also problematic is the fact that manipulations of respectability
involve varying an entire constellation of characteristics simultaneously, thereby confounding a number of factors that may exert very
different effects on people's judgments. By operationalizing victim
respectability as marital status, for example, researchers have confounded the effects of the perceived severity of the consequences of
rape for the victim, the victim's prior sexual experience, and perhaps
the victim's presumed physical appearance. In expanding the range of
victims to include prostitutes or topless dancers and nuns (e.g.,
Luginbuhl and Mullin 1981; Smith et al. 1976), researchers have further confounded occupational status, religiosity, social class, and
characteristics of dress, at the very least. To the extent that any
of these variables are differentially related to judgments about rape,
such confounding can only serve to increase the variability of subjects' responses and decrease the interpretability of any consistent
findings that do emerge.

The impact of a few of the characteristics that may underlie victim respectability has been investigated empirically. It has been
argued, for example, that providing information about a victim's prior
sexual history has detrimental effects on perceptions of the victim
(Borgida and White 1978). Indeed, L'Armand and Pepitone (1982) found
that the more sexually experienced a victim was, the more she was
blamed for the rape, the less the rape was viewed as serious and damaging to her, and the less the defendant was blamed for the assault.
Similarly, Burt and Albin (1981) found that a victim with the reputation of being "easy" was evaluated more negatively and considered more
likely to have precipitated the rape than a victim who had been a virgin prior to the incident.

It has also been hypothesized that there might be a strong bias
associated with the physical attractiveness of the victim. Empirical
evidence suggests, however, that the impact of physical attractiveness
on perceptions of the victim is quite limited. Perhaps because rape
is commonly believed to be a crime of passion, attractive women are
seen as more likely targets of rape and unattractive victims are rated
as more likely to have done something to provoke the rape (Seligman
et al. 1977). Nevertheless, attractive and unattractive victims are
held equally responsible for rapes (Kanekar and Kolsawalla 1980; Seligman et al. 1977; Thornton 1977) and are seen as equally credible
(Thornton 1977). Evidence regarding the impact of the victim's attractiveness on punitiveness toward the assailant is inconsistent.
Seligman et al. (1977) and Kanekar and Kolsawalla (1980) obtained no
significant relationship between the attractiveness of the victim and
the sentence assigned to the assailant. Thornton (1977), however,
found that while verdicts were unaffected by a victim's attractiveness, a man who raped an attractive woman was generally assigned a
harsher sentence, especially by male subjects.

Research on the impact of victim provocativeness has been inconclusive. Although provocatively dressed rape victims may be seen as
more at fault than unprovocatively dressed victims (Kanekar and Kolsawalla 1980), the effects of this variable on attributed victim blame
seem to be moderated by other factors, including victim respectability
(Kanekar and Kolsawalla 1980), victim status (Kanekar et al. 1981),
and sex of subject (Kanekar and Kolsawalla 1980; Kanekar et al. 1981).
Moreover, the provocativeness of a victim's dress does not appear to
influence the severity of the sentence assigned to her assailant
(Kanekar and Kolsawalla 1980; Scroggs 1976).

Investigation of the effects of other victim characteristics has
been minimal and generalizations based on single studies are not very
fruitful (Vidmar 1979). So far, then, it appears that subjects do
consider at least some of the victim's characteristics relevant to
their judgments and attributions of responsibility for rape. To what
extent do comparable *defendant* characteristics influence subjects'
evaluations of rape victims? This question constitutes the focus of
the next section.

Defendant Characteristics

Not suprisingly, little research has addressed the impact of defendant characteristics in rape cases and that which has been conducted has yielded conflicting results. Kahn et al. (1977), for example,
operationalized defendant respectability in terms of occupational
status and found no differences in the sentence recommended for the
defendant or the amount of fault attributed to the victim, regardless
of whether the defendant was described as respectable or somewhat unrespectable. Deitz and Byrnes (1981), by contrast, found that both
the defendant's occupation and his physical attractiveness were predictive of subjects' perceptions of the victim and the defendant.
Similarly, Ugwuegbu (1979) found that white subjects treated a black
defendant more harshly than a white one, yet Oros and Elman (1979)
used the same trial summary and obtained no significant effects associated with the defendant's race.

In light of the inconsistency of these findings, no conclusions
about the role of defendant characteristics should be drawn at this
time. Instead, the next section will consider those characteristics
of experimental subjects which may influence perceptions of rape victims.

Subject Characteristics

One of the more intensely researched hypotheses involving subject
characteristics is that women and men will differ in their perceptions
of rape victims. Legal lore has it that female jurors are *a priori*
biased against male defendants in rape trials, readily believing the
victim and advocating severe punishment for her alleged assailant.
On the other hand, it has been suggested that because women find rape
threatening, they may try to increase the psychological distance between themselves and the rape victim in order to assure themselves
that it could never happen to them. This would result in a tendency
for women to cast blame and doubt on the victim rather than on the
defendant. Such reasoning, it should be noted, often underlies defense attorney tactics during *voir dire* in rape cases.

Research confirms the existence of widespread sex differences in
this domain. Men and women exposed to the same information regarding
a sexual assault often interpret and evaluate it quite differently.

For example, both sexes tend to identify most strongly with the rape victim, yet females identify more with the victim than do males, and males identify more with the defendant than do females (Kahn et al. 1977; Krulewitz and Nash 1979). Consistent with this pattern, men are more likely than women to attribute responsibility for a rape to the victim's character (Calhoun et al. 1976), to view the rape victim as the kind of person who gets herself into those situations (Calhoun et al. 1976; Cann et al. 1979), and even to believe that the victim had an unconscious desire to be raped (Cann et al. 1979). Men are also more likely to believe that the woman's behavior contributed to her rape (Calhoun et al. 1976; Cann et al. 1979; Selby et al. 1977), that perhaps she was being careless (Smith et al. 1976), or was behaving in a suggestive manner (Cann et al. 1979).

Women, by contrast, tend to view a rape as more due to chance (Luginbuhl and Mullin 1981) and attribute more responsibility to the rapist than do men (Krulewitz and Nash 1979; L'Armand and Pepitone 1982). Not surprisingly, the sexes also seem to view the consequences of rape somewhat differently; women tend to rate the crime as more serious (Feldman-Summers and Lindner 1976; L'Armand and Pepitone 1982), more damaging (L'Armand and Pepitone 1982), and as having more psychological impact on the victim (Feldman-Summers and Lindner 1976) than do men.

Underlying some of these sex of subject effects may be differences in male and female beliefs about the dynamics of rape. There is some evidence that rape stereotypes are gender-specific, varying, for example, in the extent to which rape is seen as sexually versus aggressively motivated (Heilbrun 1980). Furthermore, men and women maintain opposing beliefs regarding the most appropriate way to respond to an assault. Whereas men believe that rape is most likely if a victim does not physically resist an attack, women believe that rape is most likely if a victim does resist (Krulewitz 1981). In fact, the more a victim resists, the more intelligent and less at fault she is likely to be considered by men. Women, by contrast, attribute more fault and less intelligence to a victim the more she resists (Krulewitz and Nash 1979).

It thus appears that men and women indeed maintain different perspectives on rape, each of which is associated with some fairly consistent beliefs about its causes and consequences, the most effective means of coping during an assault, and the extent to which an assailant is responsible for a rape. The nature of sex differences on some of the more legally pertinent dimensions is less clear, however. Some studies have found no differences between male and female ratings of defendant guilt (Kaplan and Miller 1978; Lenehan and O'Neill 1981). Others have found that women are more likely to believe that the defendant is guilty (Thornton 1977) and others have found that the subject's gender interacts with factors such as victim respectability (Feldman-Summers and Lindner 1976) to produce these judgments. Sex differences in sentencing are equivocal as well. In at least one study, males delivered harsher sentences than females (Thornton 1977), yet other researchers have found either that females are more punitive than males (Feldman-Summers and Lindner 1976; Kanekar and Kolsawalla 1980; L'Armand and Pepitone 1982; Smith et al. 1976), that there are no sex differences (Jones and Aronson 1973; Kahn et al. 1977; Kaplan and Miller 1978; Oros and Elman 1979), or that there are interactions between the subject's gender and characteristics of the victim (Luginbuhl and Mullin 1981) or the case under consideration (Richardson and Campbell 1982).

Finally, attempts to determine whether men and woman differ in the tendency to hold the victim responsible for her rape have produced completely inconsistent results. Empirical evidence has supported all possible conclusions; that men blame the victim more, that women blame the victim more, that there are no sex differences, and that the effects of a subject's sex depend on a whole host of other variables.

The existence of such inconsistencies is both disturbing and puzzling. It is disturbing because the inconsistencies tend to emerge on the most common dependent measures, such as recommended sentence and victim blame, rather than the more idiosyncratic measures used by only a few investigators. It is also puzzling because the most immediately available explanations for these inconsistencies are clearly inadequate. It is plausible, for example, that as mass media attention to the phenomenon of rape raises men's general level of awareness to the problem, many sex differences in reactions to rape and its victims will begin to disappear. There are no evident temporal trends across studies, however. Studies published in 1982 are no less likely to exhibit sex differences than those published in 1973. It is equally plausible that task differences across studies might account for the obtained differences on outcome measures. It should be noted, however, that many studies in this domain were intended to be literal replications of Jones and Aronson (1973), and thus utilized virtually identical stimulus materials, dependent measures, and experimental procedures. Any task differences, then, must have been very subtle, no doubt too subtle to be ascertained from standard published reports of the research.

A more promising explanation for the inconsistencies in this research area may lie in the failure of most researchers to control for other subject characteristics which may be less than perfectly correlated with gender and differentially distributed across subject populations.

Numerous attitudinal, personality, and experiential variables have been investigated and there is evidence that some of them are significantly related to evaluations and judgments regarding rape. Kaplan and Miller (1978), for example, hypothesized that identification with a rape victim would lead to an anti-defendant bias. They reasoned that parents of females, aware that their daughters are potential victims, would identify more strongly with a rape victim and deliver harsher sentences than would parents of males. Consistent with predictions, parents of females delivered stronger guilt ratings and harsher sentences, but only when the rape occurred in a setting which they believed their daughters were likely to encounter. When the rape occurred under somewhat unusual and risky circumstances, the responses of all parents were the same. Similarly, Deitz et al. (1982) have presented evidence that the tendency to empathize with a rape victim, as measured by the Rape Empathy Scale, is a significant predictor of harsher sentencing, greater certainty of defendant guilt, and attributions of responsibility to the defendant rather than the victim.

Others have hypothesized that attitudes toward women and endorsement of sex-role stereotypes play an important role in subjects' judgments and evaluations regarding rape (Weidner and Griffitt 1983).

Evidence on this point is mixed. Thornton et al. (1982) found that attitudes toward women were significantly related to attributions of responsibility to the victim. Deitz et al. (1982), however, replicated this effect in a sample of college students, but found no such relationship in a random sample of adults from a local jury roster. Burt (1980) obtained evidence that sex role stereotyping, along with distrust of the opposite sex and acceptance of interpersonal violence, are strongly related to the acceptance of stereotyped, false beliefs about rape, rapists, and rape victims. Acceptance of these rape myths leads to more restrictive definitions of rape, a tendency to believe a victim provoked her rape, and a tendency to evaluate the defendant more positively (Burt and Albin 1981). This suggests, then, that the effect of attitudes toward women and sex roles on rape evaluation is indirect, operating through its impact on acceptance of prejudiced attitudes toward rape.

Personality variables, on the other hand, appear to be largely unrelated to rape evaluations and attributions. Although subject dogmatism may predict attributions of victim responsibility (Thornton et al. 1982), the tendency to believe in a just world (Kerr and Kurtz 1977; Thornton et al. 1982), and locus of control (Thornton et al. 1982) do not, and evidence for the impact of personal versus environmental attributional style is equivocal (Thornton et al. 1981; Thornton et al. 1982).

In sum, the data suggest that subject characteristics are important determinants of evaluations and attributions regarding rape. Of those subject characteristics investigated, the effects of *attitudinal* variables appear to be the most consistent and important. To the extent that subjects maintain biased and stereotyped beliefs about what constitutes rape, one might expect evaluations to be sensitive to the context in which the rape occurred. The focus of the next section is on the impact of such contextual variables.

Contextual Characteristics

Research on the impact of contextual factors suggests that stereotypic beliefs about rape affect evaluations and interpretations of particular rape cases. Evaluations of rapes may differ according to the degree of correspondence between features of a particular rape and subjects' notions of the "prototypical" rape. Most subjects, for example, are more certain that a rape has actually been committed, the more physical force the rapist uses (Krulewitz and Payne 1978) and the more the victim resists (Krulewitz and Nash 1979). For feminist women, however, extreme physical force is not a defining characteristic of rape, as they are equally certain that a rape has occurred at all levels of force (Krulewitz and Payne 1978).

If one believes, as do many, that "true" rape involves strangers, information about the prior relationship of the victim and the defendant may also significantly influence judgments. There is evidence that rape by an acquaintance is judged as less serious and damaging (L'Armand and Pepitone 1982), and more due to provocation by the victim (Smith et al. 1976). On the other hand, women raped by strangers may be seen as more careless (Smith et al. 1976). Depending on the circumstances of the rape and, perhaps, the plausibility of carelessness versus provocation explanations, the victim of rape by a stranger may be seen as either more responsible (Smith et al. 1976), or less responsible (L'Armand and Pepitone 1982) than the victim of rape by an acquaintance. More generally, the impact of prior relationship

may often depend on other fairly specific features of the rape under
consideration, such as the time and place of the assault (Bolt and
Caswell 1981), and the number of previous rapes in the area (Calhoun
et al. 1976).

Implications
      Social psychological research on the social perception of rape
victims suggests that the process of evaluating victims is complex.
Subjects do not process the facts of a particular case in a logical
and detached fashion. Instead, they seem to integrate information
from a variety of sources in light of their own biases and attitudes
about rape. This may lead them to weigh heavily certain data that
are of questionable legal relevance, such as the attractiveness or
prior sexual history of the victim or the race of the defendant.
The research reviewed thus far in the chapter highlights some of the
variables that subjects seem to view as pertinent to their experimental tasks and provides evidence on the impact of these variables
on attributions of responsibility for rape. These research findings,
however, must be interpreted with caution. Although most studies
have focused on only a few variables at a time, there are numerous
signs that the effects of most factors are actually interactive; the
impact of a particular victim characteristic may depend on characteristics of the defendant, contextual details, and most important, the
subject's own attitudes and beliefs about rape. Because few studies
have investigated these interactions explicitly, what is known about
the operation of various victim, defendant, case, and subject variables may be quite context-specific or crime-specific (Myers and La-
Free 1982).
      Moreover, what this research suggests about how jurors in court
actually assess evidence in a rape trial is questionable. Very few
of the social perception studies have considered judgments and evaluations about rape in a legal context. Instead, the rape case has
typically been used as a convenient context within which to study
person perception and attributional processes by researchers who often have only a peripheral interest in legal questions. Although
such research may yield results which are quite informative with
respect to basic social psychological theory, problems arise when
such researchers claim that their findings are policy relevant
(Weiten and Diamond 1979).
      The courtroom setting may constitute a unique attributional and
judgmental context (Penrod and Borgida 1983). Very little is currently known about the extent to which attributions are constrained by
the contexts in which they are made, but the little evidence that
does exist suggests that these concerns about context are warranted.
Using records of actual juror verdicts, for example, Myers (1980)
found support for only a subset of hypotheses about attributions of
responsibility derived from the experimental literature. She argues
that her analysis "raises the possibility that qualitatively different attribution processes occur and, within empirically specifiable
limits, reflect the operation of contextual constraints that shape
attributions in complex and unanticipated ways" (p. 415).
      No research better illustrates this interactive, contextual com-
plexity than the study conducted by Feild and Bienen (1980) who examined the impact of various juror, victim, defendant, and case characteristics on reactions to a hypothetical rape case. A number of
features distinguish this work from most other research in this area.

First, the investigators were sensitive to the legal issues underlying their inquiry, and concerned with both the practical and legal implications of their findings. Accordingly, subjects were asked to examine a more extensive case summary than other researchers have typically used, including synopses of the prosecuting and defense attorneys' cases and photos of the victim and the defendant, as well as a general description of the rape. After reading the summary, subjects were asked to render a verdict, to indicate their degree of confidence in that verdict, and to recommend a sentence for the defendant. Thus, an attempt was made to simulate the adversarial nature of a rape trial, and to include legally relevant dependent measures.

Second, Feild and Bienen acknowledged the wide array of factors that potentially contribute to juror verdicts, and incorporated as many of them as possible into a single research design. Six factors were varied systematically through modifications in the case summary and litigant photographs: (1) victim race; (2) physical attractiveness of the victim; (3) moral character of the victim (sexually experienced versus sexually inexperienced); (4) defendant race; (5) type of rape (non-precipitory versus precipitory); and (6) strength of the evidence. The resulting sixty-four versions of the case enabled examination of the effects of every factor independently and in combination. Furthermore, subjects completed a number of individual difference measures assessing attidues toward rape, attitudes toward women's roles and women's rights, knowledge regarding the phenomenon of rape, and various background characteristics. This facilitated the search for interactions among juror, victim, defendant, and case characteristics.

Finally, unlike previous research which relied almost exclusively on college student subjects, Feild and Bienen utilized a large sample of non-student adults drawn from four subgroups: citizens, patrol police officers, rape crisis counselors, and convicted rapists. In addition to enhancing the external validity of their findings, this permitted examination of subgroup differences in levels of knowledge and attitudes toward rape.

What did Feild and Bienen find? Comprehensive treatment of the plethora of results generated in the course of this research is beyond the scope of this chapter, so discussion of the Feild and Bienen data will be confined to findings of direct relevance to juror decision-making in rape cases. One of the most stiking features of Feild and Bienen's data set is the prominence of interaction effects. For example, on the average, black defendants were given harsher sentences than white defendants, but this was because black men who raped white women were given especially long prison terms. When the rape was of a black woman, the defendant's race had no impact on sentencing. This effect was further moderated, however, by the attractiveness of the victim. This relationship obtained for attractive victims, but only the defendant's race affected sentencing for unattractive victims.

Similarly, the defendant's race had no impact on sentencing when the victim was sexually experienced. When the victim was both sexually inexperienced and unattractive, on the other hand, jurors were more punitive toward black defendants.

In total, there were seven significant interaction effects, and each independent variable was involved in at least two of them. Without examining interactions, one might have come to very different con-

clusions. Considered independently, for example, the victim's physical attractiveness and her moral character appeared unrelated to sentencing, yet they were clearly influencing jurors' decisions in combination with other factors; the effects of physical attractiveness
depended on the defendant's and victim's race and the victim's moral
character, while the victim's moral character interacted with all
five of the other independent variables under investigation.

Juror characteristics were also significantly related to sentencing. Higher educational attainment and a belief in severe punishment for the crime of rape predicted harsher sentencing, while
increasing age and beliefs that women are responsible for preventing
rape, that victims tend to precipitate rapes, and that rapists are normal, predicted leniency. Interestingly, the attitudinal variables
were by far the most predictive juror characteristics; adding background variables accounted for little additional variance in sentencing.

Not surprisingly, juror characteristics interacted with characteristics of the defendant, the victim, and the case. For example,
jurors who believed that women precipitate rape gave shorter sentences to men who raped sexually experienced women than jurors who did
not believe that women cause rapes. Jurors who believed in severe
punishment for rape were more punitive toward black defendants than
white ones. And, in general, jurors tended to treat a defendant of
their own race more leniently than a defendant of the opposite race.

Taken together, Feild and Bienen's findings highlight the complexity of people's reactions to, and evaluations of, rape victims,
and the drawbacks associated with investigating the impact of only
one or two variables in isolation. It also provides us with a basis
for making some generalizations which may prove to be valid in a
legal setting. Markedly absent from the entire program of research,
however, is any consideration of victim credibility, thus severely
limiting the kinds of generalizations that can be made. This omission was intentional. Although they acknowledged its probable impact
on juror judgments, and its importance for attorney decisions regarding how to present a case in court, Feild and Bienen avoided measuring perceptions of victim credibility.

Similarly, virtually none of the social perception studies discussed thus far have directly addressed the question of victim credibility. A number of researchers have assumed that perceptions of
credibility mediate attributions of responsibility for rape, but
this hypothesis has not been tested directly. Within the general
attribution research area, in fact, the role of cognitive mediators
also is often assumed but rarely investigated (Taylor and Fiske 1981).
To be fair, given the goals of some attribution researchers, the role
of victim credibility may have been of limited theoretical interest.
Perceptions of victim credibility, however, are so central to juror
decision-making in rape cases that determining its status as a mediator may constitute the most important line of investigation for
psycholegal research on rape trials. An understanding of victim
credibility is critical in order to increase the proportion of rape
cases that go to trial, to increase conviction rates once they get
there, and to improve the treatment on rape victims throughout the
justice system. In the next section of this chapter, therefore, a
program of research that increases our understanding of victim credibility in rape trials will be discussed.

VICTIM CREDIBILITY IN THE COURTROOM

Statutory reform
     At the outset of this chapter, it was noted that various evi-
dentiary reforms have been legislated over the past decade to protect
rape victims in court. In fact, over forty jurisdictions have enacted such statutory "rape shield" laws since the passage of Michigan's
Criminal Sexual Conduct law in 1974. In most instances, these new
laws shifted the burden of proof to the defense by prohibiting the
admission of third party prior sexual history evidence and eliminating
resistance and consent standards. In so doing, these new laws assumed
that more victims would be willing to pursue their cases to court and
that prosecutors' chances for achieving convictions would increase.
But recent legal impact studies of the law reforms in Michigan (Marsh
1981; Marsh et al. 1982) and in the state of Washington (Loh 1980,
1981) provide mixed empirical support for the validity of these assumptions. Whereas Marsh and colleagues (1982). using a combination
of interrupted time series analysis and interviews, report an increased conviction rate for original charges of rape since law reform
was introduced in Michigan, Loh (1980) found that in King County,
Washington, the increase in convictions since law reform in 1975 was
entirely attributable to changes in the labelling of rape convictions.
     However, conclusions about the impact of law reform as measured
by legal impact data (e.g., arrests, convictions, pleas, and sentencing) must be tempered by the fact that different states have adopted
different types of law reforms, with different standards of rape.
Loh (1980, 1981), for example, classified the different law reforms
along a continuum of "victim-actor orientation." He placed common
law statutes at the victim end of the continuum because they require
some degree of victim resistance to prove the crime of rape. Law reforms like Michigan's anchor the other end of the continuum because
they define rape in terms of the defendant's conduct. Washington's
law reform, which Loh systematically evaluated, would be located in
the ambiguous middle of this continuum because it considers the conduct of both victim and defendant. Therefore, Washington and Michigan clearly have different types of law reforms according to Loh's
scheme. In fact, the Marsh et al. (1982) Michigan study suggests
that the impact of one type of law reform (e.g., one that emphasizes
defendant conduct) should not be expected to (and apparently does not)
predict the impact of other types of law reform.
     Borgida's (1980) classification of the various law reforms in
terms of the extent to which they restrict the admission of third
party prior sexual history evidence explicitly suggests that it is
crucial to consider type of law reform in determining legal impact.
His "Common Law" category included those jurisdictions without an
exclusionary rule and assumes the comparatively unlimited admissibility
of third party prior sexual history testimony. In contrast, his two
categories of reform statutes reflect the arguments put forth by critics
of traditional rape laws. The critical difference between the reform
statutes rests in the amount of discretion which is left to the trial
judge in determining the admissibility of third party prior sexual
history evidence. In those jurisdictions governed by a "Moderate
Reform" exclusionary rule (e.g., Washington), such evidence is generally excluded unless the court determines the evidence to be material

to a fact at issue. Laws of this type allow the trial judge considerable discretion in weighing the probative and prejudicial aspects of the evidence in question. As a result, the impact of law reform in Moderate Reform jurisdictions may be no greater practically than in Common Law jurisdictions (although the *intent* of such law reforms is clearly to screen the admissibility of prior sexual history evidence as compared to the Common Law). Finally, a number of jurisdictions (e.g., Michigan) have adopted more restrictive "Radical Reform" statutes that require the exclusion of third party prior sexual history evidence. The view in these jurisdictions is that such evidence is more prejudicial than probative when offered to prove consent and therefore should be excluded.

This reformist assumption that evidence of prior sexual history is inflammatory and prejudicial, and that the admission of such evidence in rape trials would bias juries to acquit the defendant on issues not directly relevant to his guilt, was tested in a jury simulaion study by Borgida (1981; Borgida and White 1978). Qualified adult jurors sampled randomly from the Twin Cities metropolitan area viewed and then deliberated one of six different versions of a videotaped trial (*State v. McNamara*) which presented a consent defense (for procedural details, see Borgida 1981). In each version of the trial the complainant maintained that she had been forcibly raped and the defendant claimed that the complaintant had voluntarily consented to sexual intercourse.

Particularly in rape cases such as *State v. McNamara*, certain features of a fact pattern (e.g., location of the assault, prior relationship between the complainant and defendant) may combine to suggest to jurors complainant consent or contributory behavior. The presence of such features in any given case, therefore, could reduce the likelihood of conviction, whether or not evidence of prior sexual history had been admitted. Consequently, one-half of the *State v. McNamara* trials embodied an "Improbable Likelihood of Consent" fact Pattern and the other half embodied a "Probable Likelihood of Consent" fact pattern. The same core scenario was included in both fact patterns, but certain critical features were varied between fact patterns. Whereas the complainant and defendant "hardly knew each other" in Improbable Likelihood of Consent, for example, they were "very close friends" and had been physically affectionate with one another in Probable Likelihood of Consent. Testimony by the defendant about the complainant's failure to resist was emphasized in Probable Likelihood of Consent. Furthermore, the complainant and defendant had met earlier on the evening in question at a bar-disco in Probable Likelihood of Consent, whereas in Improbable Likelihood of Consent they both just happened to visit the trailer home of a mutual friend earlier in the evening.

The type of exclusionary rule applied to evidence of the victim's prior sexual history was the second factor which was varied in *State v. McNamara*. In accordance with Borgida's (1980) classification of the evidentiary reforms, the defense testimony of a prior sexual history witness whose testimony would have been admissible was included in the Moderate Reform versions of both Probable and Improbable fact patterns. In the Common Law versions of both fact patterns, the defense also presented the testimony of a second prior sexual history witness whose testimony would only have been admissible under the Common Law rule. No prior sexual history evidence was added to either fact pattern in the Radical Reform versions.

Thus, the simulation experiment examined the extent to which the types of legal rules (and, by implication, types of law reform) affect not only juror perceptions of the complainant, but also the conviction rate in *State v. McNamara*. In addition, the study examined the extent to which the varying degrees of implied victim consent moderate the efficacy of the different exclusionary rules. An interaction between type of exclusionary rule and likelihood of consent was expected. Since Improbable Consent fact patterns are less suggestive about the complainant's moral character and propensities than Probable Consent fact patterns, juror verdicts were expected to show the highest likelihood of conviction when the restrictive Radical Reform rule governed the Improbable Likelihood of Consent fact pattern.

In *State v. McNamara*, jurors were indeed reluctant to convict the defendant when any testimony about the complainant's third party prior sexual history was introduced by the defense in support of the consent defense. Only the Radical Reform rule, when applied to an Improbable Consent fact pattern, increased the likelihood of conviction. By contrast, the admission of third party prior sexual history testimony under the Moderate Reform or Common Law, in an otherwise conviction-biased case, was clearly detrimental to the prosecution's case. Neither type of legal reform enhanced the conviction rate when the trial fact pattern conveyed probable consent.

In general, when third party prior sexual history evidence was introduced in *State v. McNamara*, jurors readily inferred complainant consent, more carefully and unfavorably scrutinized the complainant's character than the defendant's character, attributed more responsibility to the complainant, and even denigrated the skill and competence of her attorney. Rather than weigh the facts in this particular case, jurors seemed to use the complainant's prior sexual history with men other than the accused to impeach her credibility as a prosecution witness and by inference to impugn her veracity.

In order to examine further this notion that "prior promiscuity imports dishonesty"--that jurors perceive a direct causal link between complainant credibility and culpability in *State v. McNamara*--Borgida (1981) conducted a path analysis. The direct causal effects of complainant credibility and various personality, attitudinal, experiential, and demographic predictors on individual juror verdicts, as well as the direct causal effects of these predictor variables on complainant credibility, were examined. The best predictor of verdicts in *State v. McNamara* was not any juror socioeconomic characteristic, or whether they had prior jury experience or acquaintance with a rape victim or, for that matter, their authoritarianism or sex role identification. The strongest predictor of verdicts was jurors' perceptions of the complainant's credibility. In fact, 64 percent of the verdict variance was accounted for by the complainant credibility predictor.

In addition to the central importance of complainant credibility, jurors' attitudes toward women and rape also reliably predicted verdicts in *State v. McNamara*, accounting for 12 percent of the verdict variance. Jurors whose belief systems incorporated a high number of stereotypical beliefs and cultural myths about rape (e.g., "In the majority of rapes, the victim is promiscuous or has had a bad reputation") were much less likely to find the defendant in *State v. McNamara* guilty of sexual assault. Such jurors apparently maintain rather restrictive intuitive definitions of what constitutes rape (Burt and

Albin 1981) and therefore were more likely to acquit the defendant in *State v. McNamara*.

Implications

To the extent that statutory reforms alter juror perceptions of victim credibility, as the simulation data strongly suggest, noticeable improvement in the conviction rate for a consent defense rape case like *State v. McNamara* can be expected. Interestingly, criminal justice officials who were interviewed by Marsh et al. (1982) in their impact study of the Michigan law reform largely attributed the documented increase in the rate of original rape convictions and the reduced courtroom harrassment of rape victims to the new law's evidentiary prohibition on the admission of the victim's prior sexual history. Such corroborative field data, it should be noted, can only enhance the external validity of the jury simulation approach (Borgida 1981).

Several legal scholars, however, have raised cogent arguments against the "presumptive inadmissibility" of Radical Reform as well as the Moderate Reform statutes because, in certain cases, exclusion of the complainant's prior sexual history may violate the due process clause of the Fourteenth Amendment and the confrontation and compulsory process clauses of the Sixth Amendment. Some have acknowledged that there may be prejudicial effects associated with prior sexual history evidence, but question whether such evidence is any *more* harmful than similar types of evidence like prior record of the accused or the prior criminal record of any prosecuting witness which traditionally have been admissible (Tanford and Bocchino 1980).

But thus far, the rape shield laws have fared remarkably well in the appellate courts. Both Moderate and Radical Reform statutes have been upheld. Moderate Reform statutes have been examined by appellate courts in New York, Washington, New Jersey, and Kansas. In each case the court recognized the state's legitimate interest in protecting the privacy of the rape complainant and concluded that the exclusion of prior sexual history evidence did not deprive the defendant of any constitutionally protected right. It is no doubt more significant that the Radical Reform statutes have been able to withstand constitutional challenge. Decisions in California, Oklahoma, Louisiana, and Michigan have refused to set aside Radical Reform statutes as unconstitutional. The opinions uniformly express the view that evidence of a complainant's prior sexual history is not probative of her credibility or her tendency to consent, and that such evidence, as the results of the simulation study suggest, is highly prejudicial.

Although these appellate decisions thus far have upheld the constitutionality of the new rape shield laws, legal scholars continue to argue that the absolute prohibition of even third party prior sexual history in some cases may deprive the defendant of his constitutional rights (Tanford and Bocchino 1980). Defenders of the law reforms continue to respond that evidence of a complainant's prior sexual history is not probative of consent nor is it relevant to any other issue. A defendant has no constitutional right, in this view, to present evidence that is arguably probative and highly prejudicial. "The problem," therefore, as Berger (1977) has observed, "is to chart a course between inflexible legislative rules and wholly untrammeled judicial discretion: the former threatens the rights of defendants; the latter may ignore the needs of complainants" (p. 69). A non-statutory approach that bears on the charting of this course is discussed in the concluding two sections of the chapter.

Countering Rape Myths Through Expert Testimony

Despite the statutory reforms designed to increase conviction rates and protect the interests of victims, the general public maintains numerous myths (Burt 1980), stereotypes (Heilbrun 1980), and misconceptions (Feild and Bienen 1980) about rape that may adversely affect perceptions of the rape victim's credibility in court. For example, although research indicates that in about 40 percent of all rapes, the victim is at least casually acquainted with her assailant (Amir 1971; National Commission on the Causes and Prevention of Violence 1969; National Institute of Law Enforcement and Criminal Justice 1978) it is commonly believed that "true" rape involves strangers. Similarly, people often view a woman's reluctance to go to the police as indicative of a fabricated rape report, despite the fact that only an estimated 10 to 30 percent of all rapes are ever reported to the police (Amir 1971; National Criminal Justice Information and Statistics Service 1979).

Stereotypes and misconceptions such as these contribute to juror bias against the victim by providing grounds for questioning her credibility and by restricting the range of incidents that are defined as rape (Burt and Albin 1981). In fact, the research by Borgida and his colleagues (1978, 1980, 1981) on statutory reform, as well as the previously reviewed research on social perception of rape victims, indicates that a very good predictor of juror verdicts is the extent to which jurors endorse these rape myths.

Aware of these biases, prosecutors have shied away from bringing to trial all but the strongest rape cases (Loh 1980). In response to this trend, rape researchers (Feild 1979; Luginbuhl and Mullin 1981) and prosecutors (Rowland 1979) have advocated the introduction of expert scientific testimony on behalf of the prosecution in rape trials. The intent behind such a strategy is, in effect, to reeducate jurors by directly confronting their erroneous beliefs with scientific evidence. It is assumed that informing jurors that their preconceived notions about rape have little scientific basis will be sufficient to keep them from using their stereotypes when evaluating a particular case, which should, in turn, increase conviction rates.

Is such an assumption warranted? Does expert scientific testimony function as an effective means for counteracting jurors' rape myths and inferential biases? What is the impact of expert testimony on victim credibility? Rowland (1979), former Deputy District Attorney of San Diego County, California, has introduced expert scientific testimony in four rape trials. She obtained three convictions and one hung jury, with eleven of twelve jurors voting guilty in the latter case. Post-trial interviews with jurors conducted informally by Rowland suggested that the expert witness had a decisive influence, but only one controlled study to date has been conducted to examine the impact of expert testimony is rape trials.

In a jury simulation experiment designed to assess the influence of expert testimony on juror judgments in rape trials, Brekke and colleagues (1983) randomly assigned college students to juries of balanced sex composition. Juries listened to an abbreviated, audio-taped version of the *State v. McNamara* case used by Borgida and his colleagues (1981; Borgida and White 1978). The basic fact pattern was exemplary of a "casual acquaintance rape" with a consent defense.

Both parties knew each other prior to the incident and both agreed
that intercourse had taken place. The major point of dispute was
over the issue of consent. The complainant claimed that she had
been raped; the defendant contended that the complainant had been a
willing participant. The basic trial stimulus lasted slightly over
an hour and contained all the structural features of an actual rape
trial. This version was presented to jurors in the control condition.

Four additional versions of *State v. McNamara* were constructed
which included testimony by an expert witness. The expert was identified as a male university psychiatrist who had conducted extensive research in the area of rape, counseled rapists and rape victims, and
taught courses on human sexuality. In his testimony, the expert addressed the low level of public awareness regarding sexual assault
and attempted to debunk a number of widely held misconceptions about
rape. For example, using empirical evidence to support his claims,
he testified (a) that few women falsely accuse men of rape; (b) that,
in fact, rape is one of the most under-reported of all crimes; (c)
that many rapes involve acquaintances rather than strangers; (d) that
rape is a crime of violence rather than a crime of passion; and (e)
that it may be better for a woman to submit to her attacker than to
risk the additional violence that may result from ineffective attempts
to fight back. The expert also described common behavior patterns exhibited by rape victims during and following their sexual assaults.
On cross-examination, the expert admitted that he was being paid for
testifying by the county and that he had discussed the facts of the
case with the prosecuting attorney prior to his court appearance.

The four versions varied according to the type of expert testimony employed and the timing of presentation of that testimony during
the trial. In the "general information" condition, the prosecuting
attorney asked a series of leading questions that enabled the expert
to dispense his testimony in essentially a lecture format. In the "specific-hypothetical" condition, jurors listened to the general information, followed by an explicit attempt to point out the connection
between the expert testimony and the case under consideration. Specifically, the prosecuting attorney posed a hypothetical example to
the expert, incorporating in it the essential facts of *State v. McNamara*. The expert was then asked to comment on the reasonableness of
the hypothetical victim's behavior, given the situation she was in.
The expert highlighted features of the example that were typical of
casual acquaintance rapes and argued that the hypothetical victim's
behavior was quite predictable and reasonable, when viewed in light
of scientific knowledge of typical behavior in such circumstances.
It should be noted that inclusion of the hypothetical example provided
no additional information beyond that already given to jurors; it
merely enabled the expert to comment more directly on the case at hand.

Each type of expert testimony was presented half of the time
early in the trial (i.e., as first prosecution witness), and half of
the time *late* in the trial (i.e., as last prosecution witness).

Thus, type of expert testimony was crossed with timing of presentation in a 2x2 factorial design with an independent no-expert testimony control group. Six juries listened to each version of the trial.
Following the case, jurors deliberated to unanimous verdicts or for
thirty minutes, whichever came first. Jurors then completed questionnaires assessing verdict, recommended sentence, and evaluations of
various trial characters and pieces of evidence.

Brekke et al. (1983) hypothesized that the expert testimony would be most effective when it was linked directly to the trial by means of a hypothetical example, especially when it was presented early in the trial. The rationale behind this hypothesis was two-fold. First, given the inferential tendency to underutilize abstract, statistical information in favor of more vivid case-specific information (Nisbett and Ross 1980), it seemed likely that jurors would tend to disregard the general information expert testimony and base their judgments on the more vivid information available to them (e.g., testimony by the litigants and jurors' own personal experience). Brekke et al. reasoned, however, that using this lecture format to educate the jury followed by a hypothetical example to highlight key points in the actual trial, would allow maximum dissemination of information and would provide some assurance that jurors would understand how to apply their newly-acquired knowledge to the case at hand. The danger, of course, was that this type of expert testimony would be viewed as too directive and explicit, and that psychological reactance would set in, leading jurors to rely even more strongly on their own erroneous preconceptions.

Second, Brekke et al. expected early presentation to be most effective because it provided an opportunity to reeducate jurors before their preconceptions and biases had had a chance to influence their perceptions of the complainant and her behavior. Once jurors had formed negative impressions of the complainant, expert testimony should have relatively little impact on judgments.

Results of the Brekke et al. study were generally in accordance with predictions. Including expert testimony clearly influenced the percentage of jurors who rendered guilty verdicts. Without expert testimony, only 11 percent of jurors voted guilty. When general information expert testimony was included, conviction rates jumped to 38 percent, a statistically significant increase. Even more effective, however, was the specific-hypothetical expert testimony; 65 percent of jurors who listened to that version of the trial rendered guilty verdicts (again, a highly significant increase).

Results on other dependent measures pointed to the importance of considering the type of expert testimony employed. Compared to jurors who received general information expert testimony, specific-hypothetical jurors recommended harsher sentences for the defendant, considered it less likely that the complainant consented to have sex, saw her as more credible and moral, and attributed less responsibility to her for the events on the night in question. Post hoc comparisons with the no expert testimony control group revealed that except on the verdict measure, general information expert testimony means did not differ significantly from no expert testimony control means. In other words, expert testimony appears to have affected perceptions of the litigants only when it included a hypothetical example relating the information directly to the case.

Timing of presentation tended to moderate the effects of type of expert testimony. The timing by type interaction reached statistical significance only on measures of recommended sentence, attributions of responsibility to the complainant, and likelihood of complainant consent, but a clear pattern emerged on all those dependent measures with type of testimony main effects. The expert testimony always yielded the strongest effects when it was linked to the case via the hypothetical example and presented early in the trial.

The introduction of expert testimony thus appears to be an effective means of counteracting the otherwise pervasive effects of rape myths and inferential biases on juror judgments. It is crucial, however, that the testimony be linked explicitly to the case at hand, rather than presented as generally relevant to an understanding of rape. Without this link, jurors seem unable or unwilling to apply the information to the facts of the case they are considering. In addition, it seems advisable to present the testimony early in the trial, before jurors' biases have affected their interpretations of the evidence and influenced their impressions of the litigants.

The admission of expert scientific testimony in rape trials, however, has recently become the subject of considerable controversy. A particular type of expert testimony, rape trauma syndrome evidence (Burgess and Holmstrom 1974), seems to be at the heart of this controversy. The scientific reliability of such testimony has been questioned, and there has been some concern expressed that its use by the prosecution may be prejudicial to the defendant. In the concluding section of this chapter, the current legal status of expert testimony on rape trauma syndrome is discussed.

Rape Trauma Syndrome Evidence in Court

Broadly defined, "syndrome evidence" consists of a description of particular physical or emotional conditions which manifest themselves in certain situations (Coleman 1982). Such evidence has been introduced by the prosecution in cases involving battered women, battered children, family incest, and rape. Rape trauma syndrome, in particular, represents a predictable sequential pattern of emotional reactions typically experienced by a rape victim as she attempts to cope with the post-traumatic stress associated with rape (Burgess and Holmstrom 1974; see also Chapter 4 in this volume). In order to improve the conviction rate in rape cases, prosecutors across the country have begun to introduce expert testimony on rape trauma syndrome in court. Rowland's (1979) use of expert testimony was essentially prompted by a judicial instruction (CALJIC 10.23) that emphasizes the *defendant's* state of mind at the time of the assault. Jurors are to decide the case on the basis of the defendant's "reasonable and good faith belief" about victim consent. The rationale behind expert testimony, then, is to direct jurors' attention toward the rape victim's perception of the situation, and to explain how the victim's behavior in the situation constituted a normal coping response as defined in part by rape trauma syndrome. As discussed in previous sections of the chapter, jurors bring to trial numerous misconceptions about a rape victim's perceptions and behavior; expert testimony could serve to corroborate the victim's testimony in a consent defense rape case and, in turn, increase the likelihood of conviction.

The admission of expert testimony on rape trauma syndrome, however, has proven controversial (Frazier and Borgida 1983). Thus far, there are published appellate court opinions in five criminal sexual conduct cases that were appealed on the basis that expert testimony on rape trauma syndrome was improperly admitted at the trial court level. The first decisions on this issue were made by the Minnesota Supreme Court in August, 1982 (*State v. Saldana*; *State v. McGee*). The Minnesota Court's opinion was that the expert testimony on rape trauma syndrome was inadmissible and constituted reversible error (the *Saldana* case has since been re-tried and the defendant was acquitted). A Kansas court (*State v. Marks* 1982) decided, however, that rape trauma syndrome evidence is relevant and proper testimony (*People v. Bledsoe* 1983; *Delia S. v. Torres* 1982). Because the courts are divided at this time over the admissibility of rape trauma syndrome evidence, it is instructive to examine each of these cases more closely in order to evaluate the current status of rape trauma syndrome evidence in court.

State v. Saldana provides the most detailed discussion of the admissibility of rape trauma syndrome evidence. The appellant in *Saldana* had been charged with first degree criminal sexual conduct and alleged at trial that intercourse had been consensual. The state called a rape victim counselor as an expert witness to rebut his claim. The witness (a) described the typical behavior of rape victims, (b) stated that she definitely believed that the complainant had been raped, and (c) stated that she did not believe the rape had been fantasized. On appeal, the Court evaluated each aspect of this testimony according to the criteria for admitting expert scientific testimony.

Briefly, under the Federal Rules of Evidence, there are several criteria that govern the admissibility of expert testimony. First, the trial judge must determine that the proferred evidence is relevant and that its probative value is not outweighed by "the danger of unfair prejudice, confusion of the issues, or misleading the jury, or by considerations of undue delay, waste of time, or needless presentation of cumulative evidence" (Rule 403). Second, under Rule 702, the expert must be qualified on the basis of "knowledge, skill, experience, training or education ..." Additionally, Rule 702 requires that the expert evidence must assist the trier of fact in determining the truth (the helpfulness requirement), which has been conservatively interpreted in one leading opinion (*Dyas v. United States* 1977) to mean that the expert must provide knowledge that is "beyond the ken of the average layperson." Finally, the courts have traditionally required that the expert's testimony be scientifically reliable and generally accepted in the scientific community (Giannelli 1980; Imwinkelried 1981; McCormick 1982).

In regard to the scientific reliability of rape trauma syndrome testimony, the Court in *Saldana* held that the evidence was not sufficiently established in either the medical or psychiatric community. However, the thrust of the Court's argument seems to be that even if such evidence were reliable, it would not be helpful to the jury because it is not the kind of evidence that "accurately and reliably determines whether a rape occurred." The Court also stated that the post-traumatic stress symptoms associated with rape could follow *any* psychologically traumatic event and that not every case of rape will result in the symptoms described in the syndrome. Thus, the Court held that evidence concerning how some, or even most, people react to rape is not helpful to the jury; rather, the jury must decide each case on the basis of the facts at hand. Although rape trauma syndrome may be a useful counseling tool, the Court reasoned, it is prejudicial in the courtroom.

The expert witness in *Saldana* also testified that, in her opinion, the complainant had been raped. As to whether an expert may offer an opinion of this kind, the Court held that although the expert may testify in the form of an opinion, a majority of the courts ruling on this issue have decided that admission of a physician's opinion that a rape had occurred was in error because it involved a legal conclusion. The Court did note three cases in which physicians had been

allowed to give an opinion (based on their physical examination of
the complainant) that intercourse had not been voluntary. But the
Court rules that the *Saldana* expert's testimony would have been erroneous in any case because the witness was not a physician, had not
physically examined the complainant, and had not in fact met the complainant until ten days after the incident.

The third aspect of the expert's testimony examined by the Court
in *Saldana* was an assertion by the expert that she did not believe
that the complainant had fantasized the rape. Generally, such credibility judgments are regarded as in the province of the jury. Expert
testimony on this issue is only allowed in unusual cases (e.g., a
mentally retarded witness). The Court saw no special circumstances
warranting the testimony in this case, ruling also that the witness
was not qualified to testify whether the complainant could distinguish
fantasy from reality.

The Minnesota Court also reversed a criminal sexual conduct conviction in the companion case to *Saldana*. In *State v. McGee*, a physician had been allowed to testify that in his opinion the complainant's
behavior after the incident was consistent with the symptomatology of
rape trauma syndrome. The Court ruled that admission of this testimony constituted reversible error for the reasons outlined in the
Saldana case.

However, a noteworthy dissenting opinion was submitted in the
McGee case. Justice Wahl maintained that there is indeed a substantial data base in support of rape trauma syndrome, thus making it
sufficiently reliable within the scientific community. Arguing that
the physician was an expert and that the subject matter of the testimony was not within jurors' common knowledge, Justice Wahl argued
that the crucial question was whether the evidence was helpful to the
jury. As distinguished from the expert in *Saldana*, the physician in
McGee did not give his opinion as to whether a rape had occurred.
He described the complainant's symptoms after the incident and stated
that he found these to be consistent with rape trauma syndrome. Justice Wahl found this testimony to be probative on the issue of consent
and thus helpful to the jury in resolving the conflicting facts of the
case.

Probative value, as mentioned earlier in this section, must be
weighed against the danger of unfair prejudice. In this regard, Justice Wahl compared rape trauma syndrome evidence to other kinds of
syndrome evidence; notably, battering parent syndrome (*State v. Loebach* 1981) and battered child syndrome (*State v. Loss* 1973; *State v.
Goblirsch* 1976). Battering parent syndrome was proscribed in *Loebach*
because it directly attacked the character of the defendant. Rape
trauma syndrome evidence, however, is more closely akin to battered
child syndrome evidence (which was upheld in *Loss* and *Goblirsch*) because it is victim-oriented and non-prejudicial to the character of
the defendant. Thus, according to Justice Wahl, the prejudicial effect of the evidence does not outweigh its probative value.

The decision of the Kansas Court in *State v. Marks* (1982) reflected the same thinking as the dissenting opinion in *McGee* in its
judgment that the admission of rape trauma syndrome evidence was not
reversible error. In *Marks*, a psychiatrist testified on the basis of
his evaluation of the complainant that she had been the victim of an
attack and was suffering from rape trauma syndrome. The appellant
did not challenge the expertise of the witness. Rather it was argued

that rape trauma syndrome evidence, whether reliable or not, is inadmissible where consent is a defense because it invades the province of the jury. The Court, however, argued that if rape trauma syndrome is detectable and reliable as evidence that an assault took place, then it is relevant when a defendant alleges consent. The expert opinion does not invade the province of the jury but is offered as any other evidence with the expert open to cross-examination and the jury left to determine its weight. In regard to reliability, the Court concluded that rape trauma syndrome evidence is generally accepted within the scientific community and therefore admissible when the defense is consent.

In *People v. Bledsoe* (1983), the defendant argued that the testimony of the complainant's rape counselor was irrelevant, based on previous decisions in *People v. Clark* (1980) and *People v. Guthreau* (1980). However, the inadmissible evidence in *Clark* and *Guthreau* concerned the reasonableness of the victim's resistance rather than rape trauma syndrome evidence. The *Bledsoe* decision distinguished between these two types of evidence and concluded that rape trauma syndrome evidence was relevant to whether a rape occurred.

Justice Wiener dissented from this ruling, asserting that the testimony in this case could not be distinguished from that in *Clark* and *Guthreau*. His opinion maintained that the expert merely corroborated the subjective state of mind of the victim and provided circumstantial evidence to support the inference that the complainant had been raped. Justice Wiener also criticized the Court for its failure to address the issue of the reliability of the evidence. Citing *Saldana*, *McGee*, and *Marks*, Wiener concluded that the question of scientific reliability was still highly debatable. Without an answer to this question and a definition of the scientific body of knowledge, Justice Wiener stated that it would be impossible to determine if an expert had the requisite qualifications. This opinion concluded, in line with *Saldana*, that the testimony was not beyond the common knowledge of the jury and that the danger of unfair prejudice outweighed any probative value.

In another California case (*Delia S. v. Torres* 1982), the expert testified concerning the reactions of rape victims and the characteristics of rapists. The defendant argued that this testimony improperly validated the complainant's testimony, thereby constituting prejudicial error. But the Court (a) held that the testimony was proper because the subject matter was not within the common knowledge of the jury; (b) affirmed the qualifications of the expert, who was a clinical social worker with considerable experience in rape crisis centers; (c) affirmed the relevance of the testimony concerning common reactions of rape victims on the basis that the defendant sought to show that the complainant's behavior was inconsistent with that of most rape victims (adding that the expert in this case only provided general information on rape victims and did not give an opinion that the complainant was psychologically motivated to act in a certain way); and (d) recognized the potential danger of testimony regarding the characteristics of rapists, yet concluded that its admission was warranted due to the defendant's claim that he was not likely to be a rapist because of his status in the community. The expert did not express an opinion as to whether the defendant fit the profile of a rapist. Thus, the testimony did not attack his character, but provided a means by which the jury could determine the probative weight

to be given to the fact that he had status in the community. Thus,
prejudice was not outweighed by probative value and there was no a-
buse of discretion, according to the decision. The Court, however,
did not discuss the issue of the scientific reliability of the evidence.

Implications

Courts recently faced with expert testimony on rape trauma syndrome have been divided over the admissibility of such testimony.
This is rather clear from the five appellate opinions on rape trauma
syndrome reviewed in the previous section. Three key issues have
been and no doubt will continue to be central to determining the legal status of expert testimony on rape trauma syndrome: (1) whether
its probative value outweighs any prejudicial effect; (2) whether
such testimony is beyond the ken of the average juror; and (3) the
scientific status of rape trauma syndrome. This chapter concludes
with a brief assessment of each issue.

Prejudice vs. Probity. Particular case facts may render the
expert testimony more prejudicial than probative and it is the trial
judge who has discretion over the admissibility decision. With respect to expert testimony on rape trauma syndrome, the problem of prejudice is most likely to arise when the testimony is seen as pointing
an "accusatory finger" at the defendant. This point was made by Justice Wahl in her dissenting opinion in *McGee* and is further discussed
by Coleman (1982). Like battered child syndrome, rape trauma syndrome should address victim behavior rather than the defendant's character. Furthermore, in comparison to battering parent syndrome, no
opinion need be expressed as to who inflicted the injury. In fact,
rape trauma syndrome testimony will be challenged less often if the
expert does not offer a legal opinion on whether the victim had been
raped. Thus, expert testimony on rape trauma syndrome may be admissible when its focus is limited to victim characteristics. To the
extent that the expert testimony has such a focus, the danger of undue prejudice to the defendant is minimized considerably.

The "Helpfulness" Requirement. To what extent is expert testimony on rape trauma syndrome beyond the ken of the average juror?
Does the expert testimony "assist the trier of fact" in understanding
the evidence in a consent defense rape case, or is rape trauma syndrome commonly understood? *Saldana* and *McGee* both ruled that the evidence was within jurors' common knowledge. In *Torres*, which upheld
the admissibility of the testimony, it was argued that while jurors
indeed may have opinions about the common reactions of rape victims,
these opinions are often quite erroneous; hence, *Torres* ruled that
expert testimony on rape trauma syndrome did not invade the province
of the jury.

Other arguments regarding the helpfulness requirement also relate to whether the evidence on rape trauma syndrome is misleading or
invades the province of the jury. In *Saldana*, for example, it was
argued that inclusion of such testimony may lead to a time-consuming
"battle of the experts" which could distract the jury from its task.
A more common argument is that rape trauma syndrome evidence, rather
than corroborating complainant credibility, improperly *bolsters* complainant credibility (Cade and Imwinkelried 1983). Corroborating evidence is routinely admissible because it is relevant to the case
facts and only indirectly addresses, in this context, victim credibility. The argument against admission of testimony on rape trauma syn-

drome, however, is that such evidence functionally bolsters victim credibility. Because it is originally based on the complainant's self-reports, to admit such testimony would de facto bolster the credibility of the victim's perspective. Evidence that bolsters complainant credibility, according to this argument, invades the province of the jury. Proponents, however, have plausibly argued that rape trauma syndrome evidence is introduced only to corroborate the victim's testimony about case facts, i.e., that she did not consent. The expert should not testify that the complainant was a truthful person; only that the complainant exhibited symptoms common to other rape victims.

   Scientific Status. As is the case for expert testimony on battered woman syndrome (Walter 1982), the courts have disagreed over the "state of the art" standard required for admitting expert testimony in rape cases. In *Saldana*, the Court argued that such syndrome evidence has not been reliably established in the psychiatric community, but the Court in *Marks* argued that rape trauma syndrome was a well-documented example of a post traumatic stress disorder. Cade and Imwinkelred (1983), writing for the National Association of Criminal Defense Lawyers, have argued that expert testimony on rape trauma syndrome should, like any other scientific evidence, meet the controversial *Frye* test (*Frye v. United States* 1923). Under the *Frye* test, scientific evidence must be "generally accepted" within the scientific community. But the *Frye* test has been criticized for a variety of reasons, including the extent to which it is an ambiguous standard (what, for example, constitutes "general acceptance" in the scientific community?). And, in many jurisdictions, the *Frye* test has been superceded by the relevancy approach embodied in the Federal Rules of Evidence (Giannelli 1980).

   Cade and Imwinkelried (1983) also argued that although the diagnosis of post traumatic stress disorder is generally recognized in the psychiatric literature, the specific application of that disorder to rape trauma is not yet altogether accepted. However, it has been suggested that the admissibility of rape trauma syndrome evidence need not be determined by this general acceptance criterion (Coleman 1982; Frazier and Borgida 1983). The court in *Ibn-Tamas v. United States* (1979), for example, has emphasized that admissibility should only be based on general acceptance of an expert's methodology. That is, scientific evidence could be evaluated by the court in terms of the methodology used in a particular study or the scientific soundness of the studies on which the expert bases his or her testimony (Imwinkelried 1981). "The accessibility of the conclusions and theories ordinarily is the function of the jury, i.e., a determination of which side to believe. Requiring the conclusions to be generally acceptable ignores the adversarial nature of our system ... and the jury's ability to make a proper ascertainment of the truth" (Walter 1982, p. 293). As the research base on rape trauma syndrome continues to expand, questions about its scientific status should begin to abate, leaving juries to determine the weight of expert testimony in the context of all the facts at trial.

REFERENCES

Amir, M. *Patterns of Forcible Rape.* Chicago, Illinois: University of Chicago Press, 1971.

Berger, V. "Man's Trial, Woman's Tribulation: Rape Cases in the Courtroom." *Columbia Law Review* 77 (1977): 1-101.

Bolt, M., and J. Caswell. "Attribution of Responsibility to a Rape Victim." *Journal of Social Psychology* 11 (1981): 137-138.

Borgida, E. "Evidentiary Reform of Rape Laws: A Psycholegal Approach." In *New Directions in Psycholegal Research*, edited by P.D. Lipsitt and B.D. Sales. New York: Van Nostrand Reinhold Co., 1980.

Borgida, E. "Legal Reform of Rape Laws." In *Applied Social Psychology Annual*, Vol. 2, edited by L. Bickman. Beverly Hills, California: Sage Publications, 1981.

Borgida, E., and P. White. "Social Perception of Rape Victims: The Impact of Legal Reform." *Law and Human Behavior* 2 (1978): 339-351.

Brekke, N., E. Borgida, and D.K. Mensing. *Expert Scientific Testimony in Rape Trials.* Paper presented at the annual meeting of the Midwestern Psychological Association. Chicago, Illinois: May, 1983.

Burgess, A., and L. Holmstrom. "Rape Trauma Syndrome." *American Journal of Psychiatry* 131 (1974): 980-986.

Burt, M.R. "Cultural Myths and Supports for Rape." *Journal of Personality and Social Psychology* 38 (1980): 217-230.

Burt, M.R., and R.S. Albin. "Rape Myths, Rape Definitions, and Probability of Conviction." *Journal of Applied Social Psychology* 11 (1981): 212-230.

Cade, B., and E. Imwinkelried. "Rape Trauma Syndrome Evidence." *The Champion* 3 (1983): 2-4.

Calhoun, L.G., J.W. Selby, and L.J. Warring. "Social Perception of the Victim's Causal Role in Rape: An Explanatory Examination of Four Factors." *Human Relations* 29 (1976): 517-526.

Cann, A., L.G. Calhoun, and J.W. Selby. "Attributing Responsibility to the Victim of Rape: Influence of Information Regarding Past Sexual Experience." *Human Relations* 32 (1979): 57-67.

Coleman, N. "Syndrome Evidence Cases." *Seventeenth Annual Criminal Justice Institute* 1982: 279-294.

Deitz, S., K.T. Blackwell, P.C. Daley, and B.J. Bentley. "Measurement of Empathy Toward Rape Victims and Rapists." *Journal of Personality and Social Psychology* 43 (1982): 372-384.

Deitz, S.R., and L.E. Byrnes. "Attribution of Responsibility for Sexual Assault: The Influence of Observer Empathy and Defendant Occupation and Attractiveness." *Journal of Psychology* 108 (1981): 17-29.

Elwork, A., B.D. Sales, and D. Suggs. "The Trial: A Research Review." In *The Trial Process*, edited by B.D. Sales. New York: Plenum, 1981.

Feild, H. "Rape Trials and Jurors' Descisions: A Psycholegal Analysis of the Effects of Victim, Defendant, and Case Characteristics." *Law and Human Behavior* 3 (1979): 261-284.

Feild, H., and L. Bienen. *Jurors and Rape: A Study in Psychology and the Law.* Lexington, Massachusetts: D.C. Heath, 1980.

Feldman-Summers, S., and K. Lindner. "Perceptions of Victims and Defendants in Criminal Assault Cases." *Criminal Justice and Behavior* 3 (1976): 135-150.

Frazier, P., and Borgida, E. *Rape Trauma Syndrome Evidence in Court.* Unpublished manuscript, University of Minnesota, 1983.

Giannelli, P.C. "The Admissibility of Novel Scientific Evidence: *Frye v. United States,* a Half-Century Later." *Columbia Law Review* 80 (1980): 1197-1250.

Heilbrun, A.B., Jr. "Presumed Motive in the Male and Female Perception of Rape." *Criminal Justice and Behavior* 7 (1980): 257-274.

Imwinkelried, E.J. "A New Era in the Evolution of Scientific Evidence." *William and Mary Law Review* 23 (1981): 261-290.

Jones, C., and E. Aronson. "Attribution of Fault to a Rape Victim as Function of Respectability of the Victim." *Journal of Personality and Social Psychology* 26 (1973): 415-419.

Kahn, A., and I.A. Gilbert, R.M. Latta, C. Deutsch, R. Hagen, M. Hill, T. McGaughey, A.N. Ryan, and D.W. Wilson. "Attribution of Fault to a Rape Victim as a Function of Respectability of the Victim: A Failure to Replicate or Extend." *Representative Research in Social Psychology* 8 (1977): 98-107.

Kanekar, S., and M.B. Kolsawalla. "Responsibility in Relation to Respectability." *Journal of Social Psychology* 102 (1977): 183-188.

Kanekar, S., and M.B. Kolsawalla. "Responsibility of a Rape Victim in Relation to her Respectability, Attractiveness, and Provocativeness." *Journal of Social Psychology* 112 (1980): 153-154.

Kanekar, S., M.B. Kolsawalla, and A. D'Souza. "Attribution of Responsibility to a Victim of Rape." *British Journal of Social Psychology* 20 (1981): 165-170.

Kaplan, M.F., and L.E. Miller. "Effects of Jurors' Identification with the Victim Depend on Likelihood of Victimization." *Law and Human Behavior* 2 (1978): 353-361.

Kerr, N.K., and S.T. Kurtz. "Effects of Victim Suffering and Respectability on Mock Juror Judgments: Further Evidence on the Just World Theory." *Representative Research in Social Psychology* 8 (1977): 42-56.

Krulewitz, J.E. "Sex Differences in Evaluations of Female and Male Victims' Responses to Assault." *Journal of Applied Social Psychology* 11 (1981): 460-474.

Krulewitz, J.E., and E.J. Nash. "Effects of Rape Victim Resistance, Assault Outcome, and Sex of Observer on Attributions about Rape." *Journal of Personality* 47 (1979): 557-574.

Krulewitz, J.E., and E.J. Payne. "Attributions about Rape: Effects of Rapist Force, Observer Sex, and Sex-Role Attitudes." *Journal of Applied Social Psychology* 8 (1978): 291-305.

L'Armand, K., and A. Pepitone. "Judgments of Rape: A Study of Victim-Rapist Relationship and Victim Sexual History." *Personality and Social Psychology Bulletin* 8 (1982): 134-139.

Lenehan, G.E., and P. O'Neill. "Reactance as Determinants of a Judgment in a Mock Jury Experiment." *Journal of Applied Social Psychology* 11 (1981): 231-239.

Lerner, M.J. "The Desire for Justice and Reactions to Victims." In *Altruism and Helping Behavior*, edited by J. Macaulay and L. Berkowitz. New York: Academic Press, 1970.

Loh, W.D. "The Impact of Common Law and Reform Rape Statutes on Prosecution: An Empirical Study." *Washington Law Review* 55 (1980): 543-654.

Loh, W.D. "What Has Reform of Rape Legislation Wrought?" *Journal of Social Issues* 37 (1981): 28-52.

Luginbuhl, J., and C. Mullin. "Rape and Responsiblity: How and How Much is the Victim Blamed?" *Sex Roles* 7 (1981): 547-559.

Marsh, J.C. "Combining Time Series with Interviews: Evaluating the Effects of a Sexual Assault Law." In *Methodological Advances in Evaluation Research*, Vol. 10, edited by R.F. Conner. Beverly Hills, California: Sage Publications, 1981.

McCormick, M. "Scientific Evidence: Defining a New Approach to Admissibility." *Iowa Law Review* 67 (1982): 879-916.

Miller, G.R., and F.J. Boster. "Three Images of the Trial: Their Implications for Psychological Research." In *Psychology in the Legal Process*, edited by B.D. Sales. New York: Spectrum Publications, 1977.

Miller, G.R., and J.K. Burgoon. "Factors Affecting Assessments of Witness Credibility." In *The Psychology of the Courtroom*, edited by N.L. Kerr & R.M. Bray. New York: Academic Press, 1982.

Myers, M. "Social Contexts and Attributions of Criminal Responsibility." *Social Psychology Quarterly* 43 (1980): 405-419.

Myers, M., and G.D. LaFree. "Sexual Assault and Its Prosecution: A Comparison with Other Crimes." *Journal of Criminal Law and Criminology* 73 (1982): 1282-1305.

Nagao, D.H., and J.H. Davis. "Some Implications of Temporal Drift in Social Parameters." *Journal of Experimental Social Psychology* 16 (1980): 479-496.

National Commission on the Causes and Prevention of Violence. Washington, D.C.: U.S. Government Printing Office, 1969.

National Criminal Justice Information and Statistics Service. *Rape Victimization in 26 American Cities*. Washington, D.C.: U.S. Department of Justice, 1979.

National Institute of Law Enforcement and Criminal Justice. *Forcible Rape: Final Project Report.* Washington, D.C.: U.S. Government Printing Office, 1978.

Nisbett, R.E., and L. Ross. *Human Inference: Strategies and Short-comings.* Englewood Cliffs, New Jersey: Prentice-Hall, 1980.

Oros, C.J., and D. Elman. "Impact of Judge's Instructions upon Jurors' Descisions: The 'Cautionary Charge' in Rape Trials." *Representative Research in Social Psychology* 10 (1979): 28-36.

Penrod, S., and E.Borgida. "Legal Rules and Lay Inference." In *Review of Personality and Social Psychology*, Vol. 3, edited by L. Wheeler. Beverly Hills, California: Sage Publications, 1983.

Richardson, D., and J.L. Campbell. "Alcohol and Rape: The Effect of Alcohol on Attributions of Blame for Rape." *Personality and Social Psychology Bulletin* 8 (1982): 468-476.

Rowland, J. "Rape Experts Dispell Jurors' Preconceptions." *Prosecutors' Brief* 5 (1979): 21-25.

Rumsey, M.G., and J.M. Rumsey. "A Case of Rape: Sentencing Judgments of Males and Females." *Psychological Reports* 41 (1977): 459-465.

Scroggs, J.R. "Penalties for Rape as a Function of Victim Provocativeness, Damage, and Resistance." *Journal of Applied Social Psychology* 6 (1976): 360-368.

Selby, J.W., L.G. Calhoun, and T.A. Brock. "Sex Differences in the Social Perception of Rape Victims." *Personality and Social Psychology Bulletin* 3 (1977): 412-415.

Seligman, C., J. Brickman, and D. Koulack. "Rape and Physical Attractiveness: Assigning Responsibility to Victims." *Journal of Personality* 45 (1977): 554-563.

Smith, R.E., J.P. Keating, R.K. Hester, and H.E. Mitchell. "Role of Justice Considerations in the Attribution of Responsibility to a Rape Victim." *Journal of Research in Personality* 10 (1976): 346-357.

Tanford, J.A., and A.J. Bocchino. "Rape Victim Shield Laws and the Sixth Amendment." *University of Pennsylvania Law Review* 128 (1980): 544-602.

Taylor, S.E., and S.T. Fiske. "Getting Inside the Head: Methodologies for Process Analysis in Attribution and Social Cognition." In *New Directions in Attribution Research*, Vol. 3, edited by J.H. Harvey, W. Ickes, and R.F. Kidd. Hillsdale, New Jersey: Erlbaum, 1981.

Thornton, B. "Effect of Rape Victim's Attractiveness in a Jury Simulation." *Personality and Social Psychology Bulletin* 3 (1977): 666-669.

Thornton, B., M.A. Robbins, and J.A. Johnson. "Social Perceptions of the Rape Victim's Culpability: The Influence of Respondents' Personal-Environmental Causal Attribution Tendencies." *Human Relations* 34 (1981): 225-237.

Thornton, B., R.M. Ryckman, and M.A. Robbins. "The Relationship of Observer Characteristics to Beliefs in the Causal Responsibility of Victims of Sexual Assault." *Human Relations* 35 (1982): 321-330.

Ugweugbu, D. "Racial and Evidential Factors in Juror Attribution of Legal Responsibility." *Journal of Experimental Social Psychology* 15 (1979): 133-146.

U.S. President's Task Force Final Report. *Victims of Crime.* Washington, D.C.: U.S. Government Printing Office, 1982.

Vidmar, N. "The Other Issues in Jury Simulation Research: A Commentary with Particular Reference to Defendant Character Studies." *Law and Human Behavior* 3 (1979): 95-106.

Walter, P.D. "Expert Testimony and Battered Women." *Journal of Legal Medicine* 3 (1982): 267-294.

Weidner, G., and W. Griffitt. "Rape: A Sexual Stigma?" *Journal of Personality* 51 (1983): 152-166.

Weiten, W., and S.S. Diamond. "A Critical Review of the Jury Simulation Paradigm: The Case of Defendant Characteristics." *Law and Human Behavior* 3 (1979): 71-94.

Whobrey, L., B.D. Sales, and A. Elwork. "Witness Credibility Law." In *Applied Social Psychology Annual*, Vol. 2, edited by L. Bickman. Beverly Hills, California: Sage Publications, 1981.

CASE CITATIONS

Delia S. v. Torres (1982) 134 Cal. App. 3d 471.

Dyas v. United States (1977) 376 A.2d 827, 832 D.C.

Frye v. United States (1923) 293 F. 1013 (D.C. Cir.).

Ibn-Tamas v. United States (1979) 407 A.2d 626 (D.C. Cir.).

People v. Bledsoe (1983) Daily Journal D.A.R. 556.

People v. Clark (1980) 109 Cal. App. 3d 88.

People v. Guthreau (1980) 102 Cal. App. 3d 436.

State v. Goblirsch (1976) 309 Minn. 401, 246 N.W. 2d 12.

State v. Loebach (1981) Minn. 310 N.W. 2d 58.

State v. Loss (1973) 295 Minn. 271, 204 N.W. 2d 404.

State v. Marks (1982) Kan. 647 P. 2d 1292.

State v. McGee (1982) Minn. 324 N.W. 2d 232.

State v. Saldana (1982) Minn. 324 N.W. 2d 227.

CHAPTER 20

CRIMINAL PROFILING RESEARCH ON HOMICIDE

Robert K. Ressler, Ann Wolbert Burgess,
John E. Douglas, and Roger L. Depue

Statistics over the past decade from the FBI Uniform Crime Reports clearly indicate that violent crimes represent a serious national problem. Those Americans who feel we live in an increasingly
violent society have support for that belief through mortality statistics.

Public pressure is great on law enforcement officials when a
community member is victimized by a violent, senseless, "motiveless"
crime. In the case of a homicide, a community is generally shocked
over the crime and demands swift and positive action from law enforcement in investigating and identifying a suspect. And once a suspect
has been arrested and charged, the public then looks to the behavioral sciences for an explanation of the murderer's mental state.

The advancement of law enforcement investigative techniques requires a knowledge base of the criminal personality. However, there
are major problems inherent in the study of criminal personality.
First, it is difficult to gather sufficient numbers of cases in an
unbiased manner. More frequently, single cases are reported often by
forensic clinicians. Second, although murder can be classified as an
interactional situation involving at least two parties, the literature contains more reports on the murderer than on the victim. Third,
prior to trial as well as after conviction, offenders rarely will cooperate in an interview because the material may serve to incriminate
them as they continue the appeal process. Fourth, there is a paucity
of data from staff managing offenders in their daily institutional
routine that could lend significant understanding to the state of
mind of the offender. And fifth, the various disciplines whose work
brings them into contact with offenders focus on only one part of the
total picture. They concentrate only on the problem from their specialty perspective. Interagency cooperation through sharing of information and collaborating on cases is not practiced. Mental health
staff are not knowledgeable about the details of the crime or how the
suspect acted during initial arrest or interrogation. Clinicians see
the suspect when his frame of mind is different because the clinical

Robert K. Ressler, M.S., is a Special Agent at the FBI Academy, Be-
    havioral Science Unit, Quantico, Va., and the director of the Crim-
    inal Personality Research Project.

Ann Wolbert Burgess, R.N., D.N.Sc., is Associate Director of Nursing
    Research, Department of Health and Hospitals, Boston, Ma.

John E. Douglas, M.S., is a Special Agent at the FBI Academy, Behav-
    ioral Science Unit, Quantico, Va., and the director of the Criminal
    Profiling and Crime Scene Assessment Program.

Roger L. Depue, M.S., Unit Chief, Behavioral Science Unit, FBI Acade-
    my, Quantico, Va.

This research is supported in part by a National Institute of Justice
grant #82-IJ-CX-0065

environment is unlike the crime scene, the police station or prison.
Similarly, investigators do not see the offender within the structure
of a prison or hospital to note adaptive or maladaptive behavior.

An Approach to the Problem? Psychological Assessment

As the violent crime rate continues to spiral and as criminals
become increasingly sophisticated with their crimes, so must the investigative tools of law enforcement be sharpened. Over the past
years, one tool being developed at the Behavioral Science Unit of the
FBI Academy is criminal profiling--the psychological assessment of a
crime.

As used in this paper, psychological profiling (Teten 1981) is
defined as the process of identifying the gross psychological characteristics of an individual based upon an analysis of the crimes he
or she committed and providing a general description of the person
utilizing those traits. This process normally involves five steps:
(1) A comprehensive study of the nature of the criminal act and the
type of persons who have committed this offense; (2) A thorough inspection of the specific crime scene involved in the case; (3) An in-
depth examination of the background and activities of the victim(s)
and any known suspects; (4) A formulation of the probable motivating
factors of all parties involved; (5) The development of a description
of the perpetrator based upon the overt characteristics associated
with his/her probable psychological makeup.

It is not known who first used this particular process to identify criminals, however, the general technique was used in the 1870s by
Dr. Hans Gross, an examining judge in the Upper Styria Region of Aus-
tria, and according to some, the first practical criminologist. More
recently a similar approach to criminal investigation was popularized
by Dr. James Brussel, a New York psychiatrist, who provided valuable
information in such famous cases as the Mad Bomber, the Boston Stran-
gler and the Coppolino murders.

The procedure, as described, was first used by the FBI to assist
local police in finding the perpetrator of a homicide in 1971. Though
the profiling was done on an informal basis in connection with classroom instruction, the analysis proved to be accurate and the offender
was apprehended.

In the following years profiles were informally prepared on a
number of cases with a reasonable degree of success, and as a result
the requests for the procedure by local authorities increased steadily.
The requests for profiling, provided by the Behavioral Science Unit,
Training Division, have continued to increase since that time and today represent a significant commitment of agent-power.

In 1981, the Institutional Research and Development Unit of FBI
Training Division was asked to initiate a cost-benefit study to determine the extent to which the service has been of value to the users.
Specifically, the analysis was undertaken to examine two questions:
(1) what was the nature and extent of any assistance provided by psychological profiling; and (2) what were the actual results of utilizing a psychological profile in terms of offender identification and/
or savings in investigative man-days.

A review of the material submitted by the various field divisions
for analysis revealed that requests had originated within the juris-
dictional areas of fifty-nine Field Offices located within the United
States and two FBI Liaison Representatives assigned to American Em-
bassies abroad. While the majority of these submissions were from
city police (52 percent) requests came from all levels of law en-

cluding county police or sheriff; FBI; state police; state investigators; and state highway patrol.

As might be suspected, most of the requests for psychological
profiling were submitted in an effort to identify the individual(s)
responsible for one or more murders (65 percent). The second highest
offense requested was for rape (35 percent) with other offenses including kidnapping, extortion, threat/obscene communication, child
molestation, hostage situation, accidental death, suicide and other.
Most of the cases submitted involved a single victim (61 percent) although 10 percent involved at least two, and 17 contained six or more
victims.

Based on the total requests (N=192), the suspect(s) were identified in a total of eighty-eight or 46 percent of the cases. In these
cases responding agencies indicated that psychological profiling was
useful in the following ways: (1) focused the investigation properly;
(2) helped locate possible suspects; (3) identified suspects; (4) assisted in the prosecution of suspect(s). Only in fifteen cases was
the profiling stated to be of no assistance.

In attempting to document the cost-benefit aspect, the study
suggested that the use of psychological profiling resulted in a total
savings of 594 investigative agent-days. That number is considered a
substantial figure when such matters as salaries, support costs and
availability of personnel for other assignments are considered.

THE CRIMINAL PERSONALITY RESEARCH PROJECT

Concurrent with the development of the Criminal Profiling Project, the Training Division of the FBI issued a mandate in 1978 to
its staff to conduct original, in-depth research in order to advance
the state of knowledge in areas relevant to the law enforcement community. In response to the mandate, Special Agent Robert Ressler
proposed and received permission to initiate a long-term research
project in conjunction with FBI training schedules to conduct interviews of criminal personalities serving sentences in various penal
institutions across the United States. The question remained as to
whether incarcerated offenders would cooperate in such research and
whether the staff at the correctional institutions would be willing
to participate with the interview project.

The response by correctional staff was most encouraging and
eight convicted offenders were approached and asked if they would be
willing to be interviewed in regard to their crime. All but one
were willing to be interviewed. Following this pilot project, plans
were developed for an extended ongoing systematic study of convicted
offenders in order to better understand the patterns of dynamics of
criminal behavior. Sexual homicide cases were selected as the initial area of focus and concentration, given that it is a lethal type
of crime which attracts a great deal of public attention. Special
Agent John Douglas who directs the Criminal Profiling and Crime
Scene Assessment Program, joined Ressler in conducting the interviews
with the first seventeen murderers for the study. A research protocol was used for the interviews in addition to the collection of
crime scene photographs, psychological and court evaluations, victim
background profiles and supplementary reports. The research proposal
was developed initially by Ressler, Douglas, Special Agent Robert R.
Hazelwood, also of the FBI Behavioral Science Unit, and Dr. Ann Burgess, a clinical specialist in psychiatric nursing and Dr. A. Nicholas Groth, a clinical psychologist.

In October, 1981, the Training Division completed its first Special Agent In-Service class in Criminal Profiling. There were two objectives of the two-week intensive course. First, was to place in every FBI field office Special Agents in possession of the latest information and research regarding the psychology of the most violent criminals in the country. This course was the result of years of experience of the Bureau's Behavioral Science Unit in crime scene analysis and interpretation, in criminal personality profile construction, and in conducting intensive interviews of the perpetrators of crimes of violence such as serial homicide, assassinations, and multiple sex offenses. The second objective of the course was the assignment for each of the fifty-nine Special Agents to plan and conduct interviews of violent criminals from their state. The agents were furnished with research interview protocol forms and voluntary consent forms to be executed for the interviews. The interviews were to be conducted of incarcerated felons for whom the legal appeal process had been exhausted and in correctional institutions who wished to collaborate in the research process.

Objectives of the Research Project

The research project on serial murderers of sexual homicide has the major aim to analyze data systematically collected by FBI Special Agents on incarcerated murderers. The study seeks to address the following questions:

> (1) What clues relating to the location of the victim's body, type and sit of injury, amount of mutilation, evidence of sexual assault, type of weapon and aggression, cause of death, position of body might indicate a personality configuration of the murderer?
>
> (2) What are the similarities and differences of crime scene in serial murder cases and how can the components be analyzed by investigators?
>
> (3) What are the cognitive, emotional, social, economic, and attitudinal characteristics of the serial murderer as well as the circumstances and conditions associated with the offense?
>
> (4) What physical, psychological, social and educational symptoms develop in childhood, adolescence and young adulthood, what symptoms persist, and what correlation is there with psychiatric history and criminal behavior.

The specific objectives of the project include (a) developing statistical models and companion computer software to discriminate between patterns of homicide crime scenes; (b) identifying patterns of criminal behavior and personality traits of the murderer that correlate with evidence and clues found at the crime scene; (c) broadening the based of empirical understandings about sexual homicide and the violent person.

Collaboration and Interdisciplinary Significance

This research project requires team work and interdisciplinary cooperation and collaboration. Correctional staff are crucial in aiding the interviewing process. Insight gained by staff from dealing with the offenders being interviewed will significantly improve the validity of the data obtained. The project should encourage correctional staff to report their observations of behavior patterns in these offenders.

This information can provide future data to help cross check the results of the study. Correctional staff will be encouraged to contribute from their perspective information specific to the offender's reaction to the social system in which he lives, his demeanor and attitudes, his social network in prison as well as his response to family, friends, and visitors.

This research project has been designed to benefit the various disciplines whose work brings them into contact with either the criminal or the victim in the following ways:

1. For criminal justice agents, it will test a cost-effective technique to use in focusing an investigation and identifying potential suspects from crime scene data.

2. For the behavioral scientists, it will strengthen the knowledge base regarding criminal behavior in regard to sexual homicide by establishing a data base from which information can be retrieved.

3. For crisis staff providing victim services, it will suggest information for treatment as well as prevention.

4. For correctional staff, it will provide an opportunity to contribute their perspective of convicted murderers.

It is envisioned that this research program will expand from homicide cases to include a broader variety of felony crimes such as rape, child molesting, arson, hostage taking. The research represents the combined approaches of law enforcement, victim specialists, behavioral scientists, statisticians, computer programmers, mental health clinicians and correctional agency staff as well as the participation and contribution from convicted felons to better understand the dynamics of violent acts in order to consider strategies for early detection and apprehension as well as management of the dangerous person and ultimately prevention.

National Center for the Analysis of Violent Crime

On January 11, 1983, the Director of the Federal Bureau of Investigation authorized the Training Division to explore the concept of creating a National Center for the Analysis of Violent Crime (NCAVC) to be located at the FBI Academy in Quantico, Virginia.

On July 12, 1983, testimony before the Subcommittee on Juvenile Justice by Pierce Brooks, originator of the VI-CAP concept, Roger L. Depue, Unit Chief of the Behavioral Science Unit, and others, generated enthusiastic support by Senator Arlen Specter, Subcommittee Chairman, who indicated he was going to express support for the concept in a letter to the Attorney General. A Workshop on Sexual Abuse and Exploitation of Children and National Missing and Murdered Children and Child Murder Tracking and Prevention was conducted at Sam Houston State University on July 12-14, 1983. During this meeting estimated cost figures and organizational structure of the NCAVC were proposed. On June 6, 1984 The Behavioral Science Unit received initial funding support for NCAVC from The National Institute of Justice and The Office of Justice Assistance, Research and Statistics, both Department of Justice agencies. On July 10, 1984, NCAVC was publically unveiled at the FBI Academy. The conceptual model of the Center is outlined.

The National Center for the Analysis of Violent Crime (NCAVC) is a law enforcement oriented behavioral science and data processing resource center which consolidates research, training and investigative support functions for the purpose of providing expertise to any legitimate law enforcement agency which is confronted with unusual, bizarre and/or particularly vicious or repetitive violent crime. It is administered by the Behavioral Science Unit and consists of four

programs: Research and Development, Training, Criminal Personality
Profiling, and Violent Criminal Apprehension Program (VI-CAP).

The Research and Development Program is responsible for conducting research into violent crime areas to support the other three
programs. The soon to be completed serial murder research project
serves as a good example. A 57-page coded-for-computer research
protocol has been completed on 36 killers who have each committed a
series of murders. The research protocol contains data on physical
characteristics, background development, offenses committed, victimology, and crime scenes. Each killer was personally interviewed by
a behavioral science trained, experienced Special Agent investigator
regarding why and more importantly how he committed his crimes. A
great deal of insight into the minds of these killers has been obtained as well as information regarding their modus operandi (MO) and
"successful" techniques. This information has been applied to the
analysis and profiling of unsolved homicides in the Criminal Personality Profile Program, and to the course curricula in the Training
analysis and classification data base of the computers of the VI-CAP.

The Training Program is responsible for converting the information received from research, profiling and VI-CAP into curricula,
publications and presentations for appropriate dissemination to the
law enforcement community. It will also be necessary to educate law
enforcement officers about the functions and purpose of NCAVC and to
train them about how to avail themselves of the NCAVC resources and
assistance. Successful investigative techniques and other useful information obtained from training interaction will be incorporated into the other programs, as appropriate.

The Criminal Personality Profiling Program is responsible for
the behavioral and investigative analysis of unsolved crimes of
violence for the purpose of creating a profile of the unknown offend-
er(s), and to furnish consultation to criminal justice agencies regarding investigative strategy, personality assessment, preparation
of seach warrants, arrest and interview, prosecutive strategy, etc.
Information obtained from case analysis and successful techniques resulting from consultation experience will be incorporated into other
programs, as appropriate.

The VI-CAP is responsible for the intake of the crime report
forms which are then analyzed by violent crime specialists and the
data entered into computers. The VI-CAP computer will have a data
base consisting of all previously entered case reports and programs
developed as a result of state of the art crime analysis technology,
research projects and reports, training program feedback, actions
previously taken, and profiling experiences. The programs will
enable the computer to analyze and classify the data and report
out patterns, linkages, trends, etc. The computer will also be programmed to review existing strategies, techniques and successful profiles in its memory bank and report possible proactive approaches,
risks to be avoided, and prevention suggestions. If the case is determined to be appropriate for further analysis by the profiling program, it will be forwarded there. The submitting police agency will
be contacted by telephone regarding relevant findings and for additional information as warranted. Agencies working identical or similar cases will be notified, the investigations will be coordinated,
and further assistance rendered as possible.

Police investigative interns from major law enforcement agencies
will be selected to work in the NCAVC for a period of six to nine
months to learn the programs and to develop skills enabling them to

return to their agencies to implement similar operations and technology.

Selected Special Agents will serve in the Research and Profiling Programs for three-year periods to assist in the operation of the programs and to obtain knowledge and skills useful to field division investigations.

Specially trained FBI Special Agent field profile coordinators will facilitate interactions with user agencies.

A nationwide network of approximately 60 police agencies will eventually be set up, each of which will designate a Law Enforcement Network Coordinator who will be trained by the Special Agent field profile coordinator to function as a member of a field VI-CAP team. This team of a Special Agent and a police officer will be responsible for area training and updating of VI-CAP operations, coordinating submission of cases and dissemination of reports, following and reporting results of center analysis, providing other relevant feedback and other coordination functions.

CHAPTER 21

TREATMENT OF PARAPHILIACS, PEDOPHILES, AND INCEST FAMILIES

Mark F. Schwartz
William H. Masters

The Paraphiliac

The term paraphilia literally means "substitute love." This meaning suggests that there is a critical pathonemonic feature com-comprised of a multiplicity of cognitive, affective, and behavioral patterns that constitute this syndrome. In cases of paraphilia, there has been an interference with or displacement (a "placing be-side") of the establishment and maintenance of intimacy between two adults. Common features among paraphiliacs are the inability to cope with closeness and attachment to other adults and the inevitable lone-liness that is an integral part of social separation. Paraphiliacs usually cope with their social pathology by withdrawing into the com-fortable world of fantasy.

Paraphilia involves obsessive-compulsive behavioral patterns and appears to have a number of clinical similarities to addiction. The paraphiliac engages in obsessional sexual thinking and compusively acts out these fantasies. The illicit compulsion may involve cross-dressing, fetishes for leather, undergarments, inanimate objects, pornography, exposing the genitals, making obscene telephone calls, peeping into windows, or fondling children. Generally, unresponsive to nondeviant, affectional sexual stimuli, the paraphiliac becomes dependent on highly specific imagery and/or socially inappropriate, external stimulation to achieve sexual arousal.

Like other addicts (Peele and Brodsky 1975) the paraphiliac ex-periences almost a "trance-like" sense of relaxation, relief, and homeostasis when involved in the illicit sexual activity and, converse-ly, exhibits social unease when not sexually acting out. Acting out becomes an escape from distasteful aspects of life. The paraphiliac usually evidences adolescent-like narcissism which results in his fre-quent attempts to extract unrealistic demands from his environment. Since he usually fails in this effort, he is continually frustrated and frequently angry. Finally, chronically low self-esteem, self-depreciatory preoccupation, and poor assertiveness skills result in the paraphiliac repetitively feeling victimized. One exhibitionist, for example, became furious on a daily basis for over a year because his office mate played the radio and his wife asked his help with her college work. A male pedophile was so enraged that the parking lot near the clinic was closed that he could not participate in the thera-py session. These individuals feel an overwhelming sense of inade-quacy and lack of control. The paraphiliac's acting-out experience thereby may become an expression of rage or an attempt at control, giving him a temporary sense that "he is calling the shots."

Paradoxically, this illusion of control quickly abates, leaving a residual overwhelming feeling of inadequacy. Some sexual addicts, pushed by their "sickness," spend hours each day searching for the right situation in which to act out. The paraphiliac becomes unable to make decisions based on the personal morality and rarely recog-nizes potential harm to himself or to others. What follows is fur-ther internalization of "why bother?" "I can't," "I'm sick," and other cognitions indicative of an absence of a sense of mastery and self-responsibility. Such cognitions then generalize and result in a myriad of other manifestations of self-sabotage which in turn fuel the addiction. Alcohol abuse may further this pattern by providing still another factor for rationalization.

Proceptive, Acceptive, and Conceptive Deficits

Paraphilia typically presents as a primary proceptive, acceptive and conceptive disorder (Schwartz, Money, and Robinson, 1981). Proception refers to all aspects of pair-bonding and eroticism that lead to copulatory behavior. Acception refers to genital interaction and copulation. Conception includes pregnancy, birth and parenting. Proceptive disorders include difficulties with all aspects of pair-bonding and self-esteem including touching and sexual and social interaction with a potentially erotic partner. Proceptive difficulties also arise from problems with continuing attachment to and ultimately with separation from the primary care givers, who often have been either distant and unloving or overtly erotic and possessive in interaction with the paraphiliac as a child. Subsequently, the individual fails to establish peer relationships and dating experiences and finds himself socially isolated.

Manifestations of proceptive difficulties, therefore, include uneasiness with touching, poor social and dating skills, low self-esteem, and difficulties with gender role/identity. Also evident may be fears of adult females and of intimidation by adult males, poor communication and negotiation skills, and difficulties with all aspects of intimacy such as self-disclosure, trust, empathy, and commitment. Finally, deviant imagery and arousal are primary signs of proceptive difficulty. Identification of these symptoms of the paraphiliac during treatment provides a basis for directive forms of intensive psychotherapy aimed at decreasing destructive and increasing constructive thoughts and behavior.

Acceptive disorders usually result from punishment and taboos associated with sexual unfolding during childhood and adolescence. Both sexual arousal and sexual behavior may be so traumatized that the adolescent boy is cognitively unable to rehearse erotic partnerships in masturbation and dream fantasy. For many boys in this culture, eroticism is associated with specific characteristics of the nude female body; yet the range of imagery that enables sexual arousal is often quite narrow, because the parameters seem to be shaped by societal channeling before, during, and after puberty. For the paraphiliac, adult females may be too threatening even to appear in imagery; adult males also may provoke social anxiety. Therefore, erotic relationships with adults of either sex are difficult for the paraphiliac to establish and/or maintain. Eroticism is left to emerge without typical societal channeling, so that the unusual or the bizarre is often allowed to intrude or displace societal norms (Money 1970, 1977; Schwartz and Masters 1983). For example, one five-year old boy who was sexually abused by his mother, could only feel safe when masturbating by focusing on the knot on the bathroom wall (Lang feldt 1983). All "human-contact" fantasy patterning was rejected. From this example, one can see how sexual arousal may become dependent on an external stimulus. The intrusive image becomes indelibly "programmed" in similar fashion to the range of "enabling" erotic stimuli that are socially programmed in nonparaphiliac boys. During childhood and adolescence repeated pairing of sexual pleasure with deviant

enabling stimuli make these erotic stimuli particularly resistant
to change in the adult paraphiliac.

Conceptive deficits of paraphiliacs emerge only in those cases
in which the individual established a pair-bond. The most dramatic
examples of these deficits can be found in incest families. Similar
to Harlow's (1963) and Suomi's (1977) monkey infants deprived of
parenting ("motherless"), these individuals are generally incompetent
as parents and tend to transmit many of their problems to the next
generation. In both monkeys and humans, the quality of parenting
early in life usually affects adult parenting competency.

Successful rehabilitation of paraphiliacs requires the therapist
to focus on proceptive, acceptive, and in the long run, conceptive
components of eroticism. Reducing heterosexual anxiety through repeated exposure to a woman in a nonthreatening, socially safe setting
can compensate for developmental proceptive deficits. Repeated nonsexual touching or sensate focus with the female partner is also
critical. Once greater psychosocial comfort levels are accomplished,
the next therapeutic step is to utilize various techniques to decrease the paraphiliac's arousal to deviant imagery or activity and
to increase his arousal to consenting female partners. Permission-
giving and information-giving about sexuality encourage the uninter-
rupted unfolding of adult sexuality. The eventual goal, of course,
is to help the paraphiliac male establish and maintain an intimate
relationship with a consenting female.

Biosocial Contributing Factors

Paraphilia is almost exclusively a male disorder. This suggests
a high likelihood of mulitple biosocial etiologic contributions. It
is intriguing to parallel this factor of male dominance in the incidence of paraphilia with the findings of Harlow and his colleagues
(1963) that the male rhesus monkey's affectional and erotic systems
are more vulnerable to early deprivation than those of the female.
Maclean (1973), in studying the neuroanatomy of primate sexual systems, also notes that the male's differentiating sexual system is
more vulnerable to insult. Similarly, the human male's psychosexual
system may be more vulnerable to biosocial deprivation.

Possible organic etiologic contributions are suggested by numerous reports of increased paraphilia in men with temporal lobe deficits (Epstein 1960, 1969; Krafft-Ebing 1931; Davis and Morgenstern
1960; Petritzer and Foster 1955; Yawger 1940; Blumer and Walker 1975;
Mitchell et al. 1954; Hunter et al. 1963; Walinder 1965). In paraphiliacs, abnormal EEG's from the temporal lobe have been noted by
Mitchell et al. (1954).

Pedophilia and Incest

For the paraphiliac uncomfortable in sociosexual interaction
with adult males and females, eroticism may emerge in response to an
object (fetishism); through sexual interaction with an adult conducted at a safe distance (voyeurism, exhibitionism, obscene telephone
calling); or by a sexual act with a nonthreatening child (pedophilia).
Since the pedophile's social development has been impeded, he typically verbalizes a sense of uneasiness with other adults. Usually
the only time he can feel comfortable and 'be himself' is with a
child. Psychosocial trauma has caused a fixation of or an impediment
to cognitive maturation, so the pedophile often thinks, feels and
acts like a child. As eroticism emerges it becomes compulsively at-
tached to the only "safe" human being.

   The pedophile often appears clinically as an inadequate, passive individual, burdened by guilt and self-hate. Mohr and coworkers (1964), report that 4 percent of pedophiliac victims are age three or under, while 18 percent are age eight to eleven. They also report that the victim is a complete stranger to the pedophile in only 10.3 percent of cases.

Incest Families

   Incest offenders may or may not be paraphiliacs. But since so many are pedophiles, and those who are not pedophiles are clinically so similar, the incest family will be included in this discussion. Many incest offenders are pedophiles who have married and continued their pedophilia with greater safety by sexually approaching their own child or step-child. Although most incest offenders deny being sexually aroused by children, plethysmography studies in which the man's erection is measured with a mercury stain gauge in response to visual stimuli suggest that many of these men have greater arousal to children than they are willing to admit even to themselves (Laws and O'Neill 1981). Another reason incest is included in this discussion is that in our experience, incest offenders require very similar treatment to that of the paraphiliac, with the major difference being that intervention for the incest offender also includes a family therapy component.

   The husband and wife relationship in the incestuous family often evolves into an immature, undifferentiated couple creating confusion, conflict habituation, and other types of destructive dependent relationships (Bowen 1974a, 1974b, 1978). The homes of these men and women reflect any combination of the following: chaos (few rules are consistently followed): enmeshment (everyone is involved in one another's business); disengagement (no one cares what the other says or does); and rigidity (extreme authoritarianism) (Ingerbritson 1983). In about 40 percent of reported cases, the incest offender and/or wife are alcoholic. According to recent data (Ingerbritson 1983) and our own clinical experience, the nonalcoholic offender may actually display more psychopathology than the alcoholic.

   Some incest offenders are extremely rigid and authoritarian, sometimes even physically abusive to the other family members. The rigidity protects the offender from overwhelming feelings of inadequacy in dealing with daily transactions. The incest perpetrator is often intimidated by other men and uneasy in his work and social interactions. One perpetrator who dropped out of school at sixteen and had recently been promoted to an administrative position, stated "I feel like I have to fake it every day." He said he felt the same way with his wife--"uneasy, inadequate, incompetent" yet, without her he was unbearably lonely. At times he was overtly acquiescent with her; at other times, particularly when drinking, his rage manifested itself in physical violence. Variations on this theme are characteristic of many incest perpetrators.

   The research literature is rife with pejorative speculation regarding the wife's role in perpetuating sexual abuse in the family (Weiner 1983). The wives of incest offenders have been described as "frigid, indifferent, hostile, narcissistic, unconsciously homosexual, slovenly, dependent" (McIntyre 1981). Mothers are perceived as possessing personality traits that somehow warrant an assault on their daughters. The incest offenders' wives are described as having consciously or unconsciously contributed to the victimization of their daughters "through the non-fulfillment of their motherly or wifely roles, thereby causing the husband and the daughter to seek emotional refuge with each other" (Forward and Buck 1978).

It may be common for the wife of the incest perpetrator to have some of the characteristics described above. For successful rehabilitation of the family, many of these difficulties must be reversed. However, while the interaction patterns between the perpetrator and his wife may contribute to the incest, it is not necessarily the wife's behavior per se that is a primary etiological factor. And, while many wives are aware at some level of the ongoing incest, most women feel shocked, angry, or guilty at disclosure of the incestuous relationship and sincerely need someone with whom they can discuss the issues rationally. A large percentage of these women have been victims of sexual abuse as young girls, and are particularly upset and confused by the generational repetition.

Poorly defined and inappropriate role playing is characteristic of incest family members. Quite often the victim is "pseudo-mature" acting much older than her chronologic age in specific situations. She obtains social reinforcement by taking on what were previously "mother's responsibilities" such as caring for younger siblings, cleaning the home, and "taking care of daddy." This practice ranges from cooking his meals to tucking him in when he has had too much to drink. The mother may be pleased to relinquish these chores; while she nurses a wide range of somatic complaints or acts out her adolescent desires for the social excitement which she was deprived of during her own incestuous childhood. In other instances, she may feel threatened by the competition, and resentment and jealousy may develop between mother and daughter. The result is that two members of the family triad frequently line up against the third. For this reason, treating the incestuous husband and his wife without focusing on the mother-daughter dyad or other family dynamics can produce iatrogenically a united front between husband and wife to exclude the daughter from the home. If during investigation or treatment of an incestuous relationship the daughter feels that she is being punished for her father's transgressions, the health-care professional's efforts may have been more destructive than helpful.

Typically, other family members not directly involved in the incestuous relationship are aware of the activity and are, therefore, at least indirectly involved. Other daughters are often neglected and thus angry at father, mother, and sister. Sons often develop psychiatric symptoms or resolve their sense of neglect by becoming involved in sexual play with other siblings.

Finally, a preliminary observation of a small sample of highly sexual, young incest victims at Masters and Johnson Institute is that there may be concommitant learning disabilities and low IQ scores which do not accurately represent the individual girl's learning achievement or potential. Special attention needs to be focused on the interrelation between premature sexual awareness and learning disability in girls who are incest victims.

Intensive Treatment: The Masters and Johnson Model

There are several phases to the Masters and Johnson treatment program for paraphiliacs and incest families. During Phase One, the men participate in ten three-hour group therapy sessions. These are counseling sessions designed to establish social, dating, and intimacy skills and to improve stress management, problem-solving, and communication skills.

Phase Two entails fourteen sessions of intensive, conjoint therapy and combines the critical components of the Masters and Johnson treatment model--social isolation, daily therapeutic intervention, a dual-sex therapy team, integration of marital therapies, communication skills, experience with sensate focus, and directive psychotherapy focused on improving the state of intimacy between two adults.

Phase Three is follow-up. All clients are actively watched for a minimum of two years.

Phase Four, for incest families only, is family therapy.

If the individual has noxious paraphilia (paraphiliac behavior that is harmful to self or others), it is essential to stop the acting out as rapidly as possible. Among the many different therapeutic approaches to the problem, contracting with the patient to stop the behavior for at least three months is a primary requisite. Several techniques have been employed to assure compliance with the contract. Antiandrogen injections (depo-provera dosage titrated according to individual's body weight) have been utilized by some researchers (Money 1970; Money and Weideking 1972). Behavioral techniques such as fantasy satiation (Abel and Blanchard 1974; Abel et al. 1975; Ladd and Mize 1983) or other forms of aversive conditioning can be quite effective while eliminating concern about medication side effects. A third alternative is temporary institutionalization, particularly during Phase One of the psychotherapy program.

Phase One: Behavioral Skills Training

The most frequently encountered clinical presentation of paraphilia is that of a single man who describes very little interaction with adult partners. Despite the fact that the man may have significant sexual experience, or even if he is married, multiple behavioral skills deficits are still common. Therefore, the first phase of the Institute's rapid intervention program consists of ten sessions of three hour group therapy aimed at information giving, role-playing, and social skills training. Female graduate students act as group facilitators and role play with the patients during the last hour of the group.

Some discussion of the techniques employed to improve or implement social skills is necessary, since the techniques represent a synthesis of approaches and procedures described by others in the field (Ladd and Mize 1983; Merluzzi et al. 1981; Barlow et al. 1977). The Institute's approach conceptualizes social behavior as a network of interacting components that include the individual's cognitions, his behavior, and his social environment. The individual is seen as an active organism in which all three components mutually influence social competence (Bandura 1980; Eisler and Frederiksen 1976). This treatment model postulates a ladder approach toward modification of maladaptive behavior and the subsequent development of behavioral proficiencies. Individuals in the group therapy educational experience progress through levels of social competency at an individually tailored rate. First, the patient is taught how to start conversations. Advice is given regarding dress and hygiene and how to maintain appropriate eye contact without distracting motor gestures; the individual learns appropriate self-disclosure, how to keep a conversation flowing, how to handle silences (Zimbardo 1978), how to listen attentively, and how to terminate conversations. The second step is for the man to learn how to ask a woman for a date and to make the date fun. Paraphiliacs need to understand the complicated sociosexu-

al scripts of how the male typically initiates social interaction in
our double standard culture. A third step is to establish a moderate
level of intimacy with a consenting female partner.

A female facilitator is critical to effective group treatment.
She provides the necessary female identity on which the man can test
his irrational beliefs about women. When his misconceptions prove
obviously false, the level of his social anxiety is usually reduced.
Primary therapeutic emphasis in the group is placed on role modeling,
which permits the client to see how others perform a specific skill
to make it socially effective (Ladd and Mize 1983; Eisler and Freder-
ickson 1980). Through continuous rehearsal of his new-found skills,
the paraphiliac develops a greater sense of self-mastery and esteem
which in turn increases his confidence to use these skills in his
environment.

Some paraphiliacs may be relatively competent in their social
skills initially, but most have difficulty with moderate levels of
intimacy. At this stage men are provided with suggestions regarding
potential ways and means to meet partners. Once a partner is found,
the men are given progressively specific, but flexibly graded instructions such as a coffee date (Zilbergeld 1978), going to the movies
with a specific time to end the date, meeting in the partner's home
with no physical interaction, then kissing, petting but no intercourse, and finally, intercourse with a lot of nongenital touching.
After each date, the patient is asked to detail and evaluate his social experience and is then provided with specific suggestions regarding social, dating, intimacy, or sexual skills.

Another component of social skills is attitude change. Most sex
offenders manifest uneasiness with specific aspects of adult sexual
functioning. Early in therapy, definitive sex education is provided,
including the use of visual materials if indicated. As an integral
part of this educative process, female sexuality is discussed in
depth by a female therapist who simultaneously models the competent
woman.

Cognitive restructuring is critical to successful rehabilitation
of the paraphiliac. Therefore, destructive thinking styles require
continual reassessment in all phases of the therapy process. Cognitions which are destructive to self-esteem include: irrational beliefs, self-depreciatory preoccupation, negative self-statements, unrealistic expectations, anticipated failures, misinterpretation of
feedback, and easily elicited defensiveness (Meichenbaum and Cameron
1981; Glass and Merluzzi 1981). Negative self-esteem is maintained
by each individual's unique cognitive filtering system. During the
therapeutic process, the paraphiliac's biases in processing input
from the environment are confronted and explained by the therapist
after which reality is tested by the client. Paraphiliacs are asked
to attend to the positives rather than the negatives in their lives.

Therapists attempt to note and underscore styles of destructive
thinking in context. One client stated, "I'd rather be put in jail
than have to call my wife to tell her I won't come home tonight because I have to work. In suggesting I call, you people are taking
away all of my freedom." Obviously this man needed to test reality
to realize that the act of not calling his wife did not jeopardize
his freedom. One unmarried client stated "I am not interested in any
woman who starts a conversation with me." This man held the irrational belief that any friendly woman is a "whore." Obviously, this

irrational belief needed to be exposed to therapeutic scrutiny and tested. A married client said "When a woman speaks her mind, she wears the pants." He needed to discover that allowing his wife to represent herself was in his best interest. In group therapy, therapists and facilitators continuously need to be looking for faulty thinking styles that require reality testing.

Another common problem for the paraphiliac is the feeling of being a victim of life's circumstances, of constantly being pushed and pulled between undesirable alternatives. The socially immature offender will often respond to stress by moaning like a child, complaining, and blaming others for his problems. As previously noted, he evidences little capacity for self-responsibility or for taking positive action. Such individuals often display personalities that are unattractive to potential partners or tend to attach themselves to partners who will "mother" them, but who may not be erotically stimulating. In response to even minor stresses, such as traffic jams, the paraphiliac may exhibit rage and then retreat into his fantasy world. Instead of changing the situation or finding a constructive means of stress reduction, that is, taking the "front door" by confronting and managing the stressful situation, the man retreats through the "back door" into deviant sexual fantasy or behavior.

In group therapy sessions clients are encouraged to set small, attainable goals to facilitate confidence that "I can create and support the environment I live in." For distress that cannot be reduced, stress management techniques such as physical exercise, joining social organizations, and relaxation techniques are introduced. Stress also results from consistent passivity instead of responsible, assertive behavior. Assertiveness skills are taught and practiced in role-playing. Occasionally, paraphiliacs may cope with their helplessness and passivity with inappropriate aggression. Therefore, attention is given to mastering basic communication skills. Assertiveness skills (Lange and Jakubowski 1979), need to be coupled with a change in self-esteem so that paraphiliacs feel they have the "right" to express their desires to others. This is particularly true in interactions with new partners, since the paraphiliac's initial feeling is often "I'm lucky if she stays with a person as terrible as me, so I can't risk telling her if I'm upset or annoyed."

Problem-solving skills are also rehearsed in group therapy. The individual is helped to feel a sense of mastery over whatever problems arise. Group members are taught to function as a creative team to solve problems rather than attacking one another (Parnes, Wollner and Biondi 1977; Parnes 1967). Members use these techniques to brainstorm potential solutions to their problems.

Yochelson and Samenow (1977) have documented "errors of thinking" common among paraphiliacs and incest perpetrators. Some of these errors are discussed here briefly. First is the "closed channel." Rarely will the paraphiliac or the incest offender tell the full story (at least initially) to the health-care professional evaluating his problem. These individuals have ambivalent motivation. They despise their sexual acting out, yet fear the loss of these experiences since acting out is the one high that helps them escape their distasteful lives. Fabrication has been a way of life. Paraphiliacs and incest offenders even lie successfully to themselves; for example, some incest offenders state convincingly that they are not aroused by children until shown plethysmographic results of their erections in response to kids.

Total self-disclosure of the paraphiliac or incestuous behavior is requisite to successful therapy, much like the alcoholic who must begin his treatment program by admitting his alcoholism. Lack of trust is also significant in this context. The paraphiliac will not allow himself to even hope that change in his acting out behavior is possible. A positive attitude is necessary for change, and is initially established as the client talks with other group members and with the therapists.

Second, "victim stance"--blaming others for his behavior--is dealt with by pointing out the kinds of things done to him by society as well as the things he has done to himself as a result of this behavior. Situations in which the individual acted self-destructively are repeatedly pointed out. The therapist's style is not condemning but, rather, challenging; example, "Do you want to continue to act out or try a new approach in the future?" All aspects of directive therapy are oriented to giving paraphiliacs and incest offenders a mode of handling previously insoluable problems. By making small changes on a daily basis the man begins to realize that any effort to achieve short-term and long-term goals maximizes the probability of happiness.

Third, perhaps the most important motivating factor in eliciting behavioral change is repeatedly reminding the perpetrator of the effect of his behavior on the victim. Whenever he feels an urge to act out, he must ask himself, "How will my behavior affect this other person?" Additionally, if the behavior is potentially noxious, a second thought to be encouraged is, "What will be the possible consequences of my actions?"

Phase Two: Focus on Relationship Issues

The core of the Masters and Johnson treatment approach for sex offenders is a variation of the short-term intensive model described in *Human Sexual Inadequacy* (1970). Once the man has found a female partner and has completed the ten-week, group therapy program, he is placed in couples therapy. Some men with advanced social skills are permitted to bypass the group therapy phase of the program.

Couples therapy comprises a fourteen-day period in social isolation from daily home and job responsibilities during which the paraphiliac and his female partner are asked to devote themselves to their relationship. The couple "try-on" different ways of interacting socially and sensually. The experience of positive interchange on a daily basis increases motivation for continuing change.

Most paraphiliacs living in close quarters with a partner will evidence a myriad of resistances to intimacy. These resistances are diagnostic and can be utilized therapeutically. Confronting each partner with a single destructive transaction, describing how he or she perpetuates the specific distress, and then suggesting a way to do it differently (which they can explore in the next twenty-four hours) is the key to effective, short-term therapy. Therapeutic rapport, established through insight, empathy, and support, is particularly critical in these cases. Many paraphiliacs and incest offenders are emotionally rigid and tend to respond with a child-like defensiveness and withdrawal from confrontation with authority. In addition, they are typically pessimistic and ambivalent about their potential for change. Frequently their ambivalence about losing the excitement of the addictive aspects of the paraphilia will manifest itself as therapeutic sabotage. Since sabotage is predictable, it can be either prevented with anticipatory guidance or identified and utilized to help the individual or couple deal with their "fear of success."

When treating sexual dysfunction, sensate focus is a most effective means of eliciting factors which interfere with "natural" sexual responsiveness. In similar fashion, when treating paraphilia sensate focus is extremely valuable in eliciting factors which have interfered with heterosexual unfolding. Once the interfering factors are identified, directive psychotherapy can be utilized in an effort to neutralize the "roadblocks." Certainly, sensate focus can also be therapeutic in and of itself. These techniques are a means of gradually introducing stimuli that are potentially anxiety-provoking while allowing the individual to maintain a sense of control. Sensate focus also provides the opportunity for cognitive restructuring by encouraging individuals to be less goal oriented.

Male sex offenders inexperienced in heterosexual interaction commonly express concern about touching their female partner's breast or genitals in the "right" way. Actually pleasing the partner sexually may become an obsession. These men frequently admit anxieties about erections and ejaculation. For even the heterosexually experienced paraphiliac, the anticipation of sexual activity with a woman is usually accompanied by performance anxiety or feelings of ineptness and a sense of discomfort. The anxiety of the pressure situation is then compared by the client with the excitement of paraphiliac acting out, and the latter is perceived as preferential.

Through sensate focus experience, a man previously oriented to paraphilia is given an opportunity to interact sexually with a woman without having to contend with culturally oriented demands for male sexual expertise or performance facility. Consequently, he has the opportunity to learn a great deal about female sexual responsiveness in a non-demanding environment. In addition, he becomes more aware of his own sexuality in relation to women, and of the potential for sexual pleasure without intercourse. He begins to realize that pleasurable states of sexual excitement and sexual comfort can be attained with adult partners.

Some paraphiliacs manifest aversion to the female body. For example, one pedophile in response to a suggestion to touch his partner's genital area experienced flashbacks to childhood of his mother sitting in the bathtub with him and insisting that he put his hands on her labia and into her vagina. He required several days of non-demanding genital touching with his partner before he could focus on her body exclusively. This clinical adaptation of the sensate focus experience allowed the man to respond "naturally" to tactile stimulation without paraphiliac imagery.

The female cotherapist continually orients the female partner to be lover, friend, and companion. In turn, the woman provides an effective observer's source of continual informational feedback, not as another therapist but rather as an interested and involved party.

Obviously the female partner's appearance, personality, and sexual confidence are critical factors directly affecting the progress and ultimately the prognosis of couples' therapy. When an unmarried paraphiliac searches for a female partner to bring to therapy, he usually chooses a socially nonthreatening woman. She is often physically unattractive, and non-complementary in intelligence and personality. Frequently she is sexually unsophisticated. Yet, therapy can benefit by her presence as long as she: (1) does not evidence significant individual psychopathology; (2) is sufficiently motivated to help; and (3) does not develop overt antipathy towards the man. The sexually naive paraphiliac usually acquires a great deal of sociosexual information from this nonthreatening partner which, in due course, he transfers to other potential relationships.

Successful treatment of incest families requires a more sophisticated therapeutic process than the intervention techniques described for the paraphiliac offender. Intervention simultaneously focuses on the victim, the offender, the wife and the family. The Masters and Johnson program for child sexual abuse integrates individual, couple, group, and family therapy modalities into a rapid treatment program of fifteen to twenty weeks in duration. The specific goals of the treatment program include stopping the incest, preventing reoccurrence, minimizing trauma to the victim, and establishing a profile of offenders, wives, and victims. Alcoholics are required to continue their established outpatient support practices.

A unique characteristic of the incest offender is his extreme rigidity, authoritarianism, and defensiveness. Repeated confrontation with factors contributing to and maintaining the incest is required. For example, it may be necessary to change dramatically the family's style of living. Several men were encouraged to obtain high school equivalency degrees in an effort to reverse their hopeless, goal-less, and perceived powerless existence. Others were helped to find and maintain jobs.

The wives in incestuous families are helped to recognize how they may have had a role in maintaining the abusive sexual behavior. As a means of improving the status of the marital relationship, many wives are introduced to pleasure in sexual activity for the first time. Husband and wife are helped to feel more at ease with peers. Many wives begin to dress differently and give more attention to good grooming. Those who have resorted to adolescent, acting-out behavior are taught to interact less self-destructively.

In family therapy the following areas are explored: (a) the nature of leadership and discipline; (b) pathologic coalitions within the family triad; (c) appropriate ways of being close; (d) ability to take responsibility for parenting; (e) appropriate roles for mother and daughter; (f) family problem solving; and (g) use of the therapists for preventive assistance.

Conclusions

The psychotherapy program for paraphiliacs and incest families has not had the necessary follow-up period to document its effectiveness statistically; therefore, the concepts and principles described in this article are tentative. The initial therapy failure rate, however, has been low and major alterations have been noted in behavior and in psychological testing profiles, which have been maintained in follow-up.

Mental health professionals need to encourage cooperative arrangements with the legal system to provide efficacious, humane treatment of the paraphiliac. Research efforts are currently being focused on predicting which clients can and cannot benefit from brief intensive psychotherapy. Like the alcoholic, the paraphiliac offender can rarely be considered cured; rehabilitation may be a chronic process so that long-term follow-up is required.

Conceptualizing incest as a pair-bonding disorder generates the components of the described comprehensive, conjoint treatment program. There is little logic in offering extensive rehabilitation support for incest victims but not for incest offenders (the current situation in most cities). This is especially true since incest is readily treatable with current modes of therapeutic intervention. Symptom reversals in paraphilia and in incestuous families may have previously failed because insufficient therapeutic attention has been paid to intimate, reciprocated pair-bonding and to problems with adult sexual functioning.

REFERENCES

Abel, G., E. Blanchard, D. Barlow, and M. Movissakalian. "Identifying Specific Erotic Cues in Sexual Deviations by Audiotape Descriptions." *Journal of Applied Behavioral Analysis* 8 (1975): 247-260.

Abel, G., and E. Blanchard. "The Role of Fantasy in the Treatment of Sexual Deviation." *Archives of General Psychiatry* 30 (1974): 467-474.

Bandura, A. "The Self System in Recirpocal Determinism." *American Psychologist* 33 (1978): 344-358

Barlow, D.H., G.G. Abel, E.B. Blanchard, et al: "A Heterosocial Skills Checklist for Males," *Behavior Therapy* 8 (1977): 229-239.

Bellack, A., and M. Hersen. *Research and Practice in Social Skills Training*. New York: Plenum, 1979.

Blumer, D., and A. Walker. "The Neural Basis of Sexual Behavior." In *Psychiatric Aspect of Neurologic Diseases*, edited by D. Benson and D. Blume. New York: Grune and Stratton, 1975.

Bowen, M. "Alcoholism as Viewed Through Family Systems Theory and Family Psychotherapy." *Annals of the New York Academy of Sciences* 233 (1974a): 115-122.

Bowen, M. "Toward the Differentiation of Self in One's Family of Origin." In *Georgetown Family Symposium Papers, I*, edited by F. Andres and J. Lorio. Washington, D.C.: Georgetown University, 1974(b).

Bowen, M. *Family Therapy Clinic Practice*. New York: Jason Aronson, 1978.

Davies, B., and F. Morgenstern. "A Case of Cysticerosis, Temporal Lobe Epilepsy and Transvestism." *Journal of Neurology and Neurosurgical Psychiatry* 23 (1960): 247-249.

Eisler, R. "The Behavioral Assessment of Social Skills." In *Behavioral Assessment: A Practical Handbook*, edited by M. Hersen and A. Bellack. New York: Pergamon, 1976.

Eisler, R., L. Fredericksen, and G. Peterson. "The Relationship of Cognitive Variables to the Expression of Assertiveness." *Behavior Therapy* 9 (1978): 419-427.

Eisler, R., P. Miller, and M. Hersen. "Components of Assertive Behavior." *Journal of Clinical Psychology* 29 (1973): 295-299.

Entwistle, C., and M. Sim. "Tuberous Sclerosis and Fetishism." *British Medical Journal* 2 (1961): 1688-1689.

Epstein, A. "Fetishism: A Comprehensive View." In *Dynamics of Deviant Sexuality, Vol. XV: Science and Psychoanalysis*, edited by H. Masserman. New York: Grune and Stratton, 1969.

Epstein, A. "Fetishism: A Study of Its Psychopathology with Particular Reference to a prior Disorder in Brain Mechanisms as an Etiological Factor." *Journal of New Mental Disorders* 130 (1960): 108-119.

Epstein, A. "Relationship of Fetishism and Transvestism to Brain and Particularly to Temporal Lobe Dysfunction." *Journal of Nervous and Mental Disorders* 133 (1961): 247-253.

Forward, J., and C. Buck. *Betrayal of Innocence: Incest and Its Devastation*. New York: Penguin, 1978.

Glass, C., and T. Merluzzi. "Cognitive Assessment of Social-Evaluative Anxiety." In *Cognitive Assessment*, edited by T. Merluzzi, C. Glass, and M. Genest. New York: Guildford, 1981.

Harlow, H., and M. Harlow. "The Affectional Systems." In *Behavior of Nonman Primates, Vol. 2*, edited by A. Schrier, H. Harlow, and F. Stollnitz. New York: Academic, 1963.

Harlow, H., M. Harlow, and E. Hansen. "The Maternal Affectional System of Rhesus Monkeys." In *Maternal Behavior in Mammals*, edited by H. Rheingold. New York: Wiley, 1963a.

Hunter, R., V. Logue, and W. McMenemy. "Temporal Lobe Epilepsy Supervening on Longstanding Transvestism and Fetishism." *Epilepsy* 4 (1963): 60-65.

Ingerbriston, M. "Incest and Alcoholism: Dual Addictions." Lecture given in St. Louis, Missouri: January, 1983.

Kinsey, A., W. Pomeroy, and C. Martin. *Sexual Behavior in the Human Male*. Philadelphia: Saunders, 1948.

Krafft-Ebing, R. *Psychopathia Sexualis*. New York: Physicians and Surgeons, 1931.

Ladd, G., and J. Mize. "Cognitive Social Learning Model of Social Skills Training." *Psychological Review* 90 (1983): 2, 127-157.

Lange, A., and P. Jakubowski. *Responsible Assertive Behavior*. New York: Research, 1979.

Langfeldt, H. "Sexuality in Childhood." Lecture given at the International Congress of Sexology, 1983.

Laws, D., and J. O'Neill. "Variations on Masturbatory Conditioning." *Behavioral Psychotherapy* 9 (1981): 1-38.

MacLean, P. "New Findings on Brain Function and Sociosexual Behavior." In *Contemporary Sexual Behavior*, edited by J. Zubin and J. Money. Baltimore: Johns Hopkins University, 1973.

MacLean, P. "A Triune Concept of the Brain and Behavior." In *The Hinks Memorial Lectures*, edited by T. Boag. Toronto: Toronto University, 1970.

Masters, W., and V. Johnson. *Human Sexual Inadequacy*. Boston, Massachusetts: Little, Brown, 1970.

McIntyre, K. "Role of Mothers in Father-Daughter Incest: A Feminist Analysis." *Social Work* 11 (1981): 462-465.

Meichenbaum, D., and R. Cameron. "Issues in Cognitive Assessment: An Overview. In *Cognitive Assessment*, edited by T. Merluzzi, C. Glass, and M. Genest. New York: Guildford, 1981.

Merluzzi, T., C. Glass, and M. Genest. *Cognitive Assessment.* New York: Guildford, 1981.

Mitchell, W., M. Falconer, and D. Hill. "Epilepsy with Fetishism Relieved by Temporal Lobectomy." *Lancet* 2 (1954): 626-630.

Mohr, W., R. Tusz, and M. Jerry. *Pedophilia and Exhibitionism.* Toronto: University of Toronto, 1965.

Money, J. "Cytogenetic and Other Aspects of Transvestism and Transexualism." *Journal of Sex Research* 3 (1971): 141-143.

Money, J. "Human Behavior Cytogenetics: Review of Psychopathology in Three Syndromes--47, XXY; 47, XYY; and 45, X." *Journal of Sex Research* 11 (1975): 181-200.

Money, J. "Paraphilias." In *Handbook of Sexology*, edited by J. Money and H. Musaph. Amsterdam: Excerpta Medica, 1977.

Money, J. "Paraphilias: Phyletic Origins." Unpublished manuscript, Johns Hopkins University, 1970(a).

Money, J. "Role of Fantasy Pair-Bonding in Erotic Performance." In *Progress in Sexology*, edited by R. Gemme and C. Wheeler. New York: Plenum, 1976.

Money, J. "Use of an Androgen-Depleting Hormone in the Treatment of Male Sex Offenders." *Journal of Sex Research* 6 (1970b): 165-172.

Money, J., C. Wiedeking, and P. Walker. "47, XYY and 46, XY Males with Antisocial and/or Sex Offending Behavior. Antiandrogen Plus Counseling." *Psychoneuroendocrinology* 1 (1975): 165-178.

Petritzer, B., and J. Foster. "A Case Study of a Male Transvestite with Epilepsy and Juvenile Diabetes." *Journal of Nervous and Mental Disorders* 121 (1955): 557-563.

Schwartz, M., and W. Masters. "Conceptual Factors in the Treatment of Paraphilias: A Preliminary Report." *Journal of Sex and Marital Therapy* 9 (1983): 3-19.

Schwartz, M., J. Money, and K. Robinson. "Biosocial Perspectives on Eroticism." *Journal of Sex and Marital Therapy* 7 (1981): 4-19.

Suomi, S. "Development of Attachment and Other Social Behaviors." In *Attachment Behavior, Volume 3*, edited by T. Alloway, P. Aines, and L. Krames. New York: Plenum, 1977.

Thompson, G. "The Relationship of Sexual Psychopathy to Psychomotor Epilepsy and Its Variants." *Trans American Neurological Association* 77 (1952): 96-101.

Tollison, D., and H. Adams. *Sexual Disorders: Treatment, Theory and Research.* New York: Gardner, 1979.

Walinder, J. "Transvestism, Definition and Evidence in Favor of Occasional Deviation from Cerebral Dysfunction." *International Journal of Neuropsychiatry* 1 (1965): 567-573.

Weiner, L. "Partners of Incest Offenders." Unpublished manuscript, April, 1983.

Yawger, N. "Case study of a Male Transvestism and Other Cross-Sex Manifestations." *Journal of Nervous and Mental Disorders* 92 (1940): 41-48.

Yochelson, S., and S. Samenow. *The Criminal Personality*. New York: Jason, Aronson, 1977.

Zilbergeld, B. *Male Sexuality*. New York: Bantam, 1978.

Zimbardo, P. *Shyness, What It Is and What To Do About It*. Reading, Massachusetts: Addison-Wesley, 1978.

PART V

MASS MEDIA, PREVENTION, AND THE FUTURE

The goal of most research in rape and sexual assault, whether explicit or implicit, is to stop sexual violence. There are a number of perspectives to consider when developing strategy. The first three chapters in this section look at issues of mass media and pornography which are suggested to have some link to rape and sexual assault. Mass media is examined from a civil rights perspective and pornography is reviewed from the feminist perspective. Research studies on the cultural implications on aggression against women is also examined. The last chapter in the *Handbook* is on prevention of rape and reviews the prevention efforts over the past decade.

CHAPTER 22

MASS MEDIA AND CIVIL RIGHTS

Judith A. Reisman

"Sex before eight, or else it's too late"
-Rene Guyon Society[1]

Sexual entrapment and the use of children in sex rings and pornography rings are increasingly documented throughout the USA (Burgess 1984; Linedecker 1981). Seduction into such rings is initiated via common psychological techniques. Sexually explicit media is often shown to the selected children as justification of the appropriateness of the sex acts proposed, and as arousal stimuli for young males (Keating 1970; Lloyd 1976). "Rewards" often include candy, trips, money, affection, and, for older youth, supplies of clothing and drugs (House Select Committee of Child Pornography, Texas 1978). "Punishments" are varied, but these often include threats and acts of bodily harm to the child and his/her family (Marshall, Christie 1981), withdrawal of earlier rewards, and "sexual media blackmail"--whereby offenders gain compliance from child victims by threatening to reveal sexually explicit photos and films, in which the child appears, to un-

---

[1] Rene Guyon Society is an organization claiming up to 5,000 supporter/ members, centered in Southern California. Other public American child-sex advocacy groups include PIE (Pedophile Information Exchange), NAMBLA (North American Man Boy Love Assoc.), and CSC (Childhood Sexuality Circle).

aware parents and guardians. This blackmail is used to secure the
child into remaining in the ring, and/or into recruiting other children for active participation (Linedecker 1981; Burgess 1984).

"Mass Media Effects" can be said to be one of the most heatedly
debated social issues of our time. Based upon the evidence accumulated to date, some media do appear to be significant in the entrapment of bodies of women, and especially in the entrapment of juveniles into lives of crime and/or lives of personal and social dysfunction. Moreover, evidence is surfacing which seems to link certain sex/violent media with possible murder and mutilation of women
and children.

To date, examination of sexual media have questioned its effect
upon adult readers. And, it now seems that the media/technological/
sexual revolution may have had a significant impact upon the lives,
both short term and long term, on small children and youth.

Exploitation of Children and Youth

History does repeat itself. Until the church and women's groups
of the nation lobbied successfully for the Mann Act in 1912, both
adult and child prostitution attracted men from every class and from
every social strata. Modern pedophiles and pederasts also reflect
all strata of society but additionally, they appear to be compulsive
photographers, collectors and distributors of child pornography.
Child pornography here refers to juveniles under 18 who are described
as "sexual objects" via nude or semi-nude images in which they are
engaged in "adult" sexual behavior or, in which they exhibit biologi-
cally defined "mating" postures or gestures and the like (Battaglia
1983). This compulsion carries over to incestuous family/affinity
group child molesters as well as stranger pedophiles (Lanning and
Burgess 1984). The deluge of Scandinavian child pornography in the
mid-1970's indicated that a native adult American market existed for
child sex. With photographic equipment cheap and widely available,
broadscale marketing of American-produced child pornography became an
economically feasible profit venture. While these prospects also
drew many investors on a purely venture capital basis, the data confirm that some of these men also realized what had been private pleasure could be parlayed into profitable gains (Linedecker 1981).

For a portion of pedophile/pederasts, the transition was easy.
The transition from recreational sex offenders to business sex offenders was a "natural" process. This business enterprise provided job
opportunities for "actors," producers, etc. In fact, as disconcerting
as it may be, business history tells us that child pornography follows
age-old, traditional patterns of business development. That is, when
goods produced by an individual for personal use find a market, the
individual often attempts to increase production of such goods. If
the effort seems profitable, other entrepreneurs enter the field.
The industry then follows the well known marketing theory of supply
and demand (Kotler 1967). It is the demand for the child "supply,"
and the coercion and violence of the employee recruiting processes
involved, which has become of primary concern to those responsible
for child welfare and for curbing juvenile delinquency. The age-old
tales of the child molester as a harmless old man who merely loves
children (Martinson 1979) do not correlate with modern pederast/pedo-
phile employee recruitment behaviors involving ".... 50,000 stranger
abductions and missing children per year, 2,500 murders of juveniles
per year by serial murderers, pedophiles, child prostitution enforcers,

etc., 3,000 unidentified bodies in morgues...." (Heck 1983).

Well-known recruitment techniques of children into pornography/ prostitution have included abduction, torture, and imprisonment. In extreme cases, the end results have been death. It is hardly surprising that such a turn of events should receive serious coverage in the daily press, the TV media and women's journals (*The Ladies Home Journal*, April 1983; *Women's Day*, July 1983). Moreover, the body of research into TV violence in the media continues to indicate that types of visual experience may, in combination, trigger youthful anti-social behavior (Gerbner et al., 1970-1982; Belson 1978).

It would seem reasonable to suggest that social critics, particularly those with some sympathy to feminist theory regarding rape (Brownmiller 1975; Lederer 1980), seriously investigate the special components of mass media, to see which of these components may be facilitating an increase in rape and sexual assault of women and children. Pedophiles/pederasts, and even rapists, are still functionally seen as sexually deviant persons (Marshall, Christie 1981). Pornographers are known to "arouse" the sexual lust of sexual deviant groups via depictions of sex, still commonly seen by society as "deviant"; that is, sex acts such as bestiality, sadism, and child sex (Goldstein, Kant 1973; Abel et al. 1977; Barbaree et al. 1979). Moreover, recent research among college males indicates that when violent imagery is combined with sexual imagery, male sexual aggressivity is significantly increased, and a more positive personal view of "raping" is expressed (Donnerstein, Berkowitz 1981; Malamuth, Check 1981). Furthermore, media specialists have been documenting the increasing levels of violence in sexually explicit media such as in *Playboy/Penthouse* (Malamuth, Spinner 1980; Reisman et al. 1979, 1983).

Evidence from varied methodologies seem to confirm that sexually deviant lust murderers "are excited by cruelty, whether in books or in films, in fact or in fantasy." (Brittain 1970; Linedecker 1981). It seems quite relevant that a number of children have been victims of lust murderers. It would seem reasonable for scientists to seriously assess the relationship which may exist between some mass media fantasies which include images and symbols of raped or "sexy" children or beaten or murdered children, and real risk to the health and welfare of children. It would certainly seem to be a major scholarly responsibility to define the structure by which mass media may contribute to victimization of juveniles by adults.

Not only does the evidence support a relationship between some mass media and the seduction/abduction/murder of children (Keating 1970), but the mass media sex industry is a serious factor in the worrying growth of a teenage prostitution market in the United States. Latest statistics suggest that approximately 2.4 million American teenagers are engaged in prostitution, (U.S. General Accounting Office 1982).

Suicide among juveniles is estimated at a reported minimum of one death each 4 1/2 hours (Statistical Resources 1979), and some suicide has been traced to youthful entrapment into the sex industry at a vulnerable life stage (Linedecker 1981). Moreover, modern causes of junveile delinquency suggest that we research the possible relationship between youthful suicide and the practices of incestuous caretakers. The possibility of this connection gains significance

when we read reports of incest survivors discussing their suicidal
tendencies (Woodbury 1971) or, when we examine the research on incest
survivors who--as juvenile delinquents--had attempted suicide (Geiser
1976; Tilelli, Turek, Jaffee 1980).

Sex media may emerge as a strong incest stimuli when accredited
psychotherapists, employed by popular erotica, publicly recommend
"family sex" as a therapeutic experience (Constantine 1979).   Corre-
spondingly, incestuous caretakers regularly photograph and exchange
images, films of family sex acts (Armstrong 1978; Reisman 1979).   The
theory has been advanced that just as many juveniles have become
street runaways due to incestuous caretakers and that some youngsters
"run away" by taking their own lives.

Based upon the growing numbers of child molestation and statutory rape reports, as well as what appears to be a growth in incestuous abuse of children, there seems little indication that child sexual
abuse trends will remain status quo, that they will level off, or
that they will lessen in the foreseeable future.   Forecasting from
present data, we should anticipate severe increases in sexual and
general criminality among a significant number of American children
(Winter 1981).   We may also expect that the numbers of abused and
neglected children will rise exponentially as the current crop of
abused juveniles themselves grow into parenthood, often repeating
their own patterns of abuse (Hunner 1981).

It would seem to be in the interest of society to establish a
scientific, juridically and legislatively viable definition of mass
media imagery in terms of its effects upon women's and children's
lives, and their civil rights.   We must establish if such imagery actually serves to seriously endanger the freedom and the civil rights
of women and children, rights and freedoms guaranteed by law to every
American citizen.

Webster defined "free" as "not under the control of power on
another; having liberty; independent.... having civil and political
liberty ... able to move in any direction," and freedom similarly
as a "right or privilege."

To practice their freedom as American citizens then, women need
to be relatively free from fear of violence, particularly the sexual
violence which numerous rape studies suggest women fear the most.
It follows from this that widescale media fusion of sex with violence
may undermine the freedom of women to pursue their promised unalienable
rights.   That is, it may just turn out that widescale media fusion of
sex with violence increases women's subservience and second-class
citizenship.   There does seem to be some solid physiological precedence
for this notion.

Sex and Violence

If we are examining a physiological phenomenon, a neurological
activity in which sex and violence are fused visually and repeatedly
by some mass media, we would do well to recall Darwin's renowned
"Theory of Associated States." He documented that if two frequently
joined arousal states (say, sex & violence), are seen repeatedly and
vividly, the sight of the one stimulus (say, a violent film) will
produce the arousal felt toward the other stimulus (say, a sexy picture).   That is, if one is aroused by a (sex/violent) visual experience repeatedly (via film, television, sexually explicit magazines,

advertisements or whatever), a sexually lustful sight could arouse
the emotion of aggressivity; and a violent sight could arouse the
emotion of sexual lust ... whether we like it or not.

Some assert, alternately, that visual violence, visual sexuality,
and visually-joined-violent-sexuality, are neutral experiences for
most people. Despite this, modern neuroscience seems to agree with
the nineteenth-century Darwinian notions. As Paul MacLean, the neu-
rologist who first identified the limbic system as the brain's emotional center sees it, "There are no neutral affects, because emotionally speaking it is impossible to feel unemotional" (MacLean 1979).

If, in fact, media sexuality or violence or both in combination
does tend to physiologically arouse sex or violence against women and
children, then society may have to re-examine its priorities. For it
was no less an authority on democracy than John Stuart Mill who stipulated that one's freedoms are expected not to do harm to others (Mill
1859).

Unless the significant environmental factors which have led to
the unnatural escalation in American sexual exploitation and violence
are identified and explained in comprehensive language to the public,
legislature, and the courts, we are likely to see these developments
continue, unleashing economically and psychologically staggering bur-
dens upon the nation and the survival of the democratic process. The
renowned John Dewey addressed this issue when he spoke of the foundation of democracy as being rooted in what he saw as faith in the capacities of human intelligence and human nature and the power of
pooled and cooperative experience (Dewey 1937). These ideas are referred to in the modern vernacular as "participatory democracy."

Following these thoughts further, some types of popular, widely
consumed mass media materials do serve to undermine "the power of
pooled and cooperative experience," in so far as these media images
belittle or objectify a class of American citizens objectively defined as "women." Also, denigrating "sexist" imagery could be said
to do violence to both women and democracy in so far as such imagery
may serve to undermine faith in the capacities of women's human nature and her human intelligence.

It follows from this, that we must consider seriously whether
some kinds of media experience actually impact the brain/mind/behavior
syndrome, causing some vulnerable publics to view women (and children)
as suitable targets for their aggressive impulses. For, if this is
so, if some forms of media actually interfere with woman's safety,
then some forms of media may limit woman's pursuit of liberty, restricting her democratic participation in the playful and serious
activities of society. Now, if this turns out to be the case, to any
significant degree, would we not consider the notion that such media
materials may seriously be undermining the democratic process itself?

Therefore, it seems relevant to democracy to identify the newly
fresh factors which have increased heterosexually dysfunctional behaviors of rape, child sexual abuse, lust murder, and the like. If
these factors can be isolated, and once isolated, properly, demo-
cratically mediated against, we might anticipate, as in the Hawaii
experience from 1974-1976 (Court 1982), swift and dramatic reductions
in crimes against both women and children. Moreover, such an understanding could provide an opportunity for women and men to reach together toward the heterosexual dialogue and respect upon which the
future of any democratic nation can be said to depend.

REFERENCES

Abel, G., D. Barlow, E. Blanchard, and D. Guild. "The Components of
Rapists' Sexual Arousal." *Archives of General Psychiatry* 34 (1977):
895-903.

Armstrong, L. *Kiss Daddy Goodnight*. New York: Simon & Schuster,
1978.

Barbaree, H., W. Marshall, and R. Lanthier. "Deviant Sexual Arousal
in Rapists." *Behavior Research and Therapy* 17 (1970): 215-222.

Battaglia, N., San Jose, California Police Department. Lecture,
Sam Houston Criminal Justice Center, Conference on Sexual Violence,
Huntsville, Texas, July, 1983.

Belson, W. *Television Violence and the Adolescent Boy*. London:
Saxon House, Lexington Books, 1978.

This seems the most complete and methodologically precise analysis
of the effects of television--as a specific experience--attempted
by scholars to date. Belson has long years as a respected researcher in the management world. While his longitudinal investigation
was completed for CBS TV, the results have been denied and ignored
by the agency, apparently due to the conclusions Belson drew from
his subject population.

Brenton, M. *The Runaways*. New York: Penguin, 1978.

Brenton's historical treatment is notable for its broad view of
the contemporary "runaway" problem, as it reflects patterns of
juveniles, fathers, mothers, husbands, wives.

Brittain, R.P., is cited by Hazelwood and Douglas, "The Lust Murderer," *FBI Law Enforcement Bulletin*, April 1980. It is taken from
Brittain's article, "The Sadistic Murderer," *Medical Science and
the Law* Vol. IV, (1970): 202.

The FBI article is especially useful in its reference to the role
of fantasy in the construction of rape and murder scenarios by offenders. Hazelwood and Douglas also refer to Reinhardt's book,
Sex Perversions and Sex Crimes. The role of fantasy in the commission of sexual violence to women and children is seen here as serving as a preliminary *act* to the performance of the lust murder,
when, "the pervert ... may resort to pornographic pictures, grotes-
que and cruel literary episodes *out of which* (my emphasis) he
weaves fantasies. On these his imagination dwells until he loses
all contact with reality ... drawing human objects into the fantasy"
(pp. 221-222).

Brownmiller, S. *Against Our Will, Men, Women and Rape*. New York:
Simon & Schuster, 1975.

Burgess, A., A. Groth, and M. McCausland. "Child Sex Initiation
Rings." *American Journal of Orthopsychiatry* 51 (1981): 110-119.

Burgess, A., ed. *Child Pornography and Sex Rings*. Lexington, Mass.:
Lexington Books, 1984.

Constantine, L.L. *Love and Attraction*. London: Pergamon Press,
1979, pp. 503-507.

See the body of Constantine's articles on children and sexuality for
his arguments that children should be exposed to and could participate commercially in pornography.

Court, J. "Pornography and Sex Crimes: A Revaluation in the Light of Recent Trends Around the World," *International Journal of Criminology and Penology*, Vol. 5 (1977): 129-157.

Court, J. "Pornography and the Harm Factor." Paper delivered at the World Congress on Women's Scholarship, Haifa, Israel, December 1982.

Darwin, C. *Expressions of the Emotions in Man and Animals*. London: Murray, 1904.

Densen-Gerber, J.A. See the broad spectrum of articles and releases published by Odyssey Institute, Bridgeport, Ct. for their data on child abuse and neglect. A work of import is, "Incest and Drug Related Child Abuse--Systematic Neglect by the Medical and Legal Professions," by S.F. Hutchinson and R. M. Levine.

Dewey, J. Address cited in *Democracy* (1937), reprinted in *Readings in Philosophy*, edited by J. Randall, 1950, p. 348.

Donnerstein, E., and L. Berkowitz. "Victim Reactions in Aggressive Erotic Films as a Factor in Violence Against Women." *Journal of Personality and Social Psychology* (1981): 710-724.

Gerbner, G. See the Annenberg School of Communication, Philadelphia, Pa., for a full spectrum of reports and data on TV and violence. See especially Gerbner and Gross on "The Scary World of TV's Heavy Viewer," *Psychology Today* April 1976, pp. 41-8.

Geiser, R.L. *Hidden Victims*. Boston: Beacon, 1979.

The theme of attempted and completed suicide as closely related to a portion of incest victim responses, appears sprinkled liberally throughout the literature on child abuse. Arshack and Schmidt write of such suicide attempts in, "Incestuous Behavior as an Etiological Factor Leading to Juvenile Delinquency and Crime," 1977, Child Protection Center, Children's Hospital, Washington, D.C.

Goldstein, M., and H. Kant. *Pornography and Sexual Deviance*. Berkeley: University of California Press, 1973.

Heck, R.O. Opening statement at Sam Houston Criminal Justice Center workshop, "Missing Children and Serial Murder Task Force," Huntsville, Texas, July, 1983.

House Select Committee on Child Pornography, Texas, 66th Session, 1978, p. 87.

Hunner, R.J., and Y.E. Walker. *Relationship Between Child Abuse and Delinquency*. New Jersey: Allanheld, Inc., 1981.

Keating, C.H. *Commission on Obscenity and Pornography*, 2331 West Royal Palm Rd., Suite 105, Phoenix, Arizona 85021. September 1970.

Keating, one of the President's commissioners, has drafted a separate body of data for public consideration regarding pornography as a cause of violence to women and children.

Kotler, P. *Marketing Management*. Englewood Cliffs, New Jersey: Prentice-Hall, 1967.

See especially the Rogers model, "Diffusion of Innovation," p. 345, for a marketing perspective in which child sex or sadism (called

"bondage" etc.) may be merchandized as sex industry innovations.
See also Kotler's newer editions of this basic text.

Lanning, K., and A.W. Burgess. "Child Pornography and Sex Rings,"
FBI Law Enforcement Bulletin 53, 1, January 1984, 10-16.

Lederer, L. *Take Back the Night: Women on Pornography*. William
Morrow, 1980.

This is the only compilation of feminist essays on the issue of
pornography and violence to women and children.

Linedecker, C.L. *Children in Chains*. New York: Everest House, 1981.

Linedecker gives us some of the most up-to-date data on child
abuse in the USA. His detailed investigative reportage and annec-
dotal materials lend his argument added support.

Lloyd, R. *For Money or Love*. New York: Ballantine, 1976.

As an investigative reporter, Lloyd covered the "chickenhawk" issue
of boy prostitution in the USA.

MacLean, P. "The Paranoid Streak in Man." In *Consciousness: Brain,
States of Awareness, and Mysticism*, edited by Goleman and Davidson.
New York: Harper and Row, 1979, pp. 24-27.

Malamuth, N.M., and B. Spinner. "A Longitudinal Content Analysis of
Sexual Violence in the Best-Selling Erotica Magazines." *Journal
of Sex Research* 16 (1980): 226-237.

See additional articles by Malamuth et al., especially college
male responses to rape data, with Check 1981.

Marshall, W.L., and N.M. Christie. "Pedophilia and Aggression,"
Criminal Justice and Behavior. Vol. 8, no. 2, June 1981, pp. 145-
158.

Marshall and Christie present data from penitentiary files which
reveal that more than half of their incarcerated pedophile subjects
used threats and/or actual violence to control the children and to
gain their sexual objectives. Such objectives also included sexual
intercourse. There seems to be emerging a great deal of support
for the observation that the simple "fondling" acts of "harmless"
pedophiles and pederasts were either a) always much more violent
than investigators had suspected, or b) that the acts of pedophiles
and pederasts are increasing in their violence due to something in
the environment which is supportive of both violence and of sexual
attacks upon children.

Martinson, F.L. "Infant and Child Sexuality: Capacity and Experience."
Love and Attraction. London: Pergamon, 1979, pp. 489-491.

Martinson, quoted by *Playboy* for his comments upon the embryonic
nature of children's sexuality, here defines children as seeking/
deserving sexual activity from birth. The entire chapter of essays on children's sexual feelings, reprinted here as the Proceedings from the Wales Conference on Love and Attraction, 1978, is unusual for its group of academic males, all agreeing upon the erotic,
"sexual" view of children. L. Constantine is also represented in
this group of essays. Strangely, a joint paper which I delivered
at this conference on children as sex objects in the sex industrial

literatures/eroticas was not inlcuded in the book collection.
The exclusion was unfortunate, since this paper would have presented the only alternative information on children's sexual feelings
to that of the, for want of a better term "united" group approach
reprinted.

Mill, J.S. *On Liberty*. Bobbs-Merrill, 1956. First printed in 1859.

A thorough reading of Mill makes it quite clear that the idea of
Freedom of Speech was, to his mind, contingent upon the no-harm
principle. This is a concept he returns to again and again in this
small classic on democracy.

Reisman, J.A. (Bat-Ada), see Lederer, L. "Playboy Isn't Playing,"
plus articles/book in press; "The Kinsey Secrets," forthcoming,
1984.

Rush, F. *The Best Kept Secret*. Englewood Cliffs, New Jersey:
Prentice-Hall, 1980.

The literature on incest is sprinkled with casual references to ties
between pornography and incestuous abuse. My own work with the
International Association of Women Police confirms the sporadic
reports and anecdotal confidences of incest victims regarding the
use of pornography as a coercion tactic to force acceptance of sex
with members of the child's affinity group.

Tillelli, J., D. Turek, and A. Jaffe. "Sexual Abuse of Children--
Clinical Findings and Implications for Management." *New England
Journal of Medicine*. Vol. 302, no. 6, February 7, 1980, pp. 319-
323.

Wilson, J.W. "Thinking About Crime." *The Atlantic Monthly*.
September 1983, pp. 72-88.

Citing Glueck, Robins, McCord, Hirschi, West, Farrington et al.

Winter, C. "Prevention of Child Abuse," Videotape documentary relating childhood abuse and later criminality. The tape is based
upon a survey of institutionalized males, produced by the National
Institute of Justice, 1981.

Woodbury, J., and E. Schwartz. *The Silent Sin*. New York: Signet,
1971.

CHAPTER 23

PORNOGRAPHY AND RAPE: A FEMINIST PERSPECTIVE
Hollis Wheeler

Probably the most fundamental aspect of pornography from a feminist perspective[1] is that it is seen as but one element in a system of violence against women that is in inself also but an element in the larger social system of male dominence and female subordination. Brownmiller's *Against Our Will: Men, Women and Rape* appeared in 1975 with what most social scientists would consider a heavyhanded "theoretical" stance: rapists are the front line shock troop who serve to keep *all women* in fear for the benefit of *all men*. This is often coupled with Robin Morgan's statement that "pornography is the theory, and rape the practice" (Morgan 1978). This fundamental theme receives its latest expression from Dworkin (1981): " ... power is the capacity to terrorize ... the acts of terror run the gamut from rape to battery to sexual abuse of children to war ... there is the legend of terror, and this legend is cultivated by men with sublime attention.... Male power is the raison d'être of pornography; the degradation of the female is the means of achieving this power" (pp. 15, 16, 25). Though these statements may be too bald and simple to suit the scholar, their basic logic continues to fuel much of the feminist understanding of both sexual violence and its function in unequal social structures.

This chapter is devoted primarily to elaborating this theme. However, before beginning this elaboration, two additional aspects of the feminist perspective on pornography are fundamental and deserve mention. First, an important source of energy for feminist work is our acute sense of physical danger. This sense, which makes a luxury of strictly cerebral considerations of violence, has produced action nationally--such as twenty-four-hour hotlines, rape crisis and battered women centers, and "Take Back the Night" marches. Second, an important component of the feminist perspective on pornography and other forms of sexual objectification and violence is a profound anger, which storms through the writing of Dworkin or surfaces more quietly in a work of scholarship in *Signs: the Journal of Women in Culture and Society.*

Perspectives
The reader of feminist literature on pornography may note child sexual abuse, child prostitution, rape, and pornography are treated as though they are the same phenomenon, or see even soft core pornography referred to as "violent." They are not literally the same, of course, but in order to explain this equation, let us return to the structure of our society.

Feminists believe, and have done much to demonstrate, that we live within an unequal social environment which depends for its very existence on the subordination of women in all its class strata, in all its ethnic and racial groups, and in all its major institutions such as the family, religion, the government, and the economy. The subordination of women does not arise naturally from our biology, nor does it exist because it was ordained by God. It is humanly created and humanly enforced; it is systematic and lawful in that sense, and

its sociocultural patterns can be traced and scrutinized. Women's
economic, psychological, and emotional dependence is *formally* institutionalized through child socialization in the home, church, and
school, which produces stereotyped gender behavior; through unequal
legal and political status; through unequal educational and job opportunities; and through the actual practices of established health
care delivery and psychotherapy, to name some ways. But it requires
more than these formal institutionalized arrangements to systematically subordinate all women. Female subordination is *informally* institutionalized in such diverse phenomena as the images of women in literature and art, in patterns of conversation, and in the structure of
the English language itself. Subordinate status and unequal power of
women are also informally created and reinforced through such legally
prohibited activities as rape, wife battering, child sexual abuse,
and sexual harassment on the job and in schools. These formally prohibited acts are in actuality permitted and condoned through the behavior of socially legitimized office holders such as police, physicians, psychiatrists, educators, judges, and attorneys. In other
words, when formal structures are routinely breached, this amounts
to an informal institutionalization of the (ostensibly illegal) practices. Furthermore, these activities have become commonplace and are
tolerated by our society through ideologies which assume that most
rapes are really seduction, that marital rape cannot happen, or that
the power held by a male employer is not a relevant part of a situation in which he may be sexually suggestive to his female employee.

It is beyond the scope of this chapter to demonstrate in detail
the assertion of feminists that a continuity exists from normative
female and male sex role behavior to rape, sexual abuse, and battering. In this view, the critique is that it is "normal" for men to
use force with women or that normal heterosexual relations resemble
rape. Suffice it here to say that rape, child sexual abuse, adult
and child pornography, wife battering, sexual harassment and so forth
may look different and certainly do differ in some important ways.
However, they also share important similarities in at least three
ways. First, they all focus primarily on females--with the exception
of child sexual abuse, regarding which it is sometimes suggested that
little boys are equally at risk with little girls (Groth 1981)--and
reduce, one might say objectify, females to a single dimension: the
sexual. This objectification is the basis for actual violence and
our theoretic understanding of it. Second, they all involve men acting out coercively their superordinate positions--and men are generally superordinate to women in age, income, physical size, education,
status, and prestige.

Finally, there is a third way I propose they are linked, and
that is the affective or feeling response of women. There are remarkable similarities in the way it *feels* to be violently raped as an
adult, incestuously abused as a child, or sexually harassed on the
job--and in the way it feels to view pornography. One such emotional
response is that of being overpowered, helpless, unsafe, and frightened. This is in response to our position as prey. Another is the
feeling of objectification, of being treated as worthwhile only as an
unidimensional object, a sex object, which is degrading. Connected
with this is a feeling of being tainted, unclean, and ashamed.
There is also, I believe, often a vague sense of uneasy confusion
which arises from the contradiction between our deep true sense that

we are being wronged and harmed and the opposite sense we get from
myriad external social cues that it is all right if we are raped,
beaten, harassed, and objectified in pornography. It is this confusion that has been articulated in the literature on rape, child sexual abuse, wife battery, and sexual harassment.[2] The confusion is
currently becoming clarified as feminist analysis exposes the power
dynamics of pornography and its relation to other forms of control.
As these forms of violence against women give way to a theoretical
and practical understanding, helplessness, fright, and shame often
give way to anger.

In brief, then, this short explanation should suffice to show
why feminists argue that different forms of violence against women
form a system that is but one element in the larger social system of
male dominance and female subordination. (The interested reader for
whom these connections may seem tenuous is referred to a burgeoning,
almost runaway, body of publications in the humanities, social sciences, and women's studies which examines ethical, political, legal,
esthetic, and social questions from a woman's point of view.[3]) Pornography is viewed as part of the sexual violence system. Soft and
hard core, violent pornography, snuff films, and seductively posed
pubescent girls in popular magazines are variant forms of the same
essential phenomenon. What remains constant from one example to
another is the view of females as dehumanized sexual objects to be
used by men. What varies is the degree of exploitation, bad treatment, or brutality that is depicted and condoned.

The objectification of the female we see expressed in soft pornography is the same objectification of women which appears as violence in hard core porn. With the introduction of sexualized pre-
pubescent girls in popular magazines are variant forms of the same
in "kiddy porn," what varies is the age at which females may be used.
With the advent of incestuous pornography, what varies is the size
of the circle of females that may be exploited.

What does not vary in pornography is an expression, always, of
disrespect and even hatred for women. Furthermore, it is one of the
important mechanisms for the social control of women by men. It
teaches girls and boys, women and men, something about their reciprocal unequal roles and legitimizes the power differential to both
groups. It teaches and reinforces low self-worth in females and
some of it threatens them if they step out of line. It instructs
males in modes and methods of domination and grants them permission
to use these methods. The instructional role of pornography is more
implicit in some examples, but explicit in other instances such as a
kiddie porn magazine, *Schoolgirls*, which "instructs a father in text
and photographs as to those positions for intercourse best used with
pre-pubescent girls (in this instance a girl of 9) and still another
shows in serial photographs how to affix a lock to one's daughter's
labia so that no other man may 'get to her'" (Densen-Gerber 1980,
p. 51). Examples of these themes of disrespect, hatred and control
through intimidation and violence are developed in Dworkin's (1981)
following description and interpretation of a photo which appeared in
Hustler magazine:

> The photograph is captioned "Beaver Hunters." Two white
> men, dressed as hunters, sit in a black Jeep. The Jeep
> occupies almost the whole frame of the picture. The two
> men carry rifles. The rifles extend above the frame of

the photograph into the white space surrounding it.
The men and the Jeep face into the camera. Tied onto
the hood of the black Jeep is a white woman. She is
tied with thick rope. She is spread-eagle. Her pubic
hair and crotch are dead center of the car hood and
the photograph. Her head is turned to one side, tied
down by rope that is pulled taut across her neck, extended to and wrapped several times around her wrists,
tied around the rearview mirrors of the Jeep, brought
back around her arms, crisscrossed under her breasts
and over her thighs, drawn down and wrapped around the
bumper of the Jeep, tied around her ankles. ... The
text under the photograph reads: "Western sportsmen report beaver hunting was particularly good throughout
the Rocky Mountain region during the past season.
These two hunters easily bagged their limit in the high
country. They told *Hustler* that they stuffed and mounted
their trophy as soon as they got her home."

The men in the photograph are self-possessed ... they
are armed; first, in the sense that they are fully
clothed; second, because they carry rifles ... the
woman is possessed ...

In the photograph, the power of terror is basic. The
men are hunters with guns. Their prey is women. They
have caught a woman and tied her onto the hood of a car.
The terror is implicit in the content of the photograph,
but beyond that the photograph strikes the female viewer
dumb with fear. One perceives that the bound woman must
be in pain. The very power to make the photograph (to
use the model, to tie her in that way) and the fact of
the photograph (the fact that someone did use the model,
did tie her that way, that the photograph is published in
a magazine and seen by millions of men who buy it specifically to see such photographs) evoke fear in the female observer unless she entirely dissociates herself
from the photograph: refuses to see the bound person as
a woman like herself. Terror is finally the content of
the photograph, and it is also its effect on the female
observer. That men have the power and desire to make,
publish, and profit from the photograph engenders fear.
That millions more men enjoy the photograph makes the
fear palpable. That men who in general champion civil
rights defend the photograph without experiencing it as
an assault on women intensifies the fear, because if the
horror of the photograph does not resonate with these
men, that horror is not validated as horror in male culture, and women are left without apparent recourse....
(pp. 25-27).

Child pornography has not been sharply differentiated within
feminist analysis from pornography in general, but is seen as linked
to it in two ways: (1) through the identification of women with children, children with women; and (2) as a backlash to the women's movement. In important ways, women and children are equated or identified together (as in "women and children first" off a sinking ship)

or are treated alike (as in patterns of male conversational interruptions of females which closely resemble patterns of adult conversational interruptions of children) (West and Zimmerman 1977). In these instances of pornography women are relegated to child status (status as a girl), rather than vice versa. Rejection of this imposed child identity is at the root of feminist distaste for the term "girls" as applied to competent, able-bodied, adult women in general. We may recall the much celebrated child-like character of sex idol Marilyn Monroe as an example of the coupling of child personality with mature adult female sexuality as the ideal,[4] and notice no parallel ideal of male sexuality which combines the sexually mature adult body with the character and personality of a young boy. Florence Rush, author of a noted book on child sexual abuse (1980), remarks that "men are attracted to a woman who has the helplessness of a child. They prefer children, whether they are large size or little size. Today our society either makes the child look like a woman or the woman look like a child" (Lederer 1980, p. 71). Feminists believe that the pairing of the adult, sexually mature female body and adult "sexual cues" with little girls' dress, mannerisms, helplessness, and child-like qualities confuses young girls forming their self-images as children and later as women. The general cultural identification of women as children has been noted repeatedly, for example, in the research of Broverman et al. (1970), which found essentially child-like characteristics such as submissiveness, dependence, unaggressiveness, emotionality, and fear of math and science are associated with the mature healthy female even by mental health professionals. As women become more independent, more objective, less emotional, and break into mathematics and the sciences--that is, become increasingly less child-like--children increasingly often become replacements for women/wives to be sexually and psychologically dominated by men. Unequal power relations remain at the crux. This so-called "backlash" theory is used to explain the co-terminous rise of the women's liberation movement with the rise in brutal adult pornography, child pornography, and child prostitution. The same backlash logic has been applied to explain the rise in rape, incest, battering, and the targeting of lesbian women for rape.

We have proceeded thus far without a formal feminist definition of pornography, and will turn for that to Helen Longino, who follows the Commission on Obscenity and Pornography in defining porn as "verbal or pictorially explicit representations of sexual behavior that have as a distinguishing characteristic the degrading and demeaning portrayal of the role and status of the human female ... as a mere sexual object to be exploited and manipulated sexually" and, she adds, "in such way as to endorse the degradation [and the degradation of the female character is] represented as providing pleasure to the participant males, and even worse, to the participant females, and there is no suggestion that this sort of treatment of others is inappropriate to their status as human beings" (Lederer 1980, pp. 42-44).

In more passionate terms, pornography has alternately been called "the undiluted essence of anti-female propaganda" (p. 32); the "ideology of a culture which promotes and condones rape, women-battering, and other crimes of violence against women" (p. 19); and also "violence against women that masquerades as sexuality" (p. 92). Feminists contrast these views with both the conservative approach, which sees porn as immoral because it exposes the body, and with the

liberal approach, which approves of pornography because it is taken
by liberals as a healthy expression of human sexuality. Unlike con-
servatives and liberals, feminists distinguish porn from erotica,
which may also be sexually explicit and is also aimed at sexual a-
rousal. But erotica, whose derivation is from eros, or passionate
love, is not degrading or demeaning to women, men, or children.[5]
The derivation of pornography is "porno," meaning "prostitution" or
"female captives," and "graphos," meaning "writing about" or "description of." Most of what is generally labeled as erotica by non-
feminists is in fact pornographic by these definitions, as the power
differential exists in almost all depictions of sex (and actual sex)
and the pleasure differential exists in a great deal of the depictions of sex (and actual sex). It is surprising that so little in
erotic (in the feminist sense) art and films is generally available.
The emerging production of erotic art by feminist artists (e.g.,
Judy Chicago) may begin to fill this gap. Sex education materials
may be distinguished from erotica in that they are sexually explicit
but are not intended to arouse the viewer; they may or may not be
sexist.

   In the recent past, most American feminists have come to advocate an anti-censorship position, and of the three major activist
anti-pornography organizations nationally, all three are against efforts to make pornography involving the use of adults illegal. Pornography involving the use of children, however, is clearly taken to
constitute child sexual abuse and should be illegal on that ground
if no other.

Feminist Action[6]

   Feminist actions relating to the representation of female bodies
and sexuality, which repeatedly took the headlines during the middle
and late 1960s, were an integral element of the second wave of American feminism. "Sexual objectification of women's bodies" was what
offended the angry protestors of *Playboy* magazine and Miss America
pageants. In those years, beginning perhaps with the appearance of
The Feminine Mystique by Friedan in 1963, a contemporary feminist
analysis of sexism in society was emerging, more or less contemporary
with the "sexual liberation movement." However, the first feminist
anthology, *Sisterhood is Powerful* (which appeared in 1970), though it
considers sexist images of women in literature, art, advertising and
the like, contains not a single reference to pornography. Indeed,
soft core porn and violence against women had not yet appeared as advertising themes, though female semi-nudity and nudity had certainly
been used to sell products for decades.

   The liberal understanding of pornography as harmless, pleasurable,
and positive expressions of human sexuality too long repressed[7] by
Victorian notions was held by feminists in general as well as by liberals in general, as it had been put forward by the President's Commission on Obscenity and Pornography in 1970. When the first feminist
critiques of pornography began to emerge, many feminists were caught
in their own liberal understanding of the issue and, feeling uncom-
fortably prudish, were baffled by or did not take the critique seriously. Undeniably it is the case today that, irrespective of the existence of the anti-pornography and media violence movement within
the women's liberation movement, some feminists working actively on
issues such as reproductive rights and passage of equal rights legislation believe that porn is strictly a sexual issue, or not a problem

important enough to warrant diversion of activist energies, or hold
what is here labeled as the liberal perspective.[8]

Greater numbers of feminists took the anti-pornography position
as more extreme forms of violent pornography such as snuff films
gained an audience, and as violent pornography moved into mainstream
advertising with such examples as the "I'm black and blue from the
Rolling Stones and I love it" album cover depicting a bruised and
chained female, which stimulated action and analysis. The earliest
step of an explicit feminist anti-media violence movement was taken
when the movie *Snuff*--advertised as being"from South America where
life is cheap"--opened in New York City in January, 1976, and toured
mainstream theaters from the East to San Francisco and Los Angeles.
Snuff[9] was a simulation of actual South American films which culmi-
nate in a real woman's life being "snuffed out" in an "eroticized"
murder which is intended to be sexually arousing to the viewer. An
ad hoc group of feminist protestors arose in Los Angeles naming themselves "Women Against Violence Against Women" (WAVAW) and began to
argue that this film promoted real violence against real women. WAVAW
argued that it should be just as socially intolerable to glorify and
sell the depiction of the eroticized murder of a woman as it would be
if the murder victim were a member of a racial, ethnic, or religious
minority group. In July of the same year, when Atlantic Records
raised a billboard of the now-famous Rolling Stones album cover on
Sunset Strip in Los Angeles, WAVAW sent a press-covered delegation to
protest Warner-Electra-Atlantic (WEA) Records and organized a national
boycott of the company. In three years, with more than a dozen supporting chapters across the country, WAVAW realized its goals when
WEA agreed to stop using images of "sexual and physical violence a-
gainst women" on album covers and ad campaigns. WAVAW also created
a slide show of pornographic and violent album covers, which they e-
ventually passed on to "WAVPM."

Women Against Violence in Pornography and Media (WAVPM) was
forged in 1976 by feminists inspired by WAVAW who had worked against
media violence and by feminists who had been active in anti-snuff and
other anti-pornography in San Francisco. WAVPM launched the first feminist demonstration against pornography in the United States (and the
second in the world) with their May Day Stroll in 1977 in San Francisco's
North Beach porn district, and they developed the original WAVAW slideshow into a general advertising and pornography slideshow. Through the
November, 1978, First Feminist Perspectives on Pornography Conference,
WAVPM also launched several other anti-porn activist groups across
the country, and one of them was Women Against Pornography (WAP) of
New York City. WAVPM organized one of the first "Take Back the Night"
marches, which has been duplicated in cities throughout the country
and the world. They currently continue actions, demonstrations, and
workshops, and publish a monthly newsletter which devotes itself to
instructions for grassroots anti-porn actions and to a "Write Back!
Fight Back!" campaign which targets each month a particularly offensive example of pornographic or violent advertising and provides an
address to which to send complaints. They also conduct tours of the
North Beach porn district, and take speaking and slideshow engagements
(the slideshow is available for rent or purchase).

In early 1979 a handful of New York feminists stimulated by
WAVPM's "Take Back the Night" march, toured the Times Square porn
district. By May they began touring other people through the district.
Their program was an immediate success and provoked coverage in the

New York Times, *Time* magazine, and on television. Under the name Women Against Pornography (WAP), and assisted by an organizer from WAVPM, the group developed two major long-term goals: first, to firmly establish pornography as a feminist issue; and second, to reverse the growing public acceptance of pornography through education and attitude change. By the fall of 1979, WAP accomplished two important actions: they held an east coast conference on feminism and pornography which drew 800 conferees, and they organized 10,000 people in a march on Times Square. WAP now publishes a quarterly newsletter and plans actions in response to the pornography industry. One such action was a protest of the film *Deep Throat*, at which Linda (Lovelace) Marciano testified that she was forced at gunpoint to film *Deep Throat* and pointed out the bruises which are visible on her in the film, visual testimony to beatings she received.[10] In another action, WAP organized a protest of Edward Albee's play *Lolita* and criticized the "Lolita Syndrome," in which little girls are eroticized and portrayed as seductive and willing sexual playthings and pedophiles are sympathetic figures. WAP has also organized two major forums on "Pornography and Male Sexuality" and "Pornography and Women's Self Images."

Although not a self-avowed feminist, the anti-pornography work of Densen-Gerber should be mentioned. Based on her work at the Odyssey Institute, an international research, education, and child advocacy organization, and her work with hundreds of adult and child drug- and sex-abuse related cases (which she has detailed in one of the most persuasive and penetrating reports on empirical work done on this topic) (1980), she strenuously argues the links between adult pornography and child sexual abuse, child prostitution, child pornography, and drugs. In 1974, 44 percent of adult female addicts surveyed at Odyssey Houses (residential treatment centers) throughout the United States had a history of childhood incest victimization which occurred before the drug abuse. By 1980 this had risen to 49 percent. During the same year male addicts were also surveyed and 25 percent reported incest victimization.

It is commonly held that nude posing is harmless to children. Densen-Gerber rejects this for two reasons. First, there is ample evidence that being a subject for pornographic photography is distressing and damaging in and of itself.[11] Second, child pornography does not exist in a vacuum; it is consumed by adults who sexually use children. "We have found that the child pornographer is also often the molester. Photography is only a part of it, a sideline more often than not to prostitution, sexual abuse, and drugs" (p. 50). Densen-Gerber (1980) adds the opinion of Henry Giarretto, famous for his work in San Jose with incest families, who attributed increases in incest cases "in large measure to the burgeoning 'kiddie porn' industry" (pp. 50-51). Arguing the harmfulness of child pornography to the children being used, she states, "I grow tired of Fifth Amendment debates with people who have never treated girls who were prostituted at three and were mothers at nine" (p. 8).

In 1976, Densen-Gerber viewed sixty-four separate child sex films at the Crossroads Bookstore of New York City, some of which depicted and promoted incest, and her outrage brought her to work with legislators to draft both New York State and Federal bills which made the sale and distribution, as well as production, of such films illegal. In May, 1981, the New York State Court of Appeals

overturned the 1977 laws and ruled that child pornography could be
sold until each piece was judged separately. Densen-Gerber is now
engaged in a massive voter petition effort to have this ruling re-
pealed, as well as working with the press to encourage responsible
coverage of pornographic victimization of children. For several
years, Densen-Gerber has also collected and documented the existence
of child porn. Recently this includes "baby porn," depicting children under age three and coming out of Amsterdam, which was brought
to light at the Third International Congress on Child Abuse.

Other work includes documentation of the "sale" of children
through advertising such as the Brooke Shields, Tina Payne, and
Kristine Ohlman campaigns, and public education efforts about the
existence of groups such as the Rene Guyon Society, whose motto is
"Sex by age 8 or it's too late." According to Densen-Gerber, "There
is a growing trend to legitimize the sexual uses of children and to
impose adult sexuality on children at younger and younger ages. In
previous years sexploitation took the underground form of pornography.
Now daily advertising practices promote babies as sexual objects.
An atmosphere has evolved in the United States which allows the marketing industry to sexualize whomever they choose and thus validate
the appetite of the consumer, even when that consumer is a pedophile"
(Densen-Gerber and Benward 1976).

In addition to the three national feminist anti-pornography organizations discussed here and the Odyssey Institute, a recent dir-
ectory[12] lists seven smaller international and thirty United States
anti-pornography/media violence groups, as well as an additional
forty "progressive" anti-media violence groups, women's media groups,
related groups, individual activists, contacts, and sources.[13]

Feminist Research

Activist sociologist and writer Kathleen Barry (1979) calls
feminist research on porn "busy work" and warns us not to get side-
tracked on false issues such as freedom of speech and research to
prove what we already know (that porn is harmful to women) through
our commonsense experience. Despite her admonishment and the immediate dangers to our physical and spiritual existence which has ener-
gized feminist action, feminist research[14] is now beginning to emerge.
Most fully developed are feminist critiques of male research on pornography, and certainly some male research has begun to yield to the
pressure of feminist criticism.[15]

The feminist criticisms of male dominated research on pornography are many. Just as only men formed the Presidential Commission
on Obscenity and Pornography which did so much to shape permissive
liberal ideas on pornography and provide support for legal decisions
permissive of pornography, so only men have thus far done nearly all
the empirical pornography research. Male researchers in general take
for granted female sexual objectification and are prone to accept
commonly held myths about rape when they formulate research questions
or interpret results.

Russell (in Lederer 1980, pp. 234-235) cites work done by three
prominent male researchers who are critical of the effects of pronography but who nevertheless defined a rape involving a "forcefully
crushed," "terrified," "screaming" female in a rape-story used as a
stimulus in an experiment as a "benign rape," because the woman was
depicted in the rape-story as experiencing an orgasm.[16] The male
researchers argued that "if a pleasurable outcome for the victim is

a highly potent factor affecting the subjects' [in the experimental research] sexual arousal, then it would seem inappropriate to consider fantasy rape stories as necessarily reflecting hostile aggression...." To which Russell answers, "How can this be interpreted as a benign or non-hostile fantasy? The effect of the orgasm at the end of the story is likely to free the rapist (or the person identifying with him) from guilt, to show how powerful he is and how animal-like women are underneath their 'pure facades.'" In an opinion shared by other feminists, Russell points out that oppressive behavior is permissible toward females that would be untolerated toward other groups:

> ... after reading a violent rape story [in an experiment]
> ... women students were asked whether they were likely to
> enjoy being victimized under the same circumstances de-
> scribed in the story if they were assured no one would
> ever know ... I can well imagine what the reaction would
> be if black people were asked if they'd like to be beaten
> up by white people if they were assured no one would
> know about it! Or imagine an average man's reaction
> to a question about whether he would enjoy another man
> forcefully sodomizing him. It is a reflection of how
> oppressed we are as women that such questions can still
> be asked and asnwered (p. 235).

Another central female criticism of male-dominated research is the use of the "catharsis model": the more violent pornography seen by viewers, the less likely they are to engage in the behavior observed. In contrast to this perspective, feminists stress the "social learning" or "imitation" model: the more violent pornography seen by the viewer, the more likely he is to imitate it in his own actions. The social learning model has been shown to explain increased aggression and other behaviors in children and adults (for example, increased aggression in children viewing films which depict aggressive behavior), and there is no reason to believe that laws of learning established through decades of research would be suspended for those who observe pornography. Diamond (1980) points out that in 1969 "The Presidential Commission on Causes and Prevention of Violence concluded that media violence can induce people to act aggressively." but in 1970 the Presidential Commission on Obscenity and Pornography "concluded that pornography does not seriously [sic] promote antisocial behavior" (p. 691).

In several experiments the exact nature of the materials used as the stimulus are not detailed. However, to interpret the results it is necessary to know if the sexual materials would be classed as erotica, soft core, hard core or violent porn, or sex education materials, and to know whether genital torture, incest, bondage, etc., are depicted. Individual experiments are subject to particular criticisms-- for example, in one study "sexual deviance" was defined by lumping together homosexuality, "sex without love," rape, prostitution, exhibitionism, and transvestism. Similarly, in another experiment the use of pornography was compared among groups of rapists, homosexuals, transsexuals, pedophiles, and "heavy porn users," as contrasted with a control group from the community; however, it was not clear that the control group did not contain members from these other groups.

To counter these problems, Russell (in Lederer 1980, pp. 225-228) proposes experiments conducted by females and without the presence of

males. Ideally, some researchers should be feminists who could ask
questions and form hypotheses based on a sensitivity to sex roles
and who have an interest in and concern for female as well as male
sexuality. In her own research, Russell shifts away from the focus
on the relationship between sexual arousal and aggression in men to
a concern with pornography and its impact on violence against women.
With this special focus she elicited interview data in 1978 from a
random household sample of 930 San Francisco women, aged eighteen and
over.[17] Ten percent of these women believed that some men, as a
direct outcome of viewing pornography, attempt to re-enact pornographic scenes they have viewed by requesting, pressuring, or forcing
compliance from real women in their lives. Eighty-nine women (or 9.6
percent) in the sample of 930 answered "Yes" to the question, "Have
you ever been upset by anyone trying to get you to do what they'd
seen in pornographic pictures, movies, or books?" The women who answered "Yes" were all asked, "Could you tell me briefly about the experience that upset you the most?" A selection of the replies follows:

> He was a lover. He'd go to porno movies, then he'd
> come home and say, "I saw this in a movie. Let's
> try it." I felt really exploited, like I was being
> put in a mold.

> It was physical slapping and hitting. It wasn't a
> turn-on; it was more a feeling of being used as an
> object. What was most upsetting was that he thought
> it was a turn-on.

> My husband enjoys pornographic movies. He tries to
> get me to do things he finds exciting in movies.
> They include twosomes and threesomes. I always
> refuse.

> He forced me to go down on him. He said he'd been
> going to porno movies. He'd seen this and wanted me
> to do it. He also wanted to pour champagne on my
> vagina. I got beat up because I didn't want to do it.
> He pulled my hair and slapped me around. After that
> I went ahead and did it, but there was no feeling
> in it.

> Once he tried to persuade me to go along with anal
> sex, first verbally, then by touching me. When I
> said "No," he did it anyway--much to my pain. It
> hurt like hell.

> This guy had seen a movie where a woman was being
> made love to by dogs. He suggested that some of his
> friends had a dog and we should have a party and set
> the dog loose on the women. He wanted me to put a
> muzzle on the dog and put some sort of stuff on my
> vagina so that the dog would lick there.

> My boyfriend and I saw a movie in which there was
> masochism. After that he wanted to gag me and tie
> me up. I was nervous and uptight. He literally tried
> to force me, after gagging me first. He was hurting
> me with it and I started getting upset. Then I
> realized it wasn't a joke. He grabbed me ... and

> brought out some ropes, and told me to relax, and
> that I would enjoy it. Then he started putting me
> down about my feelings about sex, and my inhibited-
> ness. I started crying and struggling with him.

Seeming much less harmful by comparison with the assaults above, but nevertheless disturbing is even the suggestion to engage in such acts, as illustrated in a closing quote from a women who clearly stated her rejection:

> I was newly divorced when this date talked about
> S & M and I said, "You've got to be nuts. Learning
> to experience pleasure through pain! But it's your
> pleasure and my pain!"

CONCLUSION: *"But It's Your Pleasure and My Pain!"*

Pornography directly hurts real, individual women, and it also functions more indirectly in complex ways with other phenomena at a macrosocial level to help maintain male dominance and female subordination. Several themes from the feminist perspective are given voice in the spontaneous responses of the women interviewed above:

--Porn sexually objectifies women. Women feel this degradation.

--Porn teaches men that women enjoy violence. It eroticizes violence for men.

--Porn confuses some women into believing they should "experience pleasure through pain." Some men enjoy hurting women physically.

--It teaches women to endure rape and violence.

--Sometimes real women experience real rape arising directly from males viewing pornography.

Of the eighty-nine women who had been "upset" by someone trying to reenact a scene from pornographic pictures, movies, or books, fifteen of them (which is 17 percent of the subset and 1.6 percent of the original sample of 930) were victims of a sexual assault arising out of the situation: four suffered completed vaginal intercourse (rape) with force, ten suffered completed oral, anal or vaginal intercourse (rape) with a foreign object with force. Russell argues compellingly this is a conservative estimate from her sample.

These outcomes are direct. Indirectly, the wide prevalence of the physical and sexual coercion which is depicted, glorified, and legitimized in porn contribute to female subordination. Staying home at night because of fear, decreased economic success due to sexual harassment in our workplaces, and the reluctance of women in general to seek elective office are effects of this subordinate status. Feminists who feel keenly frightened or insulted or angry at the spiritual bludgeoning in soft core porn and the "licence to kill" in hard core will continue to fight by the thousands across the country, and even the world,for ourselves and for the protection of our children.

The efforts will continue in regard to feminist theoretical analysis, in regard to action, and in regard to research. The development of a general body of feminist theory has cast floodlights on our position, but left many shadows to investigate. Where this regards pornography, feminist analysis should be extended and applied. For example, there has been little consideration by feminists of patterns of sexual abuse of girls vs. boys; patterns of abuse which occur in the home vs. outside the home; the rise of incestuous abuse among military men; or heterosexual male vs. homosexual male use of chidren.

As pornography continues to proliferate, so does the geographic area covered by feminist activists and the effectiveness of their activism. For example, an anti-pornography effort has arisen in Israel, a country noted by feminists for its lack of any strong feminist movement. Here in the United States, anti-pornography activists have been successful in efforts to induce some major manufacturers to change longstanding advertising programs.

Ultimately, even without complete agreement regarding the power dynamics of pornography and its relation to other forms of control, feminists want freedom and equality for women. The interrelatedness of different forms of oppression and the commonality of our goals unite the fights of those whose efforts are directed explicitly at pornography, or at gaining ratification of the Equal Rights Amendment, or equality of opportunity and pay in the labor force, or control of our bodies' reproductive capacity, or safety from battering in marriage and rape anywhere, or a greater presence of women in the House, Senate, and Supreme Court so that it will not be so wholly men who make laws for women.

Within the feminist perspective, to combat pornography is to fight broadly for equality and freedom for women. More narrowly, it is to fight for our bodily safety, for our own sexuality, and in Gloria Steinham's eloquent words (Lederer 1980, p. 39) it is to fight also for

> our spirits that break a little each time we see ourselves
> in chains or full labial display for the conquering male
> viewer, bruised or on our knees, screaming a real or pre-
> tended pain to delight the sadist, pretending to enjoy
> what we don't enjoy, to be blind to the image of our
> sisters that really haunt us--humiliated often enough
> ourselves by the truly obscene idea that sex and the
> domination of women must be combined.

NOTES

1. This chapter relies heavily on the feminist book *Take Back the Night*, edited by Laura Lederer. The interested reader is referred to that book for a general in-depth coverage of feminist perspectives on pornography, as well as coverage of the following specific topics which receive no consideration or limited consideration herein: pornography and the first amendment rights, differences between erotica and pornography, critiques of the findings of the President's Commission on Pornography and Obscenity, pornography research in Scandinavia, lesbianism and pornography, racism and pornography, critiques of male-dominated pornography research, and the film *Snuff*.

2. For example, see "Divided Loyalty in Incest Cases" (Burgess et al. 1978); the institutional treatment of rape victims in *The Victim of Rape: Institutional Reactions* (Holmstrom and Burgess 1983); the analyses of rape in *Rape: the First Sourcebook for Women* (Connell and Wilson 1974) and *Sexual Harassment of Working Women* (MacKinnon 1979), a book that has been hailed as brilliant. Also informative is *Sexual Shakedown: The Sexual Harassment of*

Women on the Job (Farley 1973); *Battered Wives* (Martin 1976); and
Rape in Marriage (Russell 1982).

3. The Feminist Press is one of several publishing houses of inter-
    est. In addition is the National Women's Mailing List, 1195
    Valencia Street, San Francisco, California 94110 (415-824-6800).

4. The converse, the coupling of adult sexual behavior or cues with
    the immature child's body, grows more visible daily. A particu-
    larly instructive example, because it involves the recent "por-
    nographication" of a long-standing advertisement familiar to the
    eyes of Americans, is the case of a Coppertone sun tan ad. In
    this ad, a girl of about five years looks back over her shoulder
    in childish dismay, hand raised to mouth, mouth in an "O", and
    eyebrows arched as a black cocker spaniel tugs at her panties,
    exposing her buttocks. This has always been a picture of child-
    ish innocence, the girl just at an age when she is beginning to
    understand that her buttocks are not properly displayed in public,
    yet she is young enough so that neither for her nor for the adult
    viewer is there any sexual connotation to her nudity. This is
    what has always made the picture "cute" and an appealing ad.
    The caption for years has been "Tan, don't burn, get a Coppertone
    tan." Recently, however, on enormous Miami billboards the cap-
    tion has been changed to "Flash them a Coppertone tan." This
    change in ad line changes the exposure of the buttocks to an in-
    tentional sexualized display by the little girl: first by use of
    the word "flash" which has associations with "flasher" or "flash-
    ing," and second in the intentionality implied, as if it were
    said "flash them a smile." Through the change in ad line, the
    look of childish dismay has been transformed to a coquettish af-
    fection.

5. An important exception to this generally accepted feminist dis-
    tinction between the two is held by Dworkin, who calls erotica
    nothing but high-class pornography (1981, p. 10).

6. For material in this section I wish to thank the following for
    granting me telephone interviews: Bridget Wynne of WAVPM, P.O.
    Box 14635, San Francisco, California 94114; Delores Alexander of
    WAP, 358 West 47th Street, New York, New York 10036; and Jean
    Elahi, Vice President of Public Information, Odyssey Institute,
    Inc., 656 Avenue of the Americas, New York, New York 10011.

7. For treatments of the relationship of porn and repression, see
    "Pornography and Repression: A Reconsideration" (Diamond 1980).
    The author warns against an oversimplified equation of pornography
    and violence in an excellent analysis of the contrasting assump-
    tions which underlie the feminist perspective, the right wing's
    moral crusade against porn, and the male dominated research on
    porn. See also *Pornography and Silence: Culture's Revenge Against
    Nature* (Griffin 1981). For a consideration of pornography and
    repression from the English literature which approves the pur-
    ported anti-repressive role of pornography and reports on the
    written work and life of Sade, see *The Sadean Women and the Ide-
    ology of Pornography* (Carter 1978).

8. Friedan (1981), for example, states, "It seemed irrelevant, wrong
    for women to be wasting energy marching against pornography--or

any other sexual issue--when their very economic survival was
at stake" (p. 20). Ellen Willis, a feminist writer for *The
Village Voice*, is pro-pornography. In their 1982 article,
Ehrenreich, Hess, and Jacobs raise the differences on pornography and other sex-related topics to the level of a "crisis"
within the women's movement, noting among other things the split
in the lesbian and gay male communities on the issues of pornography and sexual abuse of children. Rush (1980, p. 173) also
notes the opposing positions taken on these issues by the Lesbian Feminist Liberation of New York and the North American Man/
Boy Love Association (NAMBLA).

9. Much confusion exists regarding the actual existence in the U.S.
    of a film titled *Snuff* or the existence of South American "snuff
    films." It is a real film which has shown in the U.S. and Cana-
    da. Beverly LaBell, who attended the film *Snuff* and later helped
    organize against it, gives the following information (Lederer
    1980, pp. 272-278):

    [*Snuff*] achieved notoriety because of the carnage of its
    final five-minute sequence. The film first surfaced in
    1975 shortly after the New York City Police Department an-
    nounced that they had confiscated several "underground"
    South American pornographic films containing actual murder
    footage. [In the plot, a movie crew is filming a murder
    film--which is itself a snuff film--in which the charac-
    ters, "followers of Satan," murder a beautiful blond
    pregnant woman in a film sequence clearly modeled on the
    Charles Manson and "family" murder of Sharon Tate. The
    "followers of Satan"] surround the bed where she lies ...
    with her enormous stomach protruding ... and a dagger is ...
    plunged savagely into her stomach, which explodes with
    the sounds of gushing blood and gurgling amniotic fluid....
    A pretty young blond woman who appears to be a production
    assistant tells the director how sexually aroused she was
    by the stabbing. The attractive director asks her if
    she would like to go to bed with him and act out her fan-
    tasies.... The director picks up a dagger ... and says,
    "Bitch, now you're going to get what you want...."
    He butchers her slowly, deeply, thoroughly. The observ-
    er's gut revulsion is overwhelming at the amount of
    blood, chopped-up fingers, flying arms, sawed off legs,
    and yet more blood oozing like a river out of her mouth
    before she dies. But the end is still at hand. In a
    moment of undiluted evil, he cuts open her abdomen and
    brandishes her very insides high above his head in a
    scream of orgasmic conquest. The End....

10. See Marciano's autobiography *Ordeal*, 1980, which recounts the
    years of beatings, sadistic rapes, prostitution, and captivity
    to which she was subjected by her husband, Chuck Traynor.

11. In my own work with over 100 adult women who were sexually
    abused or assaulted as children, an incomplete survey shows
    more than 10 percent were used to make pornography, either for
    the personal consumption of the offender or for commercial sale.
    All recount associations of fear or shame with this. Joyce St.
    Pierre of NETWORKS (Franklin/Hampshire Community Mental Health,

Northampton, Massachusetts) points out that pornographic photos used as court evidence should eventually be destroyed because in her experience in therapy with the child subjects, the existing photographs remain in their minds as proof of the guilt they believe they bear.

12. WAVPM Newspage, Vol. V, No. 8, Aug./Sept. 1981.

13. Some politically conservative groups do vigorous national-level work against child pornography and child exploitation which is based on anti-feminist assumptions and philosophy. One such organization is a Christian group called the "Interfaith Committee Against Child Molesters" which has issued an undated publication titled "The New Predators," published by the Community Church of America, P.O.B. 20, Glendale, California 91209. For research on feminist anti-pornography groups see the sociological analysis in "The Future of Feminist Anti-Pornography Crusades" (Kirkpatrick 1982).

14. For the reader interested in theoretical, methodological, practical, and ethical issues in feminist research, see *Doing Feminist Research* (Roberts 1981).

15. In particular, the recent work of Neil Malmuth is well thought of by feminists generally.

16. In my own work with rape and incest victims, one victim of violent incestuous rape reported her successful attempt to reach an orgasm because she believed her assailant (an adult male relative) would kill her if she did not (he had previously hospitalized her twice with injuries he had inflicted). Burgess (1974) has reported occasional rape victims in fear of their lives as nevertheless experiencing sexual response, though this did not indicate they "enjoyed" being raped. For some victims this is reported as part of a survival strategy.

17. The questions on pornography were included as part of a survey seeking to ascertain the prevalence of sexual assault in San Francisco; female interviewers trained in in-depth interview techniques obtained interviews from thirty minutes to two hours in length.

REFERENCES

Barry, K. *Female Sexual Slavery*. Englewood Cliffs, N.J.: Prentice-Hall, 1979.

Boverman, I., et al. "Sex Role Stereotypes and Clinical Judgments of Mental Health." *Journal of Consulting and Clinical Psychology* 34 (1970): 8.

Brownmiller, S. *Against Our Will: Men, Women and Rape*. New York: Simon and Schuster, 1975.

Burgess, A.W., A.N. Groth, L.L. Holmstrom, and S.M. Sgroi. "Divided Loyalty in Incest Cases." In *Sexual Assault of Children and Adolescents*. Lexington, Massachusetts: Lexington Books, 1978.

Burgess, A.W., and L.L. Holmstrom. *Rape: Victims of Crisis*. Bowie, Maryland: Robert J. Brady Company, 1974.

Carter, A. *The Sadean Women and the Ideology of Pornography.* New York: Harper Colophon Books, 1978.

Connell, N., and C. Wilson, eds. *Rape: The First Sourcebook for Women.* New York: New American Library, 1974.

Densen-Gerber, J. *Child Abuse and Neglect as Related to Parental Drug Abuse and Other Antisocial Behavior.* New York: Odyssey Institute, 1980.

Densen-Gerber, J., and J. Benward. *Incest as a Causative Factor in Antisocial Behavior.* New York: Odyssey Institute, 1976.

Diamond, I. "Pornography and Repression: A Reconsideration." *Signs* 5 (1980): 686.

Dworkin, A. *Pornography: Men Possessing Women.* New York: Perrigee, 1981.

Ehrenreich, B., E. Hess, and G. Jacobs. "A Report on the 'Sex Crisis.'" *Ms* (March 1982): 61.

Farley, L. *Sexual Shakedown: The Sexual Harassment of Women on the Job.* New York: McGraw-Hill, 1978.

Friedan, B. *The Feminine Mystique.* New York: Dell Publishing Co., 1963.

Friedan, B. *The Second Stage.* New York: Summit Books, 1981.

Griffin, S. *Pornography and Silence: Culture's Revenge Against Nature.* New York: Harper and Row, 1981.

Groth, N. *Sexual Victimization of Children: Proceedings of the First National Conference on Child Sexual Victimization,* edited by B. Jones. Washington, D.C.: Childrens Hospital National Medical Center, 1981.

Holmstrom, L.L., and A.W. Burgess. *The Victim of Rape: Institutional Reactions.* New Brunswick, New Jersey: Transaction Books, 1983.

Kirkpatrick, G. "The Future of Feminist Anti-Pornography Crusades." Paper presented at the Pacific Sociological Association meeting. San Diego, California, April 21-24, 1982.

Lederer, L. *Take Back the Night.* New York: William Morrow & Co., 1980.

MacKinnon, C. *Sexual Harassment of Working Women.* New Haven, Connecticut: Yale University Press, 1979.

Marciano, L.L., with M. McGrady. *Ordeal.* New York: Berkeley Books, 1980.

Martin, D. *Battered Wives.* San Francisco, California: Glide Publications, 1976.

Morgan, R. *Going Too Far.* New York: Vintage Books, 1978.

Morgan, R., ed. *Sisterhood Is Powerful.* New York: Random House, Inc., 1970.

Roberts, H. *Doing Feminist Research.* London: Routledge and Kegan Paul, 1981.

Rush, F. *The Best Kept Secret*. Englewood Cliffs, New Jersey: Prentice-Hall, 1980.

Russell, D.E.H. *Rape in Marriage*. New York: Macmillan, 1982.

West, C., and D. Zimmerman. "Women's Place in Everyday Talk: Reflections on Parent-Child Interaction." *Social Problems* 24 (1977): 521-529.

CHAPTER 24

THE MASS MEDIA AND AGGRESSION AGAINST WOMEN:
RESEARCH FINDINGS AND PREVENTION

Neil M. Malamuth

INTRODUCTION

In this chapter, I will describe findings from a research program on the cultural and individual causes of aggression against wom-
en. While the primary focus has been on aggression in the general
population and not on clinical or incarcerated populations, I anticipate that the findings will also shed some light on the roots of
aggressive acts that come to the attention of legal and mental health
agencies.

One of the ways we have attempted to study the role of cultural
factors in aggression is by focusing on the mass media. The media,
according to numerous writers (e.g., Brown 1981; Goffman 1979), both
reflects and shapes cultural images, values, and social scripts.
Our research in this area has to date dealt primarily with pornography. The term "pornography" is used herein to refer to sexually explicit materials without any pejorative meaning necessarily intended.
It is important to note, however, that the effects found are likely
to occur with other types of stimuli as well and that the depiction
of sexual aggression in the mass media is by no means limited to pornography. For example, a recent content analysis of sexual interactions in television soap operas (Lowry et al. 1981) indicated that
aggressive-sexual contact was the second most frequent type of sexual
interaction (with erotic touching among unmarried persons being the
most frequent). Similarly, a cover story in *Newsweek* magazine (September 28, 1981) focused on the tremendous viewer attention that soap
operas have attracted. Interviews in *Newsweek* with producers and actors from these shows stressed their beliefs that aggression against
women attracts audiences; for example, "The male population started
watching us because we no longer were wimps. When a woman was wrong,
we'd slap her down" (p. 65). Thus, although the following presentation concerns primarily empirical findings on the effects of aggressive-pornography, we expect that the conclusions also apply to many
other areas of the mass media.

Defining Aggressive-Pornography

Many feminist writers argue that pornography is "hate literature"
against women: "Pornography is the theory and rape the practice" con-
tends Morgan (1978, p. 169). The content of pornography, according
to these writers, is primarily intended to dehumanize and degrade
women, and is an expression of a "sexist ideology" in which women are
seen as the tools of men:

> The most prevalent theme in pornography is one of utter
> contempt for women. In movie after movie women are
> raped, ejaculated on, urinated on, anally penetrated,
> beaten, and, with the advent of snuff films, murdered
> in an orgy of sexual pleasure. Women are the objects
> of pornography, men its largest consumers, and
> sexual degradation its theme. (Barry 1979, p. 175).

Feminist writers do not object to sexually explicit materials that portray men and women in humanized and positive relationships. Rather, they object to what they perceive as portrayals of unequal power relations between men and women and the degradation of women. They argue that as an expression of a sexist ideology such materials "promote a climate in which acts of sexual hostility directed against women are not only tolerated but ideologically encouraged" (Brownmiller 1975, p. 444). In other words, their position is that pornography contributes to acts of violence against women by making such acts less reprehensible to people.

The distinction between aggressive versus "positive" types of pornography is often difficult to establish operationally and conceptually. For example, Steinem (1980) differentiated between what she considers acceptable erotica from objectionable pornography in the following way:

> Look at any photo or film of people making love; really making love. The images may be diverse, but there is usually a sensuality and touch and warmth, an acceptance of bodies and nerve endings. There is always a spontaneous sense of people who are there because they want to be, out of shared pleasure.
>
> Now look at any depiction of sex in which there is clear force, or an unequal power that spells coercion. It may be very blatant, with weapons of torture or bondage, wounds and bruises, some clear humiliation, or an adult's sexual power being used over a child. It may be much more subtle: a physical attitude of conqueror and victim, the use of race or class difference to imply the same thing, perhaps a very unequal nudity, with one person exposed and vulnerable while the other is clothed. In either case, there is no sense of equal choice or equal power (p. 37).

In the studies described below, aggressive-pornography refers to depictions of sex that would be considered "blatantly" coercive by Steinem. By and large, these are portrayals in which physical force is either used or threatened to coerce a woman to engage in sexual acts; rape is one example. Conclusions and implications of the research findings concerning aggressive-pornography can therefore be applied only to such "blatant" materials at this point. Effects of materials that portray coercion more subtly have not been adequately researched yet.

The President's Commission and Aggressive-Pornography

In 1967, the United States Congress established the Commission on Obscenity and Pornography to conduct a thorough investigation of this issue. Based on several converging lines of evidence, the Commission concluded in its report (1970) that there was no evidence to support contentions that pornography has antisocial effects. When the Commission conducted its research studies, however, aggressive-pornographic materials were relatively infrequent. This may partially explain why the Commission's studies almost without exception did not include stimuli that involved rape or other forms of coercive

sexuality. The only Commission studies in which more than passing
attention was paid to such materials were retrospective surveys comparing the reports of sexual offenders, sexual deviants, and comparison groups from the general population regarding their previous exposure to pornography. These studies unfortunately yielded highly
conflicting conclusions (Goldstein et al. 1971; Davis and Braucht
1971).

Although aggressive-pornography was relatively rare in earlier
years, a number of recent articles in the general media (e.g., "The
Porno Plague" 1976; "Pretty Poison" 1977) and in pornography magazines (e.g., Thistle 1980) observed that aggression has become increasingly prevalent in sexually explicit books, magazines, and films
during the 1970s. More systematic content analyses generally corroborate these observations. For example, Smith (1976a, 1976b) analyzed
the content of "hard-core" paperback books published between 1968 and
1974. He found that in about one-third of the episodes force is used,
almost always by a male, to coerce a female to engage in an unwanted
act of sex. Furthermore, he found that the average number of acts
depicting rape doubled from 1968 to 1974. Similarly, Malamuth and
Spinner (1980) analyzed the pictorials and cartoons in *Playboy* and
Penthouse magazines. While throughout this five-year period about
10 percent of the cartoons were rated as sexually violent, a change
appeared in pictorials, with sexual violence increasing from 1 percent in 1973 to 5 percent in 1977.

Theoretical Concerns

There would appear to be ample reasons for concern about the
effects of aggressively-toned pornographic stimuli. To begin with,
the antisocial effects shown to result from non-sexual depictions of
aggression in the mass media (Eron 1982; Parke et al. 1977; Thomas
et al. 1977) would seem likely to also occur when the aggression is
presented within a sexual context. However, there are theoretical
reasons for being particularly concerned about the fusion of sexuality and aggression in the media (Malamuth and Spinner 1980). First,
the coupling of sex and aggression in these portrayals may result in
conditioning processes whereby aggressive acts become associated with
sexual arousal, a powerful unconditioned stimulus and reinforcer.
In fact, current treatments for sexual offenders (Abel et al. 1978;
Brownell et al. 1977; Hayes et al. 1978) are based on the premise
that conditioning may occur by associating fantasies of socially-sanc-
tioned arousal and behavior. It is also possible that the juxtaposi-
tion of media portrayals of aggression and sexuality could lead to
conditioning and thereby increase sexual arousal to aggressive stimuli, possibly leading to concomitant changes in fantasies and behavior.
Secondly, in aggressive-pornographic depictions the victim is frequently portrayed as secretly desiring the assault and as eventually deriving sexual pleasure from it (Malamuth 1980b; Smith 1976a, 1976b).
Such information may suggest that even if a woman seems repulsed by
a pursuer, she will eventually respond favorably to forceful advances,
aggression, and overpowering by a male assailant (Brownmiller 1975;
Johnson and Goodchilds 1973).

Many subjects may recognize the fictional nature of this type of
information. Still, research on the availability heuristic (Tversky
and Kahneman 1973) suggests that such depictions may nonetheless have
a significant impact (Hans 1980). According to the availability
heuristic concept, events that come relatively easily to mind are apt

to be regarded as likely to occur. An example of research supporting
this concept is a study by Carroll (1978). This investigator demonstrated that subjects who were asked to imagine an event that they
knew was totally fictional were more likely to believe the incident
would actually occur than subjects who were not instructed to imagine
its occurrence. Similar experiments conducted specifically to examine the impact of mass media (Holloway et al. 1977; Hornstein et
al. 1975) provided additional support for the utility of the availability heuristic concept. To the extent that the media presents
images of women as responding favorably to male aggression, such
images may easily come to people's minds and affect their beliefs,
attitudes, and behavior.

This chapter will now describe research on the effects of aggressive-pornographic stimuli. I will first discuss the degree to which
such materials stimulate sexual arousal. Next, I will consider the
effects on responses other than aggression (e.g., attitudes and perceptions). Finally, the findings of studies on the effects of aggressive-pornography on behavioral aggression will be discussed briefly.

SEXUAL AROUSAL TO AGGRESSIVE-PORNOGRAPHY

Rape Index

Abel and his associates (Abel et al. 1976, 1977, 1978a, 1978b,
1980) reported that rapists showed relatively high and about equal
levels of penile tumescence to audio-tapes portraying rape and consenting sexual acts. While there was some indication that the more
violent rapists were more aroused sexually by rape than by consenting
scenes (Abel et al. 1977), the conclusion about rapists in general
was that they were as equally aroused by rape as by mutually consenting depictions. In contrast, these studies found that nonrapists
showed relatively little sexual arousal to rape as compared with consenting depictions (both in self-report and tumescence measures).

On the basis of their findings, Abel et al. (1977) developed
the "rape index," which is a ratio of sexual arousal to rape divided
by arousal to consenting portrayals. They argued (see also Abel et
al. 1978a, 1978b, 1980) that this measure serves as an objective
index of a proclivity to rape. Accordingly, an individual who shows
similar or greater sexual arousal to rape than to consenting depictions would be considered to have an inclination to rape. These investigators and others have been using this measure to diagnose and
treat rapists and have recently extended it to child molesters by
contrasting sexual arousal to child molestation with arousal to adult
consenting depictions (Abel et al. 1981; Quinsey et al. 1980). Quinsey and colleagues provided some support for the predictive validity
of this assessment technique by showing that it predicted recidivism
following discharge from a psychiatric institution.

Mass Media and Sexual Violence

As noted above, the development of the "rape index" was based on
findings that nonrapists showed relatively little sexual arousal to
rape depictions. Such data appear to be inconsistent with earlier
citations which indicated that a substantial percentage of pornography
incorporates rape themes. It seems likely that publishers' decisions
to include such violent pornography in their publications is to some
degree a reflection of buyers' interests and gratifications. This
suggests that rape themes may be quite sexually arousing to many consumers of pornography, most of whom would probably not be actual

rapists.

To account for the differing conclusions regarding nonrapists'
sexual responsiveness to rape depictions, Malamuth et al. (1980b)
suggested that the type of sexual violence found in the mass media
may differ in content from that used in the research with rapists
and that certain types of rape depictions may be highly arousing to
some nonrapists. To assess this possibility empirically, they systematically manipulated the content of rape and consenting depictions
presented to college students. Their findings and those of subsequent experiments (Malamuth and Check 1980a, 1980b) implicated the
victim's reactions within rape scenes to be of critical importance:
rape depictions were found to stimulate relatively little sexual
arousal when the victim was portrayed as continuously abhorring the
assault; when the victim was perceived as becoming involuntarily
aroused sexually, on the other hand, sexual arousal to rape was as
high, and even tended to be nonsignificantly higher than arousal to
consenting depictions (see Malamuth and Check 1980a). These data
appear to help reconcile the conflicting conclusions described above
since both content analysis studies (e.g., Smith 1976b) and somewhat
less systematic observations (e.g., Brownmiller 1975) have noted that
rape portrayals in pornography frequently depict the victim as becoming aroused sexually when assaulted.

Individual Differences

While manipulations in the content of stimuli yielded information about the type of rape depictions that inhibit the sexual arousal
of nonrapists, previous research in this area has largely ignored the
potential mediating role of individual differences among subjects.
The classification of subjects into either a rapist or nonrapist
grouping may have obscured important information. Consideration of
individual differences among the nonrapist group seems particularly
necessary (although similar analyses examing individual differences
among rapists are needed) in light of theorizing (e.g., Clark
and Lewis 1977; Russell 1975) and research (e.g. Malamuth 1981b, 1984)
which suggest that within the nonincarcerated male population there
are men with inclinations to aggress against women.

Findings in this area are well illustrated in the recent data of
Malamuth and Check (1983). In a preliminary session, male subjects
were administered questionnaires concerning their sexual attitudes
and behaviors. One of the items inquired about the likelihood that
the subject himself would rape if he could be assured of not being
caught and punished (i.e., the Likelihood of Raping or LR item). On
the basis of this item, sixty-two subjects were classified as Low LR
(a rating of 1 = "not at all likely" on the 5-point scale). Forty-
two subjects were classified as High LR (a rating of 2 or higher).
This distribution is similar to that of other studies (Briere and
Malamuth 1983; Malamuth 1981a, 1981b; Malamuth, Haber and Feshbach
1980; Malamuth and Check 1980a; Tieger 1981).

Several days later, these subjects listened to one of eight
audio tapes of an interaction involving sexual acts between a man and
a woman. The content of these depictions was systematically manipulated along the dimensions of Consent (woman's consent vs. non-consent), Pain (woman's pain vs. no pain) and Outcome (woman's arousal
vs. disgust).

The data highlighted the importance of the interaction between
individual differences among subjects and variations in the depiction

content in affecting sexual arousal to rape portrayals. The pattern of data on both self-report and tumescence measures clearly indicated that when the woman was portrayed as experiencing disgust, both Low and High LR subjects were less aroused sexually by the non-consenting as compared with consenting depictions. However, when the woman was perceived as becoming aroused sexually, a very different pattern emerged: Low LR subjects were equally aroused to the consenting and the non-consenting depictions, whereas High LR subjects showed *greater* arousal to the non-consenting scenes.

These data suggest that current trends within the mass media may indeed reflect interest among some segments of consumers. The findings show that a sizeable minority of the population (i.e., High LR subjects) are more aroused to the type of rape depiction typically found in pornography (i.e., that portraying victim arousal) than to consenting portrayals. Future research should examine the cultural and individual reasons why some men are highly aroused sexually to certain types of rape depictions.

Validity of the Rape Index

As part of research assessing the construct validity (Cronbach and Meehl 1955) of the various measures used in this area of research, Malamuth (1982, 1983) examined the relationship between the "rape index" developed by Abel et al. (1977) and an objective measure of aggressive behavior. Approximately half of the subjects in these studies were male students and half were males from the general population. This research was conducted in two phases. In the first phase, the "rape index" was determined. The second phase was held several days later and subjects were completely unaware of the fact that this latter phase was related to the same research. This procedure was used to eliminate the possible role of "demand characteristics" (Orne 1962).

In the second phase, subjects were irritated by a confederate of the experimenter. Later, within the context of a bogus ESP study, they were given the opportunity of ostensibly punishing the person who had annoyed them with aversive noise and rewarding him or her with money. In the first experiment (Malamuth 1983), the confederate was female whereas in the later experiment (Malamuth 1982, 1984) either a male or female confederate interacted with a subject.

Both experiments showed that higher levels of sexual arousal to rape relative to arousal to consenting depictions (i.e., the "rape index") for the male subjects were predictive of higher aggression against women as measured by the levels of aversive noise and reward levels administered to the confederate. In other words, men who were more aroused sexually by rape depictions were also more aggressive against women. As expected, the "rape index" was not predictive of aggression against a male victim (Malamuth 1982). These data provide support for the construct validity of this index as a measure of aggressive tendencies against women.

In the next section I will summarize the research findings concerning the effects of exposure to aggressive-pornography. I will examine whether or not the data indicate that such exposure produces *changes* in a person's sexual responsiveness to aggressive-pornographic stimuli, fantasies, perceptions, attitudes, and aggressive behavior.

CHANGES INDUCED BY EXPOSURE TO AGGRESSIVE-PORNOGRAPHY

Sexual Responsiveness

There is little evidence at this time to indicate that exposure to aggressive-pornography increases a person's sexual responsiveness to such stimuli. A nonsignificant trend in one study (Malamuth et al. 1980a) suggested that if subjects first read a sadomasochistic portrayal, their subsequent reported sexual arousal to a rape scene presented shortly afterwards tended to be heightened. Later research, however, did not confirm this finding. Failure to find a sexual arousal enhancement effect of exposure to aggressive-pornography has occurred both with single presentations (Malamuth 1981b; Malamuth and Check 1980a, 1981b) as well as with repeated presentations over a period of several weeks with five aggressive-pornographic feature-length movies (Ceniti and Malamuth in press).

Fantasies

Only one experiment to date has examined the effects of aggressive-pornography on sexual fantasies (Malamuth 1981a). Subjects were presented with either rape or mutually-consenting-sex versions of a slide-audio show. All subjects were then exposed to the same audio description of a rape incident taken from Abel et al. (1977). Later in the same session, they were asked to create their own sexual fantasies. The results indicated that those exposed to the rape version of the slide-audio show created more aggressive-sexual fantasies than those exposed to the mutually-consenting-sex version.

Perceptions and Attitudes

There are considerable data indicating that exposure to aggressive-pornography may alter observers' perceptions of rape and of rape victims. In three experiments subjects were presented first with pornographic scenes in which aggression supposedly had "positive" consequences for the female victims (e.g., victim's sexual arousal) or with other depictions (e.g., a rape with victim abhorrence or a mutually-consenting scene). Afterwards, all of these subjects were given a different depiction of rape and asked to indicate their perceptions of the experiences of the victim. In two of these experiments (Malamuth et al. 1980a; Malamuth and Check 1980a), those exposed to the "positive" outcome version of the aggressive scene, in comparison to other subjects, thought the rape victim in the second portrayal had suffered less. The third experiment (Malamuth and Check 1981a) revealed effects on general perceptions about women.

In this third study, male undergraduates were first classified as Low vs. High LR on the basis of their responses to a questionnaire administered in a preliminary session. A laboratory session was held at a later date. In this latter session, subjects were randomly assigned to listen to audio-tapes that were systematically manipulated in their content along the dimensions of Consent (woman's consent vs. non-consent) and Outcome (woman's arousal vs. disgust). Later, subjects completed a questionnaire about their beliefs regarding the percentage of women, if any, that would derive some pleasure from being raped. While ethical questions may be raised concerning such questions, the fact that much research shows that such a myth is held by many individuals (e.g., Burt 1980; Malamuth et al. 1980a) and the use of a debriefing shown to be effective at counteracting such false beliefs (Malamuth and Check in press; Check and Malamuth in press; Donnerstein and Berkowitz 1981) may justify these inquiries within a research context.

The results indicated a main effect of Likelihood of Raping reports, with High LR subjects estimating much higher percentages of women enjoying being raped in comparison with Low LR subjects (M = 24.7 percent and *M* = 6.63 percent, respectively, *p*<.0001). In addition, an interaction effect was obtained between the Consent and Outcome content manipulations. Whereas the manipulation of Outcome (i. e., woman's arousal vs. woman's disgust) within the consenting portrayals had no impact on subjects' perceptions of women's reactions to rape, manipulations of the Outcome dimension within non-consenting depictions did significantly affect subjects' perceptions. However, further analyses indicated that this Outcome by Consent interaction primarily occurred with High LR subjects. Such subjects who listened to the "rape-woman's arousal" depiction believed that more women would enjoy being raped (mean of 36.9 percent) than High LR subjects presented with the "rape-woman's disgust" depiction (M = 20.0 percent, *p*<.008). As expected, manipulation of the Outcome dimension within the consenting-sex depictions had no impact on subjects' estimation of reactions to rape for either High LR subjects nor Low LR subjects. For Low LR subjects, the manipulation of Outcome within the rape depictions did not have a significant effect either, although the pattern of the means (10.6 percent for the arousal vs. 3.8 percent for the disgust depiction) was in the same direction as the significant differences obtained for High LR subjects. These data suggest that men who are already accepting of rape myths to a relatively high degree may be particularly susceptible to the influence of media depictions of such myths.

In contrast to the previously cited studies, Malamuth, Reisin, and Spinner (1979) found no evidence of changes in perceptions or in attitudes following exposure to aggressive-pornography. In this experiment, one group of male and female subjects looked at issues of *Penthouse* and *Playboy* magazines showing incidents of sadomasochism and rape. A second group examined issues of these magazines that contained only non-aggressive pornography and a third group was given only neutral materials. Shortly afterwards, subjects watched a videotaped interview with an actual victim of rape and responded to a questionnaire assessing their perceptions of the victim and her experience. Weeks later, in what was purported to be a general survey of public attitudes, subjects indicated their views on rape. Exposure to the aggressive-pornography did not affect perceptions of rape either in response to the videotaped interview with the rape victim or to the survey of attitudes.

One of the differences between this study and the three experiments that did show significant effects on perceptions of rape concerns the content of the materials used. In the three experiments in which antisocial effects were found, the aggressive-pornographic stimuli were specifically selected because they explicitly depicted violence against women as having "positive" consequences. Malamuth et al. (1979), on the other hand, used materials that generally did not show such "positive" outcomes. At least with respect to cognitive changes, therefore, the antisocial effects of aggressive-pornography may be limited to stimuli depicting "positive" consequences of sexual aggression.

In a field experiment, Malamuth and Check (1981b) obtained perhaps the strongest evidence to date to suggest that depictions of sexual aggression with "positive" consequences can affect social per-

ceptions and attitudes. Two hundred and seventy-one male and female
students served as subjects in this investigation. Some had agreed
to participate in a study ostensibly focusing on movie ratings. They
watched on two different evenings either (1) the movies *Swept Away*
and *The Getaway*, films that show women as victims of aggression within erotic as well as non-erotic incidents, or (2) neutral feature-
length movies. These movies were viewed in theatres on campus and
two of the films (i.e., one experimental and one control movie) were
being shown by the university as part of the campus film program.
Members of the classes from which subjects had been recruited but who
had not signed up for the experiment were also used as a comparison
group. The dependent measures were scales assessing acceptance of
interpersonal violence (AIV) against women, rape myth acceptance (RMA),
and beliefs in adversarial sexual relations (ASB). These measures
were embedded within many other items in a Sexual Attitude Survey administered to all students in classes several days after some of them
(i.e., those who had signed up for the experiment) had been exposed
to the movies. Subjects were not aware that there was any relationship between this survey and the movies.

Results indicated that exposure to films portraying aggressive
sexuality as having "positive" consequences increased significantly
male but not female subjects' acceptance of interpersonal violence
against women and tended to increase males' acceptance of rape myths.
These data demonstrated, in a non-laboratory setting and thus not vulnerable to criticisms of laboratory artificiality and "demand characteristics," that there can be relatively long-term antisocial effects
of movies that portray sexual violence as having "positive" consequences.

There is also recent evidence that "heavy dosages" of exposure
to sexual violence, even if "positive" consequences are not portrayed,
may result in negative effects. Donnerstein and Linz (1984) found
that exposure to ten hours of sexually violent films caused male subjects to perceive the consequences of rape in a reenacted rape trial
as less severe. This effect may have been due to a desensitization
to violence resulting from the high levels of media exposure to sexual
violence.

Aggressive Behavior

A number of studies examined the effects of viewing aggressive-
pornography on males' aggression. These experiments used the "Buss"
paradigm (Buss 1961) in which the delivery of aversive stimuli (e.g.,
electric shock, noise) to the confederate of the experimenter constitutes the operational definition of aggression. The data show that
aggressive-pornography increases aggressive behavior against female
but not male targets, in comparison to exposure to neutral, non-por-
nographic-aggressive (e.g., a man hitting a woman) and non-aggressive-
pornographic (e.g., mutually-consenting sex) media stimuli (Donnerstein 1980, 1983, 1984; Donnerstein and Berkowitz 1981; Malamuth 1978).
Interestingly, non-pornographic films that portrayed aggression
against women were found to increase the levels of aggression against
female victims, although to a lesser degree than aggressive-pornographic scenes (Donnerstein 1980).

Increased aggression against female victims following the viewing of aggressive-pornography was found both with subjects who were
first angered by the confederate as well as non-angered subjects, although the increase tended to be greater for angered subjects (Donner-

stein and Berkowitz 1981). Interesting differences between the effects of aggressive-pornography on angered as compared to non-angered
subjects emerged when the outcome of the aggression was systematically manipulated in a manner similar to the experiments described
earlier (i.e., "positive" vs. negative victim reaction). It was
found that a negative ending to an aggressive-pornographic film did
not increase aggression for non-angered subjects. In constrast, when
the victim's reaction was portrayed as "positive," a very clear increase in aggression was found for both angered and non-angered subjects (Donnerstein and Berkowitz 1981). These data may be interpreted
to suggest that "positive" victim reactions (those that are, as noted
earlier, very common in aggressive-pornography) may act to justify aggression and to reduce general inhibitions against aggression. The
portrayal of negative victim reactions, on the other hand, may inhibit
the aggression of non-angered subjects but may fail to restrain the
increased violence of individuals in a state of anger or who are particularly inclined to aggress against women for other reasons (Donnerstein and Berkowitz 1981).

PREVENTION AND FUTURE RESEARCH

The overall pattern of the data across the various laboratory and
field experiments discussed in this chapter strongly supports the assertion that the mass media can contribute to a cultural climate that
is more accepting of aggression against women. This is not to suggest
that the mass media is the most, or even one of the most, powerful influences in this area. Rather, it may be one of the many factors
that interact to affect responses. The nature of the effects and the
degree of influence may depend, among other things, on the background
of the person exposed to the media stimuli and the sociocultural context in which exposure takes place.

If a point is reached at which we conclude that the weight of
the evidence is sufficiently compelling to justify social action to
bring about changes in the content of the mass media, how can this
be accomplished? We should be cognizant of the reality that demonstrating scientifically the existence of socially important negative
effects is unlikely to be sufficient to prompt changes when there are
strong economic and structural-institutional factors that resist such
changes. This is aptly documented in discussions of the limited success of attempts to bring about modifications in media content based
on research on the negative effects of television violence (Siegel
1980) and of children's advertising (Choate 1980).

There are a variety of strategies that may be used to introduce
changes in media content. I will discuss legal, political-economic,
and educational options, approaches that are by no means mutually
exclusive. Efforts at each of these levels are likely to be necessary
to bring about long-lasting changes. I would like to note, however,
that my primary intent here is not to advocate specific changes or
particular strategies. As an investigator conducting research in an
area relevant to social policy decisions, I believe that it is important to explore such policy options in order to highlight issues that
merit further research. Since the primary focus of the research reviewed in this chapter dealt with sexually explicit stimuli, the emphasis in the discussion that follows will also be on such media.

Legal Approach

The use of legal censorship to ban aggressive-pornography has been suggested by some (e.g., Russell 1980) although censorship is generally not advocated even by organized women's groups against pornography (e.g., Brownmiller 1980). From the researcher's perspective, it is important to consider what types of scientific evidence may be relevant to such legal measures.

In order to make a legal case in the United States for restricting the production and distribution of certain types of pornographic materials on the basis of their harmful effects, it would probably be necessary to demonstrate that such media stimuli are "... soliciting men to commit crimes of violence" (Yeamans 1980, p. 250) or that they present a "clear and present danger" (Kaminer 1980). As Kaminer points out, such a position would require the demonstration of a relationship between aggressive-pornography at the individual rather than the social level. It would be necessary to show that the individuals were incited directly to commit crimes by such media stimuli rather than demonstrating the possibility that such materials can affect various aggression-related responses, that cumulative effects may occur or that there is an impact on the general cultural climate.

The tools of social scientific research are unlikely to enable an adequate analysis of such a direct and immediate impact of aggressive-pornographic stimuli, whether one does or does not exist. For the researcher, however, this issue highlights the need to address more systematically the relationship between individuals' characteristics and the impact of aggressive-pornography as well as the possible influence of such stimuli on those who actually commit illegal acts. It is important in future research to assess the effects of aggressive tendencies, familial experiences with violence and male-female power relations, hostility toward women, previous pornography exposure, sex role stereotyping, and sexual experiences.

In concluding their discussion of research on the effects of mass media violence on children's aggression, Parke and colleagues (1977) stress the need to address the question, "How does this influence occur in naturalistic settings?" A similar emphasis is needed in research on aggressive-pornography. While laboratory experiments provide a useful framework for determining whether aggressive-pornography *can* affect aggressive tendencies (Berkowitz and Donnerstein 1982), there is a need at this point to extend the examination of influences that mass media stimuli may have on various individuals in naturalistic settings. To accomplish this goal it will be necessary to employ a multi-method approach including correlational analyses using statistical controls as well as laboratory and field experiments. An example of such a correlational study is that of Baron and Strays (1984), which analyzed the relationship between amount of readership of pornography magazines (e.g., *Playboy, Hustler*, etc.) in the 50 states of the United States and rape rates in those states. They found a strong association with higher pornography consumption correlated with higher rape crimes.

We need to obtain survey data regarding the use of aggressive and other types of pornography by differing subject populations. These data should be gathered in the context of developing theoretical models concerning the motivations for seeking such media stimuli (i.e.,

uses and gratifications) as well as concerning the effects of exposure. The development of models will require information not only
about pornography consumption, but about other aspects of the person.
The testing of these models may require experimental research to measure impact over long time periods of differing "dosages" of aggressive-pornography in the context of other media stimuli. "Causal"
modeling (Bentler 1980) may prove particularly useful in testing aspects of theoretical models not amenable to experimental manipulations (e.g., the hypothesis that childhood experiences mediate the
impact of pornography).

Political-Economic Approach
Two contrasting tactical strategies may be described within the
political-economic approach. The first might be termed "cooperative
consultation" with media industry whereas the second might be labelled
as a "pressure-confrontation" strategy.
Cooperative Consultation. Breed and De Foe (1982) reported recently successful attempts to affect media content. While to some
their efforts seem a viable model for changing media portrayals affecting aggression against women, others may consider it an unsuitable
model. These investigators reported the results of a concerted effort
to change the portrayal of alcohol drinking on television by using
"cooperative consultation." This involved working with writers and
producers in a consulting role in which changes were suggested by the
social scientists but no political or other forms of pressure were
exerted.
As Breed and De Foe note, one of the key factors that enabled
these investigators to obtain cooperation by media personnel was the
noncontroversiality of the topic in question. The media people were
sympathetic to combating alcoholism or alcohol abuse and there was no
indication that they believed that their cooperation would have ad-
verse effects on the ratings. The noncontroversial nature of the portrayal of alcohol stands in marked contrast to the highly controversial nature of the effects of pornography. Nonetheless, there may
be areas, such as in dealing with "blatant" forms of aggressive-pornography, where an "advisory" approach to media producers may result
in voluntary restrictions in the use of such stimuli. This approach
is likely to be effective if the media producers do not believe that
the use of aggressive forms of pornography are germane to economic
success.
Pressure-Confrontation. Organized groups have had some success
in using political and economic pressure tactics (e.g., boycotting of
sponsors, demonstrations) to bring about changes in media portrayals.
This occurred in areas such as sexist advertising and violent television programming (Butler and Paisley 1980), as well as in aggressive-
pornography. In fact, throughout North America there are women's
groups that have among their primary purposes the monitoring and protesting of media portrayals of violence against women. Such organizations have claimed success in many instances (e.g., LaBelle 1980;
Gever and Hall 1980). It should be noted that some of these organizations focus their protests exclusively against media portrayals of
violence against women whereas in other instances they have also pro-
tested pornographic depictions in general.
The choice between "cooperative consultation" or a "pressure-
confrontation" tactic of exerting political and economic influence
will to a large degree depend on whether those protesting the media

portrayals believe that there is a fundamental clash between their
goals and those of the media producers. If the protest is directed
at the very existence of the industry (e.g., pornography, then it
would seem that a "cooperative" approach is essentially useless. If,
however, the protest is directed against a specific aspect of the
media content (e.g., "blatant" depictions of aggressive-pornography)
then the cooperative approach may be more relevant. For example, a
cooperative approach might be used to work with magazine producers
such as *Playboy* to eliminate the depictions of "blatant" sexual aggression. As noted earlier, the content analysis conducted by Malamuth and Spinner (1980) suggested that although the frequency of such
aggressive depictions showed some increase, they remained relatively
low. It may well be that the publishers of *Playboy* would be amenable
to eliminating any aggressive depictions of this nature. (It may be
relevant to note that even prior to the actual publication of this
content analysis, the publishers of *Playboy* requested a copy from the
authors.) However, if the protest is addressed to the very existence
of a magazine such as *Playboy* that, according to various writers, objectify and dehumanize women (e.g., Brownmiller 1980), then a cooperative approach is clearly unsuitable.

For the researcher, the above discussion clearly points to the
need to investigate systematically the type of pornographic stimuli
that may have antisocial effects. The aggressive-pornographic stimuli
used in the research discussed in this chapter fall, as noted earlier,
into the "blatantly" coercive category according to the distinctions
suggested by Steinem (1980). Are the effects limited to such materials, or might similar effects be obtained with stimuli that more
subtly or indirectly portray unequal power relations between males
and females? In other words, is there a clear distinction to be made
between aggressive and non-aggressive pornography, or is it more accurate to distinguish sexually explicit stimuli that place emphasis on
"shared pleasure" (Steinem 1980) from aggressive-pornography that
varies on a continuum of blatancy? Future research should also assess
the impact of sexual materials that portray unequal power relations
between males and females without the explicit depiction of aggression.

The importance of assessing the impact of pornographic depictions
that are not blatantly aggressive is underscored by the recent findings of Zillmann and Bryant (1984). These investigators conducted
an experiment on the effects of "massive" exposure to pornography over
a period of nine weeks. The pornography consisted of unedited commercially available short films which did not generally include violence.
Nonetheless, the results showed that exposure to such pornography resulted in more calloused attitudes towards rape and a general triviali-
zation of the exposure phase of the research.

A related question concerns the type of aggressive-sexual stimuli
that are most likely to cause antisocial effects. The increased acceptance of aggression against women found by Malamuth and Check
(1981b) occurred following exposure to movies that have been shown on
national television and were clearly not x-rated pornographic films.
Moreover, the primary theme of the films was not aggressive sexuality.
It may be that a film that is explicitly pornographic is perceived as
highly unrealistic and stimulates subjects' defenses against accepting
the information conveyed uncritically. In contrast, the type of film
used by these investigators may communicate more subtly false information about women's reactions to sexual aggression and thus may have a

more potent effect on viewers who are not "forewarned" (Freedman and Sears 1965) by the label "x-rated" or "pornographic." Similarly, the portrayal of sexual aggression within such "legitimate" magazines as *Playboy* or *Penthouse* may have a greater impact than similar portrayals in hard-core pornography. Research is needed that examines specifically the impact of the context within which aggressive-pornography appears.

Educational Approach
There has recently been growing interest in educational interventions to modify the impact of the mass media on the audience (e.g., Doolittle 1976; Singer et al. 1980). With respect to the media and aggression against women, there are varied educational endeavors that could prove effective. These may be analyzed along two dimensions: (1) indirect vs. direct, and (2) individual vs. mass.
    Indirect vs. Direct. Indirect educational interventions do not address specifically the content of media depictions but deal with topics or issues that may reduce a person's vulnerability to undesirable media influence. For example, a general sex education program may make a participant sufficiently knowledgeable that he/she would be less likely to be influenced by myths depicted in media. Such educational programs should teach about similarities and differences in male-female responses, sex role rigidity and role alternatives, differences in males' and females' interpretations of various "signals" (Abbey 1982), and communication skills. The study by Malamuth and Check (1981a) discussed earlier, which suggested that some men (those already more accepting of violence against women) may be more susceptible to media portrayals of rape myths, may provide a starting point for exploring systematically, differences in educational backgrounds that affect vulnerability to media influences.
    Another example of indirect educational efforts is the creation of positive alternatives to aggressive-pornography. Scandinavian sexologists, Drs. Phyllis and Erberhard Kronhausen, produced a feature length "x-rated" film entitled *The Hottest Show in Town* which was shown in regular "adult" theatres throughout North America. This movie was designed to portray sex in a manner much more akin to the desirable erotica advocated by Steinem (1980), cited earlier in this chapter. Ironically, this movie was shown in "adult" theatres as part of a double feature with such films as *Femmes de Sade*, which focused on sado-masochistic relations between women. Nonetheless, it may be that the availability of "desirable erotica" that portrayed "shared pleasure" (Steinem 1980) could indirectly counteract the impact of aggressive-pornography by providing an alternative to those seeking sexual stimulation via media depictions.
    In contrast to indirect approaches, direct educational interventions would address specifically the myths portrayed in the media. Some recent research in this area (Donnerstein and Berkowitz 1981; Malamuth and Check, in press; Check and Malamuth, in press) consisted of presenting subjects with information designed to dispel rape myths. This information was presented to subjects with information designed to dispel rape myths. This information was presented to subjects who were first exposed to aggressive-pornography portraying rape myths as well as to subjects who were not first exposed to such pornography. Assessment of the effectiveness of such educational interventions was conducted as long as four months following research participation (Donnerstein and Berkowitz 1981) and without subjects' awareness that

this assessment was related to the earlier exposure to the educational materials (Malamuth and Check, in press; Check and Malamuth, in
press). The findings of these studies indicated consistently that
the educational interventions were successful in counteracting the
effects of aggressive-pornography and in reducing beliefs in rape
myths. These studies, however, can only be construed as a first step
in an area that requires considerable additional work
       Individual vs. Mass. Educational interventions may be designed
for individuals judged particularly likely to benefit from such interventions or to mass audiences not selected on any individual basis.
Educational programs geared to individuals who have already committed
crimes such as rape (Burt 1978) are clearly desirable. It may be
ethically questionable, however, to select individuals who have not
come to the attention of the law, but who according to attitude surveys and self-reported inclinations to aggress against women may be
particularly susceptible to media and other influences (Malamuth and
Check, 1981a). Ethical concerns arise because such selection for
educational programs may result in undesirable labels applied to the
participants.
       There is, however, clearly a need for the development of educa-
tional interventions that can be applied to individuals. For example,
educational guidelines should be developed that would help parents
to explain aggressive-pornography and related media portrayals to
both girls and boys. Such efforts may be somewhat facilitated by
parental guidelines for dealing with violence in other areas of the
media (e.g., Singer et al. 1980).
       Educational efforts addressing mass audiences are well exempli-
fied by recent media programs (documentaries, docu-dramas, and fictional drama) concerning topics such as rape and rape myths (e.g.,
Cry Rape, *Why Men Rape*, *A Scream of Silence*) and aggressive-pornography (e.g., *Not a Love Story*). These programs were designed to raise
the viewers' consciousness about these issues. Such programs may be
important in affecting large segments of the population and thereby
contribute to a cultural climate that is less accepting of aggression
against women. However, trying to reach a large audience without
tailoring the information to particular individuals may result in un-
intended and undesirable effects. For example, such films may include segments showing explicit sexual depictions and rape scenes.
These may be sexually stimulating to some members of the audience.
Such arousal may interfere with the attitude changes sought by the
film's producers. Similarly, such education films may include interviews with rapists or other men who express rape myths. In light of
research indicating that selective processing of information may lead
viewers to strengthen their preexisting beliefs if some supportive
information is presented, even when information contrary to their beliefs is emphasized (Lord et al. 1979), it is essential to investigate
the impact of such media programs. In this area as well as with other
educational endeavors described above, there is a clear need for research designed to improve the development of a program and for research concerned with judging the overall effectiveness of a developed
program.
       On a final note, in this chapter I pointed to the need for addi-
tional research in several areas. While social scientific research
in and of itself will not bring about major social changes, I firmly
believe that there is an important role for the researcher in pro-

viding scientific data that will aid those engaged in political, economic, and educational efforts to prevent aggression against women.

REFERENCES

Abbey, A. "Sex Differences in Attributions for Friendly Behavior: Do Males Misperceive Females' Friendliness?" *Journal of Personality and Social Psychology* 2 (1982): 830-838.

Abel, G.G., D.H. Barlow, E. Blanchard, and D. Guild. "The Components of Rapists' Sexual Arousal." *Archives of General Psychiatry* 34 (1977): 895-903.

Abel, G.G., J. Becker, W. Murphy, and B. Flanagan. "Identifying Dangerous Child Molesters." In *Violent Behavior: Social Learning Approaches to Prediction Management and Treatment*, edited by R.B. Stuart. New York: Brunner-Mazel, 1981.

Abel, G.G., J.V. Becker, and L.J. Skinner. "Aggressive Behavior and Sex." *Psychiatric Clinics of North America* 3 (1980): 133-151.

Abel, G.G., E.B. Blanchard, and J.V. Becker. "An Integrated Program for Rapists." In *Clinical Aspects of the Rapist*, edited by R. Rada. New York: Grune & Stratton, 1978a.

Abel, G.G., E.B. Blanchard, and J.V. Becker. "Psychological Treatment of Rapists." In *Sexual Assault: The Victim and the Rapist*, edited by M. Walker and S. Brodsky. Lexington, Massachusetts: Lexington Books, 1976.

Baron, L., and M.A. Strays. "Sexual Stratification, Pornography, and Rape in American States." In *Pornography and Sexual Aggression*, edited by N.M. Malamuth and E.I. Donnerstein. New York: Academic Press, 1984.

Barry, K. *Female Sexual Slavery*. Englewood Cliffs, N.J.: Prentice-Hall, 1979.

Bentler, P.M. "Multivariate Analysis with Latent Variables: Causal Modeling." *Annual Review of Psychology* 31 (1980): 419-456.

Berkowitz, L., and E. Donnerstein. "External Validity Is More Than Skin Deep: Some Answers to Criticisms of Laboratory Experiments with Special Reference to Research on Aggression." *American Psychologist* 37 (1981): 245-257.

Breed, W., and J.R. De Foe. "Effecting Media Change: The Role of Cooperative Consultation on Alcohol Topics." *Journal of Communication* 32 (1982): 88-99.

Brière, J., and N.M. Malamuth. "Self-reported Likelihood of Sexually Aggressive Behavior: Attitudinal Versus Sexual Explanations." *Journal of Research in Personality* 17 (1983): 315-323.

Brown, B.C. *Images of Family Life in Magazine Advertising*. New York: Praeger, 1981.

Brownell, K.D., S.C. Hayes, and D.H. Barlow. "Patterns on Appropriate and Deviant Sexual Arousal: The Behavioral Treatment of Multiple Sexual Deviations." *Journal of Consulting and Clinical Psychology* 45 (1977): 1144-1155.

Brownmiller, S. *Against Our Will: Men, Women and Rape.* New York: Simon and Schuster, 1975.

Brownmiller, S. "Let's Put Pornography Back in the Closet." In *Take Back the Night: Women on Pornography*, edited by L. Lederer. New York: William Morrow and Co., 1980.

Burt, M.R. "Attitudes Supportive of Rape in American Culture." *House Committee on Science and Technology, Subcommittee Domestic and International Scientific Planning Analysis and Cooperation, Research into Violent Behavior: Sexual Assaults* (Hearing, 95th Congress, 2nd session, January 10-12, 1978). Washington, D.C.: Government Printing Office, 1978, pp. 277-322.

Burt, M.R. "Cultural Myths and Supports for Rape." *Journal of Personality and Social Psychology* 38 (1980): 217-230.

Buss, A. *The Psychology of Aggression.* New York: Wiley, 1961.

Butler, M., and W. Paisley. *Women and the Mass Media: Sourcebook for Research and Action.* New York: Human Sciences Press, 1980.

Carroll, J.S. "The Effect of Imagining an Event on Expectations for the Event: An Interpretation in Terms of the Availability Heuristic." *Journal of Experimental Social Psychology* 14 (1978): 88-96.

Ceniti, J., and N.M. Malamuth. "Effects of Repeated Exposure to Sexually Violent and Sexually Nonviolent Stimuli on Sexual Arousal to Rape Depictions." *Behavior Research and Therapy* (in press).

Check, J.V.P., and N.M. Malamuth. "Can Participation in Pornography Experiments Have Positive Effects?" *Journal of Sex Research* (in press).

Choate, R.B. "The Politics of Change." In *Children and the Faces of Television*, edited by E.L. Palmer and A. Dorr. New York: Academic Press, 1980.

Clark, L., and D. Lewis. *Rape: The Price of Coercive Sexuality.* Toronto, Canada: The Women's Press, 1977.

Commission on Obscenity and Pornography. *The Report of the Commission on Obscenity and Pornography.* New York: Bantam Books, 1970.

Cronbach, L.J., and P. Meehl. "Construct Validity in Psychological Tests." *Psychological Bulletin* 52 (1955): 281-302.

Davis, K.E., and G.N. Braucht. "Exposure to Pornography, Character and Sexual Deviance: A Retrospective Survey." *Technical Reports of the Commission on Obscenity and Pornography*, vol. 7. Washington, D.C.: U.S. Government Printing Office, 1971.

Donnerstein, E.I. "Aggressive-Erotica and Violence Against Women." *Journal of Personality and Social Psychology* 39 (1980): 269-277.

Donnerstein, E.I., "Erotica and Human Aggression." In *Aggression: Theoretical and Empirical Reviews. Vol. 2*, edited by R.G. Green and E.I. Donnerstein. New York: Academic Press, 1983.

Donnerstein, E.I. "Pornography: Its Effect on Violence Against Women." In *Pornography and Sexual Aggression*, edited by N.M. Malamuth and E.I. Donnerstein. New York: Academic Press, 1984,

Donnerstein, E.I., and L. Berkowitz. "Victim Reactions in Aggressive-Erotic Films as a Factor in Violence Against Women." *Journal of Personality and Social Psychology* 41 (1981): 710-724.

Donnerstein, E.I., and D. Linz. "Sexual Violence in the Media: A Warning." *Psychology Today* 18 (1984): 14-15.

Eron, L.D. "Parent-Child Interaction, Television Violence and Aggression of Children." *American Psychologist* 37 (1982): 197-211.

Freedman, J., and D. Sears. "Warning, Distraction and Resistance to Influence." *Journal of Personality and Social Psychology* 1 (1965): 262-266.

Gever, M., and M. Hall. "Fighting Pornography." In *Take Back the Night: Women on Pornography*, edited by L. Lederer. New York: William Morriw and Co., 1980.

Goffman, E. *Gender Advertisments*. Cambridge, Massachusetts: Harvard University Press, 1979.

Goldstein, M.J., H.S. Kant, L.L. Judd, C.J. Rice, and R. Green. "Exposure to Pornography and Sexual Behavior in Deviant and Normal Groups." *Technical Reports of the Commission on Obscenity and Pornography*, vol. 7. Washington, D.C.: U.S. Government Printing Office, 1971.

Hans, V.P. *Pornography and Feminism: Empirical Evidence and Directions for Research*. Paper presented at the American Psychological Association. Montreal, Canada, September, 1980.

Hayes, S.C., K.D. Brownell, and D.H. Barlow. "The Use of Self-Administered Covert Sensitization in the Treatment of Exhibitionism and Sadism." *Behavior Therapy* 9 (1978): 283-289.

Holloway, S., L. Tucker, and H. Hornstein. "The Effects of Social and Nonsocial Information on Interpersonal Behavior of Males: The News Makes News." *Journal of Personality and Social Psychology* 35 (1977): 514-522.

Hornstein, H.A., E. LaKind, G. Frankel, and S. Manne. "Effects of Knowledge About Remote Social Events on Prosocial Behavior, Social Conception, and Mood." *Journal of Personality and Social Psychology* 32 (1975): 1039-1046.

Johnson, P., and J. Goodchilds. "Pornography, Sexuality, and Social Psychology." *Journal of Social Issues* 29 (1973): 231-238.

Kaminer, W. "Pornography and the First Amendment: Prior Restraints and Private Action." In *Take Back the Night: Women on Pornography*, edited by L. Lederer. New York: William Morrow and Co., 1980.

Labelle, B. "Snuff--The Ultimate in Woman-Hating." In *Take Back the Night: Women on Pornography*, edited by L. Lederer. New York: William Morrow and Co., 1980.

Longino, H.E. "Pornography, Oppression and Freedom: A Closer Look." In *Take Back the Night: Women on Pornography*, edited by L. Lederer. New York: William Morrow and Co., 1980.

Lord, C.G., L. Ross, and M.R. Lepper. "Biased Assimilation and Attitude to Polarization: The Effects of Prior Theories on Subsequently
Considered Evidence." *Journal of Personality and Social Psychology*
37 (1979): 2098-2109.

Lowry, D.T., G. Love, and M. Kirby. "Sex on the Soap Operas: Patterns
of Intimacy." *Journal of Communication* 31 (1981): 90-96.

Malamuth, N.M. "Aggression Against Women: Cultural and Individual
Causes." In *Pornography and Sexual Aggression*, edited by N.M. Malamuth
and E.I. Donnerstein. New York: Academic Press, 1984.

Malamuth, N.M. *Erotica, Aggression and Perceived Appropriateness.*
Paper presented at the Annual Meetings of the American Psychological
Association. Toronto, Canada, September, 1978.

Malamuth, N.M. "Factors Associated with Rape as Predictors of Laboratory Aggression Against Women." *Journal of Personality and Social
Psychology* 45 (1983): 432-442.

Malamuth, N.M. *Predictors of Aggression Against Female as Compared
to Male Targets of Aggression.* Paper presented at the Annual Meetings of the American Psychological Association. Washington, D.C.,
1982.

Malamuth, N.M. "Rape Fantasies as a Function of Exposure to Violent
Sexual Stimuli." *Archives of Sexual Behavior* 10 (1981a): 33-47.

Malamuth, N.M. "Rape Proclivity Among Males." *Journal of Social
Issues* 37 (1981b): 138-157.

Malamuth, N.M., and J.V.P. Check. "Debriefing Effectiveness Following
Exposure to Pornographic Rape Depictions." *Journal of Sex Research*
(in press).

Malamuth, N.M., and J.V.P. Check. *The Effects of Exposure to Aggres-
sive-Pornography: Rape Proclivity, Sexual Arousal and Beliefs in
Rape Myths.* Paper presented at the Annual Meetings of the American
Psychological Association. Los Angeles, California, 1981a.

Malamuth, N.M., and J.V.P. Check. "The Effects of Mass Media Exposure
on Acceptance of Violence Against Women: A Field Experiment."
Journal of Research in Personality 15 (1981b): 436-446.

Malamuth, N.M., and J.V.P. Check. *Factors Related to Aggression
Against Women.* Paper presented at the Annual Meetings of the
Canadian Psychological Association. Montreal, 1982.

Malamuth, N.M., and J.V.P. Check. "Penile Tumescence and Perceptual
Responses to Rape as a Function of Victim's Perceived Reactions."
Journal of Applied Social Psychology 10 (1980a): 528-547.

Malamuth, N.M., and J.V.P. Check. "Sexual Arousal to Rape and Consenting Depictions: The Importance of the Woman's Arousal." *Journal of Abnormal Psychology* 89 (1980b): 763-766.

Malamuth, N.M., and J.V.P. Check. "Sexual Arousal to Rape Depictions:
Individual Differences." *Journal of Abnormal Psychology* 92 (1983):
55-67.

Malamuth, N.M., S. Haber, and S. Feshbach. "Testing Hypotheses Regarding Rape: Exposure to Sexual Violence, Sex Differences, and the "Normality" of Rapists." *Journal of Research in Personality* 14 (1980a): 121-137.

Malamuth, N.M, M. Heim, and S. Feshbach. "Sexual Responsiveness of College Students to Rape Depictions: Inhibitory and Disinhibitory Effects." *Journal of Personality and Social Psychology* 38 (1980b): 399-408.

Malamuth, N.M., I. Reisin, and B. Spinner. *Exposure to Pornography and Reactions to Rape.* Paper presented at the Annual Meetings of the American Psychological Association. New York, 1979.

Malamuth, N.M., and B. Spinner. "A Longitudinal Content Analysis of Sexual Violence in the Best-Selling Erotic Magazines." *The Journal of Sex Research* 16 (1980): 3, 226-237.

Morgan, R. *Going Too Far.* New York: Vintage Books, 1978.

Orne, M. "On the Social Psychology of the Psychological Experiment: With Particular Reference to Demand Characteristics and Their Implications." *American Psychologist* 17 (1962): 776-783.

Parke, R.D., L. Berkowitz, J.P. Leyens, S.G. West, and R.J. Sebastian. "Some Effects of Violent and Non-Violent Movies on the Behavior of Juvenile Delinquents." In *Advances in Experimental Social Psychology*, edited by L. Berkowitz. New York: Academic Press, 1977.

"The Porno Plague." *Time*, 5 April 1976, pp. 58-63.

"Pretty Poison: The Selling of Sexual Warfare." *Village Voice*, 9 May 1977, pp. 18-23.

Quinsey, V.L., T.C. Chaplin, and W.F. Carrigan. "Biofeedback and Signaled Punishment in the Modification of Inappropriate Sexual Age Preferences." *Behavior Therapy* 11 (1980): 567-576.

Russell, D. *The Politics of Rape.* New York: Stein & Day, 1975.

Russell, D. "Pornography and the Women's Liberations Movement." In *Take Back the Night: Women on Pornography*, edited by L. Lederer. New York: Wiliam Morrow and Co., 1980.

Siegel, A.E. "Research Findings and Social Policy." In *Children and the Faces of Television*, edited by E.L. Palmer and A. Dorr. New York: Academic Press, 1980.

Singer, D.G., J.L. Singer, and D.M. Zuckerman. *Teaching Television: How to Use TV to Your Child's Advantage.* New York: Dial Press, 1980.

Smith, D.G. *Sexual Aggression in American Pornography: The Stereotype of Rape.* Paper presented at the Annual Meetings of the American Sociological Association. New York City, 1976a.

Smith, D.G. "The Social Content of Pornography." *Journal of Communication* 26 (1976b): 16-33.

Steinem, G. "Erotica and Pornography: A Clear and Present Difference." In *Take Back the Night: Women on Pornography*, edited by L. Lederer. New York: William Morrow and Co., 1980.

Thistle, F. "Hollywood Goes Ape Over Rape." *Game 7* (1980): 23-25, 84.

Thomas, M.H., R.W. Horton, E.C. Lippencott, and R.S. Drabman. "Desensitization to Portrayals of Real-Life Aggression as a Function of Exposure to Television Violence." *Journal of Personality and Social Psychology* 35 (1977): 450-458.

Tieger, T. "Self-Reported Likelihood of Raping and the Social Perception of Rape." *Journal of Research in Personality* 15 (1981): 147-158.

Tversky, A., and D. Kahneman. "Availability: A Heuristic for Judging Frequency and Probability." *Cognitive Psychology* 5 (1973): 207-232.

Yeamans, R. "A Political-Legal Analysis of Pornography." In *Take Back the Night: Women on Pornography*, edited by L. Lederer. New York: William Morrow and Co., 1980.

Zillmann, D., and J. Bryant. "Effects of Massive Exposure to Pornography." In *Pornography and Sexual Aggression*, edited by N. Malamuth and E. Donnerstein. New York: Academic Press, 1984.

CHAPTER 25

THE PREVENTION OF RAPE

Carolyn F. Swift

Prevention in the health field is an idea whose time has come (Klein and Goldston 1977). Prevention theory is also alive and well in a variety of behavioral applications (Cowen 1982; Heber and Garber 1975; Spivack and Shure 1973; United States President's Commission on Mental Health 1978). But in the field of sexual assault, primary prevention is an idea that has never been tested. This paper outlines the application of primary prevention concepts to rape, reviews activities traditionally cited as preventive for this field, and evaluates research bearing on the effectiveness of these activities. Rape and sexual assault are used interchangeably to refer to sexual activity in which the person attacked is coerced or pressured into participation.

While services to rape victims have increased in quantity and improved in quality in the last decade, no such breakthrough has been achieved in preventing sexual assault. There is no indication that increased consciousness about the crime of rape has reduced the number of rapes that occur. Conventionally, prevention of rape has focused on altering the behavior of the victim. Through proscriptions of behavior resulting in vulnerability to attack (e.g., don't go out alone at night, don't walk through parks alone, don't leave car doors unlocked), women are cautioned to restrict their activities to make themselves less accessible to rapists. Few efforts have been directed to preventing the development of the behavior of rape in males. Conventional efforts have identified the rapist after the fact and focused efforts on treatment at that point.

Primary prevention is first defined, below, and the appropriate target for rape prevention efforts discussed. The next section reviews the findings of epidemiological research on rape. This is followed by a review of rape prevention activities, with an emphasis on strategies aimed at systems change. Activities considered include legislation, law enforcement policies and practices, skill training, educational interventions, and media strategies.

Prevention means to stop something from happening. In the health field, primary prevention refers to activities that reduce the number of new cases of a disorder (incidence) in a population. The prevalence of a disorder refers to the total number of cases in the population. Prevalence includes new cases as well as cases of long standing. Prevalence is a function of both the rate of production of new cases and the duration of the disorder. Two ways of reducing prevalence, then, are to reduce incidence and reduce duration. Reducing duration through early case finding and treatment are activities classified as secondary prevention. Prevention in this paper refers to primary prevention.

THE TARGET OF PREVENTION EFFORTS: STRESSOR OR HOST?

Golda Meier outlined the parameters of this controversy in her challenge to the Israeli Parliament (Bart 1980). In response to a wave of rapes in the community, members of the Parliament suggested locking all females in their homes after dark. Why not lock up the males instead, the Prime Minister countered, since males were commit-

ting the rapes. Whether prevention efforts should be targeted on
males to stop the development of sexually assaultive behavior, or on
females, to teach them resourcefulness in escape and avoidance techniques, is an issue that has led to confusion in designing prevention
strategies.

Reference to classic prevention theory clarifies the issue. In
the public health model (Bloom 1971; Bloom 1981) disease is seen as
the dysfunctional outcome of an interaction between the environment
(stressor) and the person (host). The model projects two basic prevention strategies: (1) eliminate or change the environmental stressor,
or (2) strengthen the host. For example, spraying swamps in tropical
countries gets rid of malaria-carrying mosquitos. In this prevention
effort, the stressor is eliminated. In other diseases, innoculating
the potential host prevents the development of the disease by strengthening the host's defenses against the stressor's impact.

When physical environmental stressors are pitted against human
hosts, the calculation of prevention resources is theoretically
straightforward. The choice of targeting stressor or host is a pragmatic one. Questions such as: which is more accessible, which strategy is less costly, or which more effective, determine the selection.
Yet when the environmental stressor is another human being, preventive
strategies become blurred (Cassel 1974). This is the case in the act
of rape. Two human beings are involved: the stressor is the assailant,
the host is the victim. Should prevention efforts be focused on altering the behavior of the human in the stressor role, or on strengthening the defenses of the human in the host role?

The choice of focus is critical. Applying classic prevention
theory to rape leads to radically different strategies, depending on
whether the stressor or the host is targeted for prevention efforts.
The paradigmatic prevention model involves five steps (adapted from
Klein and Goldston 1977).

1. Identify a behavior or health status judged to be dysfunctional.
2. Document the incidence of the dysfunction in the general
   population.
3. Identify a population at risk--one in which the incidence exceeds that for the general population.
4. Intervene with the risk population so as to arrest
   or stop the development of the dysfunction prior to
   the occurrence of negative outcomes.
5. Assess the effectiveness of the intervention.

Walking through the prevention model point by point, using rape
as the behavior to be prevented, highlights the distortions of logic
and values that have historically plagued the field. The problem is
simple as seen in Table 1: in order to stop sexual assaults, sexually
assaultive behavior must be prevented. However, no programmatic interventions with the general population of males have been attempted
to prevent the development of sexually assaultive behavior. In practice, prevention activities have been almost exclusively devoted to
interventions with the host population.[1]

[1] Early identification and treatment of sexually victimized boys has
been suggested to arrest the development of abusing behavior (Swift
1979). This is based on evidence that boys who are sexually victimized are proportionately more likely to be sexual abusers as adults
than boys who have not suffered victimization (Burgess et al. 1981;
Groth 1979; Swift 1979). While such efforts may be effective, they
are directed to secondary rather than primary prevention.

TABLE 1

Application of prevention theory to rape: targeting
the stressor or the host population for intervention.

STRESSOR		HOST
	STEP ONE	
1. The act of rape is a dysfunctional behavior.		1. The trauma of rape victimization results in short-term and/or long term dysfunction.
	STEP TWO	
2. Incidence unknown. Rapists are predominantly male.		2. Incidence unknown. Victims are predominantly female.
	STEP THREE	
3. Males are a population at risk for the development of sexually assaultive behavior.		3. Females are a population at risk for sexual victimization.
	STEP FOUR	
4. Intervene with males to prevent the development of sexually assaultive behavior.		4. Intervene with females to prevent sexual victimization.
	STEP FIVE	
Assess the effectiveness of the intervention.		

THE EPIDEMIOLOGY OF RAPE

The science of epidemiology provides the research base and
methodology for primary prevention efforts (Bloom 1971; Schwab and
Schwab 1978). Epidemiologists trace the distribution of disease in
a population in an effort to identify cause. It is an empirical
finding that disorders are not randomly distributed in populations.
The pattern of cases across time, place, and persons suggests cause.
Armed with this information, hypotheses can be tested and preventive
interventions designed and implemented.

Epidemiological analyses of rape in the United States have produced a wealth of statistics (Amir 1971; Boggs 1965; Chappel et al.
1977; Rabkin 1979). The most significant finding, for prevention,
is the sexual split between assailants and adult victims. Over 90
percent of rapists are male (Groth 1979). Adult victims are primarily female (the sexual victimization of children is addressed elsewhere in this volume). Stopping the cause of rape translates to
identifying and eliminating the variables that maintain sexually assaultive behavior in males.

The second thread that forms a constant across these studies is
the rapist's readiness to use violence as a form of sexual expression.
The incidence of rape is higher in neighborhoods and subcultures that
condone personal violence (Amir 1971). This readiness appears to be
an integral part of male socialization, not just an attribute of a
small group of offenders. Recent research based on self-reports
suggests that a relatively high proportion of male college students
would rape if they had the opportunity to do so without being caught

(Malamuth 1981a, 1981b; Tieger 1981). These studies provide evidence
that rape "proclivity" in males is associated with high levels of
aggression, belief in rape myths, and attributions of blame to rape
victims--a pattern similar to that found in convicted rapists (see
especially chapters 18, 19 and 24 of this volume).

The principal message of epidemiological studies is that the
highest predictor or rape victimization is female status, and the
highest predictor of sexual assault in males is membership in a culture and/or subculture that condones interpersonal violence and deni-
grates women's roles. Cross-cultural studies support these findings.
Sanday (1981) surveyed a standard sample of 186 societies for information relating to rape. Of the 95 societies for which information
was available, 47 percent were classified as rape free, 18 percent as
rape prone, and 35 percent as intermediate. Rape-prone societies include those with a high incidence of rape, and those in which rape is
a ceremonial act or an act used to punish or threaten women. Rape-
prone cultures are characterized by male dominance, a high level of
interpersonal violence, and sexual segregation. Rape is linked with
a pattern of violence that views women as property, evidenced by pay-
ment to the wronged husband, and the use of tribal women in exchange
systems between men.

The cultural profile suggested by these studies matches that
identified by Burt (1980). In interviews with a random sample of
Minnesota adults, she found that acceptance of rape myths can be predicted from attitudes of sex role stereotyping, adversarial sexual
beliefs, and acceptance of interpersonal violence. The more extreme
the stereotypes, the higher the acceptance of rape myths.

Epidemiological and sociological studies support the feminist
view that prevention strategies directed to equalizing the power
balance between the sexes and reducing society's practice and tolerance of violence have the most promise for reducing the incidence of
rape.

RAPE PREVENTION ACTIVITIES

Policies or activities that have implications for rape prevention include legislation, law enforcement policies and practices,
skill training, educational interventions, and strategies utilizing
the media. Rehabilitation programs with identified rapists are not
considered in this review, since these efforts fall under secondary
or tertiary prevention.[2]

Legislation
The only formal population-wide rape prevention "program" focusing on the population at risk for developing sexually assaultive behavior is rape legislation. Rape laws define the act and specify
consequences for violations. Given that the confinement of convicted

---

[2] It is notable that according to the traditional view, in which
rape victimization--rather than the development of raping behavior--
is the goal of prevention efforts, successful rehabilitation of convicted rapists would indeed reduce the overall incidence of victimization, since a high proportion of offenders are recidivists (Groth
et al. 1982), but would not have an impact on the incidence (new
cases) of sexually assaultive behavior in the non-offender male population.

rapists takes them off the street and prevents them from committing
further rapes, the more important question for prevention is whether
legal sanctions discourage sexually assaultive behavior in males who
have not been convicted of rape. Laws command obedience through two
channels: fear of punishment, and codification of moral standards.

Is punishment an effective deterrent for rape? The cumulative
research indicates that certainty of punishment is effective in reducing crime rates, but severity of punishment is not. Bailey (1974)
found that capital punishment did not affect homicide rates. Since
many rape murders are officially classified as murder only, this
finding has relevance for rape. The spectre of capital punishment
also discourages juries from convictions for sexual offenses (Andenaes 1975). Using a variety of methods--from correlations of crime
rates with length of sentences to econometric studies--researchers
have confirmed the efficacy of the certainty of punishment in reducing
crime (Erikson and Gibbs 1973; Gibbs 1968; Tittle 1969; Silver 1975).

Punishment, however, is far from a certainty for rape. The
dismal record of rape laws for preventing this crime has been well
documented. It is estimated that as many as 90 out of 100 cases go
unreported (Groth 1979) and that only two convictions result for
every 1,000 cases of rape (MOCSA 1980). Proportionately fewer arrests
for rape result in convictions than arrests for murder, robbery, or
burglary (Williams 1978). One caveat: most of these studies failed
to take account of the difference between the incapacitative and the
deterrent effects of punishment (Andenaes 1975). Locking up rapists
prevents them from raping for the period of their sentence, whereas
the fear of probable punishment may prevent a prospective rapist in
the community from committing the act.

In prevention terms, research on punishment supports reform
legislation and policies of enforcement and prosecution that increase
the certainty of punishment for sex offenders. Rigorous enforcement
of legal sanctions against rape would signal strong public sentiment
that rape is unacceptable, and thus influence behavioral norms.

The last decade has seen sweeping reforms in rape legislation
in the United States (Geis and Geis 1978; Deming and Eppy 1981).
These reforms cover three general issues: the definition of rape, the
penalty, and the rules of evidence covering rape corroboration and
the victim's prior sexual history ("rape shield" laws). While it is
premature to draw definitive conclusions about the effectiveness of
these reforms, certain trends are clear. Reform legislation appears
to (1) increase the number of convictions for crimes labelled rape,
and (2) increase the certainty, but not necessarily the severity, of
punishment (see especially chapters 14, 15, 16, and 19 in this volume).
The prevention of rape reform laws in increasing the certainty of
punishment can only be effective with a public that is aware of the
change. Public information and education campaigns are an integral
part of rape prevention strategies focusing on legislative change.

A second preventive effect of legislative change is in the codification of cultural norms: "The legislation of one generation may
become the morality of the next" (Walker 1964). Loh (1981), in assessing rape reform legislation- echoes this point:

> The role of rape law as catalyst for attitude change may
> be greater than any immediate impact on the criminal
> justice system. The criminal law serves not only a
> general deterrent function. It also has a "moral or

sociopedagogic" purpose to reflect and shape moral
values and beliefs of society.... The new rape law
symbolizes and reinforces newly emerging conceptions
about the status of women and the right of self-de-
termination in sexual conduct.... Conviction of rape,
rather than of some surrogate defense, is a dramatic
lesson about society's disapprobation of the act,
and helps to strengthen the public code (p. 50).

Reform of rape laws is only a small part of the legislative
agenda of those who subscribe to the theory that rape is a function
of the power differential between the sexes. Legislation directed
to the codification of women's equality and rights in the educational,
economic, political, and social arenas is an integral part of a comprehensive prevention strategy for eliminating rape.

Skill Training

The primary skill training relevant to prevention activities is
rape avoidance (Bart 1980, Burgess and Brodsky 1981; McIntyre 1981).
These techniques, based on the prevention strategy of strengthening
the host, are designed to prevent sexual victimization. They have
the potential for significantly reducing the incidence of victimization for certain host populations. Paradoxically, these measures may
not result in the prevention of either sexual assault or victimization in the general population. There is evidence that assailants
abandon attacks on resistant women and seek locales and victims offering minimum resistance and threat of detection. The net effect
of successful rape avoidance, then, may be to displace victimization
from informed women, prepared women, and women proficient in self
defense to the very young, the physically or mentally disabled, or
the elderly.

A series of studies have solidly established the effectiveness
of resistance in avoiding rape. Once faced with an attacker, women
who opt for aggressive responses such as fleeing, screaming, and
kicking, are much more likely to avoid being raped than women who cry,
plead, or do nothing (Bart 1980; McIntyre 1981; Queen's Bench 1976).
These studies refute the view that cooperation is the optimal response
when confronted with an attacker (Storaska 1975). A second piece of
conventional wisdom put to rest is that resistance will escalate the
attack and increase the probability of the victim's mutilation or
death. While resistance seems correlated with an increased level of
victim injury, these injuries are generally not serious, and appear
to be preferred to the trauma of a completed sexual assault.

Bart's (1980) results are an example. Her sample consisted of
forty-three women who had been raped and fifty-one who had avoided
rape, recruited through a variety of sources, including newspaper advertisements. Through interviews, data were collected on the subject's background and on situational variables associated with the
rape or rape attempt. Bart's major finding is that resisting increases the chances of avoiding rape. The most effective strategy
was fleeing from the rapist. Over 80 percent of the women who tried
this avoided being raped. It's not clear why this was the least used
strategy; perhaps fleeing was not a realistic option for many of the
women. The second most effective strategy was physical resistance.
Almost 70 percent of the women who fought their attackers avoided
rape. Verbal resistance was almost as effective when it was directed

to rational arguments or attempts to con the rapist. Pleading turned out to be the least effective strategy. Women who tried this had a greater chance of being raped than sample probability alone would predict. Avoiders used an average of two and one-half times as many strategies as raped women.

Fear was a significant variable in outcome. Over half of the women who avoided rape reported they were motivated primarily by fear of rape, compared with only 7 percent of the women who were raped. Death or mutilation was the primary fear reported by 65 percent of the raped women, compared with 37 percent of the avoiders. Situational variables positively associated with rape confirm the results of other studies—that is, most rapes occurred at night, inside rather than outside, and to women living alone. A review of background variables that differentiated avoiders from raped women points to variables clustering around independence as key for rape avoidance. Women who were taller, heavier and more physically active, never married, employed rather than students, and more highly educated more often avoided rape than their shorter, lighter, dependent, married, less educated sisters.

Self-defense training for women has become a standard rape prevention strategy promoted by a broad spectrum of sponsors, from feminist groups to police departments. The feminist movement has legitimized women's efforts to control their own bodies. These efforts are reflected in their increasing participation in sports, bodybuilding activities, and self-defense classes. That women can be taught to defend themselves against attack is no longer in dispute. The results of rape avoidance activities go beyond their potential for preventing subclasses of women from sexual victimization. These activities have significance for host-focused interventions in both the microenvironment of the rape event, and the macroenvironment in which systems change takes place. Resistant women have empowered not only themselves, but all women, in demonstrating that female status and victim status are not inevitably paired. To fight back is to claim power over oneself for oneself—an act that women must replicate at ever-widening circles of social interaction.

Educational Interventions

The prevention of rape in our culture requires change in the social system. Alternatives to violence as a means of resolving interpersonal and intragroup conflicts must be found. The current process of sex role socialization prepares women for inferior status and sexual victimization (Albin 1977; Miller 1976; Rose 1977; Sparks and Bar On 1982; Vance 1977), and men for the expression of power through violence, particularly sexual violence. To eliminate rape, society's major institutions must begin to reflect a revaluing of women's contributions and an expansion of women's roles to include accepted access to the public arena. Critical to this effort is the cooperation of schools in eliminating sexist curricula and teaching practices.

An experiment by Guttentag (1977) illustrates both the problems and the promise of this approach. Three large school systems in Boston were the research sites. Using curricula, teacher training, and peer group involvement, Guttentag attempted to modify the sex role stereotypes of five, ten, and fourteen-year-old children (kindergarten, fifth, and ninth grades). Material for the six-week intervention was designed to fit children's cognitive stages. Books,

plays, special projects, and records were integrated into English
and social work studies (for fifth and ninth graders) and into the
kindergartner's day.
     Guttentag found sex role stereotypes of children to be *independ-
ent* of social class, ethnic background, and the employment status of
the mother. She suggests that the pervasive influence of television
and peers are more powerful than family influences in determining
cultural stereotypes. Boy's sex role stereotypes about women's
roles were stronger initially than those of girls and showed less
change. Most attitudinal change occurred in the area of occupational stereotypes. Girls--and boys to a lesser extent--broadened their
views about multiple career options for both sexes, but did not
change traditional views of family roles. Rather than becoming less
stereotyped, the views of ninth-grade boys became more rigid, suggesting that interventions should be scheduled as early as possible
in the educational process to be effective. Not surprisingly, more
change occurred in classrooms where the teachers were committed to
the goals of the project. Rape prevention requires educational interventions countering sex role stereotypes, introduced in the earliest grades, and taught by teachers trained and committed to promoting
nonstereotypical views.

Media Strategies
     A major barrier to the widespread implementation of prevention
programs has been the difficulty in reaching target populations.
One of the most effective means of reaching the general population
is through the medium of television. Children in this country watch
an average of three to four hours of television daily (Comstock et
al. 1978). By the age of eighteen, today's children will have spent
more time watching television than hours in the classroom (Liebert
et al. 1973; Lyle and Hoffman 1972). We are only beginning to understand the effects of viewing on children.
     In addition to providing entertainment, television is both a
social support and an educator. As a social support it is a baby-
sitter, a companion for the lonely, and a catalyst for social interaction. As an educational took it teaches everything from the alpha-
bet to highly technical scientific material. The parameters of
learning through television have only been marginally explored to
date. The five volumes of the technical reports to the Surgeon General's Scientific Advisory Committee on Television and Social Behavior (1972) and the updated version of that work (Pearl et al.
1982) document the role of television in teaching aggressive behaviors to children. Research indicates that the linking of sex and
violence in the media contributes to the public acceptance of violence against women as a norm (Malamuth and Check 1981; Tieger 1981).
     Additional findings that have been experimentally demonstrated
are that television is a major influence on children's learning of
sex role behavior, and that for some children, TV has taken over the
role of sex educator as well (Pearl et al. 1982). The following stereotypes are projected daily into the nation's living rooms: TV women
rarely grow older--most are in their twenties or thirties; most are
married; few are employed outside the home, and few are minority
women. TV males outnumber TV females by three to one. While women
are underrepresented on television as lawbreakers, they are overrep-
resented as victims (Greenberg 1982).

On television, for men the emphasis is on strength,
performance, and skill; for women, it is on attractiveness and desirability. Women characters are more likely than men to use their bodies seductively, according
to a survey of sexual behavior on prime time television
(citation omitted). Many of the plots and stories require erotically enticing costumes on the women, and
the camera often focuses on particular parts of their
bodies ... Sex is commonly linked with violence. On
dramatic and action shows, discussions of sex are often
in the context of rape or other sex crimes.

... These content analyses show that on television
male and female sexuality is characterized by a double
standard and by stereotyped definitions of masculine
and feminine traits and roles (Pearl, Bouthilet &
Lazar 1982, p. 55).

While television's capacity to teach violence and sex role
stereotypes has been experimentally explored and confirmed, less attention has been given to exploring the medium's capacity to teach
prosocial behaviors, although the available research indicates that
learning of prosocial behaviors does take place (Harvey et al. 1979;
Liebert and Poulos 1975; Liebert et al. 1975; Sprafkin and Rubenstein
1979, 1983).
The power of television as a teaching tool can be mobilized for
positive as well as negative health and behavioral outcomes (Johnston
1983; Keegan 1983; Lovelace and Houston 1983; Solomon 1983; Swift 1983).
One of the major primary prevention television studies aimed at a
mass audience, and targeted to changing behaviors with an impact on
health, is the Stanford study (Maccoby and Farquhar 1975, 1976;
Solomon 1983). Researchers at Stanford University conducted a study
using the mass media and individual instruction to reduce susceptibility to heart disease. Three California towns were selected for participation. The behaviors targeted for change were smoking, diet, and
exercise. Results indicate that target behaviors and attitudes in
the two towns receiving the mass media programs changed in the predicated direction more than those in the control town. In addition,
those in the high risk group receiving the media intervention plus
special instruction showed more change after the first year than those
who received media messages alone. After the second year, however,
the media-alone group had caught up with the media-plus-instruction
group in all areas except smoking reduction.
These findings demonstrate what large advertising firms have
known all along, but what prevention professionals are just beginning
to find out: bombarding viewers with a simple message gets results.
It sells cereal, toothpaste, and cars. It also sells violence. The
critical question here is whether rape prevention advocates can command the resources to mobilize the power of television to counter sex
role stereotypes and reduce television violence. Alliance with other
groups seeking these goals (such as parents and senior citizens) is a
beginning strategy.
No one of the strategies explored above will effect the desired
change. Like any social movement, rape prevention will require simultaneous changes in political, economic, educational and social institutions:

A variety of rape prevention measures have been proposed. Unfortunately, too many ignore the cultural or
systemic factors which support or even promote rape,
such as the glorification of violence against women in
some advertising. In the case of rape, this has meant
that women's victimization implicitly has been attributed to traits or behaviors of the rape victim (e.g.,
seductiveness) or to psychological disorders of the
rapist; consequently, preventive strategies involving
changes in the social system have been overlooked.
When substantial energies of our society's institutions are focused on eliminating rape, both men and
women living in our cities will have less to fear
(Gordon et al. 1980).

REFERENCES

Albin, R. "Psychological Studies of Rape." *Signs: Journal of Women
in Culture and Society* 3 (1977): 423-435.

Amir, M. *Patterns in Forcible Rape.* Chicago, Illinois: University
of Chicago Press, 1971.

Andenaes, J. "General Prevention Revisited: Research and Policy
Implications." *Journal of Criminal Law and Criminology* 66 (1975):
338-365.

Bailey, W. "Murder and the Death Penalty." *Journal of Criminal Law
and Criminology* 65 (1974): 416-423.

Bart, P. *Avoiding Rape: A Study of Victims and Avoiders* (Final Report). National Center for the Prevention and Control of Rape,
National Institute of Mental Health, 1980.

Bloom, B. "Strategies for the Prevention of Mental Disorders." In
Issues in Community Psychology and Preventive Mental Health, edited
by G. Rosenblum. New York: Behavioral Publications, 1971.

Bloom, M. *Primary Prevention: The Possible Science.* Englewood
Cliffs, New Jersey: Prentice-Hall, 1981.

Boggs, S. "Urban Crime Patterns." *American Sociological Review* 30
(1965): 899-909.

Burgess, A., and S. Brodsky. "Applying Flight Education Principles
to Rape Prevention." *Family and Community Health* 4 (1981): 45-51.

Burgess, A., N. Groth, and M. McCausland. "Child Sex Initiation
Rings." *American Journal of Orthopsychiatry* 51 (1981): 110-119.

Burt, M. "Cultural Myths and Supports for Rape." *Journal of Personality and Social Psychology* 38 (1980): 217-230.

Chappel, D., R. Geis, and G. Geis. *Forcible Rape: The Crime, the
Victim and the Offender.* New York: Columbia University Press, 1977.

Cassel, J. "Psychosocial Processes and "Stress": Theoretical Formulation." *International Journal of Health Services* 4 (1974): 471-482.

Comstock, G., S. Chaffee, N. Katzman, M. McCombs, and D. Roberts.
Television and Human Behavior. New York: Columbia University Press,
1978.

Cowen, E. "Special Issue: Research in Primary Prevention in Mental Health." *American Journal of Community Psychology* 10 (1982).

Deming, M., and A. Eppy. "The Sociology of Rape." *Sociology and Social Research* 65 (1981): 357-380.

Erickson, M., and J. Gibbs. "The Deterrence Question: Some Alternative Methods of Analysis." *Social Science Quarterly* 54 (1973): 534-551.

Geis, G., and R. Geis. "Rape Reform: An Appreciative-Critical Review." *Bulletin of the American Academy of Psychiatry and the Law* 6 (1978): 301-312.

Gibbs, J. "Crime, Punishment and Deterrence." *Social Science Quarterly* 28 (1968): 515-530.

Gordon, M., S. Riger, R. LeBailly, and L. Heath. "Crime, Women, and the Quality of Urban Life." *Signs: Journal of Women in Culture and Society* 5 (1980): 144-160.

Greenberg, B. "Television and Role Socialization: An Overview." In *Television and Behavior: Ten Years of Scientific Progress and Implications for the Eighties*, vol. 1, edited by D. Pearl, L. Bouthilet, and J. Lazar. DHHS Pub. No. (ADM) 82-1195. Washington, D.C.L U.S. Government Printing Office, 1982.

Groth, A.N. *Men Who Rape: The Psychology of the Offender*. New York: Plenum, 1979.

Groth, A., R. Longo, and J. McFadin. "Undetected Recidivism Among Rapists and Child Molesters." *Crime and Delinquency* 28 (1982): 450-458.

Guttentag, M. "Prevention of Sexism." In *Primary Prevention of Psychopathology*, vol. 1, edited by G. Albee and J. Joffee. New Hampshire: University Press of New England, 1977.

Harvey, S., J. Sprafkin, and E. Rubenstein. "Prime Time Television: A Profile of Aggressive and Prosocial Behaviors." *Journal of Broadcasting* 23 (1979): 179-189.

Heber, R., and H. Garber. "The Milwaukee Project: A Study of the Use of Family Intervention to Prevent Cultural-Familial Mental Retardation." In *The Exceptional Infant: Assessment and Intervention*, edited by B. Friedlander, G. Sterritt, and G. Kirk. New York: Brunner/Mazel, 1975.

Johnston, J. "Using Television to Change Stereotypes." In R_x *Television: Enhancing the Preventive Impact of TV*, edited by J. Sprafkin, C. Swift, and R. Hess. New York: Haworth Press, 1983.

Keegan, C. "Using Television to Reach Older People with Prevention Messages: The Over Easy Experiment." In R_x *Television: Enhancing the Preventive Impact of TV*, edited by J. Sprafkin, C. Swift, and R. Hess. New York: Haworth Press, 1983.

Klein, D., and S. Goldston. *Primary Prevention: an Idea Whose Time Has Come*. DHEW Publication No. (ADM) 77-447. Washington, D.C.: U.S. Government Printing Office, 1977.

Latessa, E., and H. Allen. "Using Citizens to Prevent Crime: An Example of Deterrence and Community Involvement." *Journal of Police Science and Administration* 8 (1980): 69-74.

Lester, D. "Rape and Social Structure." *Psychological Report* 35 (1974): 146.

Liebert, R., J. Neale, and E. Davidson. *The Early Window: Effects of Television on Children and Youth*. Elmsford, New York: Pergamon, 1973.

Liebert, R., and R. Poulos. "Television and Personality Development: The Socializing Effects of an Entertainment Medium." In *Child Personality and Psychopathology*, edited by A. Davids. New York: Wiley, 1975.

Liebert, R., J. Sprafkin, and R. Poulos. In *Twentieth Annual Conference/1974 Proceedings*, edited by W. Hale. Advertising Research Foundation, 1975.

Loh, W. "What Has Reform of Rape Legislation Wrought?" *The Journal of Social Issues* 37 (1981): 28-52.

Lovelace, V., and A. Huston. "Can Television Teach Prosocial Behavior?" In R_x *Television: Enhancing the Preventive Impact of TV*, edited by J. Sprafkin, C. Swift, and R. Hess. New York: Haworth Press, 1983.

Lyle, J., and H. Hoffman. "Children's Use of Television and Other Media." In *Television and Social Behavior*, edited by E. Rubenstein, G. Comstock, and J. Murray. Washington, D.C.: U.S. Government Printing Office, 1972.

Maccoby, N., and J. Farquhar. "Bringing the California Health Report Up to Date." *Journal of Communication* 26 (1976): 56-57.

Maccoby, N., and J. Farquhar. "Communication for Health: Unselling Heart Disease." *Journal of Communication* 25 (1975): 115-126.

Malamuth, N. "Rape Fantasies As a Function of Exposure to Violent Sexual Stimuli." *Archives of Sexual Behavior* 10 (1981a): 33-47.

Malamuth, N. "Rape Proclivity Among Males." *The Journal of Social Issues* 37 (1981b): 138-157.

Malamuth, N., and J. Check. "The Effects of Mass Media Exposure on Acceptance of Violence Against Women: A Field Experiment." *Journal of Research in Personality* 15 (1981): 436-446.

Marsh, J., and N. Caplan. *Law Reform in the Prevention and Treatment of Rape* (Final Report). National Center for the Prevention and Control of Rape, National Institute of Mental Health, 1980.

McIntyre, J. *Victim Response to Rape: Alternative Outcomes* (Final Report). National Center for the Prevention and Control of Rape, National Institute of Mental Health, 1981.

Metropolitan Organization to Counter Sexual Assault. *Rape Prevention*. Kansas City, Missouri: MOCSA, 1980.

Miller, J. *Toward a New Psychology of Women*. Boston, Massachusetts: Beacon Press, 1976.

Pearl, D., L. Bouthilet, and J. Lazar. *Television and Behavior; Ten Years of Scientific Progress and Implications for the Eighties*, vol. 1, DHHS Publication No. (ADM) 82-1195. Washington, D.C.: U.S. Government Printing Office, 1982.

Queen's Bench Foundation. *Rape: Prevention and Resistance.* San Francisco, California, 1976.

Rabkin, J. "The Epidemiology of Forcible Rape." *American Journal of Orthopsychiatry* 49 (1979): 634-647.

"Rape Program Improves Conviction Record." *Concern* 6 (1979): 4.

Rose, V. "Rape As A Social Problem: A Byproduct of the Feminist Movement." *Social Problems* 25 (1977): 75-89.

Sanday, P. "The Socio-Cultural Context of a Rape: A Cross-Cultural Study." *The Journal of Social Issues* 37 (1981): 5-27.

Schwab, J., and M. Schwab. *Sociocultural Roots of Mental Illness: An Epidemiological Survey.* New York: Plenum, 1978.

Silver, M. "Punishment, Deterrence and Police Effectiveness: A Survey and Critical Interpretation of the Recent Econometric Literature." As cited in J. Andenaes, "General Prevention Revisited: Research and Policy Implications." *Journal of Criminal Law and Criminology* 66 (1975): 338-365.

Solomon, D. "Mass Media Campaigns for Health Promotion." In R_x *Television: Enhancing the Preventive Impact of TV*, edited by J. Sprafkin, C. Swift, and R. Hess. New York: Haworth Press, 1983.

Sparks, C., and B. Bar On. "A Social Change Approach to the Prevention of Sexual Violence Toward Women." Paper presented at the National Institute of Mental Health Staff College Course, *Mental Health Services for Women: Treatment and Prevention.* Washington, D.C., July, 1982. Available from Community Living for Women, Box 265, Edgewater, Maryland 21037.

Spivack, G., and M. Shure. *Social Adjustment of Young Children: A Cognitive Approach to Solving Real-life Problems.* San Francisco, California: Jossey Bass, 1973.

Sprafkin, J., and E. Rubenstein. "A Field Correlational Study of Children's Television Viewing Habits and Prosocial Behavior." *Journal of Broadcasting* 23 (1979): 265-276.

Sprafkin, J., and E. Rubenstein. "Using Television to Improve the Behavior of Institutionalized Children." In R_x *Television: Enhancing the Preventive Impact of TV*, edited by J. Sprafkin, C. Swift, and R. Hess. New York: Haworth Press, 1983.

Storaska, F. *How to Say No to a Rapist and Survive.* New York: Random House, 1975.

Surgeon General. *Television and Growing Up: The Impact of Televised Violence* (Summary Report). The Surgeon General's Scientific Advisory Committee on Television and Social Behavior. Washington, D.C.: U.S. Government Printing Office, 1972.

Svalastoga, K. "Rape and Social Structure." *Pacific Sociological Review* 5 (1962): 48-53.

Swift, C. "The Prevention of Sexual Child Abuse: Focus on the Perpetrator." *Journal of Clinical Child Psychology* 8 (1979): 133-136.

Swift, C. "Applications of Interactive Television to Prevention and Programming." In R_x *Television: Enhancing the Preventive Impact of TV*, edited by J. Sprafkin, C. Swift, and R. Hess. New York: Haworth Press, 1983.

Tieger, T. "Self-Rated Likelihood of Raping and the Social Perception of Rape." *Journal of Research in Personality* 15 (1981): 147-158.

Tieger, T., and J. Aronstam. "'Brutality Chic' Images and Endorsement of Rape Myths." Paper presented at the Annual Meetings of the American Psychological Association. Los Angeles, California, August, 1981.

Tittle, C. "Crime Rates and Legal Sanction." *Social Problems* 16 (1969): 409-423.

United States President's Commission on Mental Health. Report to the President, vol. IV. Washington, D.C.: U.S. Government Printing Office, 1978.

Vance, E. "A Typology of Risks and the Disabilities of Low Status." In *Primary prevention of Psychopathology*, vol. 1, edited by G. Albee and J. Joffee. 1977.

Walker, N. "Morality and the Criminal Law," 1964. As cited in J. Andenaes. "General Prevention Revisited: Research and Policy Implications." *Journal of Criminal Law and Criminology* 66 (1975): 338-365.

Williams, K. *The Prosecution of Sexual Assaults*. PROMIS Research Project, Publication 7. Washington, D.C.: Institute for Law and Social Research, 1978.

Abel, G.G., 166, 242, 395, 397-98
Abrahamsen, D., 64, 301
Adolescents:
coping by, 132
development of, 130-133
family response, 172-173
victimization of, 117-138
Ageton, Suzanne, 129, 124
Albee, Edward, 381
Albin, R.S., 303, 317
Alcocer, Anthony M., 15
Alton, A., 142
American Psychiatric Association, 305
Amir, M., 124, 225, 227, 296, 303
Anderson, Linda, 15, 65
Anderson, W.P., 238, 266
Anger rapist, 153, 249-251, 252, 279
Anthony, Susan B., 4
Anti-rape slogans, 5
Apfelberg, B., 228, 229
Armenti, N., 301
Aronson, E., 314-16; 316
Ashton, N.K., 162
Ashworth, C.D., 190
Atkeson, B.M., 176

Bailey, W., 417
Baluss, M., 40
Bard, M., 36, 41-43, 49
Baron, L., 402
Bart, P.B., 23, 29, 63, 415
Barry, Kathleen, 382
Bassuk, E., 54
Bay Area Women Against Rape, 5
Becker, J.V., 23, 29, 182
Behavioral Science Unit, FBI
Academy, 343, 345, 347
Bell, A., 99, 102, 107
Berger, V., 328
Bernard, C., 46
Bernstein, M.H., 163, 164, 182

Biener, L., 322-324
Blashfield, R.K., 275
Borgida, E., 325, 326, 327, 329
Boverman, I., 378
Bowman, K., 300
Breed, W., 403
Brekke, N., 329, 331
Broncale, R., 228, 300
Brooks, Pierce, 347
Brown, Marilyn T., 16
Brownmiller, Susan, 2, 146, 374
Brussels, J., 344
Bryant, J., 404-05
Burgess, Ann W., 16, 40, 48-50,
124, 133, 140, 141, 144,
161, 165, 166, 171, 175,
180, 182, 183, 189, 248,
308, 345
Burt, M.R., 317, 321, 416
Byrnes, L.E., 318

Cade, B., 337
Calhoun, K., 176
Canavan, W., 106
Cannon, W.B., 46
Caplan, N., 24, 30, 195, 196
Carpenter, J., 301
Cavallin, H., 86
Chandler, S.M., 55
Chappell, D., 47
Check, J.V.P., 396, 399, 404, 405
Child Abuse, 61-65, 89, 110, 203
Child Molesters, 221, 293, 366
assessment of, 350, 269
characteristics of, 231-236
homosexual molesters, 231-233
MMIP, 235-241, 266
subtyping, 269-281
types of, 253-260
Child Sexual Abuse Treatment
Program, 202
Child pornography, 110-114, 117-
122, 366, 368, 374, 375-382
commercial, 113

law enforcement response, 117-
    130
pedophilia, 113, 221, 228, 232,
    233, 241, 255, 257, 278
Child prostitution, 114, 115, 117,
    336, 374, 378
Child Protection Act, 110, 113
Child Protection Service, 302
Children's Hospital National
    Medical Center, 32
Christie, M.M., 230, 231
Churches, 7, 374, 375
Cognitive-behavioral model, 54,
    55
Cohen, M.L., 246-270, 279,
    297, 299
Coleman, N., 336
Commission on Obsenity and
    Pornography, 278-283, 386,
    393, 394
Common Law Rule, 326, 327
Compensatory rapist, 251-252,
    263, 268, 270, 279
Consciousness-raising groups,
    1, 3, 4
Cowna, S., 164, 181
Cowden, J.E., 240
Crime Victim Assistance Fund, 12
Criminal Justice System, 7, 160,
    189-197, 199-207
    child victims, 199-208
    expert testimony, 205
    police, 191-193, 201
    prosecutor, 193-195, 201, 205
    rape victims, 189
Crisis intervention, 41, 54, 90-
    92, 178-181
Cross, Phyllis O.D., 16

Darwin, C., 368, 369
Davenport, J., 183
Davies, M.A., 178, 183
DeFoe, J.R., 403
Densen-Gerber, J., 381
Depue, Roger L., 347
Diamond, I., 383
Dietz, S.R., 318, 320, 321
Displaced Anger-Aggressive rapist,
    252-253, 262, 264, 279
Dewey, John, 369
Donnerstein, E.I., 400
Douglas, John E., 345
Dworkin, A., 376, 387

East, W., 297
Egidio, R.K., 181

Ellerstein, N., 106
Ellis, A., 228, 300
Ellis, E.M., 176
Ellison, K., 49
Elman, D., 318
Elmer, E., 62
Endicott, J., 273
Engle, B., 300
Equal Rights Amendment, 11, 386
Erikson, Erik, 131
Etherington, C., 182

Family violence, 61-69, 73, 79,
    335, 336
    adult violence, 62
    child abuse, 61, 336
    cultural factors, 64
    incidence studies, 61-62
    intervention, 64
    parent education, 66
    patterns of abuse, 63
    prevention, 65, 66, 67
    social variables, 63, 64
    stress producing factors, 62,
        63
    treatment phases of, 65
    wife battering, 61, 64, 85,
        146, 149, 150, 304
FBI Uniform Crime Reports, 46,
    139, 340
Federal aid, 9
Federal Rules of Evidence, 333,
    337
Feild, H.S. 191, 322-324
Feldman-Summers, S., 164, 165, 182,
    190, 191, 308, 315, 316
Felice, M., 173, 183
Feminists, 4, 5, 306, 307
    perspective on rape and pronog-
        raphy, 374-387
Ferenczi, S., 134
Feshback, S., 307
Financial support of victim
    services 8, 9
Fine, R., 297
Fischman, A.M., 190-196
Fisher, G., 233
Fitch, J.H., 253-259
Filklehor, David, 19, 25, 63,
    70, 83, 100-102, 106, 128,
    147, 148, 150-154
Fletcher, C., 300
Fogarty, C., 300
Fojtik-Stroud, K.M., 55
Foley, T.S., 172-175, 178, 180,
    183

Frank, Ellen, 22, 28, 29, 163, 167, 173-175
Freud, Sigmund, 42, 47, 297
Friedan, B., 379, 387
Frieze, I., 147-149, 166
Fritz, G., 101
Frye vs. United States, 337
Furst, S.S., 47

Gager, Nancy, 2
Garmezy, N., 130
Gearing, M.L., 237
Gebhard, P.H., 229, 230, 232, 247-249, 253-256, 265-267, 274, 279
Geis, G., 47
Geist, A., 195, 196
Gelles, R., 53, 149
General Adaptation Syndrome, 38, 39
Giarretto, Henry, 65, 126, 381
Gil, D., 61, 64
Gilberto, S.J., 172, 182
Giles-Sims, J., 149
Glaser, D., 306
Glueck, B.C., 228, 229, 233
Glueck, S.S., 295, 290
Goodwin, J., 134, 164
Gordon, L., 86
Griffin, S., 106, 306
Gross, Hans, 344
Groth, A. Nicholas, 50, 63, 106, 140, 152-154, 246, 248-259, 263, 266, 274, 435
Guertin, W.H., 236
Guttentag, M., 419
Guttmacher, M.A., 246-248, 253, 296-301

Haber, S., 307
Halleck, S., 305
Halpern, S., 163, 164
Hammer, E.F., 236, 299
Handicapped victims, 139-145
Hanneke, L., 154, 155
Harlow, H., 352
Harrell, S., 128
Haver, A.L., 237
Hazelwood, Robert R., 345
Heiman, William, 16
Herman, Judith, 20, 26, 70, 75, 76, 91. 126
Hiberman, Elaine, 42, 49, 305
Hirschman, Lisa, 20, 26, 126
Hollander, B., 304
Hollingshead, D., 308

Holmes, K.A., 134
Holmstrom, Lynda L., 48-50, 124, 133, 140, 141, 144, 161, 165, 166, 171, 175, 180, 182, 183, 308
Homicide, sexual, 343-349
Horney, K., 303
Horowitz, M., 37, 38, 47, 55
Howell, L.M., 233, 241
Hunt, E., 165, 181

Ibn-Tamas v. United States, 337
Impulsive rapist, 253
Imwinkelred, E.J., 337
Incest, 25-27, 42, 70-82, 134, 228, 297, 303, 350
  brother-sister, 78
  definition of, 70-71
  family constellation, 84-87
  family structure, 79, 84, 85, 353, 354
  father-daughter incest, 70, 72, 83-96
  identification, 89
  incest history, 87-88, 134
  intervention, 89-92
  kinship position, 74
  offenders, 72-77, 84-87
  prevalence, 83-84
  resistance to, 73, 74, 78
  secrecy, 87
  stress factors, 77, 78
  treatment of, 92-93, 354-361
Indian Health Service, 15
Institutional Responses, 2, 3, 4
Investigation of sex crimes against children, 110-122

Jacks, I., 299
James, Jennifer, 20, 26
Jones, C., 314, 315, 316, 320

Kahn, A., 317, 318
Kaminer, W., 402
Kanekar, S., 315, 317
Kaplan, M.F., 320
Karpman, B., 297, 299
Katz, S., 174
Kempe, C.H., 61
Kilpatrick, D.G., 22, 27, 165, 166, 182
Kinsey, A.C., 83
Kolsawalla, M.B., 315, 317
Kopp, S.B., 246, 247, 252, 253-258, 266
Kromer, R., 64

Kronhausen, E., 405
Kronhausen, P., 405
Kruleqitz, J.E., 161, 162
Krupnick, J., 38, 55

Lafree, G.D., 195
Landis, J., 83
Largen, Mary Ann, 16
L'Armond, K., 317
Latham, T., 182
Law Enforcement Assistance
    Administration (LEAA), 199
Lederer, Laura, 386
LeGrand, C., 302
Leppmann, F., 299
Lerner, M.J., 314
Lerner, R., 123
Levinger, G., 62
Lindemenn, E., 37, 54
Linder, K., 315, 316
Linz, D., 400
Little, C., 306
Little, Joan, 10
Littner, N., 299, 301, 303
Loh, W.D., 194, 195, 325
Lona-Wiant, Magdalena, 16
Longino, Helen, 378
Luginbuhl, J., 316
Lystad, M.H., 134

MacLean, Paul, 352, 369
Malamuth, Neil M., 307, 396,
    397, 399, 404, 405
Mann, E.M., 173, 183
Marciano, Linda, 381
Marital rape, 146-158, 191, 375
    definition, 146-147
    law of, 156-157
    offender, 152-157
    prevalence, 147-149
    wife-beating, 146, 149-150,
    152
Marsh, J.C., 195, 196, 325,
    328
Marshall, W.L., 230
Massachusetts Treatment Center
    (MTC), 274, 275, 278-281
Masters and Johnson Treatment
    Model, 354-360
Mathias, Senator Charles M., 1,
    9
Mazur, M.A., 175
McCaghy, C.H., 254, 257, 258,
    263, 302
McCahill, T.W., 167, 190, 192,
    194, 196

McCall, George J., 16
McClure, Florence, 16
McCombie, S., 180
McCreary, C.P., 238
McIntyre, J., 30
Meagher, J., 164, 182
Media, influence of, 64, 67, 202,
    305, 306, 365-373, 376, 392,
    395, 402, 403, 413, 420
Meehl, P.E., 277
Meier, Golda, 413
Mental health needs of victims,
    35-43
Meyer, L.C., 190, 192, 193, 194,
    196
Michigan Criminal Sexual Code,
    123-124
Midlorsky, E., 47, 55
Mill, John Stuart, 369
Miller, L.E., 320
Miller, W.R., 163, 182
Millon, T., 275
Mills, C.W., 294, 306
Mohr, J.W., 227, 228, 231, 233
Mokran, A., 64
Morgan, Robin, 374, 392
Monroe, Marilyn, 378
Montgomery, Mary Ann, 16
Morolla, J., 298, 302
Morse, E.L., 240
Moss, C., 316
Myers, M., 322

Nadelson, C.C., 49, 167, 176, 182
National Association of Criminal
    Defense Lawyers, 337
National Center for the Analysis
    of Violent Crime (NCAVC), 347-
    348
National Center for the Prevention
    and Control of Rape (NCPCR),
    14-34, 197
    Advisory Committee, 31-32
    films and publications, 32
    research efforts, 14, 25
    research portfolio, 18-24
    research priorities, 16
National Center on Child Abuse
    and Neglect, 61, 110, 200
National Clearinghouse of Mental
    Health Information of NIMH,
    14
National Coalition Against Sexual
    Assault (NCASA), 11, 12, 15
National Crime Survey, 127

National Incidence Study, 103, 110, 128, 129
National Institute of Mental Health, 1, 10, 14, 31, 33
National Organization for Victim Assistance (NOVA), 11, 15, 197
National Organization for Women (NOW), 3, 9, 10
New York City Radical Feminists, 4
Niederland, W. , 47
North Carolina Rape Crisis Association, 32
Notman, N.T., 49, 176, 176

Ochberg, F.M., 37, 38, 55
Orem, R., 128
Oros, C.J., 318

Paraphilia, 350-364
treatment of, 354-360
Pagelow, M., 149
Panton, J.H., 237
Parke, R.D., 402
Pawl, G.L., 54
Pawlson, M., 64
Pedophiles, 113, 219, 228, 232, 233, 241, 255, 257, 258, 278, 279, 350, 366
People Against Rape, 27
People vs. Bledsoe, 326
People vs. Clark, 335
Pepitone, A., 317
Peters, Joseph J., 189
Pierce, D.M., 236
Pinto, Jody, 4
Ploscowe, Judge, 302
Pornography, 366-368, 374-392, 393-412
Post-Traumatic Stress Response, 49-60, 337
definition, 49
intrusive imagery, 50, 55
subtypes, 53, 54
symptoms of, 51-53
treatment of, 54-55
Power rapist, 153, 249-251, 263
Prandoni, J.R., 236
Prentky, R., 275
President's Commission on Crime, 305
Prince George County study, 3
Psychological profiling, 344

Quinsey, V.L., 242, 262

Rabkin, J.G., 124
Rada, R.T., 230, 300, 302
Randall, S.C., 192
Rape
anti-rape movement, 1-13
anti-rape squads, 4
definition of, 46
epidemiology, 415-416
group rape, 50
history of anti-rape movement, 12
law reforms, 30, 31, 325, 326
marital, 146-158
prevention, 29, 413
psycholegal research, 313-342
rape empathy scale, 320
theories of, 294-312
vocabularies of motive, 294-308
Rape Crisis Centers, 5-11, 46, 143, 201, 374
Rape trauma syndrome, 46-60, 332, 335-337
phases of, 48, 49
recovery from, 55
response patterns, 46
treatment of, 54, 55
Rape victims, 35-45, 163, 196, 219, 228, 250, 302-307, 313-342
coping behaviors, 140-142
family response, 159-188
handicapped, 139-145
immediate needs, 40-43
mental health needs, 35-43
partner's repsonse, 161-167
precipitation, 302-307
provider's response, 41-43
response to, 28-30, 314-342
sexual dysfunctions, 39, 167
treatment for, 27-29
Rader, C.M., 237
Redlich, F., 308
Reisin, I., 399
Resick, Patricia A., 22, 27, 182
Reskin, B.F., 195
Ressler, Robert K., 345
Rich, R., 40
Robertson, D., 181
Robins, J., 273
Robinson, Jane, 16
Rose, V.M., 192
Rosenberg, R., 235
Rowland, J., 329, 332
Ruch, L.O., 55
Ruff, C.F., 241

Rush, Florence, 378
Russell, D.H., 84, 107, 146, 147,
    150, 154, 155, 191, 382-385
Sadistic rapist, 153, 249-251,
    258, 262, 279
Saminow, S., 357
Sanday, Peggy R., 18, 26, 416
Santiago, Jose, 16
Saunders, Frances F., 16
Scherl, D., 48
Schmidt, A.M., 172, 183
Schneider, B., 235
Schultz, L.G., 127
Schurr, Cathleen, 2
Schwartz, M., 39
Scully, D., 298, 302
Seattle Rape Relief, 190
Seghorn, T.K., 246, 251, 253,
    262, 269, 279
Seligman, C., 317
Selye, H., 38, 39, 46
Sex offenders, 49, 50, 153,
    219-293, 297-307, 315,
    321, 359, 397, 415, 417
  assessment of, 260-269
  boy victims, 104-107
  characteristics of, 225-227,
    230-236
  classification of, 245-260,
    269-273
  criminal justice, 200-208
  drug treatment of, 120-122
  marital rapists, 152-154
  MMPI, 235-241, 266, 299
  social variables, 63-64
  style of attack, 50, 230,
    248
  subtypes, 269-281
Sex rings, 106, 129, 365
Sexual abuse of boys, 97-109,
    128
  definition, 97
  offenders, 104-107
  pedophiles, 98
  prevalence, 99-101
  scope of abuse, 101-103
Sexually dangerous person, 269,
    280
Shafer, G., 65
Shields, D.A., 128, 171
Siegel, H., 55
Skinner, L., 166
Smith, R.E., 315
Smithyman, S.D., 298
Spates, C.R., 37

Specter, Senator Arlan, 347
Spiegel, D., 55
Spinner, B., 399, 404
Spirer, J., 296
Spitzer, R.L., 273
Sprung, S., 55
Stanko, E.A., 193
State v Loebach, 334
State v. Marks, 334, 335, 337
State v. McGee, 334-336
State v. McNamara, 326-330
State v. Saldana, 333-337
Stein, J., 41
Steinem, Gloria, 386, 393,
    404, 405
Steinmetz, S., 63
Sterling, Joanne W., 16
Straus, Murray, 19, 25, 61, 63
Substance abuse, alcohol, 62,
    65, 76, 79, 86, 87, 135,
    150, 226, 232, 235, 246,
    249, 278, 280, 301-303,
    358, 403
Suomi, S., 352
Sutherland, E., 306
Sutherland, S., 48
Swanson, D.W., 254, 257, 258,
    268
Swift, C., 63, 128
Symonds, M., 36, 40, 41, 42
Szaz, T.A., 296, 301

Task Force on Victims of
    Violence, 56
Thorne, F.C., 241
Thronton, B., 317, 321
Traub, S., 306
Treacy, E., 166
Tremblatt, W.E., 236

Ugwuegbu, D., 318

Veronen, Lois J., 22, 27, 165,
    166, 182
Victim and offender relationship,
    124-126
Victimization, 35, 36, 41, 42,
    47, 98, 143, 313, 416, 419,
  adolescents, 123-138
  boys, 101, 128
  criminal, 46
  definition, 123
  incest, 89
  stages of, 36
  theoretical models, 37-40

women, 63
Vietnam veterans, 42
Violence in the home, 61-67
Violent Criminal Apprehension
    Program (VI-CAP), 347-349
Virkkuner, M., 233
Visher, C.A., 195
Von Hentig, H., 302, 205
Von Krafft-Ebbing, H., 49

Walker, L., 61, 63
Weihofen, H., 246-248, 253, 296-
    301
Wienberg, M., 99, 102, 107
Weis, K., 125
Wenger, D., 300
Werner, A., 48
Williams, A.M., 163, 164, 182
Williams, J.E., 134
Wilson, B., 156
Women Against Pronography, 380,
    381
Women Against Violence Against
    Women (WAVAW), 380
Women Against Violence in Porn-
    graphy and Media (WAVPM),
    380, 381
Women's Movement, 1, 66, 97,
    201, 378, 379
Wright, E., 241

Yllo, K., 147, 148, 150, 152,
    153, 154
Yochelson, S., 357

Zakcman, H., 167, 176
Zalba, S., 61, 62
Zellman, G.L., 125
Zillmann, D., 40, 404